A to Z

OF ALL OLD DUBLIN CINEMAS

By

George P. Kearns
&
Patrick Maguire

For further information, please contact:
George at (01) 8345 811 or
Pat at (086) 2065 867

TABLE OF CONTENTS

Title: **Page:**

FOREWORD

This book is very much an A to Z of all, old Dublin cinemas, and to the best of our knowledge Pat Maguire and yours truly have included all of the cinemas that operated in the Dublin area during the years 1896 to 1975.

While films were shown in many venues over the years we write only about premises that were known to the public as cinemas, be it a shed, mobile fit-up cinema, converted building or a purpose built cinema

Films were also shown in school halls and clubs like the "St. John Bosco Youth Club", on Davitt Road, a hall in St. Ita's Hospital Portrane, the shed in the back garden of the late Albert Kelly's home, where Albert showed films for a penny a go when he was in his early teens. They were also shown in the John Player Theatre in Players Wills on the South Circular Road, the De La Salle School in Ballyfermot. In my own area in Finglas a local man showed films in a shed in his back garden where all my kids were regular customers. We mention the above, just to let you know that we were well aware of the existence of these venues but as they were not proper cinemas we did not include them in our list of cinemas.

While we found quite a bit to say about some of the cinemas on our list, others left us with nothing to write home about and in consequence we simply tell you the name of the cinema, where it stood, perhaps a small ad. or two from a newspaper and hopefully its opening date.

The most outstanding cinema of our research had to be the "Assembly Picture Hall" on Serpentine Avenue, Sandymount, which in the minds of all the people that we spoke and had contact with, it simply never existed. Nobody it appeared had ever heard of this Picture House, yet Patrick and I had proof positive that it did indeed exist. Hopefully our story will awaken a memory or two in someone's mind.

We put advertisements in the windows of local shops, ran articles in newspapers, including the Garda Review and took part in a number of radio interviews. We stopped fellow Golden Oldies in the streets, and probed the minds of some of our fellow researchers in the libraries and archives of Dublin's repositories, but we never once came across anybody that had even remotely heard mention of the Assembly Picture Hall on Serpentine Avenue.

By the time we have this book finished, published and on the shelves of Dublin Libraries, which is our immediate goal, we just might come across somebody with a memory in connection with this picture hall or perhaps we might even stumble on a picture in some newspaper or magazine. In light of this possibility we will reserve a page at the back of our book for updates on this or any other story in our book.

Yours truly,

George P Kearns and Patrick Maguire

HOW THIS BOOK CAME ABOUT

By George P. Kearns.

Patrick Maguire {retired} and yours truly, George Kearns {retired} met in the upstairs section of Pearse Street Library, which houses the Gilbert Library and Dublin City Archives, in January of 2005.

Patrick, I learned, had taken up the research of times past as a hobby and I must say I have never met a person more dedicated to a hobby than Patrick At the same time I was researching the history of some cinemas in relation to my attempt at writing a book about the history of the "Princess Cinema" where I had worked in the 1950s.

At one point in time, I was looking for some information on the showing of "Gone with the Wind" in the Savoy cinema many years ago and when Patrick noticed what I was doing, he started to help me with my research.

One thing led to another and soon he was coming to me with all manner of information on cinemas, and it was then that we made a pact, that when I had finished my book we would both compile the history of all old Dublin cinemas and with some luck publish this in book-form a little later. Little did we realise it at the time but that it would take us almost two years to complete this exercise!

Almost immediately we made a list of all the cinemas we knew about and Pat began his research and yours truly in a reverse role to that, in which we had met, took to feeding him with additional information.

In June of 2005 my book "The Prinner" was published and thank God it managed to make its way onto the shelves of some 52 libraries.

I then joined Patrick fulltime in an intensive research programme and when I say fulltime I mean 24/7. It was agreed from the beginning that although we would both carry out research, Pat with his vast knowledge of books and library procedures would lead the way and by the same token I would do the writing.

Our research took us beyond the beyond and our minds boggled when we came upon cinema after cinema, that most people of today had never heard of. Just to whet your appetite we will name a few, "The Trinity", "Kavanaghs Picture House", and of course, "The Assembly Picture Hall", in Sandymount.

In August of 2006, we managed at last to call a halt to our endeavours and declare the work done, although we are in no doubt, but that we will continue to find more details of cinemas in the foreseeable future.

Our efforts have been mostly enjoyable, but also exasperating, frustrating and at times disheartening, fruitless and depressing. Without exaggeration we feel we have read every newspaper that was ever printed, and visited every library and archive in Dublin including the Registry of Deeds, The Valuations Office, The Company's Registration Office, The Fingal and Dublin County Council Archives.

We have become members of the Fingal and Dublin Public Libraries, The Gilbert Library, The National Library. The Irish Architectural Archives, the National Archives and I wouldn't be at all surprised if the staff members of all those institutions on sighting us entering their thresholds wished it were their day off.

We have visited the site of every cinema that we have written about and where possible interviewed people of an advanced age in the neighbourhoods of Dublin, all local libraries where contacted for information and if we were lucky enough to find a local historian we grilled them unmercifully.

Twenty months on, we have managed to unearth sufficient information on all of the cinemas that once graced the streets of Dublin to at least fill a page on each individual building and we hope that you find the results of our findings at least interesting.

Had we gone a different road we could have earned ourselves a PhD.

In our search into the archives of cinemas past, we came across a church that became a cinema and a cinema that became a church, a building that was built as a cinema but never showed a picture and a dance hall that became a cinema. A cinema where one could gain admission for a fixed amount of marbles, and in another a few jam jars would suffice and yet in another a tram or train ticket was acceptable. We found cinemas with the screen behind the patrons as they entered the auditorium, cinemas where the projector showed the films from behind the screen rather that in front. We found a cinema with the entrance in one street and the auditorium quite a distance away in another street. We found three cinemas that most people believed didn't exist and another that resembled a train carriage, which was installed in a mock railway station complete with porter etc. We took note that some premises served afternoon tea, the price of which was included in the admission fee. We found a cinema in a cellar and another in a coal shed and yet another where the building began its life as a bus garage and waiting room.

George & Patrick

ACKNOWLEDGMENTS AND CREDITS

Where to start and where to begin?

This is without doubt the hardest part of the book to write and no matter what we write we will never be able to say thanks as earnestly as we mean it. We are also very concerned that we might forget to give credit where it's due and if we have left anybody or anything out please, please bear with and forgive us.

For starters we could not have compiled this information without the help of the staff of the Gilbert Library and the Dublin City Council Libraries and Archives. Their understanding and willingness to help us at all times is most commendable and very much appreciated.

On top of which we have been honoured by their invitation to launch our book in their Pearse Street Premises.

Without the permission of the Irish Times and the Irish Independent Group of Newspapers to copy and or paraphrase news items, advertisements and articles about cinemas in their papers over the years, our exercise would have been fruitless.

Our gratitude also extends to the "Evening Mail", "Freeman's Journal"," Irish Press", "Fingal and Drogheda Independent", "The Bioscope magazine, and books and magazines read in the library of the Irish Film Centre. The permission granted by the National Library to copy and use certain pictures and for allowing us to read and research many articles in the Library in particular "The Bioscope magazine". Ditto also to the Irish Architectural Archives, National Archives, the Registration of Companies Office and Fingal County Council Archives and Rathmines Library for the photo of the Sundrive cinema.

The New Link Pearse Street
NewsFour Ringsend
Dalkey Newsletter
Lucan Newsletter
Rush Newsletter
People group of newspapers
Newstalk 106
Anna Livia Radio

We would also like to thank all the individuals that gave us material and information to use in our book, some who allowed us to interview them and others who contributed tales of yesteryear and the many that gave us sound advice over the last eighteen months. Included were:
Jack Benton ex-operator of the Savoy and Strand cinema Balbriggan
Patrick Ging of the Ging family who were the owners of the Tower Cinema Clondalkin
Tony Byrne owner of the Tivoli Theatre Francis Street
Kevin Cunningham who once managed the Green and many other Dublin cinemas
Kevin Harrington for his photo of the Princess Cinema
Kevin Thorp Editor of the Rush Newsletter

Brendan and Raymond Langan for their photo and stories of the Blue Lagoon, Rush
Willie Price
Noel Twamley for his storyline contributions
Paul Bushe of Ranelagh
Sheila Farrell for helping us to prove, that the "Dalkey Cinema" did in fact exist.
Jack Moore for his tour of Malahide and his tales of the "Grand"
Tom Wall for the use of his photographs
Seamus Kearns for allowing us to copy old photos from his book
M. Kinsella of Albert Place
Marc Zimmerman for his photos of the Pavilion and Leinster cinema
Greta de Groat of Stanford University Library for her posters of film "Sold"
Liam and Margaret Grogan owners of the old Portrane cinema property
Bobby Grassic former operator of the Rathcoole cinema
Mary McNally writer and local historian Rathcoole
Mary Muhall Lucan Newsletter
Mrs. Ann Murray for allowing us to paraphrase her late husband Kevins' writings
Sundrive cinema photo from Newspage, Passionist's, Mount Argus
Peter Brady former operator of the Premier for his photo
Jim Sweeney of Lucan Studios for use of photo
Ronald Turner Junior son of the original owner Ronald Rice/Turner
John Carton Rush cinema operator
Kevin Cunningham cinema manager
Jason Faulkner Sketch Artist
Maurice Craig for picture
Patrick Flanagan for the copy of the 'Articles of Association' of the Brunswick
Maureen Grant Olympia for her story
Bernie Archivist Heritage Centre Swords
David Griffin Irish Architectural Archives
Bob Monks National Library
Vincent P. Lynch for his memories of the Leinster and Rialto cinemas
The late Albert Kelly

We would also like to mention our gratitude, albeit posthumously, to the DMP Superintendent of E Division Rathmines who advised his superior officers that there was indeed a second cinema in operation on Serpentine Avenue, in the year of 1922.

We also received items of news, pictures and programmes from people who knew not where they had come from, we therefore cannot credit a source, so once again we would say thanks to the anonymous owners.

We also came across a number of individuals who were of tremendous help to us but being the decent souls that they were they would not allow us to publicly thank them and of course those that we may have overlooked or perhaps mislaid their names.
Thank you, Thank you, and Thank you.

A CINEMA IN DISGUISE

We read an article in the Irish Independent, which was written by a Victor M. Wood's who proudly proclaimed himself to be an old Dubliner who was simply reminiscing about the Dublin of yesteryear and as fellow old Dubliners we follow in his well worn footsteps and retell his tale of a cinema in Henry Street in our own words.

However, when we say cinema we really should have said screen, because that was really all it was in its early days. According to the good Victor it didn't even have seats.

It would appear that back in the late 1880s there was a shop in Henry Street called Samuel's Bazaar, which was an open fronted shop and was also referred to as the $6^{1/2}$d shop. Victor believed that it was a forerunner of the famous Woolworth Store that was to follow at a later date, as the 6d shop sold all sorts of goods including light hardware, crockery, and novelties at very low prices.

The building also housed a waxworks, which was similar in lines to that of Madame Tussaud's of London and lay upstairs in a large upper room. At the end of this room was a small stage where variety turns and marionette shows were given. At Christmas time, the marionette shows sometimes included a whole pantomime.

The admission prices which also included entry to the 'Waxworks' were a penny for children and threepence for adults and of course as already mentioned, there were no seats and all had to stand. Nobody however cared or complained as great entertainment was being provided for little cost.

At the back of the stage adorning the bare wall was a small white screen where on many occasions Victor as a young boy enjoyed many an "Animated or Living Picture" as they were referred to in those early days of Cinematograph Exhibitions and he was both amazed and thrilled to be able to witness people walking around London.

The Proprietor of the premises was none other than Councillor James an American who was also High Sheriff of the City of Dublin. However, Councillor and Mrs James who had no children were very charitable people and they adopted a very pretty young woman who was a midget. She had a very sweet voice and would at times entertain an audience by singing on the stage.

In between performances and at other times, she would serve behind the shop counter and would use a high stool in order to deal with customers. She was very popular and was well known as "Marcella the Midget Queen".

The $6^{1/2}$d shop, Cinema and Waxworks were all burnt down during the 1916 Rising and nothing further is known of that happy family.

(See story on Worlds Fair Henry Street)

A FULL PAGE OF ADVERTISEMENTS
Courtesy of the "Evening Press" September 27th 1967

Gaiety
LAST 4 SHOWS
Maureen Potter
GAELS OF LAUGHTER '67
Coming Attraction !
DUBLIN THEATRE FESTIVAL
MARIE KEAN
O'FLAHERTY V.C.
THE WORDS UPON THE WINDOW-PANE
Commencing Monday, 9th Oct. 8 p.m.
DUBLIN THEATRE FESTIVAL
LAUGH BUT LISTEN WELL
ABBEY THEATRE
INTERNATIONAL THEATRE SEMINAR
GATE
LOVERS
DUBLIN THEATRE FESTIVAL
THE ORDER OF MELCHIZEDEK
JOE LYNCH
EDWIN RICHFIELD
THE GOOSE

OLYMPIA
MIXED SPICE
DUBLIN THEATRE FESTIVAL
FRANKENSTEIN
ANTIGONE
NOW BOOKING
FOR ONE WEEK ONLY
THE QUICK AND THE DEAD
By HUGH LEONARD and ANNA MANAHAN
NOW BOOKING
APOLLO, Walkinstown
STELLA
MY FAIR LADY
STELLA
ORMONDE
RITZ
HAWAII
KENILWORTH, Harold's Cross
BROKEN LANCE
CLASSIC
A Countess From Hong Kong

EBLANA
LAST WEEK
THE GOOD OLDE DAYS
EBLANA
DUBLIN THEATRE FESTIVAL
JIM NORTON
THE ZOO STORY
with O. Z. Whitehead
Mon. to Wed. inclusive
SEAMUS FORDE
LIAM SWEENEY
Please Break The Glass Gently
Thurs. to Sat. inclusive
MAY CLUSKEY
THE NOON-DAY DEVIL
EXCURSION TO BELFAST AND PORTADOWN
GRAFTON CINEMA
GO CIE
Grosvenor
BALLADS CASTLE INN
TRACY
GRAND HOTEL, MALAHIDE

METROPOLE
LAST 2 DAYS
HOW TO SUCCEED IN BUSINESS WITHOUT REALLY TRYING
FRIDAY!
GEORGY GIRL
CORINTHIAN
LAST 2 DAYS
THE HILLS RUN RED
The Beatles In HELP!
FRIDAY NEXT
Gene Barry
Elsa Martinelli
Leslie Phillips
Cyd Charisse
MAROC 7
FILM CENTRE
HOPE & BALL
FACTS OF LIFE
TERROR IN A TEXAS TOWN
PLAZA CINERAMA
Ireland's most beautiful and luxurious theatre opens with a GALA PREMIERE
"FABULOUS!"
"ELECTRIFYING!"
Grand Prix
TOMORROW at 8 p.m.
FRIDAY
SANDFORD, Ranelagh
TALK OF THE TOWN CABARET

Capitol
THE DEADLY AFFAIR
Friday Next
SHENANDOAH
Michael Caine in
THE IPCRESS FILE
AMBASSADOR
LAST 2 DAYS
THE SAND PEBBLES
Friday Next
THE GREAT ESCAPE
STEVE McQUEEN
JAMES GARDNER
RICHARD ATTENBOROUGH
ACADEMY
Dirk Bogarde
Stanley Baker
Jacqueline Sassard
ACCIDENT
REGENT
A MAN FOR ALL SEASONS
INTERNATIONAL
10.30 P.M. Summer
BALLADS
JESSE OWENS
Clontarf Castle
LIMELIGHT

SAVOY
2nd Week Of Sizzling Suspense!!
THE PROFESSIONALS
ADELPHI
FRIDAY
THE FAMILY WAY
ADELPHI
GREEN
7 BRIDES FOR 7 BROTHERS
JANE POWELL
HOWARD KEEL
PARKSIDE HOTEL

CARLTON
WARNING SHOT
FRIDAY
2 BIG GANGSTER THRILLERS
Ernest Borgnine
PAY OR DIE
Barry Sullivan
THE PURPLE GANG
Astor
LAST 2 DAYS!
THE SNOWS OF KILIMANJARO
FRIDAY NEXT
OTHELLO
It's Heaven on Earth
ROYAL STARLIGHT HOTEL
GARDA CLUB
TONIGHT
OLLIE MALONEY
ALTONAIRES
AGS
JOHNNY FLYNN
RULESTOWN FRIDAY
JACK RUANE
GLENALBYN ATHLETIC CLUB
For its OPENING TONIGHT presents THE CYCLONES
NATIONAL
SATURDAY NIGHT NEXT
JACKPOTS
NATIONAL
ALTONAIRES
ERNE HOEDOWNERS
CASINO
PALM BEACH SATURDAY NEXT
TELEVISION CLUB SAT. THE CADETS
ROSE MARIE
McGOVERNS
THE WEE FOLK

CINERAMA
NOW ON ITS 2nd YEAR!
THE SOUND OF MUSIC
CHARIOT
Charioteers
WE 4
The Ould Triangle Folk Club
EMBANKMENT
YOUR PHONE CALL

A STORY WITHIN A STORY
Begging the question "Which ship was it?"

In our search for facts on the wood panelling and doors etc. used in the construction of the La Scalla Theatre restaurant, lounge and ballroom, we came across a number of ships names and each was said to be the liner in question. However, in our search for truth, we dug into the history of the three names mentioned and the following are our findings.

THE BRITANNIA

Barney Markey retired as manager of the Capitol Cinema in January of 1967 and in an interview with a reporter from the "Evening Press" he mentioned the maple and oak wood panelling in the upstairs restaurant which, he said, once adorned the walls of the state rooms in the Belfast built "Britannia". We immediately assumed that he either meant the Britannic or that the spelling was simply a typographical error. However, true to form, we checked up on the RMS Britannia which turned out to be a Paddle Steamer in the 1840's.

This ship which was built in Greenock, Scotland and launched on February 5th 1840, made her maiden voyage from Liverpool to Halifax and was the first passenger carrying cruise ship for the Cunard Line with one of its first passengers being Charles Dickens. The Britannia travelled back and forth with fare paying passengers for many a year, but was eventually sold to the German Navy in 1849 and was renamed the "Barbarosa". Later again, having served her purpose, she was used as a target for experimental torpedo attacks and was sunk in 1880.

~~~~~

THE MAURETANIA

There were two ships of that name and both belonged to the Cunard lines. The first was built by the Tyneside firm Swan Hunter and Wigham Richardson and she was launched in 1906. She was a sister ship to the "Lusitania". She made her maiden voyage from Liverpool to New York on November 16th 1907. She was driven by a steam turbine engine, which enabled her to reach speeds sufficient enough to enter the "Blue Ribbon" records. She also did a stint as a troop and hospital ship during W.W. 1. In 1921 due to a fire she underwent repairs in Southampton where her power was converted to fuel oil. Her last Atlantic run took place in 1934 and she was then withdrawn from service. She rested in a dock in Southampton for almost a year when a decision was made in 1935 to have her scrapped. Her fixtures and fittings were auctioned off on the Southampton Docks on May 14th 1935 and were reputedly bought by Sir Charles Boot an English building tycoon.

Sir Charles Boot created Pinewood Film Studios in 1934 and they were built on the 156 acre estate of Heatherden Hall, near Iver Heath, Buckinghamshire by the Henry Boot Company of Sheffield. Sir Charles, J. Arthur Rank and the 'Jute' heiress Lady Yule formed a company to run the studios and they opened for business on September 30th 1935.
~~~~~

The first film produced at the studio was "London Melody" while "Talk of the Devil" which was directed by Carol Reed was the first film to be made entirely at Pinewood.

Heatherden Hall was a Mansion on the estate that required extensive refurbishing and it was said that the fixtures and fittings from the "Mauretania" were used in the reconstruction of this building.

It is also interesting to note that Heatherden Hall was the location for the signing of the Irish Free State Treaty in 1929.

In 1934 the White Star Line merged with the Cunard Line.

When the Elstree studios went on fire in 1936, its owners, British and Dominion film Studios, invested the insurance payout in a 50% share in Pinewood.

The first Bond movie "Dr. No" was produced by Pinewood Studios.

MAURETANIA 11

This second Mauretania, which also belonged to the Cunard line, was launched in 1938 and she too made her maiden voyage from Liverpool to New York just like her predecessor. She also was pressed into service as a troop and hospital ship in World War II. After the war she returned to her original duties, and was late scrapped in 1965.

THE BRITANNIC

The most likely candidate (in our opinion)

The Britannic was built by Harland and Wolff in their Belfast Shipyards in 1914 and was almost at the end of her fitting out period when she was requisitioned by the Admiralty for use as a hospital ship, during World War 1. Before setting sail for Liverpool where she was to be fitted out and repainted with three large red crosses as a hospital ship, Harland and Wolff stripped her of her luxury panelling and stored it in Belfast.

When refitted she was capable of carrying 3,300 casualties and a medical staff and crew of 1,000. Her maiden voyage was made from Liverpool to the Mediterranean where she began her service as a hospital ship.

As we have already told the story of the "Britannic" in our history of the "Capitol" cinema it would be unfair of us to repeat same. We would however make known the following facts and mention our source of information on the use of the fixtures of the Britannic in the construction of the restaurant, lounge and ballroom in the La Scalla Theatre Complex and the reasons for our strong belief that the fittings did indeed come from the "Britannic".

(a) The Builders of the La Scalla Theatre, J & R Thompson had offices in both Dublin and Belfast and would most likely have had knowledge of local architectural salvage yards in both counties and would surely be advised of any building materials being auctioned off in the areas.

(b) Barney Markey when interviewed by a reporter from the "Evening Press" on his retirement in January 1967, made reference to the panelling of the restaurant having been taken from the Belfast ship the "Britannia". We believe he meant to say the "Britannic" as the "Britannia" was a Scottish built ship. Of course the spelling of the name could have resulted from a typographical error.

(c) The fact that, as the "Britannic" had been built in Belfast and stripped of her luxury fittings there, which had been put in a local storage facility.

(d) The fact that, as the "Britannic" had sunk, its fixtures and fittings were no longer required by its owners or Harland and Wolff.

(e) An article in the "Irish Times" on Thursday January 4th 1923 where the writer described the La Scalla Theatre and Opera House as one of Dublin's new buildings, went on to mention that special interest attaches to the woodwork, panels and doors used throughout the building as all this material, he wrote, was originally intended for the White Star liner, the "Britannic", which had sunk at sea while on duty as a hospital during W.W.I.

(f) Hearsay and our own belief that the material did come from the "Britannic".

(g) That the fittings of the "Mauretania" had gone to "Pinewood Studio" and the fact that she had been scrapped too late for her fittings to have been used in the construction of the La Scalla Theatre.

~~~~~

OLYMPIC

It might also be interesting to note that the fittings from the scrapped "Olympic" ended up in the "White Swan Hotel" in Bondgate, Alnwick, England.

It would also appear that the fittings and fixtures from scrapped luxury liners were a major marketing item when these ships were being scrapped.

The "Olympic" was the first of three large luxury liners which were built by Harland and Wolff for their client the White Star Line. The other two of course were the "Titanic" and the "Britannic". All ships were described as "Olympic Class Ships".

The "Olympic" was launched on October 20th 1910 and was the first Transatlantic Liner to have a Swimming Pool. She too served in World War I and earned the name "Old Reliable". In April 1935 she was laid up alongside the Britannic in Southampton and was also scrapped in that year.
~~~~~

A.O.H CINEMA
31 Parnell Square

The A.O.H cinema opened on Monday night October 4th 1920 featuring a silent film drama Starring Pauline Frederick and Robert Cain.

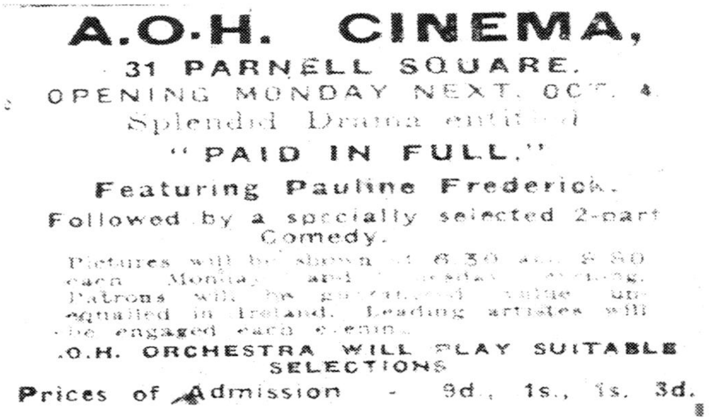
A.O.H. CINEMA,
31 PARNELL SQUARE.
OPENING MONDAY NEXT, OCT. 4.
Splendid Drama entitled
"PAID IN FULL."
Featuring Pauline Frederick.
Followed by a specially selected 2-part Comedy.
Pictures will be shown at 6.30 and 8.30 each Monday and [illegible] evening. Patrons will be [illegible] value unequalled in Ireland. Leading artistes will be engaged each evening.
.O.H. ORCHESTRA WILL PLAY SUITABLE SELECTIONS
Prices of Admission - 9d., 1s., 1s. 3d.

Paid in Full was a story about a bookkeeper (Robert Cain) who stole money from his boss and in desperation he turned to his beautiful wife (Pauline Frederick) to get him out of the mess he had got himself into.

This film which consisted of 5 reels is now considered lost and is not to be confused with similar named films made in1950 and 2002.

While not much is known of Robert Cain, Pauline Frederick is remembered in the history of film as one of the greatest and most powerful actresses of the screen. She began her acting career on the stage and was in her thirties when she got her first break in silent movies and here she excelled. She was usually cast in the roles of strong and powerful women and later as self-sacrificing mothers and these parts she made her own. While the beautiful Pauline was most successful in the "talkies" she is best remembered for her silent film roles.

The 1950 version of "Paid in Full" was a soap/drama movie. This was a story of two sisters falling in love with the same man, starring Robert Cummins as handsome Bill, Lizabeth Scott as Jane and Dianna Lynn as her sister Nancy.

The 2002 version was a drama/action movie, about the drugs scene in the 1980's Harlem District starring Wood Harris as Ace and Esal Morales as Lulu. Plotline: A Drug Baron has a crisis of conscience.

A view of the A.O.H building in Parnell Square as it stands in 2005.
Barely discernable over the first floor windows are what's left of the A.O.H lettering.

The A.O.H. didn't stay in the cinema business too long. Some years after its official opening as a cinema, management began to hold dances in the hall and as they grew in popularity, it was decided to convert to a full time dance hall.

When the initial application for a Cinematograph licence was made, Parnell was known as Rutland Square. The change of name came about on April 3rd 1933. The Irish National Foresters Co. were the then owners of the cinema which could seat 432 persons. In its favour when applying for a licence was the fact that their projector was safely contained in a fire-proof concrete enclosure and was suitably ventilated by external air.

ADELPHI
Abbey Street

On Friday January 13th 1939 Dublin's newest picture palace the Adelphi opened its door to a representative audience specially invited to this grand opening. Friday the 13th it would seem didn't cause management any concern and nobody paid any heed to this date and the opening ceremony went off without a hitch. There was seating for 2,300 people and the cinema appeared to have two entrances, the main one being in Abbey Street and the other in Princess Street, although these doors were more likely used as an exit, rather than an entrance.

The cinema also had a well appointed café which was under the management of Miss Marie Brady (formerly of the United Services Club) and the cinema provided good employment for a large staff, consisting of six cashiers, fourteen usherettes, two pages, seven ushers and eleven cleaners, not to mention the operating staff and management. J. H. Hamilton was the manager and Kevin J. Browne was his assistant.

In the Projection room were the latest Ross Projectors, which were fitted with R.C.A. sound equipment and supplementary to the film projectors were two spot-light projectors and a bi-unial lantern for showing slides. The Chief projectionist was M. O'Toole who previously held a similar position in the Green Cinema.

The opening night feature film was "The Adventures of Robin Hood" starring Errol Flynn, Olivia De Havilland, Basil Rathbone and Claude Rains.

This movie was filmed in the early days of Technicolor and was so effectively done that a movie critic felt it was safe to make a forecast that night, to the effect that within a period of three years all big pictures would be filmed in colour. Some of the scenes, he said, made possible by this new advance in colour technique are almost indescribably beautiful.

While the Adelphi was in all practical terms a cinema it did have a stage proper and over the years played host to many famous show-business people and groups including the "Beatles" on November 7th 1963.

This appearance of the Beatles caused a serious riot in the city that night when some of the hundreds of fans who failed to get in ran riot through the city streets, breaking windows, and overturning cars. The costs ran to thousands and many people were injured.

The Adelphi enjoyed a good run right into late 1969 when it was decided to convert it into a multi screen cinema, which was inline with the new trend in cinemas. The cinema closed in September of that year, work began and on October 8th 1970 the Adelphi opened in a blaze of colour with three screens, which were advertised as screens 1, 2 and 3, each with a different feature film. For the first week the films available were listed as, Screen 1 "Kelly's Heroes" starring Clint Eastwood, Screen 2 "Chisum" with John Wayne and Screen 3 "Z" with Yves Montand.

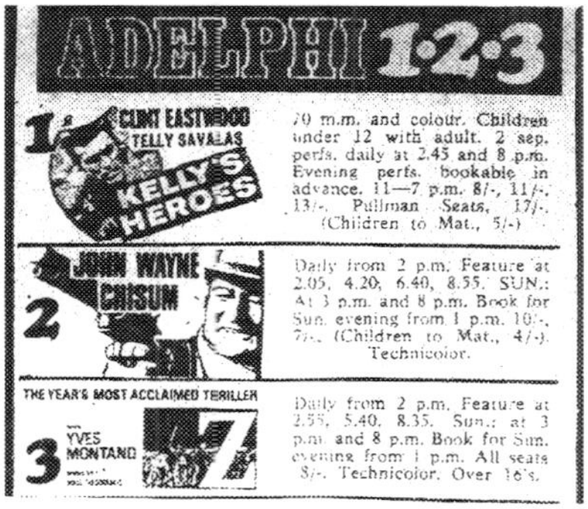

"Charmers": On the night of the Gala Opening which was attended by the then Taoiseach, Jack Lynch, was an added attraction in the shape of the final for a Charm Contest. Before the contest was held the finalists sold brochures to the members of the audience. The proceeds of these sales were in aid of the Variety Club. The three winning contestants were taken on a tour of Elstree Studios, London, stayed in the Hilton and went night-clubbing as "The Adelphi Charmers".

One of the many programmes distributed over the years by the Adelphi Management, advertising their next attraction.

Harry Lush was the new manager of the Multi-screened Adelphi

The Adelphi also provided some terrific stage shows over the years featuring names like, the "Rolling Stones" "Johnny Cash" "The Beechboys" "Gene Pitney", and many, many more.

A sketch of the layout of the new Adelphi and its three separate cinemas;

Adelphi 1, formerly the balcony, with seating for 614
Adelphi 2, formerly the stalls, seats 1,052 persons and
Adelphi 3, formerly the restaurant, held 360.

(Photo circa 1995)

Thursday, October 8th 1970 was the chosen date for the official opening of the new "Adelphi 1, 2, 3 cine-complex which was Ireland's first triple cinema. It was opened in the presence of An Taoiseach, Jack Lynch and was by invitation only. On Friday 9th it was open to the public.

Each cinema was installed with the most sophisticated air conditioning equipment, which was thermostatically controlled and it was claimed, would prove to be most beneficial to non-smokers. The projection and sound systems in these three modern cinemas were adaptable for any form of screen presentation then available and for any future screen presentations.

On Friday November 23rd 1973 a fourth screen was opened by subdividing screen 2.

In 1976 the Adelphi cinema was fire bombed along with other cinemas and pubs in the area. These explosions took place on Monday morning August 30th and political circles believed it was the work of "loyalist terrorists"

In all six premises were badly damaged in these attacks and the damage was estimated at over £1 million pounds. The Ambassador, a seventh target, escaped harm when the incendiary device failed to go off. These devices are no bigger that a 20 cigarette packet and could be disguised in any type of parcel of that size and would be most likely well hidden. The

Gardai advised caution and warned members of the public that these devices could be booby trapped.

The Premises involved were the;

Adelphi cinema, seriously damaged
Carlton cinema, minor damage
Suffolk House Pub, badly damaged
Abbey Mooney Pub, destroyed
Parnell Mooney Pub, seriously damaged
Earl Mooney Pub, slightly damaged
Ambassador cinema, no damage

Repair work began immediately on the Adelphi and it reopened ten days later on September 10th 1976.

The Adelphi closed on November 30th 1995 to make room for the expansion of Arnotts and a modern multi storied car park.

The last two films shown were "Gigi" & "High Society".

The Adelphi closed on November 30th 1995 and for its grand finale it displayed five new releases and two golden oldies.

"Clueless" (1995) with Alicia Silverstone, Stacey Dash and Brittany Murphy

"Nine Months" (1995) with Hugh Grant and Julianne Moore

"Under Siege 2" (1995) with Steven Seagal and Eric Bogosian

"Apollo 13" (1995) with Tom Hanks and Bill Paxton

"French Kiss" (1995) with Meg Ryan and Kevin Kline

And the last night "golden oldies" specials were;

"Gigi" (1958) with Leslie Caron, Maurice Chevalier and Louis Jourdan

"High Society" (1956) with Bing Crosby, Frank Sinatra, Grace Kelly, Celeste Holm, John Lund and Louis Armstrong, which left us with such musical memories as;

"Well did you Evah" by Bing and Frank, "High So-ci-ety" by Louis Armstrong, "True Love" by Grace and Bing and "Now that's jazz" by Bing and Louis.

(Pictures and programmes courtesy Dublin City Libraries)

ADELPHI
Dun Laoghaire

The Adelphi cinema Dun Laoghaire opened on Saturday night November 29th 1947 to a huge audience with the film "Night and Day" which starred Cary Grant and Alexis Smith. The proceeds of this gala performance were donated to the Vincent De Paul Society and the Mount Street Club.

This new enterprise was under the management of T.J. Lawler who had some considerable cinema experience in Dublin. It was also one of the first suburban Dublin cinemas to have a café attached.

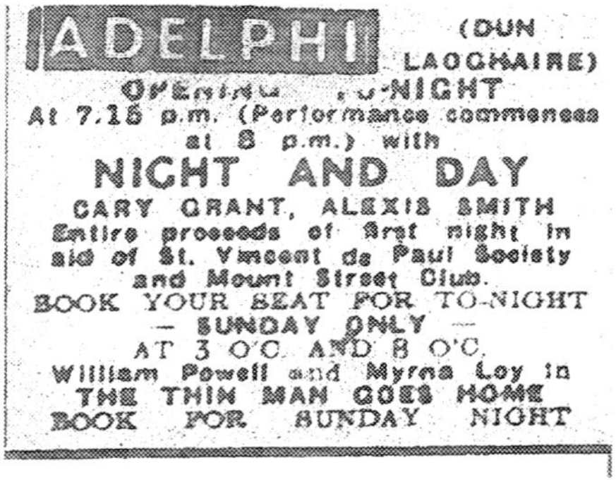

This new place of entertainment was much appreciated by the locals of Dun Laoghaire who flocked to its every change of performance, and its café was very popular

The cinema was spacious in design and had seating accommodation for 1,620 persons. A sizeable place indeed one might remark which befitted a town such as Dun Laoghaire.

The Adelphi served the community well and always showed the best of films. Management, it would appear, had excellent taste. In September 1954 it changed over to Cinemascope in order to show the film "Knights of the Round Table" starring Robert Taylor as Sir Lancelot, who was banished from King Arthur's Court for falling in love with Guinevere, played by Ava Gardner.

In 1971 after 24 years of service the Adelphi finally closed its doors on May 16th and the last film featured was "My Fair Lady" starring Rex Harrison as an elocutionist who trained and made a common young flower girl, played by Audrey Hepburn, into a Lady.

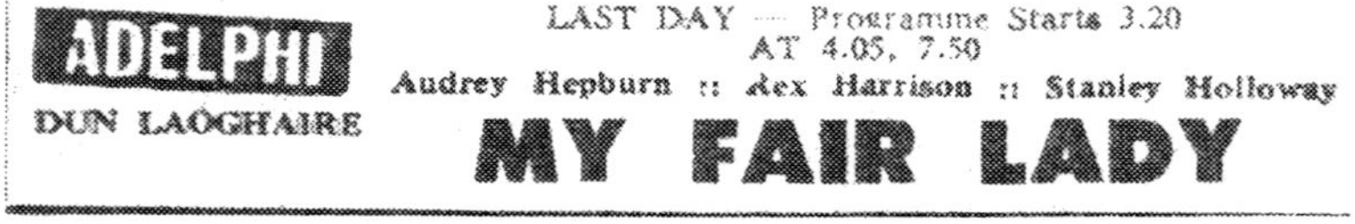

A beautiful musical with great songs such as; "On the Street Where You Live" "I Could Have Danced All Night" "Get Me to the Church on Time" and "Wouldn't it be Lovely"

The building lay idle for many years but was finally demolished in 1978.

APOLLO CINEMAS
The Apollo cinemas
Sundrive Road, Walkinstown and Dundrum

These adds for all three Apollo cinemas appeared in the Evening Herald on Wednesday May 13th 1964, and its worth noting that the Sundrive Apollo was now specialising in Bingo Games.

The Apollo cinema group may well have begun with the opening of the "Cameo" cinema in Grafton Street which may have been the first cinema venture in Dublin by the Kearns brothers, George and Leo.

On October 10th they followed their success with a new cinema in Walkinstown when they opened the "Apollo" cinema on Friday October 16th 1953.

The owners now known as "Walkinstown Enterprises Ltd." spared no expense on the building of this most modern picture house, which was on a par with any other cinema in the city.

Massive housing development schemes were well underway in the Walkinstown area at that time which will soon provided a good catchment area for this new enterprise.

On the left is an advertisement by John Smith the builder who was or is about to become a partner/director in the Kearns's company/s.

This new cinema seats 1,000 people and instead of a balcony it is styled in the manner of a stadium, which holds 300 people and the stalls 700 people.

A feature of the cinema is its cooling system. During summer months a change of air takes place eight times an hour.

The opening night film was "Never Take No for an Answer".

* * * * *

This is a film about a small boy, 'Peppino' who has a sick Donkey and was refused permission by the local Pardre to take his ailing donkey to the grave of St Francis of Assisi in search of a cure.

Refusing to take no for an answer, he makes a long gruelling journey with his sick donkey from his hometown of Assisi to the Vatican in Rome where he hopes to get permission from the "Pope" to visit the crypt of St Francis.

* * * * *

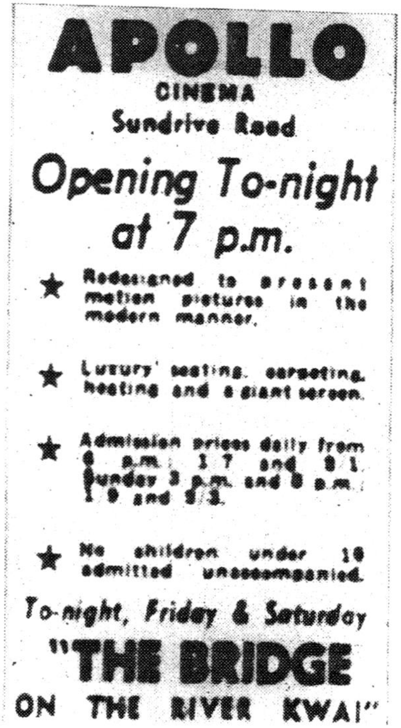

In 1954 the Kearns brothers, now trading as the Kilmainham Cinema Company with John Smith as a fellow director took over the running of the Sundrive Cinema and some years later they closed the cinema for remodelling and reopened it as the Apollo on February 7th 1959.

A new giant screen had been installed and the cinema could now present pictures in the most modern way. New carpets had been fitted, together with plush new seating and the heating and air conditioning systems were all upgraded.

The opening film was "The Bridge on the River Kwai", directed by David Lean and starred Alec Guinness, Sessue Hayakawa and William Holden.

* * * * *

The story of the film was based on a book of the same name, was fictional, but was based on the real life sufferings of Allied soldiers, who as prisoners of war, were forced to work by the Japanese Forces on the 1943 building of a railway line, that stretched for some 258 miles across Burma and Thailand.

The Bridge over the River Kwai, near Tamarkan, was just one of many such bridges that supported the tracks of the railway as it passed over river after river.

It is said that over 100,000 conscripted Asian workers and 16,000 allied prisoners of war died on the whole project.

* * * * *

Friday night April 21st, 1961, saw the company open its third and last cinema in Dublin and it too was christened the Apollo. The site of this new Apollo once housed the Odeon cinema in Dundrum, which closed on June 1st 1959.

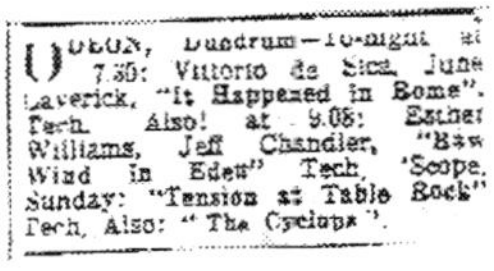

ODEON, Dundrum—To-night at 7.30: Vittorio de Sica, June Laverick, "It Happened in Rome". Tech. Also! at 9.08: Esther Williams, Jeff Chandler, "Raw Wind in Eden" Tech. 'Scope. Sunday: "Tension at Table Rock" Tech. Also: "The Cyclops".

This ad appeared in an evening paper on May 30th 1959 and as no more ads appeared after that time we could only assume that the Odeon closed on that Sunday. We are also unsure of when the Apollo group took over this cinema. Did they, for instance, take over immediately and change the name to the Apollo at a later date or did the cinema close for two years? If they had simply continued to run the Odeon as it was for a while, it would have been in keeping with their take-over of the Sundrive cinema.

Their opening film "High Time" was another easy going movie starring Bing Crosby, who mixes big business activities, widowhood, fatherhood, making the grades in college and falling in love again - a wonderful, happy and easygoing experience. One of the better feel-good movies of the time.

* * * * *

Bing plays the part of widowed Harvey Howard, a Millionaire Hamburger Restaurateur franchiser in his fifties, who against the wishes of his grown up son Harvey Jr., played by Angus Duncan and daughter Laura, played by Nina Shipman, decides to return to college where he falls in live with his French Professor, Helena Gautier played by Nicole Maurey. Fabrian and Tuesday Weld also star

Despite this being a musical comedy Bing only gets to sing two songs; the first when he falls in love and sings "The Second Time Around" and the second being "It Came upon a Midnight Clear" which he sings during a Christmas time hay-ride.

* * * * *

The Closing of the Apollos

While we don't have accurate closing dates, we have had to put two and two together and try to make four ,by searching for the last advertisements to appear in the newspapers. While some cinema owners added a rider to their last advertisement announcing the closure of the cinema, others just closed their doors.

What appears to be the last advertisement for the Apollo cinema, Sundrive Road.

The Apollo then became a Bingo hall and remained as such until its closure in 2004 when it was demolished to make way for apartments and a public house.

The Sundrive ad appeared in the "Evening Herald" on May 12th, 1964'

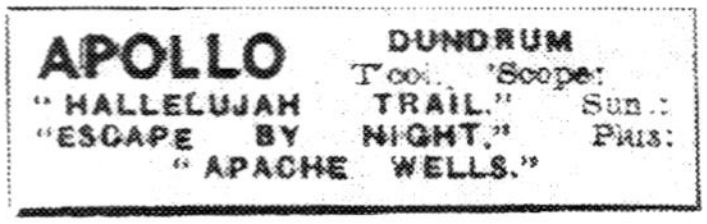

The Apollo Dundrum ad appeared on February 25th, 1967 and again we assumed it closed on Sunday, February 26th, 1967

* * * * *

Escape by night starred Terence Longdon, Jennifer Jayne, Harry Fowler and Peter Sallis; it was directed by Montgomery Tully and told the story of the hi-jacking of a bus loaded with prisoners on their way to jail, by a gang who wanted to free one of the prisoners.

Having freed their friend the gang then locked the driver of the bus and the rest of the prisoners in a barn, which they then doused with petrol and with threats of setting the place alight, they then made their escape. However their prisoner friend was killed when his car crashes and the rest of the film is about the police backtracking the gang's movements in order to rescue the people in the petrol soaked barn, before it goes on fire.

* * * * *

APOLLO, Walkinstown — "Angels From Hell". Also: "Face of Evil". Sun., "Watch Your Stern", plus "Operation Bikini".

The last ad for the Walkinstown Apollo dated Tuesday May 25th, 1974.

The new Sundrive Cinema which has just been opened at Kimmage.

The Apollo/Sundrive is now well underway to being a pub and an apartment block, the Apollo Walkinstown is long gone, while the Dundrum Apollo building pictured above still stands. This picture was taken on Sunday October 23rd, 2005.

In the early sixties, the Apollo Group provided cine-variety shows, but it would appear that there was no way of distracting people from their new found home entertainment via the television set.

ASSEMBLY PICTURE HALL
Serpentine Avenue,
Sandymount, Ballsbridge
Our Mystery Cinema

This cinema, which was one of two cinemas situated on Serpentine Avenue, Sandymount began to take on an air of mystery, simply because nobody seems to know anything about it, including George who was born and reared in the area.

He did of course know of the Ritz, known affectionately to one and all as the "Shack" and the "Regal" cinema in Ringsend, but never the Assembly Picture Hall. Asking around we were told, "ah yes the Assembly rooms, that was in Pearse Street at the back of the Palace cinema". While there was an Assembly Room in Pearse Street at the back of the Palace, it was not the one we sought. Without doubt, according to Thom's directories there was an Assembly Picture Hall in Sandymount, and here began our first serious attempt at investigative journalism. Little did we know at the time just what we were letting ourselves in for, and how difficult it would be to track down a building that nobody had ever heard of.

However, all this investigative work paid off in the end because we eventually found evidence of the existence of the Assembly Picture Hall, and in the course of our investigations we uncovered news, advertisements and articles about other cinemas that we never knew or heard of.

Our first big break came when we found this advertisement for the Assembly Picture Hall in the year of 1913.

ASSEMBLY PICTURE HALL
SERPENTINE AVENUE, SANDYMOUNT.
NOTICE—From 23rd June Continuous Performance,
SATURDAY, 3.30 to 5
Admission—6d. and 3d. .... Reserved Seats, 1s.

This is the first advertisement for the Assembly Picture Hall that we could find, and proof positive that the Hall actually existed. It also clearly states that the Hall was situated on Serpentine Avenue. We found this ad. in the "Evening Mail" of June 21st 1913. Unfortunately for us it did not give a house or building number.

Because of the way this advertisement was worded, we were of a mind that it signified the opening date of the Assembly Picture Hall. While it may well have been a notice heralding its official opening, we now know that the hall had shown pictures as early as 1912, because we came across an article written in the Bioscope cinema magazine in October 1912 that informed us that a "Izidore Isaac Bradlaw" had temporarily leased this building in 1912 in order to show pictures on an occasional basis and that may well have been the forerunner of the Assembly Picture Hall.

While it was mentioned in the Trade section of Thom's directories for many years, it was only ever referred to as the Assembly Picture Hall, Sandymount, and the reference never gave a properly numbered address.

This picture house was proving to be a hard find for us and we searched high and low in our efforts to pin point the exact address of this Picture House, a Picture House I would remind you that nobody appears to have heard of, including a firm of Film Distributors and a number of Sandymount residents of a certain age.

In sheer desperation we first put an advertisement in the Newsagency shop on Serpentine Avenue asking for help in identifying the exact whereabouts of this cinema, and we followed this up with an article in the June 05 edition of NewsFour the local Ringsend, Irishtown and Sandymount Free Community newspaper.

In late April 2005 we were invited to give a talk on the Anna Livia radio about our forthcoming book and once again we pleaded for help in finding this picture house.

We were also featured in the Northside and Southside People newspapers and met with Declan Carthy when he was out and about on the streets of Dublin on behalf of "Newstalk". We also sought the help of the Garda Siochana by featuring our missing cinema in an article in the April 2005 issue of the Garda Review, Volume 33 No 3. But all to no avail. Not a clue was found; indeed up to the time of writing this piece towards the end of August 2005 we have not had one reply that favoured the existence of the Assembly Picture Hall in Sandymount.

We stopped fellow oldies on the streets of Sandymount, paid a visit to all the libraries in and adjacent to the area, checked with the Valuations office, the National Archives, The National Library, The RDS library in Ballsbridge, and had the cheek to write and phone a number of residents on Serpentine Avenue in our search for this venue. We left nothing to chance and let nothing deter us in our search.

In the files of the Pembroke Urban District Council, which are held in the D.C.C. Archives we found written records of letters which had been sent from the Council to the cinema owners and ditto from the owners to the Council proving once again that this cinema did exist, however not one of the letters carried a street number for the premises.

One of these letters, dated August 2nd, 1913 acknowledged receipt of the cinema licence it had applied for and in the same letter the owners asked for a refund of the deposit they had lodged in regards to the supply of Electric Light .On April 29th, 1915 Thomas O Neill wrote to the Council lighting department and complained that the owners of the cinema were paying full rates for their electricity supply. He sought a reduction in the scale of charges and the Council agreed to a 12.5 % discount for motive power to the Assembly Picture Hall on condition that the account was paid weekly. In all we have photocopies of some letters, all addressed to or from the Assembly Cinema Theatre or Picture Hall on Serpentine Avenue, but not one with a street number. However because of the aforementioned letter of August 2nd we now knew that if nothing else the Assembly Picture Hall was an officially recognised and licensed cinema. Our quest continues.

We were also advised on numerous occasions that we had the wrong picture house in mind and that the "Shack" picture house was the only picture house on Serpentine Avenue - if only that had been true. However, to the best of our knowledge the "Shack" picture house was not in existence as early as 1912-1913. (See story of the Ritz).

In 1919 two cinemas were operating on Serpentine Avenue one of which was the Assembly Picture Hall managed by a James O'Neill whose residential address was given as 59a Serpentine Avenue. The other cinema was situated in the grounds of 84 Serpentine Avenue, which was also known as the Elmerville and this cinema appeared to be a simple shed where matinee pictures were shown at weekends. It would appear that this cinema was operating incognito, in so far as the officers of the local Dublin Metropolitan Police station were concerned, as they appeared to be unaware of its existence, which had to mean that this cinema was not licensed in accordance with the 1909 Cinematograph Act. This came to our attention when we were trawling through some records belonging to the Department of Justice in relation to cinema licences and we came across a file entitled "Military operations and censorship of films" dated July 1922. In this file we found details of a direction issued by the Press Censor that was to be served on all licensed cinemas in the Dublin Area.

This direction allowed for a General Beasley of Military Operations to introduce a notice of censorship on all war related films in July of 1922, which was to be served on all cinemas in the Dublin Metropolitan area without delay. He further directed that these notices were to be hand-served on the owners/managers of the cinemas by a local uniformed DMP officer and that he be furnished by return with a signed affidavit from this officer stating the name of the person so served with this notice. He also requested that he be advised of any venue showing films that were not on record as official licensed cinemas.

The notice of censorship addressed to the Assembly Picture Hall was duly served on a James O'Neill at his residence, which was 59a Serpentine Road, Sandymount by a uniformed DMP officer from the Irishtown Road Police Station and as directed, this officer returned a signed affidavit to this effect, to the Press censor. Having made no mention in his report to General Beasley of another cinema operating in the area we have to assume that this officer and, it would appear, his workmates in the Irishtown DMP station knew nothing about the Shed, which accommodated the showing of films.

However the Superintendent of the Rathmines DMP station had it seems more knowledge of the Serpentine Avenue area than did the officers of the Irishtown station as he reported in a rider to his affidavit that there was indeed a second cinema on that Avenue.

Further to our investigations we discovered that in 1914 a DMP officer, one William Henry Johnston was in residence at 59 Serpentine Avenue and there is a fair possibility that this officer was attached to the Rathmines station. Given that he lived almost on the site of one cinema and so near the Shack there was good enough reason to suppose that the information about the second cinema on Serpentine Avenue came from him.

Telegrams: "DAMP, DUBLIN."
Telephone No. 22.

DUBLIN METROPOLITAN POLICE.

G

CRIMINAL INVESTIGATION DEPARTMENT,

Dublin, 16th. July 1922.

Subject CENSORSHIP OF CINEMA FILMS.

I beg to report that on 16th. inst. I was informed by the Press Censpr , General Beasley, that he is about to introduce a censorship of all War Films exhibited in Dublin and he requests that the attached addressed letters which contain notices similar to the attached be served on the proprietors or managers of Bicture Houses in Dublin and suburbs, without deaay, by uniform Police, and that he, the Press Censor, be furnished with a return showing names ets of persons on whom service has been effected.

General Beasley requests that if there be any other Cinemas in Dublin City and Suburbs that he be supplied with names etc. so that notices can be forwarded for them.

Twentythree notices enclosed.

John J. Purcell
Superintendent.

The Chief Commr.
D.M.P.

A copy of the report from Superintendent John J. Purcell of the Criminal Investigation Department of the DMP to the Chief Commissioner outlining the directive from the Press Censor, General Beasley, Dated July 16th, 1922.

D.M.P. Form No 31.

DUBLIN METROPOLITAN POLICE.

Station Report,

Irishtown Station, E. Division.

18th July 1922.

Notice served on the owner of Picture House

I beg to state that on this date I served the notice mentioned on attached on James F. O'Neill proprietor of the Picture House in Serpentine avenue at his residence 59 Serpentine avenue.

John O'Connell
Sergt 20 E.

The Supt. E. Divn.

Submitted. Cornelius Kiernan
18-7-22 Superintendent

The Chief Commissioner
D. M. Police.

This is a copy of the Irishtown DMP Officer's affidavit, which made no mention of a second cinema in the area.

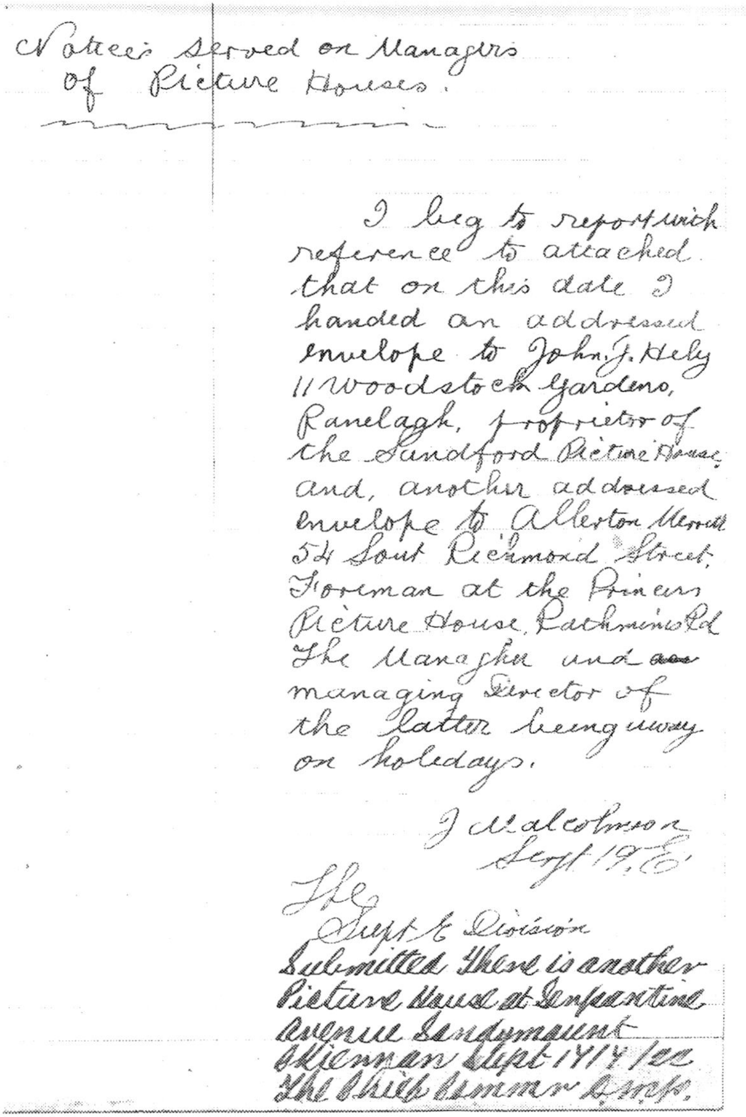
Notices Served on Managers
of Picture Houses.

I beg to report with reference to attached that on this date I handed an addressed envelope to John J. Hely 11 Woodstock Gardens, Ranelagh, proprietor of the Sandford Picture House, and, another addressed envelope to Allerton Merritt 54 Sout Richmond Street, Foreman at the Princess Picture House, Rathmines Rd The Manager and managing Director of the latter being away on holidays.

J Malcolmson
Sept 19/ 16

The
Supt E Division
Submitted There is another Picture House at Serpentine Avenue Sandymount
O'Kiernan Supt 19/7/22
The Chief Commr D.M.P.

This is a copy of the Rathmines affidavit with the rider reporting the presence of another cinema on Serpentine Avenue in July of 1922.

Whatever happened following the report by the Rathmines Superintendent of a second cinema on Serpentine Avenue few will ever know –but within a period of one year James F O'Neill leased the grounds of Elmville on which stood this second picture house from a Messrs Callow and almost immediately he sub-leased the ground to a George Mullen excluding a section measuring 41feet by 210 feet which contained the picture house thereon. O'Neill now owned both cinemas on Serpentine Avenue.

According to a young patron of this cinema, which adorned the holdings of Elmville, a Master Nash of Tritonville Road, this cinema was housed in a large shed, not unlike, I suppose, a Nissan Hut.

Below is a copy of some correspondence involving the leasing of this cinema

ALFRED E. WALKER.
SOLICITOR.
COMMISSIONER FOR OATHS.
TELEPHONE No. 4067.

St. Andrew's Chambers.
1, College Street.
Dublin 31st August 1923

Dear Sir,

re/- Elmville-Serpentine Avenue.

These premises were recently acquired under sub-demise by my Client Mr. O.Neill from Messrs Callow, who has granted a Sub-demise of the major portion of the premises to Mr. George Mullen; and I understand that the latter through his Solicitor, Mr. Fagan, is making some arrangement about the reversionary lease with you.

My Client wishes to point out that the portion of the premises viz:- A Plot 41 feet by 210 on which the Picture House stands and situate on the South East corner of the premises is excluded from Mr. Mullens sub-demise and if any reversionary Lease is being granted he desires to arrange for a further term of Lease of this excluded plot.

Would you kindly let me know what can be done to meet Mr. O:Neills wishes in the matter. If you wish I can call and discuss it with you.

Yours faithfully,

H. Vernon, Esq.,
Pembroke Estate Offices,
Wilton Place, Dublin

With James O'Neill now being the owner of two cinemas in very close proximity to each other we are none too sure of what path he followed but we do know that the Assembly Picture Hall fell into some disrepair and on the 3rd November, 1926 he was advised by the Clerk of the Pembroke Urban Council that the cinema was in need of substantial repairs.

At a further meeting of the Council, the Clerk read out the contents of his letter to the owner of the Hall and as no repairs had been carried out, the Council recommended that the Cinema Hall be closed until the required repairs and alterations be carried out. It further agreed that if the premises were closed voluntarily no legal proceedings would be taken.

We believe that James F O'Neill did indeed close the premises and according to our findings it never opened as a cinema again.

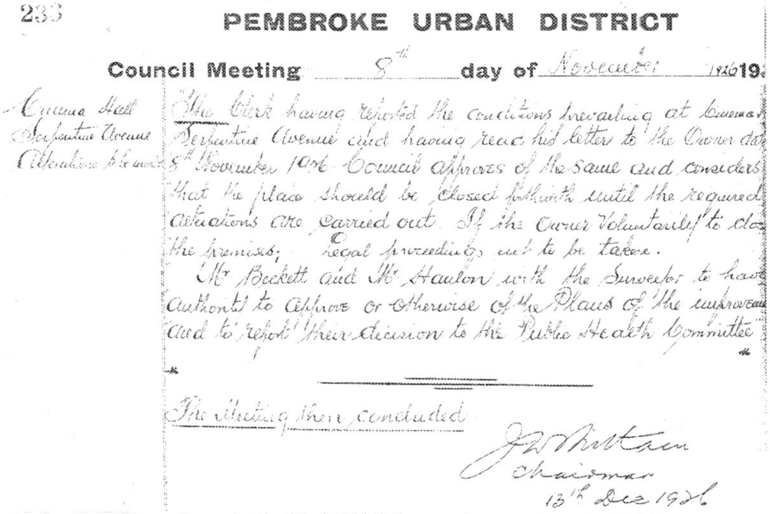
233

PEMBROKE URBAN DISTRICT

Council Meeting 8th **day of** November 1926

Cinema Hall
Serpentine Avenue
Alterations to be made

The Clerk having reported the conditions prevailing at Cinema at Serpentine Avenue and having read his letter to the Owner dated 8th November 1926 Council approves of the same and considers that the place should be closed forthwith until the required alterations are carried out. If the Owner voluntarily to close the premises, Legal proceedings not to be taken.

Mr Beckett and Mr Hanlon with the Surveyor to have authority to approve or otherwise of the Plans of the improvements and to report their decision to the Public Health Committee.

The Meeting then concluded.

Chairman
13th Dec 1926

O'Neill it would seem centred all his attentions on his new acquisition and showed pictures here for many years, at times it was known simply as the "Picture House" sometimes O'Neill's cinema, and because of his involvement with the "Assembly Picture Hall, some also referred to it as the "ASEM". There is also a fair possibility that he brought with him some old signage from the Assembly Picture Hall and hung it somewhere on this Shed of a building. I would also hazard an educated guess that it would be circa this era that the cinema earned the nickname of "The Shack".

During the course of our investigations we uncovered details of another hall on Serpentine Avenue that might at times have been referred to as an assembly hall or room, and that was situated at the beginning of the Avenue as one came in from Merrion Road and in the words of George, the other side of the tracks, referring of course to the railway line intersect on Serpentine Avenue, and a piece of the dialogue from the film "Kings Row" and that this end of the Avenue would have been viewed more as Ballsbridge than Sandymount.

This hall in which we give mention to in another section of this book housed the Olympia Skating Rink and was leased to a Joseph Mason from the Royal Dublin Society and had absolutely nothing to do with our mystery cinema.

However as luck would have it, while we were researching data on another cinema, Dublin's first cinema "the Volta" in Mary Street, we came across an online exhibition about James Joyce and Ulysses and when we hit on this article we found mention of a list of 37 cinemas in a file belonging to the Department of Justice, a list that we had missed during our search of this file many months earlier. Back we went to the National Archives and having once more requested this file we opened it and searched for this piece of paper, which we eventually found and to our joy and amazement it contained a complete list of all licensed cinemas in the Dublin area in the year 1922 which were to be served with the Notice of Censorship by uniformed DMP Officers. Lo and behold we found our mystery cinema the "Assembly Rooms" numbered 31st on the list, with its official address given as 59 Serpentine Avenue in clear and distinct print. We now knew exactly where the Assembly Picture Hall once stood in the early 20th century!

We reproduce this list on the following page as proof positive of our findings and going that extra yard we went back to the Gilbert library and found that the O'Neill family occupied at times both 59 and 59a Serpentine Avenue and further to our research we checked through old maps of the area and found that to the side and rear of these two houses stood two extensions or outside buildings either one of which could have been the Assembly Picture Hall. One quite large building was situated to the side of 59a and to the rear a smaller building, but nevertheless large enough to be a cinema.

These houses still exist on Serpentine Avenue but the outbuildings are long gone. However, on close inspection of the side-wall of 59a, one can see the markings on the outside wall where once another structure stood.

We also reproduce on the following pages some articles of interest in connection with our research on the Assembly Picture Hall, including the NewsFour story.

Now that we have brought this exercise to a successful conclusion by establishing the existence and proper address of this picture hall we are, to say the least,-at a loss for something to investigate.

George & Patrick
Special investigators with the Old Dublin Cinemas Research Team, specialising in "Lost Cinemas".

CHIEF SUPERINTENDENT'S OFFICE,
18th July,1922.

LIST OF PICTURE HOUSES in Dublin Metropolitan Police District, and the names of Proprietors or Managers upon whom the Police served notices regarding the exhibition of pictures, etc, relating to Military operations in Ireland without being passed by the Military Censor.

NO.	NAME AND LOCATION OF PICTURE HOUSE	PERSON SERVED WITH NOTICE.
1	Peoples' Picture Palace, 50 Thomas St	Percival Watson, Chief Operator
2	Camden Picture House, 55 Lr Camden St	Alfred Poulter, Manager
3	Theatre De Luxe, 86 Lr Camden St	Maurice Elliman, Manager
4	Inchicore Cinema, 39 Tyrconnell Road	Robert Pearson, Manager
5	Theatre Royal, Hawkins St	J.H.Hamilton, Manager
6	Brunswick Picture Theatre, 42 Great Brunswick St	Clifford Marston, Manager
7	Dame St Picture House, 17 Dame St	John Ahern, Manager
8	Grafton Picture House, 72 Grafton St	Michael M Richardson, Manager
9	Empire Theatre, Dame St	Edward Doherty, Stage door keeper
10	Gaumont Film Co., Lord Edward St	H Young, Manager
11	Cinema Picture House, 17 Great Brunswick St	Mr Doyle, Manager.
12	Electric Cinema, Talbot St	James Foley, doorman
13	Masterpiece House, Talbot St	James Holden, Manager
14	Pillar Picture House, Upr O'Connell St	Patk J Harling, Secretary
15	Lyceum Cinema, 45 Mary St	John Bignam, Manager
16	Mary St Picture House, 12-13 Mary St	Stephen Berkley, Manager
17	Dorset Picture House, Dorset St	Frederick Sullivan, Manager
18	Corinthian, Eden Quay	Eric Nolan, Manager
19	Rotunda Picture House	Jennie Staunton, Manageress
20	Carlton, Upper O'Connell St	Mary A Cleary, Manageress
21	Metropole, Lr O'Connell St	Abraham Elliman, Manager
22	LA-Scala, Prince's St	Fred Chambers, Manager
23	Sackville Cinema, Lr O'Connell St	May Ryan, Manageress
24	The Corona, 71B, Parnell St	Eric Nolan, Manager
25	Central Cinema, Lr O'Connell St	Patrick J Harling, Secretary
26	Pathe Film Co., 2 Lr Abbey St	Esther O'Hara, Clerk.
27	Manor Picture House, Manor St	John J Fagan, Owner
28	Bohemian Picture House, Phibsboro Rd	Richard Tanner, Manager
29	Phibsboro Picture House, Blacquiere Bridge	James Cottington, Manager
30	Phoenix Picture House, Ellis's Quay	John Ahearn, Owner
31	Assembly Rooms, 59 Serpentine Avenue	James F O'Neill, Owner
32	Sandford Picture House, 5 Sandford Road, Ranelagh	John J Healy, Owner
33	The Princess Cinema, Rathmines Road	Allerton Merritt, Manager
34	Kingstown Picture House, 10 Upr Georges St	John Toner, Manager
35	Pavilion Gardens, Kingstown	Thomas Cogan, Manager
36	Blackrock Picture House	Mary Murphy, Manageress
37	Dalkey Picture House	John Kavanagh, Manager,

Chief Superintendent.

SANDYMOUNT ASSEMBLY PICTURE HALL,
(SERPENTINE AVENUE),
Continuous Performance, 6.30 to 10.30.
ADMISSION- 6d. and 3d.

2nd ad. found November 1913

OLYMPIA RINK.
ROYAL DUBLIN SOCIETY'S PREMISES,
CLOSED FOR THE WINTER SHOW.
RE-OPEN MONDAY, DECEMBER 13th.
J. S. MASON, Managing Director.

This small advertisement, which appeared in a newspaper on December 6th, 1909, clearly links the Olympia Rink on Serpentine Avenue to the R.D.S.

SANDYMOUNT ASSEMBLY PICTURE HALL,
(SERPENTINE AVENUE).
Continuous Performance, 6.30 to 10.30.
ADMISSION—6d and 3d.

This advertisement appeared in an evening newspaper on November 22, 1913, long before it was noticed that the Shack existed.

TO-NIGHT, FRIDAY, AND SATURDAY
SIR J. FORBES-ROBERTSON and MISS GERTRUDE ELLIOTT and Full Company [illegible]
"HAMLET."
PERFORMANCES, [illegible] MATINEE [illegible] at 3.
O'NEILL'S PICTURES,
SERPENTINE AVENUE, SANDYMOUNT.

The Hall also often referred to as O'Neill's Pictures

The side wall area of 59 Serpentine Avenue which we believe was the site of the "Assembly Picture Hall", In the Ordnance Survey Map of that time a shed is clearly marked to the side of this building.

For a brief month in time, we prepared to put on our own show, and then the door opened.

Great Craic

Yours truly, and Patrick being interviewed by Pat and Sarah on Anna Livia Radio in early 2005, while only months into our research, we were already encouraging great attention.

THE FORCE MAGAZINE SINCE 1923 VOLUME 33 NO. 3 APRIL 2005

GARDA REVIEW

ONE OF OUR CINEMAS IS MISSING

George P Kearns and Pat Maguire are putting together the history of all Dublin cinemas, from the time of the first showing of a cinematography exhibitions in the Star of Erin Theatre in 1896, and the opening of the Volta by James Joyce in 1909 to some of the late sixties.

However, they have lost a cinema, and were wondering if a retired member of the force might have a clue as to where it was. In 1922, the Film Censor had to write to the managers of all Dublin cinemas, informing them that all future showing of war films were subject to strict censorship. This was done by way of a notice that had to be served on the proprietor of a cinema by a uniformed member of the Dublin Metropolitan Police (DMP). The serving of this notice had to be recorded by way of a signed affidavit by the DMP officer to the censor press officer. This direction also required any DMP officer to report on his affidavit any information he might have of a cinema that was not on the list and one DMP officer duly recorded that two cinemas existed on Serpentine Avenue, Sandymount.

The Irishtown DMP station served his notice on the Assembly Hall on Serpentine Avenue as directed, the so named cinema being on the list, an officer attached to the Rathmines station reported that there were two cinemas on Serpentine Avenue, and here the puzzle begins. While the Assembly Hall was a listed venue, known to the Film Censor's office that showed pictures in 1922 - the notice was duly served by the Irishtown DMP officer on its proprietor, Mr James O'Neill, whose address was given as 59a Serpentine Avenue, Sandymount. The other cinema referred to by the Rathmines DMP officer could only have been a shed that was used to show pictures circa that time.

There is little doubt that this shed was the pre-runner of the Astoria and later the Ritz Cinema that had the loveable nickname of the "Shack"; which no doubt stemmed from its days as a shed. However, while the Shack is remembered by one and all, nobody seems to remember the Assembly Hall. This hall has been mentioned many times over the years in Thom's directories as a picture house, in the trade section, but never in the section detailing the premises on Serpentine Avenue. Nor was its actual street number ever mentioned. Can anybody help solve the mystery?

INFORMER

20 GARDA REVIEW APRIL 2005

When we placed this notice in the Garda Review we had great hope that some retired Garda might just remember the Assembly Picture Hall, but unfortunately once again no one came forward to assist us in our investigations.

THE MYSTERY OF THE 'ASSEMBLY PICTURE HALL'

By George P. Kearns and Patrick Maguire

In 1922 the Press Censor ordered that a notice of censorship on all war films be served by hand on the owner/managers of Dublin cinemas by uniformed DMP Officers. When served, the DMP Officer had to file a signed return to his station's superintendent stating that he had served this notice and to further state to whom he had handed it.

The DMP Officers were further charged that should they have any knowledge of a cinema not on the list of cinemas that came with the notices to each station, then the Press Officer should be immediately notified.

While a DMP Officer from the Irishtown station duly served the notice on Mr James F. O'Neill of 59a Serpentine Avenue the stated owner of the Assembly Picture Hall which was on the Press Officer's list, a fellow officer from the Rathmines Station informed his superior officer that there were two cinemas on Serpentine Avenue, and here the mystery

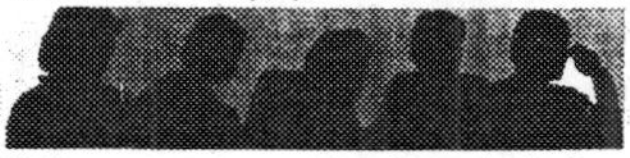

began.

We have made extensive enquiries and to date have not found one person from the Sandymount area who remembers or knows anything about the Assembly Picture Hall cinema. We cannot pin-point exactly where the Assembly Picture Hall stood, although all our findings are leaning towards 59a Serpentine Avenue. There is, however, definite proof of its existence on Serpentine Avenue, as there survives an advertisement from an evening newspaper paper of the time.

The Assembly Hall was owned by a Mr James F. O'Neill who also had an address at St Helen's Avenue, Booterstown and we know for sure that this cinema existed between the years 1913 to 1923.

The other cinema referred to by the DMP Officer could only have been the 'Shack' situated at 78 Serpentine Avenue. The 'Shack' was the forerunner to the Sandymount 'Astoria Cinema' which later changed its name to the 'Ritz' which in time became the 'Oscar' cinema and theatre.

The building concerned still stands and now houses a Mosque. The 'Shack' was in effect a shed, where films were shown and we know that it was operating in 1919 in direct competition with the Assembly Picture Hall. On one occasion it offered its patrons an episode from the 'Pearl White' adventure series and a feature film entitled 'Elmo the Mighty', both of which were released in 1919.

James F. O'Neill also founded the 'Astoria' and the 'Ritz' Cinemas. While some may care to differ, we also have knowledge and records of the Whittle family and George Jay's involvement with this cinema. As a matter of interest, the entertainment on Serpentine Avenue didn't centre on cinemas alone, because there once stood a skating rink at number 3, owned and managed by Joseph Mason.

We would welcome contact with any relative of James F. O'Neill the founder of the Assembly Picture Hall and the Astoria/Ritz cinema, and by really pushing our luck any relative of the owner of the original 'Shack' cinema.

We are in the process of compiling the history of all old Dublin cinemas which we hope to publish in book form. We are interested to hear about any cinema or venue that showed pictures from that historical 20th day of April 1896 when a moving picture was shown in the 'Star of Erin' Theatre, right up to any cinema that was built in the late sixties.

We would be very interested in any information NewsFour readers might have and maybe a copy of any old photos of cinemas or advertisements. Perh[...]
might even have a [...]
about their local cine[...]

The fact that we [...]
past a skating rink a[...]
cinema in the Sandy[...]
which nobody now [...]
remember, is proof [...]
a good part of our k[...]
is dying with the ol[...]
tion. We would sugg[...]
body with details of [...]
tory should take a li[...]
record this in writing
on.

George Kearns has [...]
book on the history [...]
cess Cinema. Rath[...]
some other Dubli[...]
Copies at €25 are a[...]
contacting him at 83[...]
book is a limited ed[...]
size and consists of [...]
and is available onl[...]
come, first served ba[...]

If you have any kn[...]
impart on the myster[...]
sembly Picture Hall
of Dublin cinemas [...]
in touch either thro[...]
Four, by telephoning
8345811 or by email
cinelore@hotmail.co[...]

JIMMY AND MARIE HOPKINS celebrated their 50th Wedding Anniversary with their extended family, nurses and patients on 10th April at the Royal Hospital, Donnybrook. Jimmy who are from Stella Gardens, were mar[...] April 1955.

This story appeared in the June issue of NewsFour the Free Community Newspaper serving Sandymount, Irishtown, Ringsend, Docklands, Ballsbridge and Donnybrook.

George has written a story or two for this newspaper over the years.

(Unfortunately photocopying once again is at fault)
(Promise, if we make a couple of million each out of this labour of love, we will purchase our own equipment)

4 May 2007 West

LOST CINEMAS BACK IN THE FRAME!

ÁINE KERR talks to two Dubs working on a book on the city's movie theatres of yesteryear

'Stories of jam jars being accepted as an entrance fee, the shed that was used as a cinema or the screen which was back to front are only some of the humorous tales uncovered.'

A FORGOTTEN city, in which some 70 cinemas were once subjected to bombings, shootings and countless calamities, is being rediscovered and documented by two earnest Dublin retirees.

After months of researching material, George Kearns, from Finglas, and Pat Maguire, from Crumlin, share what they aptly call a "labour of love" for stories about Dublin's lost cinemas.

Stories of jam jars being accepted as an entrance fee, the shed that was used as a cinema or the screen which was back to front are only some of the humorous tales uncovered.

Their shared passion was only realised in the confines of the Gilbert Library when George was completing work on his book about the history of the Princess cinema of Rathmines.

Since beginning the laborious task of wading though documentation, they have discovered cinemas that few knew existed, and all with the most grandiose of names.

The Astoria, Regal, Royal, Ambassador, Palace, Ritz and Corinthian are only some of the mystery picture houses without a recorded history.

Miniscule advertisements in the daily newspapers are often all George and Patrick have to confirm that these cinemas once existed.

The Assembly Picture Hall on Serpentine Avenue, in Sandymount, which survived from 1913 until 1923, is one such cinema which intrigues both George and Patrick. It stood in direct competition with the 'Shack', which was once the site of a cinema in a shed.

Thus far they have established that in 1922 the Dublin Metropolitan Police was summoned to forbid the Assembly from showing any films, which contained war references.

"Nobody remembers it," says George. "People who would have been seven or 10 at the time know nothing of it."

The Cosy/Corona cinema that once graced Parnell Street is also another which the two determined researchers seek more information on.

Other cinemas such as the Bohemian, which opened in 1914, have been researched in-depth. Having survived a fire in 1921, a second fire in 1922 into which a bomb was thrown forced its closure for seven years.

A retailer's shop which was converted into a picture house in 1909 was the first dedicated cinema in Dublin. This famed cinema, the Volta was opened by Joyce opened on Mary's Street and is credited with giving rise to the dramatic number of cinemas built in Dublin in the ensuing decades.

George Kearns and Pat Maguire with a press cutting featuring one of Dublin's lost cinemas, the Leinster, Dolphin's Barn

George Kearns reasons that it was doomed to fail because they weren't "picking the right films", showing mainly Italian movies.

The Princess in Rathmines was, however, the first purpose built cinema in Dublin.

In later years, cinemas such as the Theatre Royal would be home to royal visits and be witness to a battle riot after Lord Lieutenant Wesley instructed people not to place seats on the statue of King William on Dame Street.

According to Patrick Maguire, Trinity College students were known to "cause mayhem" in the picture houses across the city.

In Cabra, one cinemagoer was renowned for arriving on a horse and had to be constantly instructed to return without his favoured mode of transport. Other cinemas, such as the Classic in Harold's Cross, which opened in 1953, showed the Rocky Horror Show every Friday night for 21 years.

During this period, however, Dublin's legion of cinemas were starting to disappear.

George reasons that suburban cinemas found it difficult to acquire decent films promptly and the advent of television obliterated the need for so many picture houses.

Some of what he describes as "beautiful, the best of architecture" still survives in furniture shops or bingo halls across the city but cinemas or fast food restaurants have replaced most of them.

Where once three cinemas stood on O'Connell Street - the Sackville, Pillar Room and Grand Central - a bank and two Mc Donalds restaurants now reside.

"We are out to show the people that the local history that was out there is being brought back to them," explains Patrick.

George adds that bringing the past back to people is their simple objective.

Presently, the two retirees are still conducting their research and hope to publish the results of their hard toil in a book in August. They claim that their findings have been in-depth and consistent because they have gone right to the heart of the story.

"We are not just going out and writing a book and saying 'this is it'," says Patrick. "We are going right to the core to make it something people will understand."

Bonded by a "labour of love" the two joke that they have spent an incalculable amount of money on photocopying cards and arguing with each other. But still, a love for Dublin's history prevails and they share a determination to bring the past back to a city that has forgotten its glorious past of picture houses.

'A retailer's shop which was converted into a picture house in 1909 was the first dedicated cinema in Dublin.'

A limited number of copies of George's book on the Princess cinema and George and Patrick's forthcoming book on the history of all of Dublin's cinemas can be ordered at cinelore@hotmail.com or by writing to George Kearns at 23 Griffith Parade, Dublin 11. Also, people are asked to contact them on these addresses should you have any information on

The Grand Cinema in Whitehall is now a bingo hall

'In Cabra, one cinemagoer was renowned for arriving on a horse and had to be constantly instructed to return without his favoured mode of transport.'

Ann Kerr, Ace Reporter for the Northside, Westside and Southside People interviewed us about our labour of love and gave us great coverage and exposure. This feature story ran more than once in each of the abovementioned editions.

It also led us to be interviewed by Pat and Sarah on Anna Livia Radio and by Declan Carthy on Newstalk 106.

Pictures of Declan interviewing us outside the old "Shack" is included in the story of the Ritz Cinema.

The Dalkey Community Council Newsletter no 354 also ran an article for us in our search for the Dalkey cinema, which for a while became our second mystery cinema.

THE CINEMA HUNT GOES ON!

In the case of Dalkey we have been lead to believe that a cinema once stood on the site of 37a Convent Road, Dalkey and that this cinema belonged to one John Kavanagh, a builder whose address was St Bridget's Convent Road.

This cinema was established circa the 1920s and was mentioned in Thom's Street Directories in the years 1923/4/5.6.7. The owner was also the recipient of a notice which was hand-delivered by a uniformed D.M.P Officer from the Dalkey Police Station in 1922. This notice was from the Government Censor Office and a signed affidavit from the serving officer was required by returned as proof of delivery. {We have a copy of same}

The fact that the cinema was on the delivery list was proof enough that it was a bona-fide premises and operating under a license which was issued in accordance with the Cinematograph 1909 Act by the U.D.C.

However we now have a dilemma, simply because very few people know of this cinema and to-date we have found nobody who could stand firm and point to the actual site on which it once stood.

Despite the fact that we have established that the summons / notice as previously mentioned was served on John Kavanagh at St Bridget's, Convent Road by a uniformed D.M.P. Officer in 1922.

That 37a Convent Road was given in Thom's directories as the address of the Dalkey Picture House in the 1920s. {1922 - 1927}

That the Dalkey Picture House was the 37th cinema listed on the official cinema list from the Chief Superintendent's Office of the Dublin Metropolitan Police District.

It has been suggested to us that the cinema was {A} a myth; and {B} an old Cow-shed situated to the rear of the house, which we very much doubt as the cinema was licensed.

However there is another possibility and that would be that the actual cinema was situated in the Town Hall as was the Clontarf cinema in Clontarf.

Hopefully your readers will be able to tell us exactly where it was, and just maybe supply us with a picture or sketch of same.

We would also mention that we have trawled the Dublin evening newspapers and the Bray Herald but never found an advertisement for this cinema.

George P Kearns / Patrick Maguire
c/o 22, Griffith Parade, Finglas East, Dublin 11.
Ph. 01-8345811 Email; georgemamie@eircom.net

By now we were beginning to feel like a couple of celebrities and we began to wonder if we should charge a fee for these interviews, or maybe we should get ourselves an "agent" after all we now had a taste of fame but not a lick of fortune.

A chap named Noel Twamley who had purchased a copy of George's first book, "The Prinner" wrote a very nice little review of same and sent it to the Editor of "The New Link" magazine who duly published it in the Christmas 2005 issue.

George is a regular contributor to the contents of this magazine, which is edited by Patrick McGauley and published and distributed free by the St Andrew's Resource Centre, Pearse Street.

Noel and George have since met and correspond regularly. In consequence Noel has contributed a couple of stories for inclusion in this book.

DEAR EDITOR

Dear Editor

As an occasional reader of your "New Link" magazine which features from time to time wonderful stories and pictures of the thirties, forties and fifties Dublin I would like to tell you that I have just finished reading a real 100% page turner of a book, no! Dear Editor I am not referring to the "Di Vinci Code but to "The Prinner" by one of your writers George P Kearns. This is a 206 page large format book about the "Princess Cinema" in Rathmines where George actually worked as a young man and he tells the story the way it was. I myself spent many hours in the Princess and George describes it exactly as I remember it.

This book is not just about the "Prinner" the author paints on a broader canvas and he tells gems of stories about the Stella, Sundrive, Carlton, Bohemian, Tivoli and many more. I had forgotten how large some of these cinemas were, the Carlton held 2,000, the Savoy 3,000 and the Royal a staggering 3,850 people. This book is a genuine "Tour de Force"; he covers Dublin cinemas from the early 1900's right up to last years closing of the "Stella" which was also in Rathmines. It is a time capsule of Dublin's post war years and is simply un-put-downable. I am constantly dipping into this book and every time I do I seem to find something new.

George must have spent years researching this book, it is full of information and there are dozens of pictures and hundreds of newspaper cuttings and advertisement, telling us what was on and where. I would like to thank George for bringing it all back to me, the Camden, Stella and of course the "Prinner"

This book is I believe on the shelves of most Dublin libraries; check it out for yourself and you will surely want your own copy. I warmly recommend this book and believe that everybody young and old will be captivated by it.
Enjoy Noel Twamley,

Editor,
The New Link

Dear Sir,
Thank you for informing me of the fact that one of your readers has written a very flattering review of my book "The Prinner" for the next publication of The New Link magazine. Needless to say I am quite chuffed and thrilled to have this happen to me, fancy that, poor auld George Kearns from Irishtown having a book reviewed in a magazine, heavens knows, just what he will get up to next. I can just imagine my old neighbours saying – yea that was Millie Bashfords son or Nellie Murphy's grandson, remember him, he was always a very delicate lad who was always muffled up in an overcoat and scarf.

My book which tells the history of the "Princess Cinema in Rathmines" which was known and loved by all as the "The Prinner" was successfully launched in the lecture room of the Rathmines library on June 29th last and most all of the copies printed have been sold. 52 of them were bought by the Four Dublin Councils for distribution and availability in their branch libraries, and quite a few were sold directly to private individuals who sought a copy. These copies were all first edition.

My book was self-published and although a very expensive exercise it was well worth the effort of having it adorn the shelves of all Dublin libraries and ditto in the reference areas of Ireland's main University's such as Trinity Dublin, D.C.U. U.C.D Maynooth, Galway, Cork and Limerick. It also found its way into Britain's four main Universities'. Fame indeed has touched yours truly.

The book which was a labour of love and told the history of a number of cinemas was never made available to any book shops; sales were privately executed and conducted only through myself. However I believe that there are some people still anxious to obtain a copy of my book without knowing how to go about purchasing it, and so for the purpose of making a copy available for them I decided I would have a further limited batch of 1st Edition copies printed and made available for sale in the next month or two through one outlet only.

The printers of my book, "The Rathmines Business Depot" has very kindly agreed on a once off basis to host the sale of the book for a short period leading up to Christmas 2005 and it will be available on a first come first served basis or it can be ordered by cash in advance. Only a limited number will be printed and this will be the last 1st Edition print of my book, which may well become a "collectors item".

George P Kearns

Dear Editor,

We have recently received a report about a retired member who was encouraged to avail of the cheaper telephone and electricity services being offered by certain operators.

She was greatly dismayed to subsequently receive a bill which excluded her usual ESB allowance, and adding insult to injury another bill for a €150 for her T.V. licence On querying the matter she was informed that this was because she had transferred her accounts. The matter is being challenged as those allowances are from the Department of Social Welfare and not from the companies concerned. The moral is that before transferring to these "cheaper" providers, get cast iron assurances that your allowances will not be lost!

Retired Members Section – SIPTU

When the Editor of New Link told George about the review he had just received, George hurriedly wrote a response and the editor published both in tandem.

(Map, from the Map Library, Trinity College Library, Dublin; Reproduced from a map in Trinity College Library Dublin, with the permission of the Board of Trinity College)

This is a copy of part of a 1909 Ordnance Survey Map of the district of Sandymount and in particular a section of Serpentine Avenue where it crosses the railway line.

We took the liberty of marking two spots on the map with (A) depicting Oakland's where a small block of houses which face onto Serpentine Avenue stand. Just to the right of the (A) are No's 59 & 59a and alongside 59a which is at the beginning of the block can be seen an outbuilding clearly shown as an outbuilding by its x type roof markings and this is the building that we believe housed the Assembly Picture Hall. With the use of a magnifying glass one can see a series of steps leading into the building.

X marks the spot or almost. Just beyond the area marked with an (X) lies the small estate known as "Elmville" where the Shack Cinema was sited. "Story of the "Shack" is outlined in another story in this book under the heading of the "Ritz Cinema"

ASTOR CINEMA
'The first'
51 Lower O'Connell Street Dublin

The Astor cinema first opened on O'Connell Street on Saturday, March 27th 1937, replacing the old Sackville and Picture House cinema that once adorned that street when it was known as Sackville Street.

Its opening film was a musical extravaganza that left all musicals previously filmed at the starting post. This was the story of the "Great Ziegfeld" and it was claimed to be the "Worlds Greatest Entertainment Film" which has never been equalled before and some would say since.

William Powell played the part of Florenz Ziegfeld and Myrna Loy his wife Billie Burke.

Flo Ziegfeld was known the world over as a producer of extravagant stage revues and was famed for his spectacular parade of beautiful girls towards the end of each show. These beauties were known as the "Ziegfeld Girls"

This film ran for a good ten weeks and was followed by another block buster "Romeo and Juliet"

The new Astor cinema, whose proprietors were the Capital Theatre Company, was one of Dublin's smallest cinemas, and the price of admission was fixed at 2/6. Despite its size it was classed as a first run cinema and therefore had a right to pick its fair share of the newest films to arrive in Dublin, which they could run for as long as they attracted full houses. These films, just like those in other "first run" houses were then rationed out to the suburban cinemas by the "Film Renters", which was the popular trade nickname given to all the companies involved in the import and distribution of film material.

This practice, which it appears began in the 1930's, was considered most unfair by the owners of cinemas which were situated outside of the town area, and remained a bone of contention for many a long day. It was claimed by many that this practice helped in no small way to bring about the decline of cinemas in the sixties.

Only the best of material and equipment were used in furnishing this little cinema and it was said to be most comfortable and restful. It also had the latest Western Electric Mirrophone Sound System installed which assured its patrons of perfect sound reproduction.

Three complete performances were on offer each day with the first at 1.20, the second at 4.40 and the last house at 8 o'clock, all seats were bookable in advance.

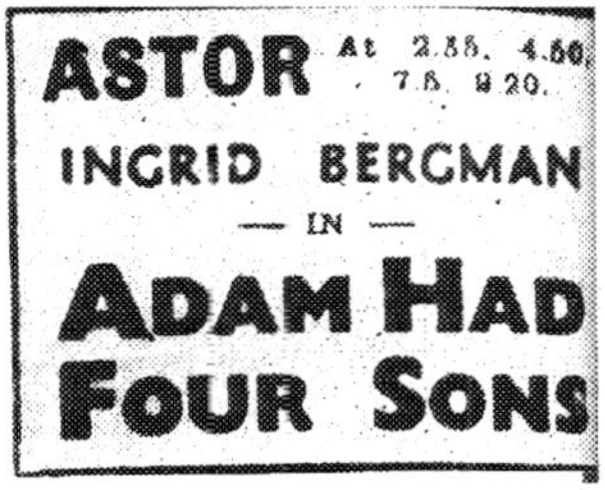

The Astor enjoyed great success and ran to full houses for quite some time, but for some reason, unknown to us, it closed down after seven years on Saturday, December 21st, 1946.
Its last picture show was "Adam Had Four Sons" starring Ingrid Bergman and Warner Baxter.

At the time of closure Bertie McNally was in charge of the cinema.

Seven years later a new Astor cinema was built on Eden Quay and once again Bertie McNally was at the helm. This new cinema opened on Friday March 13th, 1953 and management didn't feel the least bit perturbed about opening on a Friday the 13th, but rather looked upon this date as an omen for success.

This was a 300 seater cinema with all the seats on the ground floor. There was no balcony area, and it was considered to be one of the smallest cinemas in the country. Just as in the old Astor on O'Connell Street this new cinema had a fixed admission price, which this time around was 3/6.

Though Friday 13th was the official advertised opening date for the cinema, a formal opening was held on Thursday, March 12th and admission was by invitation only and those that accepted these invitations included members of the Government and Diplomatic Corps. The opening film was "Bicycle Thieves".

This film is an Italian Classic, which won an Academy Award for Best Foreign Language Film.
(Italian dialogue with English Sub-Titles)

The film was at the time the best known neorealist film which was directed by Vittorio de Sica, and told the story of a man who gets a job posting fliers around the town, to do the job the man needs the bike that he had pawned some time earlier.

To redeem the bike his wife sells her wedding sheets. Having got his bike and secured the job, the bike is stolen, and the rest of the film sees the man and his son searching for his bike.

Failing to retrieve the bike and desperate to save his job the man steals a bike, is caught and humiliated in front of his son.

The owner of the bike refused to press charges, believing that the humiliation suffered by the man in front of his son was punishment enough.

The film ends with the now depressed man and his family facing a bleak future.

No professional actors were used in this film. Instead de Sica used ordinary working class people with no acting experience whatever and the leading man was Lamberto Maggiorani, a factory worker.

The new "Astor" cinema which was converted from an auctioneer's premises was a credit to W. O' Dwyer the architect and the builders that carried out the conversion. The entrance to the cinema was said to be the most decorative in the country. The doors were made of solid mahogany with highly polished brass fittings. The floor was laid in green and red rubber and one wall in the vestibule area was completely covered with a mirror. In the centre of the ceiling was a beautiful large chandelier.

The manager, John R. Bools, said that a steady clientele would be attracted to the Astor for great emphasis will be placed on acquiring cultural films for which there is quite a demand in Dublin. It will also be a first run cinema.

The Astor survived the decline in cinemas in the sixties and seventies but finally closed its doors on June 15th 1984 and its last feature film was the "Adventures of a Private Eye"

This building, which now houses a McDonald's restaurant, was once the Picture House which opened on April 9th 1910.

The Picture House was the first cinema to open on Sackville Street and paved the way for a grand parade of cinemas in the first half of the 20th century.

This Dublin Cinematograph Theatre which was also know as the "Sackville", was initiated by an English company called the "Provincial Theatre Company Ltd who had recently acquired the "Volta" cinema in Mary Street from James Joyce.

This was a small intimate cinema with seating for only 350 and for its opening night it presented a magnificent display of pictures of great interest, which included one about Irish Fishermen off the Howth coast, Pathe's New Gazette and scenes of beauty and interest.

Prices for admission to the cinema would be 6d and 1/- and afternoon tea would be served from 3:00 pm to 5 30 pm.

On the left the Astor after its closure. When interviewed, following its closure, Mrs McNally the widow of Bernie who had passed away eight years previously, said that "sad and all as it was she could no longer afford to keep the cinema open in these present difficult times."

ASTORIA
GLASTHULE
Dun Laoghaire

In December of 1939 James F O'Neill leased a plot of ground in Glasthule on which to build a cinema and work began on this site early in the following year. He made and laid these plans while he was still in ownership of the "Astoria" cinema in Sandymount.

In 1940 he leased his Sandymount cinema to a newly formed company called the Ritz Cinema Company Limited, whose Managing director was Percy Winder Whittle. It would appear that a part of the agreement made called for the Sandymount cinema to be renamed and that he, James F. O'Neill, would be allowed to retain the name "Astoria"

On August 5th 1940 O'Neill opened his new Picture Palace with the retained name "The Astoria" and the first movie shown was "The Real Glory" starring Gary Cooper and David Niven.

The Astoria Cinema Company Limited was incorporated on April 18th, 1942 and its directors were as follows:

James O'Neill of 66 St Helens Road, Booterstown a Cinema Proprietor had 800 shares.
Robert Gerard Kirkham, a Cinema Agent, had 600 shares; and
Vernon Alfred Walker, Solicitor had 100 shares, which were later taken over by Kirkham.

Kirkham later retired and O'Neill took over all his shares and was now sole owner of the company.

The Astoria cinema, which was a most welcome addition to the area attracted good patronage and enjoyed a comfortable trade until 1957 when it was temporarily closed following the death of James F O'Neill on February 17th at his residence at 66 St Helen's Road, Booterstown.

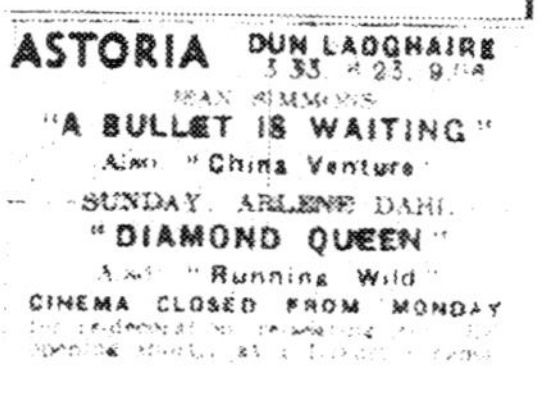

The cinema closed on September 17th and while closed, it underwent extensive decorations. In September of 1957 Kirkham's son took over the ownership of the cinema and reopened it on October 14th 1957 with the showing of the film "The Happy Wanderer".

The name remained unchanged.

This advertisement announced the re-opening of the cinema with the film "The Happy Wanderer".

A happy film claimed the management for a happy occasion.

But unfortunately these happy times were to be short lived for a lot of Dublin cinemas and the Astoria, like many others, closed its doors in the sixties.

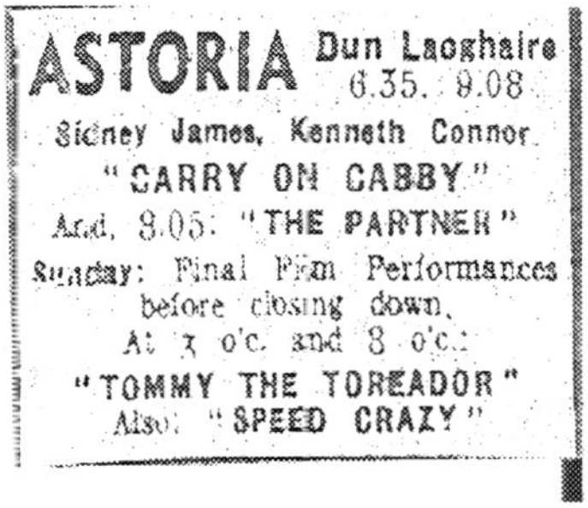

Saturday evening newspapers of June 13th 1964 announced the closure of the Astoria cinema and its last performance took place on Sunday night the 14th of June.

On that night it featured two films, beginning with the lovable Tommy Steele in "Tommy the Toreador" singing his way around the world as a sailor on a ship, who lands in the 'ships'. When on shore leave in Spain he gets mistaken for a bullfighter.

The other film being "Speed Crazy" 1959 with Brett Halsey as Nick Barrow a hot headed delinquent hot rodder, who belts out the title song and speeds his way through the whole movie.

The building remained closed for quite some time and for a while it was used as a dance hall by the Caroline Club. In 1971 it re-opened as a cinema under the direction of Barney O'Reilly and was renamed the "Forum".

The "Forum" opened on December 7th 1971 with the above advertised film;

This was a zany crazy film with no plot and seemed to centre on a football game, a trip to Tokyo to perform an operation, and an effort to find out if the head nurse "Hot Lips" of this mobile surgical hospital was a natural blond.

FORUM Dun Laoire 3 & 8 p.m.
(Sun. 3 p.m. only)
John Cleese THE TIME BANDITS
L/S 11 p.m. 18's WOODSTOCK
Sun 8 pm THE PROFESSIONALS
Also THE OUTLAW IS COMING
(Same prog. Sun. 7.30)

Some ten years later, on Sunday August 26th 1981, the Forum closed for twinning and just over two months later it re-opened on Monday, November 16th 1981 with two big screens.

FORUM DUN LAOIRE
RE-OPENING MONDAY NEXT WITH 2 BIG SCREENS
FORUM 1: PROG. 8 P.M. FEATURE 9 P.M. (18's)
HISTORY OF THE WORLD PART 1
FORUM 2: PROG. 8 P.M. FEATURE 8.50 P.M. (18's)
A CHANGE OF SEASONS
LIMITED SEATING AVAILABLE FOR MONDAY NIGHT

If you like Mel Brooks you will like the film "History of the World Part 1" as he wrote the screenplay, directed the movie and played the part of five characters including Moses, Comicus, Tomas de Torquemada, King Louis XV1 and Jacques the "Garcon de Piss"

A "Change of Seasons" tells the story of a University Lecturer who takes a young student as a lover and gets upset when his wife does likewise, with a jobbing carpenter.
Well told, with a good cast including Shirley MacLaine, Anthony Hopkins, Bo Derek and Michael Brandon.

FORUM DUN LAOGHAIRE
FOR BOOKING INFORMATION/TIMES
Tel: 01 28 07 574
15 MICKEY BLUE EYES Nightly 8.30
15 AUSTIN POWERS THE SPY WHO SHAGGED ME nightly 8.00

The Forum Closed on September 2nd 1999 and the building is now a food and grocery shop.

BLACKROCK, TOO POSH?

According to the Right Hon., the Recorder of the City Sessions on Monday, March 29th 1911, Blackrock was a residential place with very few working people and he therefore refused an application from Jacob Elliman ,for a Sunday licence for his new cinema. Instead, he offered a six day licence. Elliman refused to accept a six-day licence.

By way of explanation the Right Hon. Recorder, said that he had no objection in granting licences for Sunday openings in cinemas that were situated in working class districts where people were unable during the rest of the week to amuse themselves. But he did not understand how this could apply to Blackrock.

When Elliman refused to accept the six-day licence the Recorder said he would not grant any licence at all. Later Elliman changed his mind and accepted the six day licence.

~~~~~

In respect of a previous licence application for a similar type licence for the Dame Street Picture House, which had been refused, the proprietors took 'French Leave" and soon found themselves summoned before the magistrate and reprimanded.

~~~~~

No Morgue in Blackrock in 1913

At a meeting of the Blackrock Urban Council on Wednesday June 18th, the Township Surveyor submitted, for the consideration of the council, plans in connection with the proposed Picture Palace in the township.

McCabe a member of the council mentioned that the Coroner had made another terrible attack on the council for not having a morgue in the township and as the Coroner had some connection with this place he jested, that it instead might be turned into a morgue.

While the cinema plans were not rejected, further information was requested.

~~~~~

THEATRE INSPECTRESSES

On Monday, 15th January 1917, there was a mention of a recent report in that paper that told of the Dublin Vigilance Committee being invited by the Public Health Committee of Dublin Corporation to submit the names of five lady members of that association who would be willing to act without payment as inspectresses of theatres, music halls and cinemas in the city and report as to the class of entertainment in those places. Not surprisingly, there were plenty of applications made.
~~~~~

THE BOHEMIAN CINEMA
Phibsboro Road, Dublin 7

The "Boh", as it was popularly known, opened on June 8th 1914.

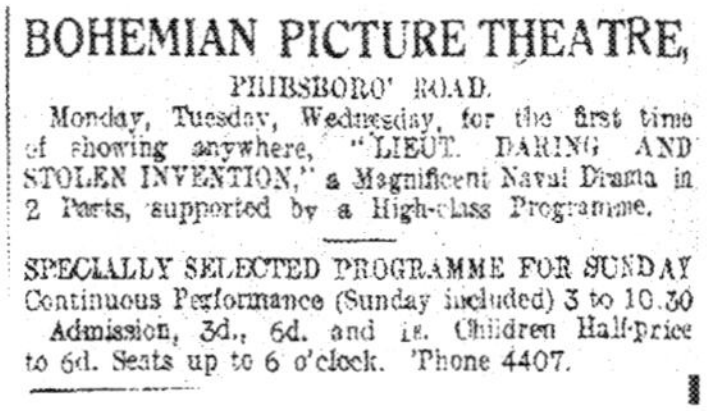

BOHEMIAN PICTURE THEATRE,

PHIBSBORO' ROAD.

Monday, Tuesday, Wednesday, for the first time of showing anywhere, "LIEUT. DARING AND STOLEN INVENTION," a Magnificent Naval Drama in 2 Parts, supported by a High-class Programme.

SPECIALLY SELECTED PROGRAMME FOR SUNDAY
Continuous Performance (Sunday included) 3 to 10.30
Admission, 3d., 6d. and 1s. Children Half-price to 6d. Seats up to 6 o'clock. 'Phone 4407.

On June 13th 1914, the "Boh" featured the film "Lieut Daring and the Stolen Invention", which was the films first showing anywhere. Lieut. Daring was a Navy Spy-catcher and it might be worth mentioning that said spies were always bearded and spy-like in their movement and appearance and were never a match for our super-hero.

The Lieut. Daring Adventures, were about one of a couple of super comedy-like hero's created by brothers Fred and Joe Evans and over one hundred films were made about them. The other hero's name was, I believe, Lieut. Pimple and if we are not further mistaken the film, "In the Hands of London Crooks", may well have involved one or the other of this duo

It is also worth noting how easy it appeared at the time for the management of the Bohemian to secure first time releases, a practice that the film importers and distributors soon put an end to in the 1930s.

The Boh, as it was popularly known to one and all, earned a place in cinema history when it was chosen to show the first film produced in Ireland by an Irish Company and Irish players The film was entitled "O'Neill of the Glen" and was adapted by the well known director W.J. Lysaght from a novel by M.T. Pender, the famous Ulster Novelist.

The film was made in Ireland in 1916 by The Film Company of Ireland Ltd., whose offices were in Dame Street, Dublin. This was an all-Irish company and the cast were all Irish actors.

This silent film was a thrilling and romantic story, that told the tale of the Tremaine and O'Neill families, where the father of one family shot the father of the other, over a row about money.
It would appear that Tremaine, a solicitor, had defrauded O'Neill out of a large sum of money, and when O'Neill challenged Tremaine, Tremaine, unable to repay the money, shot O'Neill. Many years later Nola Tremaine met Don O'Neill and they fell in love with each other.

Starring in the film were two well known Abbey actors, J.M. Kerrigan and Fred O'Donovan, plus Miss Nora Clancy, a charming young actress, together with J M. Carrie and Brian Magowan, two gifted actors.

This proprietor of the Bohemian cinema was ecstatic with this production, and had never anticipated such wholehearted appreciation from the people that had seen the movie. This new company, he said, is sure to create a thirst amongst patrons and proprietors of picture houses. During the run of this film the Bohemian had enjoyed packed houses for the full week

For a film company that was not that long in the business, it had already produced five films, and following the success of their first creation, which had drawn huge crowds in its weeks run in the Bohemian, the other four, which were comedies, were ready for release.
The Film Company of Ireland, incorporated in 1916, was to become the most important Irish Production Company during the silent picture era, and amongst its great productions were adaptations of Charles Kickham's "Knocknagow" in 1918 and "Willy Reilly and his Colleen Bawn by William Carleton in 1920. They also produced many, many dramas and comedies.

The next film to be released, immediately after the showing of O' Neill of the Glen, was the first ever comedy production by an Irish Company.

"The Miser's Gift".
A very brief synopsis of this silent film, informed us, that a young couple get a very mean father so drunk in order to get him to dream of gold.
Cast:
Fred O'Donovan, Kathleen Murphy, J.M. Kerrigan

The Bohemian Cinema also had its fair share of problems, in the shape of a bomb.

The Bomb, if it was a bomb.

Sunday night, May 12th 1935, an explosion rocked the Phibsborough Road area at its junction with the North Circular Road. Fortunately this incident occurred at midnight and nobody was hurt. The bomb, it appeared, was lobbed into the vestibule area of the Bohemian Cinema, and when it exploded, it damaged the ticket office, all the entrance doors and shattered all the glass windows. The police and emergency services were on the scene within minutes, and sealed off the area. The resulting fire from the explosion was minimal, and was easily controlled by the fire service.

Management was called and having accessed the damage, which was not as bad as first thought, organised repair crews for a dawn start the next morning. The repair teams worked furiously, as workers did in those days, and the Bohemian was ready for business that evening, as if nothing had ever happened.

The situation was thoroughly investigated and a report in an evening newspaper the following Tuesday, hinted that the cause of the explosion may have been caused by the fusing of electrical wires, while at the same time, not ruling out a bomb.

The Boh at one stage used metal tabs instead of the usual light cardboard tickets, which were common to most cinemas.

The Site where the Bohemian once stood, this picture was taken in 2005.

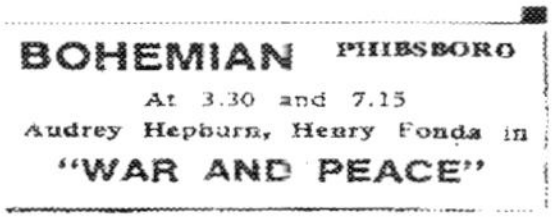
BOHEMIAN PHIBSBORO
At 3.30 and 7.15
Audrey Hepburn, Henry Fonda in
"WAR AND PEACE"

The Bohemian, which once claimed to have the finest orchestra in Ireland closed on Saturday March 30th 1974. Its last film "War and Peace" was an adaptation of Leo Tolstoy's epic novel about the life of a Russian family during the war of 1812. It starred Audrey Hepburn, Henry Fonda, Mel Ferrer with Herbert Lom as Napoleon.

BRUNSWICK CINEMA THEATRE
30 South Great Brunswick Street.
(Now Pearse Street)

On November 29th 1911, a roving reporter attached to the "Evening Herald", when taking a stroll down Great Brunswick Street, took note of the finishing touches being applied to Dublin's latest cinema, which was opening on the morrow. The new cinema he reported is a most comfortable, commodious building, which has been handsomely fitted out on the most approved principles. It is well ventilated, lighted throughout by electricity and seating has been provided for 350 persons.

Management, it would appear, had done everything possible to add to the comfort and enjoyment of their patrons.

A continuous performance will be given each day from 2.00 pm until 10.30 pm, and prices of admission will be 6d, 4d and 3d.

GRAND OPENING
OF THE
"BRUNSWICK"
CINEMA THEATRE,
30 GREAT BRUNSWICK STREET,
THIS DAY (THURSDAY), NOVEMBER 30, 1911.
Proceeds will be devoted to
THE BUILDING FUND OF
ST. PATRICK'S CHURCH,
RINGSEND.
CONTINUOUS PERFORMANCE,
From 2.30 to 10.30 p.m.
ADMISSION............... 3d and 6d.
PROGRAMME UP-TO-DATE

Thursday, November 30th 1911, was the day for the opening of the new "Brunswick Cinema Theatre, which was situated at 30 Great Brunswick Street.

It may be of interest to note that the site for this cinema had been purchased by Izidore Bradlaw, who was better known for his involvement with the Assembly Rooms on Serpentine Avenue.

~~~~~

The proceeds of the opening nights show were donated to the building fund of St. Patrick's Church, Ringsend.

~~~~~

This was another superb place of entertainment to grace this beautiful thoroughfare, that extended from D'Olier Street and led to Ringsend, Sandymount and places further south. The others being, of course, the "Queens Theatre", which was situated just across the road. Further down the road, was the "Antient Concert Rooms", which many years later became the "Palace Cinema".

The "Evening Mail" cinema correspondent of the time, wrote in his column on Friday, December 1st that this new handsome picture theatre which had opened in South Great Brunswick Street on the previous day, had enjoyed good attendances at the continual performances which took place, from 2.30 to 10.30 pm.

Good programmes of music were contributed by the Ladies Orchestral band, and the seating accommodation, which is all on the ground floor, was most comfortable. The pictures that were shown were of a most up-to date description and represented the latest in this class of entertainment. Nothing, he wrote, is left undone by management to secure the comfort and convenience of their patrons.

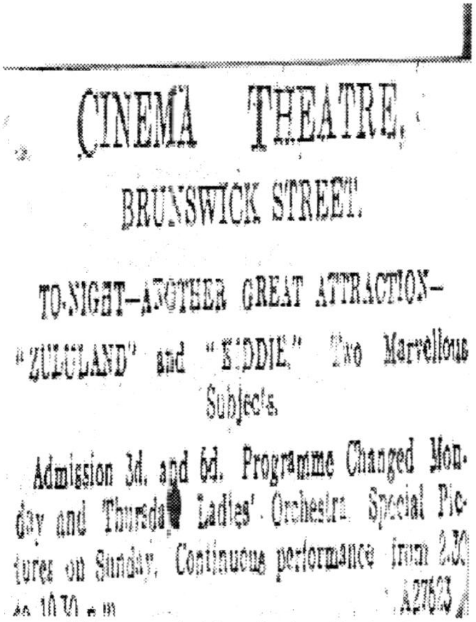

Among the first films to be shown in the "Brunswick" were "The Delhi Durban", "The Colleen Bawn" "Kiddie" and "Zululand".

Captain John R. Smallman was the manager and "Irish Amusement Limited" were the proprietors.

For a cinema of its size at the time, it advertised regularly in the National newspapers and on one occasion ran a rather large advert in the "Evening Mail".

This advert appeared on April 18th 1912.

In 1913, when the directors of the company made an application for the renewal of their Cinematograph licence, it was granted on the condition that an additional exit would be provided into Spring Garden Lane, together with the provision of extra ventilation vents. This work was carried out, inspected and the licence was issued.

While we have mentioned in the opening page that the premises were acquired by Izidore Bradlaw, we later came across the Memorandum and Articles of Association of a new company, which was incorporated on the 3rd day of December 1914, in order to purchase the Brunswick Cinema.

This new company was known as "The Brunswick Cinema Theatre", Limited, and three of its directors were named as, William Petrie, a Merchant of Glasnevin, Joseph Harris, a Merchant of South Anne Street and Maurice Elliman, a Picture Theatre Manager of Dufferin Ave, South Circular Road.

Below we re-produce a copy of the front cover of the Articles of Associations Booklet.

"THE COMPANIES" ACTS 1908 and 1913.

COMPANY LIMITED BY SHARES.

Memorandum of Association

OF

The Brunswick Kinema Theatre, Limited.

1.—The Name of the Company is "THE BRUNSWICK KINEMA THEATRE, LIMITED."

2.—The Registered Offices of the Company will be situated in Ireland.

3.—The objects for which the Company is established are:—

(*a*) To acquire and take over certain premises situated at South Great Brunswick Street, in the City of Dublin, and known as The Brunswick Kinema Theatre, and with a view thereto to enter into and carry into effect an Indenture of Assignment which has already been prepared and engrossed, and by which the said premises are to be assigned to the Company.

(*b*) To carry on the business of Cinematograph or other Theatre or Music Hall proprietors or managers, and in particular to provide for Cinematograph Shows and Exhibitions, and for the production, representation and performance, either by Cinematography or otherwise of Operas, Stage Plays or Operettas, Burlesques, Vandevilles, Ballets, Pantomimes, Spectacular Pieces, Promenade or other Concerts, and other Musical and Dramatic Entertainments and Performances, Boxing and Wrestling Competions and Exhibitions, and generally to engage in any undertaking for Public or Private Amusement, Instruction or Entertainment, and to carry on any other business connected with the Manufacture, Sale and Licensing, Renting, Production, Manupulation or Exhibition of Films or the Cinematograph Industry or the Production or Manufacture of any article or thing now or hereafter required in connection with such industry or applicable thereto, or in Dealing, Renting, Hiring, Licensing, and Handling any such articles or things.

Following this take-over, the Brunswick carried on as usual with no obvious changes. However, it can't have been doing all that well, as it closed four years later, in1918. We have no proper date for this closure, nor do we have a last advert, as the Brunswick appears to have ceased advertising in its latter years.

In the year 1919, the Brunswick Cinema Theatre was gone and the Brunswick Motor Exchange Company operated from those premises. That too, is now long gone and today, in 2006, a large modern red brick office building, which houses the Drug Treatment Centre Board, now occupies that site.

On the left of the Drug Treatment Board Centre Building, lies Spring Garden Lane with the no-entry signs on either side. This was where the additional exit had to be built by the Brunswick management in 1913, in order to qualify for a Cinematograph licence.

CABRA GRAND
Quarry Road, Cabra.

The Cabra Grand cinema opened on Saturday April 16th 1949 with the film "Sitting Pretty, starring Maureen O'Hara, Robert Young and Clifton Webb.

This film told the story of a suburban couple, Tracy and Harry, who had three young sons, who were totally out of control and in sheer desperation they hired an efficiency control expert, Lynn Belvedere (Clifton Webb), who soon had the little devils under control.

Having introduced the character of Belvedere, which proved very popular, they used this character in a number of other films including, "Belvedere Goes To College".

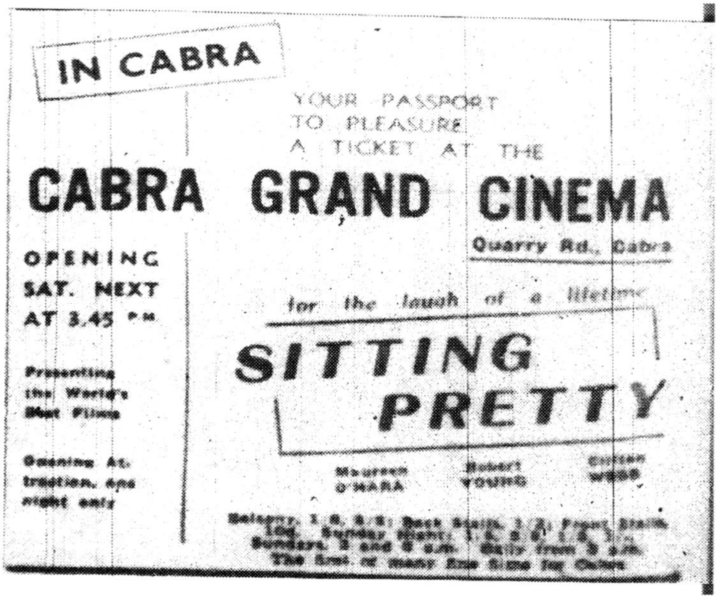

Nothing untoward came to our attention about the Cabra Grand, other than that on one occasion in September of 1951, a serious disturbance occurred, when an usher caught a young man behaving very improperly with a female companion. When asked to desist the young man attacked the usher and beat him about the body, at the same time, friends of the young man who were sitting in the balcony area began to add to the disturbance and the police were called. The young man in question was charged and the next day, when he appeared in court, he was seriously admonished by the Judge and heavily fined.

The Grand after it closed, now served the community as a Bingo Hall.

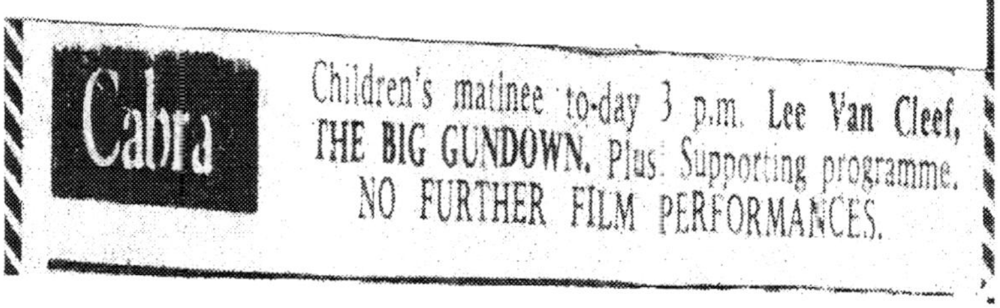

The Cabra Grand closed on January 31st 1970 and the last film shown was; "The Big Gundown" starring Lee Van Cleef in another Spaghetti Western, as a Lawman/ Bounty Hunter, who always gets his man.

The Cabra grand building in late 2005 which still appears to be in business as a Bingo Hall.

DUBLIN EMPLOYMENT PROMOTIONS LTD.

NEWS FLASH

GALA VARIETY CONCERT

MONDAY 7th OF JULY 7.30 P.M.

CABRA GRAND CINEMA

M.C. JIMMY GREALEY, RADIO 2.
Producted and directed by BILL KEATING, R.T.E.
ARTISTS: BRUSH SHIELS, PHILOMENA BEGLEY, IRISH FEDERATION OF MUSICIANS' BIG BAND, THE LIBERTIES MUSIC & DRAMA GROUP, THE JOLLY BEGGARMEN, TOM FLANAGAN, INNER CITY SCHOOL OF IRISH DANCING CAPIN, FRIEDA BANON. Host of surprise Guest Artists. Tickets £6, £4, £3. Help us to create jobs in the Cabra Inner City Area by giving us your support.

This news flash appeared in the "Evening Herald" on Friday July 4th 1986, which advertised a concert on behalf of "Dublin Employment Promotions Ltd., who were making a gallant effort to create much needed jobs at that time.

It would appear that although now in use as a bingo hall, that the Cabra Grand was willing to come out of retirement now and then, to promote concerts etc for good causes.

~~~~~

Another venue for Edison Pictures in the pioneering days of the Kinematograph was the Kingstown Town Hall (Now Dun Laoghaire).

Advertised in the "Evening Telegraph" for the evening of August 25th 1902 at 8.00 pm and for the rest of that week was The Original Irish Animated photo Company series of Edison's Celebrated Animated Pictures.

Included in the offerings were:

The Funeral of Dr. Croke
(Dr Croke retired as Archbishop in 1896 and died in 1902.
He was buried in the Cathedral of the Assumption, Thurles).

The arrival of the Mail Boat in Kingstown

Together with the Grand Coronation pictures of Edward V11 being Crowned King of England in 1902 and his wife Alexandra as Queen.

Matinee Programmes were available at 3.00 pm on the Wednesday, Friday and Saturday of the following week.
~~~~~

CAMDEN PICTURE HOUSE

The Camden Picture House 55 Lower Camden Street opened on Friday, 25th October 1912.

Two good views of the Camden Picture House
(The bottom view would have been taken after the cinema closed in 1948, as the poster on the left states "Cinema Closed")
Admission prices 3d & 6d.

The plans for the construction of this cinema were at first disallowed by the Corporation Councillors committee because of a dispute as to where exactly a fireproof door and wall should be positioned. However, agreements were reached between the owner and Councillors and the plans were approved.

It would appear that, as a caretaker would be living on the premises, the Councillors wanted a staircase leading to the living quarters completely enclosed by a wall of brick and concrete. This was to be done to the entire height of the ground floor, and subject to these recommendations being carried out, the plans were approved.

Following the article by Anne Kerr that featured us and our forthcoming book in the People Group of Newspapers we had many letters, emails and phone calls from readers of those papers, all wishing us well, some with tit-bits of information, advice, many simply with orders for our book, its availability etc and one or two with tales to tell.

Noel Twamley of Balrothery and formerly of the Old Camden Street area tells me that the Camden was one of his local cinemas and also a favourite venue of his uncle Tommy Grace of Old Camden Street.

Noel tells me of one occasion when his uncle Tommy visited the "Camden" to see the film "Picture of Dorian Gray" starring George Sanders and Hurt Hatfield, circa. 1947, When he was shown to his seat, he found that it was an ordinary free standing wooden kitchen chair. It would appear that the original seat had to be dismantled and taken away because it had been broken beyond repair and that the kitchen chair was simply a temporary replacement. Tommy, however, was none too happy as his rear end was a little sore having had to endure a hard seat for some 3 hours. On his next visit, he insisted that because of the circumstances of his last visit, that this time he should have a choice of seats.

Noel also tells me that The McGuinness family of Charlemont Street ran the Camden Picture House during that period and that two of the McGuinness sisters acted as usherettes, while their brother Christy assisted his father in the management of the premises.

When the Camden closed ,Christy acquired a position in the Carlton Cinema.

Noel also tells me that a very well known writer was once heard to proclaim "That the Fleas in the Camden wore Boots"

The Camden had the unique distinction of having its screen back to front, and when you entered the cinema proper you did so in a tunnel-like entrance that brought you directly under the screen. As you entered the auditorium, the projection lights would hit you in the eye and it was more prudent to walk backwards up the aisle until you found a seat of your choice. It was also very embarrassing for the more timid type of person because as you walked up the aisle you felt as if everybody was watching you.

The Camden's opening film was said to be "Dante's Inferno", by a reporter in the "Evening Herald", but we believed it was the "Charge of the Light Brigade". But we could not verify this. There were two versions of "Dante's Inferno" released within a year of each other and it's now difficult to determine which one was shown in the Camden. The 1911 version which was directed by Guiseppe de Liguoro, who also starred in the film, was the first full length Italian feature film ever made and it took over three years to make and grossed over $2m in the U.S. It was also the first film to be released in America in its entirety.

The 1912 version was the first film to show male frontal nudity, which didn't happen again until "Women in Love" 1969.

The Camden closed on August 28th 1948 with the film "Macomber Affair", which starred Gregory Peck, Joan Bennett and Robert Preston.

THE CAMDEN PICTURE HOUSE,

55 Lower Camden Street.

IS OPEN DAILY FROM 2.30 to 10.30 p.m.

String Orchestra from 3 to 5 and 7 to 10.30 p.m.
A continuous performance of all the latest and most up-to-date pictures.

Admission 6d. and 3d.

CREDIT WHERE CREDIT IS DUE.

If you find something in this book that we should have given you credit for and didn't, or at least requested permission for its use and didn't, we can only apologise and should we have re-produced a photograph without permission we would ask your understanding and plead ignorance and amateurism.

All our information came from reading, word of mouth and a little self-experience. We were inundated with snippets of information and received many gifts of programmes and pictures, so much so that we honestly cannot remember where half of it came from.
At all times we were overwhelmed with good wishes and goodwill and in our innocence we never once gave a thought to recording the source of the material we received, e.g. about twelve months ago we came across a photograph of the old Carlton cinema and while we made every effort to remember or locate the source, we failed in our endeavours.

Before publication of this book we wrote to the editors of all the newspapers we had read, the directors and archivists of the libraries that we had made use of and on a special page of this book, which we reserved for acknowledgements we thanked everybody that helped us. If we have inadvertently left you out of this list please, please forgive us.

George P Kearns & Patrick Maguire September 2006.

CAPITOL
4-8 Princes Street

The Capitol Cinema began life as the "La Scalla Theatre and Opera House" and was renowned for its lavish performances, which also, at times, included boxing exhibitions.

It opened on Tuesday August 10th 1920, and the main interest of the night was the appearance of John Clarke who thrilled the audience with the most popular songs of the time, which included two firm favourites "Dear Old Pal of Mine" and "Eily Mavoureen".

The main film chosen for its opening night was "Parentage" a six part selected masterpiece telling a story about two families in a small town in America which starred Lois Wilson as Mrs Melton the wife of the local banker. A supporting film was a two-part Max Sennett comedy entitled, "When love is Blind", starring Marie Provost.

The La Scalla was built on the old site of the Freeman's Journal in Princes Street off Sackville Street and just to the left of the G.P.O. It was built as an opera house but was seldom used as such. Its principle proprietors were Frank William Chambers and George Peter Fleming both of whom were said to be directors of the Carlton cinema.

The theatre was awesome in size and layout the likes of which was never before seen in Dublin. On the Saturday before it opened Thomas Quinlan the world-famed Impresario, said to the proprietors: "I have been in every theatre of note in almost every part of the world. I have seen La Scalla from floor to ceiling and I cannot make one single suggestion. Let it go at that."

T. Arthur Senior was resident manager and W.T. Mortimer musical director.

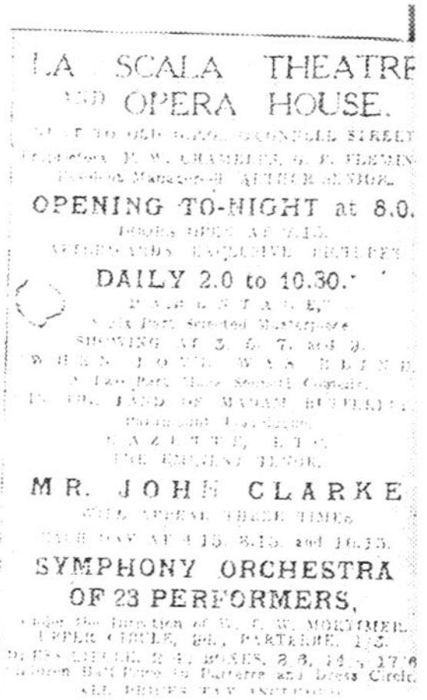
LA SCALA THEATRE
OPERA HOUSE.
OPENING TO-NIGHT at 8.0.
DAILY 2.0 to 10.30.
MR. JOHN CLARKE
SYMPHONY ORCHESTRA
OF 23 PERFORMERS,

Prices of admission were as follows: Upper Circle 9d,
Parterre, 1/3, Dress Circle, 2/4, Boxes 8/6. 14/-, 17/6,
Children half price to Parterre and Dress Circle.

The complex also boasted a restaurant, café, lounge and ballroom and some of the ornamental woodwork and carvings used in the building were said to have been rescued from the luxury White Star liner, Britannic, that was said to have been commandeered before completion and utilised as a hospital ship that was torpedoed in the Aegean Sea.

The ship was built in the Harland and Wolff shipyard in Belfast and was originally to be named the "Gigantic" but following the sinking of the Titanic in 1912 this was changed to the "Britannic".

Built to carry some 2,500 passengers and a crew of 950 she was launched in February 1914. However, before completion, she was requisitioned by the Admiralty for other uses. On Tuesday November 21st 1916, as she sailed through the Kea Channel in the Aegean Sea, under the command of Captain Charles Bartlett, she sank, as a result of an explosion caused by a mine or torpedo. To this day historians have not found out which. Despite the effort of Captain Bartlett to beach her on Kea Island, she sank within the hour with a loss of 30 lives.

Today, she lies on the bed of the channel, almost intact, and is the largest liner on the Ocean floor. She is also the largest liner to have been sunk in World War I and her sinking heralded the end of the White Star line. She never carried a fare-paying passenger and never crossed the Atlantic. A crew member, Violet Jessup, also worked on the Titanic and she survived both sinkings.

The wood panelling and doors, all beautifully carved and ornamented, which were to adorn the halls and concert rooms of the Britannic, were all stored and later purchased for use in the building of the Capitol.

The theatre had seating for nearly 1,400 people, had two balconies and numerous private boxes. On the top floor balcony one could feel dizzy looking down upon the stage.

The La Scalla Theatre opened in a week of unrest and shootings were taking place all over Dublin. It appears that the Royal assent had just been given to the Coercion Act for Ireland and to add fuel to the fire, the Most Reverend Dr. Mannix, Archbishop of Melbourne, later to become Cardinal, had been forcibly removed from a ship at sea by British naval forces, so that a champion of freedom might not visit his homeland. Theatregoing was rather a hazardous undertaking in those days.

In that same week, people queuing for admission to the Empire Theatre were shot at by parties of military, who had broke out from the castle and ran amok. More than fifty shots were fired in their general direction, as the variety lovers took to their heels.

In that week of August, the newspapers were full of reports of inquests on civilian shootings and reprisals. The La Scalla opened in the shadow of the then shell-shattered G.P.O.

Two interior views of the La Scalla

On St. Patrick's Day 1923 the world light heavyweight boxing championship fight between Mick McTigue and Baye Phal, otherwise known as Battling Siki, took place live on the stage of the La Scalla Theatre. While hundreds queued outside for admission, a bomb went off in nearby Moore Lane, which blew the heavy back doors of the Pillar Picture House. The detonation of this bomb was, it was thought, an effort to destroy the electric cable that fed power to the La Scalla Theatre.

Mc Teague beat Battling Siki in a 20 round contest which he won on points. In the audience that night was Georges Carpentier who had lost the title to Siki the previous year.

Outside, armed military patrolled the streets and their only diversion was the landmine in Moore Lane.

On September 5th 1926, a terrible tragedy occurred in Drumcollogher, County Limerick when 48 people were burned to death in a cinema. A disaster fund was established and Will Rogers, who was in Dublin at the time, gave a special concert in the La Scalla in order to win support for the effort.

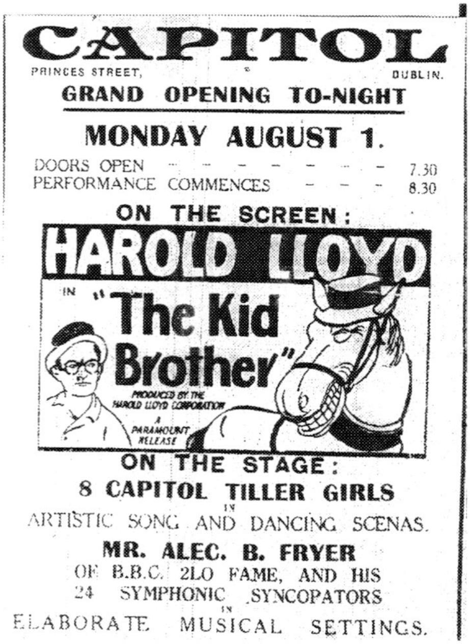

In 1927, Paramount took over the lease of the Theatre and renamed it the Capitol Cinema. The musical director of the London Rialto Cinema Alec B Fryer was brought over and he introduced the "Tiller Girls" to the stage of the Capitol and Tony Reddin was appointed manager.

With a star studded stage and two big films the Capitol announced that it was the "Mecca of entertainment in Dublin".

For its opening night, it presented "The Kid Brother" with Harold Lloyd.
While the cinema had a name change, the ballroom retained the name of La Scalla.

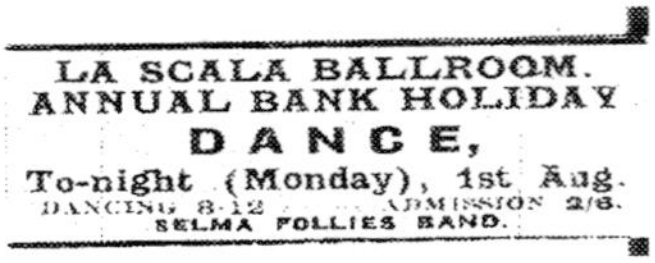

In the film "The Kid Brother", Harold Lloyd plays the part of the younger son of the town sheriff and timid brother to his two older big muscular brothers, Leo and Olin, and lacking in muscle he has to depend on his wits to hold his corner.

When his father the sheriff is falsely accused of some wrong doing, Harold and Mary, the love of his life, conspire and catch the real crooks red-handed.

Harold claims that while this was one of his favourite movies, it was also the last time he would play opposite his best leading lady Jobyna Ralston, who played Mary. Jobyna had played opposite Harold in six movies and had now found fame and stardom in her own right.

* * * * *

On Sunday April 21st 1929 Ireland's first talking picture was presented in the Capitol Cinema which was entitled "The Singing Fool"

As thousands were expected to flock to see this picture there was no continuous performances instead seats would be available before the picture started and the doors would open one half hour before the show started, admittance would cease when the programme began and at the end of each programme the house would be cleared.

There would be 4 performances daily

A reporter from the "Irish Independent" who was in attendance on that first night wrote a long piece about the film and we would mention some bits and pieces from that column.

We were he wrote, witnesses last night to things that a few years ago we could not conceive possible.

We saw and heard people on the screen walk and talk, sing and dance, laugh and cry. We saw and heard doors open and windows shut, corks pop out of bottles, telephones click, bands play and crowds roar applause.

This was all film work. There was no fake about it and most touching of all we saw little Sonny cough and sneeze just as any little delicate child in a nursery would do.

Al played the part of Al Stone a singing waiter in "Blackie Joe's "café who also wrote songs. Al was separated from his gold-digging, wife who ran off with a gangster and had taken darling little Sonny, Al's pride and joy, with her. However, little Sonny is very delicate and ends up in hospital where he dies. His heartbroken dad is there when he passes on to a better life. Gasping for breath, as he lies in his hospital bed the tiny lad asks his dad to sing "Sonny Boy" and as Al sings the song, the child sighs his way to peace.

The song "Sonny Boy" made the film famous.

"The Singing Fool" Jolson's second talking movie, "The Jazz Singer" being the first, was an instant success and helped to popularize talking movies to a wider audience. It also paved the way for a wider acceptance of sound.

* * * * *

However, not all were happy with the arrival of the "Talkies" and in particular the Directors of the British Broadcasting Corporation, in so far as they began to experience a mass resignation of their sound technicians who were being head hunted and offered luxurious contracts from firms that were devoting all their activities to the production of talking films.

Following the desertion of a dozen or so technical experts, the problem really came to the boil for the B.B.C. with the departure of R.E Jeffery's, their director of dramatic production, who had just taken up a position with one of those company's which required his services for the purpose of technical work in connection with the talkies.

They also feared that artists who were trained for recording by means of the microphone, will be tempted away by the "talkie" producers, more particularly now as their names were no longer broadcast when they take part in a studio play and are therefore deprived of the publicity which means so much to the theatrical profession.

Jeffery's was of the opinion that these microphone artists, with their finely trained voices will supply the demand for "talkie" actors and actresses.

When Scanlan, who was chief research engineer with the B.B.C., left with five others to take up employment with the same firm, the Directors of the B.B.C. concluded that they could not compete with private enterprise.

Theatres were also threatened by these new talking picture and Sir Alfred Butt, the well known theatre magnate, urged that the only way to fight the talkies was to build larger theatres, with seats at lower prices.

* * * * *

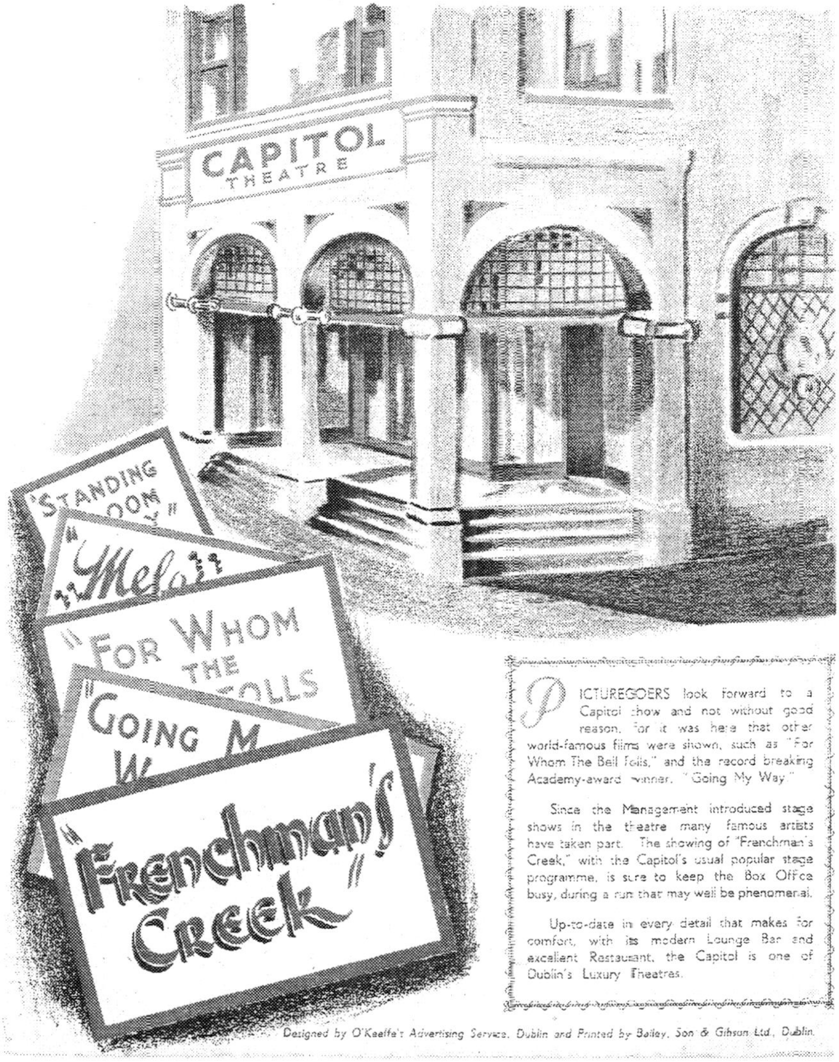

A view of some Capitol posters.

CAPITOL THEATRE

Prince's Street, - Dublin.

General Manager: - - - THOMAS C. REDDIN.

- WEEK COMMENCING MONDAY, OCTOBER 3rd. 1927 -

GENERAL LEW WALLACE'S IMMORTAL STORY—

MIGHTY "BEN HUR"

with RAMON NOVARRO

CARMEL MYERS, MAY McAVOY.
BETTY BRONSON, FRANCIS X. BUSHMAN.

A SCENE FROM MIGHTY "BEN HUR."

A scene from Ben Hur.

Sophie Tucker, the American burlesque, vaudeville and music hall singer filled the house in April 1929. Sophie was often billed as the Queen and First Lady of Show Business and was also known as the "Last of the Red Hot Mamas". The film for that week was "Shadow of the Law", starring William Powell and Marion Shilling.

Geraldo and Jack Hylton, with their orchestras, packed the theatre and Hilton Edwards sang in the Capitol in 1927 before the Gate Theatre was founded.

In 1934, the lease of the Capitol once again changed hands and the new owners planned to specialise in films only. However, the late Harold Holt organised some celebrity concerts there and at long last, having been built as an Opera House, the Dublin Operatic Society finally managed a few seasons there. Holt also brought many celebrities to the Capitol, including Count John McCormack and Paul Robeson.

In 1943, cine-variety began again in the Capitol with Frank Doherty as musical director and it continued as such until 1953, when once again, the Capitol said farewell to stage shows for good. On Thursday night, October 29th 1953, the Capitol played host to its last stage show and sad farewells were said all round.

Barney Markey, manager of the Capitol bade goodbye to Terry Rogers, the stage manager, and Jimmy Banks, the resident pianist. Johnny Keyes sang "To-nights the Night" and "Poor Little Lambs", Phyllis Power gave us "I'll Be Loving You Eternally" and Sean Mooney belted out "I'm Off to Philadelphia in the Morning". Crowds hugged and danced on the stage and Jack Kirwin wove in and out cracking his last Capitol jokes with Cecil Nash and some of the old Capitol Troupe were among the dancers.

At the closing moments the performers and audience sang "Auld Lang Syne" and numerous gifts were passed around and the players on the stage took it in turns to lean down and shake hands with Frank Doherty the conductor and fellow members of his orchestra. At 9.15 pm exactly the great maroon curtain fell on the last Capitol stage show.

Two old advertisements for the La Scalla in November of 1925

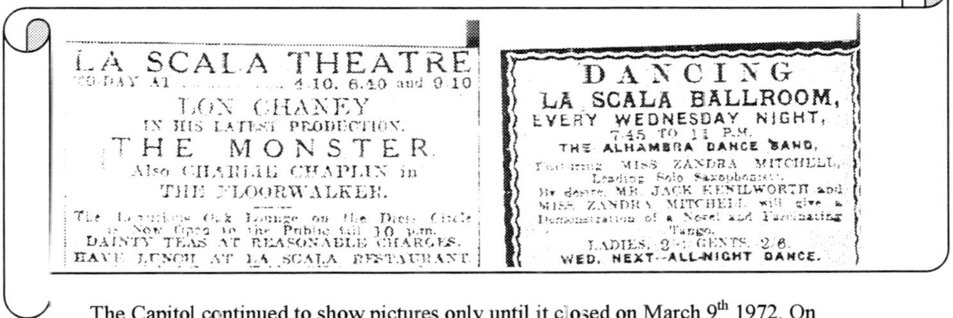

The Capitol continued to show pictures only until it closed on March 9th 1972. On March 10th its business was transferred to the "New Elec" in Talbot Street. Shortly after the Capitol closed ,the building was demolished.

CARLTON

The New Carlton cinema opened at 52 Sackville Street on Monday December 27th 1915 and was said at the time to be one of the finest cinema-theatres in Dublin. While its proprietor was one F.D. Chambers we did somewhere come across a mention of a cinema or company entitled the "Irish National Picture Palace" but reference and records are hard to trace.

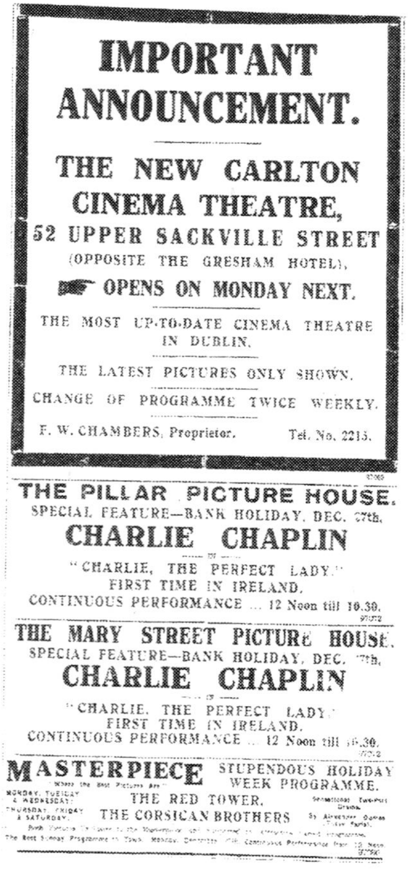

IMPORTANT ANNOUNCEMENT.

THE NEW CARLTON CINEMA THEATRE,
52 UPPER SACKVILLE STREET
(OPPOSITE THE GRESHAM HOTEL),
OPENS ON MONDAY NEXT.

THE MOST UP-TO-DATE CINEMA THEATRE IN DUBLIN.

THE LATEST PICTURES ONLY SHOWN.

CHANGE OF PROGRAMME TWICE WEEKLY.

F. W. CHAMBERS, Proprietor. Tel. No. 2215.

THE PILLAR PICTURE HOUSE.
SPECIAL FEATURE—BANK HOLIDAY, DEC. 27th,
CHARLIE CHAPLIN
"CHARLIE, THE PERFECT LADY."
FIRST TIME IN IRELAND.
CONTINUOUS PERFORMANCE ... 12 Noon till 10.30.

THE MARY STREET PICTURE HOUSE.
SPECIAL FEATURE—BANK HOLIDAY, DEC. 27th,
CHARLIE CHAPLIN
"CHARLIE, THE PERFECT LADY."
FIRST TIME IN IRELAND.
CONTINUOUS PERFORMANCE ... 12 Noon till 10.30.

MASTERPIECE STUPENDOUS HOLIDAY WEEK PROGRAMME.
MONDAY, TUESDAY & WEDNESDAY: THE RED TOWER.
THURSDAY, FRIDAY & SATURDAY: THE CORSICAN BROTHERS

Its opening film was "His Wife's Story" and it too we found to be untraceable. It was said to have been well-received by the audience and that it was its first screening in Dublin. There were many other fine films on show that night and all were accompanied by suitable music from a most competent group of musicians employed by the Carlton management.

This advertisement appeared in the "Evening Telegraph" on Christmas Eve, Friday December 24th 1915 announcing its grand opening on the following Monday.

It's also amusing to note that both the "Pillar Picture House" and the "Maro" are advertising the same film for the coming Bank Holiday and that both claim that it is the films first run in Ireland.

The Film, "Charlie, The Perfect Lady" starring Charlie Chaplin makes its debut in both cinemas, on the same day and at the same time.

While Charlie starred in this film, we believe, he also wrote the script and directed the film.

The building was badly damaged during the 1916 up-rising and underwent serious repairs, as it did during the Civil War when it once more came under attack. However it survived and remained in business until 1936 when it was closed in July of that year. The advertisement reproduced here is probably its last, at that time.

This advertisement is from the "Evening Herald" dated Friday July 10th 1936 and is reason enough for us to assume that the last performance in the Carlton occurred on the following Saturday July 11th.

It then closed and soon afterwards it was demolished and the site was prepared for a new cinema, the plans of which included the acquisition of two adjoining properties, No's 53 and 54, in order to build a larger cinema.

THE BIRTH OF THE CARLTON CINEMA

Dublin's new Café Cinema, the "Carlton", opened on Easter Saturday, April 16th 1938 at 2 o'clock in the afternoon and the directors of the company donated the first £100 taken at the box-office that night to the Society of St. Vincent de Paul. There was no formal opening and no advance bookings were accepted for that day.

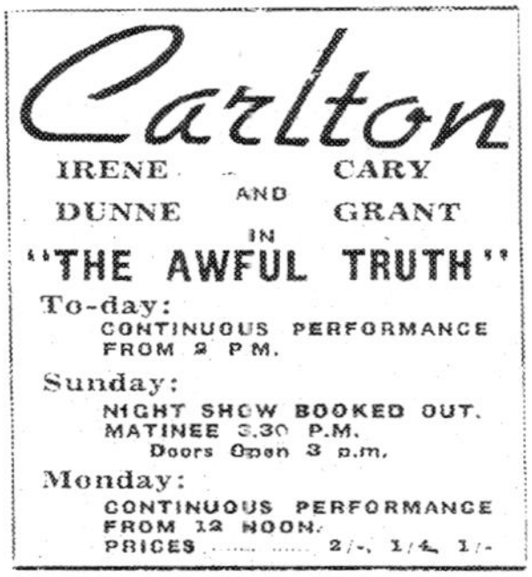

The company was a private one, long established and the directors were all local.

Tommy Gogan, a brother of Paddy Gogan the manager of the Queen's Theatre, is the manager of this new enterprise and he comes with some 20 years cinema experience, having been manager of the Pavilion Gardens, Dun Laoghaire, publicity manager of the Coliseum cinema in Henry Street and had also served as Vice-President and President of the Theatre and Cinema Association of Ireland. He was also the recipient of a presentation from that Association as a token of their appreciation of his services as a trade negotiator, and he was very much to the fore in introducing and establishing the Apprenticeship Scheme for Projectionists.

As can be seen from the display above, the front of the Carlton was ablaze with light and it was claimed that it had the largest Neon display in the country.

The building also sported a beautiful café-restaurant where you could enjoy your 'elevenses', lunch, afternoon tea or an evening meal. Prices were reasonable and the service second to none.

The Carlton however was not just a cinema it also had a well equipped stage and from time to time staged great concerts featuring world renowned artists such as Tom Jones, who appeared live in concert on Friday March 8th 1974.

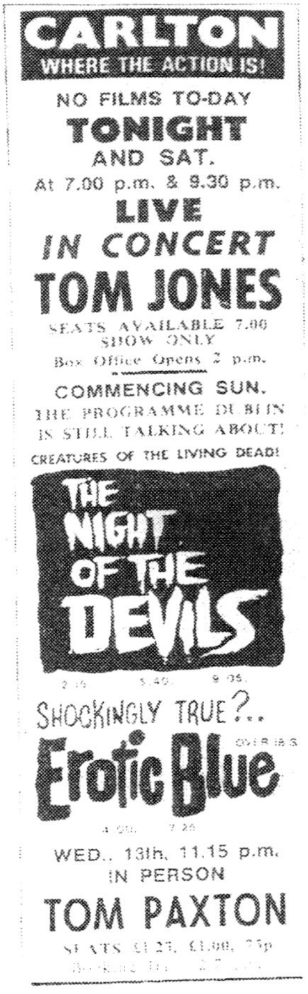

This was actually a return visit for Tom Jones as he had been in Ireland some three years previously. On this tour he was booked for two nights at the Carlton,

Tom stayed in the Gresham hotel which faced the Carlton from across the road and there, before making his appearance in the Carlton Tom was interviewed and asked about the circulating rumour that linked him with Marjorie Wallace, the shortest reigning "Miss World" ever.

In reply Tom said that he felt that Marjorie was badly treated when she lost her crown following her involvement with George Best. As for the rumours linking him with the ex Miss World he explained that she was a guest of his on a B.B.C. television special which was made in Barbados and in one sequence she and Tom exchanged a kiss, and that led to the alleged romantic links being reported.

When asked what his wife's reaction to the rumour was, Tom said she is used to those kinds of stories now.

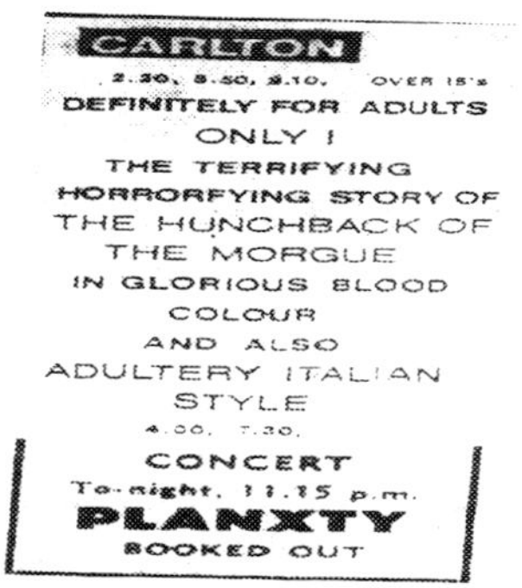

Planxty made a return visit to the Carlton on January 9th 1974 with newly married Christy Moore and to name but a few other famous artists who performed live in the Carlton I would mention; Rory Gallagher, Manitas De Plata the Gipsy guitarist and The Chieftains.

In the seventies the Carlton earned the nickname of the "House of Horror" because it appeared to specialise in featuring horror movies. Take note of the films on offer in the advertisements on the previous page and you will understand why.

* * * * *

On Friday afternoon, February 5th 1967, bullets began to fly in the Carlton cinema during the screening of the film "Where the Bullets Fly". This film was a British film company parody of a James Bond movie and starred Tom Adams as a British secret agent who had to outwit the notorious double agent "Angel" who was helping to organise a communist take-over of the British Parliament. Dawn Addams provided the love interest as 'Felicity Fiz Moonlight' and deadpan Sydney James played the part of a mortuary assistant

However the bullets flying in the Carlton that afternoon were in the auditorium and not on the silver screen. It would appear that two young men in the audience had possession of a .22 calibre pistol and having caused some disturbance they fired off some shots. Both were arrested and in court the next day they were charged with wantonly discharging a firearm, using insulting words and behaviour with intent to provoke a breach of the peace.

* * * * *

1956 "Rock around the Clock" hits town

On Friday, June 15th 1956 the Carlton cinema featured the rock and roll film "Rock Around The Clock" starring Bill Haley and his Comets.

This was the films first screening in Europe and it played to packed houses every night of its fourteen day first run.

The film told the whole story of Rock'n Roll and featured many hit tunes of the day, tunes which had the young in the audience, dancing in the aisles,

In all, there were 17 top tunes featured in the film including:
Rock Around the Clock
The Great Pretender
See You Later Alligator
Only You
A.B.C. Boogie
Razzle Dazzle
Rudy's Rock
R-O-C-K
Mambo's Rock
Giddy up a Ding Dong
We're Going to Teach You to Rock and teach them they did, in the aisles, between the rows of seats along the passages and even in the toilets.

Rock Around the Clock was a major impact film that brought about unruliness in the youth of the country that had never been witnessed before and in the opinion of George, it brought about a change in youthful attitude and behaviour for ever.

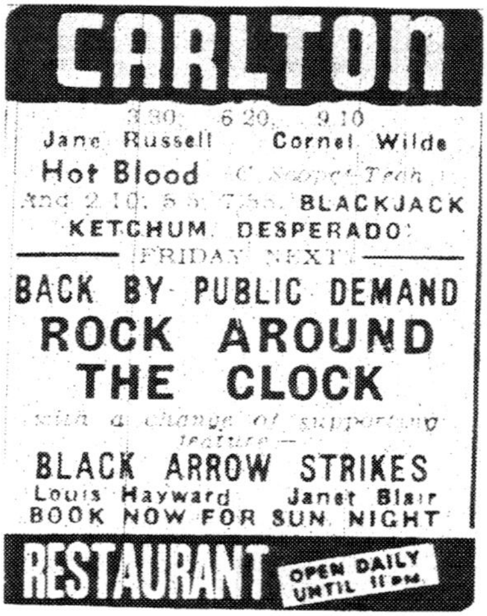

It also encouraged a film critic to become a 'Daddyo' as he termed it, and write his report in "Heptalk". Dig This, You Cats; he headlined his column as he reported his Friday night experience in the Carlton.

The film proved to be a box office success and by public demand the Carlton brought it back for a second weeks run on July 3rd 1956.

Sometime later the film went on general release and reports of trouble in cinemas abounded. We also read a book written by Lugs Branigan the well known Dublin Garda of that period, who claimed that in the course of duty he had to attend the showing of the film on some sixty occasions in order to ensure peace and quietness amongst the audience. See our story on the Star cinema.

As to rock and roll music and dancing we would tell you of the concerns of the Councillors of the Kilrush Urban District Council in 1957 when they were discussing the lack of attendances in their local hall. One Councillor suggested that they allow Rock'n Roll in their hall in order to boost attendances. Another Councillor claimed that if Rock'n Roll was allowed there would be no floor left, as when the dancers rocked, the floor would roll.

Having failed earlier to find an opening day advertisement for the Carlton, we eventually stumbled on this one quite by accident in the "Evening Telegraph" Monday, December 27th 1915.

However, the "Carlton" survived the Rock,n Roll era and continued to enjoy full houses with its concerts and films, be they horror films or not. In keeping with modern trends, the owners decided to close down the cinema and convert to a multi screen house, and on March 28th 1976, after the final performance, the Carlton closed.

The Carlton cinema, a 2,000 seater was last of the big picture houses in Dublin to finally give way to the giant ball of the demolition crew. However, its passing gave birth to three smaller Carlton's, the likes of which provided a wider choice of films. While one of the new screens could continue with the Carlton's reputation of showing horror films the other two could diversify with musicals, westerns, comedies and dramas.

"Enter The 7 Virgins" one of the last films to be shown in the Carlton cinema.

This was a film about 7 western girls captured by Chinese pirates, that promised the audience 'plenty of hanky panky' and the other film "The Sweet Body Of Deborah", was a thriller with Carol Baker.

Unfortunately however, the closing of the Carlton also signalled the end of its concert programmes.

The last concert featured the "STYLISTICS" a full orchestra and guest, Joe Cuddy.

In 1956 the Carlton was the first cinema in Dublin to experience an audience screaming, singing and dancing in the aisles when Bill Haley and his Comets Rocked Around The Clock. This was also a feature of its last night on Sunday March 28th when the Stylistics had the audience dancing in the aisles.

The Carlton and its 2,000 seats

In an interview with an Evening Herald reporter a week after the cinema closed the manager of the Carlton, Michael Nerney, recalled a number of happenings in the cinema which including two births and many near misses. The Rotunda ambulance, he said, became a part of the scene around the Carlton. Another tragic incident, he recalled, was that of a young boy who had come to the pictures with his father, and apparently the father had dozed off. Failing to wake up his father, the boy sought help, and when the staff went to investigate they found that the unfortunate man had died.

Some of the articles found in the cinema include: false teeth, a roast of beef and a dress? On one occasion, we found £850 and the owner didn't collect it for six months afterwards. He was a cattle dealer and when asked why he left it so long to collect, he replied that he knew it was in safe hands.

Some finds really intrigued the management, such as the number of single shoes which were left behind by women. How did these people not notice that their shoe was missing? How did they manage to hobble home, with one shoe on and the other off?

Michael also wondered about the spotless condition of the carpet in the cinema when he reckons that over 20,000 people a week had walked across its surface over the years. It took ten cleaners, six hours every day to clean and prepare the cinema for its early afternoon opening and in the course of their days work they would fill about 28 large bins with discarded rubbish.

George gets his spoke in here when he recalls the days when he worked in the Princess cinema in Rathmines and towards the end of his time there he tried hard to get a job as a cleaner in one of the first run town houses. These cleaner jobs were much sought after and were considered a well-paid day-job, as the hours worked were usually from 7am to 1pm. However, he claimed he hadn't a ghost of a chance because he was no good at football. It would appear that a good footballer stood a better chance of getting a cleaners job in the town houses, because all of them ran a football team and good players, it seemed, were scarce.

When the subject of horror films came up, Michael smiled and said that they had shown so many horror films that starred Vincent Price that they christened Vincent the "Chairman of the Board"

The Carlton also staged many a talent contest and quite a few well known names got their first real chance at stardom there.

Some of the biggest bands and orchestras in the world graced the stage of the Carlton at one time or other, including "Benny Goodman and his Big Band", "James Last and his Orchestra" and the "R.T.E Symphony Orchestra".

Duke Ellington beat out "Skin Deep". Gene Pitney claimed "It was only twenty four hours from Tulsa". Gary Glitter invited us to be in "His Gang" and Gilbert O'Sullivan told us about "Clair".

When George launched his book "The Prinner" on June 29th 2005, in the Rathmines library courtesy of the chief librarian Hugh Comerford and Breege his assistant, he met with Paul Bushe who used to frequent the Princess cinema. Paul told him that when Rock Around The Clock was on in the Carlton cinema in 1956, he encouraged his then girl friend, now his wife, to take a day off work and come with him to see the film.

Phoning in sick she accompanied Paul to the pictures and when the film was over and they were exiting the cinema, who was at the head of the queue for the next performance but her 'boss', who spotted her immediately and fired her on the spot!

* * * * *

When we attended school many years ago, we were totally misinformed. It was drilled into our heads that three into one wouldn't go – but, how wrong our mentors were. 3 went into 1 went perfectly well in the Carlton and many other like places.

This advertisement appeared in the evening papers on Thursday, August 26th 1976 announcing the grand opening of the Carlton 1, 2 & 3 cinemas on the following Friday.

Dublin cinemagoers were quite pleased with this new cinema offering, when they considered that they could easily have lost the Carlton completely to an office block or some other such building. Another plus in the favour of the picture-goer, was the fact that the Carlton and Adelphi shared the same management team and with so many screens to fill they had strong purchasing power assuring that only the best of films from the world's markets would be made available.

Friday, August 27th 1976, opening night of the Carlton 1, 2 and 3 cinemas, with three of the best newly released films from the worlds market, including Hitchcock's latest masterpiece "Family Plot" on Screen 1, "All The President's Men" with Robert Redford and Dustin Hoffman on Screen. Screen 3 had Al Pacino in "Dog Day Afternoon".

These multi screen cinemas also brought about a change in the queuing pattern of cinemagoers,. No longer would one see separate queues outside these multi screen cinemas for the Stalls, the Pit or the Balcony, now with uniformed prices for each screen, one would instead see queues for Screen 1, 2 or 3 and more in some cinemas.

On the Halloween Bank Holiday of 2005 George went to a multi-screened cinema complex in Parnell Street where he and his wife had a choice of 17 screens. The modus operandi there was to join a queue in the foyer in order to purchase a ticket for the screen of ones choice from one of the many ticket operators that sat behind a large counter alongside one wall.

George and his wife chose screen 11 and having purchased the tickets they were ushered up two escalators to the second floor where he was again directed to a long corridor, which contained some 9 cinemas.

Being a little early, George and his wife had a choice of sitting in the 2nd floor vestibule area, visiting a café or bar, where they could have ordered a drink, or food, or simply sit or stand on the floor of the corridor with hundreds of other cinemagoers, while awaiting admission. One could also purchase large buckets of pop-corn, sweets galore, minerals, ice cream and platters of a Mexican type food, which they could bring with them into the cinema and munch to their heart's content.

When George and his wife entered screen cinema 11 they found it quite spacious and George reckoned there were about 225 seats.

* * * * *

Three days after the opening of the three screened cinema, the Carlton along with a number of other business premises were firebombed by armed raiders on Monday morning Friday August 30th 1976. Fortunately, it only suffered slight damage to screen 3, where some 20 seats were burned. In early 1980, the Charcoal Grill restaurant was closed and a new screen was added to the Carlton. On Friday June 27th 1980, Screen 4 opened with James Caan in the film "Hide In Plain Sight"

For the next fourteen years the Carlton multi-screened cinema enjoyed a relatively peaceful existence until 1994 when a fall off in business heralded the end of its career and it closed its doors on October 20th 1994.

For its final week, the management of the Carlton ran a number of classic movies such as "Rock Around The Clock", "Grease" and "Singing In The Rain" as a farewell gesture. They referred to this last week as Nostalgia week, which was their way of saying "Goodbye".

Admission to any of these films was free of charge, provided one came dressed in 50's style clothing.

However, on one of their screens they also featured one of the latest releases "The Last Seduction" 1994.

The closure of this much loved cinema didn't warrant a lot of attention and appeared to fade quietly away without too much fanfare.

A small article appeared in the Front-Line column of the "Evening Press" bemoaning the loss of some 30 jobs and the passing of a popular land mark that had served the public for some 55 years, although we estimated it was actually 79 years.

For quite some time the building lay idle and derelict, and then the foyer was used for the retail sale of luggage, sports and raingear. George vaguely remembers a Palmist or Fortune-teller in business there, but he can't be all that sure.

There were many rumours of plans and developments that were about to take place but so far the building remains almost unchanged. The retailers are now gone and the building appears to be well sealed off and secured.

Over the years mention was made of a Millennium Shopping Mall that would have extended into Moore Street. Plans were aired for a Concert Hall that never matured and a new Multiplex Cinema was the talk of the town. The Abbey, it was said, would take it over as their new home, but this rumour also died in time. Circa. 2000, a Japanese Bamboo scaffolding was erected and covered the whole front of the building and we all wondered "what next?" This, we were told, was a work of art.

A Touch of Nostalgia

Bearing fruit to a rumour of an International Convention Centre.

The Carlton, well and truly closed in the year 2005

FIN

CASINO
North Road Finglas

The Casino cinema opened on the 25th November, 1955, and was situated on the site where the Superquinn Supermarket now stands. A part of the original building is still in evidence.

This cinema was a subsidiary of the St Stephens Green Company, owners of the Green cinema, and they claimed that the Casino was one of the largest suburban picture houses in the City. The Stalls area had seating for 1,418 people and the balcony 492 giving a grand total of 1,910.

The main contractors for this building were Maher and Murphy Ltd of Aughrim St and the architect, one John E. Collins.

The opening ceremony was performed by Mgr, R.J. Glennon .P.P and its first film was "The Student Prince" starring Edmund Purdom as Prince Karl and Ann Blyth as Katie. This film was said to be the world's greatest love musical.

Mario Lanza was contracted to play the part of Prince Karl, but it would appear that he had had a falling out with his studio bosses and he walked off the set. Following injunctions against Lanza by the studio for damages and losses which went on for some fifteen months, an agreement was reached, whereby Mario allowed his voice to be used, while another actor played the part of Prince Karl.

It seemed that Mario Lanza had already recorded the complete soundtrack of the film as early as 1952 and therefore no further work was required of him. Edmund Purdom had to lip-synch Lanza in the film and he was said to have done a marvellous job.

It was said that when Edmund replaced Mario Lanza in the Student Prince it secured him an unwanted reputation as a last minute replacement actor, as he had much earlier replaced Marlon Brando in the 1954 film the "Egyptian". Far from enhancing Edmund's opportunities, these replacement parts simply thwarted his career.

Mario Lanza made three other films before he died at the young age of 38 years. "Serenade" (1956) "The Seven Hills of Rome" (1958) and his last film "For the First Time" (1959)

STAR Frank Sinatra, Dean Martin, 4 FOR TEXAS, 5.08, 8.50. Deborah Kerr, MARRIAGE ON THE ROCKS, 3.20, 7.01. Sunday: James Mason, Lilli Palmer, TORPEDO BAY; Fess Parker, DAVY CROCKET AND THE RIVER PIRATES.

GALA John Wayne, THE GREEN BERETS, 3.15, 5.40, 8.40. Also: BUGS BUNNY No. 6. 5.28, 7.0 Sunday: Lucille Ball, Henry Fonda, YOURS, MINE AND OURS. Peter Cushing, THE EVIL OF FRANKENSTEIN.

CASINO Yul Brynner, Robert Mitchum, VILLA RIDES, 8.40. Jerry Lewis, THE NUTTY PROFESSOR. Over 18's. 6.49.

INCHICORE Paul Newman, Robert Redford, Katharine Ross, 6.25, 8.45. BUTCH CASSIDY AND THE SUNDANCE KID. Under 12's with Adult. Sunday: John Mills, Hayley Mills, Deborah Kerr, CHALK GARDEN. Barbara Shelly, SECRET OF BLOOD ISLAND.

The Casino's last advertisement.

The Casino closed, September 28th 1979

The Casino Building in 2005 and its Iron Canopy, which is still intact.

* * * * *

A Fireman's Axe

On Friday evening July 4th 1941 the body of Richard Robert's, the 50 year old manager of the Plaza Cinema in Dover, England, was found in an outside lumber shed, which was attached to the side of the cinema.

When the police arrived they found evidence of a struggle in the manager's office which also doubled as his living quarters. The manager slept on the premises and it would appear that the killer had murdered the manager by striking him with a fireman's axe, and then bundled the body out through the window of the office / bedroom and hid it in the lumber room.

Some of the previous nights takings were missing and the body was found shortly after the afternoon's performance had finished.

On July 19th 1941, a Scotland Yard Detective arrested a Leslie Hammond, an 18 year old cinema operator who worked in the cinema and charged him with the murder of Robert's

* * * * *

CINEMA ROYAL
6 Townsend Street

This building was formerly a tenement building, Temperance Hall, Coffee Palace and Palace Picture Theatre, all of which began in that order.

In 1875, The Dublin Total Abstinence Society took over this now vacant tenement building, which was situated at 6 Townsend Street and converted the building and spacious ground area to the rear into a public meeting house and entertainment hall. In 1882 they introduced coffee rooms and later again a dining area where one could partake of a light repast. Later again it entered into the hotel business.

The hall initially was used for meeting purposes, small recitals and get-togethers but very soon musical concerts, recitals and variety shows were introduced and it quickly became the custom of the principles of the society to hold such a concert every Monday evening. An integral part of this weekly entertainment would be a Temperance address that would be read out by a member of the Society.

The façade of the building was very imposing but in our opinion it projected an image more suited to a Public House than it did to a Coffee shop and Picture Palace. Most misleading was a sign on the left hand side supporting pillar, which advertised a public bar, of course it did mean a "coffee bar".

There were two entrances to this complex, the one on the right led into the dining and tea rooms while the one on the left led to the concert hall, meeting rooms and hotel. The sign writing on the shop front was neat and accurate and obviously carried out by a professional. Midway up on the façade were the words "TEMPERANCE HALL", which were carved in stone.

These premises were well placed at the beginning of Townsend Street, almost facing the "Crampton Statue" which stood on an island at the junction of D'Olier Street, College Street, Great Brunswick Street (Pearse), Townsend Street and Hawkins Street and were quite central to the city centre.

In late 1908 Cinematograph Exhibitions were introduced in the hall to the rear of the Coffee Palace and when these pictures began to attract greater numbers to the hall they became a regular feature.

In March of 1909 the Coffee Palace had a change of management and closed for a short while, in order to have a make-over. Under the direction of Erskine the theatre re-opened as "The Palace". Erskine was a most courteous person, who for many years had been connected to the "Daily Express" newspaper and was now entering the cine-variety business full of life and fresh ideas.

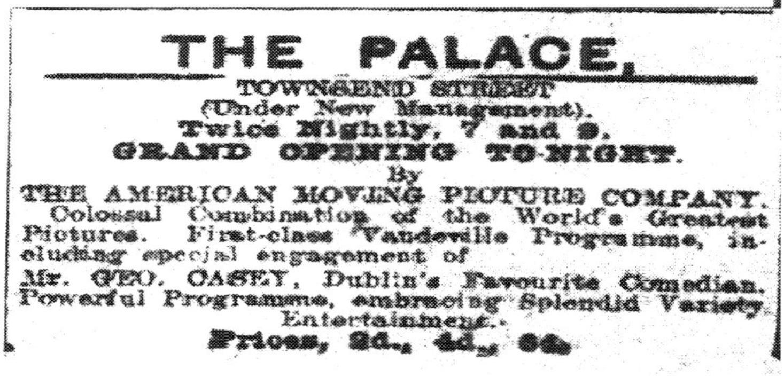

THE PALACE,
TOWNSEND STREET
(Under New Management).
Twice Nightly, 7 and 9.
GRAND OPENING TO-NIGHT.
By
THE AMERICAN MOVING PICTURE COMPANY.
Colossal Combination of the World's Greatest Pictures. First-class Vaudeville Programme, including special engagement of
Mr. GEO. CASEY, Dublin's Favourite Comedian.
Powerful Programme, embracing Splendid Variety Entertainment.
Prices, 2d., 4d., 6d.

For its "Grand Opening" on Tuesday night March 30th 1909, Erskine invited the "The American Moving Picture Company" who had a large collection of the "Worlds Greatest Pictures" in hand, to exhibit their pictures in his new "Palace Theatre". He also contracted George Casey, Dublin's favourite comedian, to provide and promote a first class vaudeville and variety act.

On Wednesday, March 31st. the "Evening Herald" theatre critic reported that the "Grand Opening" of the new "Palace Theatre" was attended by a large and appreciative audience and that a splendid selection of pictures had been shown. Some of Dublin's favourite variety artists, he said, were also on stage last night and they contributed some interesting items to an enjoyable performance.

Success breeds success, and so it went with the "Palace Theatre" in Townsend Street. Great motion pictures attracted full houses and the cream of Dublin's entertainer's craved auditions there. In April of 1913 a reporter from the "Bioscope"magazine visited the theatre one afternoon during a matinee performance hosted by Erskine for the children of a local school. He was most impressed when he found the theatre packed with a young audience who, judging by their laughter and applause, were thoroughly pleased with the show.

A small selection of films that graced the screen of the "Palace Theatre" during its short reign; "A Burglar Against his Will", "The Villagers Quarrel", "A Policeman for an Hour", "A Martyrdom of Louis XV11", "An Evil Spirit" in a Girls Boarding House" and "A Voice from the Dead".

However, showbusiness, like any other business, had its ups and downs and it would appear that the "Palace Theatre" suffered the latter towards the end of 1913. when it closed down.

In December of 1913, W. Butler of G. Butler and Sons, Monument House, O'Connell Bridge. took over, the then closed, the "Palace Theatre" and reopened it on Tuesday 23rd December 1913 as the "Cinema Royal" Townsend Street.

G. BUTLER & SONS
MUSICAL INSTRUMENT MAKERS
Issue three catalogues, post free
Monument House
O'CONNELL BRIDGE

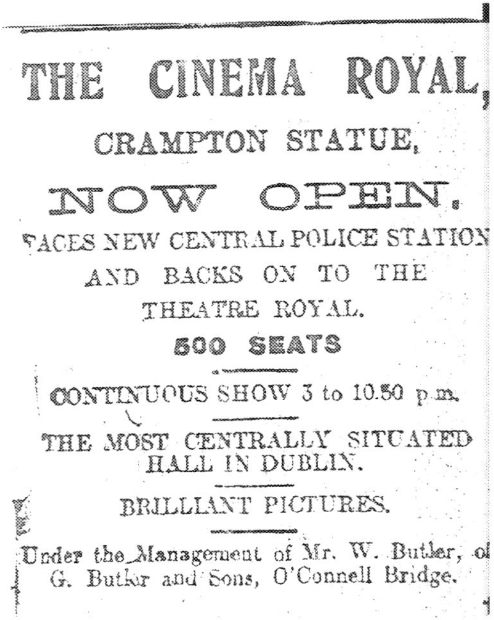
THE CINEMA ROYAL,
CRAMPTON STATUE,
NOW OPEN.
FACES NEW CENTRAL POLICE STATION
AND BACKS ON TO THE
THEATRE ROYAL.
500 SEATS
CONTINUOUS SHOW 3 to 10.50 p.m.
THE MOST CENTRALLY SITUATED
HALL IN DUBLIN.
BRILLIANT PICTURES.
Under the Management of Mr. W. Butler, of
G. Butler and Sons, O'Connell Bridge.

It was noticed that this new cinema had opened in a hurried manner, most likely in order to cash in on the Christmas trade and at the time management apologised for this urgency by promising that a projector of the newest design would be purchased and fitted as soon as time permitted, together with comfortable lounges etc.

The brilliancy of the pictures and the selection of films they said will be similar to those that have given the good name to the Thomas Street Picture House, which is also under the ownership of the same management.

In their rush to open the cinema in order to cash in on the Christmas trade it would seem that the management neglected to secure a Cinematograph licence and in the first quarter of 1914 the Dublin Corporation officials instructed the Law Agent to prosecute. A little later on the situation, it would appear, was sorted and a licence was granted to the "Cinema Royal".

On January 14th 1914 the above advertisement was displayed in Dublin newspapers and as the management claimed that their pictures were perfectly projected without flicker, they must have kept their promise by installing the newest projector available, and hopefully the comfortable lounges were also included in that re-fit.

On one of his many tours of inspection, the Inspector of Cinemas advised the Coffee Shop management to take steps and have their projection equipment encased in iron. He further demanded that panic bolts be fitted on all doors.

Dublin Coffee Palace, 6 Townsend St.

The Cinema Royal, however was not destined to have a long life, as the Incorporated Dublin Total Abstinence Society was wound-up in 1915, following a petition to the courts from its creditors because of its insolvency and inability to pay its debts.

The court hearing took place on November 9th 1915, and when the Master of the Rolls issued a winding-up order, a liquidator was appointed. As a consequence to this action, the building once again became vacant in 1916 and in 1917 it became the offices of the "Freeman's Journal".

CINEMA SITES

It may come as a surprise to Dubliner's to find that there were many applications made to Dublin Corporation seeking cinema sites or a licence to build cinemas in many parts of Dublin. Dublin Corporation also had on offer selected sites for cinemas, such as the one on Decies Road Ballyfermot in 1956, which never attracted a really serious entrepreneur or interested company. While it did attract a few tenders, they were never followed through.

Advertisements seeking tenders for this site appeared in the Irish Times, Irish Independent and Irish Press on Tuesday October 6th 1956.

According to a Codd, Principle Officer, Housing Department Dublin Corporation there were no agreeable offers to build a cinema on the site, and he suggested that other alternatives should be found. Later a pub was built on the site.

Objections to Dublin Corporation plans to build a cinema on this site were made by the directors of the Gala cinema who had spent £80,000 on the building of their cinema and as the Gala could accommodate some 2000 picture-goers they felt that the needs of the community were well and truly catered for.

There was also mention of a cinema site on Sarsfield Road, Ballyfermot.

There were also many plans and applications made for cinemas in other parts of Dublin, including areas such as;

Donnycarney, Howth Road, Keeper Road, Herberton Road,

South Circular Road (near Kelly's Corner),

Georges Street (see Georges Street Picture House story),

Parts of Finglas, Cabra,

9 & 10 Summerhill.

Plans for a cinema on Northumberland Road were rejected in 1906, as were similar plans for 94 Talbot Street. However, many years later, the "Masterpiece Cinema" was built on the site of 99 Talbot Street.

Ireland was highly rated as a cinema-going nation.

CINEMATOGRAPH ACT 1909

While we won't even try to define the legalities of this act we will simply tell you that the "Act" was brought into being for the security and safety of picturegoers. For some ten years prior to that date, cinematographic exhibitions had taken place in some very unsuitable buildings, particularly considering the fact that highly unstable nitrate film-stock had caused some serious fires.

This new "Act" was introduced by the British Government and was immediately placed under the control of local authorities who would lay down the strict rules and regulations pertaining to the use of any building for the purpose of these film exhibitions. These rules and regulations would be policed by the local authorities and if a building which was built or converted for the purpose of showing films passed a rigorous inspection by a specially appointed cinema inspector then a licence under the "Cinematograph 1909 Act" would be issued for period of one year on payment of a fee of £1.

These premises would also be subject to unannounced inspections at any time and if found to be in breach of the "Act" the licence could be revoked. The licence had to be renewed annually and would again be subject to a rigorous inspection before it was renewed.

(Full details of the Cinematograph 1909 Act can be accessed on the internet.)

Here for your perusal is a word for word copy of what it said on the licence that was issued to the Sandford cinema on December 2nd 1914, and we would believe that most other licences for other cinemas would be similarly worded.

RATHMINES AND RATHGAR
URBAN DISTRICT COUNCIL

(9 Edward V111 Chap, 30)

A Licence is hereby granted to the Sandford Cinema Company Limited having their registered office at 27 Westmoreland Street in the City of Dublin to use the premises known as 1 Cullenswood Road within the Urban District of Rathmines and Rathgar for the purpose of an exhibition of pictures or other optical effects by means of a Cinematograph or other similar apparatus under the following conditions for the period of one year from the date of the licence.

~~~~~Conditions~~~~~

1-No building shall be used for Cinematograph or other similar exhibitions to which the above Act applies unless it be provided with an adequate number of clearly indicated exits so placed and maintained as readily to afford the audience ample means of safe egress.

2-the Cinematograph apparatus shall be placed in an enclosure of substantial construction made of or lined with fire resisting material and of sufficient dimensions to allow the operator to work freely.
~~~~~

3-The entrance to the enclosure shall be suitably placed and be fitted out with a self-closing, close-fitting door, constructed of fire-resisting material.

4-The openings through which the necessary pipes and cables pass into the enclosure shall be sufficiently bushed.

5-The openings in the front face of the enclosure shall not be larger than is necessary for effective projection and shall not exceed two feet for each lantern. Each such opening shall be fitted with a screen of fire resisting material, which can be released both inside and outside the enclosure so that it automatically closes with a close fitting joint.

6-The door of the enclosure and all openings bushes and joints shall be constructed and maintained as to prevent, so far as possible, the escape of any smoke into the auditorium. If means of ventilation are provided they shall not be allowed to communicate direct with the Auditorium.

7-If the enclosure is inside the Auditorium, either a suitable barrier shall be placed around the enclosure at a distance of not less than two feet from it or other effective means shall be taken to prevent the public from coming into contact with the enclosure.

8-A plan and description of the Building hereby licensed, approved of by the Rathmines and Rathgar Urban District Council is attached to this licence.

9-If any alteration is made in the Building or the enclosure without the sanctions of the Rathmines and Rathgar Urban District Council this licence will forthwith lapse.

Given under the seal of the
Rathmines and Rathgar
Urban District Council
Second day of December
One Thousand Nine Hundred
and Fourteen

Unfortunately, many operators did not apply for such a licence and some took a chance and exhibited films in unlicensed and sometimes unsuitable premises and in so doing put their audiences at risk.

One such building in a small Limerick village was used for this purpose and the consequences were horrific, as the film stock burst into flames and set the premises alight causing forty eight people to be burnt alive.

George tells the story of this cinema in his book "The Prinner"

~~~~~

We also reproduce on the next two pages a copy of the then official licence, as issued by the Public Health Department of Dublin Corporation.
~~~~~

PUBLIC HEALTH DEPARTMENT

Licence under Cinematograph Act, 1909

LICENCE is hereby granted to ....

of .... to utilise the premises

....for the purpose of the exhibition of pictures and other optical effects by means of a Cinematograph or other similar apparatus for a period to terminate on the 31st day of October, 19........, subject to the terms, conditions, and restrictions following, and to the regulations made by the Lord Lieutenant in Council on the 20th April, 1910, and the 23rd July, 1913, under the said Act, or subject to such regulations as may at any time hereafter be substituted therefor.

1. No alteration shall be made in the building or the enclosure or the seating arrangements without the sanction of the Corporation.

2. The premises shall not open on Sundays save between the hours of 2.30 p.m. to 6.30 p.m., and 8.30 p.m. to 10.30 p.m.

3. No known improper character, reputed thief, or other disorderly person, or any person in a state of intoxication, shall be admitted into, or permitted to remain on, the licensed premises.

4. The licensee shall be responsible for the maintenance of good order and decent behaviour in the licensed premises.

5. No child of school-going age shall be admitted to any exhibition or performance during school hours on any school-attendance day, unless accompanied by a parent or guardian.

6. No child under 14 years of age shall be admitted into, or permitted to remain on, the licensed premises after 9.30 p.m. unless accompanied by a parent or guardian.

7. A separate portion of each part of the auditorium shall be exclusively reserved for children under 14 years of age who attend entertainments unaccompanied by parents or guardians.

8. The premises shall at all times, while open to the public, be in telephonic communication with the Central Fire Station.

9. At all times when the premises are open to the public there shall be sufficient light in the auditorium to enable any person present, and any person visiting the premises, under Section 4 of the Cinematograph Act, 1909, to see clearly to all parts of the auditorium from any part thereof.

10. A seat shall be provided for each attendant in the licensed premises, and the licensee shall not place any obstacle in the way of any attendant using the same.

11. The stipulations contained in Articles 2 and 5, (1) (*a*), (*b*), (*c*), (*d*), (*e*), and (*f*) of the regulations dated 20th April, 1910, made by the Lord Lieutenant under the Cinematograph Act, 1909, shall be carried out to the satisfaction of the Corporation.

12. The electric installation in the licensed premises shall always be maintained in good and safe working condition to the satisfaction of the City Engineer. No addition or alteration to the electric installation, whether such addition or alteration be permanent or temporary, shall be made without the approval of the City Engineer.

13. The means of ventilation provided for the licensed premises shall be efficiently maintained and used.

14. The several lavatories and urinals in the licensed premises shall at all times be kept in good order and repair, and be properly and effectually cleansed, ventilated, and disinfected, and supplied with water and all proper requisites, and the doors leading to them shall be suitably marked.

15. At all times between sunrise and sunset, when the premises are not open to the public, the windows, skylights, and other openings lighting the auditorium shall be kept uncovered, and shall be so used as to permit the free access of light and sunshine into the auditorium.

16. All doors, windows, and skylights shall be opened each morning for at least three hours to admit fresh air into the auditorium.

17. The premises shall be kept thoroughly clean.

18. The premises shall be entirely closed on Christmas Day, and on the Wednesday, Thursday, and Friday preceding Easter Sunday.

19. The relative positions of the picture screen and the seating shall be such that undue eyestrain is not caused.

(*Any special terms or conditions to be inserted here.*)

In the event of any breach of the foregoing, this licence may be revoked.

The issue of this licence shall be without prejudice to the right of the Corporation to exercise any powers which may be vested in them under any other Act or Regulations relating to Places of Public Resort.

CLASSIC
Terenure

Dublin's newest cinema, the "Classic" that was built on the site of the old Dublin and Blessington Steam Tramway Company, by the Sundrive Cinema Company Limited, which was opened informally on Friday July 1st 1938.

This new cinema, although purpose built as a cinema, had a fair sized stage with all the necessary equipment needed to put on a variety show if the need arose. The seating, which was divided into three sections and arranged on the stadium style, had accommodation for 750 persons and admission prices were as follows: front stalls 9d, back stalls 1/4 and stadium section 1/10.

The main contractor was Thos. Kennedy of Library View Terrace, Phibsboro, who had also built the Sundrive cinema some years earlier. The Classic had its own private car park, which would hold over fifty cars and a special feature of this new cinema was a spacious waiting room, with ample seating for patrons waiting for admission. No longer would one have to queue on the outside footpath.

The seats within the cinema are of crimson plush with rubber arm-rests and of the automatic tip-up style. Warm air is circulated throughout the cinema from grilles situated on either side of the stage and the used air is then drawn up and out through vents in the roof. Sanitary accommodations are provided for in four compartments.

There are three exits from the cinema, each with wide doors, which allow the cinema to be cleared at the end of the show, without delay.

The film "I'll Take Romance" was chosen for the opening attraction.

The three main directors of the Sundrive Cinema Group are: William Callow, Chairman, H. Croskerry and M.A. Heron, who is also manager of the cinema.

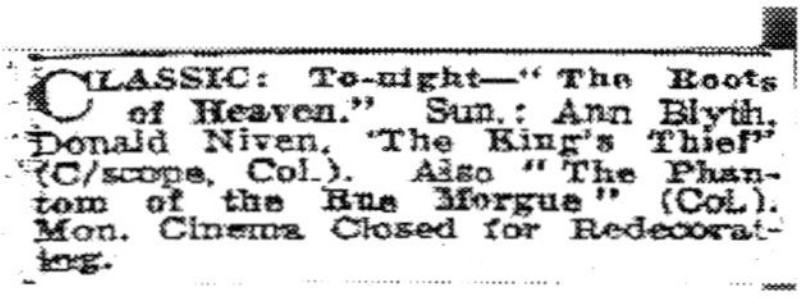
CLASSIC: To-night—"The Roots of Heaven." Sun.: Ann Blyth, Donald Niven, "The King's Thief" (C/scope, Col.). Also "The Phantom of the Rue Morgue" (Col.). Mon. Cinema Closed for Redecorating.

The Classic catered well for its patrons and in return it attracted well attended houses. In 1959, management decided the cinema was in need of some decoration and in July of that year it closed for renovations.

On Sunday, August 2nd 1959, the Classic re-opened with a new look frontage and some important interior changes, which added to the already great comfort of its patrons. The frontage was now re-decorated in Wedgewood Blue with touches of Burgundy Red. The large foyer was re-done in oak panelling which contrasted well with some modern wall coverings, which had white stars almost sparkling on a red background. New entrance doors, of the swing sound-proof type were installed and the seat-cushioning was totally refurbished. The heating and cooling system had been completely overhauled and improved upon and heavy drop curtains in rose velour completed an artistic effect together with new carpeting also in rose red with white motifs dotted here and there. In all, the Classic was now among the foremost of modern luxury cinemas and once again Thos. Kennedy was the main contractor.

The film chosen for the re-opening on Sunday night August 2nd was "Night in Havana" starring Errol Flynn and the supporting film was "Revolt in Laramie". Errol plays the part of Ned Sherwood, a dealer in a Havana casino, who gets involved with counterfeiters.

On Monday the August bank holiday they featured "The Inn of the Sixth happiness" starring Ingrid Bergman, who as Englishwoman Gladys Aylward in China, leads her charge of children to safety when the Japanese invade.

Some five years later on April 30th 1964, Matthew Albert Heron the manager of the Classic and Sundrive Cinema Company Ltd. died in his office in the Classic cinema Terenure and Albert Kelly took over as manager of both the Classic Terenure and its sister cinema, the Kenilworth, in Harold's Cross.

The cinemas business in Dublin was in decline in the sixties. In particular, the suburban houses and one of the reasons for this decline was the difficulty in getting first rate films, first hand. To counteract this problem Albert Kelly decided to import and show French and Russian arty type films such as the Kirov Ballet Companies "Sleeping Beauty" and these films proved a great success and attracted ballet enthusiasts from all over Ireland.

With a little persuasion from a film critic friend of his, Albert introduced the cult film "The Rocky Horror Show" to the Classic and it attracted so much attention that he ran it every Friday night in the late night film slot, where it attracted its own regular followers who danced and acted out the complete film in the aisles of the cinema.

"Jump to the right, step to the left, hands on your hips and knees up tight, and lets do the time warp again", went the chant.

Albert Kelly now managing two cinemas found the dual roll somewhat demanding and he hired an assistant who managed the Classic for him. This was Michael Keegan, one time manager of the Princess cinema in Rathmines, who was later to become the front manager of the Gate Theatre.
In 1976 the directors of the Sundrive Cinema Company decided to opt out of the cinema business and instead focus their energies on other activities and they closed their cinemas in July 1976.

This was the last advertisement for the Classic/Kenilworth cinemas both of which closed on Saturday June 19th 1976.

The Classic in the process of conversion into a retail showroom sometime after it closed as a cinema.

The Classic Building in October 2004.

Picture taken outside the Classic cinema, Terenure in 1970

Albert Kelly on the left, Hilton Edwards, Michael Keegan and Michael MacLiammoir We have no name for the person on the right.

During the month of June 2006, George received a call from a good lady in Harold's Cross who wished to purchase a copy of his book "The Princess". On delivery of the book he was invited in for one of his favourite brews ' a cup of instant coffee' a brew which he claims 'keeps him ticking.

The lady in question who wishes to remain anonymous knew quite a bit about cinema and through her late mother and father she knew of March and his Henry St Coliseum Theatre and she added, he (Marsh) once owned this house. (See Coliseum Story)

She also knew about the Classic and its owner and manager and when George mentioned his old pal of the "Prinner" days Michael Keegan, she said 'have I got a surprise for you' and with that she produced the above picture with Michael centre stage.

Pity about the flash, but beggars can't be choosers. George was overwhelmed with delight with his gift as he had searched high and low for a picture of his old friend for many a long time.

CLONTARF ELECTRIC THEATRE

The cinematograph came to Clontarf on July 18th 1913 in the shape of a cinema situated within the walls of the Clontarf Town Hall. This cinema was officially opened by Sir Charles Cameron, who, during his speech, let the audience into a little secret.

I have he said some shares in a company that is paying a nice little dividend to the tune of 20% and I am sorry now that I didn't sell out the entire stock and invest the proceeds in a picture house.

Sir Charles was a much liked and respected personality and Alderman Maguire having presented Sir Charles with a beautiful gold mounted umbrella on behalf of the promoters, made a witty little speech.

Alderman Maguire, in congratulating the cinema promoters on their choice of a gentleman to open the picture house, said that Sir Charles always reminded him of the saying of a great Roman Orator, who once remarked, " Give me the young man who has something of the old man in him and the old man who has something of the young man in him" He need not say which of these categories Sir Charles belonged, indeed he belonged to both for they would go very far to find such a graceful and amiable blending of the good qualities of youth and age.

(Source Freeman's Journal July 19th 1913)

In his opening speech, Sir Charles remarked that it was only a couple of years since the first cinema opened in Dublin and now there were almost forty of them that were giving great pleasure to thousands of patrons and providing employment for many people.

The picture house was a neatly appointed and commodious hall with the latest available equipment and up to-date ventilation with safety precautions to the fore.

Prior to July of 1913 The Estates and Finance Committee of the Clontarf Town Hall were approached by a couple of businessmen who proposed the opening of an Electric Cinema within the confines of the Town Hall and following a meeting the proposal was accepted on the condition that the Promoters obtain a Cinematograph licence from Dublin Corporation.

Having made an application to the appropriate department in Dublin Corporation, which initiated an inspection of the premises, the Inspector of Cinemas reported that under the Cinematograph Act the plan showing the proposed alterations to the building were in accordance with the Bye-Laws. However he did suggest that if they intended to use the premises continuously for cinematograph performances then the machine enclosure should be fixed outside the building.

The Inspection Committee paid a visit to the Town Hall and made a number of suggestions which included a separate entrance to the sanitary accommodations for males and females, together with a proviso that panic bolts be fitted on all exit doors with illuminated notices over these doors. They also advised on the positioning of the projection machine enclosure on the outside of the hall.

The Clontarf Town Hall Building is still in existence and this is the rear view, which was taken at the end of March 2006. The reason for a rear end view will become apparent as the story unfolds.

~~~~~

Clontarf in the 19th century was a separate township onto itself, with its own Town Hall and District Council completely separate from Dublin City. However, the 1900 City Boundaries Act brought all such townships together under one Dublin Authority and from that time onwards the Clontarf Town Hall was no longer needed to house the township offices.

Now obsolete, as far as official uses were concerned, the hall was used for concerts, dances, meetings and public assemblies and it was said that the premises were regularly used by the leaders of the 1916 Rising. It also doubled as a library and as you can see from the opening page of this story, a cinema.

We also read in a book entitled "the Meadow and the Bull" by Dennis McIntyre that the hall was the said to be the 'fermenting ground' for the hatching of the plot that produced the 1916 Rising.

The hall was now a liability to Dublin Corporation and wasn't really earning enough for its up-keep and when the idea of using it as a cinema was put to the Estates and Finance Committee of the Corporation it was hoped that this would solve the problem and bring about some much needed finance.
~~~~~

Situated at 61 Clontarf Road, in an area known as Strandville, which faced the beach front, the hall was in an attractive and prominent position to not only cater for local trade, but also a good passing trade, as this was the main road leading to Howth, Sutton, Baldoyle and Portmarnock and the trams that serviced those areas passed the front doors of the cinema.

This is a copy of the opening advertisement which appeared in the "Evening Herald" on Friday evening July 18th 1913.

This new cinema was welcomed by the citizens of Clontarf and in its early years it was well attended, however trade appeared to drop off after a few years and the cinema closed for a while. Fortunately, a new proprietor took over the lease and the cinema re-opened under new management on September 19th 1917.

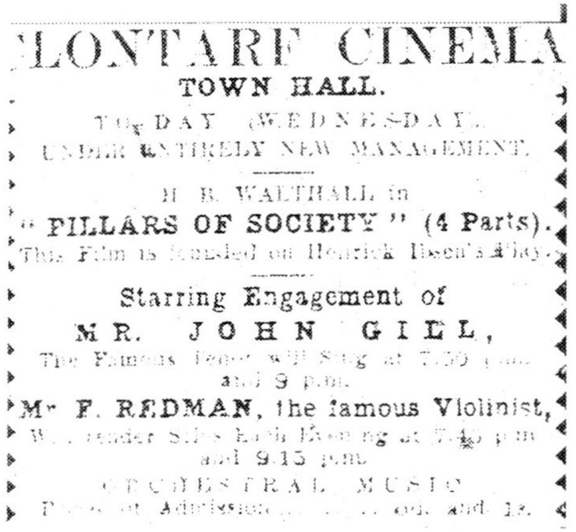

This is a copy of the advertisement that announced the re-opening of the cinema, now simply called the "Clontarf Cinema"

The opening film was an adaptation of Henrik Ibsen's play "Samfundett Stotter" This German drama, told the story of municipal corruption which was carried out by the towns elite citizens, on a large scale and brought about great tragedy in the township. Yet these Pillars of Society blamed everyone but themselves for this terrible state of affairs.

However once again this new enterprise failed and the cinema again closed after a short period of time and once again the hall was proving to be a serious liability and a drain on the resources of the Estate and Finances Committee. Those circumstances brought about a proposal in 1918 to sell the Corporation's Interest in this property.

This proposal did not, it would seem, broker well with some, as evidenced in a letter sent to the City Clerk by the Rev. J.L. Morrow, Chairman of the Clontarf Citizen's Association, in which the City Council was reminded of an agreement that had been made in London between the representatives of the Corporation and the Township of Clontarf, when a promise was given that the Clontarf Town Hall would be kept for the use of the people of Clontarf. Together with the late Lord Ardilaun the writer of that letter had been a party to that agreement.

This letter was read at a Meeting of Council on June 10th 1918 and the report on the proposal together with the letter from the Rev, J.L. Morrow, was referred back to the Estates and Finance Committee on a motion by Councillor Sir Patrick Shortall which was seconded by Councillor Gately.

No doubt many more motions were put, carried, proposed, rejected and referred to and fro between one and another, but at the end of the day the Clontarf Town Hall was sold.

In the years between, however, the cinema once again opened its doors on October 10th 1921 under the proprietorship of a Forte, but this time around no licence was applied for, which soon brought the attention of the Dublin Corporations law Agent upon the unfortunate Forde. When approached Forde was all apologies and claimed that as he was not making sufficient funds and had already lost a considerable sum of money on the venture, he was closing the cinema on November 5th 1921. In those circumstances the Law Agent suggested that procedures should not be taken against him.

This cinema opened and closed so often that it proved impossible for us to track its exact history and it could well have opened and closed on occasions that did not come to our attention. In situations of this kind we were very dependant on news items or advertisements.

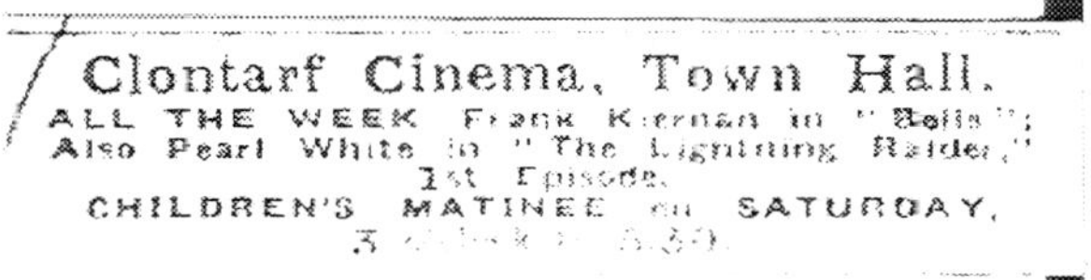

A good example would be this advertisement which appeared in the evening papers of Friday, May 6th 1921, during a period of time that we believed the cinema to be closed.

This was also the last advertisement we found.

A contributing factor to the continuous failings of the many enterprises that were put together in order to make a success of this cinema, may well have stemmed from the fact that the auditorium area could only accommodate a small number of persons.

This fact came to light when we read a report from a cinema Inspector to the Licensing Committee of Dublin Corporation that explained why the seats in the hall were battened together rather than secured to the floor as directed under the terms of the licence. The lease from the Estates and Finance Committee, he explained, only allowed the cinema to operate on six days a week (Monday being the exception), as the Committee let the Hall for dancing on Mondays and this prevented the securing of the seats to the floor. Furthermore, he added, the hall could only accommodate a small number of persons.

~~~~~

Reversing the trend

In another part of this book we tell the story of the Bethesda Chapel building that was converted into a cinema in 1911 and now we can tell you of a reverse situation when a cinema building was converted into a Church.

When the "powers that be" finally made up their minds to sell the Clontarf Town Hall it was bought by Father Dempsey circa. 1926, and converted into a chapel of ease for St John The Baptist's Church in 1927.

The Town Hall building was built of red brick and had two very large windows and a double door entrance at the front.

There were also some office-type extensions to the left of the building with widows facing streetwise.

As part of the conversions Father Dempsey had these side offices removed and a new cut stone façade, as befitting a church, was added to the building.

The hall, which was oblong in shape, was also extended.

On August 28th 1927 it was blessed and officially opened as St Anthony's of Padua by Dr. Byrne, the Archbishop of Dublin.
~~~~~

Although no longer serving as a church, the building as it stands today in 2006.
(To the rear of the building can be seen a section of the new St. Anthony's Church)
First opened as a chapel of ease to St. John the Baptist's Clontarf, it later became a parish church on July 1st 1966, when it was constituted from St. John the Baptist's. In 1975 a new St, Anthony's church was built in the grounds to the rear of the old church and once again the Town Hall Building, one of the last of Clontarf's genuinely historic buildings, became redundant.

Not for long though, for just like an old soldier, it soon rallied as a much valued community hall, serving as a Bingo hall and a host to Bridge parties. It also served as a meeting place for the local youth clubs. It is also available for community activities and theatre Groups etc.

An impression of the Clontarf Town Hall buildings original façade, by Jason Faulkner, a young and budding artistic acquaintance of ours, before the building was fitted with a cut-stone frontage befitting a church.

A Narrow Escape

On October 22nd 1917, we found details of a fire that had occurred in the operating box of the Clontarf Electric Cinema that were recorded in the Dublin Corporations Reports. This fire began at 9.28 am, long before the cinema was open for business. The lessee at the time was one David Morrison and the owners of course were Dublin Corporation.

The fire began in the operating chamber, which was situated over the porch and was contained within that area. Patrick Cullen escaped through the doorway but a young boy Anthony Cassin found himself cut off from this exit and he had to squeeze himself out through a very small window. He had a very narrow escape.

The fire was extinguished with the use of a hand pump, but all of the films were destroyed.

~~~~~

Remembering four of Dublin's great cinema entrepreneurs

James J. Jameson, who pioneered motion pictures in Ireland and exhibited animated pictures in the Rotunda and Rathmines Town Hall for many years and later developed the business to many centres throughout the country, passed away at his residence on April 3rd 1930. He was also sole agent for Warner Brothers, the film producers.

~~~~~

Albert Kelly, a true champion of independent cinema, died on July 6th 2005. Albert was the proud owner of the Classic cinema in Harold's Cross, which was formerly named the Kenilworth cinema. It was here that Albert broke all Irish cinema records by running "The Rocky Horror Picture Show" every Friday night for over twenty-one years.

~~~~~

Izidore Isaac Bradlaw, Managing Director of the Rathmines Amusements Company, who built Dublin's first purpose-built cinema, "The Rathmines Picture Palace", later to be re-named the "Princess Cinema. He was also a part of many more cinemas, including, the "Assembly Picture Hall", Sandymount, "Balbriggan Town Hall cinema", the "Olympia Theatre, the "Brunswick cinema" and many, many more. Izidore Bradlaw, a dentist by profession, died on October 22nd, 1933.

~~~~~

Alderman J.J. Farrell, one time Lord Mayor of Dublin and Managing Director of a large number of Dublin cinemas, a list of which could not be accommodated on the space left on this page. Alderman J. J. Farrell died on May 31st, 1954.

THE COLISEUM THEATRE
24 Henry Street
Aka "The Picture Palace Theatre"
"open and shut" on EASTER MONDAY

According to our findings the Coliseum Picture Palace on Henry Street opened its doors for the first time on Easter Monday, April 5th 1915 and closed them for ever on Easter Monday April 24th 1916. The building, like a lot of others in the area was destroyed during the 1916 Easter Rising.

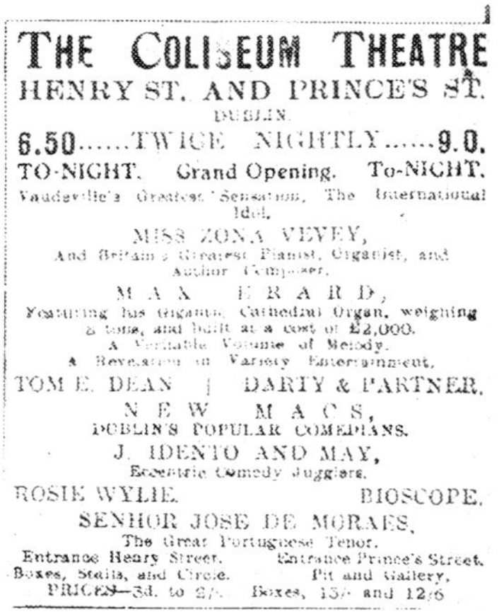

Well what more excuses can we make for the quality of reproduction of this ad, other than to point out that had you been born in 1915, you too would be a little faded by now!

By coincidence, The Coliseum was a namesake of another Dublin cinema that came and went in the space of a year.

The Coliseum Picture Palace was the latest addition of a Cine-Variety enterprise to make its appearance in Dublin City and it opened its doors to the public on Easter Monday evening, with an exceptionally brilliant performance, which included the International Idol Miss Zona Vevey and her assistant Max Erard.

Between them, they presented a charming and novel vaudeville scene, the likes of which had never before been seen in Dublin. It was Miss Vevey's custom to introduce distinctly original songs of humour and sentiment in her act and these artistic renditions won her a unique position in the world of variety, while Max Erard, a high-ranking British composer, acted as Miss Vevey's accompanist. The theatre is also equipped with a magnificent grand organ, which possesses a full range of stops, weighs eight tons and costs over £2,000.

Also included in the opening nights performance were Dublin's well-known and most popular comedians, who performed their latest successes to a most enthusiastic audience.

There were also splendid acrobatic acts by the Italian group, Darty & Partners, a fantastic juggling display by J. Idento and May, a duo of comedy jugglers and a beautiful vocal performance by the Portuguese tenor, Senor Jose De Moraes.

When the variety show had finished, the Bioscope exhibition began, with a top budget of topical up-to-date current events, comedy acts, short films etc.

This is one of the many films advertised by the management of the Coliseum Cine-Variety Palace

This film was shown on Christmas Eve, December 24th 1915.

Prices of admission ranged from 3d to 2s, with boxes costing 12/6 & 15/- Performances took place every evening, at 6.30 and 9 o'clock.

This picture was taken from a book that was published by Hely's Limited of Dame Street entitled "Sinn Fein - Revolt. 1916", the photo was taken by a T.W. Murphy.

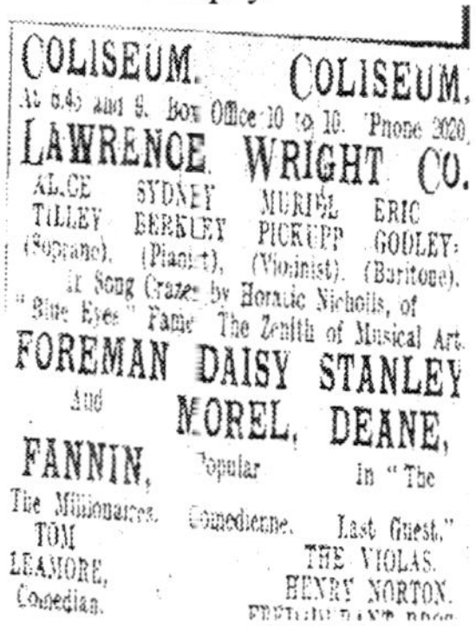

This was the last advertised show for the Coliseum Picture Palace, which was to have taken place the night of Easter Monday, April 24th 1916. This was a complete Variety show and no film was advertised for that night.

Following the disastrous closure of his beloved Coliseum Theatre and Cinema, Marsh, the owner manager, salvaged a number of items that lay about the rubble and had them incorporated, as decorative pieces of memorabilia, in various parts of his, then, home in the Harold's Cross area of Dublin. Fortunately, George had an opportunity to photograph some of them in July of 2006.

A pair of decorative tiles were stored in a tool-shed, and some panes of squared glass were used on the upper side of the ground floor bay windows and in the fan light above the hall door, while two cornice pieces were fitted as supports of the hall ceiling.

A photo of one of the tiles, a section of a window pane & a cornice piece.

THE COLISEUM PICTURE HOUSE
16-17 Redmond's Hill, Dublin 8.

This cinema was situated on Redmond's Hill, where now sits the premises of the Fannin Healthcare Shop. It opened for business circa. March 1910.

However. its existence was very short-lived as it was burned to the ground on August 28th 1911. Tthis despite the fact that assurances were given a little over a year earlier that such a risk was, to say the least, negligible.

I would mention here, that all picture houses in the early 20th century had to, apart from the need of a licence under the 1909 Cinematograph Act, apply to the courts for music and dance licences. This was because musical accompaniment was necessary to the showing of silent films.

Maurice Elliman together with his solicitor J.W. Davis duly made an application to Drury the local Magistrate sitting in the Southern Police Court, for one such licence for his latest venture , "The Coliseum", and here I will recount an amusing little repartee that took place in the courts on that day of March 15th, 1910.

When Davis had explained to the courts that the premises had been much improved and constructed for the purpose of showing cinematograph picture shows, his "Worship", Drury, pointed out that cinematograph performances were the most dangerous of openings that might be allowed.

However, Davis counter-claimed that this cinema was one that nobody could object to, because the apparatus for the showing of the films was affixed to the outside wall and that the pictures were shown through a hole in this wall, thereby implying that there was little or no risk of danger from this source, and that the pictures would in no way be objectionable.

In reply, Drury asked if the said pictures would be "strictly ecclesiastical".

"Yes, indeed", answered Davis.

"I have been greatly surprised at some cinematograph pictures", said Drury.

"Surely not in Dublin?, replied Davis, amidst plenty of laughter?
"Oh no", said Drury, "in Scotland" (more laughter).

The local D.M.P. Inspector raised no objections to the application for a licence, and it was duly granted.

A little later, in March of 1910, Davis, again on behalf of Maurice Elliman applied to the Honourable Recorder of the Green Street Courthouse for a similar licence and because of objections from the police who claimed that the premises were too small, he was nearly refused. However, he pointed out that the police objection did not hold, as Dublin Corporation had already passed the building.

The Recorder granted the licence on a temporary basis until July of that year and observed, that he would rather see the poor of the city going into cinematograph entertainments, than into the nearest public house. He was, he said, anxious to see the humble amongst them enjoying themselves in such a way, and that he did not like to interfere with any project that would give enjoyment to the worker.

(No reason was given as to why Davis applied for a second licence for this cinema; perhaps it had to do with dual jurisdiction).

However many licences the cinema had, it was not destined to survive, and on August 28th 1911 a report appeared in the "Evening Telegraph" of the fire, that totally destroyed the cinema and the dreams of its owner.

At 3.00 p.m. on that fatal afternoon, the Coliseum Picture Hall burst into flames. Fortunately, there was no performance that afternoon, and nobody was hurt. It did however have a live-in caretaker at the time, who occupied the upper portion of the building, but he succeeded in escaping.

The Fire Brigade arrived in quick time with a Captain Purcell in charge, however there was little they could do to save the building which was already burning rapidly, and by half past four the roof and upper floors had caved in. Captain Purcell had his men continually pour copious amounts of water on the building and the mobile escape was used to dowse down neighbouring roof tops that were in danger of catching fire. One of the reasons put forward for the fire gaining such a quick hold on the building was because the front of the premises mainly consisted of pitch pine and varnished wood.

In 1911, Redmond's Hill was a narrow thoroughfare, laid with tram tracks and the trams and all other traffic were brought to a standstill. The fire naturally enough caused great excitement and drew large crowds, which hampered any possibility of any through traffic. However, to add to the confusion, merciless rain began to fall with lightning flashing across the skyline and thunder pealing in the heavens, and this soon dispersed the crowds.

By half past five, Captain Purcell and his men had entirely extinguished the fire, which had at one period threatened to be of a terrible magnitude, but the building was completely gutted.

Trams and other traffic began to move and normality soon resumed.

No reason ever surfaced as to the cause of the fire, and the usual speculations were in abundance, but the Coliseum cinema was never re-built.

CORINTHIAN
4-6 Eden Quay

The Corinthian Picture Theatre opened on August 8th 1921 during Horse Show Week and by pure coincidence many, many years later it earned the popular nickname of the "Ranch", so called because, for some time, the cinema seemed to specialise in western pictures.

It opened with a most exciting silent film drama entitled "Torn Sails", starring Milton Rosmer as Hugh Morgan and Mary Odette as Gwlady's Price, who are adrift in a ship with torn sails following a fire.

Early Friday morning, on April 13th 1923, while the cinema was being cleaned, the Corinthian suffered its own little drama when two armed men held up the doorman of the cinema and planted a land mine under one of the seats.

"We're going to blow up the cinema", they told the doorman and he replied "you can't do that there are women and children on the premises".

"We can't wait", they said and having planted the bomb, they ran off. The doorman immediately ran upstairs to the managers living quarters and warned him about the bomb. The manager then ushered his family, who lived on the premises with him, out of the cinema and down the road, out of harms way.

THE CORINTHIAN.

(O'CONNELL BRIDGE).

DUBLIN'S LATEST AND MOST UP-TO-DATE PICTURE THEATRE,

OPENING

TO-DAY (Monday) AUG. 8th,

WITH A SPECIAL

HORSE SHOW WEEK

PROGRAMME:

ALLEN RAINE'S FAMOUS STORY,

"TORN SAILS."

CONTINUOUS PERFORMANCE.

PRICES..........2/-, 1/6, 1/-.

When no explosion took place, the manager returned to the cinema and found the unexploded bomb beneath one of the seats. It appeared that the fuse had burned out, just two inches from the mine!

The authorities, who were summoned by the doorman, arrived soon afterwards and took away the land-mine.

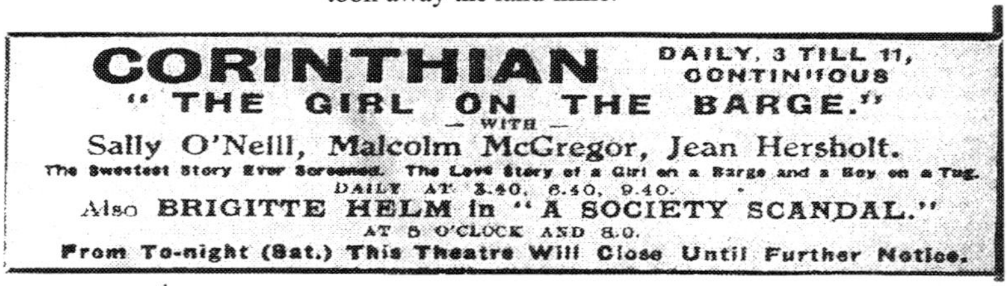

On January 18th 1930, the cinema closed for renovations with the film "The Girl On The Barge" which was claimed to be the sweetest story ever filmed.

Erie McCadden (Sally O'Neill), only child of McCadden (Jean Hersholt), a barge owner, falls in love with a young boy called Fogarty (Malcolm McGreggor), who works on a tugboat. McCadden, a strict and over-protective father, tries to stop the romance and fails. He beats his daughter and attempts to kill Fogarty. However, all is well that ends well, when Fogarty saves the barge from destruction when it is accidentally set adrift. In an act of atonement, McCadden allows them to marry.

Advance notice for the re-opening of the cinema, which appeared in the "Evening Herald" on May 12th, 1930;

While it may have had an official opening on the Friday, as promised, the following advertisement appeared in the papers on Saturday May 17th 1930.

All seemed to go well for the Corinthian and nothing untoward happened until the cinema closed in 1975 for major reconstruction although it did have a slight name change in 1956 when the word "New" was added to its name. This came about on Wednesday January 4th 1956, and at the time it simply closed for one day for a quick repaint.

On Thursday July 3rd 1975, the Corinthian closed it doors as the Corinthian for the last time.
The films shown that night were,
"Their Breakfast Meant Lead"
&
"Three Bullets For A Long Gun"

This is an Italian Western that was made in Africa.

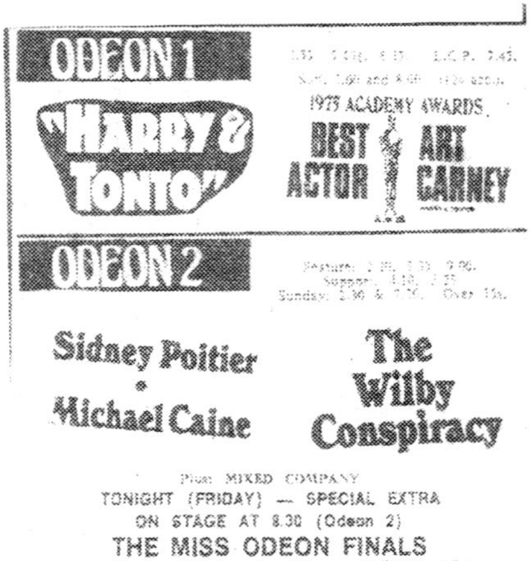

On Friday, October 17th 1975, the cinema re-opened as the Odeon with two screens and, it would seem, a serviceable stage was also available in Screen 2.

Screen 1 opened with the award winning film "Harry & Tonto".

This is a beautiful story about a retired and widowed school teacher who was now in his seventies.

Having been evicted from his apartment in New York in the name of progress and thus feeling sad, lonely and unwanted, he sets off with his cat "Tonto" on a journey across America, with a view to visiting his two married children. On the way he has many adventures. Art Carney starred, and in 1975 he won an Oscar for best actor in this film.

Screen 2 offered "The Wilby Conspiracy", starring Sidney Poitier and Michael Caine, in a story set in Apartheid South Africa.
And for good measure a special, live performance entitled "Mixed Company" was performed that night, which included the "Miss Odeon Finals".

While the official opening did take place on Friday October 17th, the new twins actually opened on Thursday the 16th , when the two new cinemas were handed over to the organisers of two charity premieres, where the proceeds from the showing of "Harry and Tonto" went to the Society of St, Vincent de Paul and the takings from the "Wilby Conspiracy" benefited the Brothers of St, John of God, Islandbridge.

On November 13th 1987, the cinema again had a name change to the "Screen" and in 1993 it closed on Wednesday March 3rd.

Some years later, it was converted into Murphy's Laughter Lounge and in the year 2002 the building was demolished and the site was redeveloped.

Based on the release date for the film on show at the time of taking this picture, "Rob Roy" starring Richard Todd, we would date the year of this photo as 1954.
The movie was said to be the best family entertainment version of "Rob Roy" ever filmed.

Ditto with this picture of the "Screen" which featured "Up Close and Personal", starring Robert Redford and Michelle Pfeiffer. This movie, which was reputed to be a story of "Jessica Savitch", the first woman anchor newsperson of seventies America, was released in 1996 and as this was the June Satzenbrau Premier, as advertised on the cinema's billboard. We would say that this photo was taken in June 1996.

The cinema building, now housing Murphy's Laughter Lounge, circa 2001.

~~~~~~~~~~~~

Where better to tell a cowboy story, than beneath a story about the "Ranch"
America 1912.

Gilbert M 'Bronco Billy' Anderson the famous American Director, Producer, Writer Actor and Creator of the world famous "Bronco Billy", the worlds first real cowboy hero, who was popularly known in Ireland as "Andy", very nearly lost his life while filming a scene for one of the Bronco Billy episodes entitled "Bronco Billy's Bible".

It would appear that during the shooting of the climax of a thrilling hand to hand struggle between Bronco Billy (Anderson) and the Baddy which was taking place at the edge of a great yawning chasm, Anderson called a break and as he was about to move forward from the edge of the cliff face, he stumbled and fell over the edge. His fellow actor a Church screamed with horror at seeing Anderson disappear over the edge of the cliff. Throwing himself forward on his face, Church peered over the precipice and then gave a shout of joy, when he saw that Anderson had been saved from an awful death by an outgrowing tree root, that had broken his boss's fall.

When they pulled Anderson to safety, in true grit cowboy style he pluckily sent the camera man back to his post to finish taking the fight scene between himself and Church, before acknowledging that that was the narrowest escape of his life. Anderson and his company "Essanay", made hundreds of these short western pictures, which were shown all over the world.
~~~~~~~~~~~~

COSY CINEMA
71b Parnell Street, Dublin.

Not an awful lot is known about the Cosy cinema, which sat right next door to Conway's pub on Parnell Street at number 71b. For a while, it appeared to be taking the shape of another mystery cinema because once again we met with few who remembered it.

Prior to being converted into a cinema, the premises was occupied by the "Rotunda Cigar Stores".

This cinema belonged to a company called the Cosy Cinema Ireland Limited, which was registered on March 9th 1914 and its main directors were R.L Boyd G.E. Lee and a T. Mason. It opened in March of 1914.

Building a cinema in such close proximity to the Rotunda cinema which lay just across the road was considered foolhardy by some, but the Cosy being a small, neat and compact little picture house, with a good turnout of popular films, held its own.

A reporter from the Bioscope magazine was a frequent visitor to this cinema and he once remarked that he always found a goodly crowd of people in attendance and the best of films on display. Their films were in the main, supplied by the "General Film Supply Company" of Talbot Street, and to name but a few of them he went on to mention, "Satan's Castle", "The Wreck", " Judgement of the Jungle", "The House of Discord" and "The Love of Mabel".

The Cosy was a most appropriate name for this little cinema which had seating for some 250 patrons and a ventilating system second to none. On another occasion the Bioscope reporter while writing of a visit to the picture house remarked that while the streets of Dublin sizzled during a recent heatwave, the inside of the Cosy was cool.

The films were shown with the aid of two Kamm machines, which were in the charge of and operated by the brothers Moiselle, and these machines being the most modern available displayed some great film. The Kammatograph machine discovered by Leo Kamm was a camera-projector with miniature images arranged on a spiral on a glass disc which contained some 350-550 pictures.

Another unique feature, instigated by Manley the manager of the Cosy cinema, was the introduction of very attractive handbills, which advertised and highlighted future films to be shown in the Cosy and these he distributed nightly amongst his patrons.

The Cosy opened at 6 pm during the summer months and with three changes of programmes every week, good attendances were assured.

Manly once invited his patrons to answer the following conundrum;
"Why is the Cosy cinema like a young tree he asked?"
and the answer was -
"Because the Tree changes every week and the Cosy gives three changes every week".

The site of the Cosy Cinema in November 2005, which is in the process of being re-developed into a Delicatessen and will most likely open in the near future.

Some years later the cinema had a name change to that of the "Corona" and, who knows, perhaps even a change of ownership.

THE CORONA CINEMA
OPENS WEDNESDAY NEXT at 4 o'clock p.m., with the Famous Super De Luxe Film:
SEVEN ACTS **"A TALE OF TWO CITIES"** SEVEN ACTS
Charles Dickens' Immortal Story of the French Revolution, featuring the Star Actor William Farnum.
COMEDIES
Roaring Lions and Those Wedding Bells, with Up-to-date Travel Programme.
High-class Orchestral Music.
SELECT, COMFORTABLE, THOROUGH VENTILATION.
PRICES ……

The Cosy cinema re-opened on Wednesday March 26th 1919 under the new name of the Corona and we were most fortunate to find this advertisement for its opening night and its opening film "A Tale of Two Cities", which stars William Farnum in both the parts of Charles Darnay and Sydney Carton.
William it would seem lost his head twice in this film. First, when he decided to save the life of his love rival and then when he did the 'far better thing', but then of course we now know, that he was only saving himself.

There was, however, no mention of a change of management.

CORONA CINEMA.
(Opposite the Rotunda).
LAST 3 DAYS OF
"THE ACROBAT OF DEATH."
Sansonia the Sensational.
USUAL PRICES. … Come Early.

Once again, we show an advertisement, which is not good in quality but unfortunately there is no substitute.
Dated February 26th 1920, for some reason beyond our understanding, some old newspapers do not scan well, besides which some cinemas like the Corona and Cosy did not advertise all that much in the newspapers and therefore we consider ourselves lucky for finding any ads at all.
The bottom lines of this advertisement read as follows:
"This is a wonderful film of courage and daring ever produced. Full Programme. Orchestral Music. Usual prices. Come Early."

~~~~~~

CORONA CINEMA
(Opposite the Rotunda).
LAST DAY OF
TORMENT,
TO-MORROW (SUNDAY), 3 O'C. P.M.,
The Edge of the Law,
A splendid five-act Film.
Until further Notice this Theatre will Open at 8 o'c. p.m. on SUNDAYS, showing Specially SELECTED PICTURES.

Some time later, we came across this advertisement on Saturday, July 12th 1919, that told us that until further notice it would be showing "Specially selected pictures on Sundays", and we would believe that, prior to that, the cinema didn't open on Sundays.

We have no closing date for this cinema.
~~~~~~

THE CRAZE FOR PICTURES

A typical scene at a picture palace. An article describing the marvellous growth in number of cinematograph entertainments appears on this page.

This sketch, which appeared on the front page of the "Evening Herald", on Tuesday, December 24th 1912, accompanied an article elaborating on the phenomenal growth of cinema throughout Britain and Ireland in such a short time span, as only a few years earlier cinema was almost an unknown quantity.

It would seem as if, at the touch of a magic wand, picture palaces sprung up in every town and village, both in Britain and Ireland. In Dublin alone there were now 27 cinemas.

Even in out of the way places, where previously a visit from a third rate circus was the occasion of a mild dissipation, now pictures houses are all the rage and no town is too lowly to have its own picture hall.

This history of the rise of modern picture theatre is a romance of modern invention and skill.

Whether it will continue to attract the masses for a prolonged period is uncertain, but in view of the fact that the possibilities of the films have not been exhausted, it would be reasonable to suppose that there will be developments in the future that will leave the present entertainment far behind in wonderful novelties

* * * * *

The above aforementioned article also told of the fabulous amounts of money been paid
to actors who took parts in these films and in particular it told the story of a seven year old boy in France who was paid the astronomical sum of £700 a week for appearing exclusively in films for that company.

No doubt, this superstardom and rather handsome remuneration affected the boys sense of importance, because on reading further, we learned that he was dismissed by the company for refusing to take part in a film with another precocious youngster and that an action was taken to restrain him from using the name "Baby".
While the writer of the article didn't elaborate on this name restraint, we can only assume that the name "Baby", was a creation of the studio.

* * * * *

Of course the fees paid to that boy in 1912, pale into insignificance when we hear what some stars of today's silver screens are earning and we have no need to tell you that figures in terms of 'hundreds' and 'thousands' never ever enter present day negotiations for top stars, as all figures on the bargaining table appear to be in millions.

How right those reporters and writers of long ago were when they supposed that there might be future developments in their world of cinema that would leave their experiences in the ha'penny place.

Apart from the massive and mind boggling advances made in film technology would they have ever envisaged a movie costing $200m to make?

Would their imagination have stretched far enough into the future to visualise a gigantic glass fronted building, like the one pictured below, that held within its doors not one, but seventeen individual cinemas?

Could they have dreamt of huge escalators that would carry one to the upper floors of the building where on one floor alone, one would find a long corridor, which contained the entrance doors to seventeen individual cinemas? With another floor laid out with cafes and bars, shops that sold popcorn in buckets rather than an old newspaper rolled into a cone, trays laden with Mexican food that one could bring with one into the cinema, and would they have ever understood the no smoking rule?

The foyer of a modern day multiplex with a vast array of mouth-watering goodies on display

However, like all good things in this life, there was also a dark side to the world of cinema and this manifested itself in horrific fires, which usually began in or near the operating or projection rooms of cinemas. A lot of these fires were brought about by the use of highly inflammable nitrate film stock and a lack of control on how these films were stored.

The Inspectors of Cinemas and Theatres under the Cinematograph Act of 1909 played a big part in the prevention of fires in these venues, by strictly enforcing the rules and regulations pertaining to their licensing under that act, but we won't elaborate on this act as we have given it great mention in other parts of this book.

We would however give mention to a number of theatre fires, which took place in many parts of the world, just to give you an idea of how widespread this danger was, and the need for ever-vigilant inspections on places of such entertainment.

~~~~~

This is a small list of cinema disasters that took place across the world which were caused by fires and in many cases from the smoke that ensued after a fire had been successfully extinguished; many of these tragedies were also brought about by sheer panic

~~~~~

During the showing of a film on Sunday night December 22nd 1912, in a cinema in the small Village of Baraques, near Flanders, it would seem that a reel of film caught fire and though the projectionist managed to extinguish the flames, a panic occurred. The result of which, caused the deaths of 12 people, most of whom were children, and another 20 were quite badly injured.

~~~~~

The fire in Paisley, Scotland on Tuesday, New Years Eve, 1929, was a prime example of this happening, which resulted in the deaths of 71 children. This fire, which began in the operating room of the Glen cinema, was disposed of quite quickly by a junior operator and the cinema manager, when they threw the smouldering film and its steel container out a side door in the vestibule area, onto a piece of waste ground, which ran along the side of the cinema. However, the smoke from the burning film drifted back into the cinema and filled the auditorium with black smoke and pandemonium ensued, causing the deaths of many children. The great tragedy of the whole affair was that this was a fire that never was.

~~~~~

Ireland too, had a tragic cinema fire in a small village named Drumcollogher in Limerick County, when a local businessman opened up a cinema in premises that was most unsuitable and ill prepared for a cinematograph exhibition, with a large audience in attendance. This tragedy took place on Sunday night, September 5th 1926 and the fire occurred when a loose reel of film which had been left on a table near two lighted candles suddenly burst into flames, that spread so rapidly, that within minutes the premises was a raging inferno. With an audience numbering between 150 and 200 people it was a wonder any of them escaped. There was only one small door leading in and out of the hall, which was situated on the top floor of a two storey barn-like building and entry and exit through this door was serviced only by a wooden ladder-type stairs, which was totally inappropriate. In all, 48 people, some of them children, perished that night in this fire. With a 49th victim dying ten days later from the injuries he had sustained that night.

A year later, Canada joined the tragic list of cinema fires, when on the Sunday afternoon of January 9th 1927, at least 77 children lost their lives, when a fire occurred in the Laurie Palace Cinematograph Theatre. It would appear that this Montreal cinema was host to a packed matinee audience, which consisted mostly of young boys and girls who were enraptured in a comedy film entitled "Get Them Young". When the fire broke out in a section of the ground floor area, just under the balcony, the children in the ground floor area began to file out of the cinema in an orderly manner, but the children in the balcony area panicked and made a wild rush for the exits. Many were killed when the narrow stairway collapsed.

It would appear, that almost all of the deaths occurred in this area and it was said that when help arrived, they found dead and dying children crushed together in such a solid mass that considerable force had to be used to extricate the bodies. One police constable, who had been called to the scene, had the harrowing experience of finding the bodies of his own three children.

This tragic fire led to a law been enacted in Quebec, that prohibited children under 16 years of age from attending cinemas. This ban lasted until 1967.

~~~~~

Many years earlier a fire at the "Colonial Theatre" in Chicago, which was also called the "Iroquois Theatre", came as a surprise to many, as this theatre was considered absolutely fireproof and was also furnished with an asbestos fire curtain. The disaster occurred just after Christmas 1903, a matter of weeks after the theatre had opened, and some 600 men, women and children perished in the fire. On this occasion, the fire was caused by a painted back-drop, which was positioned too close to a spot lamp and caught fire.

The fire spread quickly and as the asbestos curtain was lowered it jammed half-way down. At the same time, panicking people rushed out the stage door, which let in a blast of air, which fed the fire and it quickly spread into the auditorium, where it began reaching for the balconies. The theatregoers ran to the exits and with the crush of bodies, the exits were hard to open, as they opened inwards. Some were said to have been bolted from the outside. Many of the 600 were trampled to death and some died when they jumped from the balconies.

There were many, many theatre/cinema fires right across the globe and one of the latest to come to our attention was the one that occurred on December 8th 1994 in the city of Karamay in the Xinjiang Region which caused 324 deaths, most of whom were school children attending a matinee.

We have mentioned the above disasters just to highlight the fact that cinemas and theatres could bring about death and destruction just as easily as they could bring joy and happiness if not adequately staffed, supervised, and otherwise protected against fire and panic situations, together with mandatory in-house fire fighting equipment and sufficient functioning easily-reached exits that could empty a fully attended house in minutes.

~~~~~

The above is a mere handful of the theatre/cinema disasters that took place over the years, and we would estimate that there were enough theatre fires across the world to justify a book on that subject alone.

CURZON PICTURE HOUSE
Middle Abbey Street, Dublin 1.

This cinema was situated right next door to the Adelphi cinema and faced the Cameo cinema which was just across the road.

The Curzon opened on August 8th 1968 and will probably be one of the latest cinemas which we will write about as we don't expect our history of Dublin Cinemas will include any cinemas that opened after 1970.

Curzon and Light House Cinema.

This is the opening advertisement from the previous day's newspaper, announcing the opening of the "Curson" picture house.

This latest addition to city cinemas is a fine example of the trend towards the small intimate cinema of the luxury type now becoming more popular with present day cinemagoers.

Cinema audiences have changed greatly over the years and with televisions or home cinemas if you like, going to the pictures is now considered a night out, rather than just a place to go.

Audiences were now also much more discerning in their choice of entertainment and films. They also expected and demanded the height of comfort and luxury.

This new small and intimate luxury Cinema had been converted from a large warehouse within a matter of 14 weeks and will most certainly cater fully to the needs and desires of the cinema going public.

It has seating for 400 and according to its manager, Collins, it was the beginning of the new cinema world in Dublin.

For its opening night, it chose the film the "Whisperers" starring Dame Edith Evans, which was described as Dame Evans' 'tour de force 'as an actress. This film was directed by Bryan Forbes, the actor, screenwriter, producer, novelist, critic and director, whom I believe was once married to our own Connie Smith who, though born in Limerick, was reared in the Ranelagh/Rathmines area, where, having won a film star lookalike competition, then made her way to film stardom.

* * * * *

This cinema had two screens and it was one of the first cinemas in Dublin to introduce a ban on smoking by reserving one of its screens as a strictly non-smoking area. This action appeared to work and management suffered no loss of business as a consequence, a brave move indeed and one that was way ahead of its time.
In 1988, the cinema had a name change to that of the "Light House Cinema" and it began to specialise in the showing of foreign language films, which attracted quite a following.

Howeve,r it was soon to suffer the same faith as its neighbou,r the Adelphi, and be demolished to make way for the expansion of Arnotts department store, the owners of the site.

The Light House closed its doors on Saturday September 28th 1996, and the owners immediately began a search for another venue.

For its special closing presentation management gave us 3 award-wining films.

"The Jar", A Middle Eastern story about a struggle of good and evil, this film won the Film Advisory Board Award for Excellence

* * * * *

"Dean Man", by Jim Jarmusch 1995 starring Johnny Depp as William Blake, who was on the run for murder, met an old Indian called "Nobody" who helps prepare William for his journey into the spiritual world.

* * * * *

"Beaumarchais the Scoundrel"
A very witty and farcical comedy /drama that plays fast and loose with historical facts.

A selection of film titles from 1988 & 1989 that were shown in the Light-House, some of which ran for a full week.

Adventures of Reinette and Mirabellie, Directed by Eric Rohmer
This would appear to be an adventure by a naïve provincial girl who meets up with her street smart Parisian counterpart, and this leads the duo into various dramatic situations.
The film covers four adventures in all.

* * * * *

Law of Desire
By Pedro Almodovar.
Pedro Almodovar was born in La Mancha, Spain, and it is said that he is the most international acclaimed Spanish film maker since Luis Bunuel.

Starring in his film are, Eusebio Poncela, as Pablo, Carmen Maura as his sister Tina, Antonia Banderas as Pablo's new lover Antonia and Miguel Molina as his ex-lover Juan.

When Juan, Pablo's young homosexual lover moves off to a distant town. Pablo meets up with Antonia, a male model in search of a film career. The story line is mostly about a love triangle between three gay men, one of whom is murdered. To further complicate matters, Tina, Pablo's sister reveals that she was once a man who had a sex change operation and had had an affair with their father.

* * * * *

Wings of Desire
By Wim Wenger,
This was a highly acclaimed and multi award winning film, starring Bruno Ganz, Solveig Dommartin and Otto Sander.
This story is about a number of trench-coated angels, that hover over war-ravaged Berlin and listen to the tortured thoughts of the mortals below, with a view to comforting them. One angel, played by Bruno Ganz, falls in love with a beautiful circus performer and wishes to become mortal like her.

This film was remade and renamed in 1998 with Nicholas Cage and Meg Ryan in the lead roles. Its new title is "City of Angels"

* * * * *

COLISEUM.

The name Coliseum, it would appear, was ill-chosen for a cinema in Dublin, because over the years there were three in total in the city and none of them survived for a period longer than 27months.

The first Coliseum was built on Redmond's Hill and opened in April of 191. Twelve months later, it went on fire and needless to say closed in April 1911.

The second Coliseum opened in Henry Street on Easter Monday 1915, and was blown to pieces on Easter Monday 1916 during the "Rising".

The third Coliseum came about in August 1924, when the Sandford cinema, which had closed sometime earlier for renovations, re-opened as the Coliseum and in a reverse operation, the cinema again closed and re-opened as the Sandford, in November of 1926.

DALKEY CINEMA
37a Convent Road, Dalkey

My God! Another mystery cinema, "never heard of it" said most; "we never had a cinema" said others; ""it never existed said one, and another told a member of the Dalkey Castle and Heritage Centre that it was "a myth". But, just as in the case of the Assembly Picture Hall in Sandymount, which nobody had ever heard of, we have proof that a cinema did indeed exist in the Village of Dalkey.

The Dalkey cinema almost became our second mystery cinema (see Assembly Picture Hall Sandymount) but with tenaciousness and perseverance we managed to trace down a number of people who knew of the venue.

Patrick paid a visit to Dalkey in February of 2006 and found few who new of its existence and the one or two that did, referred to it as a shed. One in particular, said it was a simple cow-shed, but that can't be true as it was licensed by the Local Council.

I got in touch with the Dalkey Castle and Heritage Centre and they having questioned a local historian on the subject were told that it was simply a myth. However we had absolute proof that it was no myth and we wrote a letter to the Castle and Heritage centre informing them of this. On Thursday, March 23rd 2006, I paid a visit to Dalkey and I took this picture of 37 and 37a Convent Road, Dalkey.

The house nearest to the camera is 37a.

These two houses belonged to a John Kavanagh, a building contractor, as did a piece of land to the right of the house and it was on this land that Kavanagh built the Dalkey Cinema. 37a was also known as St Bridget's and it was here that John Kavanagh and his sister, Kate, lived. Both were single at the time

On one of my trips to Dalkey, with the hard neck that I had developed, I knocked on a number of doors on Convent Road and when I knocked at number 44, a Kellady gave me a number of names that I should make contact with, one of which was a Ms. Farrell. She very kindly responded to the letter that I wrote her and it was she who pointed out to me exactly where the Dalkey Cinema had stood and described it to me in detail.

A rough - very, very rough sketch of the cinema, as described by Shelia Farrell

The cinema, said Ms. Farrell, was a large oblong-shaped wooden building with an A-shaped corrugated iron roof, which had two large windows on either side. Just inside the door, stood a pink cubicle where Rita Kelly sat behind a small table and sold the admission tokens, which Sheila believed cost about 2d. Sheila could not be all that sure of the price because she and her brothers always got in for nothing. Her brother, Gus, grew up to become a Royal Liver insurance agent and her other brother, Peter, became an Irish Football Great, who at one time captained Everton. Peter was capped by both the Republic and Northern Ireland in the days of dual international representation. He played for the Republic 28 times and Northern Ireland 8 times.

The Screen consisted of a large white square of cloth which could be rolled up and down on a long pole as required and the projection machine sat on a large wooden table just inside the entrance door. When all the patrons had settled down, Kavanagh would extinguish the gas lights and operate the projection machine, which would project the pictures onto the white screen. Rita's mother, Annie Kelly, was the pianist and sitting at the piano, which sat at the right hand side of the screen, she would accompany each picture with appropriate music.

The seating consisted of long wooden benches that would stretch forever from one end of the hall to the other and while the pictures on display were memorable Sheila Farrell found Charlie Chaplin particularly unforgettable.

Annie Kelly was the wife of the well known tramway time keeper Johnnie Kelly who was in charge of the Tram Office in Dalkey Village.

Sheila Farrell was born in Ruby Cottage, which once stood on the site of 35 Convent Road and John Kavanagh, who was a great friend of her mother and father, was their nearest neighbour. Sheila has since moved to Leslie Avenue and on Tuesday, June 6th 2006 she very kindly invited me to her home for tea, where she told me all about John Kavanagh and his cinema. She also brought me to the carpark which was situated to the rear of the Club Bar on Coliemore Road and which ran parallel with the back gardens of 43 and 44 Convent Road. It was on this site, she said, that the Dalkey Cinema had once stood.

In this picture Sheila is standing in the rear carpark of the Club Bar on Coliemore Road, with her back to the rear of 44 Convent Road. She told me that the shed began where she stands and stretched almost as far as the small wall at the end of the yard. Had she stood there on the same spot in 1920, she would have been facing Rita Kelly sitting in her pink cubicle.

John Kavanagh had a blue motor car and when Sheila's father was ill and in hospital, John would drive her and her family there and back to visit. John, she said, married late in life to a Welsh girl and had two children and when he died, his wife returned to Wales with their two children.

~~~~~

We ran an article in the Dalkey Community Council's Newsletter in June 2006 issue no 354 (Volume 12), detailing our search for the Dalkey Cinema and we had one reply from a James McClure of St Patrick's Square, and he too remembered the Dalkey Cinema.
~~~~~

James very kindly drew us a map that his mind recalled from 1928 and he described the cinema, which was situated on a piece of ground to the side of 37a, all of which belonged to John Kavanagh. It was, he said, a big shed and opened on three nights a week. Three gaslights were sited on the two side walls and these were put out when the show began.

The shed, he told us, was always clean and tidy and regularly painted. It held about one hundred people who would sit on long wooden forms of which there were ten, and each form would hold ten persons. The front five forms cost 3d and the rear five were only 2d.

God, he wrote, I remember our hero's Ken Maynard, Buck Jones and Tom Mix and I am sure of one thing in my life and that is that there was a cinema on Convent Road.

Pat and I knew of Buck Jones and Tom Mix but Ken Maynard didn't ring any bells, but we since discovered that Ken was indeed a super cowboy hero who made the transition from silent films to talkies. We also read that although he was not a great singer he was the first to record Western music.

We also received a phone call from a Comerford, who also remembered Kavanagh's Picture House on the waste ground next to No 37a Convent Road.

George recalls his efforts to meet with Sheila Farrell, and mentions that on receipt of his letter she immediately phoned him and told him all she knew about the cinema, but as for meeting him for a photo session, life was not all that easy. Sheila, he claims, is a very busy person and involved in many community activities, so much so, that making a date to meet was not all that easy. I am, she told George very busy and since I retired I am in everything but the Christmas Crib. A delightful and knowledgeable person and it was well worth the wait to eventually meet with her.

In our search for news of the Dalkey cinema we trawled through many old newspapers of the times including the appropriate copies of the Bray Herald but we could find no sign of an advertisement for the Dalkey cinema. We could only surmise that, being the only cinema in the area, local posters would have been sufficient advertisement.

We did find the cinema listed in the Thom's Street Directories of the time and in an official list of cinemas in the Dublin Metropolitan Police District which was drawn up by the Chief Superintendent's Office in 1922. This list of cinemas (A copy of which is re-produced in the Assembly Picture Hall story) was used by local Police Stations to cros- check the delivery of summons's which had to be hand-delivered by a uniformed D.M.P. Officer to the owner or manager of every cinema in Dublin at that time. A copy of the notice served on John Kavanagh by an Officer from the Dalkey Police Station is hereby re-produced for your perusal. On the official cinema list, the "Dalkey Cinema" was numbered 37th.

This copy of the summons or notice was to inform cinema proprietors that films of a Military nature were not to be exhibited without permission of the Films Censors Office.

F

Dalkey Station
17 " 7 " 22

Notice Served Re. Films and Posters

I beg to state that at 10 " 30 P.M. 17th. inst. the notice mentioned on attached was served by me personally on John Kavanagh, St. Bridgets, Convent Road, Dalkey, Building Contractor

Richard Grant.
Sergt. G.S.

The Supt.
F. Division

Submitted

J Doran Supt 18/7/22

The C [illegible]

This notice is further proof that the Dalkey Cinema not only existed but was in itself an established bona-fide building, fully and properly licensed under the Cinematograph 1909 Act.

Sheila is convinced that the cinema was built circa 1919 and lasted through to 1931. It was gone, she said, before the "Eucharistic Congress" was held in Dublin, in 1932.

DAME STREET PICTURE HOUSE
17 Dame Street

This small cinema opened for business on Tuesday, December 24th 1912, and closed some eight years later in early 1920.

This is a view of Dame St in the years when the cinema was open for business.
(picture courtesy National Library)

If you squint real hard, you just might be able to make out a small white sign on the right hand side at headroom height that partially shows the word picture. This would be the entrance to the Dame Street Cinema.

Today, Noble House Restaurant occupies the Site.

The cinema was managed by M. Lean.

The Dame Street Picture Palace, was a work of wonder in itself, as it was converted into a picture palace from an old ruin of a building in a matter of nine weeks. This was down to the competence of its builder Alderman William Doyle of 49 Portland Row.

The building was designed by Francis Bergin, a renowned architect from Westmoreland Street, and only Irish material and Irish labour were used in its construction. The finished building was said to be one of the most comfortable picture palaces in the City, well worthy of the metropolis and compared favourably with any other of its class in Dublin, or for that matter in the United Kingdom.

The cinema was officially opened by Sir Charles Cameron CB MD, and on taking the stage he was gifted with an exact golden replica of the key of the main entrance door by the Contractor Francis Bergin. He stated, that were it not for his workmen and fellow contractors, he would not have been able to complete the job in such a short nine-week period.

Sir Charles, who was greeted with great applause, said the golden key with which he had been just presented was only a symbol –otherwise how could they account for asking him to open a picture palace, which, when he had arrived, he had found to be packed with such an appreciative audience. This drew loud laughter. However, he said, he had great pleasure, metaphorically speaking, inserting the key, turning it in the lock and declaring the Picture Palace open. This of course brought more laughter and applause.

With the cinema now declared open, the much appreciative audience was treated to an admirable programme of attractive and character films for the rest of the evening.

The Dame Street Picture Palace didn't last all that long and it closed its doors in the early part of 1920 and lay idle for many years.

In 1927, the building was taken over by the State where it was used by the Irish Film Censor and his staff to view all films entering the country, before being released for general viewing. Quite a few films failed to pass muster here and were considered un-fit for an Irish audience.

DAME STREET PICTURE HOUSE

WILL OPEN ON

TUESDAY, DECEMBER 24th,

AT 2 P.M.

CONTINUOUS PERFORMANCES DAILY DURING XMAS WEEK FROM 11 A.M. TO 10.30 P.M.
SUNDAY 3 TO 10.30.

MOST COMFORTABLE & UP-TO-DATE PICTURE HOUSE IN THE CITY.

DE LUXE CINEMA

One of our contributors, Noel Twamley related a little tale to us about "Bananas". It would seem that one day, in 1947, Noel was making his way down to the De Luxe to see the film "Crash Dive", starring Tyrone Power, when he stopped at one of the many fruit and vegetable stalls that adorned Camden Street to buy a banana.

These bananas had just come off the first fruit boat to arrive in Dublin since 1939 and "yer wan" at the stall said to Noel, "and wha would ye know about bananas ya little chiseller".

"Well", said Noel, "I know all about bananas because Carmen Miranda wears them on her hat with loads of other fruit". I purchased my banana and as I skipped off I heard "yer wan" at the stall laughingly say to another stall holder, "Jayus" Carmel did you hear wha he said, Carmen Miranda wears my bananas on her head."

The Theatre-De-Luxe cinema when it first opened on December16th 1912.

The Proprietor of this new cinema was Maurice Elliman who had also opened a cinema just down the road on Richmond Hill, a couple of years earlier which was destroyed in a fire in 1911.

The builders of the Theatre De Luxe, which was situated at 85 Lower Camden Street, were George Squires of Upper Abbey Street and the architect was Frederick Hayes M.R.I.A.I.

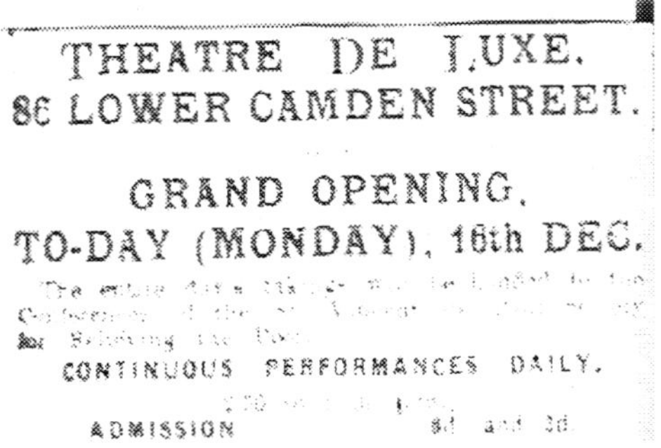

THEATRE DE LUXE.
8C LOWER CAMDEN STREET.

GRAND OPENING.
TO-DAY (MONDAY), 16th DEC.

[illegible]

CONTINUOUS PERFORMANCES DAILY.

ADMISSION [illegible]

The first advertisement for the De Luxe. The illegible print informs us that the entire days takings will be handed over to the St. Vincent de Paul Society.

Admission prices were 6d and 3d.

In March of 1920, the cinema closed for extensive restructuring and number 86 Lower Camden Street was incorporated into its expansion programme. Six months later, it re-opened on Saturday, September 4th, 1920.

After the Sunday night performance on June 3rd 1934, the "De-Luxe" once again closed down and faced major renovations.

The last picture show in the old De-Luxe was "Cross Country Cruise" with Lew Ayres and Sue Knight, which told the story of a Cross Country bus trip, with an escaped killer on board.

• * * * *

The newly renovated "Theatre De-Luxe" re-opened on Friday, October 19th 1934, replacing the old De-Luxe which had stood there since 1912.

The reconstructed building had seating for 1,500 persons and an unusually large parterre. The balcony had also been considerably enlarged and the entrances were beautifully carried out in marble and red porphyry with black and green borders, some of which can be seen in a large picture following this page.

Both the interior and exterior represented the latest ideas in artistic design and the lighting system was equally up to date,

The latest in Neon lighting was ablaze on the facade and the entire was most welcoming.

The stage was forty feet wide with a depth of thirty feet, with a grid, flies and the most modern equipment, a special feature.

The general building contractor was Messrs. Murphy of Rathmines and the architect was A. E. Jones of Messrs. Jones and Kelly.

Two views of the Vestibule area, which were beautifully laid out in marble and porphyry.

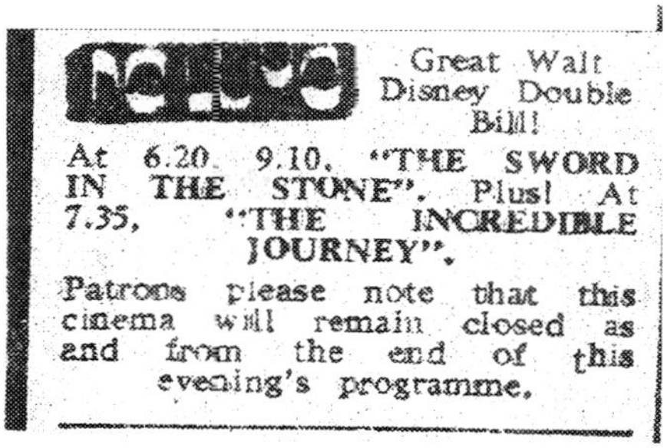

Great Walt Disney Double Bill!

At 6.20. 9.10. "THE SWORD IN THE STONE". Plus! At 7.35, "THE INCREDIBLE JOURNEY".

Patrons please note that this cinema will remain closed as and from the end of this evening's programme.

"A Sign of the Times".

The De-Luxe cinema along with five of its sister Dublin cinemas closed on Saturday June 29th 1974
The last films screened there were two 1963 offerings from the Walt Disney Studios.

"The Sword in the Stone"

A classic animated version of Merlin, the late King Arthur's Magician, who, on learning that the King had died without leaving an heir, trains a young boy to be King, provided he has the will and strength to pull the Sword from the Stone.

In an old London Cathedral appears a Sword embedded in a Stone anvil and inscribed on the stone are the words.

"Who so pulleth out this sword from this stone and anvil
Is rightwise King of England".

* * * * *

"The Incredible Journey".

A Sad and Happy tale, wonderfully filmed of two dogs and one cat who having been stranded and lost in the wilds of Canada, eventually find their way home.

* * * * *

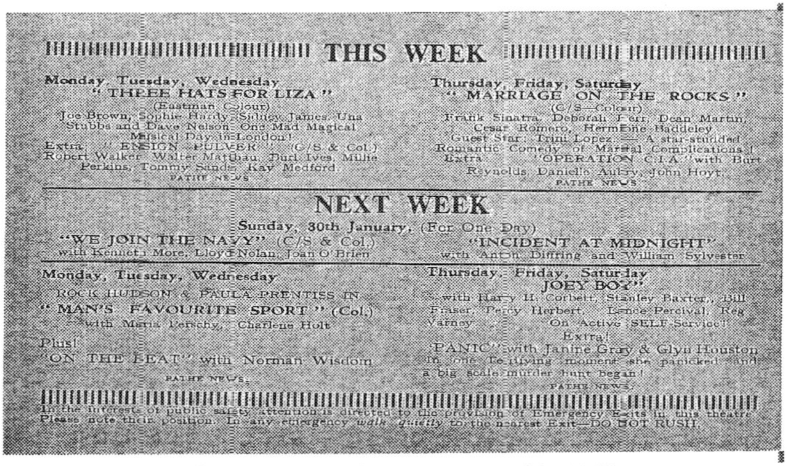

THIS WEEK

Monday, Tuesday, Wednesday
" THREE HATS FOR LIZA "
(Eastman Colour)
Joe Brown, Sophie Hardy, Sidney James, Una Stubbs and Dave Nelson. One Mad Magical Musical Day in London!
Extra " ENSIGN PULVER " (C/S & Col.)
Robert Walker, Walter Matthau, Burl Ives, Millie Perkins, Tommy Sands, Kay Medford.
PATHE NEWS

Thursday, Friday, Saturday
" MARRIAGE ON THE ROCKS "
(C/S—Colour)
Frank Sinatra, Deborah Kerr, Dean Martin, Cesar Romero, Hermione Baddeley
Guest Star: Trini Lopez. — A star-studded Romantic Comedy of Marital Complications!
Extra "OPERATION C.I.A." with Burt Reynolds, Danielle Aubry, John Hoyt.
PATHE NEWS

NEXT WEEK

Sunday, 30th January, (For One Day)
"WE JOIN THE NAVY" (C/S & Col.)
with Kenneth More, Lloyd Nolan, Joan O'Brien
"INCIDENT AT MIDNIGHT"
with Anton Diffring and William Sylvester

Monday, Tuesday, Wednesday
ROCK HUDSON & PAULA PRENTISS IN
" MAN'S FAVOURITE SPORT " (Col.)
with Maria Perschy, Charlene Holt
Plus!
"ON THE BEAT" with Norman Wisdom
PATHE NEWS.

Thursday, Friday, Saturday
JOEY BOY"
with Harry H. Corbett, Stanley Baxter, Bill Fraser, Percy Herbert, Lance Percival, Reg Varney. On Active SELF-Service!
Extra!
"PANIC" with Janine Gray & Glyn Houston
In one terrifying moment she panicked and a big scale murder hunt began!
PATHE NEWS.

In the interests of public safety attention is directed to the provision of Emergency Exits in this theatre
Please note their position. In any emergency *walk quietly* to the nearest Exit—DO NOT RUSH.

A copy of one of the many free programmes of the 1960's.

Shortly after its closure, the cinema became a snooker hall and later a hotel.

The building was also used in 1990/1 as settings for the Dublin-made film "The Commitments", which was based on a book by Roddy Doyle and directed by Alan Parker. This film was released in 1991.

The De-Luxe building in early 2006.

Courtesy Dublin City Archives and the Irish Builder

We believe that this picture was taken circa. 1934, we made this assumption on the basis of the two films that were on display at that time, both of which were released in 1934.

"She was a Lady" starred Helen Twelvetrees as a beautiful young girl who moved to America with her father after he had been disinherited and there she fell in love with a young man played by Donald Wood's who had been born into the ranks of America's High society. In consequence, his father would not allow them to get married until she could prove that she was indeed a lady.

* * * * *

"Virginias Husband", starred Dorothy Boyd as a ruthless young man-hater, who was mind-full of her inheritance and married in haste, when she heard that her very rich Aunt and benefactor, who was of the belief that her favourite niece was happily married, was paying her a surprise visit.

DRUMCONDRA GRAND CINEMA

The Drumcondra October 1934

The Drumcondra picture house, or to some the "Drummer", opened on Friday October 19th, 1934.
The opening ceremony was performed by the Lord Mayor of Dublin, Alfie Byrne T.D., and the film selected for the opening performance was;
"Paddy The Next Best Thing", starring Janet Gaynor and Warner Baxter in one of the early talkies which tells the tale of a feisty Irish lass, who when finding out that her sister was marrying a wealthy man that she did not love, marries him herself, which covers the 'next best thing' part of the title. Before the film ends, they both find that they are madly in love with each other and are thereby the "Best Thing" for each other.

The supporting programme was a "Laurel & Hardy" comedy'!

Many weeks before the Drumcondra had its official opening it ran advertisements in the evening newspapers inviting the people to guess the name of the new Drumcondra Cinema. It didn't mention any prizes and we wondered if anybody guessed the name correctly. With Dublin wit being what it is, we would love to see some of the entries.

OPENING OF NEW CINEMA
CAN YOU GUESS
THE NAME OF THE
DRUMCONDRA CINEMA
WHICH WILL BE OPENED VERY SHORTLY?

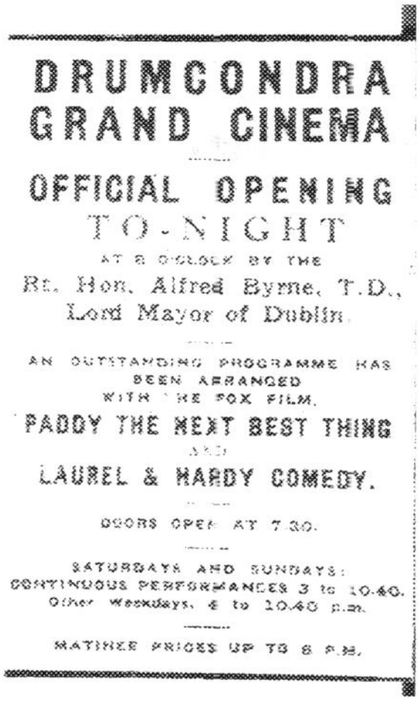

This was the official opening advertisement:

Other than its opening and closing dates, we have little or no further information on the "Drumcondra",

It closed on Sunday March 24th 1968 and the last feature film to be shown was:
"White Feather".
Starring Robert Wagner as Josh Tanner, a land surveyor and John Lund, as Colonel Lindsey, in charge of the U.S troops that are escorting the Cheyenne Tribe to a new settlement.

Geoffrey Hunter plays the part of an Indian named "Little Dog", whose fiancé", Appearing Day" (Debra Paget),
begins to make eyes at Josh Tanner, much to the displeasure of "Little Dog" and his friends, who are not at all that keen on leaving their homeland.

When the cinema closed, the building was converted into a supermarket for the 5 Star Chain and the façade of the cinema was removed and replaced with a shop front. Quinnsworth took over 5 Star and it in turn was taken over by Tesco.

While the façade was replaced, the main body of the cinema was simply fitted out as a supermarket and the outside of the building remained almost unchanged.

Picture taken Sunday, November 20th 2005

As luck would have it, just before we closed the book on this story, we got this photo of the Drumcondra from Tom Wall, who had it stored on a slide.

ENEMIES OF CINEMAS

It would appear that cinemas had enemies as well as friends in those early days of cinematograph entertainment. According to a report in the "Evening Herald" January 4th 1927, this new type of business could have a harmful effect upon the growing eye of young children.

Prior to the war, a deputation was waited on the Home Office to urge the necessity of an inquiry into the effects of the "Flicker" on the eyes of the young. The inquiry however was never held or if it was, the results were never made known.

At a conference of the Incorporated Association of Headmasters held in London on the day of this report, one of the speakers, a R.F. Cholmeley, made this subject a feature of his address and thereby issued a strong condemnation of the cinema in relation to the child.

In his opinion he felt, in the absence of a suitable inquiry into the effects of the cinema on children, that it was conceivable that children below a certain age, ought never to go to the pictures at all. Until the truth of that is known nobody has any business to talk of the use of the cinema for educational purposes.

I further quote his claim that he would not like to be a shareholder in Hollywood at the Day of Judgement. This cinema, he said, seems to be typical of all that deserves our most vigilant hostility, as protectors of the young.

Whenever we find anybody, he went on to say, or any business that has discovered children as a market or as a paying proposition of any kind, or as a means to any end that is not their education, we ought to regard that with the profoundest suspicion.

At their best, he said, they are always in danger of the temptation to lower their standards in order to extend their markets, and at the worst they are enemies of the human race. I believe he said that we can beat them, for the simple reason that our education is much more intelligent now that it was, and getting more intelligent every day.

End of quotes, end of story, and simply another interesting little piece of newsy type article in connection with the world of cinema, selected, edited and rehashed for your perusal and pleasure.

For those of you who would like to read the full report of this address, by R.F. Cholmeley, entitled, "Foe of Cinema", please read the "Evening Herald" January 4th 1927.

FAIRVIEW "The Fairo"
Opened 1929

The Fairview cinema was opened to the public by Senator Alfie Byrne on Monday night November 18th 1929. The opening coincided well with the great progress in housing schemes made by Dublin Corporation around that time, which brought thousands of people north-side of the city.

The cinema, which was luxuriously furnished and most comfortable had seating for 1,000 people and was bound to play a big part in the social life of the people living in the area, both old and new residents alike.

The feature film for the opening night was, "Trail of 98" and John Moody, a most popular orchestra leader, was in charge of the musical entertainment. The proceeds of the opening night were to be split between St. Vincent de Paul and the Herald Boot Fund.

The "Trail of 98" was an epic black and white silent film, starring Dolores del Rio as Berna and Ralph Forbes as Larry, the romantic leads. It tells the story of a bunch of prospectors seeking their fortune in the gold fields of the Klondike. Released in 1928, and directed by Clarence Brown, it was said that the Alaskan winter scenes were so real that some patrons shivered in their seats. It was also claimed that three stunt men had lost their lives during the take of the Cooper Rapids Scenes.

FAIRVIEW GRAND CINEMA

(FAIRVIEW).

FORMAL OPENING TO-NIGHT (MONDAY)

By SENATOR ALFRED BYRNE,

AT 8 P.M. (Doors open 7 p.m.).

The Proceeds will be distributed between ST. VINCENT DE PAUL SOCIETY and the "HERALD" BOOT FUND.

ON THE SCREEN: The Wonderful Story of

"THE TRAIL OF '98"

(FOR THREE DAYS.)

MUSICAL DIRECTOR: JOHN MOODY.

POPULAR PRICES: NIGHT, 8d., 1/-, and 1/3.

PLEASE NOTE: From TO-MORROW (TUESDAY) and each Afternoon from 3 to 5.30, PRICES 4d., 6d., and 9d.

BOOKING FOR SUNDAY NIGHTS. NO EXTRA CHARGE.

The Fairview cinema, when it was built in 1929, was a single storied building, with its main entrance in Fairview Avenue. The screen backed onto the Fairview Strand wall.

It was said of the Fairview cinema that management had at one stage implemented their own censorship policy, by separating the boys and girls as they entered the cinema one Sunday night. (Time of this happening - unknown).

The following week, with a near empty house they quickly learned the error of their ways.

~~~~~

In 1938, the building underwent major reconstruction which totally transformed the single storied building into a new and modern picture palace with new projection rooms, stair wells, landing and new balcony, which greatly increased the seating capacity of the cinema.

The position of the screen was reversed and a complete new entrance fronting onto Fairview Strand Road was constructed which changed the whole facade of the building.

The original entrance to the cinema from Fairview Avenue was retained, but used only as an emergency exit.
~~~~~

At the beginning of March 1970, the Fairview again closed for about three weeks, in order to have a complete renovation in decoration, seating, flooring and the construction of enlarged toilet facilities.

Following this renovation, which included a new screen and reefer curtain, the circle re-seated and the aisles luxuriously carpeted the cinema reopened on Friday March 27th 1970, with George Kerns as manager (No relation to the author).

The "Fairo", as it was usually called, was now billed by management as the "Cinema with the Sunshine Windows", as can be seen from the 1934 advertisement below.

The opening film was Alistair MacLean's "Where Eagles Dare" and needless to say this thrilling war adventure brought in packed houses.

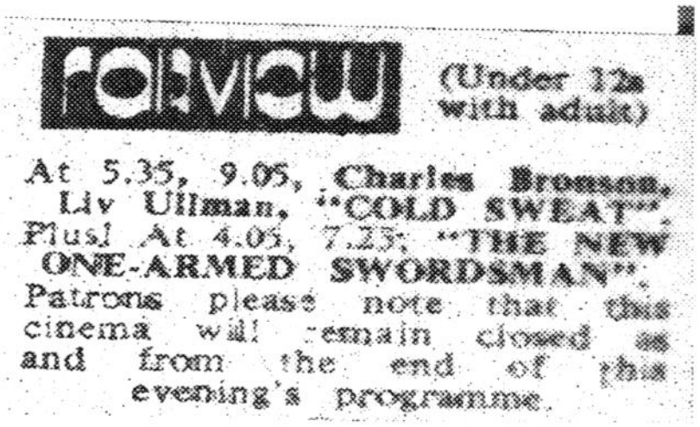

In spite of all the renovations, the Fairview closed four years later, on Saturday June 29th, 1974.

On this day, all the companies' cinemas closed, including the "Royal Bray", "Pavilion Dun Laoghaire", "State", "De-Luxe" and "Whitehall".

This photo of the Fairview building was taken in 2005.
While the building is now in use for other enterprises, we recently learned that a part of the cinema is still in use for film reviews and presentations etc., for trade purposes only.

~~~~~

Snippets

A Long Ad.

Extract from the "Letters to the Editor" column "Evening Herald" December 3rd 1925,.

"Sir - at one of our principle cinemas I attended this week, a picture was shown telling us of the comforts of somebody's heating appliance. This occupied the best part of a quarter of an hour. Later on in the programme, no less than seventeen advertising slides were shown, occupying about ten minutes. This form of advertisement seems to be growing and it is not at all favoured by cinemagoers. We pay for an evening's entertainment and not for 25 minutes of other people's advertisements. A little protest, say by clapping our hands when these items are exhibited might remind cinema managers that the audience is their first consideration." The letter was signed Rudolph.

* * * * *
~~~~~

FATHER MATHEW HALL
CHURCH STREET
October 23 1909.

While Church Street did not have a cinema proper, it did have the "Father Mathew Hall", and here on many a night, cinematograph exhibitions took place.

In the breaking of this news item, we were very fortunate to have come across a newspaper advertisement announcing its first venture into film shows and we reproduce it here for your perusal.

While the advertisement is for an exhibition by James Jameson's "Animated Picture Company", whose headquarters were in the "Rotunda" it does mention films for future display. With admission prices at 3d, 6d and 1/- one gets the impression that films will be on display in this hall for some time to come.

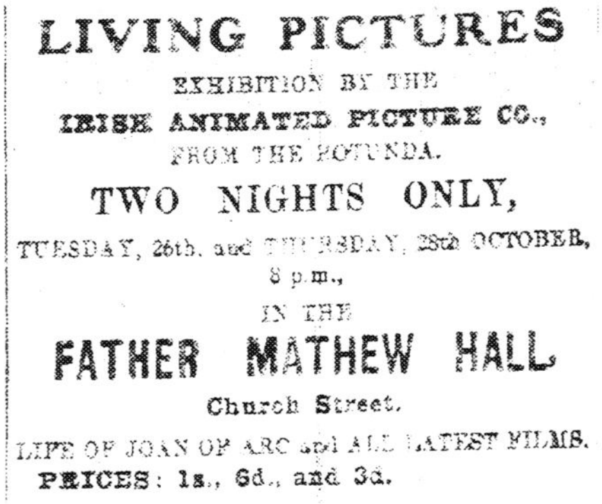

It should be noted here, that these cinematograph exhibitions were taking place all over Ireland and that as yet Dublin did not have a cinema proper. It was to be another month before James Joyce came back to Dublin and opened Dublin's first ever cinema, the "Volta".

The Rotunda Rooms and Gardens, Rathmines Town Hall, Empire Theatre, the Waxworks in Henry street and the Antient Concert Rooms, were only some of the many venues for these most popular Cinematograph Exhibitions. Many theatres, like the Tivoli on Burgh Quay, the Queens theatre on Sackville Street, the La Scalla in Princes Street, also played their part by programming some of these exhibitions.

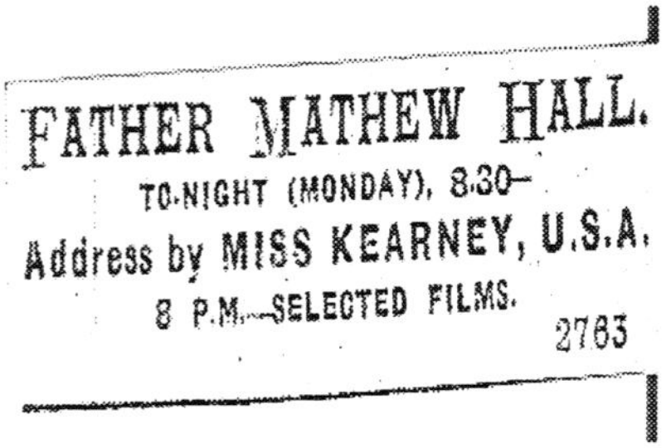

During our research on another subject, we came across this advertisement for the Father Mathew Hall, announcing selected films for display on Easter Monday, April 24th 1916, which gave substance to our earlier impression that these cinematograph exhibitions were to be a feature of this hall for the foreseeable future.

Now long closed; picture taken November 27th, 2005

FATHER MATHEW HALL
CHURCH STREET

TO-MORROW (SUNDAY) AT FOUR O'CLOCK
SESSUE HAYAKAWA IN
THE GREAT HORIZON
Splendid new seating accommodation has been installed and in the reserved portion, plush-covered tip-up seats are available.

We found an advert in the "Evening Telegraph" on Saturday, November 13th 1920, but it would not photocopy in readable form so we copied the main details into the scroll shape above. This advert, which advises us of its new seating, leads us to believe that the cinema-side of its business appears to be flourishing and that they are in business for the long haul.

FILM BLAZE IN ABBEY STREET

Tuesday morning February 6th 1923, saw a number of young men entering the offices of Pathe Freres at 2 Lower Abbey Street, where they demanded from terrified staff a Film Gazette.

We can only guess that the Gazette they were after was the current Pathe Gazette, which contained filmed news stories and was about to be released to cinemas all over Ireland.
Obviously this issue had to contain some news item that was not to their liking.

Not finding what they wanted, the men who were armed with revolvers bundled the staff of five young ladies and one man into another room and then proceeded to sprinkle petrol from cans, which they carried over furniture and fittings. They then set fire to the place and fled.

The staff members imprisoned in another room were ignorant of the men's intention to set fire to the building and panicked when smoke belched into their room. Crashing out of the room and dashing down the stairs they were lucky to have escaped with their lives, but not before some of them were badly burned on their hands, head and face.

The Pathe Freres Film Company offices were situated in rooms above the shop of C. Butler & Sons, the musical instrument makers company, who were, coincidently, also proprietors of some Dublin cinemas. A O'Brien, who worked for C. Butler, also made his escape from a top floor room, where he was working.

The arrival of the armed men, the starting of the fire, and the escape of the staff all took place in a matter of minutes, but in that short space of time the fire had made rapid progress and when it entered a store room that was stocked with reels of very inflammable film, the premises turned into a furnace.

The staff members were gathered outside the premises in an excited manner, as were some members of the public, when there was a massive explosion and the front windows on the first floor were blown out and fell, with a terrible force, on those standing on the footpath.

The injured were all ferried to Jervis Street hospital by private cars and the city ambulance, which had been called to the scene.

In all, seven people were injured, including some passers by. The names of the injured treated in Jervis Street hospital were as follows:

Miss Gladys Clancy, Miss C. Flynn, Miss Mary Lennon, Miss Mary McCabe, James Cullen, James Desmond and John Bailey.

Three sections of the Fire Brigade, under Captain Myers, were quickly on the scene and within an hour they had extinguished the fire, and saved the shop section.

INCENDIARY FIRE IN DUBLIN

The premises of Pathe Freres, at Lower Abbey street, Dublin, were entered by armed men about 9 o'clock yesterday morning, who, ordering the staff out, set fire to the building. Five of the staff and two of the passers-by were injured by the explosion, which destroyed the premises. (Freeman Photo.)

Other than the Butlers' shop, which miraculously escaped with some minor damage, the rest of the premises were gutted, with not a single article having escaped the flames.

Much sympathy was felt for the popular manager of Pathe, Gordon Lewis.

FILM CENTRE
O'Connell Bridge House
D'Olier Street, Dublin.

Which story also includes the Cameo cinemas of Grafton Street and Abbey Street.

The Film Centre opened in O'Connell Bridge House on Friday October 14th 1966.

The story of this cinema really began in Grafton Street, when Leo Kearns opened a small 16mm cine-café there, circa. 1949 and called it the "Cameo and Cine Café".

Some time later, it seems, he sold his interests in this cinema in order to pursue his interest in the Sundrive cinema. The cinema remained open under its new management and with the same name.

Circa. 1966, the owners of the Cameo vacated their premises in Grafton Street and moved to a new location in O'Connell Bridge House, D'Olier Street and there they opened up as the "Film Centre".

In 1973 on November 23rd, the cinema closed for repairs and some alterations.

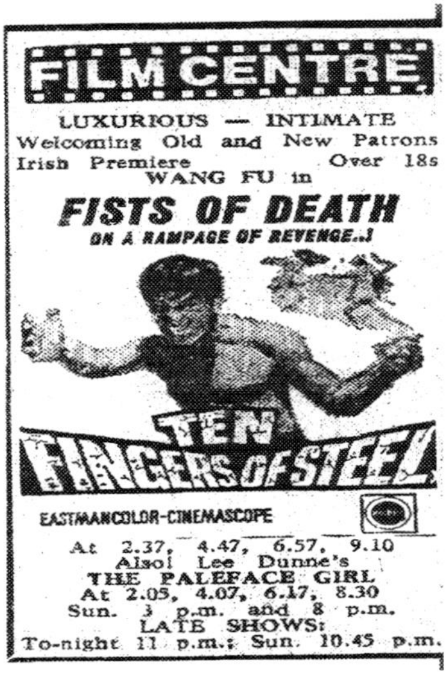

On December 22nd 1973 it re-opened and welcomed old and new patrons alike.

Ownership of the Film Centre, which was one of the most popular small cinemas in the central city area, was in the hands of Michael Butler, who was well known in the cinema business.

The Film Centre was well sited and drew full houses and in 1976 Butler and company expanded their business by opening a new cinema in Middle Abbey Street which they named the

"CAMEO"

While it wasn't our intention to mention any cinema which opened after 1970, we felt that, with the story of the Film Centre beginning with a Cameo, it should end with one.

Dublin's newest luxury cinema the "Cameo" in middle Abbey Street had a gala opening on Friday night July 30th 1976, with the film "The Sellout", which is having its first showing in Ireland.

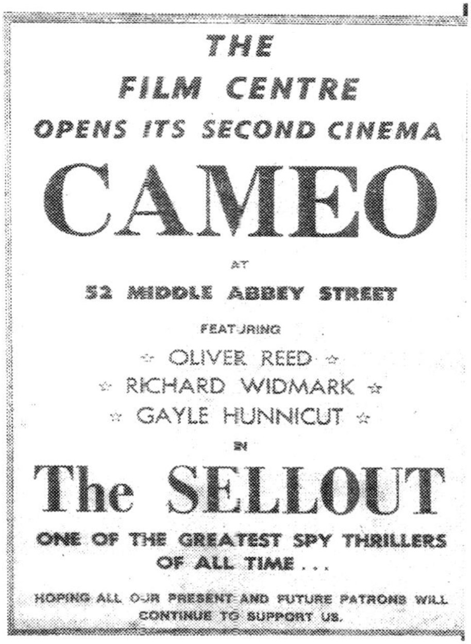

The Film which is one of great suspense and dramatic action sees retired CIA agent Sam Lucas (Richard Widmark), save his friend and protégé Gabriel Lee (Oliver Reed), from being killed by the KGB.

Someone has set up retired Sam for assassination and Gabriel is suspect.

The action and hunt takes place in Israel and Israel security are not happy being involved.

However, Deborah (Gayle Hunnicut), Sam's girl friend, is also a double agent and it was she that had set up friends, Sam and Gabriel.

As Sam, very much in love, can't do the obvious, Gabriel shoots Deborah.

Richard Widmark and Gayle Hunnicutt in a terse moment from the film "The Sellout."

A terse moment for Sam and Deborah.

The Cameo, which faced the Adelphi in Abbey Street, thrived for many years – but - unfortunately closed on March 15th 1990.

We believe that this was the last advertisement for the Cameo and also for the closing of the Film Centre on February 2nd 1984.

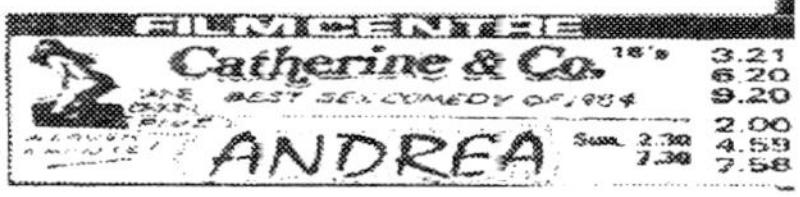

This is the building that once housed the Cameo cinema. Photo taken early 2006.

Leo Kearns opened his Cameo and Cinema Café here in October of 1949 and we believe that the following advertisement may well have been its first.

On offer that night was a film of the Royal Wedding, Dancing on Ice, Sports Parade and New England Calling. This ad. appeared October 21st, 1949

In 1952, the cinema closed for a make-over and re-opened on Friday, July 11th as the "Cameo", which promised the last word in comfort and entertainment.

For its opening performance, it offered Victor Hugo classic story "Ruy Blas" starring Danielle Darrieux and Jean Marais, which told the story of a dashing nobleman-turned-bandit, and his love for the Queen of Spain.

FINE ARTS
Eblana Theatre, Busaras, Store Street.

In 1946 it was agreed by members of the Government, that Dublin was badly in need of a central bus station and, having acquired a suitable site in Store Street, plans were drawn up and work began in 1946. However, with the dithering that can go on in Government circles when involved with undertakings of this sort, the project wasn't finished until late 1953, which belies a little joke that did the rounds in the glorious fifties, which went more or less as follows.

It would seem that a taxi driver on the O'Connell Street rank was approached by a very boastful American holiday maker who was wearing a large Stetson, a western type fringed denim jacket, jeans which were tucked into cowboy boots and a state of the art camera hanging from a strap which circled his big bull like neck. All that was missing was a holstered six shooter.

Whipping off his massive Ten Gallon Stetson the American opened the rear door of the taxi and stooping his huge frame he flopped backwards into the nearside rear seat of the taxi. "Howdy son", he drawled flashing his dollar clip, "take me on a tour of Dublin and show me the best of your old city".

Passing Nelson's Pillar, the tourist said to the driver, "what's that?" And the driver told him that it was our tallest monument. "Shucks", said the tourist, "we have tooth picks larger than that at home". The Liffey, he compared with a fish pond that ran the length of a piece of pastureland on the eastern side of his ranch in America, and the Phoenix Park was no bigger than his younger son's starter ranch. The Custom House was like a little old Houston court house and the Mater Hospital was no bigger than a downtown Dallas medical facility.

Now, totally cheesed off with this exasperating loud mouth, who believed that everything in Dublin was less in style, height and quality to their counterparts in Texas, the driver did a u-turn in Phibsboro to head back to the rank and in a last ditch effort to please the Cowboy and give him value for the dollars he was about to spend, he took the scenic route via Swords, Malahide, Portmarnock, the Hill of Howth and Dollymount back to O'Connell Street.

Having come down Clontarf Road and motoring along Amiens Street, the driver took a right into Store Street and passed the new Busaras building where the working men were topping off the roof of the new Central Bus Station. "What's that?" said the cowboy looking at the massive new building. "Don't know", said the driver staring poker faced at the American, "it wasn't there this morning".

~~~~~

The Busaras was opened on Monday, October 19th, 1953, by the Minister of Industry and Transport, Sean Lemass.
~~~~~

The complex, which was said to be one of the largest in the world, cost over £1,000,000, had a huge public concourse, which housed all manner of amenities, including comfortable seating areas, which could accommodate 240 persons, left-luggage offices, toilets and washrooms, four telephone kiosks, and other circular type kiosks, one of which sold books, magazines and newspapers, another watches, jewellery and souvenirs. There were also four shops in the arcade, which ranged in style from a tobacconists, confectionary, sweets and ice cream to a chemists shop.

As the far end of the arcade stood a first-aid station ready to cater for any small emergencies that might arise in such a busy complex.

While waiting to board any one of the fifty-plus routed long distance buses, one could also avail of a meal in the well-appointed restaurant, which rests on the mezzanine floor, or a simple cup of tea and a sandwich in the snackery, further along the floor, or perhaps a quiet drink in the bar which is situated near the restaurant.

Near the Beresford Place entrance to the large bus park is a sloping ramp which leads to a bicycle parking area and above the concourse and public areas are five floors of offices which were leased to the Department of Social Welfare.

Should one expect to have a long wait for a bus, one could always spend an hour or so in the News Cinema, which lies in the basement area some twenty feet below Store Street.

Down two flights of stairs, one would find oneself passing through a brightly lit public foyer with doors leading to various facilities, which included the public toilets. The walls of this well laid out area, were lined with bronze and stainless steel frames, displaying all manners of advertisement for various firms and at the end of the foyer, down another wide staircase, one will find the entrance door to the Busaras Cinema, which has seating for some 230 patrons.

This cinema sits two feet below mean sea level and as one watches a film buses will be passing to and fro overhead in the concourse. However, no outside sounds will permeate through the walls or roof of this basement cinema because the cinema is a completely self-contained air-cushioned unit within the larger unit of the building. Noise-deadening material, consisting of layers of quilt and cork, completely surround the cinema which also rests on a bed of cork so that "noises are most unlikely".

Though having said all that, in the early opening days of the central bus station, those passengers that sought some refreshment, a little more potent than tea, experienced some difficulties, as a liquor licence for the bar had as yet to be obtained.

The cinema must also have encountered some difficulties as it appeared to have remained idle for a period of some six years. As far as we could make out the first opening occurred in September 1959 when it opened as a theatre rather than a cinema as planned.

Sitting on a stool at the bar in Busaras, which by now had most obviously secured a liquor licence, sat a man quietly nursing a pint, when all of a sudden the doors swung open and the bar began to fill with a load of 'toff's' who were said to have been 'got-up' like the graduates of a dancing academy, the likes of which had never been seen in Busaras before.

This was the night of Tuesday, September 22nd 1959, and on enquiring of the bar staff the man discovered that the cinema, which was located in the basement area, had at long last opened its doors to the public, but not as the planned cinema, but rather as a theatre.

Apparently, this rush for the bar was brought about by the first interval of the four act play which was taking place in the new theatre. Amongst those present were Tod Andrews, Eoin O'Mahoney, John Ryan, Bikram Shah the Indian Charge d'Affaires, and Joe Lucy.
Also in attendance were Brendan Behan and Dermot Kelleher and anybody who was anybody. This gathering was described as "one of the best dressed occasions of recent times". Everybody was togged out in dress attire, everybody that is except Brendan Behan and a few reporters, including Frank Lee of the "Evening Herald",

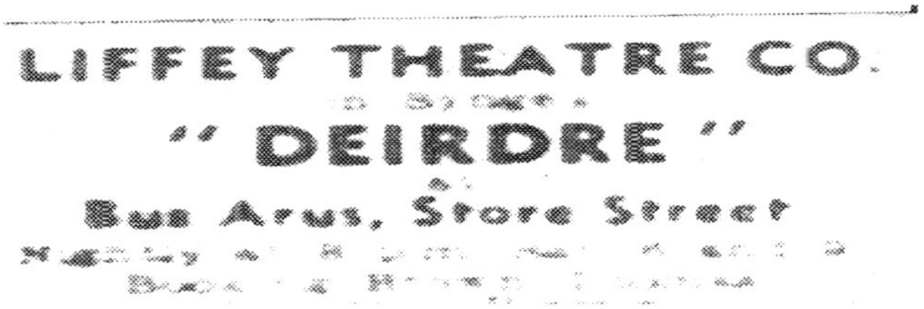

The Theatre opened with the above notice which was inserted in many evening newspapers. There was no mention of a name for the theatre, but we can confirm that it was called the "Eblana".

The Liffey Theatre Company was a new theatre group whose directors were Mairin O'Farrell and Eamonn O'Higgins, who had taken residency of this new fringe theatre. Their first offering was John Millington Synge's tragedy", Deirdre of the Sorrows".

By coincidence, another version of the Legend of Deirdre was on show in another Dublin theatre that very night, "Spider Lady" in the Pike Theatre.

The "Legend of Deirdre" is a tragedy that tells the tale of a beautiful young Irish woman who was reared in the confines of the Palace of the King of Ulster and groomed to be the wife of the King when she became of age. However, she loved another, and they both made their way to Scotland, where they lived happily together for a while. The King, blinded with jealousy, has them followed, her lover destroyed and she was returned to his Palace where she committed suicide by refusing to eat.

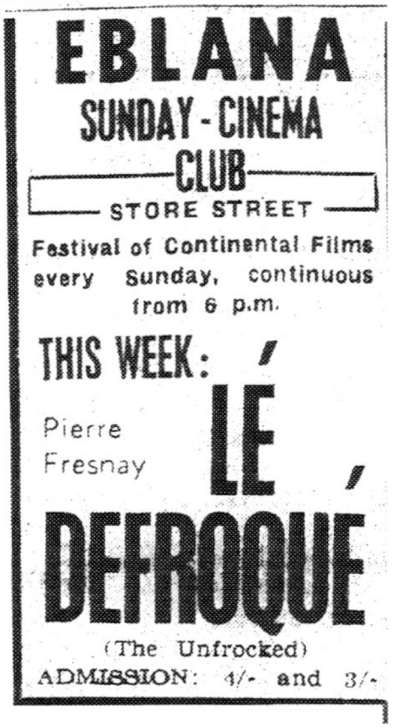

The Eblana Theatre did well, and some great Irish productions were held there. The Cream of Irish actors continually trod its boards and great comedies brought laughter to Busaras.

In 1962, the cinema, at long last, came to the theatre via a Sunday Cinema Club, which would present a Festival of Continental Films every Sunday.

As can be noted from the advertisement on the left of this page, which appeared in a Dublin newspaper on Saturday, December 28th 1962, the cinema in no way interfered with the theatres normal activities during week nights. It simply filled an empty house on a Sunday, when no plays were taking place.

These continental films seemed to attract a strong following and the Sunday Club enjoyed a successful run for many years.

On Sunday, January 26th 1963, the "Fine Arts" cinema club took over the Sunday night cinema performances and their first offering was "The Loves and Music of Johann Strauss".

They had many a box office hit over the years and to name but two we would mention "La Grande Illusion", which was retained by public demand in 1967, and Bergman's "Summer Interlude" 1964.

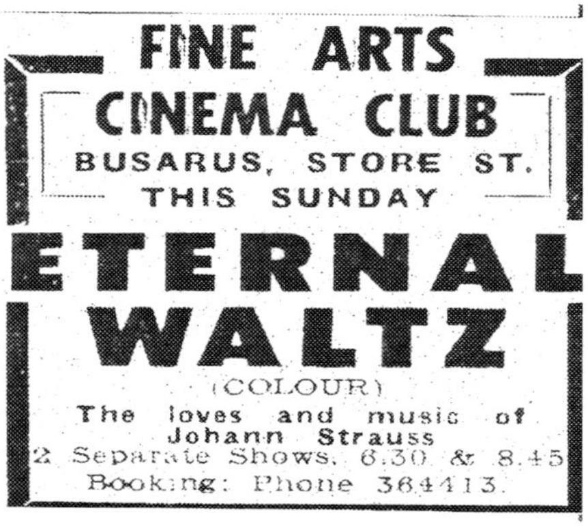

1964

1967

However, declining audiences also affected the Fine Arts Sunday Club and the club ceased showing Sunday pictures in 1969.

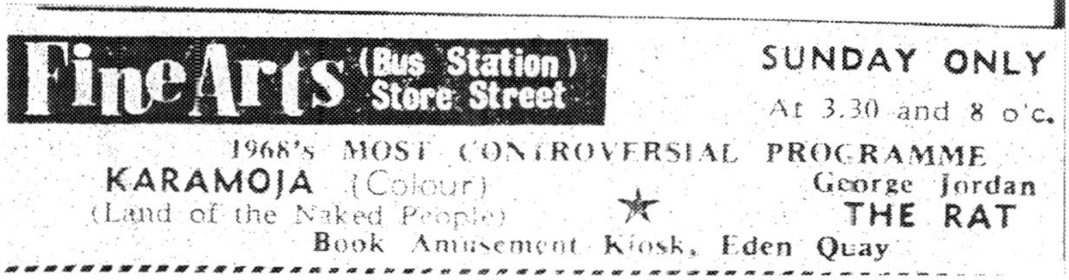

This was, we believe, the last advertisement for the Fine Arts Sunday Club, which appeared on Friday, April 19th, 1969.

The club went out on a high note when it showed "Karamoja",. 1968's most controversial picture, which not only filmed naked people but introduced and pictured their thousand year old customs of scarification, piercing and body mutilation. These were a primitive tribe who lived as their ancestors did, over one thousand years earlier.

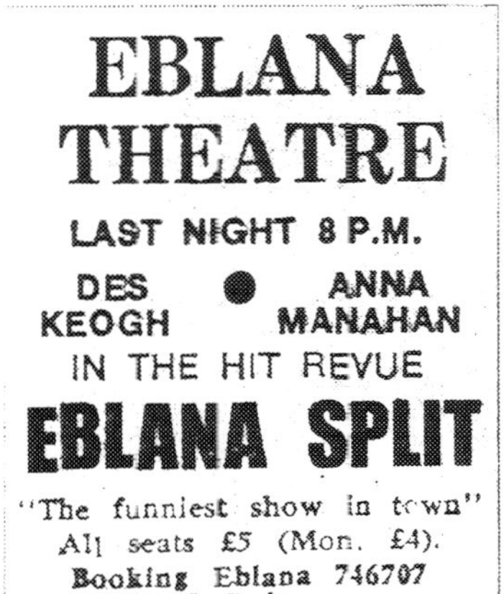

The declining attendances did not, it would seem, affect the Eblana, as this theatre appeared to survive, if not thrive, for the next twenty five years.

∼∼∼∼∼

A Tit-Bit or Two

On November 10th 1962, the "Dublin Theatre Workshop", which had been recently formed by John Franklyn the actor and dramatist, and Andrew Flynn, the publisher, gave their first production in the Eblana Theatre.

This production was Rodney Ackland's thriller, "The Three Old Ladies", which had Anna Manahan, Cathleen Delaney and Pamela Mant as the three characters. The Dublin Theatre Workshop's declared object was to help new dramatists access their work in private presentations.

∼∼∼∼∼

The theatre closed for a while in the early nineties and was re-opened in October of 1994 by the Northside Theatre Company. However, it didn't do too well and, to the best of our knowledge, the Eblana closed in 1995, with its last show being Lee Dunne's "Return to the Hill".

We believe that there was some attempt made to re-open the theatre in the late nineties, but nothing ever came of it. We heard that the breakdown in negotiations centred on the bar and the back exit. It would appear, that as Busaras closed down operations at 11 pm, the theatre bar would have to do likewise, and this would result in a serious loss of earnings.

The would-be proprietors, we were told, proposed a new exclusive entrance into the theatre, from where the emergency exit steps and gate were situated on the Amiens Street side of the complex, as pictured on this page.

This would allow for private and exclusive access to the bar and theatre and would provide for late night shows and bar extensions.
This proposal, however, appeared to be rejected and negotiations came to an end.

∼∼∼∼∼

On the left is a picture of the entrance into the Eblana. This photo was taken from the wide staircase leading down into the theatre, but the photographer couldn't venture any further because there was no lighting and the area was full of junk.

The theatre still lies there, almost intact and just possibly awaiting an entrepreneur.

∼∼∼∼∼

The Eblana was said to be unique in that it was a theatre without wings.

∼∼∼∼∼

The name Eblana may well have been used in honour of Dublin's first known settlement on the site of Dublin.
That would have course have been in the days long before the good old days.

∼∼∼∼∼

Here we would advise our readers that details about the attempted re-opening of the Eblana are really only hearsay. We have no proof that these negotiations took place or if they did, that the refusal of an exclusive entrance was the cause of a breakdown in the talks. We are simply repeating what we heard.

While the building of Busaras was an undertaking by Coras Iompair Eireann the company then in control of Irish transport, trains and buses, it is now under the control of Bus Eireann which came into being after the parent company split-up and was sub-divided into smaller more manageable companies. However C.I.E. offices are, we believe, still operational in the Broadstone complex.

FOUNTAIN PICTURE HOUSE
James Street

The Fountain Picture House opened on Monday February 26th 1923, and was said to be a thoroughly comfortable and well-equipped theatre, with fittings in the best modern style.

A new company named the "Irish National Picture Palaces Limited", was formed to build this new picture house, which according to the plans of its directors, was to be the first of ten cinemas which they would build in different parts of Ireland. High on their list of sites already earmarked for construction were Thurles, Cork, Carlow, New Ross, and Mullingar.

Whilst these were all towns of considerable importance, their principle cinema was the Fountain, which was built on the site of the former Phoenix Brewery in James Street, an area without cinema at that time.

It was a palatial structure in every sense of the world and decorated on a lavish scale with a stupendous balcony area that also accommodated a café lounge. There was seating for 1,200 patrons.

The Irish National Picture Palaces Limited was a company within a company, so to speak, and it was founded and incorporated by the Midland and Northern Industries Limited with a share capital of £50,000. Its objectives were to carry on the business of picture theatre proprietors and public entertainers. Its principle directors were, as yet, to be determined.

The opening programme featured the film "Jim the Penman", a screen adaptation of the famous novel of that name. The film was released in 1921, a remake of the 1915 version, and starred Lionel Barrymore of the Barrymore acting dynasty. Lionel was the first Barrymore to appear in silent movies and he made his debut in 1908.

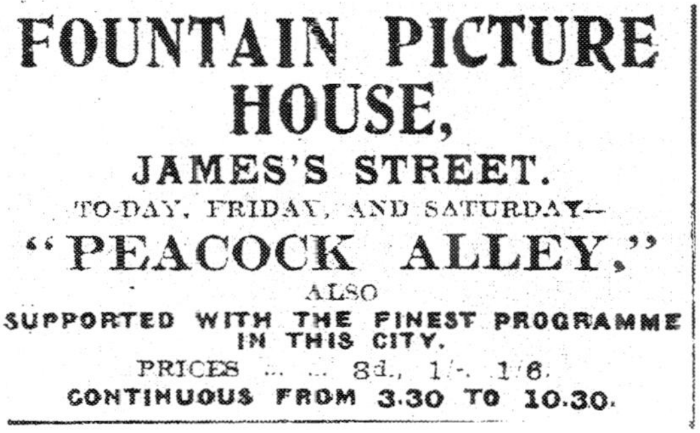

The Orchestra was under the direction of Archie Rafter, and C. Marston was overall manager.

Marston was formerly manager of the Brunswick Picture Theatre.

A small advertisement for the film featured for the 1st March 1923.

The site of the Fountain.

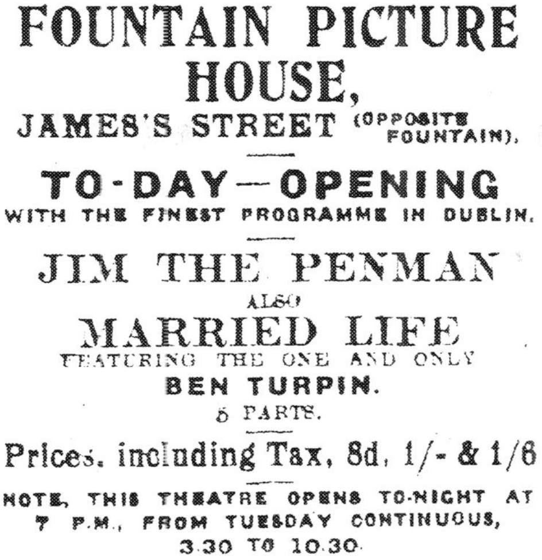

However, these were dangerous times and civil war was raging across Ireland. Only a month after it opened, the Fountain Picture House was nearly blown to smithereens, when a bomb was placed on the stone steps, against the outer iron gates of the building.

This took place at about 7.30am on Thursday morning March 19th 1923, and the bomb exploded with considerable force, smashing several of the iron bars in the gate and the overhead verandah and windows above. It would seem that little other damage was done, as the bomb appeared to be defective and failed in its objective.

The picture house remained closed for the next few days in order to carry out the necessary repairs and clean the place up. The Fountain wasn't unique in this attack, because explosions were taking place all over the city at that time and only two days earlier the Pillar Picture had had its rear doors blown off by a landmine.

Having carried out the necessary repairs, the cinema reopened some days later and continued on with the business of showing pictures. The Fountain was well placed and enjoyed good attendances, which carried it into the 1940's. In 1941 it closed down for renovations and the installation of new sound equipment. On Sunday night March 2nd, after the last performance the Fountain closed. Its last picture show was, "The Invisible Man Returns".

This movie starred Vincent Price and Sir Cedric Hardwicke and told the story of a man who when wrongly found guilty of murder, drinks a magic potion, which makes him invisible and, as such, enables him to escape from gaol and successfully track down the real killer.

Seven months later, having undergone total refurbishment, the cinema reopened as the Lyric Cinema on Sunday, September 28th 1941, with two main performances, one at 3pm and the other at 8pm.

By pure coincidence, management picked another film with a similar plot line to the one selected for the closing night of the Fountain Picture Palace many months earlier, which once again told the story of a man on the run having been wrongly accused of murder.

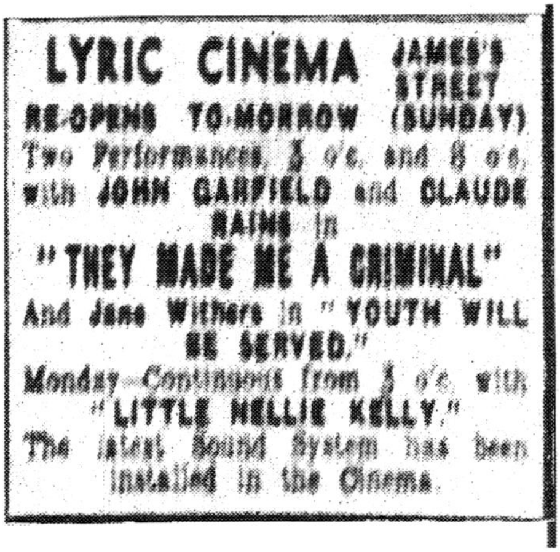
LYRIC CINEMA JAMES'S STREET
RE-OPENS TO-MORROW (SUNDAY)
Two Performances, 3 o'c. and 8 o'c. with JOHN GARFIELD and CLAUDE RAINS in
"THEY MADE ME A CRIMINAL"
And Jane Withers in "YOUTH WILL BE SERVED."
Monday Continuous from 3 o'c. with "LITTLE NELLIE KELLY."
The latest Sound System has been installed in the Cinema.

This time, it was the turn of John Garfield, who played the part of Johnny Burns, a tough hard drinking prize-fighter, who, having just won the title fight for the Lightweight Championship, was wrongly accused of having killed a reporter during the after fight party.

Garfield lams it out of New York and finds himself working on a chicken farm in another state which is run by a mother and daughter team who run the farm as a half-way house for young delinquents (played by the "Dead End Kids). Garfield falls in love with the daughter (Ann Sheridan) and becomes actively interested in rehabilitating the wayward boys. However, he is still being pursued by a relentless Detective Phelan, who finally catches up with the boxer, when Johnny returns to the ring and takes part in a fight in order to raise money for the farm. But Phelan, (Claude Rains) has a change of heart when he realises that Burns in now a changed character intent on making the farm a success.

This film was John Garfield's first starring role.

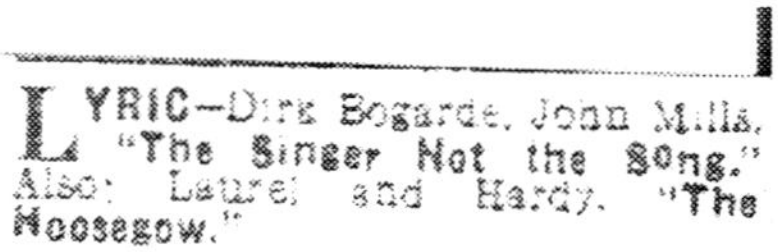
LYRIC—Dirk Bogarde, John Mills, "The Singer Not the Song." Also: Laurel and Hardy, "The Hoosegow."

This advertisement for the Lyric would appear to have been its last and as it was dated Friday June 22nd 1962 we would believe that the cinema closed on the following Saturday, June 23rd. 1962.

"The Singer not the Song", is a story about a Mexican Bandit, "Anacleto" (Dirk Bogarde), who tries to outwit. Father Keogh (John Mills), a catholic priest in a small Mexican village. The gunslinger, Anacleto, ruled the terrified villagers prior to Father Keogh's arrival and now fears he will lose control.

How lucky can we get, a last minute find albeit a night shot of the Fountain/Lyric cinema. (Picture courtesy of the Irish Architectural Archives).

In late July 2006 we met with Kevin Cunningham, one time manager of the Lyric cinema and he told us of one of those special little character stories about a little old woman who came to the pictures every Monday and Thursday nights. She was always dressed in black in the very old Dublin style with a large black shawl which would be wrapped around her upper body. Having settled herself comfortably in a seat of her choice she would sit there quietly with her arms folded until the main feature began and then she would reach into her shawl and take out a bottle of wine, which she would sip contentedly for the rest of the night. When the show was over, the empty bottle was returned to whence it came from within her shawl and off she would toddle into the darkness of the night.

GAIETY
South King Street

The Gaiety Theatre opened on November 17th 1871.
While the Gaiety theatre is not really a cinema, in the accepted sense of the word, it did involve itself by showing some spectacular movies circa the 1916 era. So much so that management had to completely refurbish the premises, in order to accommodate a masterpiece by W.D. Griffiths.

This movie, "The Birth of a Nation", which was billed in Ireland as the 8th Wonder of the World, told a story of the Post-Civil war in America and featured the Ku Klux Klan and the routing out of the Carpetbaggers.

Carpetbagger was the name used to describe outsiders who came to the post-war Southern States of America, who, it was said, were looking for opportunities to advance themselves either financially or politically. The name was derived from their habit of using cheap bags made of a carpet type of material as inexpensive luggage.

It was said that the Ku Klux Klan would lynch any carpetbagger that came to their attention.
The film had a cast of 18,000 and featured 5,000 horses and was a box office success, taking in $10m when it was released in 1915. The movie cost $100,000 and took eight months to make. This was an epic film, which ran for 3 hours and was said to be an awe-inspiring story pf Romance, Love and Patriotism.

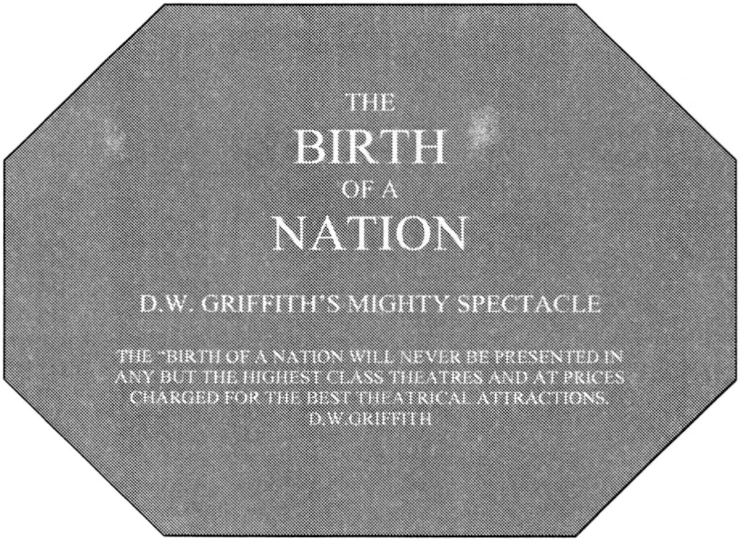

Two views of the Gaiety in 2006

On March 11th 1918, the Gaiety once again featured another blockbuster by D.W. Griffith entitled "Intolerance", which was billed as his Gigantic Production and was said to be the greatest film of its age.

Just like "Birth of a Nation", it had a cast of thousands, 125,000 in all and it was claimed that in one scene alone there were 67,000 people.

This film ran for one week only and had the backing of a full orchestra.

~~~~~

This film was considered to be one of the masterpieces of the silent film era, and it was said that it was made by Griffiths in response to critics who felt that his "Birth of a Nation" was racist, by glorifying the Ku Klux Klan.

The film consisted of four stories, which demonstrated mankind's intolerance during four different ages, as follows:

The "Babylon" period (539 BC), depicts the fall of Babylon as a result of intolerance which arising from a conflict between devotees of different Gods.

The "Judean" era (27 AD), recounts how intolerance led to the crucifixion of Jesus.

The French Renaissance (1572), tells of the failure of the Edict of Tolerance that led to the St Bartholomew's Day massacre.

"Modern America" (1914), demonstrates how crime, moral puritanism, and conflicts between ruthless capitalists and striking workers helped ruin American lives. (This analysis is from the Wikipedia Free Encyclopedia).
These stories were all intermixed throughout the film and brought together with a view of emphasising mankind's intolerance over a span of 2,500 years.

It cost in the region of $2m to make in 1915, had lavish period costumes, monumental sets and ran for three hours. However, the cost and size of the film, it flopped at the box office and brought about the bankruptcy of Griffith's Triangle Studies.

Some of the leading stars included:
Douglas Fairbanks
Lillian Gish
Mae March
Robert Harron
F.A. Turner
Sam de Grasse

This film is now recognised as a unique work of art and is preserved by the United States National Film Registry.
~~~~~

On Monday, October 20th 1914, the Gaiety opened up with another box office success for a six night run and two afternoon matinees. This was the story of Scott's Expedition to the Antarctic, which would be told by way of Pointing's Moving Picture Lecture, with Captain Scott in the Antarctic, which would be delivered by a member of the expedition.

The pictures were of an absorbing interest and many of them were quite unique at the time. They were presented to the accompaniment of explanations and comments. The general story of the great journey was told, in excellent style and in such a manner as to give the audience a vivid idea of the wonderful experiences of intrepid men in the awe-inspiring region of perpetual snow and ice.

The "Terra Nova", which was Robert Falcon Scott's second choice of a ship for the expedition, with the "Discovery" being his first, but which was not available to him at the time, was seen leaving Lyttleton, New Zealand on the beginning of its journey to the Antarctic.

On its way, it encountered mountainous seas and pitched and rolled in unbelievable storms. During one of these storms huge waves ravaged the ship and it was said that one of the dogs was most unfortunate when it was washed overboard by a fierce wave and incredibly lucky when another big wave washed it back onboard. Nearing the Antarctic, massive icebergs floated by and one of them was said to have measured some 33 miles long. Remarkable pictures were shown of the ship charging and breaking through ice floes and fantastic pictures were taken of terrible monsters known as "killer whales" that invest those desolate regions.

Beautiful pictures were shown of the landing of the expedition and the unloading of the dogs and Siberian ponies, as were excellent scenes of a football match taking place between members of the expedition on a ten foot thick layer of ice, which covered some 600 fathoms of water. There were also some entertaining illustrations of the habits of seals and penguins.

~~~~~

The Gaiety management in conjunction with Herbert Pointing's team ran a special competition for children under fourteen with 5 prizes ranging in value from £1, 10/- 5/- 4/- and 3/- for the best essays written on the subject. With H.S. Doig and a Professor Teegan, prepared to act as adjudicators.

Herbert C. Pointing was a highly-skilled photographer and quite a lot of his work is regarded as classic to this day.

~~~~~

Having made its filmic foray in the early 20th century, the Gaiety appeared to lose interest in showing films soon after that period and concentrated instead on producing plays, musicals, stage shows and pantomimes and is still alive and well in 2006.

GALA

The Gala Cinema 361-363 Ballyfermot Road, was built in 1955 and was officially opened by Canon Troy on Wednesday November 23rd, with the first ever Cinemascope Musical film, "Lucky me", starring Doris Day and Phil Silvers.

This was a large suburban cinema of 1,900 seats, with 350 of them in the balcony. The cinema was built by G.T. Crampton Ltd., and the architect was J.F. McCormack, and the building commenced in 1954. The manager in those days was J. Kelly, and for some 25 years the people of Ballyfermot enjoyed a run of top movies every week in the Gala.

The opening film "Lucky Me", starring Doris Day, Phil Silver's and Robert Cummings was in Technicolor and Cinemascope and admission prices were 1/6 in the stalls and 2/- in the balcony. Sunday prices differed slightly with Stalls at 1/8 and balcony 2/3. Seats had to be booked in advance for Sunday night shows.

The Gala was one of the biggest suburban cinemas at that time and its screen was one of the largest in the city.

In 1956 when the Housing Department of Dublin Corporation were seeking tenders for the erecting of a cinema on Decies Road, Lower Ballyfermot, the directors of Republic Cinemas Ltd., the then owners of the Gala, strongly objected to the building of a second cinema in Ballyfermot. Daniel McAlistaire, M.D., argued that it was better to have one cinema giving first class service to the community, rather than have two cinemas in financial difficulties.

In the year 1980 almost every home in the country had a television set, and this marvellous home entertainment unit brought about a huge decline in cinemagoers all over Ireland and like a lot of other cinemas the Gala cinema closed in that year.

The Gala Cinema taken in 2005.

Following its closure, the Gala was converted to a Roller Rink and later again, it became a leisure centre with snooker and other activities available. Later again, it held Bingo sessions, as did many other suburban cinemas, and to day in early 2006 it is still providing those services.

Bingo, it would appear, was a type of saving grace for many a cinema, community-type halls and old dance hall buildings.

GEM
Malahide Coal & Gasworks Yard.

Back in the thirties, circuses, carnivals, road shows, travelling theatres and a fit-up cinema used to visit Malahide and set up on the Green. The proprietor of the fit-up cinema was one Pop O'Brien, who would usually come along after the circus and theatres had left and fit-up his cinema.

Pop would arrive with a caravan and trailer and the fit-up cinema would consist of wooden framed sides with a canvas roof, canvas flap type side panels and a canvas door, all of which would be secured with tie ropes. This structure oblong in shape, and although much smaller, would for all the world resemble the surrounding wooden frame, canvas sides and roof of the average carnival bumper car attraction.

When erected this makeshift cinema might hold some 30-40 persons who would be seated on backless wooded forms which were lined along the centre of the building in rows and these were entered from an narrow aisle on either side. Pop with the help of his daughter would collect the admission fee as you entered the tent and when all were seated he would set up his projector and the picture/s would begin. He only had one projector and when a reel had run its length there would be a gap in the film until the old reel was taken out and the next reel was fitted. This would bring about a good-humoured clapping of hands or cries of "we want out money back". As this break in the continuity of the film was a regular occurrence, his customers were a patient and understanding lot.

The Ammonite.

This picture of Niall O'Neill's work of art, "The Ammonite", which now sits in the centre of the Green, could well mark the spot of Pop O'Brien's Fit-Up Cinema.

After a time, Pop made the acquaintance of the owner of the gas works yard who allowed him the use of a reasonably large shed in the yard which measured some 21ft x60 ft and Pop immediately wrote to Ryan, the County Surveyor, on August 1940, and asked if the shed would be suitable for conversion into a cinema for the winter period. He further mentioned that the shed had two very large doors that opened outward on one side and invited opinions and recommendations from the surveyor.

It would appear that the recommendations which included an outdoor projection box were carried out and a six month licence was granted. In granting the licence Ryan made it clear that this arrangement would not necessarily be continued and that the six month period was given to allow O'Brien time to re-organise his business to enable him to go back on the road again with his travelling cinema.

The cinema could now hold a larger audience and Pop invested in some more backless benches, but still continued to show his movies with the use of only one projector.

The Malahide Coal & Gas Works Yard.
Pop O'Brien's cinema would have stood somewhere in the vicinity of where the excavating machine is working.

Time passed and when his licence expired, he applied for an extension, again and again and on each occasion the County Surveyor inspected the premises and granted a six-month extension.

The County Surveyor also spoke with the Sergeant of the Guards in Malahide and when they voiced no objections to the renewal of the cinema licence, Ryan, continued to renew the licence. The last time Ryan inspected the premises was in 1944 when he recommended that the licence be extended for a further six months.

~~~~~

It was also said that this cinema was instrumental in bringing fish'n chips to Malahide in so far as when one O'Rourke, who had a shop in Killester heard about the cinema he started to sell fish n chips from a van on the road outside the yard. These, he would cook on a coal burning stove in his mobile chip van.

Perhaps he bartered fish'n chips for a bucket of coal from the Coal Yard.

~~~~~

It would then appear that O'Brien submitted an application and plans to the Council for a new cinema on the site near the Gas Works, circa. 1946, and we re-produce here a section of the drawings contained in the application.

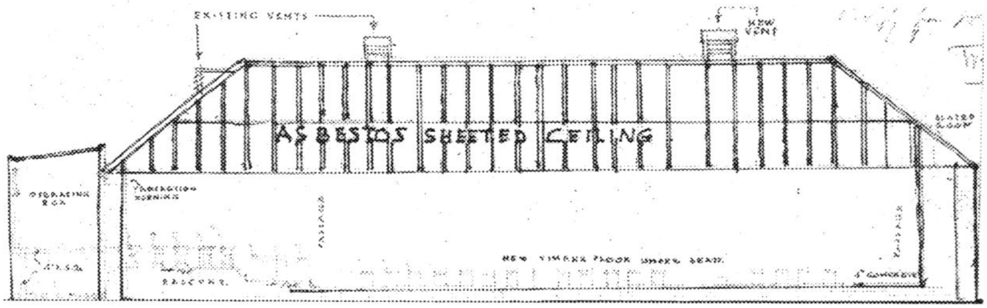

As can be determined by this illustration, the operating box would be outside the end wall of the building, which would suggest that the screen would be situated over the entrance doors. The floor appears to be of the stadium-type, with eight rows of plush seating leading down to the stalls area, where there were a further three rows of plush seats, with the rest of the stalls and pit area having backless forms.

We don't know if these plans were ever carried out or for that matter what happened to the cinema in its latter years, but we did come across a report from the then Assistant Co. Engineer to the County Secretary on May 9th 1949, which condemned the use of the building as a cinema and that he did not consider that any reasonable expenditure would make the building completely suitable and that it should not be licensed.

GEORGE'S HALL
Dublin Central Mission
South Great George's Street.

Some time around 1920, the George's Hall applied for a Cinematograph Licence in order to show occasional pictures and below we re-produce a copy of one of its first advertisements, which may well have heralded its first venture into the world of cinema.

This advertisement appeared on Friday October 1st 1920, and informed the public that a film show would be available on Saturday October 2nd.

George's Hall was a Mission house and any show or gatherings held there were usually of a religious nature. We would imagine that their venture into the cinema business was purely an exercise in fund-raising.

While it didn't come across to us as a regular picture house, it nevertheless held a Cinematograph Licence under the 1909 Act, advertised films and was open to the public and we therefore felt it was worth a mention.

Admission prices were reasonably set at 6d into the Parterre and 9d into the Balcony with children at 3d. Special Music was on offer and strangers were cordially welcomed.

Once again, we apologise for the condition of the advertisement, and once again, we would ask you to bear with us.

As you can just about see from the wording of the advertisement, the management went to great lengths to inform the public that the pictures on offer were 'Clean and Healthy' and it further stated that they were free from 'sensationalism . With this in mind we made it our business to find out exactly what type of pictures they intended to display and we wondered if they would be of a religious nature or perhaps straight laced travelogues and simple cartoons etc.

However, the results of our search were that the pictures on display were of the same type and variety that were available to all picture houses.

Here we list some of the films advertised during the months leading up to Christmas 1920.

"First Men in the Moon"
"Her Great Chance" starring Alice Brady
"The Man Who Was Beaten"
"Less than the Dust" starring Mary Pickford.

However, what did surprise us was the fact that management was advertising a picture programme on Christmas Day and this at a time when al the religious leaders in the Dublin area were bemoaning the fact that Sunday night cinema performances were interfering with church attendances and religious ceremonies.
Though on a point of technicality we feel honour bound to inform you that Christmas day fell on a Saturday in 1920, which was the halls usual day for showing pictures.

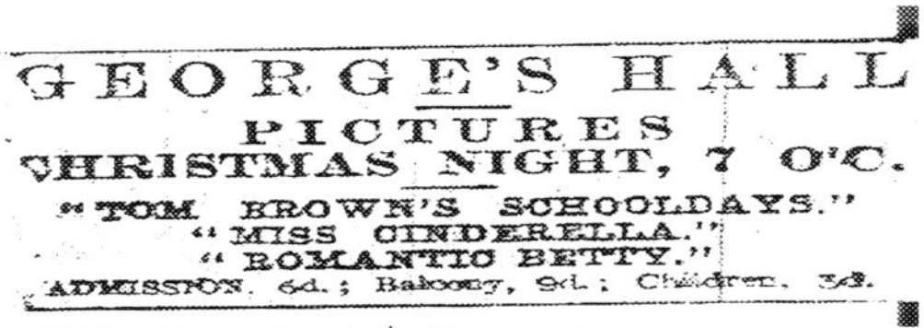
GEORGE'S HALL
PICTURES
CHRISTMAS NIGHT, 7 O'C.
"TOM BROWN'S SCHOOLDAYS."
"MISS CINDERELLA."
"ROMANTIC BETTY."
ADMISSION. 6d.; Balcony, 9d.; Children, 3d.

On the same day Friday December 24th all other picture houses were advertising their films for that day and the coming week, but none advertised a film for Christmas Day.

DORSET PICTURE PALACE
THE KINSMAN WITH Chrissie White
&
Charlie Chaplin in the
JAZZ WAITER

PALACE CINEMA
FOR A WOMAN'S HONOUR
Friday only
Change of programme for Sunday

PANTOMINE
BALL
&
CARNIVAL
A NIGHT OF FUN
St Stephen's night

PALACE BALLROOM
ANTIENT CONCERT
ROOMS
42 Brunswick Street

THE MISSION BUILDING
5 Townsend Street
Monday 27th
A Christmas Story

METHODIST CHURCH
St Stephen's Green
CHRISTMAS DAY 1920
CHRISTMAS HYMNS AND
CAROLS

Other than religious services, nowhere else did we find entertainment advertised for Christmas Day. The small ads. that we found were, once again, in a faded condition so we made up our own banners and copied the printing word for word.

The Theatre De-Luxe featured "Secret Service" with Robert Warwick
The Queens "Babes in the Wood" pantomime
The Tivoli Burgh Quay planned the "Dixie minstrels" for the 27th and
The Abbey Theatre "Candle and Crib", a play for the following week.

GEORGES STREET PICTURE PALACE.

One of the many cinema dreams that fell by the wayside.

In 1914 on August 28th, a company was incorporated under the name of the "Georges Street Picture Palace Company", with a capital sum of £10,400, which was made up £1 shares, This capital sum was set aside to acquire a corner site situated at the junction of Georges Street and Upper Stephen Street where the directors planned to build a cinema.

Some of the company's principle directors were Alfie Byrne, a publican of 17 Talbot Street, J. Harris, H. Molloy 7 Church Avenue Rathmines and H. Wigoder, B. Lynch, H. Cowan and N. Rubenstein.

Howeve,r with the site bought, the cinema was never built and the ground was either sold off, or used by the company for other purposes.

* * * * *

Here we would give special mention to Alfie Byrne, one of the abovementioned directors who at the time was a landlord of the "Verdon Bar" in Talbot Street. In later years, when he became an elected representative in the Dublin area, he became very involved in performing the opening ceremonies of Dublin cinemas on behalf of their owners. In his capacity as Lord Mayor of Dublin, a position he held for nine years, he opened the Green Cinema and many others.

While a publican, he invested in the above company, with a view to building a cinema, but unfortunately it never materialised, He was a public house landlord up to 1915, when he became an elected M.P. for Dublin and in 1922 he was an elected T.D.

Alfie, during his political career, was in alphabetical order, an Alderman, Dail Deputy, Lord Mayor of Dublin, an M.P. a Senator and a T.D.

He was the elected Lord Mayor of Dublin from 1931 to 1939. Though he retired in 1939, he was again elected Lord Mayor of Dublin in 1954.

* * * * *

FAIRVIEW CINEMA
Opened by
Senator Alfie Byrne

DRUMCONDRA
GRAND
Opened by
Lord Mayor
Alfie Byrne

LEINSTER & RIALTO CINEMAS
Opened within days of each by
Alderman Alfie Byrne T.D.
Lord Mayor of Dublin

GOD BE WITH THE DAYS

God be with the days when tea or coffee was served with biscuits during each performance, and were all, we might add, 'free of charge'.

This, of course, was in the early days of cinema and in particular the "Volta" which was Dublin's first cinema and the Sackville, which was O'Connell Streets first cinema.

The first picture show in Ireland was said to be the famous Poole's Myriorama at the Rotunda in the autumn of 1897 and it consisted of two subjects, which lasted a total length of five minutes. Although it was crudely presented, the show was considered a wonderful novelty albeit more for the amusement of children rather than adults.

However we also have reference to a visit by the Lumiere brothers in 1896 when they were said to have screened a film in the "Star of Erin Theatre" at that time and again we have mention of a Professor Jolly, who, it was claimed, presented the first filmed Irish subjects, which included "People walking along Sackville Street", "Traffic on Carlisle Bridge" and the "13th Hussars Marching through the City", in 1897.

The Lumiere brothers, Augusta and Louis were regarded as the inventors of cinema, following a presentation of their work in a Paris basement, where they displayed their first film to members of the public, which was a take of workers leaving their father's factory.

Yet it was said that Edison in 1888 demonstrated his first movie and talkie when he married his discoveries the "Kinetoscope" and the "Phonograph".

So what indeed was first, and who indeed was ahead of the Posse?

The more we researched, the deeper the plot and contradiction followed upon contradiction, we could take you back through the years and mention William Friese Greene and John Rudge with their "Magic Lantern" in 1886,
Etienne Jules Marey and his "Chronophotographic Camera"
Emile Reynard with his "Mirrors and Slots"
Eadweard Muybridge and his "Multiple Photographs" and
William George Horner with his "Zoetrope" in 1834 and with William we would place our bets.

Whichever way it was, we got pictures and from 1909 onwards we could watch a full 2 ½ to 3 hour performance in a cinema as often as we liked, sometimes for as little as a penny or as much as 1/-, and as often as desired.

These performances were continuous from morning to late evening and programmes usually consisted of travel scenes, filmed scenes from pantomimes, sporting events, comedy capers and newsworthy events, civic meeting and gatherings or simply showing a group of people leaving a church, etc. In one of Edison's displays it was said to be the simple movement by a Dickson, when he tipped his hat.

All the films, of course, were silent and were usually introduced by a spokesperson that would most likely read from a prepared script and talk one through the scenes. The films would also be musically accompanied, with either a single instrument player or an orchestra.

However, the movie world moved forward in leaps and bounds and in no time at all there were feature-length films with heroes and heroines in abundance, great romantic lovers, adventurer's, and lovable comedians, most of whom went on to become 'stars and household names'.

The movie makers catered for all tastes, be it stories of love and romance, war, gangsterism, piracy, cowboy's, musicals, comedy, sports, horror, murder, mystery, you name it, they made it, be it in outer or inner space, underneath the sea, down the road in the Jungle or even within the human body. Such as "Fantastic Voyage" with Stephen Boyd, and "Innerspace", with Denis Quaid.

The Talkies came in 1927 and from that year onwards we were entirely hooked on films, whether they were on show in cinemas or on our television screens. Few people in Ireland passed a week without seeing a film of one type or another.

The method of film distribution in Ireland has also changed much over the years and now a projectionist in an Irish cinema can download a film from a satellite station overhead in the sky, by simply pressing a button and of course you can make a simple movie on a mobile phone and watch it or forward it on to a friend.

Technology it would seem, knows no bounds.

~~~~~~~~~~

Snippets

In 1953, it was announced in Hollywood that members of the Communist Party had been barred from membership of the Screen Actors Guild by a majority of 3,769 to 15 votes.

* * * * *
~~~~~~~~~~

GRAFTON

The Grafton Picture House opened on Easter Monday April 17th 1911, under the management of a H. Huish and it had luxurious seating accommodation for 620 patrons. This new addition to the world of Dublin cinemas, at 72 Grafton Street, attracted large numbers of people on its opening night and all were in awe of the plush surroundings, which included carpeting of thick green material and red plush seats.

For the convenience of its patrons, the floor gradually rises from the front of the cinema to the entrance doors, giving everyone a perfect view of the pictures being shown, and all pictures were accompanied by music, played by a wonderful orchestra.

Management chose for its "gala opening" the film, The Siege and Fall of Troy, which had a cast of hundreds of people and, it was said, they acted in a wonderfully realistic manner. There were also some capital travel pictures shown that made one wish that they were there, together with films on current events.

The proprietors of this new enterprise were the Provincial Theatre Company Ltd who had recently purchased the "Volta" and built the Sackville Picture House. The cinema entrance hall also contained a lounge, tea-rooms and a reading room which was open to the public, whether or not they were paying in to see the pictures.

This latest cinema is not to be confused with a namesake place of entertainment that was once situated just around the corner, in South Anne's Street, which was known as the Grafton Theatre.

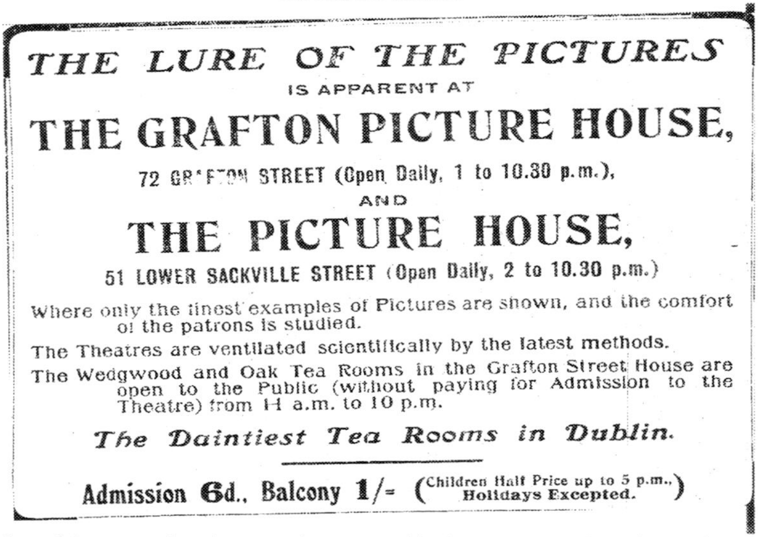

One of the many advertisements that appeared in the newspapers from time to time.

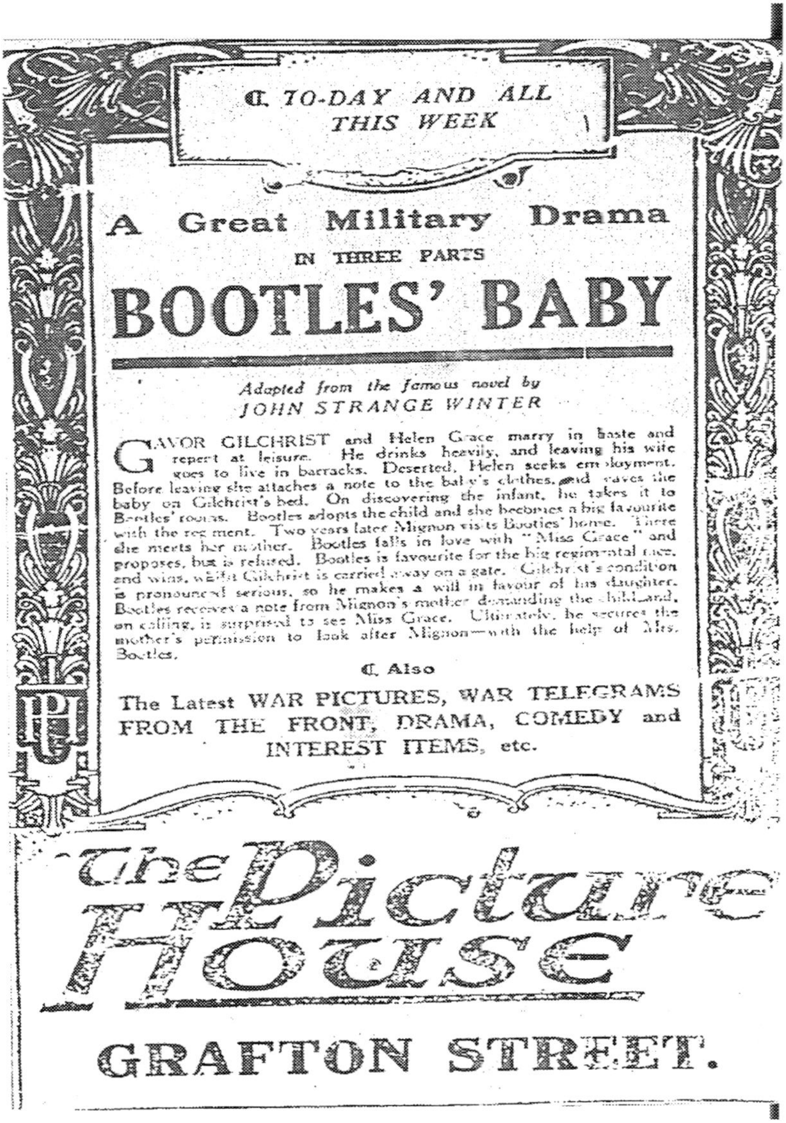

¶ TO-DAY AND ALL THIS WEEK

A Great Military Drama

IN THREE PARTS

BOOTLES' BABY

Adapted from the famous novel by
JOHN STRANGE WINTER

GAVOR GILCHRIST and Helen Grace marry in haste and repent at leisure. He drinks heavily, and leaving his wife goes to live in barracks. Deserted, Helen seeks employment. Before leaving she attaches a note to the baby's clothes, and leaves the baby on Gilchrist's bed. On discovering the infant, he takes it to Bootles' rooms. Bootles adopts the child and she becomes a big favourite with the regiment. Two years later Mignon visits Bootles' home. There she meets her mother. Bootles falls in love with "Miss Grace" and proposes, but is refused. Bootles is favourite for the big regimental race, and wins, whilst Gilchrist is carried away on a gate. Gilchrist's condition is pronounced serious, so he makes a will in favour of his daughter. Bootles receives a note from Mignon's mother demanding the child and, on calling, is surprised to see Miss Grace. Ultimately, he secures the mother's permission to look after Mignon—with the help of Mrs. Bootles.

¶ Also

The Latest WAR PICTURES, WAR TELEGRAMS FROM THE FRONT, DRAMA, COMEDY and INTEREST ITEMS, etc.

The Picture House

GRAFTON STREET.

This advertisement appeared in the "Evening Telegraph" on September 7th 1914, which billed the cinema as the "Picture House", but we could find no explanation for this occurrence.

During the years 1913-14, the British Army ran some recruitment films in the Grafton and these were seriously disrupted by some members of Countess Markievitz's "Boy Scout" movement.

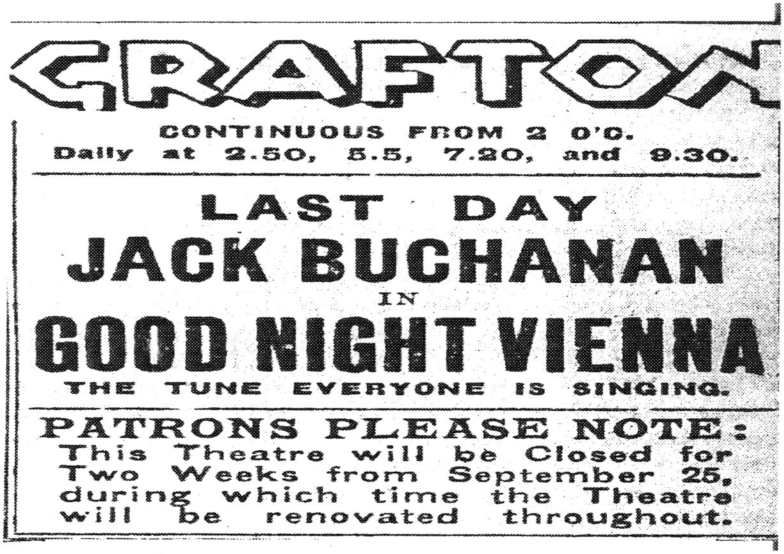

On September 25th 1932, the Grafton Cinema closed for two weeks for a complete renovation.

On October 14th 1932, the Grafton having been completely renovated had a grand re-opening with the supreme film achievement of the year "Kameradschaft".

This was the story about a band of French miners who, when working in a mine shaft below the French/German border, were trapped by a cave-in, their only hope of rescue lying in an old disused tunnel coming in from the German side, which had been buried since World War I.

Ignoring the political and ethnic differences that had separated the two countries for so long, a group of German miners began to pick their way towards the entombed Frenchmen.
When the rescue mission was accomplished, the German miners were asked why they had taken such a risk to rescue the Frenchmen, they replied -

"Miners are Miners".

OUR FIRST ALL-GAELIC FILM

A delightful scene from the first all-Gaelic film, "Oidhche Seanchais." The film with the cast of "Man of Aran" was produced under the auspices of the Department of Education, and will be shown as an Irish Week feature simultaneously at the Grafton and Carlton Cinemas, Dublin, and the Palace Theatre, Cork.

The Grafton, along with the Carlton Dublin and Palace Theatre Cork, shared the honour of showing Ireland's first All-Gaelic Film "Oidhche Seanchais", during "Irish Week" in 1935.

In the late fifties, the Grafton changed to a News and Cartoon cinema, which was well-patronised for many a year and in the late sixties it again reverted back to the showing of feature films, but this time, to the delight of many, the management specialised in the reruns of "Golden Oldies" and many a happy patrons flocked to see films such as:

"How Green was my Valley" (1941) with Walter Pidgeon and Maureen O'Hara.
"Wuthering Heights" (1939) with Merle Oberon and Laurence Olivier.
"Random Harvest" (1942) with Ronald Coleman and Greer Garson.
"Casablanca" (1942) with Humphrey Bogart and Ingrid Bergman.
"Rebecca" (1940) with Laurence Olivier and Joan Fontaine.

In the late sixties the management of the Grafton cinema decided to close their News and Cartoons cinema and following a major renovation and rejuvenation of the premises, which cost in the region of £5,000 they planned to present the greatest films ever made

On Friday May 3rd 1968 the new look Grafton presented a magnificent opening with the epic film "War and Peace" a three hour classic which starred Audrey Hepburn, Henry Fonda and Mel Ferrer

After "War and Peace" which was billed as the motion picture of the century, had run a season of twice daily showings, together with a late show every evening at 11am management followed on with a regular avalanche of top films some of which we have already listed above.

The picture of the Grafton cinema earlier in this story is of the New look Grafton.

The manager James McCarthy also mentioned that he intended from time to time to present special "seasons of notable actors" films such as Humphrey Bogart, Betty Davis, Dirk Bogard, Spencer Tracy and Kathryn Hepburn

The new look Grafton was fitted with a special cinemascope wide screen with very expensive new lenses on the projectors which gave greatly improved clarity and better picture size to these "Golden Oldies"

However despite the popularity of these films the Grafton closed down on December 1st 1973 with Eric Rohmer's "Love in the Afternoon" And "Me Natalie"

"Love in the Afternoon" starring Bernard Verley, Zouzou and Francoise Verley The story of a man that has to make a choice between his new love and his wife and family; this is one of six moral tales by Eric Rohmer.

* * * * *

"Me Natalie"
Starring
Patty Duke and James Farentino;

A story of an ugly duckling seeking love and romance

Al Pacino made his first screen appearance in a minor roll in this movie

While we laboured on the Grafton being a cinema, few people today will remember that the Grafton, which was situated in the heart of Dublin's street of vanities, also presented its fair share of stage shows and when it closed on December 1st 1973 its long-disused dressing rooms were still intact.

It is another feature of old Dublin vanishing said its manager Jim Thorpe when he was interviewed by a Herald reporter on the eve of its closure.

The passing of the Grafton wrote the Herald reporter recalls the silent days of the screen, an era that had all the enchantment of novelty, for moving pictures were a new, brash excitement, and Dublin, never slow to jump on the bandwagon of entertainment had been, in its own way, a pioneering city as far as the cinema was concerned. Dublin it was said was one of the most cinema conscious towns in the world.

The Grafton's first manager H Huish was also manager of the Volta cinema in Mary Street, which was owned by the same company, and when the Grafton opened, Huish was put in charge of the new cinema.

In its early days this cinema was advertised at the "Picture House" Grafton Street and the management spared no expense on advertising their feature films and below we re-produce a couple of their large display advertisements for perusal.

A delightful cockney romance February 5th 1917 in which it was said Miss Florence Turner is seen to great advantage.

January 25th 1917

GRAND
Townyard Lane, Malahide

Townyard Lane in the Mid 1940s was a hive of activity and was the central stabling area for all the local merchants to store their carts and have their horses liveried. It also housed the sweet shop and factory belonging to Sammy Well's, a pub, lounge, dance hall and a cinema belonging to the Walshe family.

The cinema which was called the "Grand" opened in the middle of March 1945 and was under the management of Mrs Walsh and it was commonly known as Ma Walsh's cinema. While the pub, lounge and dance hall went by the name of the "Claddagh and was managed by Ma Walsh's daughter. The main entrance to the cinema was on the Mall.

The name "Claddagh" came about because the lounge area was decorated with scenes of Galway and in the centre of the lounge was a large pond with a mock bridge. It bore the nickname "Snakepit", where one local claimed that he often drank himself silly. This nickname came about just after a film bearing the name "Snake-Pit", which starred Olivia de Havilland and Leo Glen had been shown in the Grand cinema.

The Mall site of the Claddagh and Grand

Jack Moore taking George on a tour of Malahide & Portmarnock
The Riverside Cinema once stood to the rear and right of where Jack is standing.
Jack Moore, a local historian, who provided us with a lot of information about the two cinemas in Malahide, knew quite a bit about the Grand and Claddagh as he used to help out Ma Walsh and her daughter when he was a young teenager. Jack would mind the bicycles parked outside in the yard and double as cloakroom attendant as required, and for this he would receive a wage of 3/6 and a free admission to a cinema show.

He also knew of a cinema in Portmarnock called the "Riverside" and we tell of this in another section o this book.

Photograph showing the main entrance to the Grand Cinema in Main Street Malahide
(Picture re-produced from the Malahide Golf Club Centenary book 1892-1992 by the kind permission of the Secretary)

We found this advertisement in the "Evening Herald" on Saturday March 12th 1960 to back up our claim that the Grand was called the Malahide in its latter years.

MALAHIDE—"The Naked Hills," with David Wayne and Keenan Wynn; also **"Toughest Man Alive."** Sunday: **"While the City Sleeps."** Starring Ida Lupino and Dana Andrews. Also: **"Silver Lode"**.

The Malahide/Grand cinema and the Cladagh dance hall and bars were purchased by Albert Reynolds circa late 1962 or early1963 and closed for a period of time while it was being converted into a hotel and dance hall complex. No further cinema licenses were applied for.

The finished product was an impressive hotel and cabaret centre called the "Showboat" that could accommodate 1,000 people. Albert, it was said, often served in the bar in those hectic times.

The Showboat Cabaret proved to be a winner and with the best of and most popular Showbands available engaged to play there over the years, it attracted patrons from all the surrounding areas. On certain dates special buses ferried people from the centre of Dublin to the thriving venue.

However misfortune came to the Showboat on the morning of Monday, October 13th 1969 in the form of a terrible fire that completely gutted the beautiful cabaret and hotel complex.

It would appear, according to some newspaper reports of the time, that a mysterious fire began in the complex shortly after 3am on Monday morning, October 13th 1969 and gained such a fierce hold that by the time the firemen appeared on the scene, the building was a blazing inferno.

The fire was first noticed by some near neighbours who were awakened by a series of explosions and they immediately phoned the fire brigade. Beer casks and bottles were popping and exploding all over the place and windowpanes shattered with loud bangs, sending shards of glass flying in all directions and flames licked hungrily at adjoining buildings Residents in nearby premises were warned that that they might have to evacuate the area.

In all, seven fire brigade crews fought the blaze, four of which were from Dublin and the other three were from Malahide, Skerries and Swords, but despite their gallant efforts the three storied building was burnt to the ground. The best the fire crews could do, was to prevent the fire spreading to other buildings.

Fortunately the building was unoccupied at the time, having been securely locked up following the previous night's cabaret.

In an interview following the fire, Reynolds who came from Longford though saddened at the disaster that had befallen his beautiful cabaret rooms, apologised for all the forthcoming functions that had to be cancelled because of the fire and promised that a new complex would soon be built on the site which would incorporate a hotel, cabaret rooms, a ballroom, bars and a discotheque. He would be, he said, spending between £100,000 and £120,000 on the new venture.

As-par-for-the course, we came across this advertisement in the "Evening Herald", on March 12th 1945 and once again we found it by accident while we were researching another subject. Unfortunately, like many another advertisements, it would not photocopy well and we felt it would be better if we did one of our banners.

GRAND CINEMA MALAHIDE
SENSATIONAL ATTRACTION
COMMENCING TO-NIGHT
(MONDAY) March 12th
For seven nights at 8 .15 P.M

RADION STARS PRODUCTIONS
PRESENT THE STAR-SPANGLED REVUE

SPEED AND SPARKLE
ALL STAR CAST OF 20 WELL-KNOWN
ARTISTES, INCLUDING
THE AMAZING RAMESES
RAMON AND RAMONA AND
MAY ROYAL

PRICES 2/6 1/6 and 1/-

This was the Grand's official opening advertisement, and as can be seen from the above wording of the advertisement no film was available during its opening week. This situation was not exclusive to the Grand however, as the Premier in Lucan had a similar type opening in February of that same year.

~~~~~

On the same page we were blessed with another little snippet of information on the separation of the sexes in cinemas. As you will have read in the story on the Fairview Grand cinema they too tried to separate the sexes, but soon learned a harsh lesson.
~~~~~

However, according to the writings of an "Evening Herald" correspondent, a cinema in Clones had imposed a ban on boys and girls sitting together in their cinema and as patrons entered the cinema the separation of the sexes took place.

There were many complaints from unmarried couples and for a while the management relaxed the rule, but after a lapse of only two weeks the order for the separation of the sexes was again enforced on Sunday night March 11th 1945 and no explanation was given by management.

Again numerous complaints were made by young unmarried couples to the ushers on duty but they simply said that they had strict orders to enforce the ban.

The Cinema, which was the only one in the town, was crowded for the night's performance and all the patrons reluctantly complied with the ban.

~~~~~

Author's note: it could well be misconstrued from this correspondents report that married couples appeared to be happy enough with the ban, with there being no mention of a complaint from that direction.

~~~~~

It was also claimed by one or two people that the cinema in Malahide was also called the Coliseum for a short time, but we could find no evidence to back up this claim.

~~~~~

SOURCES OF INFORMATION

Our biggest source of information on the cinemas of yesteryear was of course old newspapers without which we could not have gathered this mine of knowledge. Friends and well wishers passed on their memories to us and ex cinema workers were a great help. Strangers wrote to us and reminded us of some cinemas that we just might have passed over and we found libraries and archives with books of reference in abundance for us to plough through and the minutes and reports of local authority meetings were a historian's delight.

We were gifted with rare programmes, pictures, and tales of the past from local historians and lovers of the cinema. We got permission to paraphrase the writings of others and one very gentle old lady, with the bearing, manners and gentility of days gone by, very kindly gave us a present of two beautiful tiles that once adorned the floors of the vestibule of the Coliseum cinema in Henry Street.
~~~~~

GRAND CINEMA
8 Sackville Street (Now O'Connell Street).

In early 1913 at number 8 Lower Sackville Street sat the Grand Hotel and Restaurant which belonged to the Kay family and on this site Mr. William Kay decided to open a cinema. As well as being an experienced hotelier, (the family had another hotel on Eden Quay) William was also interested in and performed cinematographic exhibitions in such premises as the Town Hall Rathmines and other like venues. Obviously he now thought it time to open a cinema himself, the likes of which were making appearances all over the country

It would appear that William acquired a portion of the restaurant and built a small luxurious cinema there upon, which was lavishly decorated with a beautiful thick crimson carpet spread across the floor, on which rested the best of seating finished in green plush.

The screen was set high on the wall and was surrounded with a broad black border, which gave the pictures a greater intensity.

Films were bought or hired from the Gaumont Film Supply service and the famous projectors were made and supplied by the House of Gaumont. The Motion generator was supplied by the General Electric Company.

The "Grand Cinema" opened on Tuesday October 26th 1913.

It would appear that the cinema proper was situated above the restaurant, which continued to function as such, but we cannot ascertain whether or not the hotel itself remained in business.

The performance was continuous and for its opening week it displayed fine pictures of news, items of general interest and events including scenes from the Dublin Horse Show. Many cartoons were also available. Admission was 6d.

Also situated in number 8 Lower Sackville was the "Century Club" and a café, that would appear to have their entrance in number 9.
Standing side by side with this new cinema was the Dublin Bread Company Bakery shop and Restaurant, which occupied most of 6 & 7 Lower Sackville Street.

As predicted by the owners and their well wishers The Grand Cinema did a flourishing trade as this side of Sackville Street attracted a large amount of pedestrian traffic and was said to be on a par with Grafton Street with its crowded pavements. However, in 1916 just like many another building in the city centre the Grand cinema was destroyed in the Easter up-rising as was its next door neighbour the D.B.C shop and restaurant.

The last advertisement for the Grand Cinema appeared on Monday April 17th 1916 and advertised the film, which would be on display for the next week. As it was also Holy Week no further ads would appear.

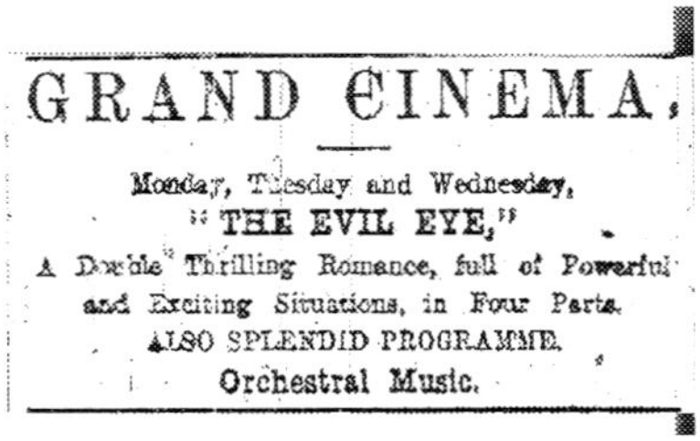

The film featured was "The Evil Eye" a thrilling romance written and directed by Romaine Fielding, who also starred in the film opposite Mary Ryan, Robyn Adair, Gladys Brockwell and Richard Wangerman.

For reasons known only to himself Mr. William Kay did not appear to rebuild his cinema and the next we heard of him was when he leased the concert hall in the Rathmines Town Hall and began to show cinematograph exhibitions there. Later again he came to our attention when he became a director of the Stella Pictures Theatre Company, in partnership with Tony O'Grady.

In the top picture to the left of centre can be seen a whitish building with 8 windows over head. This was the Grand Cinema building.

More to the centre can be seen a double building with two arched windows and two bay windows and this was the D.B.C. building.

In the picture below can be seen what's left of that section of Sackville Street and all that still stands is what's left of the D.B.C.

This site was later acquired by a J.J. O'Farrell, a former Lord Mayor of Dublin who had the ruins razed to the ground and caused work to commence on the build of a new cinema which when finished was named the, "Grand Central Cinema"

This is No. 8 O'Connell Street, which was once the site of the "Grand" cinema and the address in the early 20th century was 8 Sackville Street. This building was built long after the cinema had been destroyed. However, for a while it had us believing that it might have been the original building when we viewed its very decorative bay windows, which had a cinematic look about them.

~~~~

On February 6th 1914, the Dublin Branch of the General Film Agency held a private trade exhibition for Cinema Theatre Proprietors and Managers in the Grand cinema at 8 Lower Sackville Street at 11 am sharp, where the film "A Message from Mars" would be shown. Prior to the opening of the film the United Kingdom Films London Ltd, presented the original star cast on stage, which was headed by Charles Hawtrey, who played the part of Horace Parker.
~~~~

The shell of the D.B.C Shop and the Grand Cinema in 1916, after the "Rising".

The building to the left of the D.B.C or we should say "what's left of the building", was the site of the Grand Cinema and contrary to what people thought when the Grand Central was built on the site of these building, it incorporated the sites of No's 6 & 7 Sackville Street and not No 8. When No 8 was rebuilt it was as a retail premises and in 2006 it is the Global Internet Café.

GRAND CENTRAL
6 & 7 O'Connell Street Lower
(Formerly 6 & 7 Sackville Street Lower)

This new cinema which was built on the site of the shop and restaurant of the Dublin Bread Company, which had been destroyed during the 1916 Up-Rising, was not built as a replacement of the old "Grand" cinema which had once stood next door to the D.B.C. This was an entirely new venture by "The Irish Cinematograph Company whose chairman was Mr. J.J. Farrell, a former Lord Mayor of Dublin.

In the naming of this new cinema the "Grand Central" consideration may have been given to the old "Grand" but at this late stage who is to know.

The "Grand Central" opened on October 10th 1921 and the first film shown was "Pollyanna" starring Mary Pickford. For this superb film the company had to fork out the princely sum of £500, and a further £500 for the following feature "Mark of Zorro" with Douglas Fairbanks in the lead roll.

"Pollyanna" was said to have shown Mary Pickford at her best in this story which cast her in the roll of a young girl whose philosophy was to always look on the bright side of things when all around her is dark and dreary and her aim in life was to teach all around her that every cloud had a silver lining.

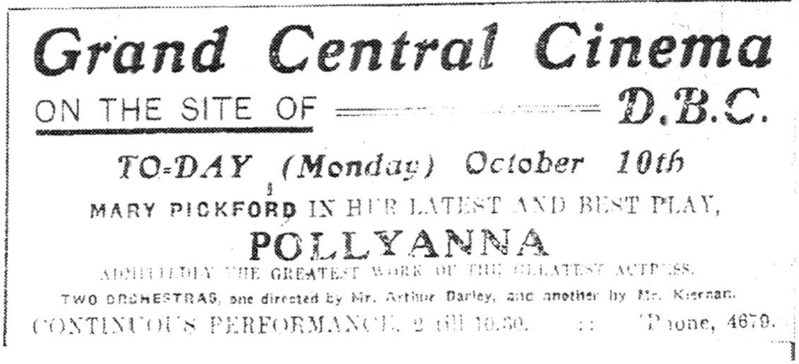

The "Grand Central" cinema was designed by Messrs O'Callaghan and Webb and Messrs Higginbottom and Stafford and its handsome front was carved out in Neo-Grec classic style and all the stonework was cut and carved in Dublin.

The spacious interior was specially laid out in order to obtain the best view and sight of the screen from every part of the house and this was as a result of the experience of Mr. J.J. Farrell's travels on the Continent and England.

The balcony was one of the most extensive in Dublin and accommodated more than half of the audience. The general contractor was H. and J. Martin.

The Grand Central building then and now.
The picture on the left was taken late in the twentieth century and the one on the right in 1923.

While looking at the front of the cinema in the photo of 1923 one would believe that the front entrance led directly into the cinema which one would take for granted as being on the ground floor level, instead of which it was on a level above the street in order to provide for a restaurant below at street level.

Business was good for the Grand Central cinema and the restaurant underneath, which gave substance to the remark made many years earlier when a "Bioscope" correspondent wrote an article on the opening of the "Grand" cinema at 8 Sackville Street and made mention that this cinema was on the best side of the street where large crowds passed daily.

However some eighteen months later on Friday, April 27th 1923 business came to a sudden halt when a mine was placed on the marble entrance steps to the restaurant and cinema and the resulting explosion caused some serious damage.

As is often the case in acts of sudden violence there were conflicting accounts on what had exactly happened, but the main consensus was that a car with four occupants, one girl and three men had drawn up and stopped outside the cinema and two armed men had taken up protection positions on the footpath while a third man had primed and placed a mine on the marble steps leading into the building.

This all happened shortly before 8 am and within seconds the mine exploded with terrific force and caused considerable damage to the walls doors and roof of the entrance and lobby area, large reinforced heavy were ripper from their hinges and the doors wrecked beyond repair. All the glass in the vestibule area and the outside canopy was shattered and rubble was piled everywhere.

The grand Central with soldiers on guard later that day

The outer and inner hallways were badly damaged as was the roof of the vestibule area and to give you some idea of the ferocity of the explosion we would tell you that there was a gaping hole some several feet in circumference in the centre of the marble steps just where the bomb had been positioned.

However, though the appearance of the front of the cinema would suggest otherwise the structure and interior of the Grand Central suffered no extensive damage.

Fortunately there were no serious casualties other than some injuries to two men who were passing by at the time of the explosion, both were taken to the local hospital where they were treated for shock and had their injuries tended to. So powerful was the explosion that another man who was walking passed the Corinthian cinema around the corner on Eden Quay at the time was thrown to the ground by the concussion from the blast.

Schedule for showing that night was the film "Lavender and old Lace (1921) starring Marguerite Snow, Seena Owen and Louis Bennison, This story was based on a novel written by Myrtle Reed and it told of a young girl who fell in love with a sea captain who had to return to the sea, promising to be true until his return she grew into a lonely old lady without ever realising that she had been jilted.

The film which was undamaged was held over for showing on another date and work on restoring the cinema began immediately. One month and three days later the cinema was re-opened on May 1st 1923 and advertised for that nights showing was "Lavender and old Lace" as second billing to "The Roof Tree" starring WM. Russel, also featured was the "Royal Wedding"

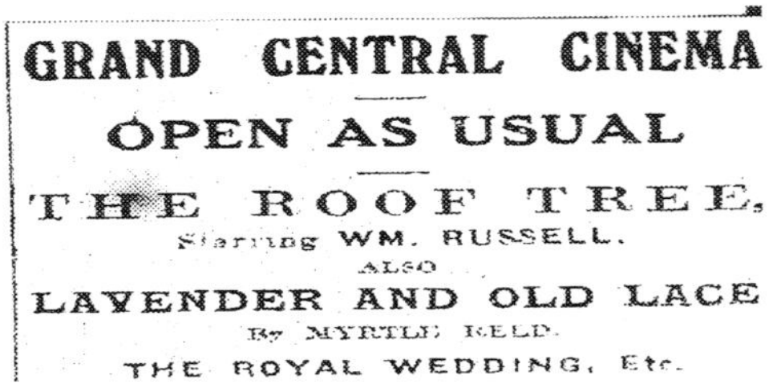

The Roof Tree tells the story of a man wrongly accused of murdering his sisters husband, then hides out in the hills, where he meets a girl, falls in love and when finally vindicated of the murder charge, marries his lover and lives happily ever after.

However good were the films available and the newsreel of the "Royal Wedding", the house wasn't pulling in the crowds and it became apparent to management that the public were afraid to enter the building for fear of injury, amid the suspicion that the premises had been structurally damaged by the explosion.

In order to combat this belief management ran a series of advertisements in the papers of the day which assured the public that though the front entrance of the cinema had been badly damaged as a result of the bomb blast the theatre proper did not suffer any lasting damage and this assurance was guaranteed in writing by the eminent architects George L O'Connor and Vincent Kelly. This seemed to convince the public and it would appear that business returned to normal.

In 1928 the "Grand Central" had its second set back when J.J. Farrell found occasion to reprimand an employee for misbehaviour and as a consequence the employee was said to have threatened physical violence to him in his capacity as Managing Director of the "Irish Kinematograph Company" and as a result of this Mr. Farrell dismissed the employee.

A lightening strike followed his dismissal and management claimed that the strikers had notified the public of their intent to strike long before they received notice by letter.

There appeared to be conflicting reports from both sides on what exactly had happened but in response to a Press report on a meeting at which it was denied that a lighting strike had taken place Mr. Farrell claimed that he knew nothing about the proposed withdrawal of labour on Sunday the 8th of July until he got a letter to that effect on Saturday night at ten minutes past eleven o'clock, a full half hour after the cinema audiences in all the companies cinemas had been advised of this dispute by way of news flashes on the silver screen.

This was a most improper action by our operators said Mr. Farrell, which was done at our expense, on our machinery and in the time for which we were paying them overtime rates.

By an agreement between the Cinema Association and the men's union a strike or lock-out notice required a months notice in writing by either side.

As to re-instating the sacked employee, Mr. Farrell informed the union that his board of directors would never keep in their employment a man who threatened physical violence to the managing Director.

This strike claimed Mr. Farrell, is not about wages or conditions of employment but about an effort to establish the right of an employee to strike his employer or manager without any danger of suffering any penalty whatever.

Picketing followed at all four cinemas belonging to the company, which eventually forced their closure and because of complaints the police became involved.

NOTICE.

OUR THEATRES, THE

GRAND CENTRAL,

PILLAR,

TIVOLI,

AND

MARY ST. PICTURE HOUSE

having been closed by a Lightning Strike, we invite our Staffs, including those on holiday, to report for duty at the Grand Central not later than 12 noon, To-morrow (Tuesday), July 10, otherwise their places will be filled.

JOHN J. FARRELL,
Chairman and Managing Director, Irish Kinematograph Co. (1920), Ltd.

THE PLAZA AND DUBLIN ELECTRIC THEATRES

give a similar invitation to that by the Irish Kinematograph Co.

JOHN J. FARRELL.

However before the lighting strike by the operating staff in all four cinema began, the offending employee must have picketed the "Grand Central" on his own, as he was arrested and charged with having unlawfully watched and beset the "Grand Central Cinema" with a view to compelling the "Irish Kinematograph Company" to take him back into their services.

Appearing in the Dublin District Court on July 7th before Justice Davitt he was convicted as charged and sentenced to two months imprisonment and following an appeal Justice Davitt reserved his decision and that night his fellow operators withdrew their labour when the last show finished in the Grand Central.

On Monday, July 9th 1928 the following display notice by the Irish Kinematograph Co" appeared in the "Evening Herald" inviting all their employee's to report to the Grand Central cinema on Tuesday 10th July and as nothing further appeared in the papers following this invitation we can only assume that the strike was then over.

As the Plaza and Dublin Electric Theatres issued a similar notice it would seem that in all six cinemas were involved in this dispute.

On the Wednesday following the issue of this notice, an article did appear in the "Evening Herald" on July 11th 1928, but this article would appear to have been a simple response by J.J. Farrell to an article that had appeared earlier in the paper and he now wanted to give his version of events.

"Unlucky for Some"

On Friday 13th September 1946 a fire began in the area between the ceiling and the roof and the cinema was completely gutted.

The fire it would seem broke out just after midnight on Thursday and despite a two hour battle by several sections of the Dublin Fire Brigade the building could not be saved.

While the full extent of the damage to the overall building had yet to be assessed it was noted that the restaurant underneath was completely water logged from the thousands of gallons of water, which had been played on the building. A director told an "Evening Herald" reporter, that it would be most unlikely that the cinema would ever be rebuilt, rather, he said, the building will be modernised and sold on.

The ruins of the Dublin Bread Company (DBC) shop and restaurant, which occupied the twin buildings at numbers 6 & 7 Lower Sackville Street pictured shortly after the 1916 up-rising. The DBC building, or what's left of it, is the large ruin on the right and next door are the ruins of number 8 and what's left of William Kay's "Grand Cinema".

(See story the "Grand Cinema").

This "Grand Cinema" is in no way connected with the "Grand Central", which is the subject of this story, other than that it once occupied the site next door.

Adverts for the film "Destination Tokyo", which was scheduled for Friday 13th and a refund offer for tickets which had been bought in advance for the Sunday nights performance.

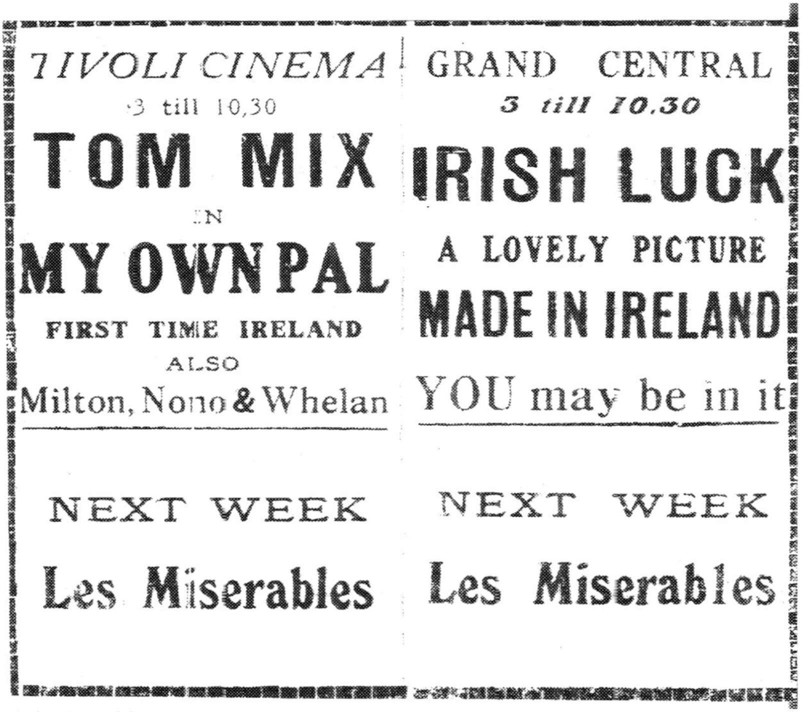

A Selection of films on offer from two of J.J. Farrell's cinemas in 1926, "Irish Luck" starring Tom Meigham was made in Ireland.

A matter of interest.

A small fire took place in the Grand Central cinema on the 16th of September 1929 and it would appear that it was not reported to the Garda Siochana. Deputy Cooney raised the matter in "Dail Eireann" on November 27th 1929 and questioned if the current precautions against the outbreak of fires in cinemas were inadequate.

According to Deputy Cooney the fire was of such a serious nature that it totally destroyed the film in the projection machine and he questioned why a prosecution did not follow. He also suggested legislation, to empower Garda authorities to inspect cinemas, to insure that regulations were complied with.

In reply to Deputy Cooney, Mr. Fitzgerald-Kenney said that he had no evidence that there was any necessity for further legislation regarding the matter.

~~~~~
~~~~~

GREEN CINEMA
The Stephen's Green Cinema Limited.

The Green Cinema opened its doors on December 18th 1935, at 127 St Stephens Green West and offered the public not only a beautiful well proportioned place of entertainment with seating for 1,500 persons but also a very comfortable café and a most enticing restaurant with panoramic views across the park.

The opening ceremony was performed by the Lord Mayor of Dublin, Alderman Alfie Byrne, T.D., and in his opening speech he declared that this new enterprise was being presented to the Dublin public as a cinema of first-class entertainment, equipped with everything that was best, and that they were to have the best type of film combined with theatrical comfort.

When Alfie finished his speech the chairman of the company Sir Thomas Robinson, presented him with a souvenir gold case which contained a perpetual pass to the cinema.

The cinema also had an extra large entrance with a specially designed queue hall, where customers could wait for admission to the cinema in a comfortable warm atmosphere
This cinema was well known for its generous supply of smallish type double seats which were in fair demand by young and sometimes not so young courting couples. It was said of some of those couples, that they were often seen to return to the cinema on the following day, but this time to see the film!
The directors of this new cinema Sir Thomas Robison, chairman, Mr. James W. Lane, Mr. William J Barnett, Mr. Robert G.H. Russell and Mr. Frank F.J. McDonnell, Managing Director had done their patrons proud. Mr. M.J. Deasy of County Carlow was the house manager and the restaurant was under the supervision of Miss Elizabeth Cullen, who was also the caterer attached to the Courts of Justice.

The Green cinema, advertising the movie chosen for its gala opening, and its fine café and restaurant.
As can be seen in its first advertisement, the "Green" was initially called the "Stephen's Green Cinema"!

The Green Cinema, which is situated on the West side of St Stephen's Green.

St Stephen's Green, one of Dublin's famous Squares and the largest Square in Europe got its name from the Church of St. Stephen, which once stood in Mercer Street. The ground for the Green, which was a marshy common, was originally filled in and levelled, in 1678 and the area was bounded by a wall with a deep ditch which was used as a receptacle for all kinds of rubbish.

The Lord Mayor held the rights of pasturage in the green and received £150 a year from the Government for damage caused by Yeomanry Corps who exercised there. In 1815 the ditch was filled in and the wall replaced by railings, which are still there to day in 2006.

In the early days, only residents of the square were allowed access to the park and the local ladies and gents partook of genteel strolls through the park after 2pm on Sundays much to the annoyance of the other residents of Dublin. However, Lord Ardilaun, Sir Arthur .E. Guinness, with the munificence characteristic of his family, encouraged Parliament to pass an Act to open the Green to the public, Lord Ardilaun paid for the laying-out of the park in its current form.

In the 18th. Century, public hangings took place in the park and many a boyo met his maker there.

In 1916, the Irish Citizen Army took up a position in the green, but had to withdraw to the Royal College of Surgeons when they found that members of the British Army had taken up sniper positions in the Shelbourne Hotel.

In 1907, an arch was erected at the main entrance to the park which almost faced the Green Cinema and this was known as the Fusilier's Arch, which commemorated those killed in the Boer War. However, it was known to Republicans as, "Traitors Gate".

As well as being one of the largest squares in Europe it now also ranks as one of the finest. The Park consists of some 27 acres and each side of the square is a quarter of a mile in length and was at one time named as follows; Beaux Walk, French Walk, Leeson Walk and Monks Walk

The park has a beautiful lake which is plentifully supplied with ducks and water fowl, and there are various stands positioned around the lake informing visitors of the various birds that frequent the area. Bandstands are well placed, as are fountains, flowerbeds and a children's playground and here you will find Dublin's other O'Connell Bridge.

Statues are in abundance, as are shrubs, trees, rockeries, walks and beautiful manicured lawns.

~~~~~~~~~~~

The Green Cinema was twinned in 1973 and the new screens opened in stages with Screen I opening on Saturday July 14th, and Screen 2 opening a week later on Friday night July 20th.

For its opening performance Screen 1 offered "Lady Caroline Lamb", which told the story of the notorious Lady Caroline wife of Lord William Lamb of Melbourne, who shocked 19th century Britain with her scandalous carry-on with Lord Byron.

While Screen 2 gave us "Butterflies are Free", starring Goldie Hawn as a very liberated young actress named Jill, who lived in an apartment next door to Don, a blind-from birth-son of an over protective mother, beautifully played by Edward Albert.

Here we learn from Don what its like to be grown-up and free, while Don learns Jill things that his mother wouldn't have taught him!!

* * * * *
~~~~~~~~~~~

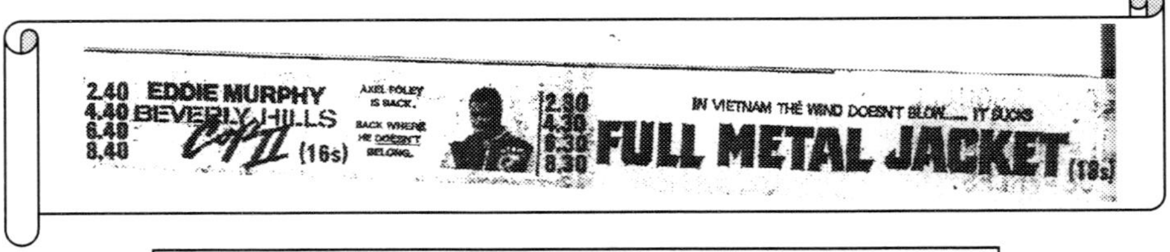

This is the last advertisement for the Green Cinema, which closed on Saturday November 7th 1987.

Screen 1 chose "Beverly Hill Cop 11", for its swan song, with Eddie Murphy playing the zany Detroit Cop 'Axel Foley', back in Beverly Hills with his former buddies solving more crimes.

And

Screen 2 gave us "Full Metal Jacket", a horrific and terrifyingly real like Vietnam-War story, about young men being trained for, and then sent to, fight in Vietnam.

Howeve,r real like this film was, the cast and crew were never anywhere near Vietnam as the whole production was put together in England. Stanley Kubrick directed this film, which cost €17million and though it only took six months to shoot, the entire production had to close down for over 20 weeks due to injuries and accidents on the set.

The Paris Island scenes were shot in a military training camp in Bassingbourne and the barracks set was located in Enfield near Potters Bar London, while the old gas works site in Becton Town by the Thames was used as the City of Hue, Vietnam.

* * * * *

We also thought it worth a mention that the Green cinema played host to a number of late night concerts during the sixties, which they billed as "Ballads at Midnight" and amongst the many who played there, were Liam Clancy and Luke Kelly.

One of the "Ballads at Midnight" advertisements.

The Fitzwilliam Hotel now occupies the site of the St. Stephen's Green Cinema.

The Fusiliers Arch, aka "Traitors Gate".
"One would want to be an earlier riser", as James Bond (Roger Moore) said to Jenny Flex (Allison Doody), in the Bond movie, "A View to a Kill", to get a clear and uninterrupted picture like this, but George picked a cold, wet and miserable Sunday morning in January 2006 to take this shot.

HALES'S TOURS
South Anne Street

While the Volta was undoubtedly Dublin's first cinema proper, it was very nearly pipped at the post by a very enterprising person who came to Ireland from the Isle of Wight in 1904, In 1905 he began to show movies in a small hall in St Anne's Street.

This hall became known as Hales Hall and it was here that Mr. Arthur Bursey introduced the first flickering shadows to a Dublin screen; prior to this it was considered something of a novelty to view a still or lantern slide.

The hall was fashioned in the shape of a railway carriage with authentic looking luggage racks overhead and to complete the illusion there was a hidden throbbing engine which beat out the rhythm of a train travelling at full speed.

The entrance was designed like a station platform with overhead telegraph wires and a ticket booking office and a uniformed guard that helped form the gathering crowds into an orderly queue.

The films shown were in effect travelogues, entitled "Hales Tours of the World" and consisted of a series of trips as would be viewed from the carriage of a train, and destinations would differ week to week. Mr. Mike Nono, a well-known Irish dancer supplied a commentary on the films.

These films, which were not only an enjoyable experience but were very educational in their content, caused great excitement. Crowds flocked to these shows and on many occasions the police had to be called to help the struggling crowd to gain admission, before the Guard on the platform waved his flag, which signified a full house.

While Mr. Bursey earned the distinction of being the first person to show a movie in Dublin his enterprise was soon outclassed when the Volta opened and introduced the silent screen which was filled with films of comedy, drama, news and "follow ups"

Mr. Bursey secured a job as operator in the Sackville Picture House when it opened in Sackville Street

* * * * *

A lot of the above information came courtesy of a letter to the editor in the July 2nd edition of the "Evening Herald" in 1963. The letter was sent by an M. Kinsella whose address was Albert Place East, Dublin and despite enquiries we could not locate him to thank him for this information.

THE HI-JACKERS And self-styled Censors.

It would appear that in Ireland circa 1925, there were a group of self-appointed film censors, who decided on what films were suitable for display in Irish cinemas.

This group very often warned the owner / manager of a cinema, against the showing of a certain movie, and if this warning was not taken seriously, swift and decisive action was taken.

(See the Masterpiece bombing on the 20th. November 1925)

On Monday morning, the 30th November 1925, a Mr. P. Founds, Manager of the Empire Cinema in Galway City was on the way back from Athenry, where he and some friends had taken the war film "Zeebrugge", to show in a local hall the night before. When the show was over, not wishing to travel home late Sunday night they stayed the night and set off home on Monday morning.

Almost home, they were approaching the outskirts of Galway City, when on a lonely country road they were held-up by a bunch of armed and masked men, and made vacate their car. The film was taken from the car by the masked men and destroyed by fire at the side of the road.

"Our instructions", they told the manager and his friends "are to confiscate propaganda war films and burn them"!

~~~~~

ZEEBRUGGE

This war film was released in 1924, and told the story of an incredible heroic raid which took place in Belgium on April 18th, 1918.

The purpose of this raid was to block off the entrance to the Bruges Canal at Zeebrugge and slow down German U-Boat traffic in the Channel.
This operation was, needless to say, "Top Secret", and code named 'Operation ZO' . (Meaning Zeebrugge/Ostende).

The plan, which was successfully carried out, but with a great loss of life, was to have three old fire burning cruisers, filled with concrete, sail across the channel to the entrance of the canal and have them scuttled there.

The sacrificed cruisers were the, "Thetis", "Intrepid" and "Iphigenia"
Each carried a minimum crew.

* * * * *
~~~~~

HOME MOVIES IN 1923

AHEAD IN TIME.

On Saturday, May 5th 1923 this advertisement appeared in the "Evening Herald".

Informing the general public that home movies were now available by mail order for the princely sum of £3.10.0.This new invention was being introduced to Ireland by the Sole Irish Distributors, Messrs Minnis and Whelan Film Company of Parliament Row.

This new invention they claimed would be a source of endless enjoyment in the home and would also be of great value to salesmen, as it would enable them to show off their goods to their best advantage. It would also be a source of education to children.

INCHICORE

The Inchicore cinema opened on Friday night November 25th 1921 and introduced two films of note; "The Breed of the Treshams" and the first run of a serial called the "Great Haigh Serial".

The cinema, which eventually became known as the "Core", belonged to Mr. John Kirkham whom it would appear lived in the area.

Sir Martin Harvey, was one of the most popular actors of his time and he tread the boards for nigh on 40 years. He was well known for his many Shakespearian parts, including Hamlet, which opened in Dublin in 1904. In all he made five films, including; "A Tale of Two Cities", where he played the part of Sydney Carton and the above mentioned "The Breed of the Treshams", which was a screen adaptation of the stage play by John Rutherford in which Sir Martin took part in on many occasions.

* * * * *

A few years after it opened, the cinema became the stage for a feud between James Larkin and Sean McLoughlin the Branch Secretary of the WUI. It would seem that this feud developed during an industrial dispute in the Inchicore Railway Works.

In early September 1924 a mass meeting was held in the Inchicore cinema by the kind permission of Mr. Kirkham. Mr. Larkin proposed the end of the strike and quoted some banalities such as, "the army that cannot retreat, cannot advance", and Sean McLoughlin opposed Larkin's proposal. While a large number of the attendance appeared to agree with McLoughlin the majority backed Larkin.

The strike ended on Monday September 15th and Sean McLoughlin led the workers who had assembled outside Kilmainham Gaol back to work. There was no sign of Mr. Larkin.

The feud didn't end there, but the involvement of the "Core" did.

This picture of the Inchicore building was taken in 2005, just weeks before it was demolished.

Another strike affected the "Core" in 1972, which caused the cinema to close for a number of months, and the 10 workers involved claimed that they were locked out by the cinema management.

The workers were on strike for overtime earnings and after two months a Union spokesman said that negotiations had taken place and a settlement had been reached on the overtime issue. However as the workers did not hear of the settlement in time they continued to picket the cinema and claimed a lock-out situation.

A management spokesman denied there was a lock-out and said that the real issue was whether or not the staff should work seven days a week; the union believed they should and management Disagreed.

Management claimed that they were prepared to bring the issue before the Labour Court and accused the union of dragging its feet.

Try as we might we could find no follow-up to this dispute, but some week later the cinema was open for business as usual.

Other than this couple of union differences nothing else of note came to our attention. However, before it closed for good in 1980 the cinema did have a couple of name changes.

In 1973 the "Core" had a name change and following a short closure for refurbishing it re-opened on Thursday. June 7th as the "Europa", with a promise of showing the best in adult films in suburban Dublin.

Author's note, we doubt that the words "adult films" would have had the same meaning then as they would have now in 2006.

Three years later it again had a make-over and re-opened as the "Pullman Studios" on Sunday, December 19th 1976, featuring "One Flew over the Cuckoo's Nest", starring Jack Nicholson

~~~~~

Unfortunately this change-over also failed to do well and the cinema closed for good on Thursday, March 27th 1980.

Sometime later it became a snooker hall, but in its latter years it was left vacant and eventually it was demolished in late 2005, possibly to make room for a block of apartments.
~~~~~

INTERNATIONAL FILM THEATRE
At Erin Foods Theatre, Earlsfort Terrace.

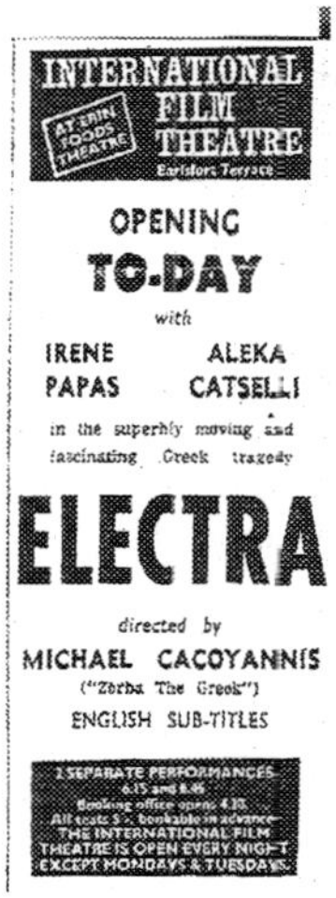

This new film theatre opened on Friday June 17th 1966 and its opening picture was "Electra" a Greek Tragedy, which was directed by Michael Cacoyannis who also directed "Zorba The Greek".
The films dialogue was Greek but it did have English sub-titles.

All seats were 5/- and were bookable in advance. It would appear that this new cinema would operate 5 nights per week with two performances per night. It would not open on Mondays and Thursdays.

It would further appear that the opening picture was indicative of the type of picture the theatre would present in the future.

Neither of us knew very much about this cinema, nor had we ever paid it a visit. However over the years it seemed to do alright as it lasted for some eighteen years. It would also appear that at one time it was a members only club; we base this observation on the wording of its last advertisement, which now invited non-members.

If this advertisement is as we believe its last then it would seemed that the theatre closed on Thursday May 31, 1984'

As you may well have guessed from the wording of the title the film is an upfront story about incest between a brother and sister in communist Hungary and stars Lili Monori as Juli and Miklos B Szekely as her brother Fodor.

The story tells of the forbidden love between Juli and Fodor and, as incest is against the law in communist Hungary, they are both thrown into prison.

The Film is directed by
Zsolt Kezdi Kovacs.

IRISH CINEMA
Capel Street.

News of a cinema in Capel Street will surprise many people, in particular a friend of George's who was born and reared in the area and claimed to know all the various businesses that had graced that thoroughfare. While he had heard of a theatre on the street he had never heard of a picture house there.

However, it was there in 1912 and it featured in an article written in the "Bioscope" cinema magazine on four different dates in that year.

The cinema which went under the name of the "Irish Cinema", was described as an excellent little cinema which was gallantly holding its own and had changes of pictures twice weekly. Admission prices ranged from 2d to 6d and on the date of this review June 6th 1912, the cinema was showing two Vitograph films entitled "Shy Pilot" and "The Thief and the Girl".

In a further review on October 3rd 1912, the writer wrote in the "Bioscope" magazine that that some improvements had taken place in this progressive little cinema which was owned and managed in a most careful way by Mr. R.H Graham. One of the two most notable improvements was the installation of a new Kamm projector, one of the most modern available, and the raising of the screen for the betterment of the viewing audiences.

Featured this week for the first time in Ireland was a picture depicting the adventures of Buffalo Bill Cody, the famous Indian fighter, Buffalo hunter and Wild West Showman.

Mr. Graham who also had connections with the "Coliseum Picture House", in Redmond's Hill, which unfortunately was burnt down in 1911, is determined to make the Irish Cinema a bigger success in the future and according to the writer of the article he appeared to be going the right way about it.

Unfortunately we could find no advertisements, pictures or any other detail of this cinema, which like the Assembly Picture Hall in Sandymount and the Corona cinema in Parnell Street they never existed in the minds of many.

* * * * *

The film, Buffalo Bill, may well have been the film in which William F. Cody played himself for the "Pawnee Bill Film Company Limited", in the year 1912, entitled "The Life of Buffalo Bill", but as no title was given for the film in the Bioscope article it is hard to know. However, Buffalo Bill played himself in many movies, which were recorded by Thomas Edison and the abovementioned film could have been any of these. Whichever one it was, we are sure it was thrilling, adventurous and most enjoyable.

We could find no mention of when this cinema closed.

Having said all that, we came across an article in the "Evening Herald" in 1913 which highlighted the lure if the cinema, which we paraphrase elsewhere in this book entitled "Craze for Pictures". This article was accompanied by a number of cinema advertisements, one of which was an advertisement for the "Irish Cinema", which we re-produce above.

Having gained admission, one could of course in those days, smoke in the cinema and with a packet of ten fags being available for 3d, one could, as the expression goes, smoke one's heart out. Little did we know it at the time, but that was exactly what we were doing.

~~~~

In the 1913 Dublin Corporation Reports, we came across two entries that told us that the owner of this cinema had been fined £5 on July 22nd 1913 for showing (spelt shewing in those days) pictures without a licence and on a subsequent occasion a penalty of £20 was imposed for disobedience of a court order.

As it is most unlikely that we will come across any more information on this cinema, we will close the story here.
~~~~

IT WASN'T ALL WORK AND NO PLAY YOU KNOW!

CINEMA BAL MASQUE

METROPOLE BALLROOM——FEB. 11th

LIST OF PRIZES.

Prizes Value.	For the Best Representation of	Presented by
£5 5 0	Most Humorous Costume	1st—METROPOLE CINEMA.
£1 1 0	Most Humorous Costume	2nd—INCHICORE CINEMA.
£5 5 0	Any Advertising Character	MESSRS. McCONNELL-HARTLEY CO., Pearse Street.
£5 5 0	Betty Balfour in "CINDERS"	CORINTHIAN CINEMA.
£5 5 0	Charity	IRISH THEATRE, CINEMA, AND AMUSEMENTS GUILD.
£5 5 0	Pat O'Malley or Laura La Plante in "THE MIDNIGHT SUN"	UNIVERSAL FILMS, LTD. Eden Quay.
£5 5 0	Best Original Costume	1st Prize—ANONYMOUS.
£1 1 0	Best Original Costume	2nd Prize—PRINCESS CINEMA, Rathmines
£5 5 0	Mary Pickford in any production	ALLIED ARTISTS CORPORATION, 71 Middle Abbey Street.
£5 5 0	Best Historical Character Costume	WESTERN IMPORT.
£1 1 0	Best Historical Character Costume	2nd—PAVILION CINEMA, Dun Laoghaire
£3 5 0	Costume representing Paramount Pictures	FAMOUS LASKY, Pearse Street.
£5 5 0	Lady's Paper Costume	1st—PHIBSBORO' PICTURE HOUSE.
£1 1 0	Lady's Paper Costume	2nd—SACKVILLE PICTURE HOUSE.
£5 5 0	Best Oriental Costume (Lady or Gent)	FOUNTAIN PICTURE HOUSE.
£1 1 0	Best Oriental Costume (Lady or Gent)	2nd—WARDOUR FILMS, LTD., Pearse St.
£3 3 0	Corinne Griffith in "INFATUATION"	GRAFTON PICTURE HOUSE.
£3 3 0	Charlie Chaplin in "THE GOLD RUSH"	ROTUNDA PICTURE HOUSE.
£5 5 0	Sport	MESSRS. HOPKINS AND CO.
£5 5 0	"Irish Independent"	INDEPENDENT NEWSPAPERS, LTD.
£2 12 6	Norma Shearer in any production	JURY-METRO-GOLDWYN, Pearse St.
£2 2 0	Estelle Brody in "MADEMOISELLE FROM ARMENTIERES"	GAUMONT FILM CO., Lord Edward St.
£2 2 0	Lady's Costume, Guaranteed Irish Linen	JAMES MONTGOMERY, ESQ.
£2 2 0	Colleen Moore in "IRENE"	FIRST NATIONAL, Middle Abbey St.
£2 2 0	Costume de Luxe	THEATRE DE LUXE.
£2 2 0	Ivor Novello in "THE LODGER"	B. COWAN, ESQ., EXPRESS FILMS, 7 Lower Abbey Street.
£2 2 0	Miss June in "THE LODGER"	B. COWAN, ESQ., EXPRESS FILMS, 7 Lower Abbey Street.
£2 2 0	Irish Colleen	LYCEUM CINEMA.
£2 2 0	Any Character from Dickens	IRISH EMPIRE PALACES.

Non Stop Dancing: 10 to 5. Messrs. Harrison's and Manahan's Bands (personally conducted).

SUPPER AND RUNNING BUFFET.

TICKETS - - - ONE GUINEA EACH.

To be had at the Metropole, or from J. J. Martin, Hon. Treasurer, 71 Middle Abbey St.

Limited number of Tables in the Ballroom can be reserved on application to Metropole accompanied by cash for Tickets.

A night at the Ball for all those poor cinema workers who never seemed to see the light of day and who spent all their working life encouraging others to enjoy themselves in palaces of luxury fit for Kings and Queens!

It would seem that a ball was held on an annual basis for cinema workers giving them a chance of dressing up and attending the Ball.

IZIDORE ISAAC BRADLAW

When I was writing the story of the Princess Cinema of Rathmines for my book entitled "The Prinner", which was the cinemas very popular nickname. I researched deeply into its history and unearthed some very useful information. However, this research was carried out in a very singular minded manner as I was only interested in the history of the Princess cinema at the time and because of this I wrongly assumed that the directors of the Rathmines Amusement Company were a group of local businessmen who were simply cashing in on a new business venture.

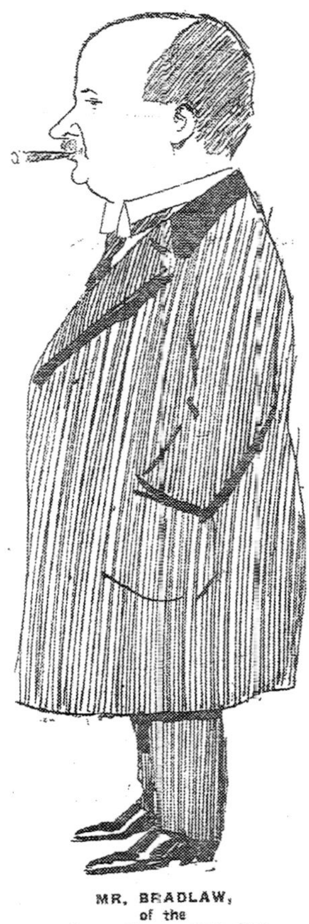

MR. BRADLAW, of the Princess Cinema, Rathmines.

Little did I know it at the time, but I had just uncovered one serious dude in the Irish World of Cinema. Mr. Izidore Isaac Bradlaw was not only a seasoned cinema entrepreneur, proprietor of many cinemas but he was also a director of numerous companies associated with the opening, and sale of cinemas. He was also the Irish agent for the "Express Ticket Machine", "The Express Projector" and the famous "Power's No 6 Projector". Not just a runner-in, you might agree.

This all came to light when Patrick Maguire and yours truly began an in-depth study of all the old Dublin cinemas and soon found Mr. Bradlaw involved in many cinema companies, including would you believe it, our mystery cinema "The Assembly Picture Hall", on Serpentine Avenue.

It would appear that Mr. Bradlaw leased the Assembly Hall in Sandymount circa 1912, in order to show films on an occasional basis.

While we couldn't find a photo of Mr. Bradlaw, we did come across this sketch of him.

Mr. Bradlaw also had a number of dental practices in various Dublin area's with the main one being in Grafton Street. This address also served as his head office and the address for a number of his cinema companies and other related businesses.

Mr. Bradlaw also had a brother, Cyril Bradlaw, who held the title of Film Manager, and I would assume that this meant that he serviced all of the cinemas under the control of his brother Isaac.

The Brothers Karmel, who were also directors of the Princess Cinema were in fact brothers-in-law of Izidore and at least one of them was involved with Izidore in the purchase of a large corner site in Grafton Street in the year 1914 where they planned to build a large picture palace that would have seating for 1000 patrons. It was estimated that this project would cost in the region of £50,000; however, this cinema was never built and most likely the site was used or sold off for other purposes.

It would also appear that Cyril Bradlaw was a shrewd and capable film manager who on more that one occasion secured the exclusive rights for Ireland of a number of top rated films, including a very early talkie movie which began its run in the Princess cinema Rathmines and no doubt did the rounds of their other holdings, before going on general release. One of these films was the Pathe exclusive "In the Grip of the Villain"

The Lord Lieutenant and the beautiful Lady Aberdeen visited the Princess Cinema to view the film taken of the Civic Procession (See George's book entitled "The Prinner")

We would tell you that Mr. Bradlaw had been entrusted with the exclusive rights to organise the filming of this procession and the opening of the exhibition by the Lord Lieutenant and that to ensure a perfect result Mr. Bradlaw had the General Film Supply Company, the Pathe and Gaumont film companies all on the spot, to take some excellent reels of film. In all there were at least twelve cameras working the scene.

Mr. Bradlaw was also involved in the Skerries Electric Theatre Company which brought cinema to Skerries, a very pretty seaside town in North Dublin. He also purchased a site for the New Brunswick Picture Palace, which he built on Great Brunswick Street. He was also involved in the Olympia Theatre in Dame Street, a cinema in Kilkenny, Dun Laoghaire, Galway and most likely many other places.

His Projectors and ticket machines enjoyed a great demand with the first orders for his projectors coming from the Seaside Picture Theatre in Clontarf, and the Picture Palace in Clonmel. The Bohemian cinema in Phibsborough was one of the first cinemas to install his Express Ticket machine and orders from some Provincial Showmen soon followed.

Mr. Izidore Isaac Bradlaw M.D.S, was a British subject of Russian origin and a well known Dublin dentist. His offices, as already mentioned, were in Grafton Street and served as his operating base.

Mr. Bradlaw was, to say the least, a prime mover in the Irish World of Cinema and was instrumental in establishing many popular Picture Palaces in Ireland. We have a lot to thank him for.

Following a long and distinguished career in the World of Irish Cinema, Izidore Isaac Bradlaw died aged 68 years on October 22nd 1933.

KENILWORTH/CLASSIC
Harold's Cross.

The Kenilworth Cinema on Harold's Cross Road, which opened on Thursday July 30th 1953, completed a trilogy of cinemas for the Sundrive Cinema Company.

This latest addition for the company took ten months to complete and over sixty men were employed in its construction. The architect was Mr. P.D. Kavanagh of Fitzwilliam Square and the main contractor was once again Mr. Thos. Kennedy of Phibsborough who had also built the companies other two cinemas, the "Sundrive" and the "Classic".

The Kenilworth, just like its sister cinema, was built on the stadium style and had seating for 1,106 with 826 seats in the parterre and 280 in the stadium section. One of the directors explained that the company's policy in having a stadium layout instead of a balcony was their idea of a family house and that it was their intention to cater for the family that liked a night out in their own local cinema.

The foyer was large and accommodating with the cash desk on one side and a kiosk where sweets and cigarettes could be purchased on the other side. There were two entrances into the cinema, with one door leading into the stadium and another into the parterre. Prices of admission were 2/3 for the stadium and 1/3 for the parterre.

The front of the building is finished in red brick with a large concrete ledge on which stands a number of well planted flower boxes and a large car park lies to the rear with room for over 50 cars with people of manoeuvring space. The entire flooring of the cinema is luxuriously carpeted and the seats are most comfortable with ample leg room.

The Kenilworth's first advertisement

A view of the Kenilworth cinema, which was taken from a newspaper cutting.

In 1954 the Sundrive Cinema Company sold their interest in the Sundrive cinema and Albert Kelly who was the Chief projectionist in the Sundrive came to work in the Kenilworth and later again became its manager.

In 1976, the company decided to sell off the Classic and the Kenilworth cinemas and Albert Kelly put in a successful bid for the Kenilworth cinema and took over the lease. As the purchaser of the Classic in Terenure intended to re-develop the property into something other than a cinema, Albert got permission to take the Classic name and he thereby changed the name of the Kenilworth to that of the Classic. He also very shrewdly continued to run the "Rocky Horror Show", as a feature of the Friday night late slot and in so doing, he drew the followers of this cult film to the new "Classic".

The Classic, in the eighties, after it had twinned.

In 1980 Albert reluctantly twinned the Classic, as he had no choice but to move with the times and instead of an eleven hundred seater cinema he now had two small cinemas one with 200 seats and the other a 300 seater. However, he could now offer a wider choice of films and attendances in both houses were good.

In the eighties with most suburban cinema closed down or now running as Bingo halls and the few that were left now had two or more screens, restrictions on the rental of first run films were somewhat relaxed and eventually disappeared altogether.

When Albert twinned the Classic, he dedicated one of the screens for the showing of "The Rocky Horror Picture Show", every Friday night and this film continued to attract good houses until the cinema closed. On Friday night, August 15th 2003, when it was last screened in the Classic Cinema, it had broken all Irish records having been continuously screened every Friday night for 23 years, not counting the number of screenings in both Classics, prior to the twinning.

Albert Kelly retired from the cinema business because of ill health and on the advice of his Doctor who told him that he could no longer continue to work the long hours involved. Without fuss and in as quiet a manner as possible, he closed the doors of the Classic cinema on August 28th 2003.

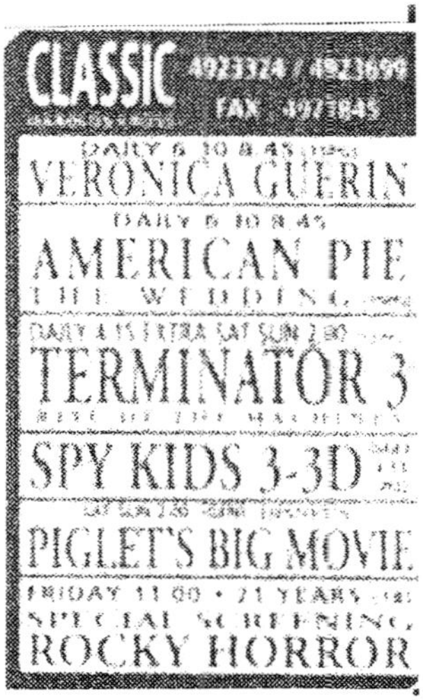

This is one of the last advertisements for the Classic cinema and the last feature films were as shown;

"Veronica Guerin"

&

"American Pie the Wedding".

Although having said that, it is only fair to point out that Albert did not forget his loyal Rocky Horror fans and two weeks prior to the closure of the Classic Albert, threw a party night for the fans on Friday night August 15th as a farewell gesture, on return the fans did not forget Albert, as at the end of the night he received a standing ovation and a beautiful engraved and mounted plaque from the fans

The fans turned out in force that night and it was most unfortunate that some 150 of them failed to gain admission.

I had two interviews with Albert in October and November of 2004 and on the second occasion he told me that if given half a chance he would buy back the building and reopen the Classic.

The Classic, taken on the Bank Holiday Monday, October 25th 2004, just before my meeting with Albert in his home in Kenilworth Square.

Picture courtesy Irish Times (photo by Cyril Byrne)

Albert Kelly outside his beloved Classic circa 2002.

KILLESTER
Collin's Avenue

The Killester cinema, which opened on Thursday, August 3rd 1950, was built by the Dublin Metropolitan Cinemas Limited, a subsidiary of the Stephen's Green Group. The building which embodies the most modern features in equipment and furnishings has a seating capacity for 1,300 persons and is one of the largest in the suburban area.

The cinema was officially declared open by Jimmy O'Dea, who deputised for the Lord Mayor, Alderman C Breathnach, and Mr. J.N Duff, chairman of the company announced that the proceeds of the night would be handed over to the local conference of the St. Vincent de Paul Society.

The building was purpose built and constructed by D.A. Cambridge from the designs of architects Munden & Purcell, while the quantity surveyors were Munden and Kavanagh.

The cinema was managed by Mr. B.G Flanagan, and admission prices were reasonable.

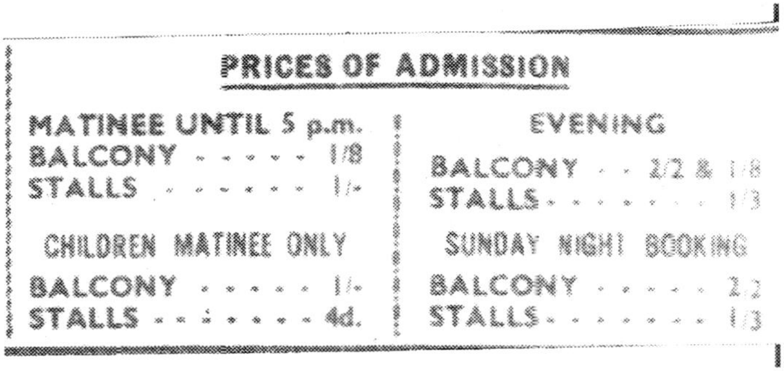

The feature film for the gala opening night was "Jolson Sings Again", with Larry Parks, who told us "You ain't heard Nothin Yet".

We have very little to impart about the Killester cinema, it seems it existed in a quiet enough manner and nothing funny, sad, outrageous, scandalous or exciting came our way.

It survived for 20 years and closed on September 19th 1970, and featured the following two movies.
"Kill Them All. Come Back Alive", with Chuck Connors and Leslie Philips in "Doctor in Love".

While we would believe that nobody needs reminding or prompting as to what a "Doctor Film" is all about, we failed to trace this Chuck Connors film.

The site of the Old Killester in Late 2005.

LANDSCAPE
Churchtown

NEW DUBLIN CINEMA

The new Landscape Cinema at Rathfornham which is expected to be opened on St. Patrick's Day. It will seat nine hundred.

—"Herald" photo (O'B.).

This picture appeared in an evening newspaper on March 11th 1955

LANDSCAPE CINEMA
Landscape Rd., Churchtown
OFFICIAL OPENING
By JOE LYNCH of "LIVING WITH LYNCH"
TO-NIGHT, AT 7.30 p.m.
WITH
3 COINS IN THE FOUNTAIN
in
CINEMASCOPE
Showing Daily 6.30, 8.30 p.m. SUNDAY 3 and 8 p.m.
ADM. 1/3, 1/8, 2/-

The Landscape cinema opened on Easter Saturday, April 9th 1955, and featured the film "3 Coins In The Fountain", starring Clifton Webb, Dorothy McGuire, Jean Peters, Louis Jordan and Maggie McNamara.

This is a story worldly and wonderful, of three lovely girls who tossed three coins in the fountain, as the Romans do and then fell in love, as women do.

Filmed in Cinemascope

Admission prices - 1/3, 1/8, & 2/.

In 1937, when Mr. James Brophy a building contractor came to live in Churchtown there were only eighteen County Council houses, two manors and five or six gate lodges in the area. But at the end of World War II, the area began to develop and houses went up on all sides.

Mr. Brophy contributed in no small way to the development of this district and as well as building houses he also built a number of shops and a garage, and noting that there was no local cinema he built the "Landscape" cinema on Landscape Road.

Having built the cinema, which had seating for 900 people, he ran the cinema as a family business which provided employment for some thirteen of a staff. The building was spacious and the auditorium was of the stadium style. The large wide screen with its four track sound was the best available and comparable with any cinema in Ireland, including Dublin's 1st run cinemas.

Business went well for James Brophy until the end of 1956 when attendances started to dwindle a little and costs began to over run. In 1957 Mr. Brophy fell foul of the Cinema Branch of the I.T & G.W. Union and the Labour Court investigated the dispute. It would appear that Mr. Brophy was in breach of union rules for replacing some operating staff with a member of his own family. The Union, it would seem, went along with Mr. Brophy employing his own son as operator providing the son attended classes in St Kevin's Technical School. However, the son did not keep up his attendances. Other problems entered the dispute and the Labour Court deliberated. In the meantime Mr. Brophy closed the cinema on May 1st 1957 and its last showing was "The Bold and The Brave"

In 1958, with the union problems obviously sorted and behind him Mr. Brophy re-opened the Landscape on November 1958 with the film "Tammy", starring Debbie Reynolds.

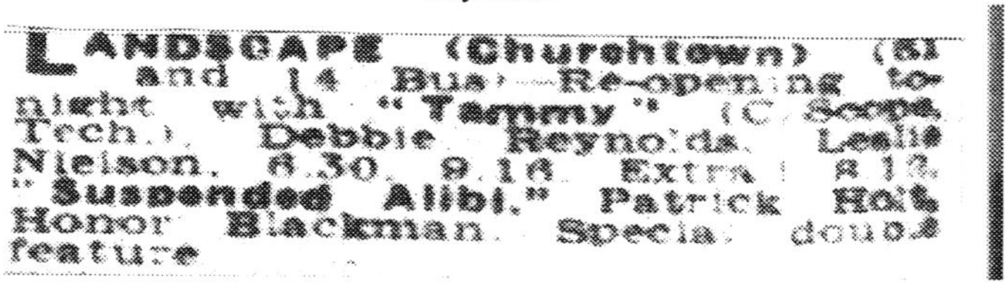

For the next seven years the Landscape seemed to operate with reasonable success until 1965, when it once again suffered dwindling attendances. On Saturday June 25th 1965 this last advertisement appeared in the "Evening Herald", and we gathered that it closed that night, with its finale film, "Please Turn Over".

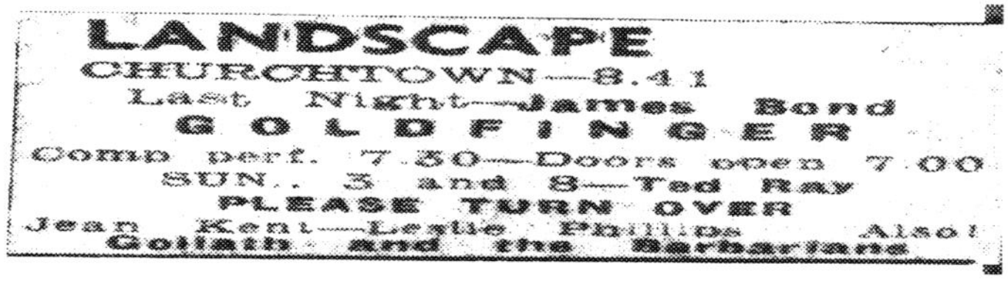

LEINSTER CINEMA,
Dolphins Barn

The Leinster Cinema opened on Tuesday November 3rd 1936, just two days before its closest rival to be, the "Rialto"

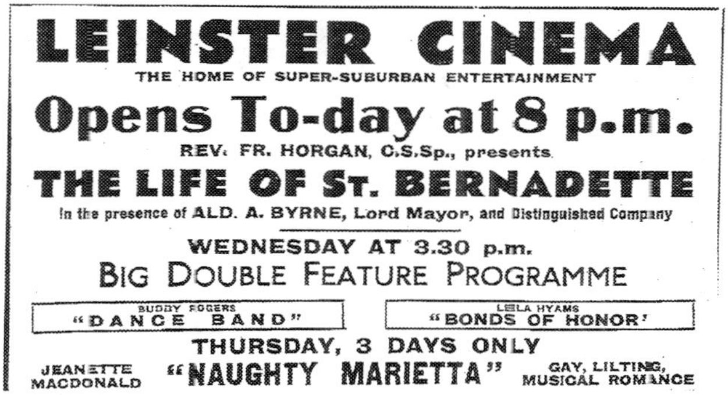

The owner was a Mr. Daniel McAlister and the builders were Murphy Brothers of Castlewood Avenue Rathmines.

The building is of modern design with a large foyer and two double-door entrances to the auditorium. One door is situated on either side of the ticket office, a fire proofed stairs led to the balcony area, where a second fire proof stairway led down to the outside wall of the cinema.

An interior view of the 1,250-seater cinema with all the uniformed staff in place.

The Picture Palace an outside view. Pity about the gaudy posters and the condition of the roadway, all of which give off a bad first impression. Hopefully it was all cleaned up before the Lord Mayor and his entourage arrived.

This was a large imposing suburban cinema, which lacked nothing in its luxurious surroundings and it had seating for 1,250 persons. It was officially opened by Alderman Alfie Byrne, Lord Mayor of Dublin, and the its first film "The Life of Bernadette" was presented by the Rev. J. Horgan C.C. Sp, and the proceeds of which were donated to the African Missions of the Holy Ghost Fathers.

In contrast to the "Life of Bernadette", the next advertised film was Naughty Marietta, which would suggest that management was prepared to cater for all tastes.

In formerly declaring the cinema open, the Lord Mayor praised the owner Mr. Daniel McAlister for having the courage to put money into this magnificent building in a hitherto neglected suburb. He also congratulated the architect Mr. Robinson and Mr. Murphy the builder and in closing, he further mentioned that management had given a guarantee that none but the cleanest and most instructive of films would be shown in his new cinema.

Two views of the Leinster.

LEINSTER 5.20 ROD TAYLOR 8.50 CATHERINE SPAAK HOTEL 3.30 FRANK SINATRA 7.10 FOUR FOR TEXAS
SUNDAY—NO SHOW

The Leinster closed its doors to the world of cinemas on Saturday May 18th 1968 and the premises later became an Ice Rink, which proved to be quite popular for a good number of years.
It finally closed completely and was demolished in 2004 to make way for an apartment block.

The last films shown were

"Hotel", starring Rod Taylor and Catherine Spaak with Rod playing the part of Peter McDermott the manager of St. Gregory's Hotel, which was situated in New Orleans, but conveniently changed location to San Francisco for the T.V. series.

The supporting programme was "Four for Texas", starring Frank Sinatra and Dean Martin and one critic remarked that the pair were so relaxed in the film that that they could have been asleep.

A WORD ON THE GROWTH OF CINEMAS IN 1912

It's hard to believe but in the year 1912 when Dublin had only just begun to build cinemas the world already had over fifty thousand cinemas up and running and it would appear that there was no evidence of a slackening of this pace.

To paraphrase a report in the "Evening Mail", on December 1912, in which a columnist wrote that, "while Rome was not built in a day, it was a long time since Rome was built and that we do things much quicker nowadays".

In the last seventeen years, he wrote, over fifty thousand picture theatres have sprung into existence and that their numbers were increasing daily." You can't get away from them"! he wrote. "You will find them in every continent of the world. Turkey has its picture theatres as has India and they flourish even in China".

"So the picture palace has come to stay", he wrote," and the superior people who look askance on every new thing and who saw in the craze for moving pictures only a passing infatuation have lived to see their predictions (as usual) falsified."

And in passing, one wonders just what he would have written today in the year 2006.

* * * * *

THE MANOR CINEMA.

A site at 60/61 Manor Street was chosen for the site of a new cinema in 1919 and work commenced immediately. On May 10th 1920, the new building opened as the Manor Cinema. This was a fair sized purpose-built cinema, that could accommodate upwards of some 630 people. Like a lot of other cinemas in the Dublin area at the time it ran two shows daily, six days a week, one evening show starting about 6 pm and a last performance at 9 pm, a matinee on Sunday afternoons and one show on Sunday nights, at about 7.30 pm.

We were told by a Manor Street local, of a respectable age, that the front rows of seating left a lot to be desired. They were, he said, wooden benches, which sat on a floor that was covered in a cheap type of lino, while the stalls had a better type of seating and the floor was nicely carpeted.

Prices of admission were; benches 9d and the rest from 1/- to 1/6.

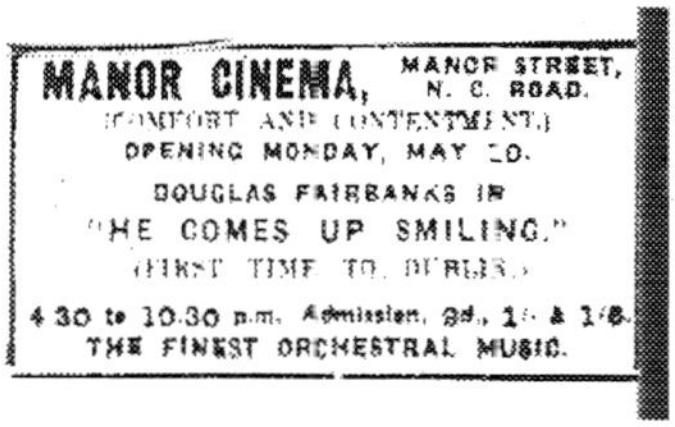

The early films were of course all silent, and its first billing was "He Comes up Smiling", starring Douglas Fairbanks and Marjorie Daw.

This was the story of a bank clerk, whose job description was to mind the boss's pet canary. The canary escapes and this leads the bank clerk into all sorts of capers, and to the love of his life.

The musical entertainment and accompaniment to the silent films was provided by a small orchestra, consisting of a pianist, a cello and two violin players. A great sufficiency, one might say, for those times.

~~~~~

There were a number of tales circulating about the Manor Cinema, and one in particular recently came to our attention, and we would relate and title it as:

"The Boozer on Horseback".

It would appear that one of its regular patrons had a little drinking habit, and when in funds he was inclined to indulge quite heavily, and so filled with drink would he be that he would go slightly mad, and do some very funny things. On one occasion having been refused admission because of his intoxicated state, the patron went off and secured a horse, which he mounted and rode up the steps of the cinema and into the foyer. Here he and the horse were stopped by the doorman and, when asked to leave, he simply rode the horse out backwards.

* * * * *

One Dubliner wrote and told us that she paid 9d entrance in to sit on a hard wooden seat to see a film starring Dianne Durbin and Jeannette McDonnell, and we wondered if they did indeed ever star together.

* * * * *
~~~~~

"Rowdies"

Like all cinemas the Manor had its share of rowdies and the only way to handle these ruffians was to take tackle them head on with a no nonsense attitude. There was no room in well-run cinemas for rowdiness.

In the Dublin Police Court on July 30th 1924 before Mr. Lupton K.C., a young man was summoned by Thomas Fagan, the Manager of the Manor Street Cinema, and he was charged with riotous and offensive behaviour, to the disturbance and annoyance of the public.

This disturbance took place on Sunday night July 20th, when the defendant and a number of other youths began to kick up as much noise as they could and throw paper streamers about the place. When this happened the manager drew the attention of a police constable who was in attendance in plain clothes and together they approached the youths. When asked for his name the youth who appeared to be the leader of the group refused, and an uniformed police constable was sent for.

Having given his name and address to the constable, the culprit was summoned to court and when he tried to smart talk Mr. Lupton he was fined 40/- and 10/- in costs. "Can I appeal", the defendant asked and Mr. Lupton told him to get out of the court or he would find himself in the dock. "You won't try any of your nonsense here, wherever else you may". The defendant then quickly left the court.

* * * * *

The Manor cinema seemed to do all right and continued to display the latest films available, however some nine years later we found that it was only advertising talent competitions and there was no mention of a film in the programme.

On March 2nd 1929, we found this advertisement telling of a forthcoming Local Talent Competition and it would appear that this was its last Advert.

While there was no mention of any films in this advertisement and no mention of the cinema closing, it would appear the Manor did indeed close.

PALLADIUM CINEMA,
MANOR STREET.

NOTICE.

THE ABOVE CINEMA HAS BEEN TAKEN OVER BY THE DUBLIN CINEMA ENTERPRISE CO., AND
WILL RE-OPEN ON SUNDAY NEXT, SEPT. 1,
SHOWING
CHARLIE CHAPLIN in
"THE CIRCUS."
The Theatre has been Thoroughly Renovated, Reseated, and Heated Throughout.
PRICES —————— **7d., 9d., and 1/3.**

Some months later we came across this advertisement on Saturday August 29th 1929, which informed its patrons that the cinema had been taken over by a new group and would re-open as the "Palladian Cinema", on the following Sunday September 1st 1929. The cinema it would seem had undergone total refurbishment and was now under new management. Admission prices had also undergone a change.

Its opening programme was a nice choice of one of Charlie Chaplin's famous Tramp stories, which this time has Charlie the Tramp working in a circus where he organises a job for his unemployed girlfriend, played by Merna Kennedy.

PALLADIUM CINEMA,
MANOR STREET.
[illegible] Continuous, 6.30 to 10.30.
Admission 4d., 7d., 9d. and 1/-.
Sundays, 3 p.m. and 8.30 p.m. Admission:
7d., 9d., and 1/3.
Children 4d. at the Afternoon Performance.
TO-MORROW ONLY—
REX LEASE & MILDRED HARRIS in a Thrilling Motor Racing Comedy Drama, "**SPEED CLASSIC.**"
Also, **TOM MIX** in "The Arizona Wildcat."
COMMENCING MONDAY, FOR ONE WEEK—
THE MOONLIGHT MINSTRELS
In their Latest Songs, Dances, Gags, Etc.
ON THE SCREEN:
RICHARD DIX in "SPORTING GOODS."

A few weeks later we found this advertisement which if we are reading it properly would suggest that the Palladian also included stage or musical acts in its very full programmes. It also gave the impression that Tom Mix was big on their list of movie characters.

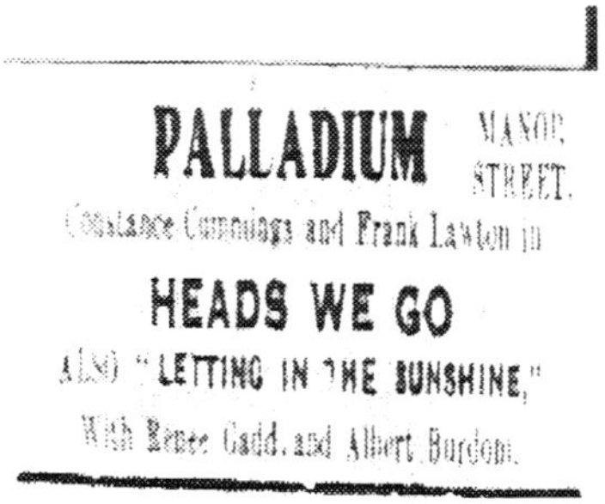
PALLADIUM MANOR STREET.

Constance Cummings and Frank Lawton in

HEADS WE GO

ALSO "LETTING IN THE SUNSHINE,"

With Renee Gadd and Albert Burdon.

Five years later we found this advertisement and it too, for good reasons was its last advert (a) because of a dispute in the newspaper industry and (b) because the next time we found mention of the cinema it was called the "Broadway".

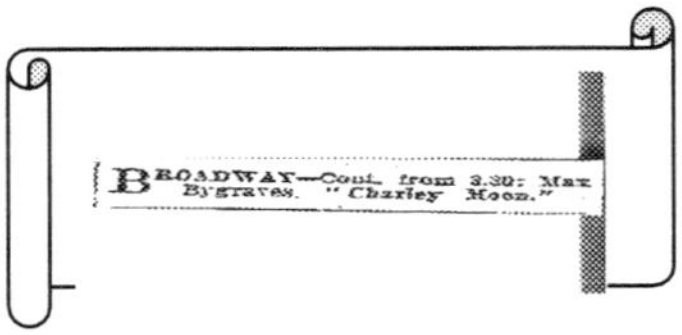
BROADWAY—Cont. from 3.30: Max Bygraves. "Charley Moon."

Last advert for the Manor Street Cinema then known as the "Broadway" was for Saturday, August 11th 1956 and we can only take it for granted that it closed that day.

From what we have read and heard the owners of the cinema had big plans for the property and wanted to enlarge it for commercial reasons. Apparently it was their intention to purchase the neighbouring premises for this purpose, but for some reason unknown to us, this initiative never materialised and for a while the building became a cooperage and later again the home of the Stoneybatter Community Training Workshop under the auspices of FAS.

MARO
The Mary Street Picture House, 12 Mary Street.

Mary Street played host to two very famous cinemas, the first being James Joyce's the "Volta" and the second of course the famous Mary Street Picture House, which became widely known as the Maro, or if you like Mero or even the Mayro.

THE
MARY ST. PICTURE HOUSE,
12 MARY STREET.
GRAND OPENING.
The Rt. Honourable the LORD MAYOR
(Councillor Lorcan G. Sherlock, LL.D.)
WILL OPEN THE
MARY STREET PICTURE HOUSE
ON
THURSDAY, DECEMBER 19th,

This cinema was opened by the then Lord Mayor of Dublin, Councillor Lorcan Sherlock in 1912 on the 19th December, and was an instant success. The opening of this cinema was a big move forward for the animated picture business, and was the first home of the Kinematograph Company limited, who's managing director was Alderman Farrell. It was designed by Mr. George O'Connor and the builder was Mr. Patrick Shorthall.

This cinema was a converted building which once housed the cabinet-making factory of Messrs Beaky's, who had moved to larger premises around the corner in 41 Stafford Street, (now Wolf Tone Street) and next door to the O'Dearest mattress factory.

The theatre was one of the best equipped venues in the country, and for a time was one of the largest cinemas around. On the ground floor alone it had a seating capacity for 800 persons, in addition to having a large balcony. Great detail was incorporated into its design and it was most suited for its role as a great place of entertainment.

It opened with a showing of "In Feudal days", in the first part of the week and for the latter part it showed "White Domino". However there was a slight hitch that week that nearly prevented the opening of this wonderful picture palace.

Having applied to the Northern Police Court for a six day music licence, which was a prerequisite to its opening on Thursday December 19th, the application was seriously objected to by the Rector of St Mary's Church, who felt that the noise from the Picture Theatre was so close to the church, that it would interfere with the conduct of the service in the church. On these grounds the application for a music licence was refused.

This refusal brought about great concern to the cinema owners, who immediately had their attorney's launch appeals. Luckily for them this worked and they received their licence in the nick of time on the day of the grand opening.

This objection by the Rector of St Mary's was noted and referred to by Lord Mayor Sherlock when he made his opening speech, but he felt that as the cinema was under the control of a gentleman like Alderman Farrell great care would be exercised. He also mentioned that this opening would be the last episode of its kind that he would be connected with, as the question of the growing number of these cinemas was one that the Municipal authorities would have to consider.

With the granting of the licence the cinema opened under the management of Mr. J.J. Eppel

The Maro

A small enough building on the outside but quite large on the inside, here you could buy a Toffee Apple for a ½ penny, and lick your way through a Tom Mix film. Toffee apples were a great favourite of the kids in those days but if one remembers correctly they were always of a very sour variety and I don't remember ever finishing one off to the last bite. Once the area of the apple with the toffee mix had been devoured the balance of the apple was often thrown away. Not very conducive, one might say, to a clean cinema floor.

~~~~~

On Monday November 26th 1923 the explosion of a "stink-bomb" in the Mary Street Picture house caused some considerable excitement among the audience. Someone shouted fire and there was a general rush for the exits. While there was no fire the sickening smell in the cinema caused some women to faint. In all there were three bombs one was a smoke bomb and the other two stink-bombs. One bomb which was hidden beneath one of the seats consisted of an electric light bulb filled with an evil smelling gas and the other two bombs were hurled into the cinema by a number of men.
~~~~~

In the ensuing panic two rows of seats were wrecked, two women injured and the exits doors were badly damaged.

The incident had a sequel in the Dublin Circuit Court on January 24th 1924 when the cinema owners sought £500 for malicious damage, Mr. Burke who represented the Dublin City Commissioners said while they could not dispute malice, he suggested that £100 would meet the damage, Mr. Finlay on behalf of his client accepted this.

During the hearing it transpired that management was in dispute with some staff members over the dismissal of one man and pickets were placed on the cinema, prosecutions had been taken against some of the workers and they came before his lordship by way of appeal. Seven days after the hearing of these appeals three men were seen talking to members of the picket-line and shortly afterwards the bombs exploded.

Judge Davitt was disgusted and found it hard to believe that the relations existing between employers and employed were such as would tolerate an action of this kind by any member of a trade union. He made a decree for £100.

~~~~

The Maro closed in1959 and we believe that the last picture shown there was"Satchmo the Great", starring of course the fabulous Louis Armstrong. This picture was featured on Friday and Saturday the 8th and 9th of January 1959.

This picture of the Mary Street premises, which now houses the offices of an insurance company was taken towards the end of the year 2005.
~~~~

(Picture courtesy of the Gilbert and Dublin city Archives)

We were very fortunate to come across this picture of the Maro before finishing the story.

In the first floor panel facing us is a poster advertising a 1952 film called "Green Gloves", and we would suppose that this more or less dates the photograph

The film stars Glen Ford, Geraldine Brooks, Cedric Hardwicke and George Macready

Glen plays the part of an ex World War 2 soldier who with his new found girlfriend scours the South of France searching for a valuable relic which some would kill for and in the process he falls in love.

Other than its nickname "The Maro" this Mary Street Picture was never gifted with an official name and it would seem that nobody ever bothered to ask why. I would have thought that one of the film critics might have raised the question but if one did, we haven't come across it.

MASTERPIECE
100 Talbot Street

The Masterpiece opened on July 27th 1914 and for its opening film it presented "Joan of Arc", that was billed as the great Savoi Masterpiece. The film was directed by Nino Oxilia, together with an up-to-date programme of pictures of comedy, drama and travel, all of which were accompanied by a first class orchestra.

MASTERPIECE THEATRE,
99 Talbot Street
(A FEW DOORS FROM THE PILLAR).
GRAND OPENING
ON
To-day (Monday), July 27th.
FEATURING THE GREAT SAVOIA MASTER-PIECE FILM.
JOAN OF ARC,
A TRIUMPH OF SPECTACULAR REALISM.
ALSO AN UP-TO-DATE PROGRAMME OF PICTURES DEPICTING TRAVEL, COMEDY, INTEREST AND DRAMA.
FIRST-CLASS ORCHESTRA DAILY.
CONTINUOUS PERFORMANCE FROM 1.30 p.m. TILL 10.30 p.m.
ADMISSION 6d.

This was one of the earliest "Joan of Arc", films made.
When we noticed that the directors had chosen The Savoia Film Companies latest "Masterpiece", for their opening number, we wondered if that fact had in anyway influenced the naming of the cinema.

While the entrance to the Masterpiece was without doubt in Talbot Street the main body of the cinema was actually in Marlborough Place. When one entered the main entrance in Talbot Street, purchased ones entrance ticket, one then had to traverse a long corridor down to the cinema proper, which turned out to be a saving grace in November of 1925 when a bomb was lobbed into the foyer of the cinema and the ensuing blast woke Dublin!

While the bomb almost completely wrecked the foyer of the cinema the main body, screen and auditorium escaped damage. The gates were blown off their hinges, the vestibule walls were badly damaged, the box office was destroyed and glass frames were left in smithereens as were neighbouring windows and doors. Directly across the road stood the large drapery premises of Moran and Son and its huge plate glass shop front was blown to pieces as were all 36 windows in the upper stories of the building, bar one small window at the top.

The bombing occurred at 7am on Friday November 20th 1925, when two men held up a civic guard that was on duty in the vicinity of the cinema and within minutes a car pulled up outside the cinema and the driver jumped out and threw a bomb into the cinema entrance.

According to eye witnesses, the car was seen to drive down Talbot Street from the direction of O'Connell Street and when the driver had completed his task all three made off in the car in the direction of Amiens Street. As the car careered along Amiens Street it broke down and the three occupants jumped out and ran down Sheriff Street.

Some little time later two guards who were on duty in the vicinity of Lower and Upper Sheriff Street saw three men running through an archway and when the guards followed them they were shot at, at point blank range; one was shot in the abdomen and left forearm and the other was also wounded in the left forearm. Both however survived the shootings and lived to tell the tale. In the aftermath, arrests were made and court appearances followed.

The cinema closed for repairs and when all the work was finished it re-opened and life carried on as normal. However it was recalled that on the Monday prior to the explosion armed men had entered the operating box and demanded in the name of the "Republic" the film reels of the "Ypres", film.

YPRES
(WIPERS)
The Story of the Immortal Salient
MASTERPIECE
LAST FOUR DAYS.
TO-DAY.
2.30, 4.30, 6.30, and 8.30.
COME EARLY.

It would appear that this film was considered British propagandist material by the republican movement and they therefore felt it their duty to seize and destroy this type of material.

While they did succeed in seizing the film, one of their comrades was detained by staff members, and, when the police arrived, he was handed over to them, charged, and detained in a police cell until he appeared in court the following morning.

The "Masterpiece" did not suffer alone from these type of hi-jacks, as only the night before the "Prince of Wales", film was seized from the Kingstown picture house.

The theft by armed raiders from the Masterpiece Cinema only served to whet the appetite of the public and packed houses were the order of the day. Management had no trouble obtaining a duplicate film and long queues formed every day for admission to view this film, which of course encouraged the armed objectors to bomb the cinema.

The name Ypres was pronounced Wipers by the British soldiers who fought there in W.W.1 and the film showed all the horrors of war, including the story of Hill 60, the coming of poison gas and the horrifying scene of a British tank crushing a brave German machinegun crew of five who continued to defend their post until death came upon them.

This bombing of the cinema was not its first attack in troubled times, as it had also suffered in the 1916 rising when it was blown up and had to be rebuilt.

One of the most outstanding features of the Masterpiece cinema were its tin chairs which were free standing and when a performance had finished the chairs would be left in disarray all over the auditorium. There were a few plush chairs to the rear of the cinema but they cost more. When an usher walked the aisle and glanced along a row of seats he would never find a row in a straight line, the chairs and their occupants would zig zag from one end to the other. Musical chairs were only in the halfpenny place!

This building in Marlborough Place once housed the main body of the cinema and on the following page the site of the front entrance.

We could trace no closing date for the Masterpiece, as it just seemed to fade out. While the front portion of the cinema is now converted into two shops the auditorium area was in use by the "Team Theatre Group", for many years and from time to time the Abbey Theatre held rehearsals there. In fact judging from the sign on the wall the Team Group are still there.

Sunday morning, November 27th 2005.
The building on the left would have been number 99 Talbot Street,
the address of the Masterpiece.

METROPOLE

This building contained a Cinema, Ballroom Room, Bars (2) and a Restaurant.

The Metropole opened on February 10th 1922, on the site of the old Metropole Hotel, which had been destroyed in the 1916 uprising. This new building was designed by architect Aubrey V. O' Rourke.

The Metropole Hotel had occupied the site of number 37 Sackville Street (now Lower O'Connell Street) since circa 1834, it was also known as Spadaccini's. Its history includes ownership at one time by the Jury brothers, who in turn sold it to a family named Mitchell.

The cinema was a 1,000 seater and most popular with Dublin cinemagoers, and up to the year of its closure in 1972 its bar and ballroom were a great scene of social activity, and a serious rival to Clery's Ballroom.

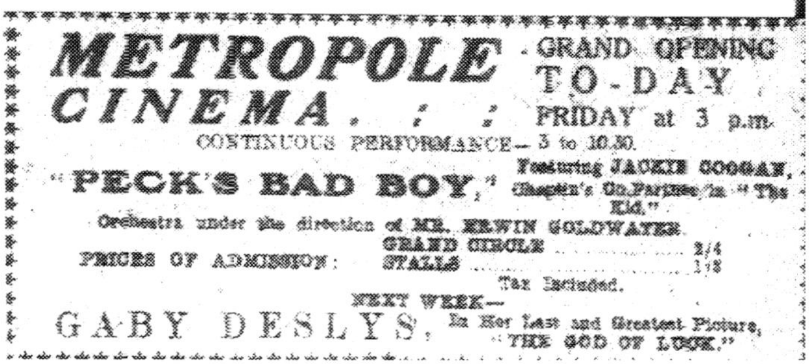

"Peck's Bad Boy", starred the loveable Jackie Coogan and this was Jackie's first released film after he had become famous as Charlie Chaplin's co-star in the "Kid".

Jackie played the part of Mrs. Peck's son Henry, who as a loveable little ragamuffin just could not stay away from trouble. Henry, his dog "Tar Baby" and Buddy his pal got into all sorts of mischief but Mrs. Peck could see no wrong in her little darling.

On one occasion when a Circus came to town, Henry let a lion out of its cage and caused a riot in the circus camp. Now hiding in the lion's cage with his pal and dog, his now frightened pal Buddy asked him why he let the lion out. Henry replied: "aw sure they said he was a man eater, how was I supposed to know he also liked little boys".

In another scene the local dog catcher had captured Tar Baby and when Henny and Buddy sprung him from the pound they let all the dogs loose and they all rampaged through the town, chasing cats, jumping through open windows, pawing out holes in freshly laid gardens and rummaging for food in waste bins.

* * * * *

The Metropole ballroom ran dances in the afternoons and during the week a late evening session would be available to those aspiring to professional ballroom dancing. Staff outings and diner dances were a speciality of the complex in the forties and fifties, and most fellows and girls attended a dinner dance there, at least once in their lifetime. Attending one of these functions, a lad had to present his date with a 'large' well-packaged box of chocolates and a Corsage, and woe betide he who didn't. It was also conditional that he wore a "monkey suit", (dress suit.).

At weekend dances in the ballroom it was customary for the lads to arrive in the main bar of the complex early. This was with the intention of getting tanked up, or if you would prefer, to meet up with your mates. After all, only dating couples met at the "Pillar", "Clery's" or under the clock at the "Ballast Office".

There was also a bar in the ballroom proper, but the downstairs bar was more popular. At times some of the lads would either drink too much in the downstairs bar or leave it too late to go up to the ballroom, and one way or the other they would not gain admission. To counteract this, the smarter lads would go up early to the ballroom, buy their ticket, enter and leave a jacket or jumper on a seat thereby booking their place and then they would return to the downstairs bar.

Photograph of a sealed frame, showing some Metropole paraphernalia, in St. Andrew's Community Centre, Pearse Street.

For lovers of old cinemas a visit to St. Andrews Resource Centre in Pearse Street would be well worthwhile. On the first floor landing they have a large display of framed pictures and paraphernalia that will surely take you back in time.

St. Andrews won two awards in the year 2005. The first being Best Old Building in the South East Area of Dublin's City Council's City Neighbourhoods Competition and the second being the Best Old Building in Dublin City.

Together with their "New Link" magazine St. Andrew's lead the way with a host of community activities.

Site of the Hotel Metropole - 1975
The scene today. The Metropole cinema and restaurants have been pulled down, along with the Capital cinema in Princes Street beyond, and the plan is to build a store on the site, but the project seems to have been held up.

A view of the site of the Metropole cinema in 1975, which was in the process of being prepared for the building of a new department store;

A view of the Metropole building, from atop Nelson's Pillar. The Metropole being the building on the right with the two buses outside and far down on the left hand side one can just about make out the canopy outside of the Grand Central Cinema.

An old programme of the Metropole, featuring one of its lounges and the restaurant.

METROPOLE CINEMA
O'CONNELL STREET . DUBLIN

Proprietors . . . The Metropole and Allied Cinemas, Ltd.

CONTINUOUS PERFORMANCE
DAILY from .. 2 to 11 p.m.
SUNDAY .. (Two Performances)
3.30 and 8.30 p.m.

PROGRAMME

Prices of Admission

STALLS	.. ..	1/3
GRAND CIRCLE	..	2/6

(Including Tax)

SPECIAL NOTE
Seats may be booked in advance for 8.30 Performance on Sundays
Advance Booking Office open daily, 2.0 to 9.30 p.m.

METROPOLE
At 3.30, 5.45 and 9.05. Over 18s.

Alsol 3.50 and 7.15 Phyllis Diller and Mile O'Shea in
THE ADDING MACHINE

● NOTE: CINEMA CLOSED FROM TO-NIGHT

Above, another copy of a Metropole Programme, and to the left, separate advertisement announcing the closure of the cinema and ballroom, on March 11th 1972.

~~~~~

★ METROPOLE BALLROOM ★
PLEASE NOTE THAT THE BARS, RESTAURANT AND BALLROOM WILL BE CLOSED FROM 2.30 p.m. TO-DAY.

The Metropole is dead; long live the Metropole!

Within four days of its closing news appears in the evening papers that a New Metropole will open on March 16th 1972.

NEW METROPOLE Townsend Street
● OPENING TO-MORROW ●
Cont. Perf. Daily from 2.00 Over 16s only
Feature at 2.05, 4.25, 6.45, [illegible]
~~~~~

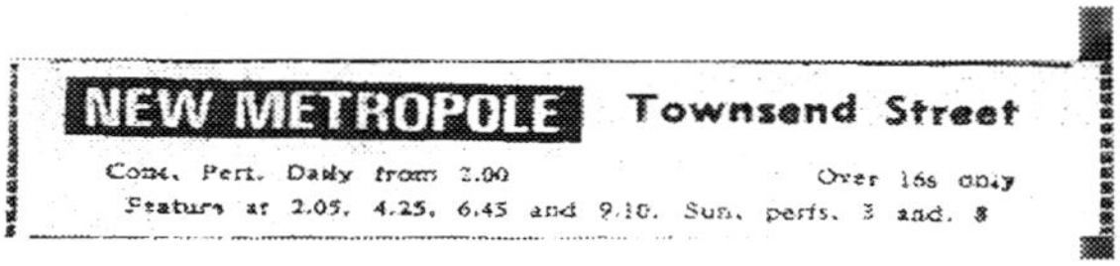
NEW METROPOLE Townsend Street
Cont. Perf. Daily from 2.00 Over 16s only
Feature at 2.05, 4.25, 6.45 and 9.10. Sun. perfs. 3 and. 8

A small advert announcing the opening of the New Metropole on Thursday March 16th, 1972.

This picture of the new Metropole cinema, which now operates as the Screen Cinema, was taken in Early November 2005.
(It might be of interest to note that this cinema, which stands in Townsend Street, was not the first to grace this site; there were two cinemas operating side by side there many years ago, namely "The Cinema Royal" and "The Coffee Palace")
or perhaps it would be more correct to say, one behind the other.
The New Metropole, which was Dublin's newest luxury cinema in 1972, was a worthy successor to the famous Metropole of O'Connell Street.

The New Metropole opened with the "Anderson Tapes", which starred Sean Connery and the cinema was managed by Mr. Trevor Berry and his assistant manager Mr. James Jordan

Some years later it converted to a three-screen cinema, and later again it had a name change to the Screen Cinema. It continues to operate in 2005.

MOUNTJOY PICTURE AND VARIETY PALACE
Rutland Place, Summerhill, Dublin

News Flash

A News Flash Circulating Dublin in 1912 heralded the announcement of a new Movie Palace that was about to grace the beautiful Summerhill area of Dublin.

This new venue which was the brain child of the directors of a newly registered company entitled the "Dublin Sporting and Picture Club Limited", is expected to be one of the most magnificently decorated and comfortably furnished cine-variety theatres ever to open its doors to the public in the Dublin area.

Work has been in progress for some time now and the opening date is planned for May

THE MOUNTJOY
PICTURE AND VARIETY PALACE,
Rutland Place, SUMMERHILL, DUBLIN,
To be Opened
FRIDAY, 17th MAY, 1912,
Under the Patronage of the Right. Hon. the Lord Mayor of Dublin (Councillor Lorcan G. Sherlock), the President and Officers of the Mountjoy Ward Branch of the U.I.L.

The Whole Proceeds of the Opening Night given to the Mountjoy Ward Branch of the U.I.L. Home Rule Fund.

SPECIAL ARTISTES. SPECIAL PICTURES.
The Very Best of Everything in the Animated Pictorial and Musical World.
NEW EVENTS. NEW TOURS. NEW FEATURES
POPULAR PRICES.
[illegible]

On Saturday May 4th 1912, this advertisement appeared in the "Evening Herald" and announced the opening of the "Mountjoy" on Friday night May 17th 1912 under the patronage of the Right Honourable, Lord Mayor of Dublin, Councillor Lorcan G. Sherlock.

Also in attendance was the President and Officers of the Mountjoy Ward Branch of the United Irish League

The directors of the Dublin Sporting & Picture Club Limited promised that the complete proceeds from the opening nights performance would be given to the United Irish League; this was the Electoral Organization of the Home Rule Fund.

The building played host to many variety and vaudeville acts and many a dancing troupe, songster and comedy act made their debut there.

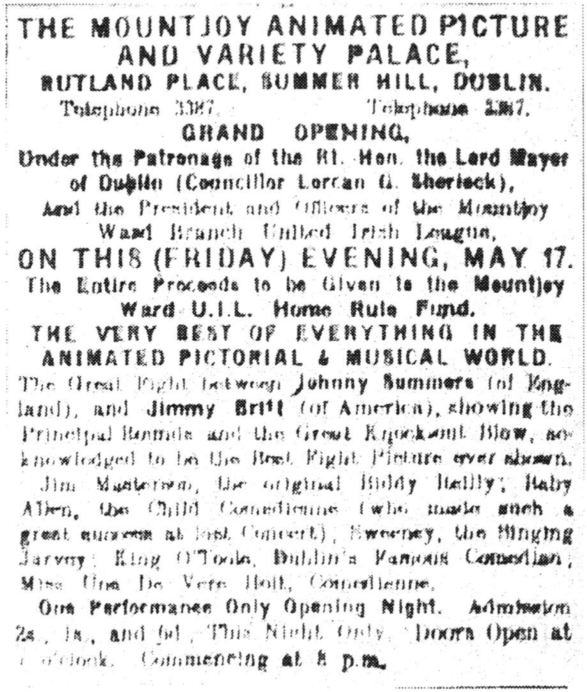

THE MOUNTJOY ANIMATED PICTURE
AND VARIETY PALACE,
RUTLAND PLACE, SUMMER HILL, DUBLIN.
Telephone 3387. Telephone 3387.
GRAND OPENING,
Under the Patronage of the Rt. Hon. the Lord Mayor of Dublin (Councillor Lorcan G. Sherlock),
And the President and Officers of the Mountjoy Ward Branch United Irish League,
ON THIS (FRIDAY) EVENING, MAY 17.
The Entire Proceeds to be Given to the Mountjoy Ward U.I.L. Home Rule Fund.
THE VERY BEST OF EVERYTHING IN THE ANIMATED PICTORIAL & MUSICAL WORLD.
The Great Fight between Johnny Summers (of England), and Jimmy Britt (of America), showing the Principal Rounds and the Great Knockout Blow, acknowledged to be the Best Fight Picture ever shown.
Jim Masterson, the original Biddy Reilly; Baby Allen, the Child Comedienne (who made such a great success at last Concert), Sweeney, the Singing Jarvey; King O'Toole, Dublin's Famous Comedian; Miss Una De Vere Holt, Comedienne.
One Performance Only Opening Night. Admission 2s., 1s., and 6d. This Night Only. Doors Open at [illegible] o'clock. Commencing at 8 p.m.

The Mountjoy would provide only the very best of everything in the animated pictorial and musical world and endeavour to obtain the best in drama and comedy films.

They would also seek out films of interest, travel, and the best of sporting films.

As proof of their enthusiasm the main feature on their opening night calendar was the film of the great fight between the British boxer Johnny Summers and his American opponent Jimmy Britt.

This film would show the principle rounds and the Great Knockout Blow and acknowledged the film as the best fight picture ever shown.

Admission prices were 2s, 1s and 6d

A few weeks later the cinema was burgled during the night of June 21/22 and despite the fact that the thief had found and taken some cash he did a fair amount of malicious damage. However, when contacted and informed of this by the D.M.P officers, Mr. Fisher the manager, said it would not interfere with the coming Monday nights big fight film.

Big fight films were big attractions in the early days of cinema life and whenever shown they always attracted large crowds of both sexes.

Live bouts were also quite common and the larger cinemas played host many times to these big fights.

On July 11th 1912, a reporter mentioned in the Bioscope magazine that the Mountjoy was closing in order to proceed with some extensive alterations, which would include raising the roof to allow for a new gallery to be built which would add considerably to the seating capacity of the cinema. It was envisaged that its new main entrance would now face onto Summerhill.

While the Bank Holiday Monday of August 5th 1912, was the target date for the grand re-opening the cinema with the "best laid plans of mice and men", never re-opened and no future plans were posted. To the best of our knowledge the venue never opened again and most likely the building was put to other uses.

~~~~~~

On a point of interest Alderman J.J. Farrell, the owner of the "Maro" had plans in hand to build a new cinema at 9/10 Summerhill in the year 1914, but failed to execute same.

~~~~~

Snippets

The granting of Music & Dance licences to some Dublin cinemas in 1910.

On Thursday March 24th 1910, the Honourable Recorder sat in Green Street courthouse and disposed of the licensing business of the Easter Quarter Sessions.

In all, there were three applications for cinema, music and dance licences.

In the case of the application for the Abercorn cinema (Picturedrome) at number 3 Harcourt Road, no objection was raised and the licence was granted.

The second application was for the premises at 52 Lower Sackville Street which the Provincial Cinematograph Theatres Limited had just secured a 21 year lease on, at a rental of £750 a year and who were spending close on £2,000 on the premises, which was about to open as a picture house. The licence was granted.

The third application was for the Coliseum cinema at 16/17 Redmond's Hill, and here an objection was raised by Mr. Ball, solicitor for the Police, claiming that the premises were small and that the proprietor was working a cinematograph instrument on the premises.

The Recorder granted the licence until July and made the observation that he would rather see the poor of the city going into cinematograph entertainments than into the nearest public house. He was, he said most anxious to see the humble amongst them enjoying themselves in such a way, and he did not like to interfere with any project that would give enjoyment to the toiler.

* * * * *

FAIR ENOUGH!
Asked in court how he felt when he came out of a pub, a man replied "Happy".

NEW CINEMA
7-9 Main Street, Blackrock.

OPENING TONIGHT
NEW CINEMA
BLACKROCK
Dublin's Newest Cinema
INTIMATE, LUXURIOUS, UNIQUE
Presenting for our Opening Programme a fantastic Double Feature ★ From Thomas Hardy's Classic Novel to the Big Screen
FAR FROM THE MADDING CROWD
(Colour)
PETER FINCH, JULIE CHRISTIE, ALAN BATES, 8.30
Plus! The World Premiere of
A JAR WITH BRENDAN BEHAN
(Colour)
7.40. Starring NIALL TOIBIN. Over 18.
NORMAL PRICES
"Would have walked away with Critic's Award at Cork Film Festival".
Ciaran Carty, S. Ind.

This advertisement appeared in the "Evening Herald" on February 1st 1973 announcing the opening of a new cinema in Blackrock.

The cinema was simply referred to as the New Cinema and no other name ever materialised.

This opening of a cinema in Dublin during a period when the cinema trade was in serious decline, appeared to be a brave move on the part of the proprietor/s. In the Sixties and Seventies, Dublin was suffering an epidemic of cinema closures.

It also brought to mind that a Judge, many years earlier had refused the owner of another cinema in the area a seven-day licence because he stated, "there were few working people in the Blackrock area and we wondered where the clientele for the new cinema would come from".

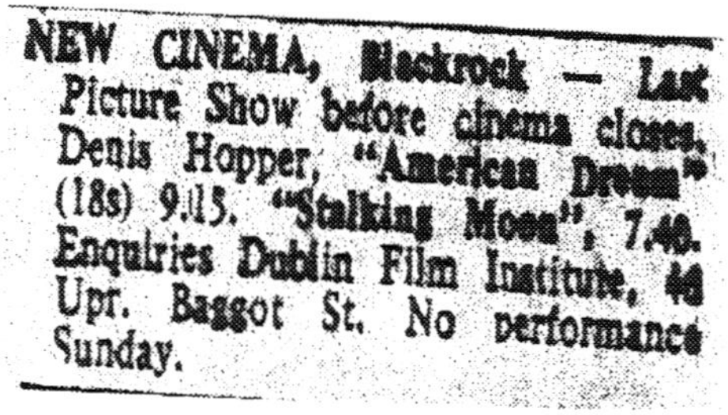

NEW CINEMA, Blackrock — Last Picture Show before cinema closes. Denis Hopper, "American Dream" (18s) 9.15. "Stalking Moon", 7.40. Enquiries Dublin Film Institute, 46 Upr. Baggot St. No performance Sunday.

As luck would have it, this advertisement appeared in an evening paper on Thursday October 11th 1973 telling of its closure a little over eight months after its grand opening.

Its last films were, "Stalking Moon" and "American Dream".

Contrary to what some people thought the "New Cinema" did not open on the site of the old Regent and Grand cinemas, rather it was a couple of buildings down the road. To be exact No's 7 & 9 Main Street

The "New Cinema", as mentioned above and" The Globe", which we are about to tell you about, would have occupied both of the properties pictured here, with Roccia Nera a restaurant at No 9 and the smaller building which is a Mexican bar & eatery at No 7.

~~~~~

The Globe Cinema

In light of the fact that the "New Cinema" had only lasted some eight months this was also a brave venture on the part of the proprietors when they opened the Globe cinema on the site of the "New Cinema" at 7 & 9 Main Street, Blackrock in the year 1974.

To the best of our knowledge it opened on May 3rd 1974 and although we found what we believe was its opening advertisement we could not re-produce it here as it was in such a faded condition. However it opened with a double feature, both of which were in Cinemascope, the first of which was "The Impossible Years", with David Niven, Lola Albright and Chad Everett, and the second was "Dirty Dingus Magee", which starred Frank Sinatra, George Kennedy and Anne Jackson.

~~~~~

On February 28th 1975, the management of the Globe began a season of five Irish made films, which were directed by Irish Directors and scheduled to run for a full week. The films and directors were as follows.

"3 Weeks in the Tower" by James Joyce

"Withdrawal", by Joe Comerford

"A Jar with Brendan Beham", by Niall Toibin

"Pobail" and "Copailology", by Louis Marcus

These films were much appreciated and attracted such good attendances that the season was extended many times to the end of March 1975. On Easter Saturday, March 29th the season concluded and the Globe closed and that was the last cinema in Main Street, Blackrock.

Just like its predecessor it only survived for a period of months, a sign of the time perhaps.

The Buildings are now all occupied by shops, restaurants, café, bars and apartments and we doubt if a cinema will ever appear again in the area of Main Street, Blackrock.

John Loder

As the ninetieth anniversary of the 1916 Rising was celebrated on Easter Sunday, April 16th 2006 just a few months before we managed to have our book published and the fact that a number of cinemas were destroyed during the Rising, we felt justified in mentioning the following.

On the Saturday afternoon of April 29th 1916, General Lowe accepted the surrender from Patrick Pearse at the top of Moore Street. While Pearse was accompanied by Nurse O'Farrell, the General was accompanied by a Junior Officer which some claimed was his son John Muir Lowe, who in later years became a very successful British and Hollywood actor.

John Lowe saw battle in Gallipoli during W.W.1 and towards the end of the war he was captured by the Germans. When the war was over he remained in Germany and ran a pickle factory as well as taking some small parts in some German movies. Later he moved back to England where he became well known in British movies. Later again he moved on to Hollywood where he was seen in Paramount's first talkie "The Doctor's Secret" (1929). When he became interested in movies in Germany he changed his name to John Loder.

John Loder married five times, and two of his wives were actresses, one of whom was Hedy Lamarr, the famous Hollywood screen Goddess.

NEW ELEC
46 Talbot Street

The "New Elec" cinema as we knew it in the fifties and sixties began life as the "Electric Theatre" and we found various openings dates for this cinema. The Bioscope magazine claimed it opened on a Sunday while someone else said it was on a Tuesday, however as ever, we focused on the newspapers and found that it had opened on Friday 19th May 1911.

Sir Charles A. Cameron, C.B. Medical Officer of Health performed the opening ceremony in the presence of the Lord Mayor of Dublin John J. Farrell, who was also Chairman of the Dublin Electric Theatres Company, and a host of distinguished personalities.

Great praise was given to Patrick Shortall, the contractor for the very excellent way that he had carried out the structural work and to George Moore the consulting architect and Mr. Storey the electrical engineer. Messrs, Farman Bros, electrical contractors and the decorator Mr. Ryan of Abbey Street were also thanked for their contribution to the excellence of the theatre.

In declaring the theatre open, Sir Charles said that he was always pleased to associate himself with any of his fellow citizens in any useful undertaking, and more especially when its object was for the intellectual and moral improvement of the people.

Following the opening speeches the audience were afterwards treated to a most enjoyable cinematograph entertainment, which included the following two short films "Stolen Pearls" and "Madge of the Mountain". The theatre had seating for some 450 and for the first week they displayed a most enjoyable show of cinematograph entertainment, which included Pathe newsreels, and scenes of some special events.

Most unfortunately this cinema was built right alongside the loop line railway tracks and many patrons claimed that they could hear a great rumbling noise as the trains passed by.

On January 26th 1911 the company was registered in the Companies Registration Office under the name of Dublin Electric Theatres Ltd (3641) and the main shareholder/director was J.J. Farrell with an address at 44-45 Talbot Street, whose name will crop up many times in connection with cinemas over the years.

The Electric Theatre was said to be Dublin's second picture house and it was generally believed in those days that the cinema business would be short lived. However Mr. Farrell had great confidence in the cinema business and as the years rolled by and he built cinema after cinema, his belief in the industry was well justified.

~~~~~

On April 25th 1912 the cinema correspondent of the Bioscope magazine writes that the Electric Theatre in Talbot Street had just re-opened having been closed for a period of time in order to have a new balcony installed in the building.
~~~~~

This new balcony, which had a capacity of 107 persons had necessitated the raising of the operating chamber and when the job was completed the entire premises was re-decorated. When all was done the correspondent described the theatre as one of the best appointed pictures houses that he had had the good fortune to see. In fact he wrote, the bills, which heralded the re-opening stated that when all the improvements were finished the hall would be one of the cosiest outside London.

~~~~~

Just to give readers an idea of what was available in cinema in the early years we would tell you that in 1916 the Manager Fred Orr ran a type of follow-up serial for a fifteen week period, showing one complete episode per week. Each episode had its own title. This serial entitled "Peg o' the Ring", was quite a crowd puller. And starred Grace Cunard as Peg. She also wrote the screen-play.
It was released in 1916 and starred Francis Ford and his younger brother John Ford who was on his way to becoming a famous director.
To the best of my knowledge these stories centred on a circus and its performers, and the titles of the fifteen episodes were as follows.
(01) The Leopards Hand, (02) A Strange Inheritance, (03) In the Lions Den, (04) The Circus Mongrels, (05) The House of Mystery, (06) Cry of the Ring, (07) The Wreck, (08) Outwitted, (09) The Leap, (10) In the hands of the Enemy, (11) The Stampede, (12) On the High Seas, (13) the Clown, (14) the Will (15) Retribution.

* * * * *

A view of the buildings, which once housed the Electric cinema, and just above the premises of Stritch & Sons Jewellers one can see a part of the brick wall of the loop-line railway bridge.
~~~~~

In 1938 some twenty-seven years after it opened the Electric Cinema was demolished to make way for a new super cinema. The "Elec" had enjoyed great popularity over the interesting years proving the prophets of doom and gloom wrong who at the time of its opening said that cinema would never last.

The new cinema was built by the Irish Kinematograph Company whose Chairman was none other than Alderman J. J. Farrell. The entire share capital of the company was Irish owner and no expense was spared in providing a theatre worthy of the district.

The new building was constructed entirely of fire-resisting materials with the main structure being mass concrete which was re-enforced by structural steel frame work. It had a floor area of 9,860 square feet, exclusive of stage, entrances and executive space available for public seating. The large stadium area was reached by a grand staircase and there were two main entrances.

The general contractors were Messrs. McNally & Co. of East Wall and the designs and supervision were supplied by P.J. Munden of South Frederick Street, ably assisted by N. Matthews, his consulting engineer.

The opening ceremony was performed by the Lord Mayor of Dublin Alderman Alfie Byrne who described the new 1,700 seater cinema as Dublin's loveliest.

Dublin's First Cinema.

Alfie Byrne, as Lord Mayor of Dublin, in his opening speech recalled his first visit to a cinema about forty years earlier. This cinema he said was an old railway carriage which sat on a piece of waste ground in South Anne Street, just off Grafton Street. The idea of the entertainment was that all the audience-(about twelve)-were being taken for a ride from Dublin to Killiney or some other County Dublin beauty spot. Pictures of the scenery on the way were shown on the screen at one end of the carriage. Realism he said was lent to the trip by the swaying of the carriage when a hill or sharp bend occurred on the route. "We have advanced a long way since those old days, he added, and the "New Electric Cinema" has travelled all the way".

(Author's note: We believe that the Lord Mayor was referring to "Hale's Cinema" in South Anne Street and having described it as Dublin's first cinema we would refer you to one of our stories entitled "We Beg To Differ".)

~~~~

On November 5th 1913 an article appeared in the columns of the "Irish Times" which informed us that the directors of the Dublin Electric Company, of Talbot Street, appealed against a valuation of £160, which had been fixed by the Commissioner of Valuation. It was stated that the Dorset Street Picture House, which was a much larger building, had been valued at £145.

The Recorder said he would not make this Picture House in Talbot Street have a larger valuation than the Picture House in Dorset Street, which was one of the finest places in the city. He reduced the valuation to £140.

~~~~

NEW ELECTRIC CINEMA, TALBOT STREET
OPENS TO-DAY

Saturday April 15th 1938

A photo from a newspaper showing one of the two new entrances.

NOW OPEN
NEW ELECTRIC CINEMA
TALBOT . STREET

This spacious modern theatre is built on the latest luxury lines, and is equipped with Western Electric Microphonic Sound Projection System; Holophane Lighting; Modern Heating and Ventilation to ensure constant flow of 30,000 cubic feet of air per minute. To seat every patron in luxury and comfort.

To-day (Easter Saturday)
EDWARD G. ROBINSON,
BETTE DAVIS
IN
"KID GALAHAD"

To-morrow (Sunday)
GEORGE BRENT,
BEVERLEY ROBERTS
IN
"GOD'S COUNTRY AND THE WOMAN"

EASTER MONDAY
(3 DAYS)
Errol Flynn, Olivia de Havilland in
"THE CHARGE OF THE LIGHT BRIGADE"

PRICES OF ADMISSION:
STADIUM (balcony)—1/-. PARTERRE—8d.
Matinee Prices Up to 5 p.m.

A CHANGE OF DAILY PROGRAMME FOR THE HOLIDAY WEEKEND. Where else, we would ask, would you get a better offer?

Kid Galahad; on Easter Saturday, Nicky Donati (Edward G Robison) a tough boxing promoter grooms Ward Guisenberry, (Wayne Morris) a bellhop, as a future champ while Fluff Philips (Bette Davis) and Turkey Morgan(Humphrey Bogart)look on. Ward falls for Marie Donati (Jane Bryan) ruthless Nicky's sister and ruthless Nicky, with his sister's happiness in mind, has a change of heart.

* * * * *

"God's Country and The Woman; On Easter Sunday", this is the story of two brothers who run a logging company in the wilds and are at loggerheads with each other in a good boy bad boy manner. Hard working Jeff Russell (Robert Barrat) tough boy makes the layabout prodigal son brother Steve Russell (George Brent)work for a living and Steve having made some serious and costly mistakes in the first week, which cost the two brothers some serious 'big bucks' makes up for his mistakes by taming the hardnosed spitfire of a woman named Jo (Beverly Roberts)who ramrods a rival company, with kisses and when they merge the companies all live happily ever after, we think.

* * * * *

The Charge of the Light Brigade; on Holiday Monday lets you ride onward and onward into the Valley of Death with the 600. With Major Geoffrey Vickers (Errol Flynn at his best) leading the 27th Lancers and Olivia de Havilland as the love of his life.

* * * * *

In true Dublin style the "New Electric Cinema" soon had its name abbreviated to the "New Elec" and at times simply the "Lec". George's in-laws were local to the "New Elec" and only had fond memories of the cinema. They also remembered a woman named Molly who used to sell apples and oranges from a pram outside the cinema. This woman had her pitch beside one of the pillars which supported the loop-line railway bridge that ran across Talbot Street at that point. She would park her pram against the pillar which had a wooden breadboard stretched across the sides of the pram and served as a table top on which she would stack her fruit. Very often a younger woman would be with her and to rest, they would sit on oranges boxes.

The years passed quietly for the "Lec" and some fantastic films made their way across its silver screen. Heroes and Heroines came and went but none were forgotten, nor were some notable baddies and many wonderful character actors. Many changes in film-making took place and great productions came our way.

On the silver screens of Dublin Picture Houses, storylines brought forth our weakest and strongest emotions, by involving us in all sorts of happenings, which at times broke our hearts and or brought about our saddest moments. They at times led us to experience feelings of great happiness and joy, made us envious and sometimes even downright jealous. We were on occasions convulsed with laughter or thrilled, mystified, enthralled, angered or excited beyond all realism. Our appetites were wheted for adventure and travel. Fantasy had no boundaries and despair no depth, while man could fly like a bird. Earthquakes and tornados were always around the corner and Moses showed us the Ten Commandments.

We witnessed murder, torture and numerous other vile acts. We experienced love, hate and debauchery in all its guises. We experienced birth with the film "Helga". We came across unbelievable kindness, acts of self-sacrifice, care and consideration. We experienced all manners of cruelty and we took part in all of the wars of mankind, and watched the wheel being invented.

We were upfront, dignified and walked tall. On occasions we hid behind the scenes and were anonymous. We lived with King's and lay with paupers. We were happy for Mickey Mouse when Walt produced Minnie and humbled when Flash Gordon led us into out space and introduced us to Emperor Ming and his daughter Princess Aura of Mongo. We scoffed when Dr. Frankenstein wanted us to believe that the transplanting of human parts was possible. We never hit a man when he was down on the ground, yet, we shot baddies in the back. Movie stories came and went and some paid more than one visit, however we enjoyed them all, whether they were good, bad or out and out trash and 'Trevor', Dublin's very own film critic kept us all a pace with Hollywood happenings.

Talking pictures became the norm and colouring techniques were for ever changing and improving. Formats changed over the years from simple black and white screens to wide-screen, we cowered in our seats when watching 3D films. We watched in wonder when Dorothy left her drab black and white home and entered "Oz", where we experienced Technicolour for the first time. We enjoyed the "Wonderful World of the Brothers Grimm" in Todd A-O and we marvelled when we saw the "Robe" in Cinemascope and listened to it in Stereophonic sound.

But nothing prepared us for the magnificence of Cinerama when it came to the "New Elec".

In the mid fifties Cinerama came to London and excited tales of the amazing scenes on film soon reached Ireland. However in order to show these Cinerama films special equipment was required including large wall to wall and floor to ceiling screens to say nothing about special projecting equipment. It also required closure of the cinema for several weeks in order to install all the necessary equipment together with some considerable investment. Fortunately for Dublin cinemagoers the owners of Dublin's Electric Cinema in Talbot Street decided to make this huge investment and in 1963 Cinerama came to Dublin.

~~~~~

Fortunately, The Irish Kinematograph Company (1920), which was chaired and managed by Alderman J. J. Farrell was quite a large investment company and had no difficulty in raising the capital necessary for converting the "Lec" into a Cinerama cinema.

Though the company and its cinemas were always associated with Alderman Farrell he was not the only director/investor in the Irish Kinematograph Company. This company which had a large number of cinemas within its portfolio also had a considerable number of shareholders including many other members of the Farrell family and other personalities from the world of Dublin cinema such as William Kay, who had once owned the Grand Cinema on Sackville Street, and had been associated with the founding of the Stella Picture Palace in Rathmines.
~~~~~

William Kay had also been connected with the Rotunda cinema and was a leasee of the Rathmines Town Hall at times. He and other members of his family who were also shareholders of company were also involved in the hotel business. Kevin Anderson and Leo Ward were also shareholders as were Frederick Croskerry (solicitor) and William Callow (Motor Engineer) of the Sundrive Cinema group. Also associated by way of shares etc were Cameo Cinemas Ltd and Capitol Provincial Cinemas Ltd.

Some of the cinemas within the portfolio of the Irish Kinematograph Company were, "The Mary Street Picture House", "The Tivoli" Burgh Quay, the "Grand Central" and the "Pillar" in Sackville Street.

Properties purchased for the expansion of the original "Electric Cinema" at 46 Talbot Street were No's 42-43-44-45.

~~~~~

1963 CINERAMA COMES TO DUBLIN.
and puts you in the picture claims an advertisement in the "Evening Press".

This second Advertisement announcing the opening of Cinerama in Ireland appeared in the "Evening Press", of Easter Monday April 15th 1963.
~~~~~

A NEW ERA IN IRISH ENTERTAINMENT

On Sunday evening, April 14, when the doors of the new DUBLIN CINERAMA Theatre in TALBOT STREET are opened, one of Ireland's finest theatres will be revealed.

From the ultra modern plush seats to the thick carpeting, from the utmost in beauty and comfort to the most advanced designs in the screen, sound and projection equipment, the new DUBLIN CINERAMA Theatre has no peer. No expense has been spared to make this opening an exciting and memorable experience in theatre going.

It is only fitting that the beautiful new DUBLIN CINERAMA Theatre should have as its first attraction the wonder that revolutionized the entertainment world — "*THIS IS CINERAMA.*" Here is an unique process, so persuasive that it actually puts YOU into the picture! When the lights dim and the curtains open—and open—and open, you are suddenly part of an entertainment experience of a lifetime! You will find yourself swept right into the picture, surrounded by sight and sound. Not one, but three projectors perform their breathtaking magic—and through twelve speakers stereophonic sound surrounds you from all sides of the theatre . . . this is a whole new world opening up and engulfing you.

THE ONLY SHOWING OF "*THIS IS CINERAMA*" IN THE WE[...] OF IRELAND WILL BE AT [...] NEW DUBLIN CINERA[...] THEATRE.

The proprietors of the DU[...] CINERAMA Theatre said:

"We want to express our app[...]tion to everyone who has wo[...] tirelessly toward the compl[...] this project. They have truly [...]plished miracles in an astoun[...] short time. And we want to [...] our neighbours — as well as friendly competitors — for thei[...] wishes and we invite one and [...] share an experience that is [...] new — the enchantment of th[...] DUBLIN CINERAMA Thea[...] the wonder of '*TH[...] CINERAMA.*'"

THIS IS CINERAMA

RESERVED SEATS NOW ON SALE

MATINEES:
WEDNESDAY, SATURDAY and SUNDAY at 3.30 p.m.
PARTY RATES: For parties of twenty-five and over for all Monday to Friday performances 10/6 Stalls for 7/6

PERFORMANCES AND PRICES

EVENINGS: Sunday to Friday 8.30
SATURDAYS and HOLIDAYS
Three separate performances 3.30, 6.0 & 8.30
MATINEES:
Wednesdays, Saturdays, Sundays 3.30
Seats will not be sold for the current performance 15 minutes after the advertised starting time

STALLS 10/6, 4/6
CIRCLE 10/6

Every Seat Bookable
ADVANCE BOOKING
OFFICE OPEN WEEKDAYS 10 a.m. to [...]
It is regretted that Telephone Bookings cannot be [...]

This advertisement appeared in the "Evening Press" on Easter Saturday April 13th 1963 and announced the opening of Ireland's first ever "Cinerama" Picture House.

By now you will have noticed that both of these advertisements advised different opening dates.

This is not the first time that we came across a situation such as this and we would tell you that in the very early days of our research we found a half-page advertisement in an evening newspaper which had a press write-up on the opening of a cinema that very same evening and having noted its details we began to move on, but as we were about to close the page we noticed quite a large block advert down at the right hand corner of the page which informed the public that the cinema in question would open on the following day.

No explanation was available for the advertising of two opening dates and we could only assume that the first opening was a private affair and admission was possibly by invitation only or otherwise the opening may have coincided with a film premier and the second opening was for the general public.

~~~~~

There were no large write-ups or reviews following the arrival of Cinerama in the next days newspapers, or at least none that we could find, except for a mention in Tom Hennigan's column in the "Evening Herald", on Monday April 15th in which he told us of his experience in the London Casino when he had viewed Cinerama there some eight years earlier. "We heard a long drawn out shriek from every throat in the auditorium", he said "and last night we heard something like that shriek again when Lowell Thomas thundered "This is Cinerama!" and the red curtains drew back from that oh-so-wide screen and we all went up the roller coaster on Coney Island together.

~~~~~

However, as often is the case when we were researching another subject, we came across this advert in the "Evening Herald" on April 4th which advised us that a Gala Irish Premier of "This is Cinerama", was planned for Easter Sunday, April 15th and that the proceeds of this event was for the benefit of the Variety Club of Ireland and St. Anthony's Rehabilitation Centre.

Now at least we had an explanation as to why two opening nights were advertised.

The film "This is Cinerama" was more of a travelogue that a film in the ordinary meaning of the world. Those films were to come later in the Shape of "How the West was Won", "It's a Mad, mad World", Grand Prix", "2001 Space Odyssey" and many more.

"This Is Cinerama" was a box office success and gave us 'never seen before' views of Niagara Falls from a helicopter, a tour of the Venice canals in a Gondola, traditional dancing in a Spanish village, Viennese Waltz's sung by the Vienna Boys Choir, Florida's Cypress gardens and a tour of America by air.

* * * * *

"This is Cinerama" finished on Saturday June 15th after a highly successful nine week run and the "Seven Wonders of the World", began a long run on Sunday, June 16th 1963.

"The Seven Wonders of the World" takes the viewers on fantastic two hour journey across five continents and only the most blasé amongst us could have left the cinema unimpressed. The trip on a runaway train in the Himalayas left many viewers dizzy. This film was made in 1954 and the aerial sequences were breathtakingly beautiful. We dropped off in Japan and watched traditionally costumed Japanese girls perform native dances and in the Belgian Congo, the Watusi Tribe, did a ceremonial dance. As he did in "This is Cinerama", Lowell Thomas narrated the trip.

* * * * *

During the run of the film, the proprietors held a Miss Cinerama contest, which was sponsored by the "Evening Herald" and the final heat took place on Saturday, July 27th 1963.

3rd Place was taken by Aisling Coogan (21) of Tudor Hall, The Hill, Monsktown.

2nd Place went to Josephine Calnan (20) of 121 Walkinstown Drive.

The Winner being 20 year old Iris Mason of 26 Portland Row, North Strand, was a buyer for a wholesale jewellery firm and a part-time model.

The prize was an extended trip to London for two

Adjudicating that night was Pat Boome and the film producer Andrew Stone and his wife Virginia.

Cinerama was said to have had a 14-year reign and in that time it was said to have been on display in 200 cinemas across the world.

Other widescreen formats, to name but a few were Cinemascope-Vista Vision, Technirama, Superscope, Superama, Panavison and Todd A-O.

Some Colour Cinematography were, Cinecolour, Technicolour, Pathe Colour Kodachrome, Kinemacolour, and gaurmont.
(N.B. We have spelt colour in the English fashion rather than the American Color)

~~~~~

On Friday March 10th 1972, the Capitol Cinema in Princess Street closed down as did the Cinerama in Talbot Street and on Saturday March 11th the Capitol cinema re-located its business to the Cinerama building in Talbot Street.

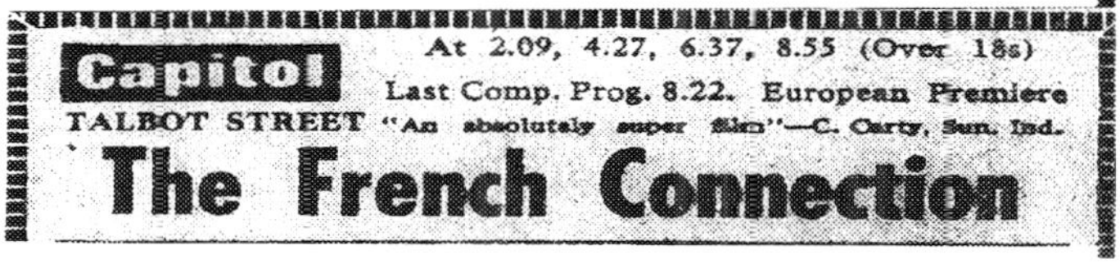

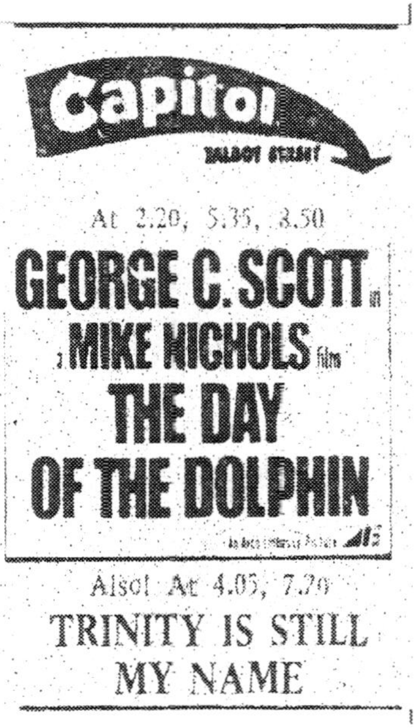

Business however mustn't have been too good as it closed down completely on Wednesday, August 28th 1974 and on the following day Thursday 29th this simple advert appeared in the evening papers.

The building remained vacant for quite a while and circa 1977 it became a music venue and later again a carpet showrooms.
~~~~~

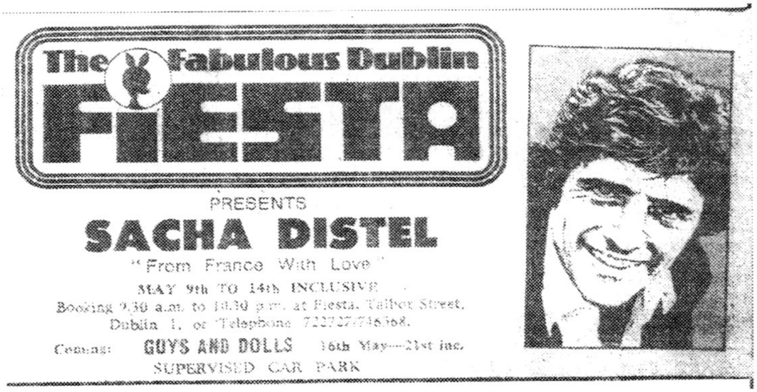

Sometime after its closure the building was taken over by a group that turned it into a music club called the "Fiesta Club" and this advertisement which appeared in the "Evening Herald" on May 14th 1977 was one of many.

~~~~~

3/- 2/6 or 1s were the type of figures used in the display of prices in the days of Pounds-Shillings and Pence or if you like L.S.D, and our printer opined that for the sake of our younger readers and or Foreign Nationals that it would be better to price all in LSD rather than the old figures as mentioned above i.e £1-3s-2d rather than 23/2d, but we declined, simply because our book was written with old Dubliners in mind and as long as they understand our writings nothing else matters. However for the benefit of those that would not know we display the prices in all their formats.

A farthing, ¼ d.
A halfpenny, ½ d.
One Penny, 1d.
One Shilling, 1s, 1/- or 1s.od.
One pound, £1. 20/- or £1.0s.0d.

~~~~~

Guinea, 21/- or £1.1s.0d.
£1. Quid, Greenback, Sovereign, 20/- 20s £1.0s.0d.
10 Shillings, 10/-, Tenner, Ten Bob, ½ note, ½ Sovereign, 10s.
Five Shilling Piece, Crown, Dollar, 5s piece, 5/-.
½ Crown, ½ Dollar, 2s.6d, 2/6d two Shillings and sixpence.
Two Shilling piece, Florin, 2/-, 2s, Two Bob.
One Shilling piece, 1/-, 1s A bob.
Sixpence, a Tanner, 6d.
A Threepenny piece, Threepence, a threepennybit, thrupence, Thrupenny piece, 3d.
One Penny Piece, Penny, Wing, 1d.
Halfpenny piece, ½ d, Make, Tosser.
Farthing, ¼ d.

£1= 2 ten shilling notes, 4 crowns, 8 ½ crowns 10 two shilling pieces, 20 shillings, pieces, 40 sixpenny pieces, 80 threepenny pieces, 240 pennies, 480 halfpenny pieces, and 960 farthings.

It was a belief in those days that a vendor had a legal right to refuse an unreasonable amount of coinage from a purchaser in exchange for goods and with 960 farthings to the pound it was easy to understand why.

NO SMOKING!

No butts . . . it's the cinema without smoke

DUBLIN'S first non-smoking cinema is doing capacity business as film goers are forced to stub out their bad habits.

After a last puff in the lobby, the customers for Oscar-winning Wall Street at the Ambassador enter a smoke free zone.

And the cinema owners predict that more cinemas will follow suit.

While some of the audience may be dying for a fag, the on-screen action in Wall Street features many smoke filled rooms.

"The trend used to be for the audience to light up when the actors started," said Ambassador spokesman Paul Ward.

The same proprietors own the Savoy, where pipes and cigars have already been banned.

"A total smoking ban will come in sooner or

AMBASSADOR
No smoking

later, probably by law," predicted Mr. Ward.

"We decided to make it sooner. After all, they've done the same on the buses."

Cinema staff have had no complaints from smokers.

This advertisement appeared in the "Evening Herald" on Thursday June 2nd 1988 and there is no doubt but that Mr. Ward's prediction was indeed shrewd, however we have to differ with him in claiming that the Ambassador was the first cinema to ban smoking, as in the story of the Curson Cinema we tell of Dublin's first cinema to impose a smoke free ban. When the Curson cinema opened in 1968 it had two screens and it dedicated one of them as a smoke free cinema.

OLYMPIA
Dame Street

According to what we have read and heard about the site on which the "Olympia Theatre" now stands it would appear that it was originally a military compound which in the early part of the 18th century housed a troop of horse soldiers and this area was simply known as the "Court". Also situated in this "Court", was a tavern that was frequented by a lot of those soldiers.

Many years later when the Military moved out, the "Court", was purchased by a bookseller named Crampton who set up his home and business there. Initially he let out the tavern to a variety of managers, none of whom made much of a success of it, until one Henry Connell came along and turned the tavern into a music hall.

In 1855 Henry Connell decided to expand his music hall and we found that on Monday, December 10th 1855, a rather large notice in the "Freeman's Journal" informed us that Henry Connell on that date begged to inform his numerous Patrons that on that Monday evening he was opening his Monster Saloon which was capable of holding some 2,000 persons.

Due regard he claimed, had been paid to the comforts of those Gentlemen who had so liberally patronised his establishment in the past and that two spacious rooms had been erected for the accommodation of Gentlemen who wished to partake of choice steaks, kidney's, oysters etc, while at the same time they would have a commanding and uninterrupted view of the entertainment in the saloon of this most popular and fashionable resort. At the bottom of this notice, Henry obviously quite confident of good attendances, advertised for twenty Waiters for his establishment.

This new music hall, with its entrance from "Crampton Court", was considered to be one of Dublin's first variety theatres and it was run along the lines of cheap music halls of the time which allowed excessive drinking and locker-room behaviour amongst its clients, with plenty of help and encouragement from the chorus girls who mingled at will with the audience who were predominantly male.

The entrance arch on the left, which leads into Crampton Court as it is in 2006. The main entrance as we know it, didn't exist until 1897.

Some years later, Henny Connell died and his wife took over the running of the business, which soon became known as the "Widow Connell's". However business slackened off and in 1878 the premises closed.

~~~~~

One year later a Mr. Dan Lowrey from Roscrea came to Dublin and bought the Crampton Court site and buildings and on December 22 1879 he opened his new "Star of Erin" music hall to the Dublin public.

STAR OF ERIN MUSIC HALL
CRAMPTON COURT
DAME STREET.

Sole Proprietor — Mr. Dan Lowrey

The above hall will open on this (Monday) Evening
With a Complete and Powerful Company
Of
Vocal and Instrumental Artistes
Prices of Admission - Body of Hall, 6d: Side Balcony and Promenade 1s.
Reserved seats - 1s. 6d

Dan was about 46 years of age at the time and well experienced in the management of places of entertainment, having once owned a tavern in Liverpool and just recently he had opened his "Alhambra" music hall in Belfast. This new enterprise was a men only venue and provided music only entertainment. A cover charge kept the riff-raff out and the hall gained quite a respectable reputation.

The Theatre critic in the "Freeman's Journal", gave this new theatre a rave review and reported, that a massive crowd besieged the doors for almost an hour before the eight o'clock opening time. When the doors opened the crowd filled the hall in every part and there was not standing room in any part of the building.

He described the hall as being the largest and finest music hall in Ireland and that it extended in length from Crampton Court to Sycamore Street and that it was of considerable width. There were, he said, three entrances from Crampton Court leading directly to a passage to the pit, bar and stairs to the promenade and gallery areas. The stage is situated at the Sycamore Street end of the building from where there is another entrance leading into the main hall, as is the stage door proper. Next to the stage are a supply of dressing rooms and all necessary accommodation for the entertainers. The long and wide hall also has three galleries on three sides and there is seating for 1,500.

The programme was a strong and well-chosen one, with some of the best talent on the music hall circuit being engaged.
~~~~~

We believe that the two arched doorways on the right, now blocked-up, might well have represented two of the main entrance doors to the "Star of Erin", in 1879. (Photograph taken 2006).

Gone were the bawdy and rakish behaviour of cheap low life music halls that was once the mainstay of the Monster Music hall and instead there were now respectable singers, instrumentalists, variety and comic acts.

In 1881, Dan now in his fifty eighth year and failing in health, found business a little too stressful and recalling his son Daniel from Liverpool where he had been managing two of the families music hall taverns in that city, he gave control of the theatre to him. With the reins now firmly in his hands, Daniel junior's first move was to close the theatre in June of that year for some changes, renovations and a chance to map out its future.

The new lay-out and face-lift took nearly three months to complete and on August 29th 1881 Daniel held a Grand Re-opening of the theatre which was now renamed;

DAN LOWREY'S MUSIC HALL.

The newly refurbished theatre was an instant success and with well planned programmes full of variety the future of the theatre was assured and as the years passed, Daniel, now shortened to Dan, soon became as well known in Dublin as his father.

DAN LOWREY'S
NEW STAR PALACE OF VARIETIES.
THIS IS THE NIGHT.
BRILLIANT RE-OPENING,
GRAND ARRAY OF STAR ARTISTES.
TO-NIGHT. TO-NIGHT.
THE GREAT PHANTOS,
In their wonderful "Gobbling Gambols."
Marguerette Fish and Charles Warren.
KARA,
The Most Astonishing Juggler in the World
MISS CORA CARDIGAN, Lady Flautist.
The Olympian Quartette of Real Coloured Glee Minstrels.
SEEBOLD and DENT.
The Brown-Kelly Combination.
Miss Jenny Venoi | Miss Annie Dunbar
Miss Flo' Morton | Mr John Williams
MONDAY NEXT, the World-Renowned
MISS KATE SANTLY.
Miss Santly does not appear till Monday.
New Doors of Admission and Prices.
Private Boxes........12s 6d to £1 1s 0d Each
Box Seats.......................... 3s 0d Each
Reserved Chairs Orchestra Stalls, 2s 6d Each
Orchestra Stalls.................. 1s 6d Each
Entrance by Sycamore street only to all above parts.
Stalls (Entrance New Door, Crampton court)....................... 1s 0d Each
Promenade and Gallery (Usual Entrance), 6d and 4d
Seats can now be booked.

Many years later in 1889, Dan once again changed the name of the theatre to Dan Lowrey's "Palace of Varieties", just months before his father died in July of 1890.

In 1892 the theatre again closed and underwent refurbishment and on Saturday, August 20th it re-opened as Dan Lowrey's "New Star Palace of Varieties", with seating for some 1,600.

~~~~~

Having heard about the Lumiere brother's showing motion pictures in Paris in1895, Dan made approaches and invited the Lumiere Brother's to come to Dublin and introduce their Cinematograph on the stage of the Star Palace of Varieties.
~~~~~

On Monday April 20th 1896, Dan Lowrey presented the Lumiere Brother's and their "Cinematographe invention", to a packed house in his "Star Theatre of Varieties" where it proved to be a dismal failure.

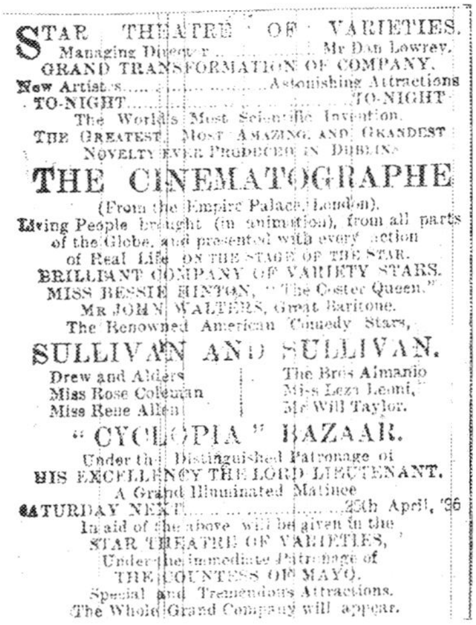

STAR THEATRE OF VARIETIES.
Managing Director .... Mr Dan Lowrey.
GRAND TRANSFORMATION OF COMPANY.
New Artistes........ Astonishing Attractions
TO-NIGHT........ TO-NIGHT
The World's Most Scientific Invention.
THE GREATEST, MOST AMAZING, AND GRANDEST
NOVELTY EVER PRODUCED IN DUBLIN.
THE CINEMATOGRAPHE
(From the Empire Palace, London).
Living People brought (in animation), from all parts
of the Globe, and presented with every action
of Real Life ON THE STAGE OF THE STAR.
BRILLIANT COMPANY OF VARIETY STARS.
MISS BESSIE HINTON, "The Coster Queen."
MR JOHN WALTERS, Great Baritone.
The Renowned American Comedy Stars,
SULLIVAN AND SULLIVAN.
Drew and Alders | The Bros Almanio
Miss Rose Coleman | Miss Leza Leoni,
Miss Rene Allen | Mr Will Taylor.
"CYCLOPIA" BAZAAR.
Under the Distinguished Patronage of
HIS EXCELLENCY THE LORD LIEUTENANT.
A Grand Illuminated Matinee
SATURDAY NEXT........ 25th April, '96
In aid of the above will be given in the
STAR THEATRE OF VARIETIES,
Under the immediate Patronage of
THE COUNTESS OF MAYO.
Special and Tremendous Attractions.
The Whole Grand Company will appear.

N.B. In this and future advertisements the word Palace was dropped from the theatre's name.

The Cinematographe, which was billed as the Greatest, Most Sensational and Grandest Novelty ever produced in Ireland, came direct from the "Empire Palace" London at a cost of £200 per week to Dan Lowrey and his board of directors.

It would, it was claimed, show Living persons from all parts of the Globe presented in real life action on the stage of the Star.

However all it did produce were flashes of light and a brief image of one or two people and then the machine broke down!

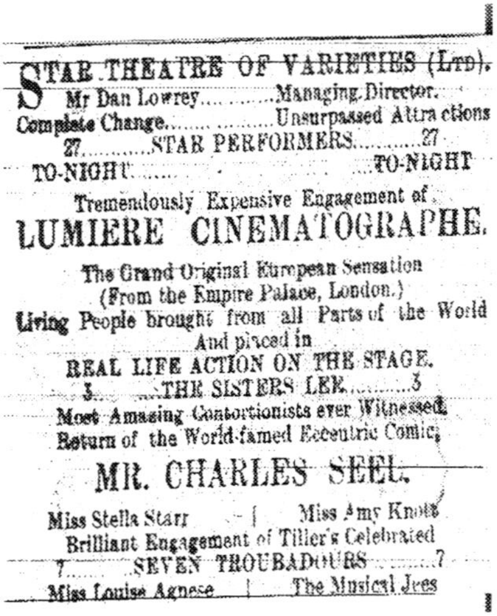

STAR THEATRE OF VARIETIES (LTD).
Mr Dan Lowrey........ Managing Director.
Complete Change........ Unsurpassed Attractions
27........ STAR PERFORMERS........ 27
TO-NIGHT........ TO-NIGHT
Tremendously Expensive Engagement of
LUMIERE CINEMATOGRAPHE.
The Grand Original European Sensation
(From the Empire Palace, London.)
Living People brought from all Parts of the World
And placed in
REAL LIFE ACTION ON THE STAGE.
3........ THE SISTERS LEE........ 3
Most Amazing Contortionists ever Witnessed.
Return of the World-famed Eccentric Comic,
MR. CHARLES SEEL.
Miss Stella Starr | Miss Amy Knotts
Brilliant Engagement of Tiller's Celebrated
7........ SEVEN TROUBADOURS........ 7
Miss Louise Agnese | The Musical Jees

However nothing daunted Dan. He held discussions with the Lumiere brothers and a further booking of the Cinematographe was made for later that year, and on November 2nd 1896 the Cinematographe returned to the stage of the "Star Theatre of Varieties" and on this, its second airing in Dublin, it proved to be a resounding success.

The theatre correspondent for the "Freeman's Journal" heaped great praise on the management of the "Star Theatre of Varieties", on their enterprise in engaging such a novel attraction as the Exhibition of the original "Cinematographe", which was displayed under the direction of Mons. Trewey from the "Empire Theatre" in London.

This very wonderful instrument, he wrote, produces with the most absolute correctness in every minute detail animated representations of scenes and incidents which are witnessed in every day life. To those who will witness this exhibition for the first time in the Star Theatre of Varieties the effect will be quite startling.

The figures, or if you like, images, were thrown on a screen which was erected on the stage in front of the audience and in one scene a busy railway station was depicted where a train was seen to arrive in the station and when it stopped passengers were seen to alight from the carriages bearing their luggage. Scenes of greetings with friends and family members were all presented perfectly true to life and the scene was an exact reproduction of life's bustle and tumult, which is everyday to be witnessed at the great railway depots of the world.

The representation of a cavalry charge, in which every motion of the galloping horses in the advancing front line was so terrifying real in its exactness that it caused more than one otherwise brave patron to cower in his/her seat.

Another scene which was wonderfully true to life was that of a group of people sea bathing and here one witnessed bathers jumping into the water and saw the spray caused by the plunge rise into the air and descend again in fleecy showers upon the surface.

The exhibition he said was altogether the finest of its kind ever seen in Dublin and the house was crowded to overflowing on its opening night.

Seven thousand people were said to have attended the theatre in the first week of the exhibition which proved beyond doubt that the "Cinematographe", was a great source of attraction.

* * * * *

The stage and private boxes, as seen from the balcony.

A view of the stage door and other entrances in Sycamore Street, which also provides a visual idea of just how extensive the premises were.

EMPIRE PALACE THEATRE,

DAME STREET .... DUBLIN.
PROPRIETORS.....STAR THEATRE OF VARIETIES, LIMITED.
GENERAL MANAGER .... MR. FRANK ALLEN.
ACTING MANAGER .... MR. A. S. FIGGIS.

BRILLIANT OPENING
TO-NIGHT . . TO-NIGHT

A PALACE OF BEAUTY
Unsurpassed in the Three Kingdoms for SPLENDOUR, REFINEMENT, COMFORT, AND SAFETY

A CREDIT TO DUBLIN.

GRAND OPENING COMPANY,
TO-NIGHT . . . TO-NIGHT

Special and Important Engagement of the
LUMIERE TRIOGRAPH,
The Perfection of the Cinematograph.
Life Size | New Pictures | Startling Sensations
And Local Views of Dublin.

WERNER AND RIEDER,
Continental Duettists and Swiss Warblers
(Direct from the Empire Theatre, London).

MISS FLORENCE ESDALE,
Charming Australian Ballad Vocalist
(Direct from the Tivoli Theatre, London).

The World-famed London Comedian,
MR. CHARLES COBORN,
In all his latest great successes.

See the Celebrated Comic Juggler,
GRIFF
(From the Palace Theatre, London.

VIRTO,
The Man of Many Instruments.

MORRIS AND MORRIS,
The Mirth-Provoking Acrobatic Grotesques.

8.........THE ELDORADOS.........8
(From Principal London Halls),
Clever Lady Vocalists and Terpsichorean Marvels.

CELESTE,
Artistic and Sensational Wire Performer.

MR LESTER KING (Popular Baritone). | DULCIE LAING, (Phenomenal Sand Dancer).

5......FRANTZ FAMILY......5
Famous Lady and Gentlemen Acrobats,
Performing in Full Evening Costume.

EMPIRE GRAND ORCHESTRA,
25.......Selected Instrumentalists.......25
Under the Direction of Mr Harry Walker.

THE BOOKING OFFICE,
12 DAME STREET (LEFT-HAND ENTRANCE),
Is Open Daily from 11 a.m. until 4 p.m.

PRICES OF ADMISSION.

ENTRANCE IN DAME STREET.

Private Boxes (to hold Four)		£1 1 0
Orchestra Stalls	(Reserved)	5 0
Grand Circle	(Reserved)	2 6
Pit Stalls		1 6

ENTRANCE IN CRAMPTON COURT.

Balcony	1 0

ENTRANCE IN SYCAMORE STREET.

Gallery	6d

NOTICE
THE DIRECTORS HAVE DECIDED TO ABOLISH THE EARLY DOORS.

Doors Open at 7 ......Performance at 7.30 o'clock.
NO PASS-OUT CHECKS.

GRAND MATINEE EACH SATURDAY,
Doors Open 1.30 Performance at 2 o'clock.
For the Convenience of Ladies and their Families
SMOKING WILL NOT BE PERMITTED
In the Auditorium during Afternoon Performances.

With great expectations of excitement and awe, we would once more astound you in true musical hall grand mastery, with the earth shattering news which we unequivocally and unambiguously impart to your goodselves with unabashed and shameless showbusiness ingenuity that once more this theatre is about to close and re-open under a new name.

"Au-Revoir", my Friends said Dan Lowrey on that last night of the "Star Theatre of Varieties", but not "Good-Bye".

STAR THEATRE OF VARIETIES (LTD),

FAREWELL NIGHT
OF THE GOOD OLD "STAR" THEATRE
PRIOR TO CLOSING FOR COMPLETE RE-BUILDING.

TO-DAY (AT 2.30) TO-DAY
LAST GRAND ILLUMINATED MATINEE.
Dazzling Attractions ...... Tremendous Company
Last Night of the Whole Company.

MR. WALTER MUNROE.
ELLIOTT TROUPE OF COSTER ACROBATS.
The 3 Castles. | St John and Dwight.
Miss Lily Marney | Mr Jesse Burton.
BONNIE KATE KARVEY,
HOWLETT'S ROYAL MARIONETTES,
And JOLY'S GRAND CINEMATOGRAPHE.

Mr Dan Lowrey says to All Old Friends,
"AU-REVOIR,"
BUT NOT
"GOOD-BYE."

On Saturday night, February 27th 1897, the last night of the old "Star Theatre", the occasion drew the largest number of people that ever assembled within its old walls and a large crowd was refused admission, for want of space.

At nine o'clock that night in response to numerous and repeated calls, Dan Lowrey came out before the curtain, where he received a standing ovation and in a thank you speech he said,:

"Ladies and Gentlemen: no doubt you are aware that this is the last occasion on which we will meet together in the old Star Theatre, and it is a source of great gratification to me to see such a splendid house. I take it as an earnest vindication of the efforts, which I have put forth during the past eighteen years, in catering for your amusement and raising the variety stage to the established position which it now holds in the city of Dublin.

I can only hope that we will all be alive and well, and that I may have the pleasure of seeing you all here on the re-opening of the new Star Palace of Varieties". Amidst tremendous cheering he also thanked the Press and the entire staff.

When Mr. Lowrey had concluded his speech the curtain was raised, and the entire company were found on the stage. In the centre was a massive Louis X1V clock, which was fully two feet high, a magnificent gift which the entire company had subscribed towards and this was presented to Mr. Lowrey.

~~~~

The theatre, now closed, underwent a massive reconstruction and major changes were made. The stage was moved from the Sycamore Street end to the Dame Street side and a new entrance was constructed in Dame Street with large overhead signs proclaiming its new name.

EMPIRE PALACE THEATRE

On Monday, November 15th 1897, the "Empire Palace Theatre", opened to a tremendous crowd of people seeking admission to the theatre, who had gathered outside the premises long before the advertised opening hour of 7pm.

In conjunction with the Police Authorities, the "Empire" management introduced a new queuing system to Dublin for the first time, This system, claimed the directors had been a great success in London and other centres and should work well in Dublin.

The Dublin public readily recognised that this new system was to their benefit and quickly adapted to this well organised scheme which gained them admission a lot quicker than otherwise might have been the case and all without the usual confusion associated with theatre going where crowds would engage in a free for all surge to the box office.

The following day Tuesday, November 16th, a correspondent from the Freeman's Journal reported on this phenomenal new system to Dublin, in which he wrote it almost worked!

This new experiment in the queue system at theatres, which was tried on Monday night at the opening of the new "Empire Palace Theatre" in Dame Street was a distinct success as far as the better parts of the house were concerned, however the same could not be said for the Sycamore Street entrance to the gallery.
~~~~

The queue for the Dame Street entrance which led to the Private Boxes, Orchestra Stalls, Grand Circle and Pit Stalls stretched along Dame Street almost as far as "Lipton's" and the would be patrons took to this new system quite naturally and queued two abreast. While some read their evening newspapers, others smoked their pipes or cigarettes and one man in particular was seen to devour a large ham sandwich.

It was noted however, wrote the reporter, that the Dame Street queue though orderly in fashion did seriously interfere with the sidewalk traffic, and he put forward the suggestion that it might be wiser to adopt the London system and put the queue not on the footpath, but on the street immediately beside it. A good deal of trouble and inconvenience would thus be avoided.

The queue for the Crampton Court entrance, which entrance led to the balcony area of the house, was also well behaved and extended right up to the end of that thoroughfare and they too entered the theatre without confusion when the doors opened at seven o'clock. Here credit must be given to the Police authorities for their help in marshalling the theatregoers in a two-abreast queue as they arrived on the scene.

On the other hand, the experiment was distinctly not a success in Sycamore Street where the queue was all right up until about a quarter to seven. The double row of people along the theatre side of this very narrow thoroughfare remained perfectly quiet except for the occasional cheer for a policeman or a loud guffaw at some joker in the crowd of people who stood by on the other side of the street, simply to watch the result of this new queuing experiment.

As the time drew near for the opening of the entrance door, however, all became confusion. There were only ten constables and one inspector in attendance in this street and such a force was quite insufficient to cope with the surging mass of humanity which at five minutes to seven wanted to get into the theatre. The result being that the "queue", which at first had been two deep, became by degrees in some places four deep, in other sections five, six and seven deep and finally an undirected and uncontrolled crowd, with each man fighting for the best place possible. The result was most certainly not a "queue;" it was chaos.

Fortunately all eventually gained entry and order ensued and with two perfectly ordered queues out of three, the experiment was deemed a success. Valuable lessons were learned that night and improvements were made as time passed on.

Charles Coburn topped the bill on the opening night and no doubt but that in the course of the evening's entertainment he would give a fine rendition of his two hit songs "Two Lovely Black Eyes", and "The Man Who Broke the Bank at Monte Carlo", which was a most famous music hall song of days gone by.

Also showing was the special engagement of the "Lumiere Triograph", the perfection of the Cinematograph.

Featuring Life Size New Pictures and Startling Sensations.

~~~~~
~~~~~

A Star of Erin programme with, we would imagine, a picture of Dan Lowrey the 1st.
(Courtesy of the Gilbert Library and the Dublin City Archives)

Grand Matinee Each Saturday.

Special matinee performances were on offer on Saturday afternoons for the convenience of Ladies and their Families who wished to see the show. For their benefit, smoking would not be permitted in the auditorium area during that time.

Doors would open at 1.30 pm and the show would begin at 2 o'clock.

Dan Lowrey died August 16th 1898.

Empire Souvenir Programme
(Courtesy Gilbert and Dublin City Archives).

The theatre survived Dan Lowrey Junior as it had done his Father and it would appear that the Findlater family who had been major shareholders in the company for many a year now took complete control of the theatre.

However, in 1915 an article appeared in the "Evening Mail" on February 15th which informed its readers that the "Empire Theatre", which it would seem had been in receivership was now being leased to a Mr. Barney Armstrong for a period of two and a half years from February 22nd 1915.

The Receiver, according to the said article, had interviewed many would-be buyers both from London and Ireland and on the 5th of February at a largely attended meeting of the Debenture holders, two offers were considered, one which was made by a Mr. George Abel and the other by Mr. Bernard Armstrong.

After some discussion a committee was appointed to go into details, and the Debentures agreed to abide by any decision the committee might arrive at. The Committee met and interviewed the two gentlemen, with the result that they unanimously agreed, subject to the sanction of the court, to accept the proposal of Mr. Bernard Armstrong and council asked that the court should sanction the arrangement. Mr. Justice Barton then made an order accepting Mr. Armstrong's proposal.

The now most popular Dame Street theatre had a new owner and on Monday, March 1st 1915, having been closed for a week while it underwent re-decoration the theatre re-opened with an all star company under the management of Mr. Barney Armstrong.

Mr. Armstrong was an Irishman and was quite well known in the city. During its closure Barney had converted the ground floor area to the parterre system and all seats were available at one price, this also done away with the old Pit area. The circle was reduced in price from 1/- to 9d thereby ensuring its popularity. He planned to show the best possible variety talent available and it was also his intention to discontinue the showing of cinematograph pictures.

It would also appear that it was customary to play the British National Anthem every night in the "Empire", at the conclusion of each performance, which many, many people found offensive and one night it was said that Mr. Peader Kearney, the composer of the Irish National Anthem hosed down the members of the orchestra for the playing of same, and we were led to believe that it was never again played in that theatre, from that day onwards. This act of protest was said to have taken place in 1915.

We have no single date for this occurrence, nor do we have proof of its happening. One or two people made mention of the story to us and we felt it was worth an inclusion.

"Votes for Women"
"No Property or Life Safe, Until We Get It".

These words were said to have been found written on a scrap of paper, which was found on Saturday, May 10th 1913 by the police in connection with a remarkable outrage in the "Empire Theatre", when an explosive parcel was found in the ladies lavatory.

This sensational evidence was given in the Southern Police Court on Monday, May 12th 1917 when a woman was charged with placing an explosive substance in a second floor ladies toilet with the intent to endanger life or otherwise cause serious injury to property.

The device consisted of gunpowder cartridges placed in a tin canister with a cotton wick that was saturated with paraffin oil, which had been set alight. Fortunately, the flame was spotted by a woman from the audience, who immediately, with great pluck, extinguished the fuse attached to the parcel.

Had the device exploded, it would have caused a panic in the crowed theatre and many lives may have been lost. A more diabolical or outrageous act would not be possible to conceive, said the magistrate when he heaped praise on the plucky and prompt action by the lady from the audience who had foiled this dastardly act.

The court was crowded for the hearing of the case and conspicuous among those present were many ladies who had long been more or less identified with the militant suffragist movement. However there appeared to be no connection between the defendant and the suffragist movement.

Having heard all the evidence against the defendant and her pleas of innocence, the Judge adjourned the case for a week and the defendant was allowed out on her own bail of £50 and two sureties of £25 each.

The case came up again on Monday, May 19th 1913, and following serious deliberations Judge Drury found that the crowns case against the defendant was not strong enough and the defendant was discharged.

~~~~~

1923 brought about many changes in the theatre, including a change of directors, another name change and the theatre closed and reopened so many time during that year that to record all the dates would be, to say the least, boring.

This advertisement appeared in the "Evening Mail" on February 5th 1923 announcing the re-opening of the "Olympia", which quite possibly might have been its first night under that name.
~~~~~

Another opening date that year that brought forth a great welcome from the theatre critic in the "Evening Mail" on Tuesday August 7th 1923 when he was thrilled to write that the "Circus was back in Town", in the Olympia theatre.

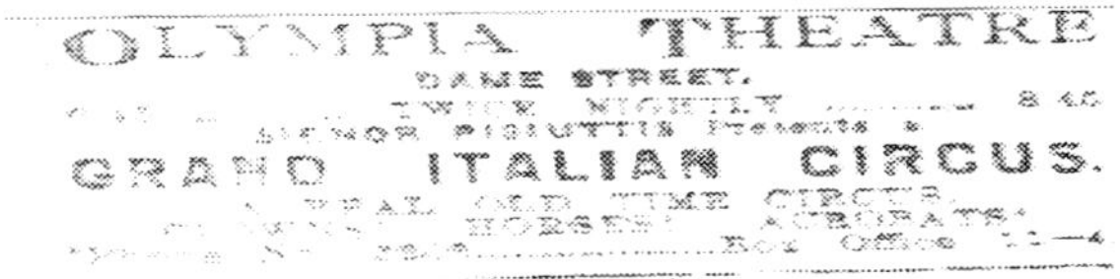

Opening August 6th 1923

This he wrote, brought us back to the good old days in Dublin when the circus was considered one of the most vital of the entertainments to have full swing for holiday periods. The revival, he wrote, even though it is on the stage and therefore necessarily cramped as compared with the old idea was exceedingly welcome and the audience the night before had relished the many items with obvious satisfaction.

The show was under the direction of Signor Pissiutti who had secured the services of a smart combination of performers which included an acrobatic team known as "The Three Winikills"; daring horsemanship by Signor Pissiutti and other members of his family; A clever mystery man, a violinist and a vocalist of great ability, dogs which did things that were almost human and a kicking donkey that provided great laughs. Indeed, he wrote, it was a marvel that so much that was clever and appealing had been executed in so little a space.

Mr. Bradlaw, a very well known cinema entrepreneur who at that time was managing director of the Princess cinema in Rathmines, joined the Olympia's board of directors that year.

While this new board of management presented drama, opera, ballet, and pantomime with a mainstay of revue and variety, a feature of the new "Olympia Theatre" was its programme of Sunday pictures, which were very popular and worth a visit.

Nothing of note came to our attention in the following years until 1970, when we noticed that the theatre had stopped advertising their Sunday night movie programmes. At first we didn't take too much notice of this because Sunday night films shows were often suspended by the theatre management, for one reason or another. However, the last advert we could find was for Sunday March 23rd 1969 and we can only assume that that was their last movie show. The titles of the films for that night were "Flight from Ashiya", with Yul Brynner and "I Saw What You Did", with Joan Crawford and John Ireland.

"I Saw What You Did", landed two very young teenage girls in a life threatening situation when, on making some silly prank phone calls to alleviate their boredom, they accidentally stumbled on a case of "uxoricide".

* * * * *

Once again while researching another cinema, we accidentally stumbled on a news item that told us that the Olympia was scheduled for auction in the autumn of 1963 and it also provided us with a very nostalgic photo which was taken circa that time.

While it thankfully continued on as a theatre we never did find out if it went to auction or if a buyer was found before hand.

This item of news should of course have preceded our 1970 story on the suspension of their Sunday night film shows but as we said, we very nearly missed this piece of news.

Neither of us are well up on theatricals or theatre personalities but we did read and took note of a number of letters which appeared from time to time in the "Letters to the Editor "columns of various newspapers which bemoaned the fact that very little credit or mention was given to Messrs. McCabe and Illsley in write-ups about the Olympia Theatre.

We would now like to make amends for those omissions and mention that according to our research Stanley Illsley and Leo McCabe were director/shareholders of the Olympia Theatre and were in control and jointly managed the same for nigh on twelve years.

This highly esteemed duo, it would appear, reigned supreme from 1951 until the year of its auction in 1963. On top of their Olympia responsibilities they also ran their own production company entitled Illsley and McCabe Productions and in this capacity they had good contacts and were able to persuade some great producers to open their plays in the Olympia, such as "Carrie" and "The Informer".

They were also responsible for the appearance on the Olympia's stage of some of the greatest names in the world of theatre including Dame Sybil Thorndike, Sir John Gielgud, Gladys Cooper, Peggy Ashford, Tyrone Power, Sir Alec Guinness, Dame Margaret Rutherford and Laurel and Hardy.

They were also instrumental in introducing great musicals to the Olympia and many star studded premieres prior to their London and New York runs.

On Tuesday November 5th 1974, the theatre once again closed its doors. However, this time around the closure was brought about by a terrible disaster, which occurred during morning rehearsals for a play that was due to open that night. The enormity of the disaster was such that had it happened forty minutes earlier, many lives might have been lost.

Morning rehearsals for the musical stage show "West Side Story", had concluded and the company had trooped off the stage for a lunch break, when some 30 minutes later the proscenium arch above the stage collapsed and tons of masonry, plaster and wood, came tumbling down onto the stage and orchestra pit.

Fortunately, only three members of the company, which numbered in all about one hundred were near the stage when the collapse occurred and they, though unhurt, were covered in grime and dust and too shocked to describe their ordeal.

The emergency services were called and between them and the theatre officials the building was cordoned off and the Fire Brigade and dangerous building experts began their examination of the rest of the building.

It would appear that the failure of a brick pier, supporting a box girder over the stage of the theatre, caused the structural collapse. A Dublin Corporation spokesman from their Dangerous Building Section, said that the structure as it stands, is still highly dangerous.

Later that evening Brendan Smith chairman of the board of directors made a statement to the effect that the collapse of the stage did not mean the end of an era, which they had strove so hard to maintain. The frame of the stage, he said, was still intact.

The building closed that day and as the weeks passed architects and building experts moved in and began making plans for the re-building of the stage. Little did they or anyone else think but that it would take some twenty-eight months before the theatre would open its doors again.

~~~~~

Backstage or should I say at some other locale, perhaps in a local hotel, frantic efforts were being made to find another venue for Dublin's latest musical production "West Side Story" because all connected knew that "The Show Must Go On".

Someone mentioned the "State" cinema which had only recently closed down on June 29th of that year and within hours the right contacts had been made and the entire production was moved to the "State", Phibsboro. In all, it took roughly 3 ½ hours to make the move and this gave the cast a chance of a twenty five minute run-through before an imaginary curtain went up on the stage of the "State" at 9.30 pm.

Some members of the orchestra whose instruments had been buried or destroyed under the tons of rubble that had fallen on the orchestra during the collapse had to use borrowed equipment and in the State cinema hastily installed amplification and lighting had to suffice, together with improvised props.
~~~~~

With the "best laid plans of mice and men" this opening night advertisement appeared in the "Evening Herald" on Tuesday evening November 5th and on Thursday 7th this one appeared for the "State"

Under the circumstances of the event, very little fault was found with the show, however it was obvious that the dancers found the stage of the State a little cramped and the inadequacies of the set were highlighted when Maria in the dialogue was heard to say: "it's dangerous", while she and Tony were perched precariously on a lighting stand which was doubling as a balcony in the makeshift set.

The "State" put on two more shows that had been booked for the "Olympia" before it closed down one more time.

OLYMPIA

GALA RE-OPENING
TO-NIGHT AT 8 P.M.
Formal Opening by
LORD MAYOR OF DUBLIN
followed by Concert featuring leading stars of the entertainment world.
PROCEEDS IN AID OF OLYMPIA RESTORATION FUND
Prices: £5, £4, £3, £2.

Commencing Tues., March 15
for limited run.
NIGHTLY AT 8 O'C.
Prices: £2, £1.50, £1.00
and Sat. Mat. at 3 p.m.
All Seats £1.00

THEY'RE BACK
Irish Theatre Company
presents

JOHN PAUL GEORGE RINGO ... & BERT

By WILLY RUSSELL
The story of The Beatles and their music.
NOW BOOKING
At Theatre, Phone 778962.
Also Switzers, Brown Thomas

On Monday, March 14th 1977, the Olympia had a gala re-opening with an address by the Lord Mayor of Dublin that was followed by a special concert, which featured leading stars of the entertainment world.

This was a special one off concert in aid of the theatres restoration fund.

Below, Albert Barden polishes the stage door sign.

Albert was one of the many staff members who were glad to see the re-opening of the Olympia Theatre. Albert as Stage doorman, was said to have had some 58 years of stage memories that began, when as a school boy, he earned a few bob pocket money, while acting as call-boy, during the pantomime season.

Tuesday night's theatregoers were in for a treat with Willie Russell's award winning musical play "John, Paul, George, Ringo and Bert" with Barry McGovern as John Lennon, Brian De Salvo as Paul McCartney, Patrick Dawson playing George Harrison, Jim Bartley as Ringo and John Olohan doing Bert. This play had just completed successful runs in Dun Laoghaire and Cork.

John, Paul, George, Ringo and Bert first opened in May 1974 in Liverpool's Everyman's Theatre where it ran for eight successful weeks. It then moved to the Lyric Theatre London and played there for a full year. In that year it won the "evening Standard and London Critic's award for "Best Musical In 1974"

* * * * *

The Continuance of an Era

Bearing in mind the words of Brendan Smith when the theatre closed on November 5th 1974, when he said that the collapse of the stage did not mean the end of an "era" and now with the stage re-built and the theatre re-opening it had to be at least for Brendan, the continuance of an "era".

All the newspapers gave a great write-up and a hearty welcome to the re-opening of the "Olympia" and the "Irish Times" dedicated its "Editorial" to its welcome. After the enormous effort to re-open the theatre, the Editorial said, it must be a small matter to work in a season of music hall before too long, as the music hall was the hub upon which the whole thing had began to spin more than 100 years ago. Then Dubliners, who have always shown great favour towards the music-hall will really feel that their old friend is fully back to life and health.

While welcoming back an old friend the "Irish Times" editorial also lamented the passing of three of Dublin's largest and most popular theatres, the Royal, the Capitol and the Queen's which had fallen to the developers hammer and left dead office blocks at night, where once there had been crowded and colourful gaiety.

~~~~~

The celebrations, interviews and write-ups surrounding the re-opening of the Olympia also brought to light a threat to the theatre just over ten years earlier when an attempt was made to establish a ballroom on the site. It would appear that in 1964 the theatre was in the possession of a London based syndicate. In order to save the theatre from re-development the Olympia company directors, which included Brendan Smith, Jack Cruise, Lorcan Burke and Richard Hallinan, took a lease on the premises and put their life savings at risk in so doing. This piece of news fits in well with our mention of the Olympia having been up for auction in the autumn of 1963.

~~~~~

Re-Building Fund.

Few members of the public would be aware of the tremendous effort put into the restoration of the Olympia by its many friends which included ordinary patrons who marched the streets in support of its restoration, its board of directors with Brendan Smith to the fore at all times, staff members who worked free of charge and actors, artists, dancers, musicians impresarios who all took a hand. Dublin Corporation and Dublin County Council also dipped deep in their pockets to help out.

The overall cost of the restoration was in the region of £250,000 and a fund was set up to raise this amount. Dublin Corporation was said to have contributed £100,000 to the kitty and Dublin County Council also made contributions. The Olympia staff and friends of the theatre organised raffles all over Dublin.

To keep the music hall going and the Olympia name alive the staff, many of whom worked without pay for almost a year, assisted in producing small musicals in a small theatre which was constructed in the stalls bar that is named after Cecil Sheridan who also helped in no small way to raise funds. This small theatre closed in September of 1977; price of admission to these shows was a mere 2/6.

Maureen Grant, a bar person in the Olympia for many a long year was to the fore in most of these fund-raising activities and on one occasion she, Eileen Buckley and Maureen Potter organised a parade across town. This parade was not meant to raise funds, but simply to keep the name of the Olympia fresh in the minds of the public. They borrowed a truck and driver and dickied it out as a float with bunting, balloons and streamers and wearing some borrowed fancy costumes from the theatre store rooms they set off across town with a view to distributing some 'support the Olympia' leaflets on the way. However as they approached Parnell Square the cheering crowds soon recognised Maureen Potter and some began to chant, "how much is a brick"? Maureen and Eileen replied 'a £1 a brick, luv' and people began to throw screwed-up one pound notes onto the truck.

~~~~~

"A Long Pilgrimage"
Monday, March 14th 1977

When the new red curtains rose and the Chairman of the Board of Directors, Brendan Smith appeared alone on the stage, he was cheered wholeheartedly even before he had spoken a word. Unquestionably it was his night, for it was he that had to be thanked for the fact that the Olympia had been given a new lease of life. "On behalf of the Olympia, said Brendan, I welcome you back". Having detailed the theatres programme for the rest of that year he described the previous two years as "A long pilgrimage" before introducing Councillor Jim Mitchel the then Lord Mayor of Dublin who officially declared the theatre re-opened.

The re-opening night was an occasion of great joy and satisfaction. The show was variety at its finest and it matched the mood of a celebratory audience. A breathtaking parade of entertainers compered by Brendan Smith, Tomas MacAnna, Vernon Hayden and Maurice Doherty entertained the crowd for three and a half hours. To mention but a few, there were the Wolf Tones playing Frank O Donovan's song "On the One Road": Siobhan McKenna gave highlights of "Cass McGuire": Maureen Potter satirised selected members of the Government: Tony Kenny sang songs from the show "West Side Story", the show that had brought the house down in 1974: Eamonn Kelly told Kerry tales: and the man who stopped the show, Cecil Sheridan who knew and loved the Olympia since he was a boy called out "Bring back music hall", for his parting words.

On the stroke of midnight there was an unforgettable scene on the stage of the Olympia with Siobhan McKenna, Rosaleen Linehan, Brendan Smith, Cecil Sheridan, Niall Tobin, Jack Cruise and about a dozen other theatre personalities chanting 'There's No Business Like Show Business' and joyously high kicking in an unbroken
~~~~~

line like the Royalettes of yesteryear. This scene marked the end of a fabulous, historic evening in which the venerable Olympia, shining like a new pin was declared open again after 28 trying months.

At 1am the Olympia was still flying and the parterre was crowed with people that didn't want the party to end.

~~~~~~

The next day, Tuesday March 6th, Dublin City Councillors each received two complimentary tickets in the post, because they had claimed that after the Council had given £100,000 to the theatres restoration fund they were snubbed by not being invited to attend the gala re-opening.
It would appear that only the Lord Mayor was invited.

(Most of the information associated with the opening night came from the "Evening Herald's "report which was written by John Finnegan and from the "Irish Times" editorial which welcomed back an old friend, some of which we copied word for word)

We believe that the Olympia Theatre is now a listed building and therefore its future is assured for the foreseeable future.

~~~~~~

Another Tragedy.

On Wednesday November 18th 2004 a truck accidentally reversed into the canopy, which fronted the Olympia and completely destroyed the structure, which had stood in that position for over a hundred years. We believed it was erected circa 1897.

The Portico was manufactured by the Saracen Ironworks Foundry in Scotland, and was considered a classical example of Victorian glass and ironwork. Fortunately the old plans of the structure were found and the entire framework and glass sections were carefully salvaged, boxed and shipped to the Heritage Engineering Works in Glasgow who had taken over the Saracen Works and contracts many years ago.

The crated canopy arrived in the Heritage Works in a thousand pieces and each piece had to be inspected, numbered and laid out on boards. While much of the ironwork could be saved a lot of the glass had to be replaced by a specialist team of glass workers. Certain sections would also have to be matched in colour and sourced and this would be very time consuming and expensive.

Initially it was expected to be fully restored in November of 2005 and a very early estimate put the cost of restoration at €100,000. However, at the time of writing this account in July of 2006 there is no sign of a replacement portico.

George took the liberty of (twice) contacting the Heritage Works seeking information but so far his emails have evoked no response.

~~~~~~
~~~~~~

Scene No 1 "The Canopy".

Scene No 2 "After the Crash"
(Courtesy "Evening Herald").

Scene No 3 "Without the Canopy" in 2006.

~~~

Maureen Grant

"An institution within an institution".

Without Maureen and her friends the Olympia may well have foundered after the stage collapsed in 1974.

Many years later as a token of appreciation the board of directors named one of their four bars after Maureen and another was named the "Sheridan" after Cecil.

"Maureen's Bar".
~~~

George took this picture of Maureen, which captured her in a reflective pose as she recalled past times.
(A copy of this picture now hangs on a wall of Maureen's Bar in the Olympia).

Maureen is one of the longest serving staff members of the Olympia Theatre who began working there as a barmaid in 1949. She now supervises all four bars and is as well known as any personality. The wall's of the bar, which bears her name, is lined with pictures of famous people who had graced the stage of the theatre over the years and all are autographed for Maureen. Many years ago, it became a custom for personalities to either have their photo taken with Maureen or to present her with an autographed photo of themselves, which would be hung on the wall of the bars.

A selection of photographs lining one of the walls.

Maureen's career in the cinema business began in the Phoenix Cinema on Ellis Quay where she worked for a year. While working there she was often loaned out to other cinemas were she worked as relief usherette.

She then moved to the Rialto cinema where she worked for two years. During those two years she married and shortly afterwards she left the Rialto and most probably just in time because as soon as news of her marriage reached the ears of management she would have been dismissed anyway, as in those days there was no room in the cinema industry for a married woman!

Some months later she was interviewed by Jim Traynor the manager of the Olympia theatre for the position of barmaid. What's you name she was asked, and she replied Maureen Grant. She was then asked if she smoked and she replied no and do you drink he asked and again she replied no. Do you think you could pull a pint asked the manager and she replied, if I am shown how I would say yes. You're too good to be true, said the manager, the jobs yours and from that day onwards she never looked back. He didn't ask if she was married and by the same token she didn't volunteer any information.

Maureen also told me that she bore eight children during her time in the Olympia theatre and nobody other than her very close friend knew about them. It would appear that Maureen was lucky enough in that she didn't show much when she was pregnant and when each child was due, she would take her annual holidays, the only remark ever made was when she returned to work and one or two staff members would mention that she had lost a little weight. She would say it was all due to the lovely sunshine.

However on her last child she was a little unfortunate because just few weeks before the baby was due she had a little accident on the upper circle. It would appear that she tripped over something and ended up in the Coombe hospital for the better part of a month. When Illsley and McCabe found out that Maureen was having a baby they were horrified and questioned other members of the staff as to who the father might be and when they asked her friend Eileen, the Chief Cashier, who the father might be, she replied knowing full well that the game was up, "her husband of course" "sure this is her eighth child" Illsley and McCabe were flabbergasted.

When Eileen visited Maureen in hospital and told her that the 'cat was out of the bag' Maureen gasped, "ah Jasus there's me job gone". However on a later visit Eileen was the bearer of an envelope addressed to Mrs. Maureen Grant and as Maureen despondently opened the envelope she expected to find a dismissal notice, but instead she found a get-well card and a cheque for a fiver.

Following the birth of the baby, Maureen paid a visit to the Olympia to see if she still had a job and Stanley Illsley welcomed her back with open arms, but he said, "promise me one thing" and "what's that", said Maureen, "don't", said Mr. Illsley, "have another baby for at least another seven years". With truth being stranger than fiction, Maureen's next and last baby was born seven years later, almost to the day!

At the time of writing this story in July of 2006, Maureen, now a widow, is supervisor of all four Olympia bars and one of her sons Jimmy is General Manager of the theatre. She also has two of her grand daughters working in the theatre, Kelly and young Maureen, who is known as 'little mo'. Some other friends and long serving staff members include Carmel McIvor, Mary Lynch and Anne Stanley.

Maureen also remember well an old friend and neighbour of George named May Begley, an usherette in the theatre, who was instrumental in introducing George to the Cinema Union and Frank Robbins the General Secretary many years ago. (See Georges book "The Prinner"). May, it would seem, was long dead and Maureen told George that poor May who had lost all her toes to Diabetes was a very brave and proud person, who following the amputation of her toes and a reasonable period of convalescence returned to her job in the Olympia.

~~~~~

George would also like to say a special thank you to Brian Whitehead, the Managing Director of the Olympia Theatre and his Secretary Serena for kindly affording him the opportunity to enter the theatre after hours to meet with and interview Maureen Grant and take a few photographs.
~~~~~

OLYMPIA SKATING RINK
3 Serpentine Ave

This rink was situated to the side and rear of number 3 Serpentine Avenue, the home of one Joseph Mason and his family, who had the property on lease from the Royal Dublin Society.

While this rink really had nothing to do with our research on Dublin cinemas it did have a little something in common with cinemas in that it was another source of entertainment available to the public at large and on more than one occasion it was wrongly suggested that perhaps this hall also housed our mystery picture house. However we also chose to mention the Rink, because we came across it quite by accident during our long and hard research on the Assembly Picture Hall and once again few if any people had any memory of it. Because music & dancing took place during its opening hours, this rink was also required to have a licence under the 1909 Act.

We would also tell you that in the early 20th century almost every district in Dublin had a skating rink and that this avenue of entertainment was also a very, very popular one indeed. Pause for a moment and visualise graceful young couples twirling and waltzing their way around the rink with beautiful musical accompaniment in the background. Wouldn't it make you wish you were there for an hour or two. The sooner they bring back time-travel the better.

The Olympia Skating Rink also appeared to have an entrance / exit on Merion Road which sometimes gave the mistaken impression that there were two Rinks in the area.

Mr. Joseph Mason who was a bazaar and ballroom decorator by trade ran this rink with the aid of his wife Annie and family, The Mason's were of English origin and in all, they had six children ranging in age from 20 years to 4 years, and I would imagine they would all have lent a helping hand.

Dorothy (20), Arthur (17) and Stanley (15) were all apprenticed to their father, while Clive (8), Walter (7) and Philip (4) were all young scholars, with Philip being the only child born in Dublin.

This enterprise began in 1909 and closed in 1916, perhaps because cinemas were making serious inroads, together with the fact that from time to time the RDS required the premises for other uses. Whichever the reason, it was closed for good in 1916.

~~~~~~~~~~

Snippets

Gaining admission using the barter system

While we learned during our research that one could indeed gain admission to certain Dublin cinemas by tendering a number of well washed empty jam jars, in either or both the 1lb or 2lb variety, one could also, we were told, gain entrance to some cinemas in country area, by bartering with a supply of potatoes, eggs, butter or even sods of turf in certain districts.

* * * * *
~~~~~~~~~~

ORIEL CINEMA(S)
CHAPELIZOD

We say cinema(s) because films may well have been shown in a number of venues when movies first arrived in Chapelizod as far back as 1922. According to one source in the village, films were shown in the Playshed of the old school building, which is now long demolished. Another source finds Father McMahon using a wooden hut on a site at the rear of Keenan's public house for the display of films and some other amenities and in 1920 a temporary licence under the Cinematograph Act was granted for the use of a portable structural in Chapelizod in which to exhibit films. (No name was mentioned).

The information that we have unearthed, points to this structure being located on a piece of ground where the Texaco garage now stands.

The wooden hut at the rear of the Mullingar House appears to have been the main venue for pictures and perhaps Father Bernard McMahon managed to secure a licence for this hut as pictures appear to have been shown there for many years before a cinema proper was built.

In 1942 Father McMahon ran occasional cinema shows in the Parochial Hall

In 1939 there was a proposal made by J Keenan to build a cinema on the site of the wooden hut at the rear of his premises and sometime later it would appear that he sold this site to a Mr. Brocklebank who received planning permission to build the cinema. This was accomplished in 1942.

NEW RITZ CINEMA, CHAPELIZOD
"She knew All the Answers"
Presenting Loan Bennett & Franchot Tone
And supporting programmes

Popular Prices   Continuous from 6.30

On Saturday August 8th 1942 this advertisement appeared in the "Evening Herald" announcing the opening of Chapelizod's first real and purpose built cinema which attracted great interest in the village and as word of this new cinema reached Ballyfermot many of the residents there made their way down Inchicore Hill Road, Ballyfermot Hill Road or Lynch's Lane to view this new attraction and many became regular patrons.

"She Knew All the Answers", is a romantic comedy where a well to do young lady almost gets taken in by a rakish lover, but her Guardian keeps a tight reign on her purse strings and in defiance she get a job in Wall Street. Soon however she realises that she is in love with her guardian and the rake gets the push.

Mr. Brocklebank didn't stay too long in the cinema business and in 1945 he sold his interest to a Mr. Mordant who lived on the Ballyfermot Hill Road and renamed the cinema as the "Majestic".

On Saturday May 19th 1945 the cinema known as the Ritz Chapelizod closed and on Sunday May 19th it re-opened as the "Majestic".

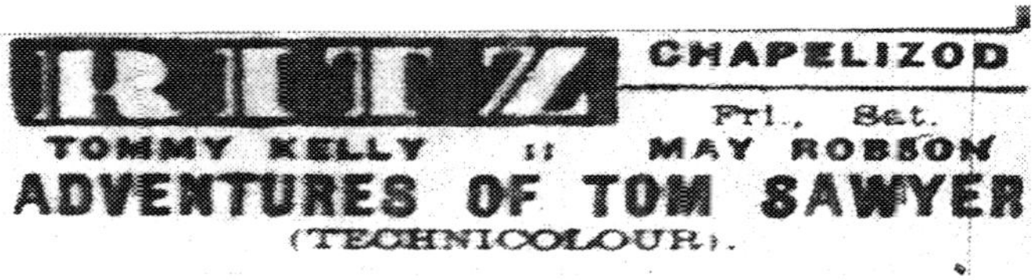

Last day as the "Ritz"

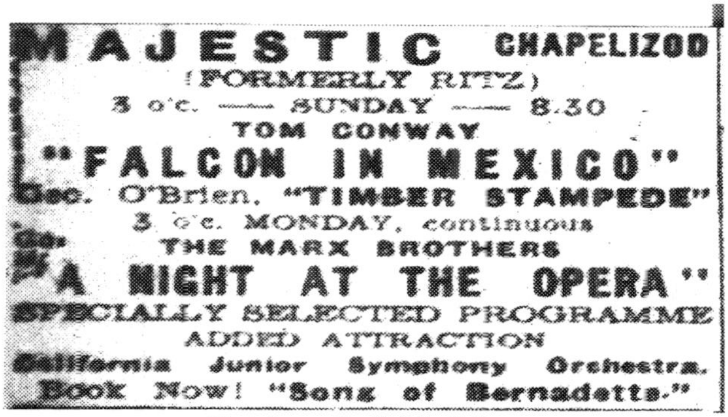

First day as the "Majestic".

The "Majestic" did well under the management of Mr. Mordant and traded for the next twelve years. However in1957 it again changed hands and it was renamed the "Oriel".

The new proprietors consisted of a partnership between Mr. Thomas O'Neil who had been the Chief Projectionist in the "Majestic" and a Mr. A Pope.

ORIEL Chapelizod
OPENING EASTER SUNDAY
With Audie Murphy, DESTRY and
Robert Newton, BEACHCOMBER
3 pm –8.30 pm
No booking for Sunday
Admission 1/- and 1/6 Children 4d.

The "Oriel" opened on Easter Sunday April 21st 1957.

The Oriel lasted well into the sixties, but with attendances in decline it closed in 1966. While we don't have an exact closing date we do believe that the advert below is its last.

ORIEL — Chapelizod
To-day from 3 o'c.
Yul Brynner, Tony Curtis.
TARAS BULBA (Col.)
Also Chuck Connors as GERONIMO (Col.).

Photograph taken early 2006.

This is the building that once housed the Chapelizod cinema.

The building, which was a purpose built cinema lies at the end of Cinema Lane, now called Old Cinema Lane and following its closure it became a small manufacturing unit and that too is now closed, although it may still be in use as a storage facility.

The entrance to Old Cinema Lane is to the left of the licensed premises Mullingar House, Chapelizod.

ORMONDE CINEMA
Stillorgan Village.

The Ormonde cinema in Stillorgan Village opened on Wednesday August 24th 1954 and although it has moved to the opposite end of the block it is still in operation in this year of 2005. (Explanation later).

The cinema which was of the most modern design in the stadium style had seating for 924 people. The building, which was designed by Mr. W.A. Maguire, cost in the region of £45,000 and the front of the building was constructed of Howth stone in mottled brown.

There is a small kiosk built into the foyer for the purchase of cigarettes, ice cream and sweets. The directors had installed the latest and most modern Zeiss-Ikon projection equipment and with a cinemascope screen measuring 33 feet in height and 34 feet in width, felt that they were well prepared for any future changes in projection or screen design. The Ormonde was the first cinema in Ireland to install this Zeiss-Ikon equipment since World War 2.

A most unusual feature about this new cinema was that the shows were to be changed four times weekly, i.e. Monday & Tuesday, Wednesday & Thursday, Friday & Saturday and Sunday. The cinema is under the management of Mr. A.J. Kavanagh whose intention is to provide good and varied programmes. With a staff of ten, the best of seating, prices of admission set at 1/6 and 2/3 patrons were well catered for.

Mr. Cosgrave, Minister for External Affairs performed the opening ceremony and the proceeds of the first night were pledged to the local church and the Cinema Benevolent Fund.
The opening film was "The Grace Moore Story", starring Kathryn Grayson.

Another feature of the Ormonde cinema was the huge car park that had spaces for no less than 100 cars. The Ormonde group were not new to the world of cinema as they also had houses in the East and South of Ireland and had earned a good reputation for providing the best of entertainment for the pleasure of their patrons.

This is the original site of the Ormonde cinema which opened in 1954 and which now houses the AIB bank. The buildings to the left and behind are all new additions which were developed when the Ormonde closed its doors on Sunday July 30th 1978.

Suffering from the decline in cinema attendances the management of the Ormonde decided to close down and sell the property to developers who built the Stillorgan Plaza shopping centre.

This advertisement which appeared in the "Evening Herald" on Saturday July 29th 1978 seemed to be the last advertised show for the Ormonde.

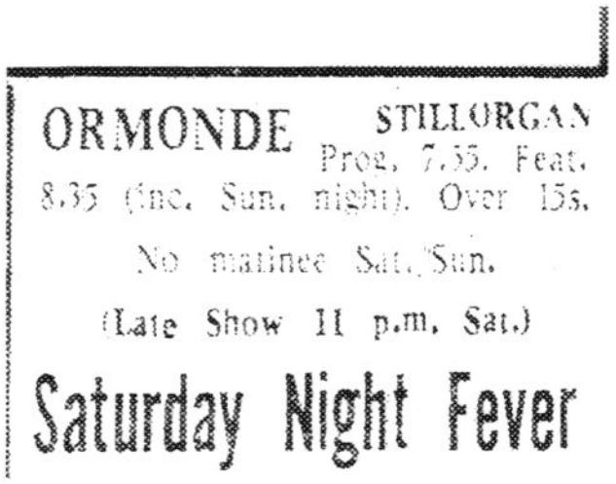

However, the developers were persuaded to include a 3-screen cinema to the rear of the shopping complex and this new cinema opened in 1983.

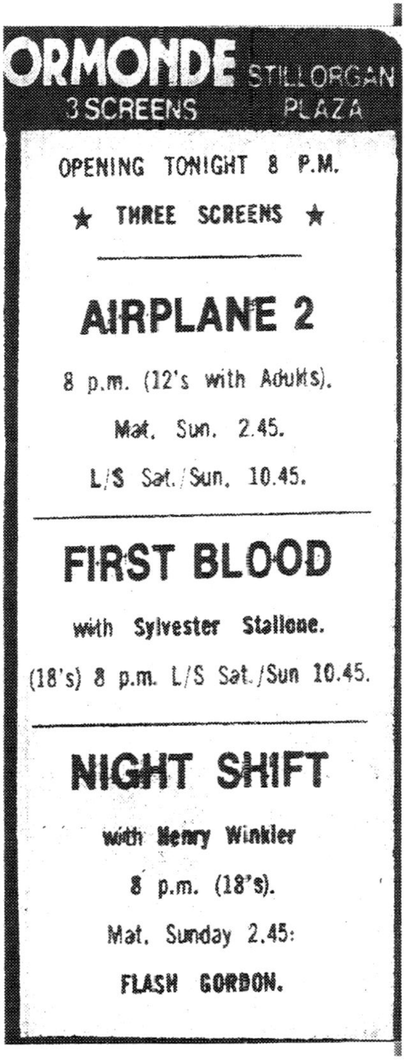

The Ormonde cinema now situated towards the rear of the Stillorgan Shopping Plaza opened on February 5th 1983 to a very enthusiastic audience.

This new cinema, with its three screens and new found ability to rent the best of 1st run films just like the "Stella", in Rathmines, the "Classic", in Harold's Cross and the "Forum", in Dun Laoghaire now stood a good chance of success.

On top of which there appeared to be a reversal of the trend of diminishing attendances and people were again going to the pictures for a night out.

Over the following years the Ormonde thrived but unfortunately the same could not be said for the shopping plaza which failed in its objective and the developers had little choice but to plan a re-development of the area.

With new plans afoot the Ormonde management had some serious discussions with the developers and it was agreed that the Ormonde would be allocated more ground for a spacious off street lobby and the building of four extra screens, bringing the total to seven screens. Having invested some £2 million, the complete cinema complex was re-developed to include luxurious armchair seating, state of the art sound and first class lighting and heating.

The Ormonde, now with seven screens, was on a par with the best cinemas in Ireland and a serious competitor for a fair share of the top films available on the world market.

The seven screened Ormonde as it stands in 2005.

Dave Fanning officially opened this multi-screened complex in April 1997 and its owner Mr. Andrew O'Gorman also allowed the use of some of his seven luxurious auditoria to be used for "Sales Presentations" and "Conferences" etc.

Cinema sizes varied from 280 seaters to as little as 80 seaters.

Patrick pictured at the well-proportioned Ticket office where one could purchase ones ticket for any one of the seven screens.

On the left is a photo of one of the many modern projection machines that are installed in the operation rooms of the Ormonde cinema complex.

To the left of the machine can be seen four big rotating dials containing large film reels on top, some of which would slowly feed a film into the projector which would then project same onto the large screen at the front of the cinema and by the same token the film having passed through the projector would be re-fed onto another reel; a simple and very modernistic method. However, this picture was taken circa July /August 2005, and by now the chances are that these machines are now obsolete as the latest method in operation is to download a film from Satellite onto a digital disk and at the press of a button one has a film in the projector.

PALACE CINEMA

Pearse St, (formerly known as Great Brunswick Street). The Palace AKA, "The Bronx", Forum, Embassy, Academy and once upon a time the "Antient Concert Rooms"

The "Academy" in the sixties.

The building, which housed the Palace cinema, was built in 1824 to accommodate the Dublin Oil Gas Company which ceased trading in 1834.
(Picture, courtesy National Library).

The building lay empty for quite some time and was later acquired by the Society of Antient Concerts who converted the building into a concert hall with seating for 800 persons. It opened in 1844 under the name of the "Antient Concert Rooms".

The hall became very well known and soon earned fame for its many musical and operatic performances. The hall featured a great organ and many recitals were held there, including extracts from "Handels' Messiah". James Joyce sang there, as did John McCormack in a competition where John won first prize. Parnell made his famous speech there when he made his plea for a free Ireland and I believe many years later the Lakes of Killarney were auctioned off there for £60,000. Top-notch boxing matches also took place in front of packed houses.

Top conductors, such as Dr; T.R. Hose and Sir Robert Stewart Baton led their orchestras through their routines in the Antient Concert Rooms and big band leaders played there as did Irelands own Bill Murtagh, in the early stages of his career. Amateur productions took place and Vaudeville acts gave way to serious Theatre Acts, some of which were directed by the Abbey Theatre Company and these in turn gave way to Burlesque and other entertaining productions. Although ever changing with the times, the building remained always a place of entertainment.

So busy were these concert rooms, that the police had to intervene and lay down strict parking and drop off rules pertaining to cabbies and drivers of private coaches, etc. Cabbies, having dropped off their fares were ordered to leave the area or proceed further down the road where they could join the local cab rank at the side of the slipway wall of Westland Row Station and ply their trade. Drivers of private cabs and coaches were directed to park on the opposite side of the road where they could await the return of their masters.

Cinema however had come to Dublin and the concerts rooms were an ideal venue for some of these cinematograph exhibitions and slowly but surely cinema shows began to establish themselves as a regular feature in the "Antient Concert Rooms".

While vaudeville was resisting cinema, cinema was pushing vaudeville and both parried with each other for many years with cinema eventually winning the day. For a while both worked together in a cine-variety type way and at one time a small orchestra was introduced and a master of ceremonies conducted community singing before the film programme started, a pre-runner I would suppose of the "Tommy Dando", singalong in the Theatre Royal many years later.

In early 1920 the premises was refurbished and converted to a cinema proper, and the Palace Cinema was born.

On Wednesday May 13th 1920, The Palace Cinema opened its doors for business to a huge audience and below we re-produce a display ad, advertising the grand opening.

Opening TO-MORROW, May 13, 1920

Dublin's Finest Cinema

Luxuriously decorated and designed throughout on the lines of a high-class theatre, the new Palace Cinema (Antient Concert Rooms) is really a triumph.

"The Antient Concert Rooms in its altered interior and seating arrangements is one of the finest in Ireland.—Evening Herald, 8/6/20.

In setting out to adapt this fine large hall to the needs of a modern Cinema, we have spared no expense in endeavouring to make it the most beautiful in Dublin. It embodies every up-to-date improvement, every innovation, that can possibly make for the greater comfort and enjoyment of the picture-loving public.

AIRY AND COOL.

The interior being large and unusually high, it is delightfully airy and cool. The outside passages are also large and provide ample seating room for our patrons. This avoids the necessity of standing queues.

COMFORTABLE.

The seats are beautifully upholstered in plush, and are so tilted as to ensure the utmost degree of cosiness and comfort, combined with a perfect view of the screen.

MODERN MACHINES.

The latest improved Cinematograph machines have been installed, thus ensuring perfectly clear pictures on the screen.

PROGRAMMES.

Only the latest and best films, selected from the foremost companies, will be shown at each performance These will include drama, comedy and interest pictures that will, in every way, be "clean" and acceptable.

THE MUSIC,

Which will be under the personal direction of Mr. John Mundy, who will play a 'cello solo at each performance, will prove an exceptional attraction to all lovers of good music. Music of the highest class only will be performed.

DR. STEEVENS' HOSPITAL.

The proceeds of the first day will be handed over to this Institution, which, as we all know, is in need of funds at present.

DON'T MISS THE OPENING PROGRAMME

Super-Production (first time in Ireland) Alice Joyce and Maurice Costello in **THE CAMBRIC MASK.** Also Charlie Chaplin Comedy, Topical Events, etc.

Popular Prices of Admission—**9d, 1/-, and 1/6.**

The Palace Cinema

Telephone 4309.

(ANTIENT CONCERT ROOMS) Near Westland Row Station, Dublin

Opening on Thursday, May 13

(The proceeds of which will go to the aid of Dr. Steevens' Hospital Dublin.)

The Most Beautiful Cinema in Dublin

ON Thursday next the new Palace Cinema (Antient Concert Rooms) will open.

This fine large hall has been luxuriously decorated and fitted as a high-class Cinema. It embodies every up-to-date improvement, every innovation, that can make for the greater comfort of the picture-loving public.

The interior, being large and unusually high, is delightfully airy and cool. The outside passages are also large and provide ample seating room for our patrons. This avoids the necessity of queues.

The films shown will be the latest and best, and will be selected from the foremost companies. The orchestra, under the direction of Mr. John Mundy, will doubtless prove an exceptional attraction to lovers of good music.

The prices are popular, the pictures the best, the music perfect, the comfort delightful. Come to the opening programme. Continuous from 3 till 10-30 p.m.

Palace Cinema

TELEPHONE 4309.

(ANTIENT CONCERT ROOMS), Near Westland Row Station.

Again we show you another advertisement reminding one and all of the forthcoming opening night.

From day one, the Palace enjoyed great success and for many long years it delighted its audiences with the best movies available which ranged from Comedies, Westerns, Thrillers, Adventure films, Gangster movies, Love stories, Detective tales and of course the most enjoyable and spell-binding Follow-uppers.

The Palace building like a lot of other picture house premises also sported a dance hall and it too was very popular in its day.

The building also had an Assembly hall, which may have doubled as the dance hall and below is a 1926 advertisement for one of the many groups that held dances there.

To night At 7.45 — OLD THIRD BRANCH — To night At 7.45

Old Dublin Brigade

Cinderella Dance

Will be held at

Palace Ballroom Pearse Street

Carnival novelties—Spot dances

O'Connor Dance Orchestra

Dancing from 7.45 to 12

Ladies 1/6 Gents 2/- Double 3/-

When the Palace cinema opened, it was under the managership of J.J. Eppel and despite his efficient capabilities, disaster struck that night in the shape of a power failure. It would appear that the electric lighting plant failed, resulting in the picture being shown in poor quality and at times almost indiscernible, however the audience appeared to be very understanding and the night passed without incident.

The Palace Cinema Ballroom also provided dancing lessons for its many patrons and these classes under the tutorship of Mr. P. Henry Greene were available every Tuesday and Thursday evenings at 7pm.

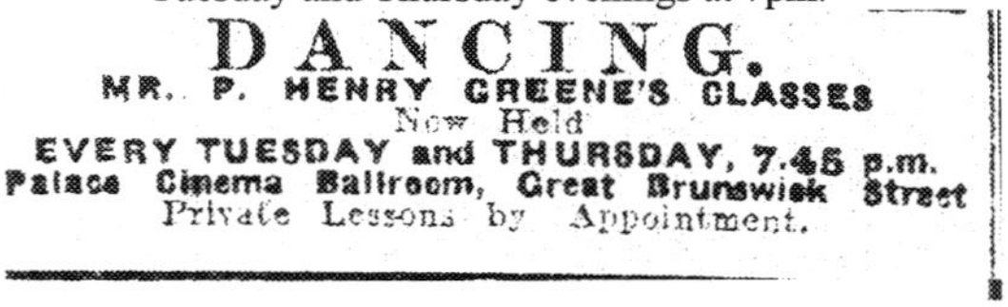

After a most successful run of some 30 years the cinema had a name change and this seemed to take place almost overnight on December 3rd /4th 1950. The picture house was now called the "Forum". Why the name was changed is not apparent, but whatever the reason the Forum it was until April 1956 when it was closed early in the month for some interior decorating with once again a name change in mind.

This advertisement although very faded is worth reproducing and recording as it was the only notice given of the proposed name change of the cinema from the "Palace" to the "Forum".

* * * * *

Other than the change of name, the cinema remained the same and continued to please its customers for the next six years by putting on the best of programmes. It closed on April 7th 1956 and its last picture show was the 1952 version of "The Story of Will Rogers", who was one of America's greatest humorists and entertaining personalities. Will was born on his families ranch in Oklahoma and it was said that he was of Cherokee descent. He died at aged 55 years in a plane crash in Alaska on August 15th 1935.

* * * * *

On April 9th 1956 having had its interior freshly painted and a large new name sign hung on the outside wall the cinema reopened for business under the name of the "Embassy". It now boldly claimed that it was fitted with Dublin's latest Cinemascope equipment and its first showing was the film" The Night Holds Terror", starring Jack Kelly and Hilda Parks.

Jack plays the part of a wealthy businessman who foolishly picks up a hitch-hiker who when he finds out the good Samaritan is wealthy, kidnaps Jack and holds him hostage with the help of some fellow baddies. However, Hilda, who plays his wife, calls in the FBI and in a joint effort they save the day. Also showing that night as part of the double bill was the movie the "Rebel", starring John Ireland.

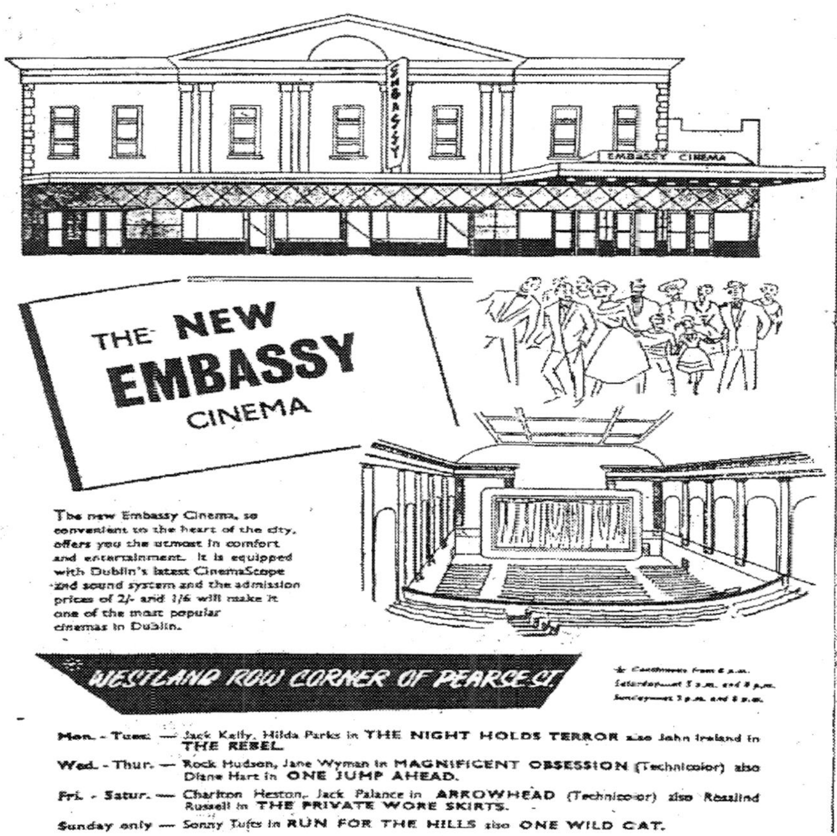

However a further change of name was in the offing when in May of 1964 the Embassy closed for a period of some ten months and having undergone total refurbishing and decorating to its interior, it re-opened its doors to the public as the "Academy Cinema", on March 13th 1965.

The owners of the "Academy" were intent on catering to serious cinemagoers that would have a real interest in cinema and in order to ensure good acoustic conditions they had installed a false ceiling and had the walls heavily draped to help bring about these affects.

It had seating for 640 persons and its first film had a limited certificate restricting admission to 16 year olds and under.

The film the "Victors", was the movie chosen by the directors for its opening night and as it was the first film to have been passed by Irelands new Censorship Appeal Board it was more or less guaranteed to attracted great interest and full houses.

The "Victors", was a much acclaimed World War 2 film telling the tale of a platoon of American soldiers battling it out in Europe in a number of short stories, based on the inhumanity of war.

It was brought to the silver screen by Carl Foreman and had a large cast of well-known names, which included;

Vince Edwards, Albert Finney, Eli Wallach, Michael Callan, Elke Sommer, George Peppard, Maurice Ronet, George Hamilton, Jeanie Moreau and many more including James Mitchum (son of Robert) and Peter Fonda (son of Henry).

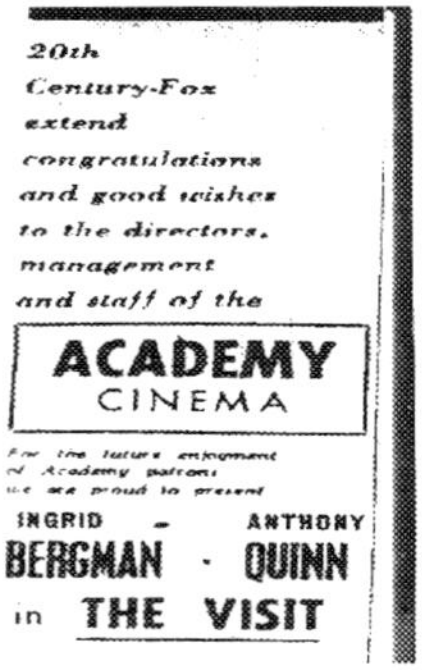

In order to keep their opening promise of providing the best films available, future box office attractions were booked well in advance as can been seen in the accompanying advertisements. Sometimes these bookings were made months in advance of the films general release.

Two of the blockbusters that were about to grace the screen of the Academy within the next year were, Dr. Strangelove and Lord of the Flies and yes we did say within the next year, because the Academy management appeared to have the gift of picking winners.

The "Victors", ran to packed houses for two full months, ending on May 13th. "Dr Strangelove", with Peter Sellers playing the parts of three men who were trying to stop a mad scientist –Jack the Ripper- from nuking the U.S.S.R., ran for seven weeks and the "Lord of the Flies", which tells the tale of a bunch of school kids turning into little savages following a plane crash in the heart of nowhere ran for many a long week as did the "Visit", for the best part of three months. "I Want My Wife Killed", ran for nine weeks, and the "Loudest Whisper", for countless weeks.

Just a small sample of the long running box office hits that came the way of the Academy cinema.

The top advertisement was for Thursday 19th and the bottom one for Friday 20th November 1981. While some cinemas advertised their closure well in advance eg: the Theatre Royal and the Carlton, others like the State and the Whitehall simply added a note to that affect at the foot of their last advertisement while quite a few just closed and locked their doors. The Kenilworth/Classic gave a party and the Carlton gave free admission.

In trying to trace the closing date of the Academy, we trawled through the advertisement columns in many papers and by a process of elimination we believe we found its last advertisement, which was on Thursday November 19th 1981. We can only assume that this was the cinema's closing date, although it could have remained open for Friday and Saturday nights performances.

As if the editor of the "Evening Herald" knew that we would be searching for the closing date of the Academy, many years on he very kindly left the space blank, where the Academy advert normally appeared in order to help us finalise a closing date.

Compare well the "Façade" of the Academy Picture House taken in 2004 long after it had closed its doors as a cinema and the picture of the Dublin Gas Oil Company building circa 1824 and you will note that little has changed.

THE DUBLIN
AMATEUR ORCHESTRAL SOCIETY
Conductor—Mr. J. F. LARCHET, R.I.A.M.
Patron—Lord Farnham. Patroness—The Marchioness of Headford. President—Sir Charles Cameron, C.B.
SEASON 1910.
FIRST CONCERT,
WEDNESDAY NEXT, 13th April, at 8.15.
ANTIENT CONCERT ROOMS.
In addition to the Orchestral Items—
VOCALIST:
MR. J. C. DOYLE.
SOLO PIANOFORTE:
MISS ANNIE LORD, R.I.A.M.
Reserved and Numbered Seats, 3s.; Balcony, 2s.; Admission, 1s. Booking at Pigott's and Cramer's.

Over the years some changes were made to the ground floor section when an overhead canopy was erected and later again a row of modern shops made their appearance there but they have all gone and when the above photo was taken the façade of the building looked very much as it did in 1824.

The building is now under construction and it is about to be converted into a block of offices. The façade I believe will be retained.

The above advertisement for the "Antient Concert Rooms" was for April 9th 1910.

While we found what we believed was its last advertisement on November 19th 1981, we do know that like its sister cinema the, "Ambassador", it re-opened on a number of occasions after that date, but finally closed its doors for good.

We would also tell you that in 1977 the Academy and the Ambassador cinemas were involved in a sit-in by their employees, because of the threatened closure of both cinemas on January 13th 1977. In all, about 40 workers were involved.

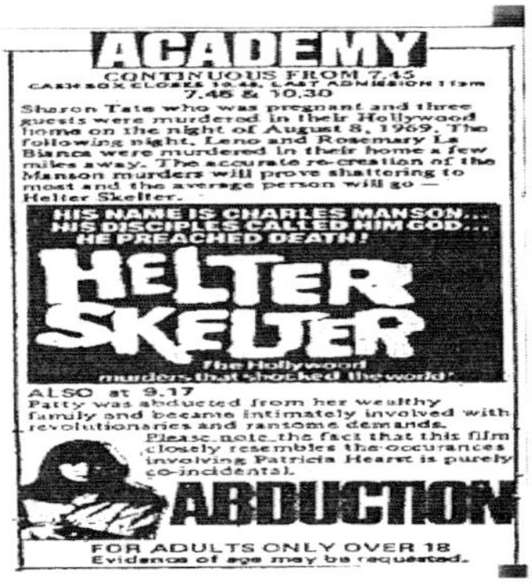

The company, which owned the Capitol and Allied Theatres Ltd., claimed that the workers had been given fair notice ten weeks earlier and that the sit-in would not alter their decision to close, which was based on the fact that they could not get sufficient good commercial films, due to the system of distribution.

Both cinemas did close as planned but the Academy re-opened on Wednesday, August 3rd 1977 and for its re-opening performance the management presented two films which told of the real life experience of Sharon Tate and Patty Hearst.

This picture of the "Embassy", taken on March 1st 1964, is courtesy of Tom Wall.

Trawling through copies of old newspapers in the interest of research has one big disadvantage in that it is so easy to allow oneself to become distracted. Most items in a newspaper have an interest to one and all and more often than not one would spot an item that rang a bell so to speak. I remember that one might think or I was there when that happened or my father told me about that, whatever the reason, one would be at least momentarily distracted.

While sitting at a micro film viewing machine one day in July 2006 searching through a 1920s newspaper, Patrick was doing ditto with the machine next to me, and suddenly I got a poke in the ribs from Patrick. Patrick 'exclaimed' look at what I have found and he proceeded to point to a small ad, which suggested that the Palace cinema had been sold. On closer inspection we realised that it was not a sold sign but an advertisement for a film named "Sold" and for a brief period we were distracted.

PALACE CINEMA,
NEAR WESTLAND ROW STATION.
"SOLD"
THURSDAY, FRIDAY AND SATURDAY,
Featuring PAULINE FREDERICK,
ALSO CHAS. CHAPLIN.
[illegible] performance at 3.30 daily. Com-
[illegible] of programme, Sunday, at 2.30
[illegible] 8.30. Phone 4308

This advertisement was dated October 1st 1920, and not only were we distracted by finding the small ad, but we photocopied it and followed through on the story. This has been a regular occurrence with us and though it adds to our storylines it also causes great delay as in this case the story of the Palace cinema was a wrap, and safely filed away and now we have to re-open it and add an extra page or two.

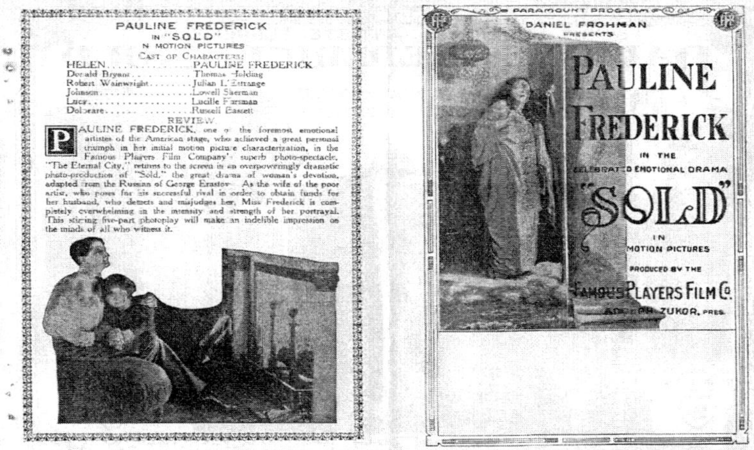
PAULINE FREDERICK
IN "SOLD"
N MOTION PICTURES
CAST OF CHARACTERS:

HELEN	PAULINE FREDERICK
Donald Bryant	Thomas Holding
Robert Wainwright	Julian L'Estrange
Johnson	Lowell Sherman
Lucy	Lucille Farman
Dolbeare	Russell Bassett

REVIEW

PAULINE FREDERICK, one of the foremost emotional artistes of the American stage, who achieved a great personal triumph in her initial motion picture characterization, in the Famous Players Film Company's superb photo-spectacle, "The Eternal City," returns to the screen in an overpoweringly dramatic photo-production of "Sold," the great drama of woman's devotion, adapted from the Russian of George Erastov. As the wife of the poor artist, who poses for his successful rival in order to obtain funds for her husband, who detects and misjudges her, Miss Frederick is completely overwhelming in the intensity and strength of her portrayal. This stirring five-part photoplay will make an indelible impression on the minds of all who witness it.

(Programme copy courtesy of Greta de Groat).

Greta de Groat is the Electronic Media Cataloguer of Stanford University Libraries and is the author of Rediscovering Norma Talmage.
Norma was the instigator of the "Forecourt of Anatomy" in front of Mann's Chinese Restaurant in Hollywood when having attended the premiere of Cecil B de Mille's King of Kings she stepped into wet concrete and began a trend that made the restaurant world famous. Many other world famous stars followed suit, including Michael Jackson and Donald Duck.

Greta is also the Creator of the "Unsung Divas" website, which included site for such stars as Alice, Clare Kimball Young, Norma Talmage and Pauline Frederick who is the star of our film "Sold".

Pauline Frederick stared in this five-reel film in 1915 which was billed as "The Drama that Reaches the Climax of Woman's Devotion". It also starred Tom Holding and Julian L'Estrange.
Pauline was regarded by her audiences and peers as one of the greatest actresses of the screen.
Her first film at age 32 was the "Emerald City" (1915) and some of her best were, "La Tosca" (1918), "Resurrection (1918)" "Ferdora (1918".
In 1920 she played her most famous role as "Madame X", with William Courtleigh, which was said to be her greatest performance in her personal history. She died in 1938 and her last role was Madame Chung mother to Peter Laurie as Mr. Moto in "Thank you Mr. Moto" (1937).

And all this dear reader, came about through distraction! It will be a wonder if we ever get to finish this history of all old Dublin cinemas.

PANIC ON THE "LIGHTER" SIDE.

According to a report in the Irish Times on Wednesday September 9th 1959, a Live Mills bomb was found in the State Cinema Phibsboro the day before by a woman cleaner and Army explosives experts who were called in by the Police, rendered it harmless.

The bomb was discovered by a cleaner, Mrs. Annie Rooney, who claimed that she got the shock of her life when, as a result of her sweeping under a seat, a bomb rolled out from underneath. "I must have disturbed it with my brush", she said, "and when it rolled out I knew immediately what it was as I had seen them during the trouble times. What terrified me most was that I appeared to have broken off the safety catch with the brush".

The following day, Thursday September 10th, another report appeared in the Irish Times newspaper with the information that Army and police experts had been called in to examine an article that looked like a hand-grenade or a Mills bomb, which had been found under a seat in the State Cinema, Phibsboro, Dublin on Tuesday and that the object had been found to be harmless.

It was discovered that the article was in fact a table model cigarette lighter fitted with a mechanism to operate a flint on top of a metal case that was fashioned in the form of a hand grenade. A police spokesman said that it contained no lighting fluid or other explosive material.

"And bang went an explosive story"

* * * * *

The Talkies

The coming of the Talkies did not bode well for everybody, as musicians all over Europe soon found themselves redundant. On Friday March 14th 1930, the "Evening Mail" ran a story about Mr. Erwin Goldwater and his nine-piece orchestra who had just received a month's notice from their employers, the Metropole Hotel Management, who no longer required their services.

In an interview with a reporter from the "Evening Mail", Mr. Goldwater had nothing but praise for the directorate of the Metropole Cinema, who he said had acted with great fairness under the circumstances. Most of the players' contracts had expired but the directorate had acted quite generously in giving them a month's notice.

However, what did deplore Mr. Goldwater was the low standard of musical taste in Dublin. If the public here insisted on getting good music, he said, orchestras would not be superceded by cheap canned melody from America.

"Nobody can blame the Dublin cinema managements for dispensing with their orchestras. They are doing it under pressure of economic circumstances. However the result is that hundreds of musicians are swelling the ever-increasing tide of un-employment".

* * * * *

PAVILION
Dun Laoghaire

We suppose the history of the "Pavilion Cinema" really began on that most beautiful day of June 22nd 1903 when the "Kingstown Pavilion" and its splendid gardens were officially declared open to the public.

The opening ceremony was gracefully performed by Lord and Lady Longford, in the presence of a large and fashionable attendance and a host of distinguished guests, which included Sir Thomas Robinson, J.P. Chairman of the Pavilion Company and some of his fellow directors. Messrs. Stevenson, the Manager and Thos Mannion, the Secretary, were also present. May Robinson, Sir Thomas's daughter presented the Countess of Longford with a beautiful bouquet and the general contractor Mr. McLoughlin presented the Earl of Longford with a Gold Key.

The Earl then declared the Pavilion open amid applause and when the company's flag was unfurled from the main flag mast, a salute of seven guns was fired by the Lifeboat crew.

What other Dublin cinema could claim to have opened in such august company and in such style and splendour?

NOW OPEN. NOW OPEN,
PAVILION GARDENS,
KINGSTOWN.
MONDAY, JUNE 22nd, AND DURING THE WEEK,
THE CELEBRATED BERLINER
ORCHESTRA,
45 Performers 45
Conductor—HERR R. MOSER.
Twice Daily, at 3.30 and 8 p.m.
Admission, ONE SHILLING.
Grand Morning Performance by the
PAVILION GARDEN'S BAND
from 11.30 a.m. to 1.30 p.m.,
COMMENCING TUESDAY, JUNE 23rd.
Conductor—MR. CLARKE BARRY.

The concert hall had seating for 1,000 and the promenades were capable of accommodating another 3,000.

Other areas included reading rooms, smoking rooms, tea rooms, ballrooms and of course its famous Marine Gardens, complete with a bandstand and waterfall, which was lit at night by coloured lamps.

John McCormack performed there in 1908 and in its first year a Viennese Evening was hosted and drew a crowd of four thousand. In a small room Bioscope exhibitions were performed on a regular basis.

As the pictures grew in popularity so too did the viewing area until it eventually became a cinema proper that was on a par with any other Dublin cinema of the time.

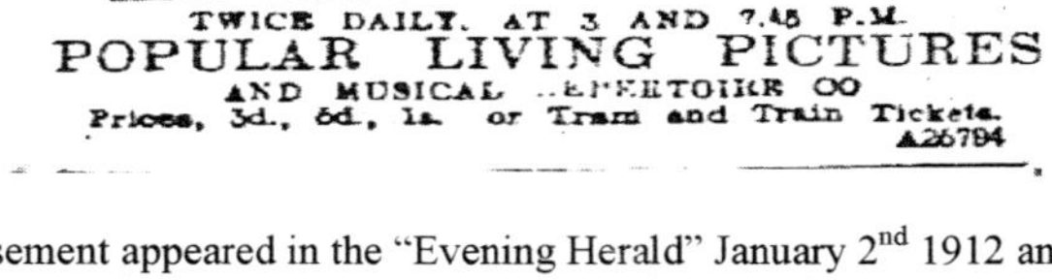
KINGSTOWN PAVILION.
TWICE DAILY, AT 3 AND 7.45 P.M.
POPULAR LIVING PICTURES
AND MUSICAL REPERTOIRE CO
Prices, 3d., 6d., 1s. or Tram and Train Tickets.
A26794

This advertisement appeared in the "Evening Herald" January 2nd 1912 and it would appear that one could gain admission free, on production of a current Tram or Train Ticket.

The Pavilion circa 1904.

Cinema destroyed by fire

At about two o'clock on the Saturday afternoon of November 13th 1915, a Mrs Page of Corrig Avenue, entered the foyer of the Kingston Pavilion Theatre with a view to booking some seats for the concluding entertainment of the Royal Irish Rifles, but found the box office closed.

As she turned to leave the cinema entrance, she noticed thick black smoke curling into the corridor from the upper portion of the theatre and she quickly made her way to alarm the constable on the beat outside on the Royal Marine Road. He, together with two coastguards and John Farrell the porter, from the Town Hall, made their way into the cinema and sourced the outbreak to be behind the stage.

The fire at this point had only a small hold and they tried to extinguish it with the use of a small bucket and water from a house type tap that was situated at the side of the stage, but the smoke was too much for them and the fire gathered momentum. At that point Mr. Ferne arrived and he tried to pull down the stage fire screen but the suffocating smoke prevented him from doing that.

He then laid the Pavilion hose but failed to get any water pressure. However, this was overcome by the arrival of the Township Fire Brigade under Captain Carroll who had two lines of hose laid to the back of the stage but by then the stage was completely engulfed by the fire. A Corporation Fire tender arrived with a Lieutenant Myers in charge who had his men lay two lines of hose from the Harbour with heavy pressure of water.

On seeing the smoke billowing from the Pavilion and before the main body of local policemen arrived, a military officer brought up a possee of armed men and placed them with fixed bayonets at the entrance and in the grounds of the Pavilion and cleared the area of mere spectators thus greatly facilitating the firemen as they arrived. At the same time a Captain Barton R.M. sent up a body of sailors who gave great assistance and did much salvage work, as did a number of officers, soldiers and members of the Royal Irish Constabulary.

By now the fire had taken complete hold of the building and glass windows were bursting with the heat and flames fanned the skyline. More Corporation fire tenders arrived as did one from the Pembroke area and between them all they did their best. Soon however the roof collapsed, walls caved in and the steel framed girders warped and twisted in the heat. For over two solid hours the firemen fought gallantly but succeeded only in containing the fire to within the Pavilion grounds. The firefighters showed such wonderful daring that oft times spectators feared for their safety. Time after time spectators had to scream warning as portions of the building showed signs of collapse.

By five o'clock having beaten out the fire, the brigades centred their efforts on hosing down the remains of the building and at 6.30pm the Dublin brigade left. However some tenders remained on duty until late Sunday evening on hosing and damping down operations as every now and then a piece of disturbed timber would glow red and flames would flicker.

Fortunately there was only one fatality that night and that was the death of a horse. It would seem that as the Township Fire tender arrived at the scene a horse that was drawing the hose wagon fell dead on arrival.

Most unfortunate and most to be regretted of the damage done, was the loss of the instruments of the band of the Royal Irish Rifles, some of which were very costly instruments. It was also understood that the premises, which had cost in the region of £10,000 to build in 1902, were substantially insured.

~~~~~

The Pavilion was rebuilt into an 800 seater theatre / cinema and it re-opened on Saturday July 7th 1917. While it held 800 patrons the opening night was so successful that twice as many seats would have been required had all the people who turned up at the theatre that night gained admission.

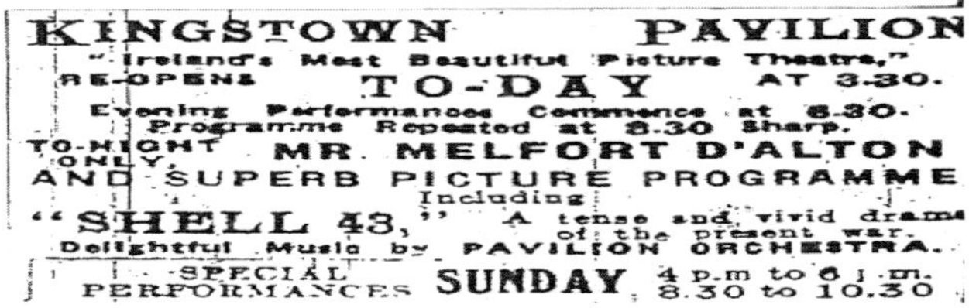
KINGSTOWN PAVILION
"Ireland's Most Beautiful Picture Theatre,"
RE-OPENS TO-DAY AT 3.30.
Evening Performances Commence at 6.30.
Programme Repeated at 8.30 Sharp.
TO-NIGHT ONLY. MR. MELFORT D'ALTON
AND SUPERB PICTURE PROGRAMME
Including
"SHELL 43," A tense and vivid drama of the present war.
Delightful Music by PAVILION ORCHESTRA.
SPECIAL PERFORMANCES SUNDAY 4 p.m to 6 p.m. 8.30 to 10.30
~~~~~

A view of the auditorium circa 1910

The opening nights entertainment consisted of a musical and picture programme both of which were suitably accompanied by the Pavilion Orchestra which was lead by Mlle. Lucy Donnelly, as too was Mr. Melfort D'Alton the distinguished tenor who appeared to be in excellent voice that evening and earned unanimous and prolonged applause following his rendition of "Love Thee Dearest". Mlle Ormonde's excellent violin solos which were also accompanied by Mlle Lucy orchestra also garnered much acclaim.

The 1916 silent Film "Shell 43", which was also known as "The English Spy", was a superb choice of Spy Drama centred on the then current World War and the hero was John 'Jack' Gilbert a leading star of many action movies of the times.

(There were many references in various writings that the Pavilion cinema again went on fire circa 1919, but we found no evidence to substantiate this claim. July 10th 2006 George paid a visit to the Pavilion to take a photo and on enquiring at the desk he was allowed read an old booklet on the theatres history and no where in that booklet was there a mention of a fire in 1919)

Some twenty two years later on Saturday April 15th 1939 the cinema closed down after the last performance for enlargement and re-decoration. The work involved was quite considerate and took all of fourteen months to complete. The Pavilion, which now belonged to Associated Picture Houses Ltd., re-opened on Saturday June 29th 1940

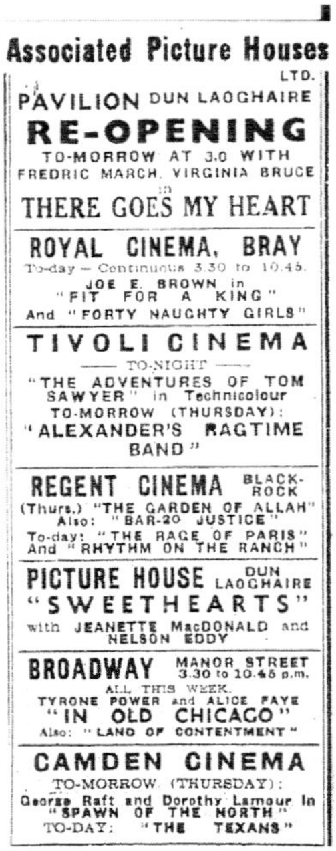

Associated Picture Houses LTD.

PAVILION DUN LAOGHAIRE
RE-OPENING
TO-MORROW AT 3.0 WITH
FREDRIC MARCH, VIRGINIA BRUCE
in
THERE GOES MY HEART

ROYAL CINEMA, BRAY
To-day – Continuous 3.30 to 10.45.
JOE E. BROWN in
"FIT FOR A KING"
And "FORTY NAUGHTY GIRLS"

TIVOLI CINEMA
— TO-NIGHT —
"THE ADVENTURES OF TOM SAWYER" in Technicolour
TO-MORROW (THURSDAY):
"ALEXANDER'S RAGTIME BAND"

REGENT CINEMA BLACK-ROCK
(Thurs.) "THE GARDEN OF ALLAH"
Also: "BAR-20 JUSTICE"
To-day: "THE RAGE OF PARIS"
And "RHYTHM ON THE RANCH"

PICTURE HOUSE DUN LAOGHAIRE
"SWEETHEARTS"
with JEANETTE MacDONALD and NELSON EDDY

BROADWAY MANOR STREET 3.30 to 10.45 p.m.
ALL THIS WEEK.
TYRONE POWER and ALICE FAYE
"IN OLD CHICAGO"
Also: "LAND OF CONTENTMENT"

CAMDEN CINEMA
TO-MORROW (THURSDAY):
George Raft and Dorothy Lamour in
"SPAWN OF THE NORTH"
TO-DAY: "THE TEXANS"

This advertisement which appeared in the "Evening Herald" on the previous Friday announced it's re-opening and the feature film chosen for the night. It also included details of all their other Dublin cinemas.

"There Goes My Heart" 1939, stars Frederick Marsh as a roving reporter after a scoop about the daughter of a Multi Millionaire, who manages to become shipwrecked on a small island with the heiress Virginia Bruce where they bicker and bicker without realising that they love each other until.....

* * * * *

However despite all the hard work that was put into the glorious re-decoration and refurbishment of the cinema more dark days lay ahead of the Pavilion and on Sunday morning November 10th 1940 shortly after 1 o'clock it once again went on fire.

Two sections of the Dun Laoghaire Brigade were on the scene within minutes, but the fire had made such rapid headway that within half an hour the roof had collapsed.

By 2 pm the house was gutted.

It was mentioned at the time that when the building had been re-conditioned and enlarged earlier in that year, that a part of the then existing roof which was made of wood, was not removed, and that this portion of the roof burnt like matchwood.

The last picture to be shown in the Pavilion was "David Copperfield", on that Saturday night and the double feature booked for the Sunday night performance was "Sworn Enemy", with Robert Young, Florence Rice and Joseph Calleia and the Dead End Kids on Dress Parade, starring,

Billy Halop, Leo Gorcey, Bobby Jordan, Gabriel, Bernard Punlsy and Huntz Hall.

* * * * *

However just like the mythical Phoenix, the Pavilion as it died, so was it reborn and soon a new Pavilion rose from the ashes.

On Easter Saturday April 12th 1941 the Pavilion cinema re-opened and continued to show pictures until it closed down in 1974.

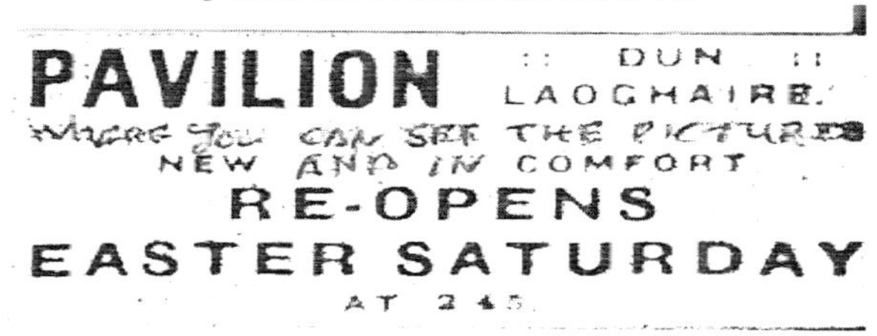

In 1974 the Associated Picture Houses Limited decided to close most of their Dublin cinemas and in their block of newspaper advertisements, on Saturday June 29th 1974 they added a note to each individual advertisement to the effect that the cinema would remain closed as and from the end of that night's performance.

We believe that the Dun Laoghaire Corporation bought the Pavilion building circa 1975 and ran it as a theatre until 1984 when it closed and fell into disuse, and in the latter part of the 20th Century the building was demolished and a new theatre was built on the site.

On Friday December 7th 2000 the new "Pavilion Theatre" opened to the public and its first production was "The Quest of the Good People".

The Pavilion Theatre July 10th 2006.

PAVILION SKERRIES
South Strand, Skerries

This cinema, which opened sometime around 1948, was said to have belonged to Leo Flanagan who was also the proprietor of the dance hall next door.

This picture of the "Pavilion" is courtesy of Maree Baker and the Skerries Historical Society as is the Writings of Paddy Halpin.

This is a picture of an apartment block named "the Tides" which replaced the Pavilion cinema some years ago.

While we don't know at this point in time when the "Pavilion" closed, we do know thanks to the unpublished writings of Paddy Halpin, a founder member of the Skerries Historical Society, that an earlier cinema also occupied this site, which began to show pictures in 1914.

Apparently this cinema, which was in effect an old recreation hall, was more suitable for promoting dances than for showing pictures, was acquired by the enterprising Mr. Flanagan who began to show "Living Pictures" in 1914.

Paddy writes, that when Mr. Flanagan took over the hall he christened it the Skerries Electric Theatre Company and fitted it out with hard backless forms, which offered no real comfort; if you wanted a plush bottomed seat, writes Paddy, you had to bring your own.

In the early stages of this cinema, performances were available on Sunday nights only and when the doors opened at eight o'clock there would be a mad scramble for the booking office, which was sited downstairs to purchase a ticket. There would be a wild rush up the stairs in order to grab a wall seat that would help support your back.

The main feature wrote Paddy, was black, white and silent and would be of a romantic kind which would always have a happy ending and a supporting programme would always consist of a hilarious slap-stick comedy that would send you home in good humour.

Paddy also remembers that on many occasions the operating machine would break down during the showing of a film, and that these exasperating delays often caused uproar in the cinema. When the machine began to roll again, the film would often appear upside down and this would cause further delays in trying to get the picture right side up.

On one occasion during a breakdown of the operating machine the uproar got a little out of hand. This caused Mr. Flanagan to put up notices around the cinema warning that he would debar from the theatre what he called 'unsophisticated louts' and that phrase haunted Paddy for many years as whenever he witnessed unruly characters on the rampage in dances halls and chippers in future years, the phrase 'unsophisticated louts' came to his lips, unbidden.

* * * * *

The mention of the Skerries Electric Theatre Company brings to mind a few items of news that we came across during our research into the history of old Dublin cinemas, one of which may well have been a simple rumour, and that was a story told to us by a couple of senior citizens in the Skerries area who told us that the indefatigable Mr. Flanagan had been responsible for the pioneering of electricity in Skerries.

It also came to our attention that Mr. Izidore Isaac Bradlaw, a well-known cinema entrepreneur who had an interest in many Irish cinemas and whose head office was in Grafton Street, Dublin, was also a director of the Skerries Electric Theatre Company Limited and was therefore also connected with the "Pavillion".

In would also appear that this company had connections with the Balbriggan Town Hall, not as we would have guessed, with the Strand cinema, but with the Town Hall proper whereby it would seem the company was in breach of the Cinematograph Act and there were three summonses against them for having at the Town Hall (01) Inadequate fire appliances; (02) Insufficient exits; and (03) No person specially appointed to look after the fire extinguishing appliances.

This prosecution took place at the Balbriggan Petty Sessions on October 22nd 1912.

The magistrates left the Court of Petty Sessions to inspect the interior of the Town Hall, the enclosure, and the fire extinguishing appliances and on their return to court the Chairman said that the decision of the Bench was, that for having inadequate fire appliances, the defendants would be fined £1, for insufficient exits, which they looked upon as a very serious matter, a fine of £2. would be imposed; while on the third summons, for having no person specially appointed to look after the fire extinguishing appliances, the fine would be 10s.

Mr. Ahern, solicitor for the defendants, intimated that steps would be taken to quash the magistrate's decision.

Marbles.

It also came to our attention, again from the writings of Paddy Halpin which came to us courtesy of the Skerries Historical Society, that in the earliest days of Skerries Cinematographic experiences one could gain admission to a picture show for the one penny or its equivalent in marbles.

These pictures were projected by a magic lantern onto a white sheet and this magic machine, wrote Paddy, belonged to a Tommy Robinson who lived almost next door to him in Church Street and who was senior to him by only a couple of years.

Some time later the "Tofts" paid a visit to Skerries. These were a touring family of amusement providers who would have many appurtenances within their group, one of which had a fit-up cinema, which consisted of a canvas like tent and a small projector. This tent was erected behind "Manning's " cottage and began showing "Living Pictures" Having peered through a slit in the tent one night, Paddy was astonished by the moving figures on the screen which appeared to be alive and from that time onwards he was a fan of cinema.

A new McMaster also toured the country with his Shakespearean Repertoire Company in a fit-up theatre and Paddy once sat through a whole week of Shakespeare's Plays.

PEOPLES PICTURE PALACE
50 Thomas Street.

Very little is known about this cinema, other than the fact that it was owned by the Butler Family, who also owned the "Cinema Royal" in Townsend Street.

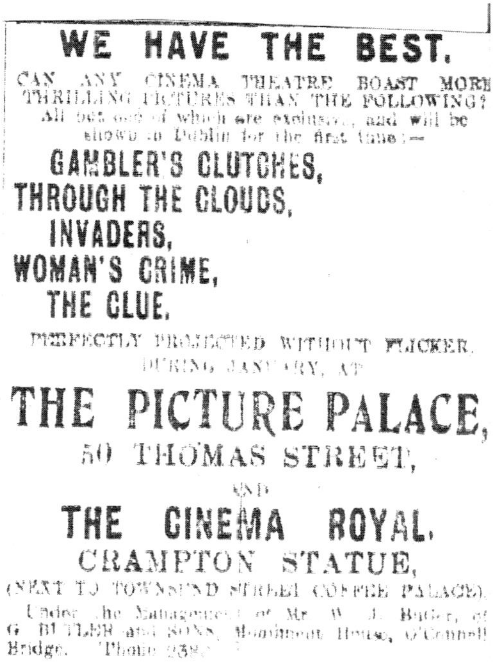

This fact is evidenced by this advertisement, which advises of one of the programmes available in both houses.

The Butler family, it would seem, were into cinemas as a side line to their main business, which was that of musical instrument makers and retailers.

Their main office was in Monument House O'Connell Street, where they had their manufacturing unit and retail showroom.

~~~~~

It should also be noted that there was no family connection between this family and Walter Butler, Dublin Corporations Inspector of Cinemas.

~~~~~

In a report to Dublin Corporation by the said Walter Butler in 1911 he advised his superiors that it had come to his attention, when the proprietors of the premises applied for a Cinematograph Licence, that they had only taken a lease of these premises for a period of twelve months and that the agreement included an option to purchase the premises at anytime within that twelve month period. He also advised them that in a letter from the Butler family's solicitor Mr. J. H. McLoughlin the Butler family agreed that if the Corporation Committee passed the plans for the cinema and issued a licence under the 1909 Cinematograph Act, that if they did exercise their option to buy the premises they would carry out any such requirements that the Corporation might demand of the premises.

It would appear that the licence was duly issued and that the cinema opened for business.

On May 11th 1912, we found an advertisement in the Evening Herald featuring details of the Nelson-Moran Big Fight but unfortunately it photocopied so badly that we couldn't re-produce it on this page in readable form, we therefore printed the details in one of our scroll shapes.

PEOPLES PICTURE PALACE
50 Thomas Street
Opposite the new Fire Station
Next Week
NELSON –MORAN FIGHT
Three minutes from College Green
Inchicore Tram passes door

Later again in the same year, we found another advertisement for a fight which we managed to re-produce in decipherable form. However, as this fight had taken place some years earlier, the film had to be a re-run, which only goes to prove that re-runs in the cinema business had an early beginning. Perhaps it was management's game plan to feature fight films as a specialty of the house.

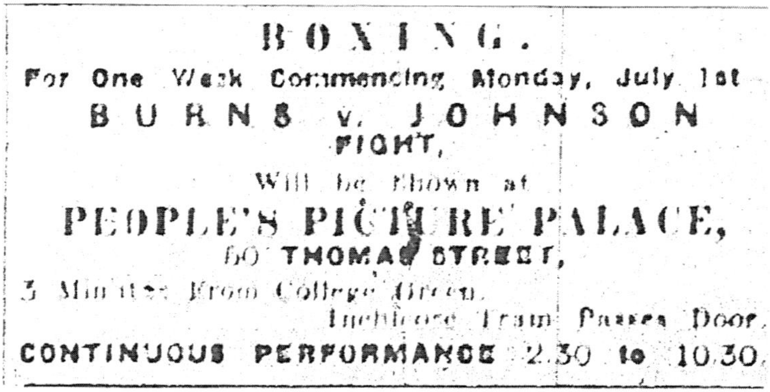

BOXING.
For One Week Commencing Monday, July 1st
BURNS v. JOHNSON
FIGHT,
Will be Shown at
PEOPLE'S PICTURE PALACE,
50 THOMAS STREET,
3 Minutes From College Green.
Inchicore Tram Passes Door.
CONTINUOUS PERFORMANCE 2.30 to 10.30.

Further to a visit to the People's Picture Palace in Thomas Street by the Corporation Committee in the latter part of 1912, in response to a recommendation which had been put to them by Walter Butler their Inspector of Cinemas, they adopted the proposal that the machine enclosure on the ground floor in its present position near the Thomas Street entrance doors, be removed to the first floor at the farthest end of the hall, in the interests of safety and the protection of persons attending exhibitions of pictures in this hall.

From its new position the machine could then project its pictures onto the wall or on a curtain placed between the two Thomas Street entrance doors.

We found no follow through to the Committee's recommendations for these structural alterations and we must therefore believe that the work was carried out and that a screen was erected above the Thomas Street entrance doors, which made the People Picture Palace the second cinema in Dublin after the Camden Picture House to have a back to front cinema screen.

Walter Butler was a man to be reckoned with in the world of Dublin theatre and cinemas in those early days and it would appear that he gave no quarter where the safety and protection of people were concerned. Were his recommendations to the Corporation Theatre Safety Committee adopted and not carried out in full then that theatre or cinema would be refused a licence or its current licence revoked. Many a 'would be cinema' that didn't conform to the standards required under the 1909 Cinematograph Act never saw the light of day.

Visits by Walter Butler to the cinemas within his jurisdictions were most frequent and his strict enforcement of the safety rules and regulation as laid down by the Cinematograph Act of 1909 were, to say the least, legendary.

Had he not been so, many accidents and fires may well have come about through acts of carelessness on the part of managers and owners as had happened in parts of Britain and America including some that were destined to happen in the distant future in a part of rural Ireland and the Town of Paisley in Scotland which caused the deaths of many. (See George's book "The Prinner" for these stories)

In April of 1913 we found another advertisement for this cinema situated at 50 Thomas Street only this time around it was called the "Dublin Picture Palace".

The People's Picture Palace now dubbed the "Dublin Picture Palace" must have been doing well, as management was now announcing refurbishing plans that would enlarge its seating capacity to 500 seats.

The quality of their advertisements have also improved somewhat, and their witticisms are without doubt amusing and attractive.

With the most comfortable of seating, rock steady pictures and the cheapest prices in Dublin, the future of this cinema must have been assured

DUBLIN PICTURE PALACE,
50 THOMAS ST.

THE HOME OF THE ROCK STEADY PICTURES.

The only vibration is that caused by laughter.

The only quiver is that caused by "thrills."

NOTICE.

Owing to the success of our carefully-chosen and brightly-projected programmes, our patrons' attendance from all parts of Dublin exceeds our seating capacity. The Company are, therefore, enlarging the House to accommodate about

500 SEATS,

and will make this Palace not only the Best in the City for Pictures but the Cheapest in Prices and Most Comfortable in Seating.

On another occasion Mr. Butler found as much as 30 persons standing in the back passage of the theatre near a point of ingress and egress and cautions were issued.

The cinema owners also fell foul of the church authorities by showing pictures on a Sunday and when chastised by the Mr. Butler they had to agree that no films would be displayed on Sundays during divine services.

50 Thomas Street as it stands in 2006.

We never did come across an advertisement that showed what type of films were favoured by the management other that those of its display of big boxing matches.

Nor could we find a closing date for same, however we somehow doubt if it survived the silent film era.

But we do have evidence that it was still in business in 1922 as it too was the subject of the censorship notice that was hand delivered to all Dublin cinemas in that year, the recipient of the notice from the DMP Officer was the cinemas Chief Operator Percival Watson at his residence, which was the Brazon Head Hotel and lodging house. (In the managers absence Mr. Hr. Watson was named as next in charge)

THERE ARE MANY PICTURES IN THE CITY
BUT
'HE PEOPLE'S PICTURE PALACE,
50 THOMAS STREET
SHOWS A PICTURE UNEQUALLED IN THE CITY FOR STEADINESS, CLEARNESS OF DEFINITION AND INTEREST OF SUBJECTS.

Call and Make a Comparison.

This advert came to us on Monday, December 23rd 1912 and it invited all to come and make a comparison. At this point in time we had not come across an advert that would give us a clue as to what type of pictures people could expect to see in the Peoples Picture Palace, but on this occasion our luck was in be cause on another part of the page we found a display of pictures that would be on display in the Picture Palace over the Christmas and here we provide you with a complete list.

Monday 23rd & Tuesday 24th December "The Iron Hand", a two-reel drama "Lieutenant Daring quells a Rebellion" and the "Vow of Isabel" a fine Western drama.

On St Stephen's Day would be Dick Turpin in "the Gunpowder plot" and the "The Ride to Death", a very thrilling subject.
On top of which will be a goodly supply of First Class Comic, Cowboy and other interesting subjects.

~~~~~

Lantern Picture Shows

From time to time the Fingal Council and Dublin Corporation showed Lantern Pictures in certain libraries and Parochial Halls in and about Dublin and on Saturday, October 23rd 1915 they took over the Carnegie Libraries in Malahide, the Parochial Hall in Killiney and St George's Parochial Hall in Dublin.

~~~~~

Jameson's Animated Picture Company was also on the move at that time and they held various displays in the Rotunda's Round Room and at the same time they opened a season at the Rathmines Town Hall. Amongst the main attractions were "Babes in the Woods", "Bronco Billy's Christmas Dinner" and to come was a fine production of the Essanay Company of America which would depict life on the Prairie and ranch. It would also include a series of pictures that would show how various Nations keep Christmas.

~~~~~
~~~~~

PHOENIX

The Phoenix Picture Palace, 7/9 Ellis Quay.

The Phoenix Picture Palace, and that was exactly what those cinemas were, Palaces, with well laid out foyers and entrances fit for a King or Queen, marble staircases and landings, most laid with the best of deep pile carpets, and walls and ceilings lined and decorated with the best designs in plaster work, together with plaques and ornaments to die for.

The Phoenix, one of the newest picture palaces to grace the City of Dublin, was opened by the Lord Mayor of Dublin on December 3rd 1912, and it was reported that it could accommodate some 750 patrons. The Phoenix Picture Palace Company was incorporated on May 31st 1912 and two of its principle directors were H. Grundy and D. Frame who was also a director of the New Electric in Talbot Street.

This was a commodious building, well equipped with the most up to date and comfortable seating arrangements, and spacious entrances and exits. The pictures were displayed by the most modern appliances accompanied by a fine orchestra.

Its manager was Mr. Cathal MacGarvey an Irishman with great business experience and artistic ability, and for its first night a most interesting series of pictures was displayed including scenes from France and Australia, together with some humorous stories.

The Feeno became famous for its Saturday afternoon "Penny Rush", where it was said, it often doubled its capacity. It closed in 1958 and today the building houses furniture showrooms.

Speaking of Kings & Queen's, isn't it ironic that this building was taken over by a Dublin firm called Kings & Queens who at their own great expense lovingly preserved and restored some of the interior fittings including the beautiful balcony, pillars and beautiful ceilings?

Isn't it also ironic when one considers the coincidences of life, there we were sitting side by side at a desk in the Gilbert Library putting together our notes for this story when in the course of a passing conversation we heard proof of something which up to now we had been very sceptical about? We refer to the use of jam jars as a means of admission to some cinemas. We never really believed that that was a possibility, but we have now been proved wrong.

Alastair Smeaton a divisional librarian in development at Dublin City Libraries was passing by the desk we were working at when compiling this story, when he stopped for a chat. Having noticed that we were writing about Kings, Queens and Palaces in relation to the Phoenix cinema he remarked that the "Ellis" was once his local cinema and that as a child he used to gain admission to the cinema in return for a few jam jars. To say the least we were flabbergasted. Here at long last we now had first hand knowledge that this method of payment was indeed a fact of life.

Site of the Phoenix,
its current occupiers - Kings & Queens

The well-preserved ceiling

The beautiful balustrade of the balcony area.

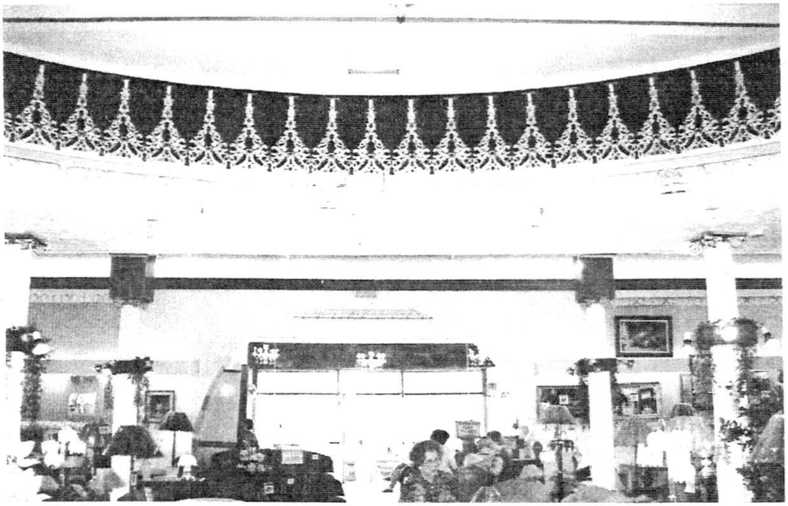

The only available picture we could find showing the Phoenix Picture Palace (White coloured building on the left of the River Liffey, with six windows).

As already mentioned, the Phoenix was usually referred to by most Dubliners as the Feeno, but to our surprise it was also known as the "Ellis" by some locals.

During the silent era, the Phoenix boasted of a first class orchestra.

It also, in a very enterprising manner, advertised special rates for school groups, football clubs, party groups etc.

CARPETS CLEANED. CARPETS SHAKEN

PRESCOTTS' DYE WORKS,

SATURDAY HERALD

6.30 FOOTBALL WHITE

£1 TO £1,000

Great Central Money Office, 53 FLEET STREET

TERENCE KELLY.

CERTIFIED NET SALES EXCEED THOSE OF ANY OTHER DUBLIN EVENING PAPER.

VOL. 22. NO. 82. DUBLIN, SATURDAY, APRIL 5, 1918. PRICE ONE HALFPENNY.

The Olympic Games

The Chariot Racing

The Bull Fighting

PHŒNIX PICTURE PALACE, Ellis's Quay (QUEEN'S ST. BRIDGE) Dublin.

THE HOUSE FOR GREAT PICTURES.

Commencing MONDAY, APRIL 7th, for First Time in Ireland.

BY ARRANGEMENT WITH THE PROPRIETORS, JURY'S IMPERIAL PICTURES, LTD.,

QUO VADIS?

An 8,000 Foot Picture. The Most Expensive Film ever produced.

Heinryk Sienkiewicz's Famous Classic Novel in Picture Form. A Realistic Portrayal of Ancient Rome at the time of Nero.

ONLY TO BE SEEN AT

THE PHOENIX PICTURE PALACE.

PERFORMANCES — WEEK DAYS—3.30 p.m., 6 p.m. and 8.30 p.m. SUNDAYS —2.30 p.m., 5 p.m. and 8.30 p.m. Doors open half an hour before each performance.

Admission—Reserved Seats, 2/- & 1/6; Unreserved, 6d. & 1/-. Children Half-price.

BOOKING AT CRAMER'S, WESTMORELAND STREET.

Hungry Lions LOOSED ON Defenceless Christians IN THE ARENA

The Burning of Rome

Gladiators in Deadly Combat

Evening Herald advertisement for the most expensive film ever produced and which was available exclusively to the Phoenix.

Well worth a jam-jar or two, doncha tink?

This is another view of the Phoenix building, which was taken towards the end of October 2005 on a Sunday morning.

The last advertisement we could find for the Phoenix cinema appeared in the "Evening Herald" on Saturday January 26th 1957 and we can only assume that it closed that night, as no film was advertised for the following day Sunday.

The final film on show was "Interlude", starring Cary Grant and Ingrid Bergman.

PICTUREDROME
Abercorn Hall, Harcourt Road.

The Picturedrome Cinema, which some referred to as the Abercorn, because of the fact that the picture house was converted from a hall known as the Abercorn, where religious meetings were once held.

This hall became a cinema circa 1911/12 and other than a large sign over a next door shop front, there was no evidence of a cinema in the vicinity. A small single doorway beside the aforementioned shop led into a long passageway that in turn led into a hall in the rear yard.

According to a reporter of the Bioscope magazine, the proprietors of the Picturedrome were the Entertainment Halls Company Limited and the manager of the cinema was Mr. Worth. Admission to the show cost 2d and the Bioscope reporter wrote that it was quite a touching sight to witness all the little bare legged urchins, their pennies grasped in grimy hands lining up on a Saturday afternoon in a long queue to wait for the commencement of the matinee.

The entrance to the Picturedrome cinema was through the single doorway on the left of the shop and its simple advertising board can be seen above the shop. Primitive and all as the cinema was, the sign above the shop was well lit up by a series of small electric lamps running the length of the board.

The Picturedrome cinema was located on Harcourt Road almost next door to the local post-office which stood on the corner of Charlotte Street, both of which are now long gone, having given way to the building of an office block, as did Old Camden Street which ran parallel with Camden Street.

The cinema proper was simply a hall that had been built in the back yard of a shop for use as a gospel hall and when converted into a cinema little or no change was necessary except to add a screen and a projector which was said to have stood just inside the entrance door and was in constant danger of being knocked over by people entering and exiting the cinema. The long wooden backless benches were already in place.

Mr. Worth was noted as a very capable manager with a good knowledge of the cinema business and being a Dubliner he had quite a knowledge of local people and their likes and dislikes, so it was not surprising that within a short space of time he was head-hunted by the directors of the about to be opened "Rathmines Amusement Palace" (Later to be renamed the "Princess Cinema" and made manager of same.

A scene of Harcourt Road in times past showing Charlotte Street on the left and what looks like a large white board over the shop where the pony and trap are passing is in fact the Picturedrome sign. The complete scene on the left is now fully occupied by the Harcourt Centre group of office blocks. (Picture courtesy National Library)

The Picturedrome was once fined 20/- under the 1909 Cinematograph Act for using a Cinematograph Machine without proper spool boxes.

The Picturedrome closed in the early 1920s and amongst other things it was used as a billiards hall and later again an amusement arcade until it was demolished along with its neighbouring buildings and re-developed as the Harcourt Centre.

PILLAR PICTURE HOUSE
62 Upper Sackville Street, Dublin (Now O'Connell Street).

The Pillar Picture House, so called because of Nelson's Pillar, which stood almost opposite it, on an island in the middle of the road, opened on December 4th 1914.

Nelson's Pillar, which was erected in 1808 to commemorate the Battle of Trafalgar, was a famous Dublin landmark and meeting place which was destroyed by explosion in 1966 the year of the fiftieth anniversary of the 1916 Rising. All that's left of that famous column is the head of Nelson and this is now on display in the Reading rooms of the Dublin City Library in Pearce Street.
The cinema had seating for some four hundred people and it was officially opened by Alderman John J. Farrell, who as the years rolled by, was to become synonymous with many cinema openings. For its opening night it offered a programme of all new pictures and an orchestra that would play all day. Prices of admission were 1/- and 6d.

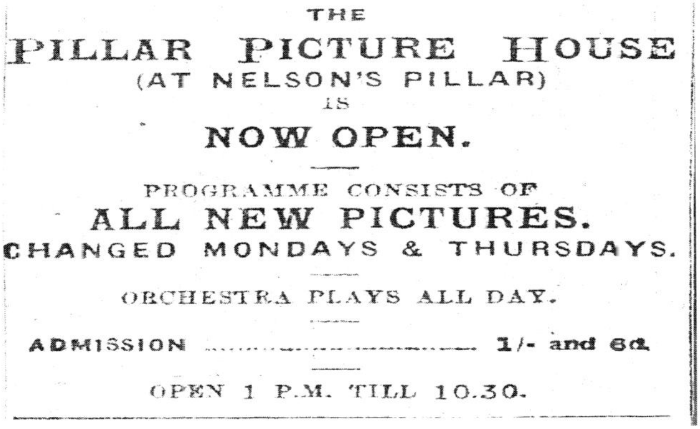

The Pillars 1st Advertisement

Like most other Dublin cinemas at that time the "Pillar Picture House", did well and enjoyed a good and steady flow of business. When feature length movies became the norm and the talkies arrived, management was well prepared for the necessary changes to be made and were most updated with their equipment. In the 1930's, like other town houses, it was designated a 1st run house and hence had the pick of the newest releases, which more or less guaranteed full house performances.

While it survived the 1916 Uprising and the War of Independence almost unscathed, it did suffer some damage during the Civil War when a group of men placed a landmine near the rear end off the building in Henry Place and the subsequent explosion blew the back doors off the cinema.

This explosion, it would appear, was not an attack on the Pillar Picture House but rather an attempt to disable a power line that supplied the La Scalla Theatre with electricity. The explosion occurred at about 7.30 pm on the night of St Patrick's Day, March 17th 1923, while a large number of people were queuing for admission into the La Scalla Theatre to watch the Championship fight between Siki and Mike MacTigue.

The devastating explosion was caused by a large landmine which was left feet away from the backdoor of the Pillar cinema and it was said had it been any nearer terrible destruction and serious loss of life would have followed. As it was the heavy exit doors opening onto Henry Place were destroyed and blown in pieces into the cinema with terrific force and caused some considerable damage. Members of the orchestra were bowled over and suffered numerous cuts and bruises from the flying debris. The ceiling of the cinema was also damaged and the plaster-work rained down on the audience. Miraculously the cinema screen was undamaged and the film continued to run for a further few minutes until the operating staff shut off the projectors.

PILLAR PICTURE HOUSE.
ALICE CALHOUN in
PEGGY PUTS IT OVER.
MACK SENNETT and SNUB POLLARD
COMEDIES, ETC.
Monday—THE CRIMSON CIRCLE.

The Advertised film for that night

On April 3rd 1938 the Pillar closed for almost three weeks for renovation and re-opened on April 16th and other than that we have no further information on the Pillar Picture House until it closed on Sunday March 25th 1945.

Its last two films were: "Gangway for Tomorrow", which starred John Carradine, Margo, William Terry, Amelita Ward and Robert Ryan which told the story of five people who worked in a munitions factory in America during World War 2. One, an ex hobo, another a racing car driver who had been so badly injured in a race track crash that he could not offer his services to the armed forces, A much disillusioned "Miss America", A French underground fighter who had come to America in order to help her fellow countrymen and an ex prison warden who had been expected to execute his own brother, and all their stories were told via flashbacks.

and

The "Red Robe", A Swashbuckling and Romantic adventure story that takes place in France during the reign of Louis X111 and starred Romney Brent, Annabella and Raymond Massey.

PILLAR
Conrad Veidt Annabella
"UNDER THE RED ROBE"
John Carradine
Gangway for Tomorrow
Ali Baba and the Forty Thieves

Very faintly at the bottom of this advert it says "Monday - Cinema Closed".

Circa 1930s (Courtesy, we believe, the National Library)

Now a McDonald's Restaurant.

PLAZA PICTURE PALACE

This cinema, which was situated on the corner of Dorset Street and Granby Row, started off its life as a small picture hall run by a Mr. W. H. Shanley, and was simply referred to as Shanley's cinema. The cinema like all other cinemas in Dublin at the time was a converted building, which originally housed the Bethesda Chapel.

This Chapel, according to our information, was built by a William Smith between July 1784 and June 1786. However, some other publications claim it was 1789. Whatever the date, it served its parishioners well for over 50 years until it was completely destroyed during the night of the big wind on January 6th & 7th 1839. The "Big Wind" of 1839 was one of the fiercest storms ever to hit Ireland and in Dublin alone over 25% of its buildings suffered some form of damage from as little as broken windows to complete destruction of property.
The chapel was rebuilt in 1840 and continued to function as a place of worship until it was desecualarised and closed in 1908. The upstairs portion of the building had been used as an asylum for female orphans for some considerable time and when the chapel closed the asylum, expanded into other parts of the building while some sections of the building served as a tenement until a fire destroyed most of the building.

Towards the end of 1910 a Mr. William Shanley from Hampstead, took over the building and converted it into a picture hall with seating for 800 people, which for a while was simply known as Shanley's Picture Hall. On May 13th 1911, now a well equipped Picture
Palace in a most up to-date manner it officially opened as the "Dorset Picture Hall". Some of the first pictures to be shown in this cinema were "The Lad from Ireland" and "How Hubby got a Rise".

The Plaza Cinema in Granby Row, off Parnell Square, in the late 1930s. It is now the Wax Museum.

The building was well equipped in the most up-to-date manner and the balcony had accommodation for 300 people. The orchestra was a four piece and always gave a good account of itself. Apart from films, the Dorset had a stage and many a fine performance was held there.

In August of 1927 the cinema closed for renovations and on Monday, September 26th it re-opened as the "Plaza" and introduced its very own "Plaza Dancing Girls".

THE PLAZA (PICTURE HOUSE) GRANBY ROW
WILL OPEN ON
MONDAY NEXT, SEPTEMBER 26TH,
WITH
"THE FLAG LIEUTENANT"
FIRST TIME IRELAND; ALSO
THE PLAZA DANCING GIRLS
PLAZA CLASSICAL ORCHESTRA, COMEDIES, ETC.

Admission prices were 1/-, 9d and 5d

Some Plaza Staff Members from times past. (needless to say, but we don't have any photos of the "Dorset" or for that matter the old Bethesda Chapel but we hope that what we have on offer will suffice).

The "Plaza" promised great entertainment and true to their word they featured the blockbuster of the day "Forest Havoc", in October of 1927 for its first run in Dublin. Starring in this film were Forrest Stanley and Peggy Montgomery, and in another first they introduced their very own "Plaza Minstrels", who provided a half hour of delight each evening.

The "Plaza" thrived and when the "talkies" were well established management in line with many other like cinema managements, sadly discontinued their wonderful stage shows, disbanded and gave notice to its orchestra and began to show pictures only.

During the following years it had many a re-paint and clean-ups but in the summer of 1958 it closed for a complete make-over and under the direction of the skilled architect Mr. H. R. Lynch it was transformed into a most modern cinema with its design based on the ideals of comfort combined with technical efficiency and contemporary décor.

The front of the building was given a modern canopy and a fascia with white neon and sodium lights, which illuminated the whole scene, and while the best and most comfortable of seating was used in the auditorium the balcony was furnished with luxurious armchair seating.

CINERAMA COMES TO THE PLAZA

Nine years later the Plaza closes down and once again it is totally refurbished and restructured and having incorporated a neighbouring building it was transformed into Irelands largest and most beautiful Cinerama Theatre. The new plaza now had a gigantic auditorium and balcony which were surrounded with towering walls decorated in gold lame and which lay under a ceiling of deep blue which was inset with port hole lighting it,
that glowed like far off stars.

The "Plaza Cinerama", Dublin's second Cinerama Theatre opened on Thursday, September 28th 1967 ushering in a new and exciting centre of entertainment to Dubliners.

For its Gala opening it presented the treble Academy Award Winning "Grand Prix" which starred James Garner, Eve Marie Saint, Yves Montand and Toshiro Mifune and tells the story of the lives and loves of a number of racing drivers during the Grand Prix Season.

Fabulous scenes were captured as the Formula one car's sped around the circuit at mind boggling speeds and the film locations are superb.

In an early scene of the film, a camera is in the cockpit of a F-1 car that spins out of control, slides off the track and crashes into the harbour scaring the living daylights out of every member of the audience.

Open House

During the first two weeks of October 1967, management invited members of the public to visit the cinema free of charge during the hours of 11 a.m. and 12 noon to get a quick glimpse of the tremendous thrills of the Academy Award winning epic "Grand Prix".

On September 28th 1967 the Plaza became Dublin's second Cinerama Theatre.

Although some great movies were made Cinerama didn't last too long and in the early seventies Cinerama movies became too expensive to make and many theatres dismantled their huge floor-to-ceiling screens and reverted back to showing ordinary films.

On January 15th 1976 the "Plaza Cinerama" showed its last Cinerama film "Earthquake" and reverted to standard type films until it closed on July 2nd 1981. The "Plaza's" swan song was a double bill from the studios of Walt Disney, "The Cat from Outer Space", and "Darby O' Gill and the Little People".

It would appear that audiences dwindled to a mere trickle in the 750 seater Plaza after the Cinerama Organisation stopped making films and as the management had suffered losses for the last couple of years it was now time to close its doors. The Plaza Cinerama had cost in the region of £100,000 to convert back in 1967 and while it was showing Cinerama films it was doing well. Once the films stopped the fortunes of the Plaza turned.
Eight people lost their jobs when the Plaza closed.

Following the closure of the cinema the building was again converted and became the "National Wax Museum", and as such it flourished until it got notice to quit in the early part of 2005.

Authors note: This was not Dublin's first "Wax Museum", as there was once a "Wax Works" situated in 30 Henry Street in the early 20th century and this "Wax Work's" was destroyed in the 1916 rising.

National Wax Museum.

The owners of the Wax Museum got notice to quit just before this photo was taken, and it would appear from this picture that Finn McColl had taken the notice to heart and was now demolishing the building.

However on Sunday morning July 3rd 2005 Dublin City Council workers arrived to take poor Finn into storage and soon brought this famous hero to his knees. All the wax figures including Finn have now been taken from the building and now lie in storage while awaiting their new home, which I believe will be situated in the Smithfield area.

For a while there was a slight reprieve and the plans to demolish the building in favour of a hotel were temporarily halted, because it seems that the long forgotten church which had once stood on that site had thrown a spanner in the works.

A Georgian Society spokesman said that any redevelopment of the site should incorporate the original chapel building in its design, however the owner of the site defended his move to demolish the building since it had been a museum since 1983 and that there was very little left of the church. He also claimed that he had decided to redevelop the site after councillors dubbed it an ugly building and that the new development would enhance the whole area of Dorset Street and Parnell Square.

Finn on his knees and having been decapitated he is now completely 'armless'.

Perhaps Finn should have read this warning, which was printed on the side of the crane-truck that lifted him from his lofty domain.

PORTRANE
Dockery's Cinema.

This cinema was sited on the upper floor of a two-storied building in Portrane and the ground floor area served as a shop. It is now a small privately owned family run supermarket and the upstairs area is their living quarters.

The upstairs section of the building still retains the original walls, windows, Stairways and wooden floors of the cinema and when I visited Portrane in October of 2005 to research the story of the cinema, the owners, Liam and Margaret, two lovely people, very kindly invited me in for a coffee and brought me on tour of their home and former cinema.

They told me that they had retained as much of the old building as possible and said that the original wooden floor, which was well preserved and lay beneath the carpet still had the screw marks where the old cinema seats were affixed to the floor.

These seats, I was informed by one of their sons, were old tram seats that had been salvaged many years ago when trams had become obsolete.

Unfortunately, there were no old posters or cinema programmes available and as the cinema had been closed long before their time they had little knowledge of it. However, they did give me a name and contact number for Peader Bates, a local historian and author, and between them, I was able to gather that the original owner was a Mr. Dockery who it would appear was a man of great entrepreneurial spirit.

Mr. Dockery it seems, had many business interests in the village of Portrane one of which was a fuel business that not only served the community but also supplied turf to the Portrane Hospital, and here I must mention that this hospital also ran cinema shows in a large hall which was used for meetings, concerts, parties etc, which were for the benefit of the patients and not the general public.

Mr. Dockery I was told, had many other interests in the village including a barber shop, a butchers and general grocery premises and of course the cinema which was simply known as "Dockery's".

I have no idea when this cinema opened or closed but I do know that it was sold on to a Mr. McAlister circa the 1950's and it would have most likely closed during his ownership, as the cinema business began to slide into decline in the late 50's.

This is a photo taken of the side and rear of the building and Liam told me that this was the main entrance to the cinema and the hand rails seen in the picture surround the concrete steps leading up to the entrance doors. When picturegoers accessed the building they would find themselves in a small lounge area that in turn led to a small cash desk where they bought their admission tickets and just beyond the desk was the cinema proper, which measured about 50 feet by some 20 feet and was fitted with line after line of tram seats. The likes of which I was told were quite comfortable.

PRE-EMPTING TELEVISION
Film Shows in your own home

The following advertisement appeared in the "Evening Herald" on October 21st 1949. Unfortunately it didn't scan well and we therefore made our own advert and quote the wording as we found it.

For the Children's Party _ _ _ A Hit-Parade

FILM SHOW
IN YOUR OWN HOME!

Treat the kiddies to an exciting film show with travel-cartoons, cowboys, adventure etc Sound or Silent films, we arrange everything.

Write or phone for details-it's really quite inexpensive

8 M.M. FILM LIBRARY

Why buy expensive 8 m.m. films
When you can hire them at low
Cost? Call and see our huge stock
of star-studded, top-liner titles.

FILM SHOWS
CORN EXCHANGE BUILDINGS
Phone 79254 or 62911.

PREMIER CINEMA
Lucan

The Premier Cinema

will open with a full Picture Programme on
THURSDAY, FEBRUARY 8th.
For attractions see Posters.

Week-night Prices :-
Balcony 1/4, Parterre 1/-, Stalls 9d, Pit 4d.
NO HALF-PRICE.

SUNDAY, FEBRUARY 11th.
Dick Foran, Irene Hervey and Fuzzy Knight
IN
"He's My Guy"
also Basil Rathbone and Nigel Bruce
IN
"Sherlock Holmes in Washington"

Sunday Night Prices :-
Balcony 1/10, Parterre 1/4, Stalls 1/-, Pit 7d.
NO HALF-PRICE
Balcony and Parterre seats can be booked in advance for Sunday Nights only.

Sunday, 11th February at 3 o'clock a Grand Matinee will be held to aid the Foreign Missions when a Variety Entertainment will be given by local children of the McCaffrey School of Dancing supported by Guest Artistes from Dublin.
ADMISSION : Balcony 2/6, Parterre 1/6, Stalls 1/- & 6d.
NO HALF-PRICE.

MATINEES
will be held every Sunday, commencing February 18th, at 3-30 p.m.
ADMISSION (children only) 3d., 4d., 7d., and 9d.
Adults usual week-night Prices.

"From quiet homes and first beginnings
Out to undiscovered ends,
There's nothing worth the wear of winning
But laughter and the love of friends."
Hilaire Belloc.

A few outstanding film attractions which will soon be coming to this Cinema :-

THE SULLIVANS.
BUFFALO BILL
SONG OF BERNADETTE.
FOREVER AND A DAY.
DESTROYER MAN.
SNOW WHITE AND SEVEN DWARFS
SALUDOS AMIGOS.
IN SOCIETY.
PHANTOM AT THE OPERA.
ROSE MARIE.
MUTINY ON THE BOUNTY.
Etc., Etc.

Souvenir Programme

THE

PREMIER CINEMA

LUCAN

Opening February 7th 1945

Two pages from the Souvenir Programme of the Premier Cinema, which opened in Lucan, "The Place of the Elm Trees", on Wednesday, February 7th. 1945.

In the 20th century it was customary to select a good picture for the grand opening of a new cinema, however the proprietors of the new "Premier" decided otherwise and they instead opened with a "Grand Celebrity Concert"

The Premier was quite a large cinema with a large stage and a pull-out section that we could extend it also had ample dressing rooms for visiting performers, as it was the intention of the proprietors that variety shows would be a big part of the theatres future. Some of the famous players to perform there, were Jackie McGowan, Dan O'Herlihy, Jack Doyle and the Mexican singer and actress Movita.

Talent contests were also a feature of the many travelling shows that would make their way to Lucan and perform for a week or two in the Premier. These contests were a source of enormous enjoyment to the patrons of the cinema and brought to the fore some great hidden local talent. One outstanding contestant who endeared herself to all the audiences was a young girl named Patty Galligan who was described by one MC as "the girl with the voice of an angel". It was said that she had such a personal magnetism that it would reach out from the stage and make you think that she was singing to you alone. Her interpretation of the old song "Marguerite", brought as many tears from the audience as it did applause. It was a just reward for her when she received the highest accolade any young singer could ask for at the time, and that was the honour of an engagement in the prestigious "Theatre Royal".

There were many other fine participants of those concerts and to name but a few we would mention Ken 'Shane' Maher the singing postman who wrote his own songs and monologues and was once offered a contract by the famous Harry Bailey. Jim Rowley, who would sing a selection of Bing Crosby's, greatest classics and a Pa Monaghan who was a brilliant exponent of the Harmonica.

~~~~

These tales of the Premier and a lot of the words used were paraphrased from the book "Some Lucan Memories" by the late Kevin Murray and permission to do so was kindly given to George by Kevin's wife Mrs Ann Murray. This book by the late Kevin also tells us of the arrival of cinema to Lucan and once again we take our information from the late Kevin's book. We are also most grateful to Mary Mulhall of the Lucan Newsletter for all her help and advice, including the copies of the two pages from the souvenir programme.

~~~~

Great excitement abounded in Lucan in the late 1930s when the first travelling cinema came to that village and dramatically transformed the social life of its inhabitants. The mobile "Picture House", as it was called in those days, came to the village in a convoy of three tractor-drawn caravans and a long dray that carried the cinema itself. The cinema was in reality a very large collapsible canvas tent which when erected was supported by individual sections of timber framework that would be bolted together. The entrance/exit would consist of a draw aside canvas flap and on one side of this entrance was a small table and chair which would be manned by one of the group in order to collect the admission fees.

The cinema, which was without any type of flooring was erected on a piece of waste land at the rear of Mary O'Mahony's shop on Main Street and lay adjacent to the side wall of St Andrew's Church. Admission prices were 4d and 8d.

The 4d seats consisted of a series of wooden planks, which stretched from one side of the tent to the other with supports at each end and one in the middle, space for a small passageway would be allowed for at both ends of each plank.

The 8d seats were of a somewhat better quality timber and would have a back rest and a foot rest which meant that your foot would not rest on the bare ground. There would also be a large free-standing iron stove whose long narrow chimney would poke out through a prepared flap in the canvas roof. This was a turf-burning stove, which would provide heat for the cinema. Music was usually provided by local talent.

Two red curtains hung from an overhead bar just inside the entrance flap and when the pictures began to roll these curtains were pulled together to block out any light that might shine through the flap and it was said that these curtains were a nest for fleas, which the owners claimed came from the stock of turf that was needed to feed the fire in the stove.

~~~

This mobile picture house belonged to an Englishman named Ronald Rice who travelled the length and breath of Ireland with his wife and a young Cork man named Danny O'Leary who was later to become famous for the breeding of Monkeys and Mynah birds in his own home. These Mynah birds were said to have achieved some type of world record because it was said that their vocabulary consisted of some thirty complete sentences which were spoken with a strong Cork accent. Danny O'Leary was also later to invent a burglar alarm which he patented under the trade name of "D.J. Alarms".

Ronnie and his mobile cinema had been touring Ireland for a good many years and initially his intended stay in Lucan was to have been for two weeks. However, they now had a young son Ronnie junior to care for and as business was good in Lucan, he and his wife decided to settle there and that was the beginning of a legitimate cinema in Lucan.

Ronnie junior was born in Terenure, Dublin in October 1937.

~~~

Many great films were shown in the Picture House which had quite quickly established itself in the village and it featured prominently in the lives of most of the villagers, not withstanding the many who walked, hitched, bussed or cycled their way to Lucan from neighbouring areas to see a picture there. Programmes began at 8 o'clock every evening with a change of film each night. Some great box office successes made it to the screen of the Picture House and they were often retained for a further day or two, but the one that broke all records was the British production "Love on the Dole", which was released in 1941 and stared Deborah Kerr in the lead role of Sally who became the mistress of a wealthy bookie in order to help her working class family who were all jobless in the bad old depression era of England. This picture broke all box office records in the Lucan cinema where it ran to a packed house for a full two weeks.

* * * * *

Mr. Rice who was a brilliant conjurer and a member of the Magic Circle in England decided to provide a little added entertainment for his patrons and with the help of some members of the audience he performed some great illusions.

One of his many tricks was to remove fresh eggs from out of the mouth of an innocent young person from the audience and he would follow this with an act that bewildered everybody in the picture house when he swallowed six 'Mack Smiles' double sided razor blades, which were strung together by a piece of string and after a long pause he would withdraw the string from his mouth with the blades still attached.

However well his illusions were appreciated by the patrons of the cinema, one of his magic tricks nearly brought about his downfall in Lucan and once again I paraphrase the writings of the late Kevin Murray.

The Black Dog

The magic acts of Mr. Rice were the talk of the village and people were saying that anyone that could do tricks like that would also be able to put a curse on the village and one local woman reported the happenings to Father Hooke and claimed that Mr. Rice had sold his soul to the devil

A lot of hysteria was being whipped up in the village and some people were claiming the sighting of a black dog that was half the size of an ass with eyes like burning coals, in the vicinity of the cinema, but others claimed that the dog had been seen before the picture house came to Lucan and that it emanated from the Church of Ireland building, which ran parallel to the picture house.

Opinions were divided, but as the winter set in a conclusion was reached and some who believed that the cinema was the cause of the manifestation burned the tent to the ground. This was of course an easy task compared to having to burn down the Church of Ireland which was built of granite blocks

Most people were devastated when they heard of the fire, but within two weeks Mr. Rice had purchased and erected a new tent and it was business as usual. This time however the owners had the good sense to have Father Hooke bless their new picture house and there were no more magic acts. The black dog was never seen again.

~~~~~

Some years later the Mr. Rice with the help of some investors incorporated a limited company named Lucan Cinemas Ltd and bought a piece of land at the East end of the village and there they built a new purpose built cinema. This cinema was built on the same style as the old Adelphi in Abbey Street. Seating was ample and comfortable and admission prices were kept to a minimum ranging from 2/6 for an early version of a Pullman type seat in the balcony area to 4d in the pits. Some of these Pullman type seats were of the double variety where a young couple could sit close together.

The new cinema was called the "Premier" and Danny O'Leary who was now a small shareholder in the company performed the opening ceremony. However like all things new the cinema had its teething problems and one of these problems lay with the sound system. It would seem that the chief operator was receiving many complaints about the acoustics and he solved the problem in a very simple manner by having the top half of the walls lined with egg cartons.
(A similar situation was brought to our attention re the Cameo cinema in Grafton Street)

Another problem, which was much more serious, raised its ugly head when the Government of the day introduced for the first time an entertainment tax which meant
~~~~~

that the owners of the Premier would have to increase the admission fees or go under. Fortunately there was a small loophole in the legislation that allowed for exemption from this tax if a stage show was incorporated in the night's cinematic entertainment.

While shows and concerts were a regular part of the cinemas activities this ruling called for cine-variety every night. Following a staff meeting a scheme was put together that would provide for this class of entertainment and Mary Joe McGovern who was the cashier in the cinema was voted in charge of this theatrical undertaking.

Mary Joe, it seems, was the founder member of the Children of Mary and although she was a leading member of the Lucan Girls Choir her only experience of arranging variety shows were organising children's concerts. This was an unpaid job and she volunteered her services solely in the interest of the local people and of course to save the cinema.

Apart from saving the cinema from going under as was the fate of other small cinemas around the country, it unearthed a wealth of great local talent and the stage experience gained from this little show proved invaluable in later years when travelling shows that were touring the country at the time stopped off to play in the Premier for a week or two.

With the cine-variety shows, the travelling show people doing a week or two, the much loved talent contests and the odd spectacular variety show with a big name showbusiness personality heading the bill, the Premier thrived, and with Sunday nights being so popular a booking system had to be introduced. Most Sunday nights would see a 'booked out' sign hanging on the wall outside the cinema.

Kevin in his writings told the tale of a very prominent politician and his secretary who approached the box office one Sunday to enquire if there were any ticket cancellations and Sadie Caples who was on box office duty that night told them there was not, but she said I can give you a box. Delighted with this good news they bought their tickets and entered the cinema to avail of their box, but what they did not realise was that a box meant a lemonade cooper which would be placed on one of the aisles between the rows of seats on the balcony. Their concept of a box was quite different from what was offered, but they accepted the box graciously.

Management also invited many of the professional touring companies to do a stint on the stage of the "Premier" such as Vic Loving, The Arco Follies, MacFadden's and the Great Ramasese's, who introduced mind reading to the patrons of the "Premier". Vic Loving's Company were also well known in the Swords and Rathcoole cinemas.

Kevin's book also tells us of the two most outstanding shows to appear on the "Premier" stage, both of which came direct from a run in the "Theatre Royal".

The first of these shows was the great New Zealand illusionist Edgar Benyon whose show was called "Bamboozlem" which it most certainly did. Edgar also introduced hypnotism to Lucan, which many locals sampled for their first time. Edgar's most remembered trick was the one which he used to close his show with every night, called the "Magic Kettle".

Each night he would invite members of the audience onto the stage and from a very small teapot he would pour into a cup any drink of their choice, no matter how obscure their choice and as a finale, while the band played his signature tune he would fill a large churn with water from his little teapot.

* * * * *

The second show broke all attendance records for the Premier and brought about the most turmoil since its opening. This show was called "Punch and Beauty" which starred the famous Mexican film star Movita and that handsome but volatile Cork man, Jack Doyle.

Jack and Movita were married at the time but 6'6" Jack had a fondness for girls and a roving eye. The family of the dancer Lollie Flanagan had to stand guard at her dressing room door in case Jack broke it down for a second time that week and tried to seduce her. Movita was also a world class soprano and she sang "Ave Maria" on the stage one night while sporting two black eyes courtesy of Jack. On another occasion during their two weeks engagement in the Premier whilst singing their duet "South of the Border" Movita stood mute beside Jack on the stage, the reason being that Jack was squeezing her hands so tightly that she couldn't open her mouth. However, it was said that Movita was also possessed of a fiery temper and could give as good as she got.

During the second week of their engagement in the Premier, Movita only agreed to continue her performance in the cinema when police protection was assured. On their last night Jack was tanked up as usual and he and Movita rowed on the stage and soon a free for all ensued and the Italian harpist Silvio was thrown bodily through the strings of his own harp .The stage manager tried to bring down the curtain, but failed and all hell broke loose. A local guard smacked Jack on the head with his baton and Jack simply shook his head and picking up the guard he dumped him head first into a large laundry basket.

A cinema usher struck Jack on the back of his head with his two foot torch, which drew blood instantly. But unfortunately for the usher Jack remained on his feet and turning he lifted the usher horizontally, walked about twenty yards to where Mr. Rice had built a large hen run and dumped him on top of it, leaving the poor usher bouncing up and down on the net wire as if it was a trampoline.

Jack, now fully enraged strode purposely through a now hostile crowd of onlookers towards a taxi and not one hero broke the ranks to try and impede him. On reaching the taxi, Jacks parting gesture was to kiss a few local girls and then he was gone, but never forgotten.

Jack was a legend in his own time and if we were to try and tell his story we would have to begin another book, but briefly we will remind you of a few highlights.

Jack was born in Cobh Co Cork in the year 1913 and died in St Mary's Hospital in Paddington, England in 1978 without any means of support. He was buried in Cobh.

Known the world over as the "Gorgeous Gael" the handsome Jack stood well over 6 feet and was a soldier, boxer, wrestler, actor, Hollywood film star, gambler, womaniser, heavy drinker, accomplished tenor and was once a contender for the British Heavyweight Championship. He also during his army career entered for and won the British Army Championship. He had notched up so many victories that for a time he was the hottest thing in sport.

His was a sell out act in the London Palladium and the Dublin Theatre Royal. He starred in at least two Hollywood movies and his successful tours of Ireland allowed him to command a figure of £600 a week. His favourite songs were "Mother Machree" and "The Rose of Tralee. He married the Mexican beauty, singer and actress Movita Castenada and it was said that they rowed continuously and that he drank, brawled and womanised at will. Jack was held in high esteem, loved, worshiped all over Ireland and women followed him everywhere, despite him being 'twice' a married man,

Following his last fight in Dalymount Park where he lost to Chris Cole, Movita left him and returned to Hollywood where she married Marlin Brando.

Drink and generosity were said to be Jack's downfall.

* * * * *

Having mentioned that Dan O'Herlihy once thread the boards in the Premier cinema we would like to tell you an amusing story concerning Dan, which was told to George by Noel Twamley who has contributed one or two storylines towards the compilation of this book.

Noel at one time worked for Mercedes Benz in Dublin and one day in 1971 he went on a callout to Dan O'Herlihy's house in Blackrock to troubleshoot Dan's imported Mercedes Benz car which had just arrived from Los Angeles where it had lain in storage for quite some time. The car would not start for Dan and hence his call for help.

When Noel arrived at Dan's house, Dan showed him to the garage where the car was housed and much to Noel's surprise the car was an absolutely magnificent 1938/39 coupe just like the Mercs that Hitler and Himmler had enjoyed during their reign of power in Germany many years earlier. It had large fenders, long running boards and left hand drive. Noel lovingly checked the car over and having made out a list of the work required to make it road worthy again, he presented a copy to Dan and told him that he would arrange to have the car towed into Ballsbridge Motors for the necessary repairs to be carried out.

Closing the garage doors Dan invited Noel in for a cup of coffee and as they sat and chewed the rag, Dan remarked to Noel, "you come across to me as a very astute young man, perhaps you could help me on another matter", and Noel replied, "sure if I can, I will".

"Well" said Dan, "I have just had a request from L.A that could save me $400 if I could find a stone from the rubble of "Nelson's Pillar" for a friend of mine, would you be able to find out for me where this rubble was buried"? Noel was astounded and wondered if he had heard right, had Dan just asked him for a stone from the rubble of Nelson's Pillar?

Seeing the look of bewilderment on Noel's face Dan reached across to a desk top and fetched a letter which he handed to Noel to read and having read it through it made Dan's request crystal clear.

The letter was from a law firm in L.A. and was written by a man called Goldberg, whom it appeared, had represented Dan on a number of occasions in an L.A court for some minor traffic offences, and attached to the letter was a bill for $400. However the letter stated that if Dan could find and return a stone to him from the rubble of "Nelson's Pillar" which he could have polished for use as a paperweight he could forget the $400 bill.

Noel found this request hard to believe, but Dan assured him that the Pillar explosion was big news in the U.S. a few years back and that such a paperweight would be an object of some great interest.

"Well", said Noel, "you have asked the right man, as I do indeed know where a part of that Pillar and statue are stored and that would be in a Dublin Corporation yard just off Cork Street". But why bother, "said Noel", "why not just nip out to the back garden and select a nice stone and post it to your friend in L.A., sure he'll never know the difference".

Dan exploded with laughter and spluttering he spilt some of his coffee on the front of his lovely shirt, my God man he said to Noel, you're a genius.

Moments later Noel took his leave of that lovely kind Irish actor and never had occasion to meet with him again. The car was towed into the Ballsbridge garage for repairs, repaired and duly returned to its owner. Noel moved on from Mercedes Benz and as Dan passed away in early 2005 Noel will never know if Mr. Goldberg of L.A. ever received his paperweight and if he did, was it from the Corporation yard or the Blackrock garden.

* * * * *

Noel himself was no stranger to the Premier and Lucan as his good wife was a Lucan girl and they enjoyed many a good film in that cinema.

The Premier cinema thrived for many years but on entering the fifties business began to slacken off a little and Ronnie went over to England to manage a family café and while there he continued to direct his business in Lucan. In the meantime Danny O'Leary had set up his D.J. Alarm business. In 1953 a decision was made to sell the Premier.

grove Cinema
1995

A side view of the Premier, courtesy Mary Mulhall, Lucan Newsletter, which was taken in 1995.

Through the kindness of Mary Mulhall, George was able to make contact with the children of Ronnie Rice who both live in England and on Tuesday morning, April 25th 2006 George met with Ronnie's son, Ronnie Junior, who was on holiday in Ireland. They met in the lounge of the Gresham Hotel where Ronnie and his wife were staying and it was here over a pot of coffee, that George learned the full story of the Rice family and their travelling cinema.

Almost word for word Ronnie Jr. told George the same stories about the fit-up cinema and the Premier that the late Kevin Murray had written in his book, but what the book didn't tell George was that Ronnie Rice's real name was Turner and not Rice, as he had led all to believe.

~~~~

It would appear that Ronald Turner was an ex British soldier who after World War 1 joined a Touring Troupe in London that did seasonal shows. One season was spent in Cobh, County Cork and it was there that the idea of a travelling show and a fit-up cinema became a feasible option for Ronald to earn a living. Ronald was an illusionist and a member of the English Magic Circle and based on these skills he put together a show that he could take on tour.

The enterprise proved a success and in the middle thirties he temporarily returned to England where he married his beautiful sweetheart Catherine. When they returned to Ireland, Catherine who was also known as Kay, was a most willing partner and one of her many contributions to his travelling show was to be the 'floating lady', of one of his famed illusions.

He took his show on tour circa 1921 just as the Civil War began and on many occasions on his travels from village to village he encountered areas occupied by either the Irish Freestaters or the Irish Republican Army and as he felt that the name
~~~~

Turner was a little too English for comfort he changed his name to Rice and never ever again mentioned that he was a retired British soldier.

He also felt that his new name helped when he was seeking permission to camp on a green site in the town or village, whether it was from a private individual or an official of the local authorities. As the years passed the quality of films improved and when the talkies entered the equation, showing films soon became his main source of income.

So as Ronald Rice and not Ronald Turner, he arrived in Lucan and introduced cinema to "The Place of the Elm Trees". While George never thought to ask, we must assume that his son Ronnie attended school under the name of Rice. In time Ronnie and his wife were blessed with three more children, Kenny, Pam and Kay.

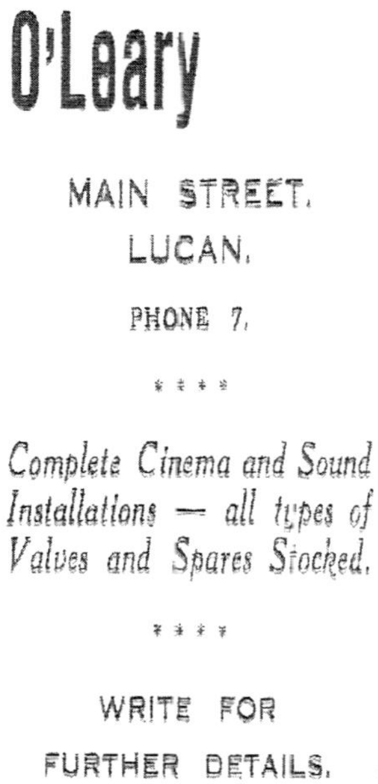

Danny O'Leary was not as most people thought, an equal partner of Ronald Rice, rather he was simply a worker that had joined the fit-up cinema family as it left Cork one evening many, many years earlier. Danny it would seem was an orphan child at the time that lived in Cork with two uncles with whom he did not like and when the Rice family set up shop one day on the village green Danny made friends with the family and when they upped and left town, so too did Danny.

Danny, Ronnie Jr. told George, was a loveable young man and a very willing worker and in no time at all he became Ronald's right hand man. In later years when Ronald incorporated the cinema business into a limited company he gave Danny 350 shares.

Danny was very mechanical minded and was always found to be tinkering with things that were faulty and eventually he would get them in good working order again. When the Premier was built Danny had the use of a room that was situated at the side of the cinema which he used as a workshop and people from the village would often call on him to fix a broken clock, doll or pram and this soon turned out to be a nice little earner.

The room, electricity and water etc were all rent free, courtesy of Ronald Rice and with little or no outgoings Danny was able to speculate a little with his earnings. As time passed he developed a simple type of alarm system that he rented out to various business premises at 10/- per week and Ronnie told George that at one stage Danny had about two thousand steady rental customers. Danny it would appear was a very successful businessman and he went on to establish a security company called D.J.Alarms Ltd., which became very well known in Ireland.

Above is a copy of Danny's advertisement, which appeared in the Premier Cinemas official programme.

This photo was taken at the end of the back garden of the house in which the Rice family lived and on the extreme left is Ronald Rice with two of his children and on the extreme right stands Danny O'Leary. We would also assume that the other little girl is Ronald's other daughter. We believe the lady standing on the rock next to Ronald is his wife.

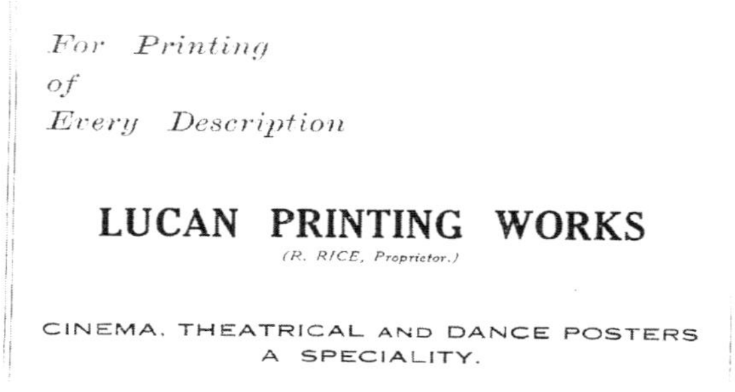

The house which was known as Lucan Bridge House was situated to the rear of the cinema as was the building that housed the Lucan Printing Works which was another flourishing business operation belonging to Ronald Rice.

When Ronald Rice incorporated the cinema business into a limited company he, as a director of the company, described himself as a Master Printer.

We would be of the opinion that all three businesses were of the same address as the cinema

This is a rear end view of the Premier Cinema that was taken circa 1945.
We would guess that the two girls in front were Pam and Kay, with Ronnie on the boiler house roof and Kenny standing on the railings behind his dad.
The doors at the rear end lead to the artistes dressing rooms and of course the one on the left was into the boiler room, on the left underneath the flight of stairs was Danny's work shop.

The photographer is most obviously standing on the Lucan Bridge
The House and printing works at the rear are long gone as is the cinema and the Ulster bank now stands on a part of the site, with a block of apartments to the rear.

St Andrew's Church, which stood next to Rice's initial site.

George took this picture of a car park that lies to the side of St. Andrew's Church in 2006 and it may well have formed part of the site behind Mary O'Mahony's shop where the Fit-Up cinema was sited in the 1930's.

Directors of the Lucan Cinema Limited
Incorporated March 22nd 1944, Ronald Joseph Rice, Secretary & Managing Director.
With the registered office being the Premier Cinema, Lucan.

Directors' names.	Occupation.	Address.	No. Shares.
Ronald Joseph Rice	Master Printer	Lucan Bridge House	1243
Daniel O'Leary	Radio mechanic	Liffey Bridge House	350
Vincent McMahon	Civil Servant	10 Kenilworth Square	50
Annie McMahon	Wife	10 Kenilworth Square	1285
Lily (Mrs) McMahon	Married Woman	1 Grosvenor Place	1285

Opening Shareholders Charles W Raynor (1) & Timothy Brophy (1)

We believe that Liffey Bridge House and Lucan Bridge House were one and the same.

In the Company returns for the year 1946 Ronald Rice's name appears as Ronald Joseph Turner Rice with an address at 108 Waterway Street, Nottingham, England and his occupation was given as a Café Proprietor.

Ronnie Junior told George that the Waterway saga was one of the worst times of his life and that neither he nor his brother Kenny wanted to leave Lucan and live in Nottingham. So bad did they feel that one night they packed most of their belongings into an old wooden tea-chest and attempted to abscond and make their way back to Lucan. However the poor innocents hardly made it to the end of the stairs with their very much overstuffed tea-chest before they were caught by their father who lovingly helped them back up the stairs and saw them safely back to bed.

According to the records in the Company's Office, in Parnell Square Ronald Turner Rice resigned his position on September 7, 1953. Lucan Cinema limited was then taken over by Kevin Anderson and Leo Ward and its new address was given as 71 Middle Abbey Street

In an email to George on 17th May 2006, Paul Anderson said that circa 1975 the cinema underwent serious renovations and Pullman Chairs replaced all the seats in the balcony area and that he changed the name to the "Grove Cinema" although he said, it was never call the Grove. The Premier was the first cinema in what was to become known as the "Ward Anderson Circuit".

Ronald Joseph Rice Turner and his family returned to England and Danny O'Leary stayed on in Lucan where he developed his alarm company.

Ronald died in the General Hospital in Nottingham on January 28th 1974, just a month short of his 77th Birthday, he was born on February 22nd 1897. Ronald being the kind and considerate man that he was, donated his body to the Local University for research and two years later his remains were returned to his family who buried him alongside his father in the family plot at Alfreton, Derbyshire. On his gravestone is the following inscription "Always the perfect gentleman"

Danny O'Leary died in Ryevale Nursing Home, Leixlip on August 9th 1986 and was buried in Esker Cemetery, Lucan.

Ronald's wife Catherine died on August 19th 1995 and her remains were cremated. Pondering on where best to scatter her ashes, her close childhood friend None Connor, who was in attendance at the church services, suggested Mount Brandon in whose shadows they had had many happy times.

Mount Brandon, on the Dingle Peninsula is said to be named after St Brendan the "Navigator", who it is told climbed to the top many, many years ago to view the Americas, before setting sail for same. Were he around today to retrace his steps and repeat that climb Ronnie tells me he would find a clump of extra green grass on the exact spot where he had scattered his mother's ashes in 1995.

Another view of the Premier cinema, Courtesy of Peter Brady who very kindly sent it to us and of course Jim Sweeney of Lucan Studios who took the photograph.

A Labour of Love

Is there really a need to tell you that our efforts during the last twenty months were that of 'a labour of love'. Sure what else could it have been when we would tell you that we funded the complete exercise from our own pockets, and that a sizable part of our expenditure was spent on photocopying documents and old newspapers in the Dublin City Archives and Gilbert libraries, which on many occasions because of the poor quality of the newspaper we were copying, the process often had to be repeated and all this at 75 cent a copy.

We journeyed all over Dublin at our own expense seeking news and clues on old cinemas and worked long into the night recording the results of the days findings and compiling these in story form. We bought all our own typing paper, ink, note books, envelopes and stamps and where possible we took our own pictures, not withstanding the costs of our computer equipment etc.

However having said all that, the final results made it all worthwhile and if we had too, we would do it all over again. As George's granny used to say when she set him a chore, if you do it today son and like it, you can do it again tomorrow.

PRINCESS CINEMA
145 Rathmines Road, Lower.
(Formerly known as the Rathmines Picture Palace).

The Rathmines Picture Palace was the brainchild of one Izidore Isaac Bradlaw a Dublin dentist who had a dental practice in Grafton Street Mr. Bradlaw was a British Subject of Russian origin.

He and three other Dublin merchants incorporated a company in Dublin called the Rathmines Amusements Company which in turn built a cinema and named it the Rathmines Picture Palace.

This cinema was unique in so far as it was purpose built as a cinema and not converted from an existing building as had all the other cinemas in Dublin at that time and it thereby earned its place in history as the first purpose built cinema in Dublin.

This new Dublin cinema opened for business on March 24th 1913 and offered to the public a stupendous performance from 3 pm to 10.30 pm every day.
Admission prices were 3d, 6d and 1/-

The films shown were of course silent movies with the accompaniment of a full orchestra, and a full and varied performance might consist of a number of news reels, comedy acts, short stories, scenes and events from home and abroad.

Similar offerings were to be had from all the other cinemas in Dublin with the only real difference being in the size of the building and orchestra; some early cinemas got by with the use of a simple piano and pianist.

The Rathmines Picture Palace appeared to thrive but for some unexplained reason it closed in its first year for a number of months and re-opened as the Princess Cinema, with no change of management or directors. The only apparent change was the new sign over the main entrance, which proclaimed its new name. The name Princess was adopted from the nickname which Joseph Karmel a director of the company had for his daughter Marjorie, whom he always referred to as his little Princess.

The Princess cinema or if you like the "Prinner" which it was lovingly nicknamed by its clientele, thrived for many years until April 30th 1937 when the Secretary of the Rathmines Amusements Company called an Extraordinary General Meeting of its directors and a resolution was passed to wind up the company and sell the Princess Cinema as a going concern.

Initially the cinema was sold to a partnership of two men which included its manager Mr Albert E Reglar, and he and his partner ran the cinema for some eighteen months when once again it was sold on to a new company.

This new company was a planned enterprise between Albert Reglar and a Mr O'Grady the managing director of the Stella Cinema, which was situated further up the Rathmines Road. No reason ever surfaced as to why the Rathmines Amusement Company was wound up, or why the partnership between Mr. Reglar and his partner decided to sell on the cinema.

However what we do know is that the new company "The Princess Cinema Limited", was equally divided in shares between two directors one being Albert E. Reglar and the other Mr. O'Grady with the share allocations being as follows, Mr. Reglar 25%, Mr. O'Grady 25% while the remaining 50% was held by the "Stella Picture Theatre Company" as security for a loan of £750.

It was so agreed that Mr O'Grady would be Managing Director and Albert E Reglar manager of the Princess cinema. This arrangement however did not last too long as on April of 1942 Mr. Reglar was no longer registered as a director of the Princess Cinema Company Limited. However he did remain on as manager of the Prinner until the very late 50's.

When Mr. Reglar left, he was replaced by the Chief Usher Michael Keegan, as manager of the cinema, and Michael remained in that position until the Prinner closed on July 2nd 1960.

In August of that year the Princess Cinema was auctioned off to the highest bidder, the "Jones Group" and having served them well for some 22 years as a metal workshop she was once again sold in June of 1981 and her new owners had her razed to the ground to make way for an office block.

This new office block stands on the site of the "Prinner, Wendy's Ice Cream shop, Wilf's Tobacconist and the Gas Company's showrooms".

It was heart-warming to hear that there was a serious attempt to re-open the "Prinner" in the mid seventies. This idea was the brainchild of Thaddeus O'Sullivan and Niall Hanggansid and the object of the exercise was to provide cinemagoers with the opportunity to see the kind of films which previously were shown only in clubs.

The plan had already been welcomed by the Director of the Arts Council, Colm O'Brian and a member of the Dublin Arts Committee Councillor Ruairi Quinn. Such a cinema it was said could probably count on support from Dublin Corporation, with their attitude towards cinemas described by Information officer Noel Carroll as a "very positive one".

Dublin Corporation policy is to "Support and assist in the provision of recreational amenities, particularly those that have a cultural element". Already that year £60,000 had been earmarked for grants to arts groups.

It was also claimed that the type of films that would be on display would provide an alternative to the traditional Hollywood blockbuster and the commercialised sex/ violence films generally available in Dublin's 15 main screens. These would include films from the "New German Cinema" movement, Continental films and films from smaller distributors.

In the previous year it was estimated that there were some 5 million admissions in central and suburban cinemas and that 80% of these admissions were in the under 34 age group and how this group would respond to alternative cinema was not as yet known.

However the plan never took off and the Princess was demolished and the site turned into an office block.

It was said at the time that Hubert McNally who had tried for years to introduce these type of art films into the Dublin scene failed and he now declared that what the public wanted was sex and violence.

George P Kearns in the uniform of the Princess Cinema circa 1954

Tall dark, and handsome then,
Now tall, grey and debatable

The Princess at the end of its tether

In one of his many offerings Noel Twamley tells me that his sister worked in Switzer's of Grafton Street and that every Wednesday she would give him 6d to go to the Princess to see a film. His favourite character in those times was "Roy Rogers" and any of the follow-uppers that might be showing on a Wednesday evening, such as "Captain Marvel, Buck Roger or Don Winslow of the Coastguard" all of which were much enjoyed by Noel.

Noel also mentioned a remark made by one well known local who was heard to exclaim that Roy Rogers never kisses the "Mott" he only kisses his horse "Trigger" so I shall go to the Stella in future.

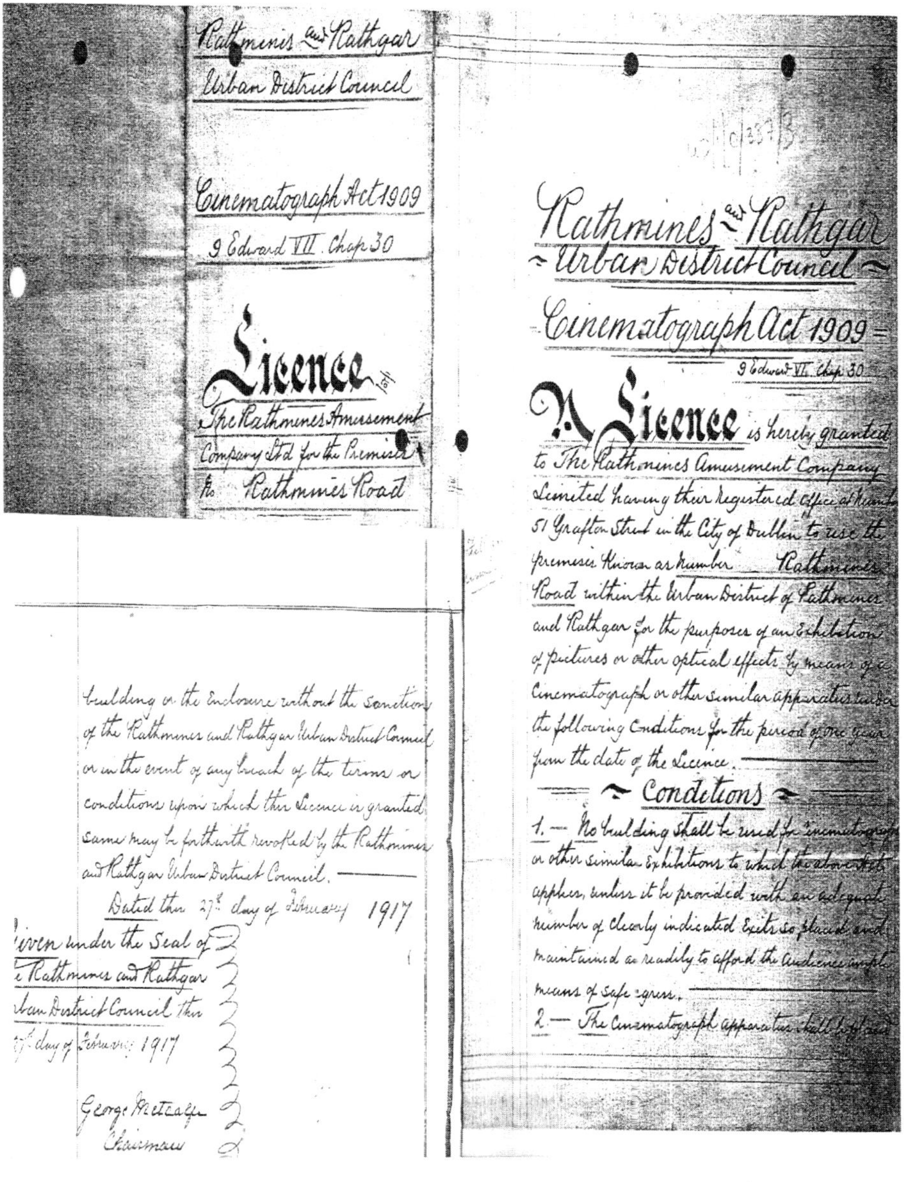
Rathmines and Rathgar
Urban District Council

Cinematograph Act 1909
9 Edward VII. Chap 30

Licence to
The Rathmines Amusement
Company Ltd for the Premises
No Rathmines Road

building or the Enclosure without the sanction
of the Rathmines and Rathgar Urban District Council
or in the event of any breach of the terms or
conditions upon which this Licence is granted
same may be forthwith revoked by the Rathmines
and Rathgar Urban District Council.
Dated this 27th day of February 1917

Given under the Seal of
the Rathmines and Rathgar
Urban District Council this
27th day of February 1917

George Metcalfe
Chairman

Rathmines and Rathgar
Urban District Council
Cinematograph Act 1909
9 Edward VII. Chap 30

A Licence is hereby granted
to The Rathmines Amusement Company
Limited having their Registered Office at Number
51 Grafton Street in the City of Dublin to use the
premises known as Number Rathmines
Road within the Urban District of Rathmines
and Rathgar for the purposes of an Exhibition
of pictures or other optical effects by means of a
Cinematograph or other similar apparatus under
the following Conditions for the period of one year
from the date of the Licence.

Conditions

1. — No building shall be used for cinematograph
or other similar Exhibitions to which the above Act
applies, unless it be provided with an adequate
number of clearly indicated Exits so placed and
maintained as readily to afford the audience ample
means of safe egress.
2. — The Cinematograph apparatus shall be placed

This is an exact copy of the licence issued to the Rathmines Amusement Company by the Rathmines & Rathgar Urban District Council which allowed them to open the

Rathmines Picture Palace for the purpose of exhibiting pictures and other optical effects through the use of a cinematograph or other similar apparatus under agreed conditions and for a period of one year only. The said licence is renewable on its expiry date for a further 12 months subject to a renewal fee and conditions.

Another view of the "Prinner" showing just above the gates on the right hand side one of the famous eight Ornamental Plaster Plaques, which adorned the walls of the vestibule area, two of which survived the demolition. One is hung on the wall of an upstairs room in the Rathmines library and the other lies in the vaults of the national Library together with a small cornice piece of plaster moulding, these plaques were said to tell a story with small children in mind...

On August 27th 1925 the Princess cinema was showing a film of the Prince of Wales tour when a woman stood up in her seat in the third row from the front of the cinema and threw a bottle of ink at the silver screen. The ink left a large black stain on the screen but did not prevent the showing of other films.
The woman was ejected and the police were informed.

Many months later the woman Nora Maguire appeared in court on the 18th December 1925 and refused to plead when she was put forward and charged with causing damage to the extent of over £5. I refuse to recognise the court she said and a plea of "not guilty" was entered.

When Joseph Lyons, an employee of the Princess cinema was giving evidence, Nora Maguire interjected and said:" This was a propaganda film. The judge warned her of possible contempt.

Miss Lily Fagan a pianist in the cinema and Mrs. Smith a cellist gave evidence of damage done to music, dresses, a cello and a cello case in the amount of £5.15s.

When the case closed, she was acquitted by the direction of the Judge and as there was no evidence put forward as to the cost of the damage done to the screen he made no order for damages.

One of the eight Ornamental Plaster Plaques

The last Pictures shown in the Prinner were "Lady from Louisiana" with John Wayne and "Tropical Heat Wave", with Robert Hutton.

If you would like further information on the Princess cinema George published a book on its history in June of 2005 entitled the "Prinner". It can be viewed in most Dublin Libraries.

George P. Kearns who worked in the Princess during the years 1952 to 1956

QUEEN'S
Great Brunswick Street.

The Queen's Theatre in Great Brunswick Street (now Pearse Street) began life as the Adelphi Theatre in 1829 and later had a name change to "The Queen's". In 1844 it was granted a patent by the Court of Magistrates which allowed it to use the word "Royal" and from then onwards it was advertised as the "Queen's Royal Theatre" and as such it produced many great musicals, drama's, play's and pantomimes under the management of Mr. Whitebread, an English playwright.

Many, many years later the "Queen's Royal Theatre" closed for a while and during that time it was totally re-designed by the architect Mr. William Stirling and when it re-opened it did so without the Royal prefix. It was then advertised as the Queen's Theatre, which soon became shortened to the "Queen's". It then had a seating capacity of 1,200.

As the "Queen's" in the very early part of the 20th century the daily programmes were of a cine-variety type and in late 1907 the theatre closed again for re-decorating and when it re-opened on March 2nd 1908 management advertised it as having the "Worlds Best Pictures", with admission prices ranging from 2d to 2/-

On March 23rd the "Queen's" was being billed as "The Peoples Popular Picture Palace". With a great variety of comic pictures on offer, and the latest in vaudeville novelties, together with a full and efficient orchestra.

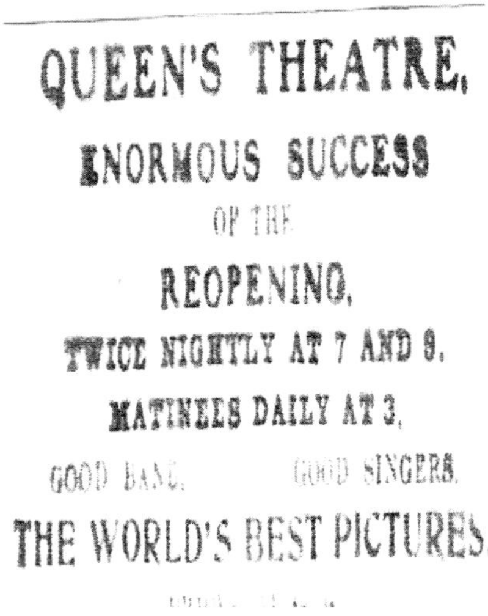

Management claimed that so popular were their shows that hundreds of would be patrons were being turned away daily.

In the 1930's / 40s the Queen's left pictures out of their weekday programmes and instead they ran feature films on Sunday's only. This was their policy right up to the time of the Abbey Theatre fire in 1951 when the Abbey Theatre Group, now without a home took over the Queen's Theatre and performed there until the building of the New Abbey Theatre was completed in 1966.

When the Abbey Theatre Group took over the "Queen's", the Sunday Film programmes ended, and when the Abbey Group moved out in 1966 the Queen's Theatre closed for good and remained in a vacant state until it was demolished many years later.

The Queen's Theatre

Some of the earlier films shown in the Queen's Theatre circa 1908:
"In the Days of the French Revolution", "Love Conquers Alf", "Poor Little Bill", "A Tramp in the Clover", "Grandmother's Bills". "A Timid Lover", "The Bandit King", "The Gentleman Highwayman", "The Cruel Stepmother", "The Tram Robbery", "A Separation Wanted" and "A Chase for a Husband".

QUALITY CONTROL.

In the course of our research we came across thousands of newspaper advertisements and articles about cinemas and having viewed these on micro film or in some cases, hardback copies, we then followed the usual guideline procedures of the libraries or archives involved, to photocopy the same.

However in quite a few situations the quality of the newsprint we were copying was not exactly compatible with the photocopying facilities available and we therefore got some poor results. The same applied when we came across an ad where some of the wording had faded in the course of time and when we photocopied them, some parts were unreadable.

We were then faced with the choice of using or not using our copies and we chose to use them because there was no real alternative. We also felt and convinced ourselves that in a way, their condition lent some authenticity to the character of the book. Ditto applied, as can be seen above, to some photographs.

~~~~~
~~~~~

RATHCOOLE CINEMA

It would appear that the Rathcoole Cinema had no name. Perhaps it was simply called Hudson's cinema after its owner or maybe the Glebe because it rested in and to the side of that property. However, name or no name, it was well patronised and showed the best of pictures.

Wednesday May 30th 2006 George took a trip out to the village of Rathcoole and by appointment met with Bobby Grassic a brother-in-law of Billy Hudson one of the three sons of Alfie Hudson the one time owner of the local cinema. Bobby took George for a walk-about in the village and showed him Tay Lane where the Hudson family first introduced their Fit-Up cinema to the residents of Rathcoole.

The site where the Hudson's erected their canvas tent was in a green area just as one entered Tay Lane from the village.

The site in Tay Lane in 2006. The wall and house were not in existence in the late 1930's.

This fit-up cinema consisted simply of large coloured poles which were sunk into the ground and covered in a tent like fashion with a heavy duty canvas, which acted as its walls and roof, with a large flap as the entrance door. The wooden floor was made up of sections of duck boarding which were laid on top of large timber joists and if nothing else it kept ones feet off the bare earth. Long wooden benches served as seats.

Alfie Hudson was a travelling showman who travelled the length and breath of Ireland with his Fit-Up Cinema and when he set up in Rathcoole, he decided to settle there for good. He had three sons, Sammy, Billy and Yankee, and they all lived in a trailer caravan which was also parked in the field on Tay Lane. There was no sign of a Mrs. Hudson and it was taken for granted that she had died some years earlier during their travels around Ireland.

Although Bobby never knew why, the Hudson's were also known as the Lynn Brothers.

Bobby told George that Alfie was a smallish type man who would take the entrance tickets at the door and that he was nicknamed the Gummy Tiger. During his first winter in Rathcoole the Gummy Tiger got many complaints from some local women who attended his film shows, about the cold conditions inside the tent and Alfie had no choice but to set up some sort of heating system inside the cinema.

It was customary for Alfie to hang framed posters outside the tent from the supporting poles, which would tell patrons of coming attractions and a couple of days later when the complaining women attended another show they were delighted to see a notice written across the posters that proclaimed central heating in the cinema.

When they entered the cinema they found that the Gummy Tiger had placed a large metal barrel, that had holes punched in its sides and was laden with fuel in the centre of the tent where he a cut a circular space in the floor of the tent and shortened the wooden seating forms to safely accommodate this barrel which rested on a few concrete blocks. When the show was about to begin he set the fuel alight and a generous fire sprung forth to the cheers of all. However Gummy hadn't allowed for the smoke and sections of the side wall canvas had to be peeled back to allow the smoke out and some fresh air in

Bobby claims that Alfie solved this problem on future nights by lighting the homemade brazier well before the cinema was to open and by the time the crowds arrived the fire in the barrel had settled down to a nice dull burning red glow with no smoke and everyone appeared to be warm and happy.

The projection machine stood on a large wooden box just inside the tent entrance flap and projected its pictures onto a large square white sheet that hung from the cross pole at the end of the tent.

Many years later the Hudson's got the offer of renting a large concrete built hall that was sited in the side yard of The Glebe House which belonged to the Church of Ireland and was ideally suited for use as a cinema. Alfie was delighted with the Minister's offer and immediately set about furnishing the hall as a cinema.

Bobby's sister married one of the Hudson boys and Bobby now one of the family began to help out in the cinema now and again. Alfie trained Bobby in the use of the projector and when required he was quite capable of taking responsibility for a full evenings performance.

Bobby Grassic showing George the building that was once the Rathcoole Cinema and The Glebe House, which we believe, is a listed building can be seen in the background.

Mary McNally a local writer and historian told George that she used to go to the pictures in the tent on Tay Lane and she remembered that on one occasion while at the pictures she opened a small box of chocolates and as she was offering some to her friends the box slipped out of her hands and fell to the floor where the sweets fell through the duck boarding onto the ground below. All was not lost however as a very chivalrous young man left his comfortable seat and going outside the cinema he crawled under the floor boards between the large wooden joists and retrieved her chocolates.

The Hudson / Lynn Brothers travelling fit-up cinema arrived sometime in the late thirties and in the forties they took over the Glebe hall, but their caravan remained in Tay Lane. Other fit-up theatres and circuses came to Rathcoole from time to time and some of the circus people like the Hudson's stayed on and settled in the village.

We could find no closing date for the Rathcoole Cinema but some claimed that it served the area well into the late forties, while others thought the early fifties. Fortunately for us the building was still in existence during George's visit and he was able to photograph it.

RATHMINES TOWN HALL.

On Saturday, December 31st 1904 Mr. James Jameson brought a bioscope show to Rathmines via his Irish Animated Picture Company where it began a short engagement in the Town Hall. The company opened with an afternoon performance and one late evening show and both performances attracted a full and appreciative audience.

The Bioscope pictures were of a good quality and included both coloured and black and white pictures. The stock of films held by this company was said to number some 20,000 and at each performance a bountiful collection was shown in great variety.

Included in their chosen pictures were scenes of leading events of the year, including war scenes from the East and much to the delight of the audiences a series of local views which showed members of the local congregation leaving the churches of Rathmines and Rathgar in which some individual portraits were easily recognisable.

There were also a fair proportion of dramatic scenes of adventure and escapes with most of them from photographs of actual happenings, together with some nicely balanced pictures of some humorous and laughable subjects.

Pantomime pictures were also exhibited with some fantastic staging effects and dances of subjects such as "The Sleeping Beauty", "Gulliver's Travels", "Robinson Crusoe" and "Puss in Boots" were all outstanding. It was said that the scenes were specially arranged for cinematograph photographs and were projected on the screen with great steadiness and remarkable definition.

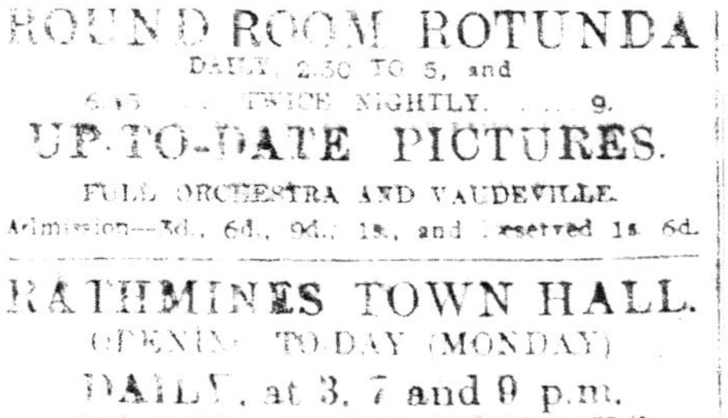
ROUND ROOM ROTUNDA
DAILY, 2.30 TO 5, and
TWICE NIGHTLY. 9.
UP-TO-DATE PICTURES.
FULL ORCHESTRA AND VAUDEVILLE.
Admission—3d., 6d., 9d., 1s., and Reserved 1s. 6d.

RATHMINES TOWN HALL.
OPENING TO-DAY (MONDAY)
DAILY, at 3, 7 and 9 p.m.
THE IRISH ANIMATED PICTURE CO.'S
MARVELLOUS PICTURES
CHARMING MUSIC AND VAUDEVILLE.

On the left is one of the many James Jameson's advertisements, which gave notice of the opening of another run of Cinematograph Exhibitions, by his Irish Animated Picture Company.

While The Irish Animated Picture Company had its head office in the Rotunda, James Jameson had a large warehouse and shop premises in Great Brunswick Street where he sold and or rented films and all things related to the cinema industry.

While the Rathmines Town Hall was not a cinema in the proper meaning of the word, it did for many years act as a venue for pictures and was available long before the thought of the Princess and Stella cinemas entered anyone's head. It also presented variety shows and pantomimes.

By the same token, mentioning the Town Hall allows us to write and tell about other venues that showed pictures which were not cinemas in their own right and here we would mention schools that would show pictures at the weekend, some for fund-raising activities and others just as a pure treat for the pupils.

The De La Salle in Finglas used to show free pictures every Friday afternoon and here the pupils had to attend, because the pictures were on show before the end of the official school closing time and therefore the pupils were obliged to attend for at least the duration of that time.

When George's children were young they used to visit a local house where a chap named Eddie used to show films at least once a week in a large shed in the back garden, and on other days he might run a disco and the local kids loved it. The entry fee was minimal and on wet or cold days it kept the kids off the streets.

The late Albert Kelly who owned the Classic cinema in Harold's Cross began his career as a projectionist in a like manner. His first initiative was to show pictures in a shed in the back garden of his father's house where he charged a fee of one penny for admission and later he toured Ireland showing pictures in village halls and centres all over the country.

The Don Bosco Boys club on Davitt Road also put on a display of films now and then, as did the proprietors of many community halls. Portrane hospital ran a cinema for its patients in their recreational hall and we are sure most prisons would have had private cinemas, at least before the advent of television.

We even have a report of a convent showing a movie on August 21st. 1913. This happened in the Sacred Heart Mount Anville, Dublin when the Sisters were occupied with a special presentation of the unique entertainment film "Natures Zoo" at the request of the Reverend Mother. These pictures of wild life which were taken in almost all parts of the Universe were projected in one of the spacious apartments of the convent, thus giving the nuns an opportunity they could not otherwise have enjoyed, or participated as it were, in Cherry Keaton's world rumble. The Lecturer of the pictures Mervyn M. Phearson, who accompanied Mr. Keaton on most of his exhibitions went to Mount Anville and gave the illustrative lecture. The whole of the arrangements for installing the projecting machines etc were in the hands of Norman Clifton the manager of "Natures Zoo".

Cherry Keaton was one of two brothers, Richard being the other, who were born in the village of Twaite in the heart of the Yorkshire Dales who found fame as the earliest wildlife photographers and writers and they were said to have been the pioneers of same. Today there are medals and other awards in their honour.

Cherry was also said to have accompanied Roosevelt on one of his wildlife trips.

"Natures Zoo" would have been Cherry's earliest attempts at filming wildlife in motion.

During another search we came across another convent experiencing an exhibition of Cinematography and this time it was the turn of Mount Sackville Convent where the

Reverend Mother allowed the Gaumont Company to present the feature film "Mary Stuart" in the convent on November 6th 1913. This entertainment was much appreciated by the Sisters and it was rumoured that the Gaumont Company intended another visit.

This we would imagine was the 1895 silent film of the "Execution of Mary Stuart" which was produced by Thomas A Edison, directed by Alfred Clark and which starred Robert Thomae as Mary

* * * * *

In the early 19th century travelling showmen brought cinemas to small towns and villages all over Ireland and the sites which were used for these fit-up theatres very often encouraged local entrepreneurs to establish proper cinemas thereupon or thereabouts those sites. To name but a few of the areas where these travelling showmen would frequent we would mention "Lucan" "Rathcoole" "Swords" and "Malahide"

Pop O'Brien was the travelling showman that brought a fit-up cinema to the "Green" in Malahide and who went on to establish the "Gem" cinema there. Vic Loving brought fit-up theatre to both Sword's and Rathcoole and most likely many more places. Undoubtedly there were many more travelling show people involved in theatre and cinema, and as they cross our paths of research we will record them.

~~~~~

As our research progresses we will undoubtedly continue to come across news items about the showing of films and as we find them we will log the details in this storyline under the heading of the "Rathmines Town Hall".

~~~~~

In 1909 Mr. Walter Butler was the appointed Inspector of Theatres and in the Dublin Corporation Reports of that year he reported on a visit to Capel Street where he inspected the premises of No 35 and found a room or hall provided with seats that were not secured to the floor and a Cinematograph Machine in the course of erection. He also found that the emergency door leading to the lane did not have a "panic bolt" but instead had a rusty bolt that required much force to displace it.

Prosecutions were instituted and the Magistrate made an order to close the premises at No 35 Capel Street as a place of public resort until the Corporations requirements were carried out, under a penalty of £25.

~~~~~

There was also a building in South Great George's Street in 1913, which traded under the name of "Joy Town" which showed Cinematograph performances without a licence and these premise were found to be totally unsuitable. However, when proceedings were instituted by the Law Agent, the parties responsible cleared out after a few days.
~~~~~

Plans for the conversion of St. Kevin's Hall in Lower Clanbrassil Street into a Cinematograph Theatre were not approved by the Corporation Committee as the premises were not considered suitable for that purpose.

The applications were one might say, judging by the following, coming out of the woodwork. When Dublin Corporation Committee rejected plans which were submitted for the conversion of the Baptist Chapel in Phibsboro into a cinema because the building had been constructed some twenty years earlier of wood framing which was sheeted on the outside with galvanised iron and had been in disuse for several years. They found that the building did not comply with the bye-laws, inasmuch as it was not enclosed by walls of brick, stone or other incombustible material.

However the Christian Brothers Schools in South Cumberland Street were more fortunate when their application to provide Cinematograph entertainments was granted a temporary permit to show films on three nights per week provided they undertook to comply with suggestions by the Inspection Committee as to seating arrangements, passages, entrances and exits, and the enclosing of the Cinematograph machine.

For a period of time the "Antient Concert Rooms" in South Great Brunswick Street abandoned the project of using the concert rooms for Cinema exhibitions, further to a visit by the Inspection Committee of Dublin Corporation in 1913. This was because of the many required improvements called for in connection with seating, an iron box enclosure for the Cinematograph machine, panic bolts and electric lighting to the satisfaction of the responsible officers, who also refused them permission to use the gallery during the performances.

The Dublin Total Abstinence Society and Workmen's Club of 41York Street also applied for a licence to exhibit pictures by Cinematograph. This Society who were also the Landlords of the Coffee Palace and Cinema Royal premises in Townsend Street planned only occasional cinematograph entertainments in their hall, perhaps on one, two or three consecutive nights when the hall would be disengaged and the speaker of the Society claimed that the proceeds would be for charitable purposes and would not profit any individual.

Mr. Butler, Inspector under the Cinematograph Act approved the granting of the licence because during a recent inspection he had found the hall greatly improved after the Society had carried out some alterations that he had recommended, which included the provision of panic bolts, a new exit leading to a back lane, better use of the electric lighting system, ventilating of the water closets and the securing of seats to the floor.

Stumbling upon a news item telling us that the "Gate Theatre" had shown a film or two over the years really surprised us, as we never would have suspected the "Gate" of going down that road.

The first film was an adaptation of Frank O'Connor's "Guest of a Nation" which told the story of a group of Irish Insurgents who were guarding their British prisoners-of-war in a remote farmhouse. As time passes the opposing soldiers come to respect and like each other and this is causing the leader of the insurgents much concern, because if the British carry out their threat to execute two I.R.A soldiers who are in their custody, then his prisoners may have to be killed in reprisal.

* * * * *

The second film "Return to Clennascaul" which was made in 1951 was written and directed by Hilton Edwards, who was also on the "Gate's" board of directors.

This film which starred Orson Wells as himself tells a tale about Orson when on a break from the filming of "Othello" is driving down a country road when he offers a ride to a man who has car trouble. While driving along the road, the man relates a spooky story about a strange event that had happened to him some time ago when he had given a couple of women a lift from the same spot.

Having driven them to their manor house he was invited in for tea and when he had left and drove down the road apiece he realised that he had left his cigarette case back in their house. Doing a u-turn he returned to the manor and when he got there he found the house deserted and decayed.

Later in Dublin the man was told by an estate agent that the two women, a mother and daughter had died years ago. Welles sufficiently spooked, drops the man off at his home and speeds off and continues on with his journey. As he does so two women try to flag him down for a lift and increasing speed he simply ignores them.

* * * * *

This film which told a haunting story was only 23 minutes long and it was nominated for an Oscar in the category 'best two reel short subject' in 1954
(This summary was by Steven Dhuey of Madison, Wisconsin, U.S.A.).

~~~~~

The Crystal Palace which we believe was an upstairs venue situated at 23 Henry was also the recipient of an unexpected visit from the Inspector of Cinemas who, on entering the premises found a cinematograph machine mounted on a wooden structure which was positioned in the centre of the floor area between the portion occupied by the audience and the exit stairs. This, claimed the Inspector, was a most dangerous arrangement which, should there be fire, would cut off access to the only stairs available for exit.

Permission to operate as a cinema was refused.

Further up the street seating plans were approved for the accommodation of 47 persons in Samuel's Exhibition Hall at No 6 Henry Street. (Also see 'World's Fair" Story).

Lourdes Hospital and Crooksling Sanatorium applied for Cinematograph Licences
Georges's Hall/ Hotel in George's Street also showed pictures.
~~~~~

JOY TOWN! JOY TOWN!
NOW OPEN,
At 48 SOUTH GREAT GEORGE'S STREET.
THE JOY WHEEL.
AMERICA'S LATEST SENSATION, AND NUMEROUS

This advertisement appeared in a newspaper on December 17th 1912. See mention of this fly by night cinema above.

~~~~~~

The De La Salle Schools in Ballyfermot were a regular source of film shows long before the Gala cinema came on the scene and for quite a while after the Gala opened they continued to show films. These film shows were not confined to pupils only, the local resident were more than welcome and well catered for.

~~~~~~

REGAL/RINN
Ringsend

Banner headlines in an inside column of the "Evening Herald" on Monday January 4th 1965 declared "Dublin Cinema to Close" and one would ask, at that time, what's new?

Another Dublin cinema, the Regal in Ringsend reads the column, is to close on next Sunday night the 10th January 1965. After 40 years the curtain will come down for the last time on this cinema, which was quite a healthy youngster in the silent days.

"Television and rising overheads", Mr. George Jay told the reporter "were the cause of the close-down", "dwindling takings", he said, "due to a fall off in attendances have left the management no option but to close".

The building has already been purchased said Mr. Jay, who also owns the Ritz cinema in Sandymount, and work will soon begin to convert it into a factory and the equipment and contents will be sold in a public auction on Wednesday January 13th.

The last film to be projected on the screen will be "The Birdman of Alcatraz", starring Burt Lancaster.

REGAL (Ringsend): Harold Lloyd, "Funny Side Of Life", 5.50, 8.58 and "The Quick Gun", 7.27 p.m. Sun.: Burt Lancaster "Birdman Of Alcatraz" and "Bugs Bunny".

This film which was nominated for many awards told the story of Robert Stroud prisoner AZ#594 who was a vicious double murderer that was so violent and dangerous that he had to be imprisoned in isolation in Alcatraz.

Stroud when allowed to keep an injured canary as a pet, which he nursed back to good health, became a renowned bird expert and while in prison he cared for and bred some 300 birds and became an authority on their existence and diseases. He was said to have written two books on the subject. Stroud although a violent killer was also an intelligent man who studied and read a lot during his 50 odd years in prison, (three prisons in all), and it was claimed that he learned a number of different languages. For the record it would seem that he was not allowed to keep birds in Alcatraz, or McNeil Island penitentiaries, his interest in birds came about in Leavenworth Penitentiary and ended there when he was transferred to Alcatraz Island, where he died aged 73 in 1962 having spent some 51 years in prison.

* * * * *

A nice little tale was told to us by one David Grundy, who as a kid was a keen patron of the Regal and Ritz cinemas. He recalled that when he was a child his uncle Leo used to sing songs about the Regal in Ringsend to him and his brother. It would appear that in the 1930's "follieruppers" were serialised week after week in certain cinemas and one of them was called "The Clutching Hand", a horror type serial and at the same time there was a popular song about which was called "An Old Cow Hand from the Rio Grande" and this song was parodied to the same air and sung by kids on their way to and from the Regal.

I'm an Old Cow Hand from the Regal Grand,
And I go to the Regal to see the Clutching Hand.
Admission free but you pay at the door,
Cushion seats but you sit on the floor.
Make any noise and your fecked out the door,
Yipee aye ay, Yipee I oh, oh

* * * * *

REGAL
Fitzwilliam Street, Ringsend.

The Regal Cinema Company was incorporated on 16th November 1936 and its company registration number was 9325. Its office address was given as 5 Marine Drive, Sandymount and the company secretary was Cissy McGrory of 48 Farney Park, Sandymount. She held 200 shares as did William Dunne the operator and assistant manager of the cinema who was a resident of St. Ann's, Newbridge Avenue. The principle director was Mr. Percy Winder Whittle who held 3,000 shares. The cinema was what you might call "Family owned" as it would appear that all the Whittle family that were old enough, participated in the running of it.

The site of the Regal cinema is now called Regal House which I believe is associated with community activities. George was born and reared in the next village "Irishtown" and knew the Regal well and if his memory serves him correct one of these shops pictured alongside the cinema was a sweet and confectionery shop which was owned by the Whittle family.

The Regal name however was not the original name of the cinema. When the cinema first opened for business on November 14th 1925 it was named the "Rinn" a most appropriate name, which was very much a part of Ringsend history. It might also further surprise Ringsenders to know that one of its most principle directors was none other than Stevedore, William Murphy of Cambridge House, Cambridge Road, Ringsend.

George will tell you here that William Murphy was a distant uncle of his through the second marriage of his maternal grandmother to one Laurence Murphy, but then who in that area didn't have a Murphy relative in the Ringsend of the 1940s. However long before George came into the world, the company had sold the cinema to the Whittle family

For the purpose of building a picture house in Ringsend, William Murphy formed and incorporated a company called the Cities Cinema Company limited on 7th August 1924 with offices at 5 Nassau St, and his fellow directors were as follows:

Michael Carrick, a Stevedore

William Byrne, a Builder

Padraig Tarrant, a Printer

John Doran, a General Manager of an Insurance Company

Peter Sherry, a Spirit Merchant

John Boyle, a General Merchant

=====

In all, the building of same cost £10,000 and the directors were more that satisfied with its excellent construction, the beauty of its design and its luxurious appointments.

The Directors, having christened their new cinema the "Rinn", opened to an invited audience, which included all the representatives of the Pembroke area, including the Chairman of the Urban District Council, the Town Clerk, Councillors and their friends.

For the grand opening the film "Quemado" was chosen, this was a fine western starring Fred Thomson as Quemado and Nola Luxford playing Conchita Rameriz his love interest Songs and dances staged by ex-members of the Carl Rosa Opera Company were also included in the opening performance, as was an excellent turn by Cathal MacGarvey.

In a report in the Irish Times in 1925 the cinema was described as one of the largest, best ventilated and most luxuriously appointed cinema theatres in Dublin.

It also said that the theatre was situated on the tram line at the three-halfpenny stage from the Nelsons Pillar.

The cinema was built by Messrs. McNally and Co. of East Wall and the architect was T.F McNamara of Pearse Street, The ornamental canopy was supplied by McGloughlin the art metal engineers of Pearse Street and Messrs Elliman and Co furnished the luxury seating. The vestibule area was laid with terrazzo and was approached by a flight of mosaic steps.

The Contractors
McNALLY & Co., Ltd.
Builders & Public Works Contractors

EAST WALL
DUBLIN

Telephone No. - 256 Drumcondra

The Central Heating and Ventilating
OF
The Rinn Cinema
HAS BEEN INSTALLED BY
THE IRISH EXPERTS,
Maguire & Gatchell, Ltd.
7-15 Dawson Street, Dublin.

RINN CINEMA.
RINGSEND.

GRAND
OPENING TO-NIGHT
AT 7 O'CLOCK.

AS THE RINN CINEMA IS THE MOST COMFORTABLE, BEST EQUIPPED, AND BEST VENTILATED CINEMA IN DUBLIN, SO WILL ITS PICTURES AND MUSIC BE ALSO THE BEST.

Opening night advertisement from the "Evening Herald" November 13th 1925

Another advertisement for the Rinn showing it admission prices.

This was an illuminated sign affixed to a public street lamp-post at the Delta opposite Fitzwilliam Street which pointed the way to the Rinn Cinema. Permission for the erection of this sign by Cities Cinemas Limited was allowed under licence from the Pembroke Urban District Council. Most appropriate, for those alighting from a tram at the three-halfpenny stage from Nelson's Pillar.

While the cinema was very welcome in the area and attracted full attendances it would appear that some difficulties arose and the cinema seemed to close and reopen on a couple of occasions. One of these occasions was circa November 1930 and on December 13th 1930 an advertisement appeared in the evening papers announcing a Grand re-opening of the cinema, which was now called the "Regal". We are also of the opinion that there may well have been a change of directors.

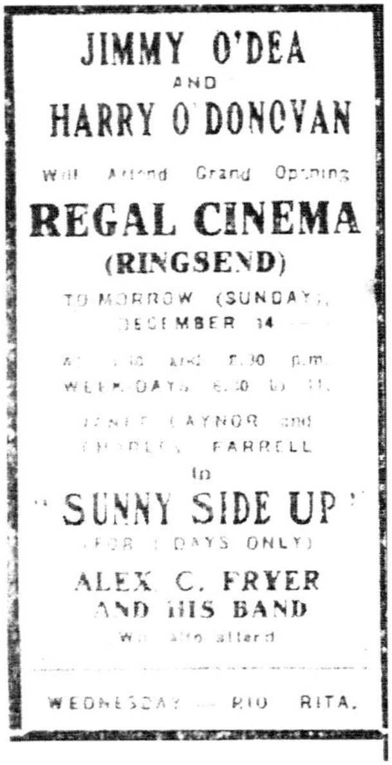

The Grand Opening, which was attended by Jimmy O'Dea and Harry O'Donovan took place on Sunday December 14th 1930 and the musical entertainment was provided by Alex C. Fryer and his band.

The feature film for the opening night was "Sunny Side Up" starring Janet Gaynor and Charles Farrell. This is a hilarious 1929 romantic comedy where Molly a poor working class girl played by Janet falls for wealthy man (Charles) who lives in a mansion.

However at the bottom of the advertisement the following Wednesday's film is mentioned and this film "Rio Rita" 1929, starring Bebe Daniels as Rita and John Boles as a Texas Ranger who chases a baddy over the Mexican Border and falls in love with the Bandits sister Rita.
Bebe Daniels we are sure will awaken many a happy memory in our fellow senior citizens.

However once again the cinema closed and on Friday August 4th 1933 another Grand Opening was announced.

The film featured for this Grand Opening was "Justice for Sale", starring Academy Award winning actor Walter Huston, father of Actor/director John Huston and grandfather to Anjelica Huston. Anjelica would be no stranger to Ringsenders as she directed and starred in the film about Brendan O'Carroll's Agnes Browne in 1999, which was filmed in Thorncastle Street, Ringsend just around the corner from the Regal Building.

The cinema then appeared to go into receivership and the following year on October 2nd 1934 Mr. Percy Winder Whittle took over the business from the Receiver. In November of 1936 he incorporated the Regal Cinema Company.

The Regal now a family run cinema appeared to thrive under the direction of Percy Whittle and in a short few years he also purchased the Astoria Cinema in Sandymount and renamed it the Ritz.

THE RINN CINEMA, RINGSEND.

Courtesy Irish Times, View of the Rinn in November 1925.

However well it was doing the Regal once again changed hands in 1949 when George Jay bought the cinema from the Whittle family.

Most of today' Ringsenders, Irishtowners and Sandymounter's would be more familiar with George Jay of the Regal and his manager Owen Dunne in the Ritz rather than the Whittle family and it was George Jay who was at the helm when the Regal closed on Sunday January 10th 1965.

~~~~

The Regal Building still stands and now houses a Community Enterprise Centre.

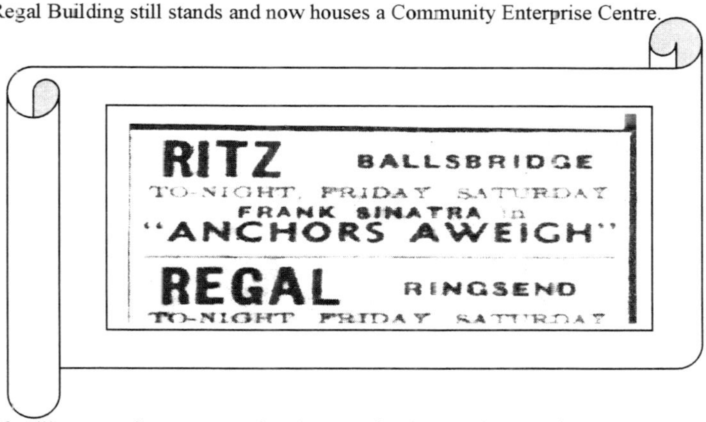

A very familiar type of newspaper advertisement for the Regal & Ritz in the 1940's.
~~~~

REGAL ROOMS
Hawkins Street, Dublin.

The Regal Rooms cinema opened on Easter Saturday 16th April 1938 with the showing of the film "True Confession" starring Carole Lombard and Fred McMurray.

This film is a hilarious comedy based on the fantasy minded wife of a Lawyer who confesses to a murder she didn't commit, and her ever-loving husband has the unenviable task of defending her.

The Regal Rooms cinema was a conversion of the Regal Rooms restaurant that had been built on the site of the Winter Gardens, which was attached to the Royal cine-variety theatre. This restaurant did not enjoy a financial success and it was decided to convert it into a cinema.

The cinema thrived and held its own until like the Royal it was closed and demolished in 1962 to make way for an office block. However it always appeared to be in the shadow of the Royal and some said they only went to the Regal Rooms when they couldn't get into the Royal. When it closed it did so without fanfare and one might say it went almost un-noticed.

On its last day it featured two films "Upstairs and Downstairs" and "Appointment with a Shadow".

This picture of the Regal Rooms Cinema is courtesy of Art Deco Ireland. This cinema was at the time described as a most intimate luxury theatre that was designed on the stadium principle, which had the most unique type of seating known as "Cheeta" seats which were hinged on ball-bearings to obviate the creaking which normally results from the raising and lowering of such tip-up seats.
The flooring was of deep red carpets, which added to the luxury of the cinema and also helped to deaden any noise. Mirrophonic sound the latest and most modern from Western Electric brought great clarity of sound to every seat of which there were 1,000 and admission prices were reasonable.

While the last advertisement for the Theatre Royal, which accompanied this one for the Regal Rooms in the newspapers, promised a "Royal Finale" the Regal Rooms left us with just a whisper and the makings of a puzzle.

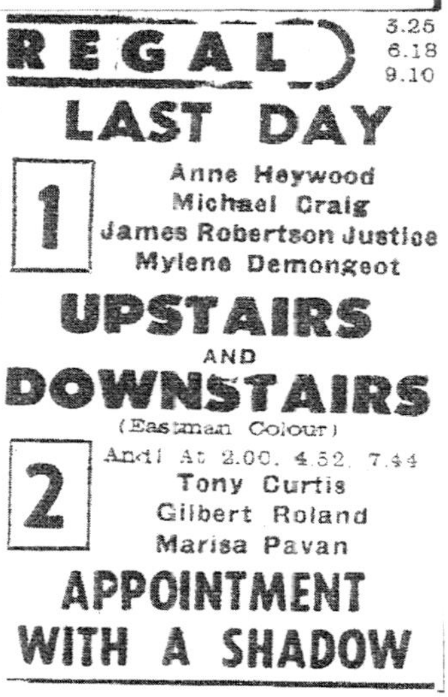

While the second film "Appointment with a Shadow" (1958) which was directed by Richard Carlson, did have Tony Curtis in its cast he was very far down the line and as far as we could tell the billing should have been as follows:
George Nader, Brian Keith and Joanna Moore
However the film was said to be aka "Midnight Story" (1957) which was directed by Joseph Pevney and this indeed starred Tony Curtis, Marisa Pavan, and Gilbert Roland.
'BUT'
They both had different storylines and we now wonder what the audience saw that night. Was it strait-laced dogged cop Tony Curtis or reformed drunk reporter George Nader?

As is our want, we researched both film titles and came upon an amazing situation that we found hard to fathom and with neither one of us a real film buff in the accepted sense of the word we found ourselves baffled.

To fill you in on our findings we would tell you that the film entitled "Appointment with a Shadow" (AWAS) which was made in 1957, (With some saying 1958) was said to be also known as Midnight Story (MS) which was also made in 1957 and this threw us completely, as did the star billings for AWAS which wrongly named actors who were character actors in the film as the lead actors, as per the advert which is reproduced on the previous page.

For starters AWAS was made one year before MS and both had different running times, with the former 73 minutes and the latter 89 minutes. While both had the same story writer Edwin Blum, the screen writers differed as did the director's. Richard Carlson directed AWAS and Joseph Pevney directed MS. While both stories told of a murder and the hunt of a murderer, the lead characters differed in each storyline, as did the lead actors.

So to all intents and purposes it would appear that we had established that the two films were completely separate productions and that the film on view in the "Regal Rooms" on its last night was either wrongly advertised as "Appointment with a Shadow" or simply credited with the wrong leading actors.

End of Story, No way!

To further confuse the issue we would tell you that the following members of the cast of both movies played the same character parts in both films.

Gilbert Roland as Sylvio Malatesta
Richard Monda as Peanuts Malatesta
Argentina Brunetti as Mama Malatesta
Marisa Pavan as Anna Malatesta
Kathleen Freeman as Rosa Cuneo
Jac C Flippen as Sgt Jack Gillen
Ted de Corsia as Lt. Kilrain
Russ Conway as Det. Sgt. Sommers
John Cliff as Father Giuseppe
Tito Vuolo as Grocer
Tony Curtis as Joe Martini
Helen Walace as Mother Catherine
Herb Vigran as Charlie Cuneo

It would appear as if the majority of the cast stood by while a second film was made.

In "Appointment with a Shadow"(1958) the leading actor is George Nader, who plays the part of a drunken reporter (Paul Baxter) who witnesses a gangster being arrested for a murder that he didn't commit and Paul goes on the "wagon" and hunts down the real Killer.

Other leading actors were; Brian Keith as (Lt Spencer), Joanna Moore as (Penny) and Frank de Kova as (Dutch Hayden) followed by the cast as already mentioned.

In "Midnight Story"(1957) the leading actor is Tony Curtis who plays the part of traffic cop (Joe Martini) and when a priest is murdered in an alleyway and the police have no clues as to who the murderer is, Joe turns in his badge and searches for the Killer on his own. His fellow leading actors in this film were: Gilbert Roland as (Sylvio Malatesta) and Marisa Pavan as (Anna Malatesta) and of course the aforementioned cast.

The Winter Gardens.

On Monday, November 23rd 1908 Mr. Fred Mouillot the Manager of the "Theatre Royal" introduced for the first time in Ireland Mr. Robert Courtneidge's entire production of the brilliant Comic Opera "Tom Jones" to the "Theatre Royal" with Florence Smithson as Sophia and Harry Welchman as "Tom Jones" and at 8pm that evening he also attended at the official opening of the Theatre Royal Winter Gardens which was annexed to the theatre.

Here in this splendid garden complex which was adorned with potted palm trees, shrubs, ferns and fountains which play at both ends of the hall which is dotted with dainty tables and comfortable lounge chairs where coffee and other refreshments can be availed of from a most courteous staff of attendants. The Garden is on a level with the theatres parterre and was approached by a broad and handsome flight of stairs leading from the dress Circle.

An "At Home" programme would be available every afternoon, which would allow for the viewing of the latest living pictures in the Theatre and afternoon tea, which would be served in the Winter Garden and all for the inclusive charge of 1/-.

The Gardens would also be available for light luncheons every day after 12 o'clock when an orchestra would play daily. However when the "Theatre Royal" closed down in 1934 for rebuilding, so too did the "Winter Gardens".

~~~~~

1935 on the same day as the opening of the new "Theatre Royal" the "Regal Rooms Restaurant" also opened for business.
~~~~~

This restaurant came about from the remodelling and restructuring of the old "Winter Gardens" and at the time seemed like a good and profitable idea, and for a while the restaurant did do well. But in 1937 trade began to slacken off and the Restaurant closed.

Later that year the premises was converted into another cinema and hence the birth of the "Regal Rooms" cinema which as already mentioned opened its doors on Easter Saturday, April 16th 1938.

Snippets.

Jimmy Campbell:
As was the custom in those happy times theatres like the Royal & Queens did not have live stage shows on Sunday nights instead of which they would show a feature film together with a supporting movie.

Nevertheless Jimmy Campbell's talents didn't go to waste as he had a resident spot in the "Regal Rooms Restaurant" on Sunday nights, with his very own "Regal Tipica Orchestra" where the Latin American beat was much appreciated by the restaurant clientele.

Jimmy was a very talented musician who began his musical career in the Scalla Cinema in South Shields, England at the tender age of 18 years and some years later he broadcast for the B.B.C as solo violinist for nearly three years from their Newcastle-on-Tyne studios. Later on he formed his own orchestra and developed a flair for orchestration, which countless visiting artists at the Royal have publicly acknowledged.

Jimmy was with the Royal from its inception in 1935 but when it closed it did not mean the end of his career as he moved on with several members of the Royal orchestra and formed a resident orchestra in the "Gaiety Theatre".

* * * * *

REGENT
Findlater Place

Or, as some would have it, Cathal Brugha Street.

Dublin's latest cinema the Regent opened on May 19th 1967 just in time for inclusion in our book about Old Dublin Cinema's as Patrick and yours truly had more or less set 1970 as a deadline for our storylines.

Not that we would be that strict with this ruling but we did have to give ourselves a guideline and cut off point as otherwise we would never get the book finished.

The Regent opened with Fred Zinnemann's award winning film "A Man For All Seasons". This film walked away with 6 Academy Awards, including "Best Picture of the Year".

But then why wouldn't it when a masterpiece maker like Fred Zinnemann's had a hand in it as he had done with other award winnings movies such as "From Here to Eternity" and "High Noon".

The film starring Paul Scofield ad Sir Thomas Moore, Robert Shaw as King Henry VIII, Orson Welles as Cardinal Wolsey and Susannah York as Margaret More, not to mention a host of other top line actors.

The film had a powerful spellbinding storyline, which told the story of Thomas Moore standing up to King Henry VIII who was rejecting the Catholic Church in order to allow himself obtain a divorce and remarry.

A masterpiece indeed and a good choice for the directors of the new Regent cinema as this film ran for over six months, finishing on January 5th 1968 when Angelique began a nine week run which finished on March 2nd 1968.

During our research into cinemas of the past nothing untoward or newsworthy surfaced in relation to the Regent other than it appeared to attract very good films, some of which ran for months, such as The Owl and the Pussycat in 1972.

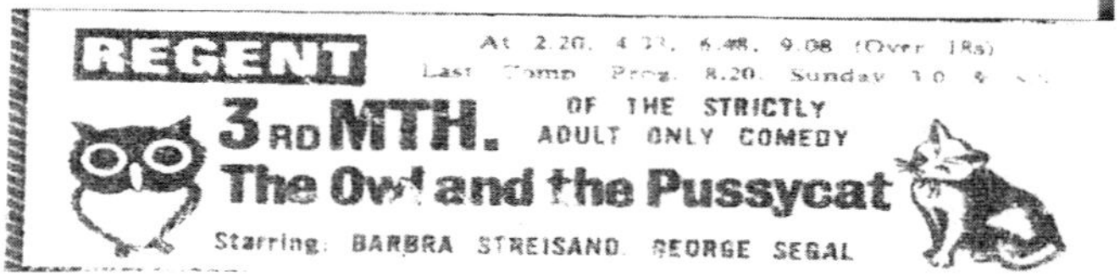

Being a town house, it obviously catered to full houses as it had a good twenty two year run and appeared to close on Sunday March 3rd 1985.

Following the closure of the cinema the building lay idle until 1996 when it was converted into a nightclub/pub called the "Back Lane". Later again it closed and was re-developed into an office block.

We found this advertisement in the "Evening Herald" on Wednesday February 27th 1985 which we believed was the last one, and it suggested to us that the Regent closed on the following Sunday March 3rd 1985.

REGENT
13 Main Street, Blackrock.

We would date this photo circa 1952 because we managed to make out the name of the film that was showing that day "which we believe was "Against all Flags" and this film was released in 1952.

This was said to be one of Errol Flynn's better Pirate films, which also starred Maureen O'Hara as Prudence "Spitfire" Stevens, a Pirate Queen and Anthony Quinn, once again playing the part of a baddie named Captain Roc Brasiliano.

Errol with his usual magnificence played Brian Hawke, a British Office on a secret mission to infiltrate the Pirate Republic of Madagascar, where he falls in love with the beautiful Queen of Pirates.

* * * * *

The Regent cinema was officially opened on February 24th 1938 by Mr. James L. Smyth, BL Acting Borough Manager and Town Hall Clerk of Dun Laoghaire.

In declaring the cinema open, he congratulated the proprietor, Associated Pictures Limited, on their enterprise in providing Blackrock with such a fine cinema. He also gave great praise to the contractors Messrs. T. and J Macken and the architect James V McGrane.

In attendance that day were five directors of the cinema, namely Mr. P.J. Whelan, managing director; Mr. J.J Hickey, Mrs.M. Hickey, Mr. J.J. Fagan and Mrs. M. Hickey .Also in attendance was Mr. M.H. J.Brunicardi the Editor of the "Evening Herald".

A unique feature of that picture house was the lack of a balcony. The air conditioning plant was of the most modern available and it was capable of regulating the heat from 212 degrees Fahrenheit down. The acoustics and lighting system were excellent and it had seating for 520 persons.

This picture of the Regent cinema was taken by an Evening Herald reporter on Friday, February 25th 1938, the day after it opened.

Judging by the stance of the chap with the sweeping brush to the right of this picture we would guess that he had just swept the pavement area in preparation for the taking of this picture.

"3 Smart Girls" was the film which was chosen for the opening night, and it was booked for one performance only.

REGENT CINEMA

BLACKROCK

GRAND OPENING OF ABOVE CINEMA THIS EVENING AT 8 P.M., with

"3 SMART GIRLS"

featuring DEANNA DURBAN.

ONE PERFORMANCE ONLY.

Proceeds Given to Poor of Blackrock.

The house was packed to capacity that night and in his opening speech Mr. Smyth, the Town Clerk said that it was a good augury and a pleasing and generous act on the part of the Associated Picture Houses Limited who planned that the entire proceeds of that nights performance would be donated to the Ladies Association of Charity and the local branch of St. Vincent de Paul for the benefit of the poor in Blackrock, and on their behalf he thanked them.

"3 Smart Girls" was a light romantic romp with Deanna Durban at her best when she performed the following three songs; "My Heart is Singing", "Il Bacio" and "Someone to Care for Me".

The story is about the 3 Craig sisters who live with their long divorced mother in Switzerland, who on hearing that their father is about to marry a gold-digging Socialite flee to New York to try and prevent the marriage and possibly reunite their divorced parents. However, romance slows down their crusade, but love triumphs.

* * * * *

The new Regent cinema, which was built on the site of the former Blackrock Grand Picture Palace in Main Street, Blackrock at a cost of £10,000 was a most attractive one. Its frontage was finished in the best modern style, in cream-coloured plaster, with tasteful decoration in Neon Glass signs, and said the Town Clerk the "population of Blackrock was large enough to justify such a cinema".

The cinema site was originally a restaurant, which was demolished in 1913 to make way for the "Grand Theatre" Blackrock, which opened on Thursday, February 26th 1914. It was sandwiched between two grocery shops William Magee's at No 11 and Hever's at No 15 Main Street where now stands O'Rourke Licensed Premises.

THE GRAND THEATRE,
BLACKROCK,
NOW OPEN.
SELECTED PROGRAMME OF PICTURES.
LADIES' ORCHESTRA.

This advertisement was taken from the "Evening Herald" Cinema listings on Thursday, February 26th 1914.

No feature film was mentioned, instead it simply offered a selection of living pictures.

The cinema was quite a large one and admission prices were from as little as 4d.

The "Grand" appeared to do well as a cinema for a period of some fourteen years, but seemed to run into some difficulties nearing the year 1931 and as a consequence it closed in that year. It then became a bicycle and gramophone shop with an arcade and billiards hall attached until 1937 when it once again was rebuilt as a cinema.

The "Regent" also traded well for some 23 years until the early sixties when the cinema trade went into decline and it closed on March 25th 1961 despite strong representations to the owners, by the Blackrock Residents Association to keep the cinema open.

The Residents Association held a meeting to this effect on February 1st 1961 when it was agreed to send a letter of protest to its owners asking them to re-consider their decision.

Its last picture show was "I'm All Right Jack" starring Peter Sellers.

This picture of No 13 Main Street, which was taken in March of 2006, shows the site where the Regent Cinema once stood. It now houses the Café Java restaurant and a block of apartments. On the left of the picture is O'Rourke's Public House at No 15 and Extra-vision on the right, which would be No 11.

Following the closure of the Regent in 1961, Blackrock was to be without a cinema until 1973 when a new cinema was built on the sites of No's 7 & 9 Main Street. The story of this venture is told elsewhere in this book under the heading of the "New Cinema".

THE RENTERS.

The name commonly used in the Dublin world of cinema to describe the Film Distributors and their contribution to the decline of the local/independent cinema

On Tuesday, June 9th 1979 a report in the "Evening Herald" said that Dublin's independent cinema owners, who for years had been strongly opposing a film distribution system that they said discriminated against them, made an approach to the Restrictive Practices Commission with their case.

In April of 1978 the Commission had issued a report on the supply and distribution of films, and made a number of recommendations, but the independent owners claim that those that relate to them were never implemented.

They said they were deprived of first-run films by the big six distributors (all of which were controlled from outside Ireland).

They also said that Odeon (Ireland) Ltd, Adelphi and Carlton (both subsidiaries of British companies) and Ward Anderson (Irish Owned) dominated the quality first-run market, leaving the independents with inferior movies.

The recommendation that particularly related to the problems of the independent owners was on the subject of "concurrencies" which was the practice where new films (particularly those likely to be highly successful at the box office) were released at the same time in several city cinemas. Concurrencies were not uncommon in Dublin at the time, and the independents claimed that they were excluded from getting a fair share of that lucrative market.

It would appear that the independents were up against a stone-wall because the system of renting films in Ireland was a complex one and the modus operandi was as follows.

The film renters worked on a percentage basis, which gives them as much as 50% in the case of a film that is expected to do well and in a prolonged run there were clauses that might have given the renter 90% of the takings after an agreed figure had been reached. Naturally enough it was in the interest of the renter to get their films into an area where the returns would be as high as possible, and this was were the independents lost out. In the city centre at that time there were only four independent cinemas and to some extent through no fault of their own they were associated with grade B. movies.

The Commission urged that the "Kinematograph Renter's Society" should encourage renters to experiment with "Concurrencies" and Gerry Duffy of Twentieth Century Fox who was also chairman of the K.R. Society said the renters would try and do something about the situation.

The independents proffered the following as a good example of their problem. Should they have placed a bid for the James Bond film "Moonraker" which had just been released, they would not have stood a chance. Many owner/managers claimed that this unfair rental system was a big contributor to the downfall of Dublin cinemas.

~~~~~

The Decline in Theatreland.

This decline in theatreland however was not exclusive to Dublin, as you will learn from a little news item, which we found in a 1967 newspaper.

According to an article we read in a copy of a 1967 "Evening Herald" newspaper which was published on April 1st of that year, we would tell, you that the decline in cinemas and theatres were not confined to the City of Dublin.

The Theatre world in the city of Paris France was also facing hard times in that year when it had suffered the closure of half a dozen of its most famous playhouses in the past few years and others were expected to follow suit as time went by.

Paris according to the article had a population of some 4,000,000 against the 8,000,000 plus in London and had twice as many theatres and it was regarded as one of the world's liveliest show centres.

It would appear from the report that figures released in 1967 by the 60-odd professionally run theatres in the French capital claim that in 1966 they attracted 152,000 fewer people to their theatres than in the year 1965.

Of the 8,350,000 seats available in that city at any given performance only 3,500,000 were filled about 42% of capacity.

On the other hand receipts were up by more than 3% but this did not keep pace with operating expenses, while this decline had nothing to do with distribution, it would appear that according to the figures given for 1965 that the world of theatre in Paris had been in decline for sometime.

No reason was proffered for this decline, perhaps television was a serious contributor. (This article can be read in full in a copy of the "Evening Herald" newspaper of April 1st 1967, which can be viewed in the Gilbert Library and Dublin City Archives in Pearse St).

~~~~~

But then like a good many other people we are also sceptical about anything we read in a newspaper, which is dated April 1st.

RIALTO CINEMA
South Circular Road, Rialto.

(Opened two days after the Leinster Cinema which was situated just around the corner). It was billed as Dublin's Suburban Super Cinema.

Nearby to most Dublin cinemas, if not immediately next door, in those good old days one would always find a shop trading in Sweets, Ice creams, Confectionery, Cigarettes and Matches, and V.P Lynch Georges accountant tells us of an amusing little happening concerning the shops adjacent to the Leinster and Rialto cinemas.

It appeared that both shops sold ice cream with one selling a coarse type of ice cream and the other a creamy soft type, catering to all tastes one might say. On Sunday afternoons there would be hundreds of children queuing for admission to the afternoon matinee performances of both cinemas and it was not unusual to see children from the Leinster queue run around the corner to the shop beside the Rialto for their choice of ice while children from the Rialto queue would do likewise for ice cream from the Leinster shop.
V.P tells me that the only real difference to him was that the soft ice cream, being real smooth went quicker. Leave it to an accountant to measure the odds, eh?

The Rialto had private car parking space for 200 cars and parking facilities for 100 bicycles.

The Lord Mayor of Dublin, Alderman Alfie Byrne, performed the opening ceremony for this new Dublin cinema, which was designed and built on super-cinema lines with most of the 1,600 seats in the auditorium .

The balcony was built over the ground floor offices and cloakrooms and rendered the overhang very small leaving only a minimum of seats under the balcony area.

V.P Lynch also tells me that when he was small and queuing for the matinee in the Rialto a tough looking usher used to walk up and down along the outside of the queue keeping it in line. With hundreds of excited kids this was no mean feat and at times two male ushers were needed.

With the queue being along the edge of the footpath on the South Circular Road and traffic being reasonably heavy at the time a strict and orderly queue was necessary and one of the ushers would regularly take off his belt and marching up and down on the outside of the queue he would keep a straight line by folding his belt in two and slapping it off the palm of his hand. The kids were scared stiff of his belt, which, added V.P, was never used to slap any child, but to simply act as a deterrent by display and in consequence no child was ever involved in a road accident outside the Rialto cinema.

The grand opening film "Everything is Rhythm" could not have been a nicer choice.

Harry Roy and his band was the hottest thing in town in the 1930s and in 1936 they decided to make a movie as a showcase for their talents.

The film features no less that thirteen of their musical numbers.

This showing in the Rialto was the film's first outing in the Irish Free State.

* * * * *

DUBLIN'S LATEST SUPER-CINEMA
AT RIALTO
Built by
DUBLIN BUILDING CO.
SWIFT'S ALLEY, FRANCIS STREET

The building was designed by F.J Macauly and built by the above.

RIALTO Kirk Douglas, Richard Harris, HEROES OF TELEMARK 7.0. Shirley Eaton, Ken Scott, THE NAKED BRIGADE.

This is the last advertisement for the Rialto, which closed on August 29th 1970.
It is now a car sales showroom.

Picture taken, Sunday morning October 23rd 2005.

RITZ
The Ritz Cinema, Serpentine Avenue, Sandymount.

The Ritz Cinema Company was incorporated on 22nd December 1940, and its company registration number is 5853 with its registered address given as 78 Serpentine Avenue.

The Directors of the company were as follows;

Percy Winter Whittle (also a director of the Regal Ringsend) 2900 shares
Home addresses 2 Oakland's Drive, Ballsbridge.
and formerly of 5 Marine Drive, Sandymount.
John Frances Stokes St. Patrick's Dundalk had 3000 shares.

David McKay 5 South Frederick St 1 share.

Premises leased from James O'Neill of 66 St Helens Road, Booterstown.

David McKay resigned shortly after the company's incorporation and gave his share to McKay. This situation is common in the formation of companies.

Stokes retired on October 4th 1946 and Whittle took over his shares, and his family now had all the shares in the Ritz, just like they had in its sister cinema the Regal in Ringsend. Both cinemas were now family owned. However it would appear that a Cissy McGrory of 48 Farney Park who was a secretary to Mr. Whittle was allocated 100 shares.

This company was formed with the sole purpose of purchasing this cinema which at the time of purchase was known as "The Astoria" and part of the agreement allowed for Mr. James F. O'Neill, its then proprietor, to retain the name Astoria, and in consequence the cinema was renamed the "Ritz".

It was also known locally as the "Shack" a nickname that it never shook to this day, and in all fairness being a purpose built cinema it looked anything but a shack. However, the cinema began its life in a shed and as it had no official title, for many years, it was often referred to by its patrons as the "Shack".

The Ritz just like its sister cinema the Regal and most other small suburban cinemas showed films twice nightly with a complete change of programme every Monday and Thursday. It would also have a special feature for Sunday nights and suitably selected children's films for its Sunday afternoon matinee. In line with all Dublin cinemas in those days, seats had to be booked in advance for the Sunday nights performances.

Owen Dunne, a relative of the William Dunne of Newbridge Avenue who ran the Regal cinema on behalf of the Whittle family, was an assistant to Mr. Whittle in his Ritz cinema and he always wore a dress suit just like his boss. Owen Dunne was the gentlest of men and was loved and respected by all the patrons of the Ritz.

This building which once housed the Ritz Cinema is now a Sikh Temple.

Yours truly with Patrick Maguire (centre) being interviewed about our efforts to record the history of all old Dublin Cinemas Outside 78 Serpentine Avenue where once stood a shed with a corrugated iron roof that served the local community as a cinema in the early part of the 20th century. Conducting the interview is Declan Carthy who was out and about the streets of Dublin on behalf of Newstalk106 FM.

This shed, which was most likely a Nissan Hut type of building was sited on a small estate named Elmville at 84 Serpentine Avenue which consisted simply of a lodge and fields. The Shed it would appear lay in the fields and may well have been partially hidden from view until the Pembroke Urban Council acquired some of the ground circa 1913 in order to widen Serpentine Avenue at that point and as a consequence of this work the Shed was now clearly visible from the road.

The Shed had no real identity of its own and was simply referred to as the Shed or Shack by its patrons. While we do know that this shed operated as a cinema in 1919 because we had found a mention of it in a book of short stories written by a William Nash of Tritonville Road. He used to attend Saturday afternoon matinee's there as a child. We were unable to find out when it first opened simply because it was never mentioned on any official documents until its existence was reported to the Press Censors Office in 1922.

Until that time it would appear that as far as the local authorities were concerned it didn't exist and this would suggest that at the time it was an unlicensed cinema. It did however put on a matinee of films for children every Saturday afternoon but whether or not it held performances during the working week is anybodies guess. Thom's Street Directories of the time never once mentioned a cinema at this address until 1936 when it gave mention to a new purpose built cinema called "The Astoria Cinema" which had opened for business in 1935 with a new address of 78 Serpentine Avenue.

Patrick Maguire my co-writer and researcher on this book about Dublin cinemas of times past is widely known in the Dublin world of historical researchers, libraries and book fairs and has a large circle of friends. One of those friends on hearing of Patrick's interest in old cinemas mentioned that he had a booklet that had been written by a Mr. William Nash who once resided in a house on Tritonville Road, Sandymount and that there was mention in this booklet of a Shed on Serpentine Avenue that had shown films on Saturday afternoons when William was a child.

Patrick borrowed the book and in turn he loaned it to me. The booklet was entitled "Danny Boy" and contained reminiscences of the author's boyhood days in Sandymount which I devoured with a hunger. Having been born and reared in Irishtown I read all and everything I come across in relation to that area.

The booklet was A5 in size and the pages were neatly typed, but most unfortunately it gave no contact details of any sort. According to the owner of the book it came from Australia some years back where the Nash family had emigrated, many years earlier.

It would appear from William's writings that as a young boy living in 7 Tritonville Road, he would often go to see a picture in a Shed on Serpentine Avenue which had to be the building known as the "Shack". While he gave no dates for these visits he did mention seeing an episode of the Pearl White adventure series and a film entitled "Elmo the Mighty". With a little detective work I was able to ascertain that the Elmo the Mighty film had been released in 1919 and I now had an approximate date for these matinee experiences.

While I knew most of the places William mentioned in his writings I never knew of this shed. When I went to the pictures in my childhood days it was either to the Regal in Ringsend or the Ritz in Sandymount, but I like everybody else in the neighbourhood always called this latter cinema "The Shack" without I might add, knowing why.

In a brief description of the cinema William told us that the seating in the "Shed" consisted of rows of long wooden benches and that the building had a slanting floor with a piano situated just below the large screen where a local pianist would hammer out suitable tunes to accommodate whatever film was on display. He also voiced his opinion that the screen was made of large white bed sheets

A few other people that we met during our research told us that in the latter years of its life the building became very drafty and that the roof had sprung leaks all over.

William and his family appeared to have moved from Tritonville Road shortly after this period, probably to Australia, but the Shack remained and carried on showing films until 1935 when it was demolished to make way for a new purpose built cinema.

Taking on board all that had been said about this shed and William's reminiscences we have to believe that this shed was the "second cinema on Serpentine Avenue" referred to by the Rathmines DMP Officer to his superior in 1922.

(Also see Assembly Picture Hall).

Researching the release dates for "Elmo the Mighty" and The Pearl White adventure series we came across the following information and we thought we might share it with you

"Elmo the Mighty" starred Elmo Lincoln a famous Hollywood he-man and this particular film was released in 1919 which helped to date William's cinematic experiences but he also made "Elmo the Fearless" the following year. Elmo was very much in demand for these muscle bound type heroes and he also starred in the "Adventure of Tarzan"

* * * * *

Pearl White was a famous silent picture heroine who kept everybody spellbound with her adventurous antics in the serials "The Perils of Pauline" and other similar adventures films.

A lot of these serials would have as much as twenty episodes and every ending bar the last one would finish with a cliff-hanger that might leave Pearl lying gagged, and bound on a railway track with a huge express train rumbling down the tracks in her direction, hogged tied on a wooden bench with a terrifying large circular saw moving slowly towards her which would surely slice her in half, or perhaps in the passenger seat of an airplane, again all trussed up, which was spiralling earthwards totally out of control as the baddy pilot had just bailed out. Whatever the ending the ever so loyal fans would have a nail biting week waiting to find out what had happened to their favourite heroine.

It was said that Pearl Fay White the daughter of a poor Missouri farmer and a most athletic type of person with looks to die for, did most of her own stunts and in so doing suffered some terrible injuries. So serious were some of these injuries that production endured many delays. Eventually, fearful for her health and of the danger she was inviting upon herself the studio had to force her to use a stunt double.

In the many adventure films she made, all of which called for some very dangerous stunts Pearl learned to fly planes, swim raging rivers, climb dangerous cliffs, ride fast horses and drive racing cars. One of her films called "The Exploits of Elaine", was selected by the United States National Film Registry for preservation.

Pearl it would seem never visited Hollywood, as all her American films were shot on the East Coast. However had she made a trip to Hollywood it was said that she would have been honoured by the film industry with a Star in the Hollywood Walk of Fame.

Circa 1923 Pearl retired from films and moved to Paris France where she bought and managed a resort hotel, casino and nightclub. She also owned a profitable horse racing stable. Having made one more film in Europe for a friend, she also took to the stage for a while, however her old injuries sustained during her American movie days came back to haunt her and the after affects of these injuries contributed in no small way to her untimely death in a Paris hospital in 1938. Pearl was born on March 4th 1889, was twice married, and died on August 4th 1938.

Despite all our efforts we could not find the name of the original owner of the Shack cinema, its opening date or any advertisements for pictures shown. The Shack it would seem depended on word of mouth to attract customers.

In 1923 Mr. James F O'Neill the owner of the Assembly Picture Hall which was also on Serpentine Avenue leased the grounds of Elmville from a Mr. Callow with the Shed cinema thereon and having sub-leased most of this small estate to another person he kept the Shed cinema and the ground upon which it was built for his own use. Mr. O'Neill was now the owner of the two cinemas on Serpentine Avenue. It would appear that he closed the Shed cinema for a period of time, perhaps for simple alterations or very possibly he may have replaced the Shed with a new building.

Whatever he did we will probably never know, but we did find this advertisement declaring the opening of the "Cinema House" on Serpentine Avenue in the "evening Mail" on July 28th 1924 and for the next twelve years he put on pictures shows seven nights a week including one or two children's matinee shows.

In late 1934 James F O'Neill again closed the cinema and had it demolished, as it had begun to show its age and was in need of serious repairs, and rather than take that road he decided that he would instead build a new cinema.

Immediately after the demolition of the Shed the building of this new purpose built cinema began in1934 and in the year1935 the new cinema was open for business. While there was no big gala opening for this new cinema named the Astoria, we believe that the following advertisement, which appeared in the "Evening Herald" on Saturday February 9th 1935, may well have been Mr. O'Neill's way of announcing the opening of his new picture palace.

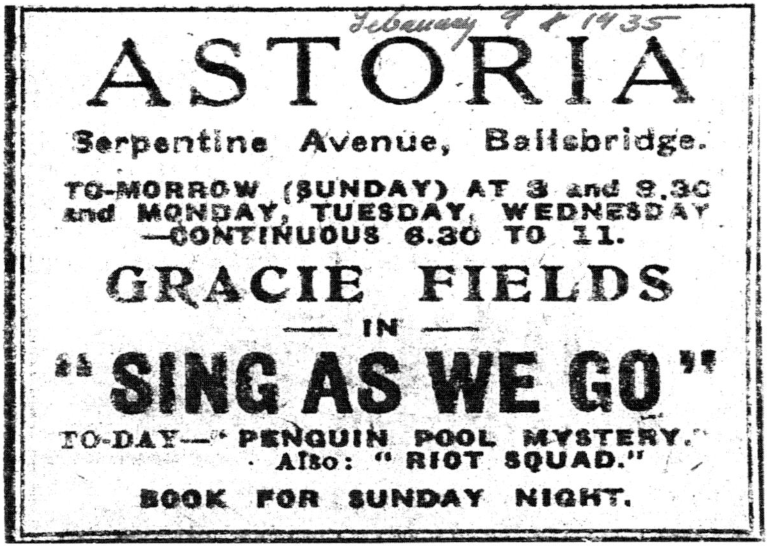

This new cinema not only brought about a new identity for itself but it also earned the right to an allocation of its own distinctive address which was now 78 Serpentine Avenue. Cinema proper had come to Sandymount and bookings were required for Sunday nights.

Now a beautiful purpose built picture palace with its own address and a new and fancy name, one would naturally assume that it had outgrown the nickname of the "Shack" but alas this did not happen. In1940 it had a name change to the "Ritz" cinema but again it was still referred to as the "Shack".

This is one of the thousands of small advertisements that would appear in all the Dublin evening newspapers over the years but the proprietors of the Ritz also advertised on billboards, one of which adorned the slip wall of Westland Row Station in Pearse Street. This billboard was situated just over the gent's public toilet which once stood there .

As to cinema advertisements, a nice little story was told to me about the "Ritz" cinema by David Grundy of Sandymount who used to patronise the "Shack" in his younger days. According to him, the Shack manager had a number of timber framed display cases situated in various places around the Sandymount area, with one fixed to the wall of the grounds of the National Vaccine Institute which was adjacent to 19 Sandymount Road, where Tesco now stands. Another adorned the wall near the Dodder River bridge in Ballsbridge and one was affixed to the outside railings of the Shack itself.

These display cases had a lockable framed glass door and each case had a number of slide in panels that located into grooved slots which were not unlike picture frames.

These panels, which were most likely made of thin sheets of plywood, were very colourfully painted in a pastel brushstroke style and were a work of art in themselves. On the panels in bright coloured text were painted the programmes for the coming week, and as there were four changes for the week, four panels in total would be on display. One for Mon-Wed, one for Thurs-Sat, one for the Saturday children's matinee, and one for Sunday night.

An usher from the Shack rode a small motorbike that was fitted with metal boxes that hung pannier style on either side of the rear wheel. These boxes were constructed so that they held the slide in panels in slots. On Saturday mornings he would do a round of all the display cases, remove the previous weeks panels and replace them with new ones for the following week. The old panels were carefully stored in the pannier boxes and no doubt recycled and repainted for the following week's advertisements. David further tells me that these glass cases were never ever vandalised or interfered with, which he rightly claimed would not be the situation today.

(Picture courtesy National Library)

The Gents toilets built into the slipway wall at Westland Row Station, where a billboard displayed the week's attractions which were showing in the Palace, Regal and Ritz cinemas. Unfortunately you can't see the billboard from this angle as it was situated a little more to the right of this picture.

This Billboard would have belonged to a professional advertising company that would have rented the space to a client/s and serviced the board regularly on their behalf. It would appear to me that the three cinemas mentioned above had each secured their exclusive section of the board, as I never remember seeing any other type of advertisement appear thereon.

David also recalls a wooden booth, which was situated in a corner of the railed and walled-in courtyard that fronted the cinema, and from this booth, which lay next to the railings an old lady sold sweets and other goodies. This would have been in the middle or the late fifties, because I remember her well, but in my time ten years earlier she sold from a rickety old baby pram. Business must have been good.

In his letter to Patrick and I, David mentioned a Mr. Dunne as being manager of the cinema. This would of course have been Owen Dunne as already mentioned earlier in the story as being Mr. Whittles assistant and this would fit in well with a change of ownership of the Ritz cinema in1949 when Mr. Whittle sold his interests to a Mr. George Jay and as Mr. Jay had also purchased the Regal cinema from Mr. Whittle it would make sense that he would have promoted Owen Dunne to the position of manager of the Ritz.

The Ritz, it would appear ran without incident, further change of management or ownership until 1973 when on Saturday September 2nd it closed its doors temporarily for alterations.

RITZ (Serpentine Ave., Ballsbridge) —Always a good show. Jack Lemmon. Barbara Harris in WAR BETWEEN MEN AND WOMEN, at 8.50. Also: THE DARWIN ADVENTURE, at 7.15. Usual Matinee on Saturday, 2nd September. WAR BETWEEN MEN AND WOMEN at 2.25, 5.30, 8.50. DARWIN ADVENTURE at 4.10 and 7.15. Cinema closed temporarily for decoration and alteration. Re-opening will be published later.

Re-opening times, said the advertisement, will be published later.

Its last feature film was "The Darwin Adventure" starring Nicholas Clay as Charles Darwin with Susan Macready supporting.

This is a biography/drama on the life of Charles Darwin and is said to be most enjoyable, well acted and very educational.

OSCAR
FILM THEATRE
(formerly Ritz)
SERPENTINE AVENUE
BALLSBRIDGE
(off R.D.S.)
DUBLIN'S MOST LUXURIOUS SUBURBAN CINEMA
Luxury Re-opening
THURSDAY
NEXT
Where picture-going and parking will be a pleasure.
PRESENTING SUPERB VALUE FOR MONEY
DOUBLE-FEATURE ENTERTAINMENT NIGHTLY
WATCH THIS SPACE EVERY EVENING

While closed, the cinema was extensively revamped and had its cavernous auditorium seriously shortened. Previously the auditorium was said to have been long and tube shaped.

On Thursday, October 18th 1973 the cinema re-opened with the new name of the "Oscar Film Theatre" under, I would presume, new ownership and management. These owners, I was later informed also owned a number of country cinemas.

For its opening night management chose the latest 'Carry On' film, "Carry on Abroad".

By attending Friday/Saturday nights show, one stood a chance of winning a free week-end break in Paris.

This was another hilarious Carry on Romp, with Sid James and Co. off on a package holiday in Elsbels, Spain where on arrival they find that the hotel has no roof. The gang further sensed something amiss when it was noticed that all the staff seemed to look alike, and then the fun began.

July 3 1976

OSCAR (Ballsbridge) — "The Carpet-baggers" (9 p.m.). Plus: "Where Love Has Gone" (7.30). Sun., 7.30 "Please Sir" plus "Twins of Evil." — Cinema closed for annual re-novations for 2 weeks from Mon. next, July 5.

This new venture however, despite an inspired advertising campaign did not, like a lot of other suburban cinemas at that time, do well. On Sunday, July 4th 1976 the Oscar cinema closed for annual renovations for two weeks.

Noting here that a period of two weeks was mentioned for annual renovations, I thought it a good opportunity to mention that that few cinemas closed for annual repairs in those days and that refitting and /or painting etc was usually scheduled for the compulsory annual three-day closure in Easter Week every year. All places of entertainment were required to close their doors on Easter Wednesday, Thursday, and Friday. Should the work involved require more time, I suppose the cinema may have closed for the full week. The Princess cinema in my time (George) closed only on the three designated days in Easter Week and of course Christmas Day.

OSCAR SERPENTINE AVE., BALLSBRIDGE opp R.D.S.
PANTHER 8.30. Prog. 7.30.
(The most successful comedy film made)
Peter Sellers, Christopher Plummer, Catherine Schell, and Herbert Lom
The Return of the Pink Panther All this week (Mon.—Sat.)
LATE SHOW 11 P.M.—SAME PROGRAMME

Having re-opened following its annual renovations in July, within another five months the Oscar cinema closed on Saturday, November 28th 1976

Following the closure of the Oscar cinema, the owners pondered their situation and decided to take a gamble and re-open the building as a Theatre instead of a cinema. This gamble they could afford as their country cinemas were all doing well. This idea was a strange reversal of a trend where heretofore theatres usually gave way to cinemas.

With the owners all for this new conversion they approached the Arts Council who also thought it a good idea and introduced them to Ronan Wilmot who had left the Abbey Theatre two years earlier and who agreed to take on the position of General Manager of the new Oscar Theatre.

Work commenced immediately on the grand transformation and the targeted opening date was for January 10th 1977, and the stage conversion which was about the same size of the Peacock theatre 20' x 28' was designed by Ruairi Quinn. The overall cost was expected to exceed £12,000 and admission prices were to be £1, and £1.50.

The Oscar cinema, during conversion to a theatre.

While Serpentine Avenue isn't exactly in the heart of theatre land, Ronan Wilmot wasn't too worried about getting people to come out there. "They'll come if the show is good enough", he claimed.

The Irish Theatre Company who were currently working in the Pavilion theatre in Dun Laoghaire were very impressed with the Oscar and were invited to regard it as "their place" for the first runs of their shows.

The future did indeed look promising for the Oscar Theatre.

OSCAR THEATRE

SERPENTINE AVE., Opp. R.D.S.
Gala Opening Tonight 8 o'c.
THE WORLD PREMIERE OF
THERE WAS A YOUNG MAN
A hilarious comedy by Matthew Dolan. With Anna Manahan, Claire Mullan, Chris O'Neill, Tom Irwin. Directed by Agnes Bernelle.
Tickets: Discfinder, Brown Thomas. Telephone Theatre: 683752.

Right on target the Oscar Theatre opened on Monday. January 10th 1977 and for its gala opening it premiered the play "There Was a Young Man".

Ronan Wilmot had great hopes for this opening show, which he described as a "grey comedy" and well done. It told the sad story of an undertaker who really wanted to be a comedian.

Eileen O'Casey was expected to open this new theatre.

The Oscar however didn't last all that long and it closed circa the 1980's and the last advertisement we could find for it was for a Saturday nights performance of a play entitled "The Long and the Short of It" which had Jim Bartley in the lead role. This was an adaptation of "Jim Crockery's Dublin" and it was scheduled for Saturday night April 16th 1983 and we believe that the theatre closed following the run, if there was a run of this play.

The Theatre/Cinema is now a Sikh Temple.

MURPHY'S LAW.

Yes Sir, it happens to the best of us and as Sir Sean Connery said of his last Bond movie "Never Say Never Again".

From the beginning of our venture we were adamant that this would be a one off book and we had no intention of ever updating our storylines or getting involved with revised editions etc. 'Enough', we said "is enough".

However with Murphy's Law working against us we may well have to swallow those words.

Having set the first week in August 2006 as our deadline to end our writings we suddenly began finding fresh items of news which we simply wouldn't have time to add to our storylines and on top of which our circle of new friends are expanding beyond belief and more and more information is coming our way. It would appear that everybody is anxious to help us

We also harbour concerns that we might have used some information or a picture without permission and we feel a need to redress that situation if it is brought to our attention. On top of which having written the history of over some 100 cinemas we must have awaken some old memories and we therefore expect some type of feed back.

We also accept that a lot of our dates clash with the writings of others and we may well be asked for some sort of clarification. So bearing all the above in mind a small booklet to set matters right may well be on our agenda for Christmas 2007.

Should you, dear reader, have anything to say, be it a question, a contradiction or a criticism please feel free to get in touch. Should you have a small story or tale of a happening about any old Dublin cinema we would be delighted to hear from you. Should you have a programme, poster or photo of any old Dublin cinema, please, please furnish us with a copy.

RIVERSIDE
Portmarnock.

This cinema which opened mostly at weekends and on the odd occasion two weekday evenings was the brainchild of one Charlie Dillon. Charlie, we are told, was a very honest and hardworking man that tried his hand at a number of enterprises.

The premises was a large wooden club house belonging to the Riverside Golf Club which we were told was built by a group of British soldiers who were stationed in the Portmarnock area. It was opened circa 1909 and closed by the end of World War 1.

The building lay empty for many a long year but was eventually taken over by Charlie Dillon who initially used it as a Turkey plucking station and possibly many other uses. In the fifties Charlie bought a projector and opened the premises as a cinema where he began to show films at weekends, much to the delight of the locals.

Hiring films wasn't as easy as it might sound and had Charlie had access to a steady supply the cinema might have been open seven days a week. As it was, weekend only openings were guaranteed. Charlie began this enterprise circa 1951 and he also used the premises for concerts, whist drives etc. His wife made toffee apples which she sold during these shows.

This enterprise began circa 1951 and Charlie, who was very much into Pitch & Putt, would set up the cinema and he would then skip off to the Portmarnock Pitch and Putt club for a quick round. Frequently the projector would break down or the reel would finish before it was expected to and one of the youngsters would have to run to the Pitch & Putt Club to fetch Charlie. The enterprise closed down circa 1957.

A picture of the Riverside Golf Club premises before it became a cinema (Picture from the Malahide Centenary 1892-1992 book, courtesy of the Club Secretary).

ROTUNDA
(Which many years later became the Ambassador Cinema).

"When did it all start"? Well, that's a good question. We trawled the internet, and could find no real answers. So we had to dig a little deeper into Dublin's history to find some sort of date or beginning, and suddenly we found ourselves in 1745.

It would seem that if it were not for the ambition of Dr. Bartholomew Mosse to establish a lying in hospital for women to have their babies we would never have had such a beautiful cinema such as the Rotunda.

Dr Mosse bought some five acres of waste ground in Great Britain Street which faced down Drogheda Street (now Upper O'Connell St.) and here he laid out a pleasure park decorated with beautiful statues , fountains , flower beds, tea rooms, pavilions and a large circular concert hall that could accommodate some two thousand people.

At the same time he had set aside a large corner of this site for his lying in hospital. The park was a huge success and attracted huge crowds. Admission was by way of an entry fee which went towards the building of the hospital, A friend of Dr. Mosse, one Richard Cassels a German architect designed the hospital building and the foundation stone was laid by the then Lord Mayor of Dublin.

The hospital cost in the region of £20,000 and much of this cost came from the funds of Dr. Mosse, with the Irish Parliament taking up the slack. Funds for fitting out this 50 bed hospital and its upkeep were raised from the takings of this most popular park and resort, and by continually putting on plays, concerts, balls, entertaining public assemblies and or hiring out the hall.

Were it not for this mans dreams we would not now have the Rotunda Hospital, Gate Theatre, the Ambassador Cinema, or for that matter the Garden of Remembrance.

Some Cinematographic Exhibitions were held in the Rotunda's Pillar rooms as early as 1897 and in 1904 it began to show pictures, but as yet it was not a cinema proper.

One film shown in the Rotunda Cinema which brought about a fair amount of controversy at the time was the movie of the World Championship fight between Jack Johnson, an African-American and James Jeffries said to be America's great white hope, which took place in Reno Nevada on July 4th 1910. Johnson won this fight on a TKO in the 15th round

The fight was referred to as "the Battle of the Century", and Johnson's victory over Jeffries sparked off race riots all across America, and many, many Afro Americans were killed. So bad was the situation that Congress barred the interstate movement of fight films less the images of Johnson beating his white opponent caused further race riots?

However James Jameson, the very popular cinema proprietor and M.D of the Irish Animated Picture Company managed to acquire the exclusive European Rights of Exhibition for this film and he programmed it for showing in the Rotunda cinema for a short run beginning on Saturday August 20th 1910.

This was the first public exhibition of this film outside of America, and when it was announced on the stage of the Rotunda cinema on the Saturday evening of August 13th at 9.40 pm that this picture was to be shown on the following Saturday there was an immediate rush for tickets, and further bookings were expected to be sensational.

There were many attempts to stop the showing of this film, as many worried that the American people might take umbrage at the exhibition of the Johnson-Jeffries fight in Ireland.

The Public Health Committee held meetings and the Theatre Inspector attached to the Corporation withheld the licence for the Rotunda to show the picture. However as Mr. Jameson rightly pointed out, that under the 1909 Cinematograph Act a licence wasn't necessary as the film used was not inflammable.

He also pointed out that many live boxing matches had taken place in other cinemas and theatres in Dublin and that quite recently the Empire Palace Theatre had staged live, the Championship fight between Jem Roche & P.O. Curran in a 10 round special fight, and no objections were raised.

Having proved his point, and the fact that he had complied with all the rules and regulations required of him under the 1909 Cinematograph Act, the Corporation of Dublin had to concede that they had no power to prevent this performance once the regulations pertaining to fire and overcrowding had been complied with. In consequence it was so arranged that Mr. Butler, Inspector of Cinemas would visit the cinema that day and upon inspection of all matters crucial to the regulations would if all was found proper, as a matter of course issue the licence.

The showing of the film commenced on Saturday August 20th 1910 and played to packed houses for fifteen days, last showing being September 3rd 1910.

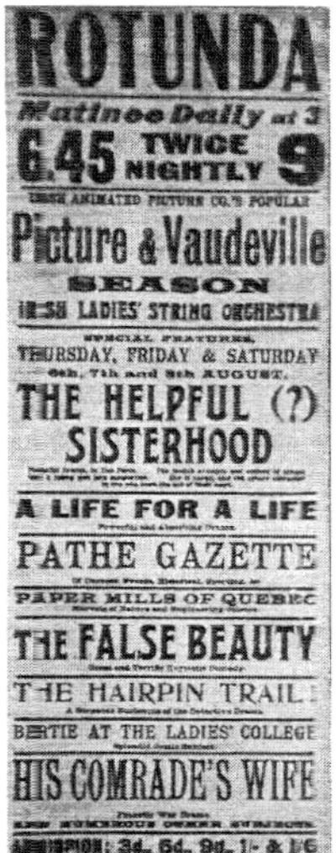

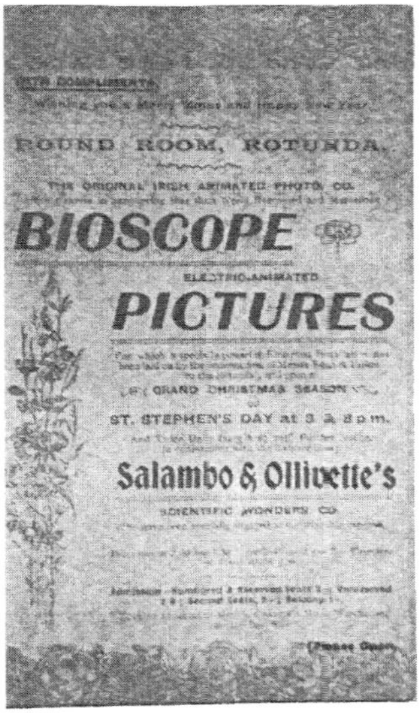

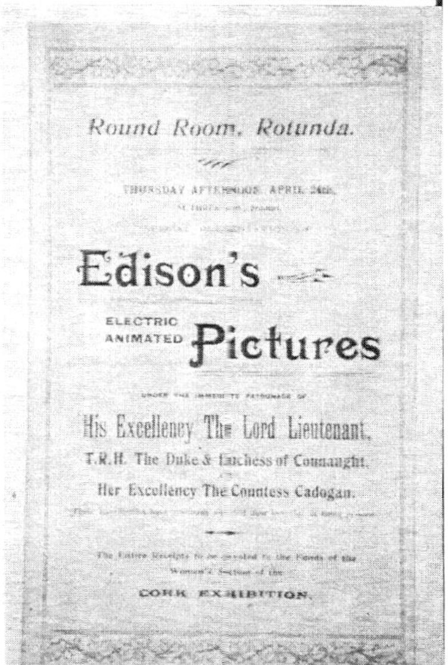

A view of the interior and a selection of posters and advertisements

James Jameson's, Irish Animated Picture Company did not in any way specialise in fight films. This cinematic company existed to provide entertainment by way of cinematograph exhibitions showing the latest displays in travel, news, comedy, pantomime and acts of drama as they became available. By 1912 film production in America was thriving and pictures were being produced in vast numbers and here I list a number of titles on display in the Rotunda for the 1912 Christmas period:

"Higher Mercy" was the title of a Vitograph subject which grips one from start to finish, wrote an "Evening Herald" critic of the time, who goes on to inform us of more of the same. "The Babes in the Wood" he wrote, was a particularly seasonable picture for the time of year and should make a strong appeal to all lovers of pantomime.

An exceptionally funny comic is that entitled "Belle of the Beach" and a thrilling and exciting encounter between U.S. troops and Redskins is shown in the film entitled "The Massacre". There was also a lively and exciting scene in "She Wanted a Boarder" which created much merriment.

While the Rotunda enjoyed great success as a cinema it would be no harm to give mention to some of the many famous people that appeared there when it was known as the Rotunda Assembly Rooms and was the haunt of fashionable Dublin when famous musicians were engaged to play there.

It opened in June of 1767 at a cost of £3,000 and was used to raise much-needed funds for the Rotunda hospital.

In 1792 John Field from Golden Lane appeared as a ten year old boy pianist, John at the time was a star pupil of an Italian piano teacher' Tommaso Gordiani' who had settled in Dublin, and he went on to become the best known Irish Composer abroad.

Johann Strauss Senior came to the Rotunda in 1838 with a 28 piece Viennese Orchestra and gave two concerts. While Franz Liszt arrived in the winter of 1940-41 and gave four concerts. Franz it was claimed was accompanied in his first concert by an orchestra of 70 performers with the Duke of Leinster playing the double bass and Sir Basil Gore Booth the cello. The Lord Lieutenant was in attendance with a Guard of Honour and the audience numbered 1,200.

P.T. Barnum presented and exhibited Charles Stratton the celebrated dwarf in 1844 together with his wife Lavinia. Both Charles, who was better known as "General Tom Thumb" and his wife were barely 25 inches high.

Lola Montez tread the boards of the Rotunda Assembly Rooms in 1858 and gave a lecture on "Beauty" "Gallantry" and "The Comic Aspects of Love". Lolo was a famous Spanish dancer who was born Eliza Gilbert in Limerick in 1818. Lolo it would appear had danced her way through most of the Capitals of Europe and was said to be one of the most outrageous woman of the times with numerous admirers amongst whom was named Franz Liszt, Alexandre Dumas, Victor Hugo, George Sand, King Ludwig, Nicholas of Russia and King Frederick of Prussia.
A Femme Fatale who was said to have died penitently of paralysis in America on January 17th 1861.

Charles Steward Parnell's first public meeting was held there on March 9th 1874
And
Douglas Hyde, who was later to become President of Ireland, appeared there in his play, "The Twisting of the Rope".

In 1915, now the Rotunda Cinema, Padraig Pearse addressed an overflow meeting, which had been called in connection with the Irish Volunteers.

Having served the cinema going public well for nearly fifty years the Rotunda Picture House closed on October 31st 1953. The last films shown was Joel McCrea's "Rough Shoot" and Angelica Hauft in "Strange World".

The owners of the building, The Capital and Allied Theatres Company whose Managing Director was Mr. Patrick Farrell, had taken over the Rotunda cinema in the late 1940s and now that they had closed the cinema they decided that it was in need of extensive alterations and upgrading. With this in mind they engaged Mr. William O'Dwyer a well know Dublin architect to redesign the building.

A new entrance was built which re-incorporated the existing Doric columns, stone urns and other interesting architectural pieces. A new balcony was installed together with a number of private boxes and this new picture palace was renamed the "Ambassador Cinema".

Mr. Joseph Keenan who had managed the Rotunda for some years was appointed manager of the "Ambassador" and Charles L. O'Malley was house manager. The cinema which was now a 1,250 seater was also equipped for 3 D films.

The Ambassador was formerly opened by the Lord Mayor of Dublin, Alfie Byrne on Thursday, September 23rd 1954.

Its choice of film for its grand opening was Danny Kaye's funniest movie "Knock on Wood" and his co-star for this spectacular was Mai Zetterling.

On a point of interest Danny's real life wife Mrs. Sylvia Fine wrote the songs for this film which is about a Ventriloquist who unwittingly becomes involved with a Spy ring.
As if his involvement with the spy ring wasn't enough trouble, Jerry Morgan the Ventriloquist, played by Danny, has to combat his Dummy's jealously whenever love and romance comes his way.

The Ambassador cinema was a popular cinema and appeared to do well during the next twenty odd years.

However we believe that it never achieved the status of a first run house which was imperative in order to obtain new releases and compete with the other town houses on a level playing field.

In the late sixties and early seventies when cinema attendances were in decline their lack of status began to show itself when they found it difficult to get good commercial films due to the system of film distribution. The owners, Capitol and Allied Theatres Limited decided to close the cinema on January 13th 1977.

The workers who were members of the Irish Transport and General Workers Union were given ten weeks notice and a redundancy package. The workers however were not happy about the closure or the amount of redundancy offered and they staged an unofficial sit-in in the cinema on New Years Eve, December 31st 1976 in protest to the threatened closure.

Management however were adamant and said that they had given the workers adequate notice and that the action taken by the workers was entirely unofficial and would not alter their decision.

The Ambassador Cinema closed on January 13th 1977 as planned.

Just three months on, the Ambassador re-opened on Friday April 29th 1977 with the film "Rocky" starring Sylvester Stallone.

This film won three Oscars for:
Best Director
Best Picture
Best editing
Not only did Stallone star in the title role but he wrote the story which made him an icon.

This was a most touching and unforgettable film and was a box office success.

An Evening Herald reporter remarked that it was ironic that while the Ambassador had closed last January for want of quality films, it should now bounce back under new management with a film that could break box-office records for this or any other town house.

After the Ambassador had closed on January 13th it was taken over by the Green Group, refurbished and re-opened but just eighteen months later it closed again on Sunday October 16th 1988 and its last offering was the 1967 version of "The Jungle Book". Although an animation classic it was not a new release film and one wondered if history was repeating itself. The Jungle Book was said to be the last film Walt Disney himself ever worked on.

However, just like the old maxim, "Never say Die" or Sean Connery when once again he played "James Bond" in "Never Say Never Again" the Ambassador once again opened for business on Friday July 22nd 1994 with the film "The Flintstones".

This was a first release film which brought to life the old T.V series with some real life characters which let us see Fred, Barney, Wilma, Betty, and babies Pebbles and Bamm- Bamm in the flesh.

This re-opening had a much longer run that its predecessor and stayed open for some five years, but alas it too closed in September 1999, featuring another new release "Varsity Blues". An American film showing their obsession with sports and winning: Starring Jon Voight and James van Der Beck.

While no longer functioning as a cinema the Ambassador is still in business as a venue for special music concerts and presentations, but with its track record, who knows what the future holds?

N.B. The Academy which belonged to this group was also involved in the 1977 dispute and it too closed on January 13th. (See Palace story).

ROYAL
The Theatre Royal Cinema and Variety Hall, Hawkins Street.

The history of the Theatre Royal dates as far back as 1635 when Dublin's first ever theatre was built in Werburgh Street and it too was named the Theatre Royal. In the 17th century the use of the name Royal was only allowed under licence by the local Magistrates Court and this licence with permission from the said Magistrates Court could be transferred or passed on to another person, provided of course that they were of good repute and that the theatre in question was found suitable.

In consequence the name Royal passed from the Werburgh Street theatre, via an Aungier Street theatre, a Smock Alley theatre, a Crow Street theatre and eventually to Hawkins Street, where a theatre was built in 1821 and rebuilt twice over the years. Once in 1897 when it was rebuilt following a fire and again in 1935 when it proved to be too small for the crowds it was attracting.

However as our interest lies only in the cinema or cine-variety aspect of the theatre we will record it history from 1910 when the lessee of the time Mr. J Collins was granted a Cinematograph licence under the 1909 Act on August 18th 1910. As this Act only came into being in 1909 the "Royal" was showing pictures long before that date.

The pictures were provided by the Paragon Bioscope Company Limited. As for a more complete history of the Theatre Royal, George had written about this in his book "The Prinner" which is available on loan by request from all Dublin Libraries.

The Theatre Royal also played host to a number of boxing contests and just prior to its involvement in cinematograph exhibitions it staged the title fight for the World Heavyweight Championship on March 17th 1908 between Tommy Burns the reigning champion and Jem Roche from Wexford, Ireland's great hope.

With its bioscope pictures, variety and vaudeville shows and visiting artists from all over the world the Theatre Royal was one of the most attractive entertainment venues in Dublin and its private boxes were in great demand by royalty, and many a Royal Command performance was held there.

The theatre was also in demand for viceregal parties and the Lord Lieutenant would at those times be given the Royal Box.

The Governor General of the Irish Free State was also a frequent visitor. In fact the Theatre Royal was so popular and so successful that in 1934 a decision was taken to demolish the cinema and build a bigger one that would be more capable of handling larger audiences.

The Royal closed on March 3rd 1934. There was no stage show that night, but simply a picture entitled "Dinner at 8".

A Theatre Royal souvenir programme.

This banner is courtesy the Irish Press Newspaper 1935.

The new Theatre Royal was formerly opened on Monday, September 23rd 1935 by Sean Lemass, T.D., Minister for Industry and Commerce. On the stage that night J.E Pearce, Chairman of the Dublin Theatre Company presented a cheque for £200 to the Lord Mayor, Alfie Byrne for the poor of Dublin.

This new cinema/theatre was the largest in Ireland and had seating for some 3,850 people. It had a huge Compton organ that would rise up on the stage from its storage place below at the touch of a button and as it slowly rose into its position on the stage Tommy Dando the resident organist would play his signature tune "Keep Your Sunny Side Up" which would start the audience off on a 15 minute sing-along.

This was the opening introduction of the evening's entertainment and it would be followed with the leggy Royalettes doing a dance routine aided and abetted by Jimmy Campbell and his 25-piece orchestra.

When the dance routine finished the girls would dance their way off the stage and the night's entertainment would begin with variety and vaudeville acts, sketches and comedy routines, juggling and circus acts and perhaps an international celebrity would be featured such as Dickie Valentine, Joseph Locke, Danny Kaye, Bob Hope or Johnny Ray.

The cream of Dublin's theatre artists made their name in the Royal and some were resident artists there for many years and we would name but a few: Jack Cruise, Cecil Sheridan, Mixer Reid, Willie O'Dea, Noel Purcell, Danny Cummins, Maureen Potter, Peggy Dell and Ireland's own Bing Crosby, Frankie Blowers.

Following the stage show, would be the feature film of the night.

Judy Garland paid a visit to the Theatre Royal in July of 1951 and because all her shows were booked out well in advance, hundreds of people who had failed to book in time, turned up outside the theatre in the hope of getting a glimpse of Judy and when Judy became aware of this she, in true showbusiness style, sang to the crowds in the street below from her dressing room window.

Tom Mix came to the Royal on Monday January 2nd 1939 and never in the history of the theatre has any star on or off the screen been given such a rousing welcome as the reception Tom received when he visited the Royal.

Tom was in town to take part in a week long Wild West Circus in the Theatre Royal and on the first morning of the week some three hours before he was due for rehearsals in the theatre crowds of adults and children gathered around Poolbeg, Townsend and Hawkins streets and as Tom arrived at the theatre he was besieged by all these fans.

As Tom left the Royal following rehearsals he mounted his beautiful grey steed "Tony" which members of his crew had waiting for him outside the theatre and set off on a much-publicised trot through College Street, Westmoreland Street and O'Connell Street where up to 50,000 people lined the way. Office workers, waitresses and shop employees leaned out of windows along the route and gave a rousing Cead Mile Failte to their hero.

As Tom and Tony careered through a crowded O'Connell Street one over enthusiastic fan tried to cut off a piece of Tony's tail.

Tom Mix and "Tony" in Dublin, January.

In the opening week of the "Theatre Royal" a group of performers known as the Frances Mangan troupe of dancers were hired for the opening performance and amongst the group was one Babs de Monte who found the dressing room facilities too cold and draughty for her liking and at the end of the week she left for the continent and never expected to dance in the Royal ever again. The Royal at the time was not quite finished and as work progressed so too did the backstage area.

However 1939 saw Babs return to Dublin with her Scottish friend Alice Dalgano another dancer and together they joined the resident group of dancers in the Royal who were then known as the "Violettes". A little later this name was changed to the "Royalettes" and under this name Babs and Alice took over and controlled and trained the Troupe. Together they forged the Royalettes into a splendidly tempered troupe of precision dancers whose fame spread beyond the shores of Ireland.

It was said that Babs and Alice broke all the rules of rigid chorus dancing routines and brought potted ballet to the masses during the years when Dublin had no visiting ballet companies whatever.

~~~~~

A Theatre Royal has stood in Hawkins Street since January 18th 1821 and over the years it had seen its fair share of life, what with, shootings, riots, attempted suicide and fires one of which reduced the theatre to ashes on February 9th 1880. However we won't repeat the history of the "Theatre Royal" as George has already outlined its history in his book "The Prinner" but we will tell you of another attempt to burn the theatre to the ground.

On July 8th 1912 during a Home Rule Meeting held in the Theatre Royal while a Mr. Asquith was addressing the attendance a Mrs Gladys Evans an Englishwoman tried to set the Royal alight but fortunately she was caught before any damage was caused and arrested.

Following a trial before the City Commissioners on August 7th 1912 Miss Evans with an address in Muswell Hill, London was found guilty. The Jury returned this verdict after an absence of only twelve minutes and Justice Madden sentenced her to five years penal servitude.

On October 3rd 1912 the Lord Lieutenant released her on serious medical grounds.

~~~~~

While Tommy Dando became world famous for his sing-along in the "Theatre Royal" with what was claimed to be the biggest choir in the world, he was not the first "Theatre Royal" organist to play the Royal's Compton Organ. This honour went to one Alan Chambers, however Tommy Dando was the most popular.

Having given special mention to the visits of Judy Garland and Tom Mix which we did because of Judy singing to her fans from her dressing room window and Tom cantering up and down O'Connell Street on Tony we must of course acknowledge the numerous other stars of stage and screen, celebrities and singing sensations that visited the Royal over the years but to try and do a piece on them individually would require another book. However, we feel obliged to mention Bill Haley and his Comets who paid a two-day visit to the "Theatre Royal" in February of 1957.

IN PERSON
BILL HALEY
AND HIS COMETS
WED, AND THURS,
27TH 28TH FEBRUARY 1957
6.40 AND 9PM

STALLS 21/-, 15/- 10/-
ROYAL CIRCLE 12/6
GRAND 7/6
CENTRE CIRCLE 5/-

Tension was high amongst the floor staff of the theatre that night as they well remembered the riots caused in many Dublin cinemas in 1956 during the showing of Bill Haley's film "Rock Around The Clock". With these memories fresh in their minds all staff members on duty on those two nights were extra vigilant. However they needn't have worried as both nights passed off quite peacefully. Jim Ferguson, Haley's manager who attended the show with his 71 year old mother, told a herald reporter that they were very grateful for the reception they had got in Dublin city and he said that what pleased them most was when they looked out of the theatre windows and saw so many hundreds of people gathered in a solid block outside in the streets, it showed he said, that they really appreciated Bill and the Boys. Of course he added nonchalantly, it's much the same the world over.

The next night however, the final night of their Irish Tour, he may have suffered a slight change of mind when he, his mother, Bill and the Boys had to slip out a side door of the theatre in order to avoid the rioting solid block in Poolbeg Street where the Guards had to draw their batons to disperse over a thousand demonstrators. Of course this sort of appreciation was probably the same the world over.

As the crowds retreated in various directions, bottles and other missiles were thrown at the Guards. Fortunately nobody was injured, but many cars were damaged, as were two plate glass windows in O'Connell Street.

Sadly the "Theatre Royal" gave way to progress and on June 30th 1962 the Royal gave its last performance.

The Compton organ hosted its last sing-along; the Royalettes opened the show with a superb dance routine and Jimmy Campbell and his orchestra brought life before death into the heart of the "Theatre Royal".

The Philharmonic Orchestra under the baton of Col Fritz Brase gave its last performance in the historic building and a host of characters arrived on the stage to give a rendition of an old song or tell an old gag. Cecil Sheridan was honoured by being asked to head the bill. Noel Purcell and Eddie Byrne who were in the "Nedser and Nuala" sketches were there as were Jack Cruise, Jimmy O'Dea and Maureen Potter and the playing of the last post had everyone in tears.

The "Theatre Royal" had one of the shortest man made lives of any playhouse in modern times, 26 and ¾ years and all the performers who were available in Dublin who at one time or another had tread the boards of the Royal stage made much effort to be there on the stage on its last night and songs like "Now is the Hour" and "There's no Business Like Showbusiness" struck a poignant note.

Jimmy Campbell who was with the "Royal" for all of those 26 and ¾ years moved to the Gaiety when the Royal closed and formed the resident orchestra there. Babs de Monte, Alice Dalgano, the Royalettes and Frankie Blowers also went to the Gaiety to take part in the Jimmy O'Dea Summer Show.

~~~~

As is the tradition in showbusiness circles "The Show Must Go On".

~~~~

Shortly after it closed the Theatre Royal together with the Regal Rooms cinema next door was demolished and Hawkins House was built on the site.

The Theatre Royal and the Regal Rooms on its left hand side (Picture courtesy Tom Wall).

SANDFORD
Aka the "Coliseum", 5 Lower Sandford Road, Ranelagh.

The Sandford cinema opened without fanfare or much ado on Monday, November 9th 1914 and its first film was "In the Bishop's Carriage" starring Mary Pickford.

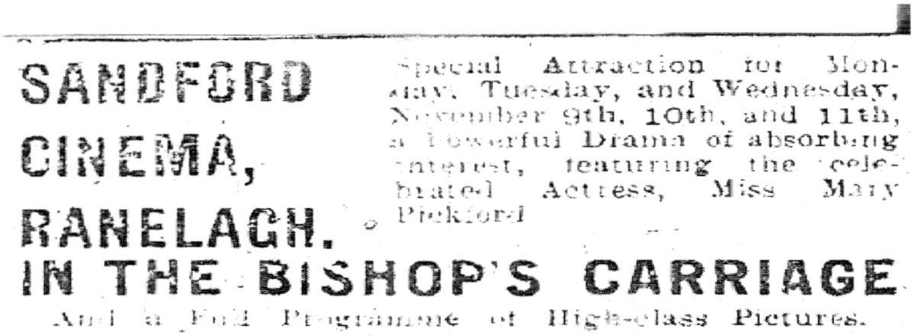

SANDFORD CINEMA, RANELAGH.

Special Attraction for Monday, Tuesday, and Wednesday, November 9th, 10th, and 11th, a Powerful Drama of absorbing interest, featuring the celebrated Actress, Miss Mary Pickford

IN THE BISHOP'S CARRIAGE

And a Full Programme of High-class Pictures.

We found this advertisement in the "Evening Mail" by pure accident while we were conducting a search on something else, because prior to that all our findings at that time indicated that the Sandford had opened on November 14th and we would never have looked beyond that date for an opening advert.

Many months ago we centred on this date and trawled the newspapers for an advertisement announcing the opening of the cinema but we could not find one and for the time being we put the Sandford on the long finger. hoping that we would read or hear something about it at a later date, which with luck on our side, we did.

When we did find the opening advertisement in the "Mail" we checked for reviews etc and again we were out of luck. In 1914 it was customary for one of the evening newspapers to produce a cinema column once a week to tell its readers what was on and where, but of course this naturally only applied to cinemas that took out advertising space in their paper and it was only then that we discovered that while the Sandford cinema did buy space for the first three nights of its opening, its advertising in newspapers after that were few and far between. That was until competition in the trade hotted-up, when cinemas began to spring up all over the city.

This was quite a high-class cinema for the time and just like the "Princess" cinema in Rathmines it was purpose built and complete with all modern conveniences. The proprietors were the "Sandford Cinema Company", with the Whittle brothers as joint managers.

The building stood on a corner site, which allowed the 3d entrance into the pit area to be separated from the front entrance to the stalls area where prices were 6d and 1/-. The 1/- seats were distinguished from the 6d seats by a square of Crochet work on the back. The front entrance doors were finished in stained glass and on entering the auditorium there was a considerable rake to the floor that enabled all patrons to have an uninterrupted view of the screen.

Twelve days in business and the owners of the Sandford found themselves up in front of Swift, K.C. Chief Divisional Magistrate in the Southern Police Court on November 21st 1914 for a breach of the 1909 Cinematograph Act.

It would appear that either the proprietors were ignorant of the fact that a Cinematograph licence was required in order to operate a cinema or they simply forgot to apply for one. Following a complaint, a summons was issued and the owners were duly brought before the court.

In their favour a D.M.P inspector told the court that he had visited the cinema premises and found them extremely comfortable and suitable in every way for a picture theatre and he added that the pictures he had seen were excellent.

A Mr. Robertson of the Chief crown Solicitors Office made mention that the Company had incurred a penalty of £20 for the first performance and £5 for each subsequent one which would have totalled some £80, but like the good chap he was, he didn't press for these penalties to be implemented

Mr. Swift, instead imposed a fine of £2.on the condition that the defendants undertook to apply for a licence as soon as was possible.

An application for a licence was immediately lodged with the Rathmines and Rathgar Urban District Council, together with the required fee of £1.The premises was duly inspected by the U.D.C cinema inspector, and a licence was issued to the Sandford Cinema Company limited on December 2nd 1914. We re-produce a photocopy of the front page of this licence in the following pages for your perusal. It was issued by the U.D.C and contained in all, three pages of rules and condition pertaining to the issue of the licence.

As the wording of this licence would be more or less standard issue we will re-write its contents word for word in another section of this book under the heading of the "Cinematograph Act 1909"

~~~~~

SANDFORD CINEMA THEATRE

RE-OPENED.

POPULAR PRICES,
NEW PICTURES,
NEW DECORATIONS,
NEW HEATING.
EVERYTHING NEW AND UP TO DATE

MOST COMFORTABLE THEATRE IN DUBLIN.

Under direct supervision of Proprietor,
JOHN J. HEALY.

In 1917 the Sandford Cinema Company Limited went into liquidation and the cinema closed.

Shortly after its closure a John J. Healy bought the interest of the company and applied to the Secretary of the Rathmines and Rathgar U.D.C to have the Cinematograph licence transferred into his name. Following some improvements to the building the Sandford re-opened on Wednesday December 26th 1917.
~~~~~

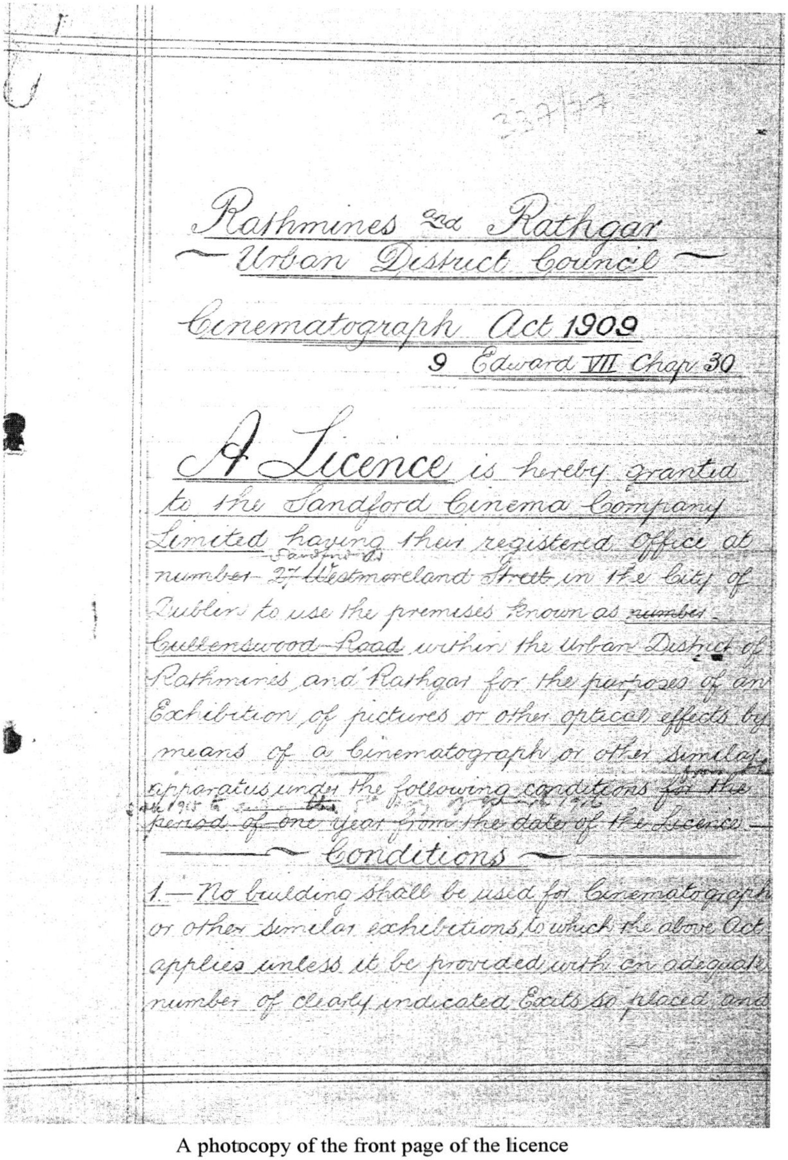

Rathmines and Rathgar
— Urban District Council —
Cinematograph Act 1909
9 Edward VII Chap. 30

A Licence is hereby granted to the Sandford Cinema Company Limited having their registered Office at number 27 Westmoreland Street in the City of Dublin to use the premises known as number Cullenswood Road within the Urban District of Rathmines and Rathgar for the purposes of an Exhibition of pictures or other optical effects by means of a Cinematograph or other similar apparatus under the following conditions for the period of one year from the date of the Licence —

— Conditions —

1.— No building shall be used for Cinematograph or other similar exhibitions to which the above Act applies unless it be provided with an adequate number of clearly indicated Exits so placed and

A photocopy of the front page of the licence

In 1924 the Sandford once again closed down and it was taken over by Dublin Cinemas limited who thoroughly re-structured the inside of the cinema and furnished it with new seating. Totally redecorated and with new operating machines installed to ensure perfect projection it was now on a par with any city cinema. On Friday August 1st 1924 Dublin Cinemas Ltd, re-opened the cinema under the new name of the "Coliseum Cinema".

This advertisement was in the "Evening Herald" on the Saturday of August 2nd and we used it instead of the Friday opening advert, which was too faded to photocopy.

As you may be able to discern from the writing in the advert, a Select Orchestra was specially engaged for the weekend opening nights, as was the celebrated Cellist Mr. Jos. Schofield.

It would appear that this company, which was only newly incorporated, had its address as 45 Mary Street which meant that it was also involved with the Lyceum cinema formerly known as the "Volta".

For whatever reason, this cinema is now fast gaining a reputation for name changes, closures and management changes and in 1925 it again closed and re-opened on Monday, October 5th 1925 with a noted drop in prices. We don't know why it closed nor if it again changed hands. We also noted that on March 5th 1925 a Mr. Kelly was issued with a licence for the Coliseum at 5 Sandford Road.

THE COLISEUM CINEMA
(SANDFORD ROAD, RANELAGH).
RE-OPENS ON MONDAY, OCTOBER 5th,
AND EVERY OTHER DAY, FROM 6 P.M. TO 10.30 P.M.
MONDAY, TUESDAY, and WEDNESDAY,
"HUTCH OF U.S.A."
Featuring CHARLES HUTCHINSON.
A POWERFUL 5-PART DRAMA.
THURSDAY, FRIDAY, and SATURDAY,
"BULL DOG JIM."
Featuring GEORGE LARKIN.
SUNDAY COMPLETE CHANGE OF PROGRAMME.
PRICE OF ADMISSION — 7d., 1/-, and 1/3.

SANDFORD CINEMA
RE-OPENING TO-NIGHT (FRIDAY) UNDER NEW MANAGEMENT.
Continuous Performance, 6.30 to 10.30.
"THE SEA HAWK," with MILTON SILLS, WALLACE BERRY and 3,000 others.
MATINEE SUNDAY

Barely had one year passed when once again the cinema underwent a change of management in the autumn of 1926 and closed down for some renovations and a new name board, which once again proclaimed the cinema as "The Sandford" which re-opened on Friday, November 12th 1926.

SANDFORD, Ranelagh
Norman Wisdom, Angela Brown
"PRESS FOR TIME"
5.50, 8.56. Also
"THE PLAINSMAN", 7.32

The cinema remained trading as the "Sandford" until the year 1968 when on Friday night, April 5th the cinema closed as usual after the last performance and re-opened the next day April 6th without fuss or notice as the "New Sandford".

In the between years of 1926 and 1968 there may have been a change or two of management, but we didn't come across any mention of same.

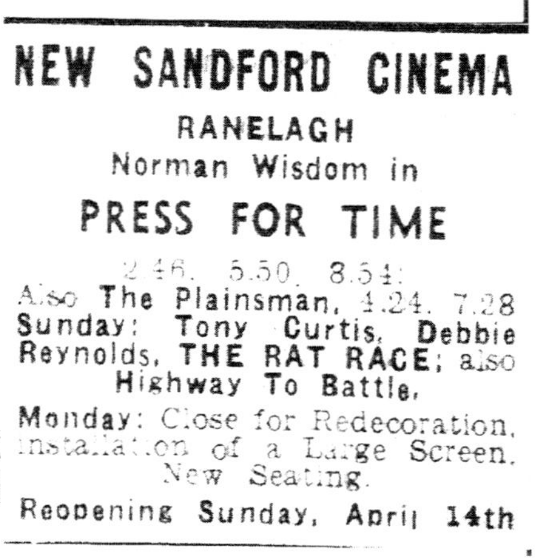

This advertisement appeared in the "Evening Herald" on Saturday, April 6th and announced the cinemas new name.

It also informed its patrons that the cinema was closing for a week after Sunday night's performance for redecoration.
While all cinemas closed for three days in Holy Week some would close for the full week in order to re-decorate or carry out some repairs etc. In Easter week of 1968 the Sandford closed for the full week and not only was the place completely re-decorated but new seating and a large screen was installed.

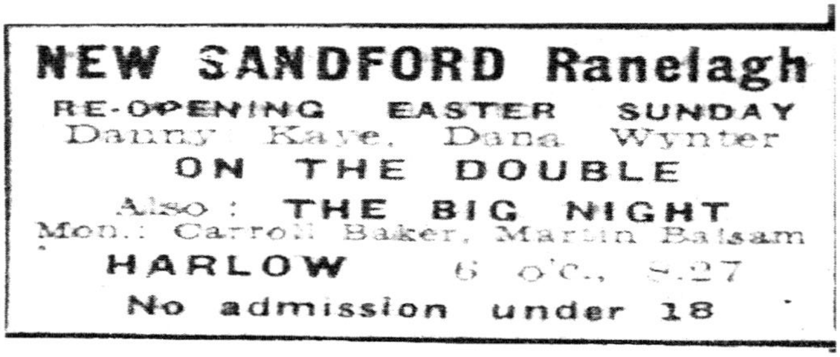

As promised the cinema did indeed re-open on Easter Sunday April 14th 1968.

It remained trading as the "New Sandford" until it closed in 1978. The advertisement on the left is the last one we could find and we believe that it may very well have closed on that Saturday, February 18th 1978

The fact that no film was advertised for the following Sunday lends strength to this belief.

Try as we might we could not find a picture of the Sandford cinema and in desperation George took this picture of the side of the building which now houses a bar and restaurant.
If nothing else the picture captures the enormity of the building, which in 1914 was a purpose built cinema.

Just as the good Walter Butler the Corporations Inspector of Cinemas might have done in 1914 Patrick takes it upon himself to inspect the fire escape. (Picture 2005)

Edison's Electric Animated Pictures.

EDISON'S PICTURES.
ORIGINAL IRISH COMPANY. DIRECT FROM ROTUNDA, DUBLIN.
TO-NIGHT. TO-NIGHT.
And during the Week.
THEATRE ROYAL, WEXFORD.
MONDAY NEXT:
THEATRE ROYAL, WATERFORD.

Edison's Pictures were so popular in the Rotunda Round Room in 1902 that the Edison management had to announce a prolongation of their programme.

People paying for admission to the early doors were guaranteed the additional advantage of seeing a series of special pictures.

SAVOY BALBRIGGAN

The Savoy, Balbriggan's second cinema, which took over from the Strand cinema was built in Dublin Street by J.J Walsh a local builder and opened on December 19th 1944 just in time for the Christmas trade. The first film to be shown was the "Phantom of the Opera" starring Nelson Eddy as Anatole, Susanna Foster as Christine Dubois and Claude Rains as the Phantom of the Opera.

The Savoy cinema building in 2005, still serving the local people as a community centre.

The auditorium, stage and screen area.

Jack Benton for a while was Chief Operator of the Strand Picture House and was in charge of its Dynamo Lighting Plant, but he left in 1947 to begin a career in motor car mechanics.

We had the great pleasure of meeting with Jack now aged 80 during August 2005 and we listened in awe to his tales of the Strand and Savoy cinemas. We also spoke with a Sally Brennan, now Mrs Moran of Drogheda Street. Jack also gave us a copy of the reference he received from the owners of the Savoy Cinema when he left their employment in 1947 and with his kind permission we reproduce it here.

TAILTEANN THEATRES, BALBRIGGAN LTD.

DIRECTORS:
A. M. CONLAN.
E. H. CONNOLLY.
T. B. CONNOLLY.
J. L. DERHAM.
E. G. SCANLAN.

Telephone 18.

DUBLIN STREET,
BALBRIGGAN.

To whom it may concern.

John Benton of Skerries Street, Balbriggan was in our employment from January 1945 to January 1947. During that time he was in charge of our Dynamo Lighting Plant and also Chief Operator. We found him very reliable and trustworthy. He left of his own accord to better his position, and I have no hesitation in recommending him for any reliable position.

FOR TAILTEANN THEATRES, BALBRIGGAN, LTD.
T. B. Connolly.
Managing Director

Jack, Started off his working life in the Strand when he got the offer of a job in the cinema simply because he had run a few errands for the cinema operator. This came about when Jack as a very young teenager was simply 'hanging out' about the cinema. "Slip down to the railway station office", said the operator to Jack one day and "fetch me the reels of film for the cinema". In return he got free admission to the film show that evening.

Within a couple of weeks he was fetching the films on a regular basis and doing this and that at the beck and call of the operator and at the end of the second week he received a wage packet. Jack it would seem was now an employee of the cinema company and he remained there until it closed. When the Savoy cinema opened in Dublin Street Jack went to work there.

"Fetching the film reels from the railway station was no easy task", Jack told us, while the steel cans in which the film reels were contained came in a large postman's like sack, Jack could only manage to carry one container at a time, as the cinema was a good walk from the Station. Besides which he would have to climb a ladder to reach the operating room at the Strand cinema.

He would also be required to rewind the films when they came off the film projector and on one occasion in the early stages of his employment he made a mess of the rewind and the film ended up in a coiled heap on the floor of the rewind room. The operator seeing his dilemma simply picked up the end piece and having inserted it on the rewind spool he then picked up the rest of the film and threw it out of the window where it uncoiled in a downward spiral. He then pressed the rewind button and rewound the film.

Jack Benton August 2005

The Savoy Cinema belonged to the Tailteann Theatres Limited and this was there third cinema, with the first being the Savoy in Kells and the second being the Savoy in Rush, County Dublin.

The cinema, which had seating for 800 persons, was built by J.J. Walsh the Chairman of the Town Commissioners in a matter of ten months. The building was Walsh's first big contract and it was said that the finished project would remain as a remarkable tribute to his ability and to that of the skilled tradesmen, all locals that he had employed. The Cinema was formerly opened by the County Commissioner and the proceeds from the first night's performance were handed over to the local branch of the St Vincent de Paul Society.

SAVOY, BALBRIGGAN

SUNDAY, 24th December, at 3.30 and 8.30 p.m.
Donald O'Connor, Susanna Foster, Richard Dix, etc. in
TOP MAN
Full of Fun, Romance and Music!

CHRISTMAS DAY, at 3.30 and 8.30 p.m.
Tyrone Power, Linda Darnell and Basil Rathbone in
MARK OF ZORRO
Powerful Drama... Glittering Pageantry... Tender Romance!

ST. STEPHEN'S DAY, at 3.30 and 8.30 p.m.
Stan Laurel and Oliver Hardy in
DANCING MASTERS
They're up to their necks in trouble—and up to their ears in fun
ALSO, Fredric March and Joan Bennett in
TRADE WINDS

WEDNESDAY, THURSDAY and FRIDAY,
December 27th, 28th and 29th.
Dorothy Lamour, Dick Powell and Victor Moore in
MELODY INN
Seven smash song hits in this Technicolor musical earthquake!

SAVOY, RUSH

SATURDAY, 23rd DEC.
Robert Page, Diana Barrymore in
FIRED WIFE
ALSO, Johnny Mac Brown in
CHEYENNE ROUND-UP

SUNDAY, 24th, at 4 and 8.30.
Lupe Velez and Michael Duane in
RED HEAD FROM MANHATTAN
ALSO, Charles Starrett in
WRONGLY ACCUSED

CHRISTMAS DAY, 4 & 8.30.
Red Skelton and Eleanor Powell, etc., in
BY HOOK OR BY CROOK

ST. STEPHEN'S DAY and WEDNESDAY, 27th Dec.
Arthur Lucan and Kitty McShane in
OLD MOTHER RILEY, DETECTIVE

Programmes for two of their cinemas for the Christmas period of 1944
Closed June 1974
Re-opened August 9th 1974 as Europa

EUROPA, Balbriggan—They're busting out again! "Carry On Girls" and "The Falling Man." Tonight at 11.30 p.m. only.

This is the opening night advert for the Europa on August 9th 1974
(See story of Tideway cinema)

It Closed in1977.

SAVOY CINEMA
In the heart of Dublin.

An artist's impression of the Savoy cinema.

Before a crowded attendance, which included many distinguished citizens, President Cosgrave formally opened the Savoy cinema on Friday night, November 29th 1929.

The No 1 Army band under Col. Fritz Brasse played the prelude, "Die Meister-singers" (Wagner) and the Hungarian Dances Nos. 5 and 6 in D minor and G (Brahms) and as the President and Mrs Cosgrave with the members of the platform party appeared on the stage they played the National Anthem.

The Savoy cinema which had cost some £200,000 to build came to us courtesy of the Associated British Cinemas Limited and it was said that the projection equipment alone cost in the region of £10,000. This equipment consisted of three magnificent Ross machines, which were the first to be used in Ireland.

In thanking the President for honouring them with his presence and opening the cinema Mr. John Maxwell, Chairman of the Associated British Cinemas made mention that the building of the Savoy cinema had been entrusted to an Irish Firm because they believed that their money should be spent where their business was to be done, and that the building was a credit to Irish craftsmanship.

One of the chief features for its opening nights production was the very interesting film "Ireland" which gave a very comprehensive idea of the many attractions of the country and this film, promised Mr. Maxwell, would be shown in over 100 cinemas in the big centres in Great Britain controlled by his company.

The film took the audience through the countries many beauty spots and centres of attraction and also includes some fine scenes at the R.D.S. Horse and Spring Shows. It begins of course with Dublin showing such places as O'Connell Street. Government Buildings, the Bank of Ireland, Trinity College, College Green and Leinster House, together with aerial views of the City, Dun Laoghaire, Dalkey and Killiney.

It followed on with views of Glendalough, Clonmacnoise, Cobh, Cork, Parknasilla, Kenmare and Killarney then along the western coast to Donegal and concludes with incidents in the Army manoeuvres and Air Force exhibitions.

This was a film that would greatly enhance Ireland as a tourist attraction

The principle film that night was "On with the Show" starring Betty Compson, Louise Fazenda, Sally O'Neill, Joe E. Brown, Ethel Waters and Arthur (Dagwood) Lake, This was an early 1929 Technicolor talkie-musical made by Warner Bros and was said to be a show within a show, where it told the backstage story behind the production of a "Broadway Musical".

Critics would have it that this film was the inspiration for the making of one of the most successful movies of its time "42nd Street" another musical made along the same lines in1933 by Warner Bros Studios. The production of which it was claimed saved the studio from bankruptcy. It was also the first major work of Busby Berkeley the now famed choreographer/director.

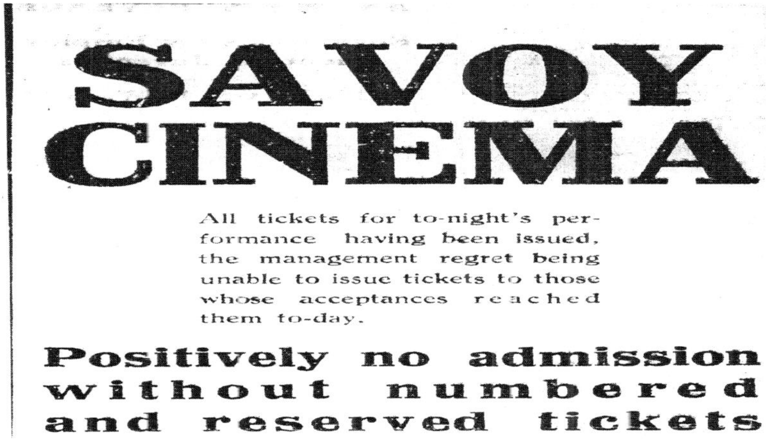
SAVOY CINEMA

All tickets for to-night's performance having been issued, the management regret being unable to issue tickets to those whose acceptances reached them to-day.

Positively no admission without numbered and reserved tickets

House Full!

A disgruntled cinemagoer.

Not all were satisfied with the way management handled the booking arrangement for seats on the opening night and one who used the pen name of "Fair Play" took them to task when he wrote a letter to the Editor of an evening paper.

While wanting to be present on opening night-but not able to afford the time necessary to queue for seats on the advertised day and time when the booking office would be open for that purpose, he arranged with a friend of his to attend in his place.

His friend arrived at the booking office at 1.30 pm on Tuesday November 26th, one hour before the arranged time of opening but found it impossible to book a seat for any part of the cinema. On hearing this from his friend, Fair Play then tried to telephone the cinema office but was told by the Post office officials that the phone had been engaged all morning, evidently for booking purposes.

Some other friends of Fair Play suffered the same fate, some of whom had queued at the cinema box office from 10.30 am and when the box office opened a staff member announced "We are booked out" and this without the issue of one ticket. On top of which, no notice to this effect was displayed until that evening at 5.30 pm.

"Why", asked Fair Play "was the general public not made aware that booking's by phone or letter was available"! In their opening notice management stated that booking facilities would be available at the cinema from 2.30pm on Tuesday 26th, but long before that hour it was impossible to obtain a seat.

Not that Fair Play could have availed of it on opening day but the Savoy also opened a Café for the benefit and comfort of its patrons.

J.M. Elliman & Son of Lower Camden Street were major players in the world of Dublin cinemas and it was they that was responsible for the Café furniture, carpets and curtains. They also provided the Savoy's luxurious seats, which were all made in Dublin.

The whole of the seats throughout this Theatre, as well as the Metropole—Rinn—Princess—Theatre-de-Luxe—Mansion House—Tivoli—Queen's, and many Cinemas throughout the Free State, were made in Dublin. The luxurious Café Furniture, Carpets, and Curtains were also supplied by us.

J. M. ELLIMAN & SON

52 LR. CAMDEN ST., DUBLIN.

We invite enquiries from Theatres throughout England and Ireland. Our Estimates are keenly competitive.

For afternoon and High Tea we believe the Café will be deservedly popular. Our aim is to establish a reputation for quick service, up-to-date equipment, and best quality food at popular prices.

No pains had been spared to render the Savoy worthy of its important position in the planning of the City and its design had been executed in conformity with the City Architect's scheme of reconstruction.

The cinema which could seat nearly 3,000 was built on the site of the old Granville Hotel and had lifts to all floors, ample cloakrooms on every floor with attendants in waiting, telephone boxes for the use of patrons, and waiting rooms for visitors should it be necessary to wait for admission to the cinema proper

The front of the building was built in the same stripped-classical style as the adjacent Gresham Hotel and Hammam Chambers and the massive interior was decorated on a Venetian theme with the proscenium done in the shape of a Venetian bridge. Decorative Venetian windows and balconies faced down on the audience and the safety curtain had a painting of the Doge's Palace.

A special staff 100% Irish, had been engaged and fully trained in the important matter of handling a large number of people so that all may thoroughly enjoy every entertainment.

An interior shot of the Savoy.

The magnificent entrance foyer.

Picture taken circa the 1990s.

One of the biggest attractions to ever grace the screen of the Savoy had to be "Gone with the Wind" which was presented in 1942 during World War 2. This film which starred Clark Gable as Rhett Butler and Vivien Leigh as Scarlet O'Hara was a box office success and ran for eight weeks in the Savoy. Both Clark and Vivien won Oscars for their performances in the film.

So popular was this film that the Savoy management had to arrange special excursions from all over Ireland to Dublin in order to give people a chance to see this beautiful love story. During its eight week run some 300,000 people had viewed the film.

~~~~~

So many good movies were displayed on the screen of the Savoy that it really seems unfair to single out any one film for special mention although we did single out "Gone with the Wind" it was more because of the excursions involved rather than the movie. The only time we plan to mention or brief on a film is when it is screened for the opening or closing of cinemas

Nothing untoward appears to have happened to or in the Savoy in the following years. As far as we know the Savoy continued to put on wonderful films for the next forty years and in so doing it enjoyed great attendances until management decided to go modern in 1969.

~~~~~

In 1969 the Savoy management made Irish history when they twinned the Savoy and on November 19th of that year Ireland's first twin screens were formerly opened by Mr. Colley T.D., Minister of Industry and Commerce, to inaugurate Dublin's "cinema-going for the Seventies.

The twinning of the Savoy was no mean feat and it took exactly 24 weeks and £400,000 to transform the old Savoy into two plush modern cinemas. Built one on top of the other the entire interior of the old cinema had to be completely rebuilt and a portion of the roof had to be raised to give greater height for both cinemas.

With safety and the utmost comfort foremost in their minds the architects had a solid concrete floor positioned between the twin cinemas which was both soundproof, fireproof and equipped with special acoustic effects. The very latest Italian projectors are installed in both operating rooms, which are slung ingeniously on a main steel girder which is built between the projection rooms.

Savoy 1 now on the top floor seats 1,072 persons and Savoy 2 on the ground floor 780. Admission prices range from 7/6 to 12/6 and children are charged 5/-. However both cinemas have a special tier of Pullman seats cum individual armchairs with deeply quilted cushions and in all there are 38 of these best seats in the house. In Savoy 1 the charge for one of these seats was17/6 and in Savoy 2, 15/-.

In addition to the new cinemas the existing bar and restaurant was totally transformed with new furnishings and cooking equipment and the entrance is now on the first floor foyer.

Viewing the two cinemas after the conversion had been completed Mr. Colman Conroy the Theatre Controller and Director of Irish Cinemas Limited which is a part of the Rank Organisation said that the two new cinemas must rank among the most modern in the world.

~~~~~

Both of the films chosen for the opening night were considered classics with Sweet Charity being commended for being a great musical and "The Shoes of the Fisherman" for its pageantry of the Vatican.

Sweet Charity tells the tale of a Taxi dancer 'Charity Hope Valentine' who is too trusting and repeatedly has her heart broken by shifty no-goods and who better to portray poor Charity than Shirley MacLaine.

* * * * *

After twenty years in a Siberian Labour Camp Kiril Lakota the Metropolitan Archbishop is set free and then finds himself in Rome where the ailing Pope makes him a Cardinal.

When the Pope dies Lakota finds himself elected Pope in a world that is in a state of crisis and he is seriously plagued by self doubt brought about by his long years in prison and by being Pope in a world that he knows nothing about.

Anthony Quinn is of course Pope Kiril.

* * * * *

In 1975 another screen was added to the Savoy and on Thursday, October 3rd of that year Savoy 3 with "The Romantic Englishwoman" starring Glenda Jackson and Michael Caine.

This new Screen had seating for 200.
~~~~~

Savoy 3 was officially opened by Councillor Patrick Dunne, Lord Mayor of Dublin and in a complete break with tradition the projection box or room was located behind the screen, which had the effect of giving shape delineation, and completely dispels the old consciousness and visual evidence of projection from behind the audience. No longer would one see that long funnel of white light from projection box to screen that would highlight thick furls of smoke arising from the cigarette smoking audience.

This new screen was constructed on the site of the old Savoy restaurant and was a most splendid and tastefully decorated little house, which would allow management to provide films of artistic and technical merit that might not have been an economic proposition in the larger 1 & 2 Savoy Screens. This was exemplified in its opening choice of film, which didn't exactly bring forth great reviews from film critics.

In 1979 a further two screens were added to the Savoy complex making a grand total of 5 screens.

On Thursday night July 5th 1979 there was a gala opening for this new complex, which, apart from the addition of an extra screen, was totally redecorated and laid with new carpeting and the most comfortable of seats. In attendance that night were the President of Ireland, Dr. Patrick Hillary and the Lord Mayor of Dublin, Councillor William Cummiskey who will view the film "Moonraker" starring Roger Moore from the new Savoy 1 screen.

It is now P.C. to refer to cinemas within multi cinema complexes as 'Screens' rather than cinemas.

The extra two screens and the total refurbishing of the Savoy complex was completed within a twelve week period and during that time two screens were able to carry on showing films without interruption.

In 1996 a sixth screen was added and this opened on July 19th 1996.

At the time of writing this piece of cinema history in December 2005, the Savoy with all her screens is still flourishing and drawing in the crowds with marvellous attractions of such magnificence and ingenuity that they would have had the chairperson of Associated British Cinemas, Mr. John Maxwell, if he were alive today, speechless.

It rather surprised us that in June 2005 following a major refurbishing programme which cost some €2 million the management of the Savoy cinema celebrated its 75th birthday when in fact it was midway into its 76th year.

As stated in the opening page of this story the Savoy Cinema opened on Friday night November 29th 1929 in the presence of President and Mrs Cosgrave and to the strains of the No 1 Army band, which was conducted by Fritz Brasse.

At midday Tuesday, November 29th 2005 we did a photo shoot on the Savoy Cinema on its 76th birthday and here we reproduce some of our pictures. Unfortunately O'Connell Street was being refurbished at the time and despite all our wishes and prayers leading up to midday on that day the road works would not go away.

Midday, Tuesday, November 2005.

RAID ON DUBLIN CINEMA.

While researching another cinema we came across a news item concerning the Savoy cinema and this was a claim for compensation by the Savoy management for criminal injury done to their property in O'Connell Street on December 3rd 1934. This claim amounted to £734.

This claim by Associated Irish Cinemas Limited and Irish Cinemas Ltd., which was brought against Dublin Corporation, was before Justice Davitt in the Dublin Circuit Court on Thursday, march 14th 1935.

Mr. Monks (instructed by Messrs Hayes and Sons) acting on behalf of the applicants, stated that on the date mentioned a picture representing the royal wedding was being shown in the cinema when the manager observed some persons at the back of the audience go out and signal to some men in the street. Immediately some two hundred men rushed into the cinema at the front entrance and another group of about one hundred came in from the back of the cinema.

They were all armed with sticks and eggshells filled with creosote. They tore up some of the seats and flung the parts onto the stage, and flung the eggshells at the front curtain. Two men rushed onto the stage and cut the screen into ribbons while others destroyed the side curtains and flower shelves. As they left the premises the intruders shouted "Up the Republic" and "Up the I.R.A".

The stage performance was interrupted and it was impossible to carry on with the show. There were 1,669 people sitting in the theatre when the invasion took place and all of these were issued with re-admission tickets at a cost of over £100.

In evidence Francis S Bowden, director of Pathe Freres Theatre Equipment Limited who had supplied equipment to the cinema when it had opened in 1929 said that it would cost in the region of £125 to fit a new screen and replacement curtains would cost over £200, apart from the damage to the seats etc.

The house manager Mr. Colman Conroy and Mr. Desmond Murphy general manager of the Savoy gave corroborating evidence that there was a serious drop in takings for several days after the raid, which was widely published in the newspapers.

Mr. T.F. Burke who appeared for the Dublin Corporation said that the damage was undoubtedly done, but he submitted that that the amount claimed was excessive.

Mr. Monks withdrew the claim for consequential damages and the Judge gave a decree for £272.11.3 with £11.5s for witness's expenses, which was to be levied off the city of Dublin.

SAVOY FANFARE

Vol. 6. No. 11 — *Free to Savoy Patrons* — Jan. 1st. 1936.

EDITORIAL

GREETINGS TO ALL OUR PATRONS!

WITH the dawn of 1936 we extend to all our patrons in Dublin, Cork and Limerick, cordial greetings that every happiness and prosperity may be yours in the New Year. For your unstinted patronage during the year that has gone please accept our sincere thanks. During 1935 our policy has been to give you only the best in film entertainment, and in this we feel you will all agree that we have well succeeded. For the New Year we have booked for your enjoyment a dazzling array of star pictures, which will afford you supreme, unalloyed pleasure.

At the Savoy, Dublin, we open on January 3rd with the greatest screen classic of 1935, a magnificent presentation of Charles Dickens' immortal masterpiece, "DAVID COPPERFIELD." The pre-view of this masterpiece to an immense gathering of Dublin teachers created quite a sensation. The Dublin press critics unanimously hailed the picture as an epoch-making event in the history of screen drama. Here is the unbiassed, straight view of the "Irish Independent" critic:

> "It is an exquisite film, bringing to life all the hidden, sombre charm of an old mezzotint. It gives us a world and an England of quiet beauty which Time tells us is lost to us. How Dickens would have loved this picture! Its two and a quarter hours are all too short."

The other Metropolitan press critics write in an equally laudatory vein.

Following "DAVID COPPERFIELD," comes a host of other superb attractions to the Savoy, Dublin, which will add much to your store of happiness in 1936.

For our patrons in Cork we have prepared an equally entrancing programme, opening on New Year's Day with "PASSPORT TO FAME," acclaimed to be the best picture Edward G. Robinson has ever made. This will be followed by such outstanding successes as "LET'S LIVE TO-NIGHT," starring Tullio Carminati, Wallace Beery in "THE MIGHTY BARNUM," and Jeanette MacDonald with Nelson Eddy in the gorgeous musical play, "NAUGHTY MARIETTA."

AT THE SAVOY, DUBLIN.

The Cinema opens for continuous performances daily at 2 p.m. The last performance concludes at 11 p.m. There are two showings on Sunday, at 2 p.m., and 8.30 p.m.

ALL seats may be booked for Sunday night. The Box Office opens daily from 2 p.m. to 7 p.m. Saturdays, 11 a.m. to 7 p.m. Sundays from 11 a.m.

ADMISSION PRICES:

GRAND CIRCLE ...	... 2/6 (including Tax).	CENTRE CIRCLE	... 1/3 (including Tax).
BACK STALLS ...	... 2/- (including Tax).	FRONT STALLS	... 1/3 (including Tax).
BACK CIRCLE ...	1/- (including Tax).		

Free [illegible] facilities for patrons of the Cinema and Restaurant. Patrons' parcels may be checked free of charge at the Ladies' and Gentlemen's Cloakrooms on either side of the Grand Circle Entrance.

The times of showing of the feature picture is published daily in both the morning and evening papers.

Before leaving the Cinema make sure that you have all your belongings. Articles lost or found should be reported to an usher and will be stored in the Lost Property Office until claimed.

The Programmes [illegible] in this issue are subject to alteration at the discretion of the Management.

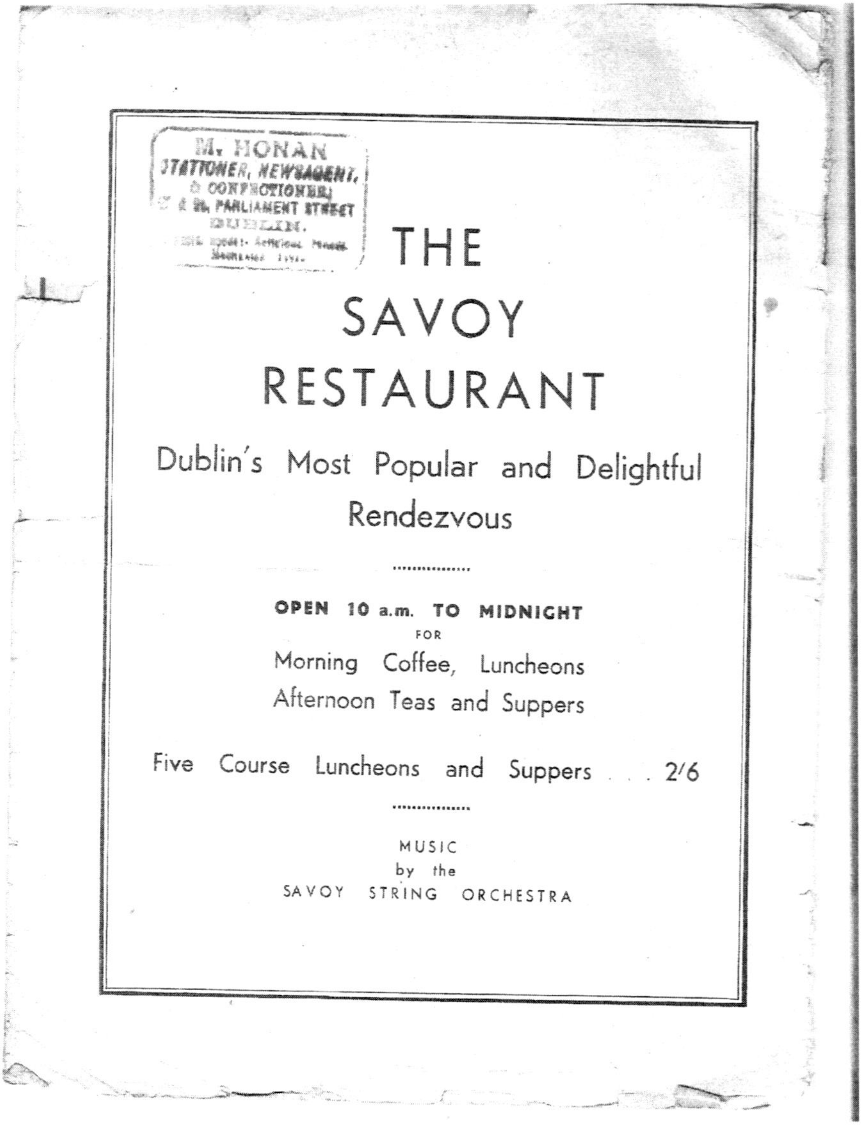
M. HONAN
STATIONER, NEWSAGENT,
& CONFECTIONER,
PARLIAMENT STREET
DUBLIN.
THE
SAVOY
RESTAURANT
Dublin's Most Popular and Delightful Rendezvous
OPEN 10 a.m. TO MIDNIGHT
FOR
Morning Coffee, Luncheons
Afternoon Teas and Suppers
Five Course Luncheons and Suppers . . . 2/6
MUSIC
by the
SAVOY STRING ORCHESTRA

SAVOY FANFARE

DAVID COPPERFIELD

THE BEST-BELOVED FILM OF THIS—OR ANY OTHER—YEAR

+ + +

Comes to the Savoy, Dublin, Jan. 3rd and to Cork, Jan. 19th

...

1935's GREATEST PICTURE

AFTER more than a year of preparation and production, "David Copperfield," the prize-winning photoplay is scheduled to open on January 3rd at the Savoy, presenting the new child star, Freddie Bartholomew, as the boy "David," supported by sixty-five stars and featured players in the major roles.

Aunt Betsey protects David from the Murdstones. A scene from "David Copperfield"

David feels his stepfather's vicious wrath. Freddie Bartholomew and Basil Rathbone

THE CAST:

Micawber	W. C. FIELDS
David, The Man	FRANK LAWTON
Agnes Wickfield	MADGE EVANS
Dan Peggotty	LIONEL BARRYMORE
Aunt Betsey Trotwood	EDNA MAY OLIVER
Mr. Wickfield	LEWIS STONE
Dora Spenlow	MAUREEN O'SULLIVAN
David, The Child	FREDDIE BARTHOLOMEW
Mrs. Copperfield	ELIZABETH ALLAN
Uriah Heep	ROLAND YOUNG
Steerforth	HUGH WILLIAMS
Mr. Murdstone	BASIL RATHBONE
Clickett	Elsa Lanchester
Mrs. Micawber	Jean Cadell
Mr. Dick	Lennox Pawle
Jane Murdstone	Violet Kemble Cooper
Mrs. Gummidge	Una O'Connor
Barkis	Herbert Mundin
Little Em'ly, The Woman	Florine McKinney
Nurse Peggotty	Jessie Ralph
Ham	John Buckler
Little Em'ly, The Child	Fay Chaldecott
Agnes, The Child	Marilyn Knowlden
The Vicar	Hugh Walpole

Etc., etc.

Directed by George Cukor. From the classic novel by Charles Dickens. Adaptation by Hugh Walpole. Screen play by Howard Estabrook.

Page Two

STAR
Crumlin.
Which was later nicknamed the 'Rats' by the local wits.

The Star cinema in Crumlin was formally opened on Thursday, January 15th 1953 by Senator Andy Clerkin, the Lord Mayor of Dublin at that time. Situated on the Crumlin Road just opposite "Our Lady's Children's Hospital" the "Star" was the last word in cinemas.

This new cinema though a local, was managed along the lines of a town house and although it was not classed as a 1st run house the very best of pictures for display were sought by management.

It was very luxuriously furnished, with the most comfortable seats and it was carpeted throughout with "Tintawn". The building, which still stands in 2005, is 90 feet wide and 120 feet long with a large attractive wide front which had two shops one on each side of the entrance doors. Management ran one of the shops for the sale of sweets, ice cream, and cigarettes and the other shop was to be put out on lease.

There was seating for 1800 persons with 1,350 seats in the stalls area and a further 450 in the balcony and included in the foyer is a most comfortable lounge area where in the future it is hoped to serve light refreshments.

Unlike most new suburban cinemas the Star also possessed a first class stage where concerts etc could be held if found necessary. There were also ample dressing rooms and cloakrooms at the back of the stage, thus allowing for management to offer cine-variety programmes should that be their wish.

The Builders were Maher and Murphy of Aughrim Street and Jones and Kelly of South Frederick Street were the architects. The building was said to have cost some £60,000.

Admission prices were reasonable ranging from 1/- to 2/2

Selected for its opening night was the film "Tea for Two" starring Doris Day, Gordon McRae, Gene Nelson and Eve Arden.

This is a beautiful musical based on a Broadway Hit entitled "No, No Nanette".

This told the story of Nanette Carter (Doris Day) a young heiress who bet her uncle $25,000 that she could say no to anything for a full forty-eight hours. If she won the bet she would also be allowed to finance and help her boyfriend (Gordon McRae) stage his own Broadway Show.

The film also featured many of Doris's great hits, including:
"I only have Eyes for You"
&
"Oh Me, Oh My!"

ROCK 'N ROLL HITS THE STAR

The film "Rock Around the Clock" did not bode well for the Star cinema when it hit their screens in late July of 1956. It would seem that on Monday July 30th 1956 when the film was in motion a bunch of "Teddy Boys" began to loudly hand clap when Bill Haley "the King of Rock 'n Roll" and his Comets were performing. When Bill had finished his rousing Rock Around the Clock number, the Teddy Boys ignored the other music and songs and began to chant "We want Haley" and bottles and other missiles began to fly.

During the disturbances exits signs were smashed, and the cushioning was torn off the arm rests on seats. Management stopped the film and a number of Teddy Boys were ejected by nine Gardai, who were on duty in the cinema while the film was being shown, a fact that made it very obvious that trouble was expected.

When the trouble makers were ejected and the rest of the patrons had settled down management continued the show with an alternative film entitled "Tight Spot" an apt choice of name you might well say for such a situation.

"Tight Spot" starring Ginger Rodgers, Edward G Robison and Brian Keith is about protecting a witness that was about to testify against her old Beau, a notorious mobster.

Most of the patrons accepted this but a number of Teddy Boys and girls left the cinema.

STAR Peter Cushing, DR. TERROR'S HOUSE OF HORRORS.
Alastair Sim, THE BELLES OF ST. TRINIANS.

The Star Closed on December 11th 1971.

The building is still standing as can be seen by the following picture taken of it on November 17th of 2005.

As can be seen in this picture the Star still flourishes as a Bingo hall, however before it entered the world of Bingo it served for quite some time as a "Roller Rink".

REVIVIFICATION

A fair amount of cinemas were re-opened sometime after their closure but once again having failed to take off they again closed down for good and we would name but a few.

The Gala Ballyfermot
Inchicore
The State Phibsboro
Bohemian Phibsboro
Star Crumlin
The Academy Pearse St, and
The Fairview Grand
Pavilion Dun Laoghaire
Although we believe that a section of the Fairview still exists for the showing of previews and press releases etc.

STATE
North Circular Road, Blaquire Bridge, Phibsboro/Phibsborough.

"The Phibsborough Picture House", sometimes called the "Blaquire" and later the "State Cinema" was opened in May 1914 by William King of Belcamp House, Raheny and was managed by his brother Jack. The cinema which became very popular not only in Phibsboro but in surrounding areas was often referred to as the "Fizzer" or the Phibo.

There were rumours at the time that Jack had such strong nationalist belief's that his family were afraid that the cinema might come to some harm. However times passed and nothing ever happened because of these strong beliefs.

However on June 4th 1914 while the film "In the Shadow of the Throne" was being shown there was a disturbance in the cinema which also caused a small riot. This came about when two men stood up in the audience and objected to the film being screened. One of the men threw ink onto the screen causing considerable damage, some of the ink landed on the blouse of one of the lady musicians and stained it beyond use, while some more landed on some music sheets and rendered them unreadable.

The other man claimed that his religion was being insulted and demanded that any Catholics in the audience should leave the premises. When members of the staff appeared on the scene and tried to eject the two men it suddenly became apparent that this was an organised gang who had come to the cinema to take the law into their own hands. Four or five more people stood up and did their best to bring about a disturbance. The management sent for the police but in the meantime the troublemakers disappeared. Later two men were arrested and ended up in court the next day where they argued their case and suggested that Ireland and England was in need of a proper censorship board to be appointed over films.

The Film it would appear was not very accurate in detail and caused a lot of controversy in the media. It told the story of a young Danish girl who had been disappointed in her love for a Prince and left the world and entered a convent. There she was professed by a group of nuns and it would appear that this was not in accordance with a profession in a Catholic convent. In another it appeared that a nun took the place of a priest and opened the tabernacle. In another scene a man was said to have made the sign of the cross.

Both defendants said that the film was objectionable and both believed that their faith had been held up to ridicule by the picture.

In his summing up the Judge fined each defendant 1s and the management of the Phibsborough Picture House booked the film for another three days such was the demand to see this film, which had caused much protest!

In 1938 the Rank Organisation bought the cinema and had it completely remodelled and its seating capacity increased from 750 to 1,330. The cinema, though it appeared to be enjoying great attendances, closed in 1951 and was later demolished. In late 1953 the site which now included a neighbouring building which had also been knocked down was prepared and work commenced on the building of a new state of the art cinema. This new building was designed by Messrs. O'Connor & Aylward Architects and the construction was carried out by the building contractors Irish Estates Ltd.

This new cinema which was named the "State" opened on April 24th 1954 with a large Cinemascope screen and the first picture to be shown on that screen was "West of Zanzibar" starring Anthony Steel and Sheila Simms. The manager was King whose father had built the original Phibsboro cinema.

"West of Zanzibar" tells the tale of a Big Game Ranger who chases ivory smugglers across Zanzibar and when he catches up with them he is shocked to the core. There is no connection or comparison between the film and Tod Browning's1928 "West of Zanzibar" where Lon Chaney plays the part of a hard done by husband, Dead Legs Phroso.

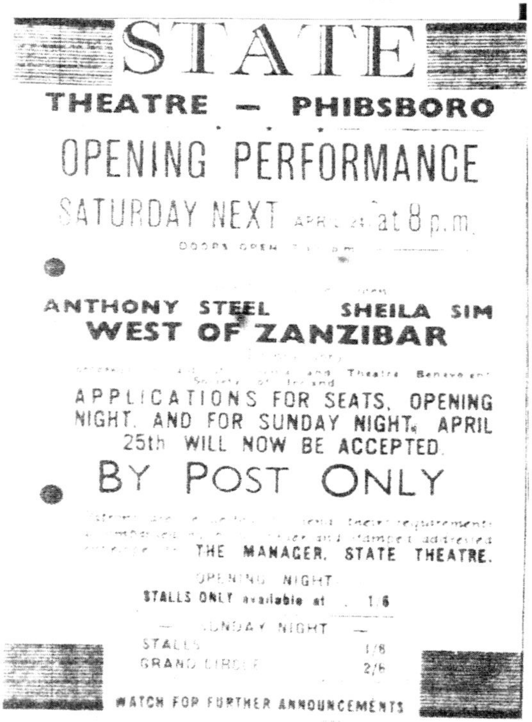

This advertisement appeared in the "Evening Herald" on Thursday April 21st 1954.

Cinemagoers welcomed this new modern cinema with great enthusiasm which had been brought to them through the courtesy of Odeon Ireland at a cost of some £75,000.

This new cinema was as near to being a town house or 1st Run house as any cinema could be and it enjoyed great patronage.

Phibsboro was a good catchment area and easily accessible from many parts of Dublin as over twelve bus routes serviced the area.

Some eight years later the "State" was awarded the status of a 1st Run House.

STATE TO BE A 'FIRST-RUN' CINEMA

Good news for northsiders. The State Cinema in Phibsboro will become a first-run house at the end of August or early in September. I confirmed this news last night with the State's manager, Mr. William D. King, who told me that all arrangements for the change-over had been completed.

To ensure more comfort for patrons, and to obviate the necessity for people standing up to allow others into seats, the seating capacity has been reduced from 1,330 to 1,222.

Incidentally, did you know that manager King's father built the original Phibsboro' Cinema in 1913 on the present site of the State.

This article appeared in the "Evening Herald" on June 30th 1962 announcing the news that the "State" cinema was about to be awarded the Status of a 1st Run house which would allow its management the right to a better choice of movie. However this entitlement would not take effect until the following August/ September.

Although this most welcome news which broke in the newspapers on June 30th 1962 brought great joy to many cinemagoers, other news on other pages in the same papers brought about great sadness and that was the news of the closing down of the Theatre Royal and Regal Rooms in Hawkins Street.

State (Over 18s) At 5.45, 9.10 Ian Hendry, "THE ASSASSIN". Plus! At 4.05, 7.30, John Cleese, Graham Chapman, "AND NOW FOR SOMETHING COMPLETELY DIFFERENT".
Patrons please note that this cinema will remain closed as and from the end of this evening's programme.

Another sad announcement which appeared in the papers on Saturday June 29th 1974, notified the public that the "State" together with another five cinemas which all belonged to the same Associated British Cinema Company would remain closed after the finale performance that night.

The State now an Ice Rink.

The State in late 2005, now a furniture showroom.

A WORD ON CINEMASCOPE AND THE STATE CINEMA

This sketch which appeared in the "Irish Times" on Saturday April 24th 1954 provides a fair description of what the Cinemascope screen looked like.

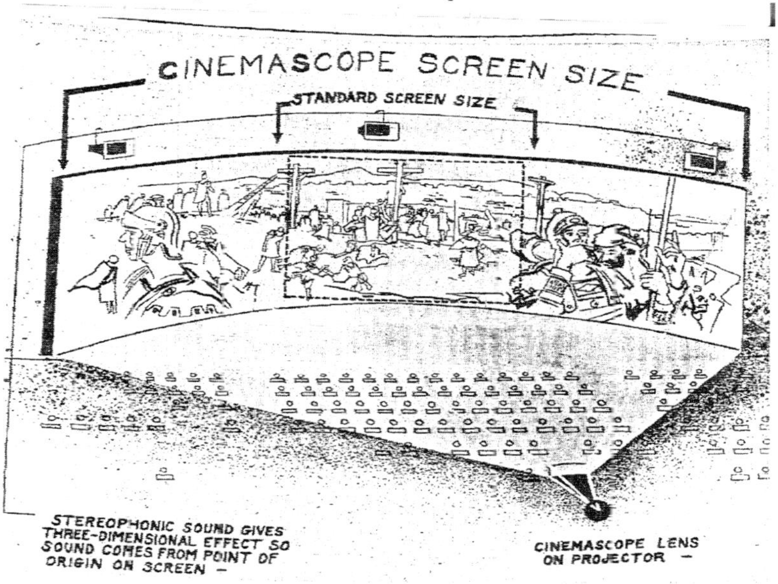

The screen is also fully retractable which enables ordinary films to be shown.

The policy in relation to the new cinema will be for it to act as a second run cinema for Cinemascope films which will have their first run in the Savoy cinema which was Ireland's first Cinemascope cinema.

"The Robe" will be the next Cinemascope presentation in the State when it has finished its run in the Savoy

Other forthcoming attractions will be;

"How to Marry a Millionaire"
Starring
Betty Grable, Marilyn Monroe, Lauren Bacall
&
"King of the Khyber Rifles"
Starring
Tyrone Power, Terry Moore, Michael Rennie, Guy Rolfe.

How to Marry a Millionaire was Twentieth Century-Fox's first Cinemascope film but for some reason it was not released until after "The Robe".

"The Robe" was the first picture to be shown on the big curved screen. All however were made in 1953.

The State Cinema in 1954

Although re-built and opened as Ireland's second Cinemascope cinema it did not open with a Cinemascope production, instead of which it featured "West of Zanzibar" on its new wide screen.

"West of Zanzibar" is a 1954 release starring Anthony Steel and Sheila Sim and should not be confused with the 1928 film of the same name, which starred Lon Chaney, Lionel Barrymore and Mary Nolan

The State had yet to advertise its first Cinemascope presentation and as "The Robe" had just begun its run in the Savoy on the same day of the State's grand opening it was a forgone conclusion that "The Robe's " next outing would be in the State.

STELLA
Mount Merion.

Another luxury cinema to grace Dublin's suburbia, and this time fulfilling a vacuum in the south city area of Mount Merrion. This is another venture by the Directors of the companies that operate and own the Stella and Princess cinemas in Rathmines to expand their business empire.

This new cinema has been built by a newly formed company called the Deerpark Cinema Co Ltd which is managed by James O'Grady who is also managing directors of the above mentioned Rathmines companies.

The cinema is well proportioned with seating for some 1,000 customers and features its very own well appointed shop in the vestibule area in the vicinity of the ticket office. No expense has been spared in the provision of spacious and luxurious surrounding and the technical equipment used for the projection of films is so up to-date that it can accommodate cinemascope at the touch of a button and by the same token cope with any future developments along those lines.

The cinema was designed by Robert Dowling and had a grand opening ceremony on Thursday July 28th 1955 which was conducted by the Dublin City Council Chairman Senator Victor Carton.

For its official opening the film "Ring of Fear" was chosen. This was a Warner Bros. Cinemascope Production, starring Mickey Spillane and Clyde Beatty.

Prices of admission were Balcony 2/6 Stalls 1/6.

The Stella Cinema building in 2005; now Flanagan's furniture shop.

The ticket office and a part of the beautiful staircase is well preserved and in good use to day. There is also a set of stairs which once led to the operating room and a number of areas still as they were in 1955.

STELLA, Mt. Merrion (12's, Charlton Heston, Ava Gardner, George Kennedy **"Earthquake"** (Prog. 8.00, Feature 8.30). Retained Sunday: Two Sep. Perfs. 3 and 8.

The Stella closed on Sunday night October 31st 1976 and on the left is a copy of its last advertisement featuring "Earthquake" as its final picture show.

Now a beautiful furniture shop it still has many touches of cinema nostalgia in and about the building, including the upstairs landing area, stair wells, and various entrances to offices and workroom sections.

STELLA RATHMINES

In the year 2004 the "Stella" was said to be the oldest cinema in Dublin with two screens. Sadly it also closed towards the end of that year.

Another little anecdote from Noel Twamley, Noel informs us with some nostalgia, that the Stella had a multi coloured lighting system which lit up the curtains on the stage and that a beautiful water fountain was situated in the orchestra pit.

He also reminded us that in the 1940's the pubs closed at 7.30 pm on Sunday nights and that quite a few of the "Garglers" would then make their way to the Stella to see a picture. Most suburban picture houses at that time would start their show at 8 pm but the Stella management delayed their opening for half an hour in order to give the boozer's time to go home, have their tea and then take in a movie.

Nevertheless, despite this clever move on behalf of the management, when the boozers did take their seats, by 9.30 pm they would be all fast asleep. The stench of sour drink said Noel and the passing of wind were staggering and, he said, "Thank God most people smoked in those days as the smell of tobacco smoke helped to curb the other foul odours".

* * * * *

The Stella cinema opened on Monday, January 29th 1923 and was considered at that time to be one of the largest cinemas to open in Dublin.

STELLA CINEMA, RATHMINES

OPENING MONDAY NEXT, JAN. 29th, at 7.30

Violet Hopson and Stewart Rome in

"The Imperfect Lover"

A MAGNIFICENT SUPER-PRODUCTION
FIRST TIME TO DUBLIN

ONE OF THE BEST ORCHESTRAS IN DUBLIN

UNDER THE PERSONAL DIRECTION OF

MISS TERRY O'CONNOR, Feis Ceoil Gold Medalist

This Cinema is one of the largest and most luxuriously appointed in Ireland

HOURS OF OPENING AFTER MONDAY NEXT—Weekdays from 3 to 10.30
Sundays from 3 to 6, and from 8.30 to 10.30. Complete Change of Programme on Sunday

PRICES OF ADMISSION — 2/-, 1/6, 1/- and 9d. (including Tax)

The Stella cinema belonged to the Stella Picture Company Limited which was incorporated on the 29th November 1921 and this company which was formed to build a picture house in Rathmines would appear to have stemmed from an idea of Anthony O' Grady, a local publican and grocer and a William Kay, a cinema proprietor, a hotelier and a cinematograph exhibitor who had at times provided cinematograph displays in the Rathmines Town Hall.

O'Grady had the largest shares in the company and was duly appointed its managing director.

The cinema was a large, comfortable and well-appointed building with the plushest seats available and it was superbly decorated. The building also accommodated a small dance hall, much to the delight of local devotees of dancing. This dance hall however went into decline in the forties, but for many years afterwards it still functioned as a venue for dancing lessons.

The cinema orchestra was under the direction of Miss Terry O'Connor a brilliant musician and a Feis Ceol Medallist.

When the talkies became the norm, orchestras and all those musicians that had provided musical accompaniment to the silent films shown in cinemas for the past thirty odd years redundant and the orchestra pits in the Stella, like cinemas now, lay idle.

The Stella management however didn't just sit back and allow the 'pit' to lie in an idle state beneath a layer of time and dust. Instead they had installed a beautiful water fountain, which would be switched on during intervals with the water sprays bathed in splendid coloured lighting provided by well placed spotlights.

STELLA BALLROOM
DANCING SUNDAY NIGHT.
MACK'S BLACK DIAMOND BAND.
USUAL PRICES AND SELECT.

STELLA RATHMINES
GARY COOPER in
"THE WESTERNER"
with Walter Brennan, Fred Stone
Doris Davenport. At 6.30 and
COMMUNITY SING."
Sunday: "I LOVE YOU AGA
with William POWELL and My
LOY, Frank McHugh and Edm
Lowe.
BOOK NOW FOR SUNDAY NIG

UTOPIA DANCES,
STELLA BALLROOM, RATHMINES
TO-MORROW (FRI.) NIGHT,
7.30 P.M. TO 11 P.M.
INTRODUCING HARRY MENDEL'S ORCHESTRA
(Late Principal Leader for the Geo. Edwardes's Daly's Theatre Productions, and Principal London Bands).
ADMISSION —— 2/-.

DANCING STELLA BALLROOM, RATHMINES.

Craoḃ Tomás Dáiḃis.
Céiliḋe
IN STELLA, RATHMINES,
SUNDAY NIGHT, 8—11 p.m. 1/-
Ceol Tomas Dáiḃis—Céiliḋe Mór
In TOWN HALL, SAT., 26/1/'35—9 to 3.
Ticéad agus Séire :: 5/-

STELLA BALLROOM, RATHMINES.
7 p.m. LILAC DANCES 11 p.m.
Under the direction of Mr. T. F. MURPHY.
OPENING CARNIVAL NIGHT ON WEDNESDAY, OCT. 6, AND EVERY WEDNESDAY.
SPECIAL ENGAGEMENT OF MR. A. VERSO NAPPER'S MELODY DANCE BAND.
LADIES, 1/6; GENTS, 2/-; DOUBLE, 3/-

STELLA MOUNT MERRION
6.5 and 9.15
GRIP OF FEAR
Glenn Ford Lee Remick
Stephanie Powers Ross Martin
Also: MURDER BY CONTRACT
Last Complete Perf.: 7.45

STELLA —— RATHMINES
YUL BRYNNER in RETURN OF THE SEVEN (C/Scope & Col.) with Robert Fuller. At 5.45 & 9.05. Extra: HIT AND RUN, Vince Edwards, Gigo Moore, Hugo Haas. At 7.40. Last Comp. Perf. 7.32. Sunday: Girl in The Headlines. Extra Calculated Risk

A selection of evening newspapers advertisements from the following years: 1925-1926-1928-1934-1967

The cinema had seating for some 1,350 patrons and at the time of closure it was the last remaining suburban cinema Dublin, which other than the twinning of same in the 1980s remained virtually unchanged.

STELLA RATHMINES (Prog. 8 p.m.) Roger Moore, Carole Bouquet
FOR YOUR EYES ONLY (8.30)
LATE SHOW 10.45: Mel Brooks, Harvey Korman BLAZING SADDLES.
Also: John Cleese MONTY PYTHON & THE HOLY GRAIL
Sun. Mat. 3 p.m.: FOR YOUR EYES ONLY. Sun. Evg. (18s) Mel Brooks BLAZING SADDLES (9.15). Also John Cleese MONTY PYTHON & THE HOLY GRAIL (7.40).

This was the last advertisement for the Stella cinema before it closed for twinning on Sunday night September 27th 1981' and the advert below which appeared in the following Mondays "Evening Herald" dated September 28th simply confirms the closure.

STELLA —————— RATHMINES
★ CINEMA CLOSED FOR TWINNING ALTERATIONS ★

STELLA CINEMA RATHMINES
TWIN CINEMA OPENING TONIGHT 7.30 p.m.
STELLA 1 Dudley Moore, Liza Minelli, John Gielgud ARTHUR (18s)
STELLA 2 Robert DeNiro, Robert Duvall, Burgess Meredith TRUE CONFESSIONS (18s)

The conversion took all of five months and on Monday February 22nd 1982 the Stella re-opened with Screen 1 & 2.

It is also interesting to note that suburban cinemas were now able to obtain 1st run films at the same time as town houses and were now playing on a level playing field.
The Film "Arthur" was also showing in the "Adelphi-Green-Forum & Fairview" and "True Confessions" was in the "Regent and Green".

The twinning of the Stella considerably reduced its seating-capacity, it now had seating for only 460 persons. Screen 1 was a 280 seater and Screen 2 had seats for 180, however these were modern times and the trend was for smaller cinemas, or as they are termed in the trade, "Screens"

The Stella left us without a whisper and you might say, caught Patrick and me off guard so to speak. While we did succeed in getting a few exterior shots of the cinema we had left it too late to get a photo shot of the inside.

This advertisement which appeared in the "Evening Herald" on Thursday August 26th 2004 is we believe the Stella's last. It would seem that the Stella closed its door on the following Saturday or Sunday for the last time.

According to a notice on the door, the cinema is closed for alterations and we also heard that planning applications had been advanced for the building of cine complex in the Swan Centre and if that goes ahead we don't see the Stella re-opening, although we would like to be proved wrong.

The Stella was Dublin's oldest cinema with two screens and in its latter days, prices of admission were €6.50 and €4.50 for matinees and concessions.

~~~~

Travelling Show People.

On September 6th 1911 Balbriggan Town Commissioners received a notice from a Thomas Harris manager of the Fair Green Picture Palace Balbriggan.

This notice which was in full compliance with section 7 (3) c of the Cinematograph Act of 1909 stated that it was his intention to give an exhibition of pictures by means of a cinematograph at the Fair Green Balbriggan in his Tent or Booth which was known as "The Electric Palace".

This performance would be given in respect of a licence, which had been granted to him by the Urban District Council of Drogheda.
~~~~

STRAND BALBRIGGAN.

The Strand cinema in Balbriggan was the first of two cinemas that catered to the needs of both the local people and holiday-makers, who used to visit this seaside town in what we all liked to call, the good old days. Train-loads of visitors would alight at the local station to spend a day on the beach as would others who would arrive by bus and on wet days, of which there were many, the local cinema was a godsend.

This cinema was said to have been the brainchild of Fr. Doherty, a local priest and it was located in George's Square next door to the Town Hall, which was built circa 1905.

The cinema thrived for many years and it was a great source of funds for the parish church, community and local schools. Good entertainment and the proceeds, all for a good cause one might say.

This is a view of the Balbriggan Library in George's Square, which is undergoing renovation at the moment and to the left is the site which once housed the Strand cinema and Town Hall and it too is under serious construction.

Children's matinees were held every Saturday and Father Doherty always made it his business to be up on the stage to welcome all the children and introduce the afternoon's films, many of which would be cartoons of the day, with Mickey Mouse being one of the most popular. When it came to the introduction of Mickey Mouse Father Doherty would only say, much to the amusement of the children, "Michael Mouse, never would he use the word Mickey".

The hall which later became the Strand cinema was situated to the rear of the Town Hall building and it was used by the local clergy to run small fund raising get togethers, dances etc and when cinematograph exhibitions and the showing of silent films began making serious inroads as a source of entertainment in Ireland, cinema arrived in Balbriggan. This came about by contracting or hiring the hall out to travelling film operators who would have their own projection equipment and a picture house was born.

This new entertainment wasn't available on a nightly basis but usually once or twice a month and the contracting operator and exhibitor of films was a Vernon who for many years delighted his patrons with his excellent choice of films.

It was during one of these cinematograph displays that the Strand cinema suffered a near fatal happening on January 28th 1929 when a reel of film burst into flames causing panic amongst the audience. In those early days of cinema it was not unusual to have the operating box located on the floor next to the stage and in front of the audience.

On this particular night the patrons had only just settled themselves into their seats when a reel of film went on fire in the operating room and immediately flames leapt out from the operating box. Vernon the operator and a travelling picture show entrepreneur suffering singeing of his face and hands rushed from the box, which was made from steel and closed the door tight. Despite this the flames threatened the nearby stage, which housed underneath its floors gas pipes which fed gas to the gas lamps which were used to light the building.

The audience was in panic as thick black smoke filled the auditorium and there was a wild rush for the exits at the back of the cinema. Some women members of the audience fainted and the shrieks and screams of others added to the panic.

Fortunately there was enough exits at the end of the hall to allow everybody safe exit thereby minimising the possibility of a conflagration. The Civic Guards were called from the nearby barracks and members of the local Commercial Club who had rooms above the barracks all rushed to help and their efforts with the help of many willing helpers from the audience saved the Town Hall building from destruction.

While there were no reports of any serious injuries, other than some minor singeing of face and limbs, the building survived with some portions of the stage and hall badly charred and the film of the night "Son of the Sheik", was totally incinerated.

Fortunately for all concerned, another cinema horror was narrowly averted and the cinema was repaired and survived into the forties.

Some years later Father Doherty a local priest took over the management of the Strand cinema as a means of fund raising for the local schools, and other community activities and he named the picture house the Strand cinema, where films were now shown nightly together with children's matinees at the weekend.

A photo taken circa 1940s, showing what's left of the Strand Cinema.

Not the best of pictures but it does show where everything was. The building on the right housed the entrance to the cinema and the dance hall, which were now two separate buildings. The doorway on the left led into the cinema and the one on the right took you into the dance hall. Upstairs was a snooker hall, and other rooms were used as offices by the Town Commissioners.

The white shed like building with the outside stairs was the operating room and the cinema proper is attached to that. Quite a large building we believe, which had a rear exit in High Street.

The celebrant taking part in the parade is Canon Hickey.

This photo is courtesy of Jack Benton who began his working life in the Strand cinema, a job it would appear that he acquired simply by accident and while we will tell you of Jack in another part of this book we would like to take this opportunity to make a plea on behalf of local historians and historical societies the world over and that is; "if you have any old photographs that you no longer want please offer them to your local historical society or the National Library".

The Strand cinema was officially opened as a cinema on Sunday, February 25th 1934 and its first picture show was the German Musical known as "Tell Me To-Night" Starring Polish Tenor, Jan Kiepura as Italian Tenor Enrico Ferraro and Magha Schnieder as Mathilde Pategg the Mayor's daughter, his love interest.

This beautiful comedy / musical love story provided Jan Kiepura a great opportunity to exercise his legendary tenor voice singing arias from La Boheme, Rigoletto, La Traviata and Martha.
There were also Travel Talks, Sing-Sing Melody and Cartoons
Prices of admission were 6d. 1s, and 1s.6d.

("Tell Me To-Night" was also known as "Be Mine To-Night" in the USA and were directed by the world famous director Anatole Litvak.

~~~~~

While we mentioned that the leasing of the cinema was the brainchild of Father Doherty the building was officially leased to Father Joseph Hickey, Parish Priest of Balbriggan on February 17th 1934 and Father Doherty managed the business. The lease, which was initially for a period of five years, was later renewed for a period of 40 years.

In 1940 Farther Hickey applied to the Balbriggan Town Commissioners for their consent to the assignment of his interest in the lease to one William Walsh and following their refusal to give their consent an action was instituted in the High Court by Father Hickey against the Commissioners for a declaration that the refusal of the Commissioners to consent to the assignment was unreasonable.

The appeal and legal arguments went on for some considerable time and it would appear that eventually it was agreed to allow the assignment of the lease to Walsh subject to an increase in rent and certain conditions.

In April 1941 the Town Hall Commissioners agreed to transfer the lease of the Town Hall cinema from Father Hickey to William Walsh under certain conditions as mentioned above and a rent increase of £200 per annum.

~~~~~

(See also Savoy Cinema Balbriggan)

STRAND CINEMA
North Strand.

The New Strand cinema had a Grand Opening on Saturday night April 16th 1938 and performing the opening ceremony was the Lord Mayor of Dublin, the Right Honourable Alfred Byrne.

Strand cinema building as it stands in 2005.

Chosen for its opening programme was the film "Love Under Fire".

—NEW STRAND CINEMA—
NORTH STRAND.
GRAND OPENING TO-NIGHT
By the Right Honourable ALFRED BYRNE, T.D., Lord Mayor of Dublin, at 8.15 p.m.
(DOORS OPEN 7.30).
OUTSTANDING PROGRAMME
LORETTA YOUNG, DON AMECHE IN
LOVE UNDER FIRE
Supporting Programme includes—POP-EYE CARTOON, COMEDY, COLOURED SHORT, SPORT ITEMS, INTEREST and PATHE NEWS.
This Programme will also be shown SUNDAY at 3 o'c and 8.30.
BANK HOLIDAY
CLAUDETTE COLBERT, MELVYN DOUGLAS, ROBERT YOUNG in
I MET HIM IN PARIS
BANK HOLIDAY Doors Open at 1.45 p.m. Spacious Car Park available for our Patrons.

THE F.S.D.S CINEMAS

FAIRVIEW GRAND
3 o'c. Sunday and 8 o'c.
Lloyd Nolan in JUST OFF BROADWAY
Also Ann Corio in SARONG GIRL
Mon. Next: ONE NIGHT OF LOVE
Also SOUTH OF THE BORDER
To-day, Last Showing, at 3.40, 6.10, 8.40: THE SULLIVANS

SUTTON CINEMA SUTTON CROSS
Sunday at 3 o'c. and 8 o'c.
David Farrar in HEADLINE
Also Roy Rogers in RED RIVER VALLEY
Mon. Next: Sabu in THE DRUM
To-day: THE GIRL IN OVERALLS
3 o'c. to 10.30

DRUMCONDRA GRAND
3 o'c. Sunday and 8 o'c.—
Mary Lee in SHANTYTOWN. Also Ralph Bellamy in Ellery Queen's PENTHOUSE MYSTERY.
Mon. next: THE GIRL IN OVERALLS and LET'S HAVE FUN.
To-day at 3.55, 6.25, 8.55: Rosalind Russell in THE BEAUTIFUL CHEAT.

STRAND CINEMA NORTH STRAND
Sunday at 3 o'c. and 8 o'c.—
Charles Bickford in THOU SHALT NOT KILL. Also Johnny Mack Brown DEEP IN THE HEART OF TEXAS.
To-day: 3 o'c.—Continuous to 10.30
MY SISTER EILEEN.
Patrons Kindly Note—On and after Monday next this Cinema will be CLOSED FOR ALTERATIONS.

As luck would have it we have little or no further news to tell you about the Strand other than the fact that it closed on Saturday September 16th 1944 for rebuilding purposes and the advertisement to the left of this page mentions its intentions to close for alterations.

It would appear that one or two neighbouring buildings were also demolished and the entire site was developed into a very large purpose built cinema.

Noting this block advertisement under the heading F.S.D.S cinemas, which also featured the films on show in the Sutton, Drumcondra and Fairview Grand cinemas makes us believe that the Strand was group owned and not as we had originally thought, an individual enterprise.

The Strand re-opened on Friday March 16th 1945 with the Spectacular Musical "The Goldwyn Girls" starring Adolphe Menjou - Kenny Baker and the Gorgeous Goldwyn Girls.

STRAND CINEMA NORTH STRAND
RE-OPENING TO-DAY (FRIDAY)
4 O'C. CONTINUOUS TO 10.30
WITH A COLOSSAL TECHNICOLOR ATTRACTION
"THE GOLDWYN FOLLIES"
Starring
ADOLPHE MENJOU, KENNY BAKER, EDGAR BERGEN and CHARLIE McCARTHY
ZORINA & THE RITZ BROTHERS
Also the Gorgeous Goldwyn Girls
Feature showing at 4.10, 6.25 & 8.40
This is indeed a Great Picture
ST. PATRICK'S DAY
DOORS OPEN AT 1.30 FOR 2 O'C PERFORMANCE

The Strand cinema closed on January 31st 1970 and the last two films shown that night were "Till Death Do Us Part" with Warren Mitchell and Dandy Nichols, and "Kiss the Girls and Make Them Die", with Dorothy Provine.

Strand Cìnema

& Theatre

NORTH STRAND, DUBLIN

Souvenìr

Souvenir of

Re-opening

AFTER COMPLETE RECONSTRUCTION

March 16, 1945

WITH THE COMPLIMENTS
OF
THE DIRECTORS

The Strand Picture Palace is no more. It has been demolished and the site is now being prepared for the building of apartments.

It would appear that the builders are retaining the façade of the building.

The lower picture shows a portion of the back of the cinema where the screen would have been.

It is not known if the section is also being retained. Only time will tell.

SUNDRIVE

The Sundrive cinema opened in 1935 but try as we might, we could not establish the exact opening date. We did however come across a small advertisement on the 19th of September 1935 in both the "Evening Mail and Evening Herald "newspapers which as far as we could ascertain was its first. This advertisement was for the feature film "West of the Pecos", starring Richard Dix and a comedy caper with the much-acclaimed double act of Wheeler & Woolsey in "Cockeyed Cavaliers".

However we must give mention to the fact that a local shopkeeper in the Sundrive area was of the opinion that it had opened a week prior to that date with the film "Dames" starring Richard Powell and Ruby Zeller.

But then we must refer to an article that appeared in the "Evening Herald" on September 25th 1935, which informed its readers about this new cinema that had just opened and had been showing excellent pictures for the past week, and this would suggest that the opening was circa the 19th.

This new cinema, which had seating for 750 persons, already had expansion plans that would add another 60 feet to the premises in the very near future. It would appear that the architect had allowed for this expansion and that the premises had been finished off in such a manner that the extension could be added on without the necessity of closing the cinema. This expansion took place in 1940.

It would seem that at this point in time we are in a stalemate situation on the official opening date of this cinema and the first film to be shown there. So if anybody knows better and has proof of the exact opening date please let us know.

Whatever the date, the cinema was built and managed by a newly formed company called the Sundrive Cinema Company which was incorporated on March 12th 1935 and its principle directors were Frederick Croskerry, Mr. William Callow (Chairman) and Mr. Matthew Heron (Managing Director) and formerly a manager with the Grand Central Cinema of O'Connell Street.

The builder was a T.J. Kennedy from Phibsborough who in time would build another two cinemas for this company.

The seats were tip-up and upholstered in rich tapestry. The auditorium is accessed by a number of Terraza marble steps leading from a well-decorated vestibule, which also houses the manager's office and the entrance to the operator's rooms ,which are enclosed in steel.

Admission prices were as follows! 4d-7d and 9d.
On a point of interest, this cinema was built on a plot of ground that was known locally in 1935 as Tongues Field and prior to that Loaders Park which faced onto Sundrive Road and was bordered to the rear by Dark Lane

The new Sundrive Cinema which has just been opened at Kimmage.

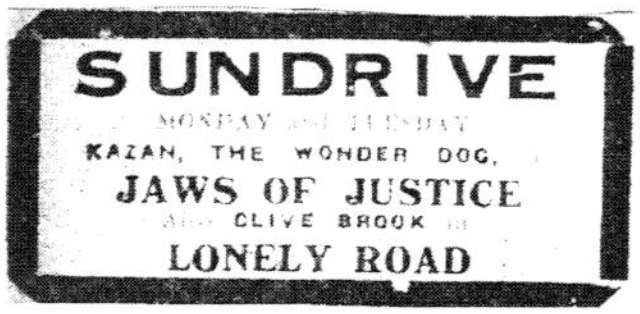

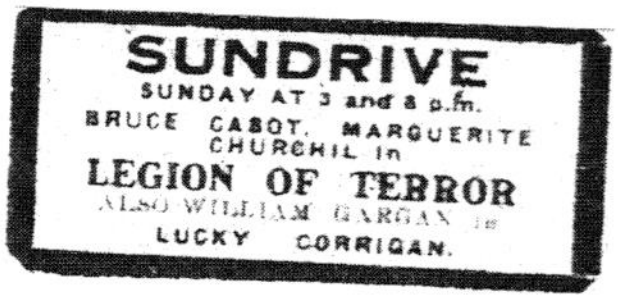

Two small advertisements, which appeared in the evening newspapers during the year of 1938

In 1954 the Sundrive Cinema Company sold the Sundrive Cinema to a company whose main directors were Leo and George Kearns and in 1958 they closed the cinema for extensive renovations and re-opened it as the "Apollo" cinema on February 7th 1959.

The story of the Sundrive/Apollo cinema continues under the heading Apollo Cinemas.

The Sundrive cinema building, under the Apollo banner.

SUTTON GRAND
Sutton Cross

THIS splendid structure was opened by the Lord Mayor on Monday last in the presence of a large and representative gathering of people from Howth, Sutton, and surrounding districts.

The Lord Mayor referred to the great lack of amusement in the district, which lack is now amply remedied by this handsome and comfortable cinema.

It is ideally situated at Sutton Cross, convenient to trains, trams, and buses. No expense has been spared to make this cinema a model in every way. Its airiness and sunshine windows ensure freedom from infection.

Space and Comfort.

Great taste has been displayed in the furnishing, while spaciousness and comfort has been kept in view throughout.

The seating capacity is 700, including a balcony to accommodate 200. There is also car parking accommodation for about 150 cars.

The heating installed is graduated to ensure an even, healthy temperature at all times, with perfect ventilation.

The screen is mathematically proportioned to the size of the house, thus guaranteeing freedom from eye strain. The sound system has been supplied by Western Electric.

The proprietors have planned to give their patrons a first-class selection of pictures chosen by experts to suit all tastes. Prices are moderate, and the hours of opening are as follows:—

Mondays to Fridays—6.30 to 10.30, continuous.

Saturdays—3 to 10.30, continuous, and Sundays—3 to 5, and 8.30 to 10.30.

At the opening ceremony last Monday, Mr. L. E. Ging, the managing director, thanked the guests for their attendance, and stated that the cinema was a credit to all concerned. The architect was Mr. H. J. Lyons, 14 Sth. Frederick St.; the contractor was Mr. William Lacy, Howth. Seating by Hilton Brothers. Artistic lighting and electrical installation by Mr. Cecil J. Lyons. Decoration by Messrs. J. G. Malcolmson and Co., Ltd.

(Display courtesy "Evening Herald)

The Sutton Grand Cinema opened on Monday January 4th 1937.

SUTTON GRAND CINEMA
NOW OPEN
TWO PERFORMANCES NIGHTLY, Commencing at 8.30 p.m.
MATINEES SATURDAYS and SUNDAYS, Commencing at 3 p.m.
FREE CAR PARK FOR 150 CARS.
PRICES:
WEEK-DAYS .... Balcony, 1/4; Back Stalls, 1/-; Front Stalls, 9d.
MATINEES—Saturday and Sunday up to 5 p.m. ...... 1/-, 9d., and 7d.
SUNDAY NIGHT and BANK HOLIDAYS 1/8, 1/4, 1/-
Change of Programmes—Mondays, Thursdays, and Sundays.
TO-NIGHT—FRED ASTAIRE and GINGER ROGERS in
"FOLLOW THE FLEET"
THURSDAY, FRIDAY, and SATURDAY—
"KING OF THE DAMNED"
Starring CONRAD VEIDT and NOAH BEERY.
CHILDREN ARE REQUESTED TO AVAIL OF EARLY PERFORMANCES

The opening film "Follow the Fleet" starred Fred Astaire and who else, but Ginger Rogers.

* * * * *

Plotline 'well' what can we tell you but that Fred and Ginger danced, danced, danced and danced.

* * * * *

"Can't Sing, Can't Dance, Can't Act". Tell that to his legion of fans.

* * * * *

See all the shows worth seeing —
SUTTON GRAND CINEMA

PRINTED MATTER

★ BUS SERVICE

Leaves SUTTON for HOWTH
7-55, 8-25, 8-55 9-25, 9-45,
10-5, 10-25, 10-45

Leaves SUTTON for DUBLIN
7-50, 8-20, 8-45, 9-20, 9-45,
10-5, 10-25, 10-45

HILL TRAM TO SUMMIT
Leaves SUTTON at 8.55, 9.55
10.55

★ TRAIN SERVICE

Leaves SUTTON for HOWTH
8-55, 9-55 10-55

Leaves SUTTON for DUBLIN
9-5, 10-5, 11-5

Subject to Alteration

Well the article from the "Evening Herald" tells all and leaves us with very little to say.

We did however manage to come across this Programme and a photograph, which was given to us by one of our many well-wishers.

As you can see in the picture our view of the "Grand" is partially blocked by an old Dublin Hill of Howth Tram passing by which brought back many pleasant memories to us.
The last Dublin Tram No 252 passed through this area on its last journey in 1949.

Unfortunately we don't know who took the photo but it would appear that it came from a magazine.

SUTTON GRAND CINEMA
HOTEL
CATHERINE SPAAK & ROD TAYLOR
ALSO
INFAMOUS CONDUCT
AND PATHE NEWS.

This was the last advert that we could find for the Sutton and we can only assume that it closed that night.

The marvellous movie of Author Haley's Hotel which was directed by Richard Quine and starred Rod Taylor as Peter McDermot, Catherine Spaak as Jeanne and Karl Malden as Keycase.

SWORDS CINEMA
Main Street, Swords.

This cinema for some unknown reason was never given a name or for that matter bestowed even with a nickname, it was simply known as a picture house or in some instances simply "Tom Bray's"

As can be seen from this photograph it was a huge warehouse like building with quite a decent looking cinema façade, together with two shops, which were never seen to open for business by those that I spoke to about this cinema. Depending on the seasons it could be cold and damp inside, or at times sweaty and suffocating. There were no toilets and when nature called one took ones chances along the side or back of the building!

According to a local historian, one Liam Heron to whom I spoke by phone at the end of September 2005, the cinema had been built in the 1950's by a local builder named Cockles McCormack, on behalf of Tom Bray.

While it showed the best of films it only opened three days a week, Fridays, Saturdays and Sundays, and remained closed for the rest of the week.

In the summers months a travelling Drama/Comedy group would come to town and put on shows which provided a great change in entertainment and were most welcome in the area. Local children would often take part in these small plays.

These shows were brought to town courtesy of Vic Loving's "Fit Up" Theatre. The format was variety turns followed by a play, and "Murder in the Red Barn", was odds on to be in the repertoire. The male lead was Vic's son "Chic Kay" who did what was considered a very daring 'Apache' dance with his wife, while her husband played the piano accordion with great panache. The chorus line (of four) was also most popular with the audience.

Tom Bray pictured outside his Swords Cinema.
(Not a great exposure but what can we do?)

It would appear from this photo that at least one of the shops attached to the cinema was open for business, despite some locals saying that they didn't remember them ever being open. Tom Bray managed the cinema with the help of his daughter Nuala and enjoyed a reasonable success for many a good year. With the general decline in cinema business it was eventually demolished and rebuilt as a Supermarket.

I believe that Tom Bray's was not the first person in Swords to show pictures. Liam Heron told me that many years before, Tom built his cinema, a travelling picture company used to set up a tent in a field or yard at the back of the Carnegie library in the Summer time and provide cinematograph exhibitions. This company was a husband and wife team known as Mr. and Mrs. Barry McDonald, and they lived in a caravan on site.

=====

Pictures are courtesy Swords Heritage Centre and information and permissions to use same and paraphrase some writings by both Bernie of the Heritage Centre and Liam Heron, a wonderful and knowledgeable local historian.

TATLER
Dun Laoghaire.

Two advertisements which appeared in the "Evening Herald" announced the opening of Irelands first "News Cinema" which opened on Monday January 16th 1950.

This new cinema replaced the old Kingstown Picture House on Georges Street.

The Tatler specialised in news-reels, and featured storylines such as the series "Passing Parade", "Fitzgerald's Travel Talks" and as fillers it showed cartoons and B&W shorts such as Joe McDoakes behind the 8 Ball series, Leon Errol and Edgar Kennedy etc. However it didn't catch on at the time and closed a short time later. In more recent times the Grafton Cinema ran a similar "News and Cartoon cinema", for a good number of years and it was highly successful for quite some time.

* * * * *

"Passing Parade", was a most popular and very interesting U.S Documentary series of short stories produced and narrated by John Nessbitt who thrilled cinema audiences with fascinating stories of touching drama revealing the lives and events of the past. These short films of human life and drama were a much-appreciated highlight of early cinema-goers.

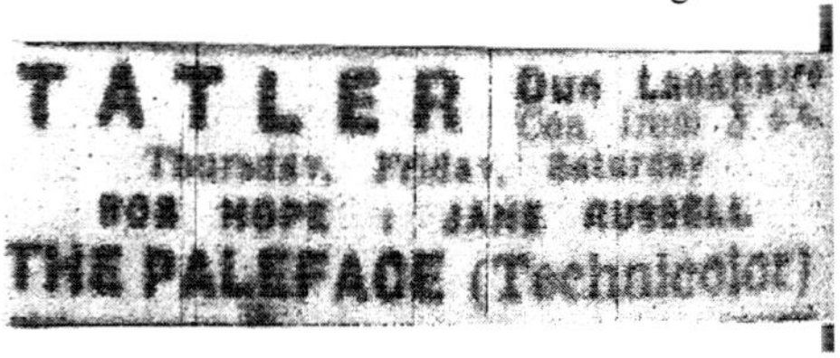

This advertisement appeared in the "Evening Herald" on Friday, May 26th 1950 and it was the last that we could find for the "Tatler".

~~~~~

Its predecessor the "Kingstown Picture House" which was also simply referred to as the "Picture House" opened on Easter Monday, April 17th 1911.

The cinema was situated on the corner of George's Street and Mulgrave Street on a site that had been vacant for some time.
~~~~~

While the building seated only 280 persons it had three exits doors in Mulgrave Street and two entrance doors in George's Street. The ground floor plan of the hall was 22 feet wide and 84 feet long and the front elevation was carried out in Ruabon brick with Dumfries stone dressings. The entrance walls and floor were tiled. The operation chambers which extended the full width of the building had a reinforced concrete floor and ceiling, in strict compliance with the requirements of the Cinematograph 1909 Act.

The General contractor was Messrs George Squire and Co., of Abbey Street and the building was designed and erected under the supervision of Charles Dunlop of St Andrew Street Dublin.

The building completed a block of buildings which had been erected in accordance with the estate design and no deviation was entertained. However the management were congratulated on having the entire building erected and fully equipped in a little over three months.

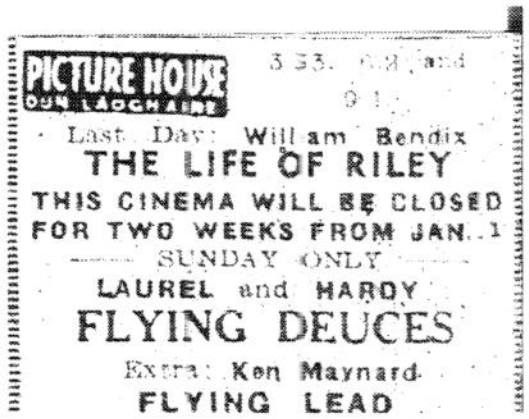

On a point of interest we would tell you that in 1911 there was no public electric lighting supply in Kingstown, which Dun-Laoghaire was known as in those times, and in order to have lighting, ventilation and heating, a 20h.p. Crossley gas engine and dynamo had to be installed. The Kingston closed for repairs on January 1st, 1950 and two weeks later it re-opened as the "Tatler".

~~~~~
~~~~~

THE BLUE LAGOON
Channell Road, Rush, Co Dublin.

Rush or if you like ROS EO, the real Irish name for Rush, which means "The Peninsula of the Yew Trees" had three cinema buildings. We say three cinema buildings, because the Palladium ,which once belonged to Anna Price and her husband B V'Bart Butterly, though built as a cinema, never showed a picture, instead of which it became a very popular dance hall.

George pictured in May of 2006 with the main body of the Palladium in the background.

This was the original entrance to the dance hall and it now displays a new shuttered steel gate.
This hall was a major attraction to the young and not so young of the area and at times it was in fierce competition with the Blue Lagoon dance hall which was situated at the opposite end of the town on Channel Road.

Both Halls attracted good crowds and both vied for the best bands available.

The Savoy which was situated on Sandy Row in Rush carried three names with the last one being the "Europa" and we tell of its history in another section of this book under the title of the "Tideway".

The Blue Lagoon dance hall which lay at the end of Channel Road began its life as a simple storage shed and was built circa 1900. The building belonged to the Langan Family and was adjacent to the quay at Rogerstown which in the beginning of the 20th century was a port of call for a number of schooner type coal boats and with the shed being so close to the Quay it became a coal storage shed. This information came to us courtesy of Brendan Langan whose father Tom was the owner.

At one time the lands to the rear of the shed were very low lying and this came about when the ships having unloaded their cargo of coal, had tons of sand excavated from the ground behind the quay to load on as ballast for their return journey. In latter years this area was used as a tipping area and this activity eventually levelled off the ground to its original height.

The Quay .

Some time later the shed was used as a petrol supply station and repair garage and the work-pit which was dug out of the ground in order to allow cars to drive across it so as to allow mechanics to work on their undercarriage was, we were told, by Brendan used by the I.R.A during the "Troubles" to hide their weapons.

He also mentions that in those days there were no petrol pumps and petrol came in 40 gallon drums which had a screw top bung at one end which when undone a tap could be screwed back in its place. The other screw type bung would be on the side of the drum and when the drum was laid atop a wooden frame this bung would be on top and before opening the tap one would unscrew the top bung a little to allow in some air that would assist the flow of petrol from the tap. The service person would then fill a gallon can with petrol as often as was required and with the help of a funnel he/she would pour the petrol into the storage tank of the car.

Later again Brendan's father Tom laid the floor of the shed with flag stones and with wooden forms as seats he opened the shed as a cinema with the help of a Daniels a travelling showman who would show films. This activity proved a great attraction to the locals. Brendan remembers well an old truck that had seen better days which was parked beside the shed with a large board that simply stated 'Show at 8'. The cinema thrived for many years until Tom Langan decided to turn the shed into a dance hall and without further ado he installed a Maple dance floor and opened for business.

The best of bands played there and crowds would cycle from miles around and they usually parked their bicycles in the ditch across the road. A shop sat to the side of the hall and here one could not only buy minerals, sweets, ice cream and cigarettes but the lads could play darts in the back room and rings in the front of the shop.

Brendan Langan tells me that the shed measured approximately 80 x 30 feet
This is one of the last pictures taken of the Shed by Raymond Langan in 2005 shortly before it was knocked down and he very kindly gave us a copy for our book. The lady in the foreground is his mother. In its latter years the shed was used as a builders providers and concrete block making plant.

Brendan tells me that many years after the Maple floor had been installed some of the flagstones underneath appeared to have worked loose and as a consequence when the dancing commenced of an evening, dust would rise up through some sections of the floor and in order to combat this, two side doors were installed with some net type covering which allowed in a slight breeze which did away with the dust.

THE PUBLIC'S TASTE IN FILMS
Ireland 1924-1925-1926.

According to a written report on the censorship of films in the "Evening Herald" on Saturday, January 15th 1927 the tastes of the Irish people are indicated in the returns of films submitted for the judgement of the film censor. The report covers a three-year period.

It would appear that pictures of a dramatic or humorous nature predominated in the demand of the public, while "interest" films, which included topical and news items were but a small proportion of the others. Educational films were in such poor demand that they were almost negligible.

It is interesting to note that thousands of Pictorial advertisements were submitted to the censor during those years and only 262 were deemed fit for viewing by the members of the public. These advertisements usually consisted of posters, slides, bills, and blocks etc.

With a view, I would suppose, to encourage the import and showing of educational films the then Minister of Justice issued an order on November 30th 1926 to the effect that censors fees and import duty would not be charged on films passed by the censor as educational. Between November and December of 1926 six such films were passed free of censor's fees and import duty.

Films submitted to the Censor Mr. J. Montgomery at the offices of the Free State Film Censor in this three-year period were as follows:

1924 Drama & Humorous films	1307	Films of Interest 318
1925	1205	552
1926	1327	392

In the total submissions of 1327 drama and humorous films for the 1925 period 121 were rejected and 166 were cut and of the 392 interest films only a few had to be cut but not to an extensive degree.

There were appeals in respect of 25 of the rejected and cut films and the results were as follows:

Decision upheld 16

Decision reversed 2

Passed with cuts 7

THE WAYSIDE

This was a small magazine/bulletin, which was produced and privately circulated by some members of the Theatre and Cinema Workers Soladality to other members.

Mostly it was confined to news items on Soladality meetings and social announcements of births, marriages, deaths, engagement and other social happenings amongst its members, including dances and outings.

Ever cinema and renting house would receive at least one copy of this bulletin each month

The WAYSIDE

BULLETIN OF THE
THEATRE AND CINEMA WORKERS SODALITY

PATRONESS—*Our Lady of the Wayside.*
SECONDARY PATRONS—*St. Francis Xavier and St. Teresa of the Infant Jesus.* Produced for private circulation among members.

February, 1959. A.M.D.G. 131st Issue

Dedication—**The Holy Family**

Sunday 1st :—St. Brigid.
Monday 2nd :—The Purification of the B.V.M.
Tuesday 3rd :—St. Blaise.
Wednesday 4th: St. John de Brito.
Wednesday 11th :—Our Lady of Lourdes. (Ash Wednesday)
Saturday 14th :—St. Valentine.
Friday 27th :—St. Gabriel of the Sorrowing Virgin.

General Meetings—Thurs., 5th; Sat., 7th; Thurs., 19th.
Mission Section—Thursday 12th.
Pioneer Council—Saturday 7th.
Council of Prefects—Thursday 26th.
Social Service Section—Tuesdays.

* ★ *

We regret to say that meetings of Prefects over the past couple of months have been very badly attended. Each Guild has a Prefect and Assistant Prefect who are expected to attend the meeting which takes place on the last Thursday of each month. We ask all Prefects and assistants to attend at the Council Room on Thursday, February 26th. at 11 a.m., as important matters are under discussion.

When our Sodality was founded in 1948, we had many contributors of articles to The Wayside. One of these was a Cinema Usher, who we are happy to say has promised to write again for us. In another page you will find a very inspiring article which was published in our March issue of 1949. For those of you who do not possess a copy and, for those of our members, who have joined our ranks since then, we are re-printing the article this month.

A-Z of All Old Dublin Cinemas

THOSE MAGICAL PICTURE HOUSES

A piece written especially for George and Patrick by Leo Magee, for inclusion in their new book about old Dublin Cinemas.

Every Sunday after dinnertime
We'd head up to Dolphin's Barn
Up to the Leinster picture house
Where they showed us many a good yarn.

To the Star, the Tivvo, and the Rialto too
They would flock from far and wide
With toffee bars and patsi pops
Right down the aisle we'd slide.
In Adelphi, Carlton and Savoy
We'd go to see James Bond
With his snazzy suits and fancy cars
And on each arm he'd have a blond.

And in the jacks we'd have a smoke.
We had woodbines, Players and Sweet Afton
When we went to see those cowboys
On the Green, Deluxe and Grafton
On invisible horses out through the doors
We'd gallop with great tenacity
For Joxer was the Sisco Kid
And I was Hopalong Cassidy.

The old mummy he would scare us stiff
And he came from the land of the Pharaoh
Stand in the way at your own peril
Of the penny rush to the Maro
And in the back row we'd kiss the girls
There was Mary, Jane and Biddyo
But those magical houses have all gone
Now it's a DVD or a Video.

All stand in line and behave yourselves
And none of your oul tricks
Fat Harry he would shout at us
As we queued for the flicks

By
Leo Magee
14th March 2005

TIDEWAY
RUSH, COUNTY DUBLIN

This cinema opened as the Savoy Cinema on Sunday, April 4th 1937 and provided the people of Rush and surrounding areas with another social amenity that was most welcome. News of its opening was received with general satisfaction and it promised to be well supported.

The cinema was sited in the old Foley Keane Hall, which was situated in a central part of town and once served the community as a dance hall. When it was converted, it blended well into a cinema. A luxurious balcony was built and the floor of the auditorium was sufficiently graded to allow for good viewing. Central heating and air conditioning was installed as was comfortable seating for some 500 persons

The Savoy's first advertised programme was as follows.

SUNDAY and MONDAY, April 4th and 5th.

PHIL REGAN, EVELYN KNAPP IN

LAUGHING IRISH EYES

Songs and Dances . . . Life and Laughter . . . The Emerald Isle, the background for a Jolly Romance.

FULL SUPPORTING PROGRAMME.

TUESDAY and WEDNESDAY, April 6th and 7th.

HERBERT MARSHALL, JEAN ARTHUR AND LEO CARILLO IN

IF YOU COULD ONLY COOK

They'll thrill you . . . Charm you . . . Win you in this glorious romantic Comedy!

FULL SUPPORTING PROGRAMME.

DOORS OPEN 8.10. COMMENCING 8.30.

The Entire Proceeds of the Opening Performance will be given to Local Charity.

NEXT WEEK: "SUTTERS GOLD."

The Savoy cinema, it would appear, is a sister to the Savoy cinema in Kells and both are owned by the same company, "The Tailteann Theatres Limited".

While the dance hall had belonged to Foley- Kean we are not all that sure of their early involvement in the cinema. However according to the record of directors, which

are on file in the Company's Office, Parnell Square the list of directors are as follows:
Margaret Scanlon, Merchant, Balbriggan,
James C Fitzsimons,
Eugene G Scanlon, Merchant, Balbriggan,
Anthony Conlon, Kells,
Joseph Rooney, Building Contractor, Balbriggan.
The Company was incorporated on November 28th 1935 and the registered office was in Kinlis Place, Kells.

At this point in time there was no evidence of a Kean connection. However there were a number of changes of directors and shareholders over the years and in June of 1937 it would appear that Margaret Kean was now listed as a shareholder with 100 shares.

On St Stephen's Day, December 26th 1953, the Savoy Cinema was destroyed by fire despite the finest efforts of the Balbriggan and Swords Fire Brigades. Two tenders under the direction of Officers McConigle and Shaw arrived to fight the blaze and centred their attention on the portion of the cinema which seemed to be the seat of the trouble and succeeded in bringing the fire under control. However the interior fittings were completely destroyed and the roof was badly damaged, but the projection room went unscathed.

The fire had been detected by two men, Alex Hoare and Mr. Brendan Dunne who were passing by the cinema shortly after midnight and they immediately raised an alarm, but as Rush did not have its own fire tender, the community had to depend on the fire services of Balbriggan and Swords. Once again demands were made for a fire station in Rush.

It would appear that the site now came into the hands of Marie Kean, the Abbey Actress and her brother Michael and they it would seem re-built the cinema and re-opened it as the "Tideway Cinema" on Sunday July 17th 1955. The cinema was so named because their father Captain John Kean, who had died at sea many years earlier on board the last ship under his command which was "The Tideway".

With Marie Kean being a part of Dublin's theatrical world, Sunday was a good choice for the opening of the new cinema, as it stood to reason that the opening would attract many of her friends from the theatre and with most actors and actresses resting on Sundays this would not be an inconvenience to them.

The opening ceremony was performed by Ronnie Walsh of Radio and Stage fame and with great aplomb he welcomed all the guests and patrons to the new Tideway Cinema. Joe Lynch also had a few words of praise for Marie and Michael which he interposed with jokes and reminiscences in his own inimitable fashion.

The film of the night was "Malaga" which starred Maureen O'Hara and Macdonald Carey and was an excellent choice of smuggling, intrigue and romance which was enjoyed by all.

We also found that Marie Kean had incorporated a company called "Tideway Productions" on July 27th 1963 but this company may or may not have had any connection with the cinema. Being connected with the theatrical world it could well have been formed in order to promote plays etc.

In latter years the cinema changed its name to that of the "Europa" in 1973 and circa 1977 it closed down and fell into disuse.

Unfortunately we failed to make contact with somebody that might have had a picture of the cinema whether it be the Savoy, Tideway or the Europa.

Some two years later, the now totally disused cinema again went on fire on the Sunday night of March 25th 1979 and was burnt to the ground. The fire which was said to have begun around 8pm was treated by the investigating Gardai as malicious.

We believe that the cinema at that time belonged to a John Mulvey a solicitor with offices in Tallaght, County Dublin.

The final curtain came down on the old Tideway Cinema, Rush on Sunday evening 25th March at 7.45 p.m., when flames were spotted belching from the building. When the drama ended at 10 p.m. the old cinema had been gutted from end to end.

The burnt-out shell must have evoked poignant memories for the older residents of Rush who spent many an exciting evening cheering on the celluloid heroes of yesteryear or hugging a loved one in the back seat and trying to cope with a choc-ice in the other hand.

The one consolation for Rush people is that the cinema was not a private house containing sleeping children, or we may have had a repeat of the terrible Skerries tragedies which occurred in spite of the fact that Skerries has a small fire-brigade. Must every building that catches alight in the Fingal area be burnt out before the fire-brigade gets there. How many more children must be incinerated before those with the power to provide Fingal with a decent Fire Service take their heads out of the sand and DO SOMETHING? Promises DO NOT get votes anymore.

A section of the front page of the Rush Community News which was published in April of 1979 which was once again bemoaned the lack of a proper fire service in the town, courtesy Kevin Thorpe, News editor.

In late July of 2006 we had the pleasure of meeting with Kevin Cunningham who was able to fill us in on a few gaps concerning the history of the Tideway, because he and his brother Adrian had leased the cinema from its owners after it had closed as the Tideway and they re-opened it as the "Europa".

This was a new and brave departure for Kevin who had began his career in the cinema business in1968 and who had during the course of his life in that trade managed some fifteen cinemas in and around the Dublin area, not to mention a few in the country.

Great auld friends.
Patrick and Kevin during our meeting in Bakers pub in late July of 2006.

When Kevin leased the Tideway cinema from John Mulvey in early 1973 he did so in partnership with his brother Adrian, who has since passed away. Between them they leased the Savoy cinema in Balbriggan from the Combined Clubs Association and the Inchicore cinema was leased from the Ward Anderson Group and all three were re-named the "Europa". They also opened up a number of cinemas in the country but we did not follow up on those.

On Easter Sunday April 22nd 1973 Kevin and Adrian opened the Europa Rush and their first film was a James Bond Movie entitled "Diamonds Are Forever" which starred Sean Connery. We used "Diamonds Are Forever" said Kevin to open many a cinema.

The Europa Rush opened first followed by the Europa Balbriggan in June 1973 and the Europa in Inchicore in August 1974. All three lasted for a few years but eventually went out of business.

Kevin was a respected manager in the cinema trade and settled many a union dispute by early negotiation and compromise. "I was always willing to compromise", he told us. He also worked in the Star cinema in Crumlin and that was, he told us, "where I met my future wife".

When the Europa's closed Kevin went to work for the Green Cinema Group.

~~~~~~

We also met with John Carton who began his trade as a cinema operator in the Savoy cinema in Balbriggan which was owned by the Tailteann Theatres at the time and for a while he worked for the Cunningham's in both the Inchicore and Rush Europa's.

We met John who is now retired from the army in the De Luxe Film Distributors in Chapelizod where he was visiting an old friend. As he lives in Cavan this was a most convenient spot for us to meet.
~~~~~~

TIV0LI
Francis Street.

The first mention of a cinema in Francis Street came about when an article appeared in the "Evening Herald" on Saturday evening October 20th 1934 which informed its readers that five men had been injured when some scaffolding collapsed on the site where a new cinema was being built in the Liberties.

It would appear that the men were working on a section of some scaffolding when a plank on which they were standing broke and they were all precipitated to the ground, a distance of some thirty feet.

Edward Clinch Upper Erne St, wounds to the head and back.
Michael Keane, Foley Street, shock and abrasions to lip & chin and hip injury.
Bernard Slowey North King Street, wounds to face and arms.
James Jones, head injuries and James O'Brien, Shock.

All five were brought to hospital by ambulance, treated and detained overnight for observation and then discharged.

The cinema was being erected at a cost of £8,000 and the contractors were Messrs McNally Ltd, Builder, East Wall Road.

The cinema was called the "Tivoli" and it was formally opened on Friday evening December 21st 1934 by Alderman P.J. Medlar, who was from the area and speaking from the stage before the screening of the first programme, he said that he had attended school in the parish forty years ago and was very proud to be there to open this the third largest cinema in the city of Dublin. Present in the audience that night was a fellow Alderman, Alfie Byrne T.D and Lord Mayor of Dublin.

Having made mention of the high quality Irish workmanship that had gone into the building of the cinema, he then praised Irish enterprise and when finished he presented a cheque from the promoters of the cinema which represented the first nights takings to the Very Rev. P. Hayden, P.P., St Nicholas of Myra's to devote to any charity he chose.

When expressing his thanks to the cinema directors for their generosity he mentioned that his parish was the poorest in the Archdiocese of Dublin and that it was still in debt to the tune of £2,000 and that he was pleased to preside at the opening of the cinema which had just contributed to the reduction of that debt.

In a short speech the Managing Director Mr. P.J. Whelan said that he and his fellow directors took pride in the fact that Irish capital, Irish labour and Irish materials had combined in the building of this new cinema that had seating for 1,700.

This feature film "Cockeyed Cavaliers" which was chosen for the opening night of the "Tivoli" also featured by coincidence as a supporting programme in the opening of the Sundrive Cinema almost a year later.

TIVOLI CINEMA, FRANCIS ST.
(DUBLIN'S THIRD LARGEST CINEMA)
WILL BE OPENED BY
ALDERMAN PATRICK JOSEPH MEDLAR
TO-NIGHT (FRIDAY), AT 7 O'C.
PROGRAMME STARTS 7.45 P.M.
FOR THREE DAYS:
"COCKEYED CAVALIERS"
With WHEELER AND WOOLSEY.
AND FULL SUPPORTING PROGRAMME.
SATURDAY: CONTINUOUS .... 3 p.m. to 10.45 p.m.
SUNDAY: AFTERNOON .... 3 p.m. to 6.30 p.m.
NIGHT .... 8.30 p.m. to 10.30 p.m.
POPULAR PRICES.

However this time around it was shown on what was claimed by the management, the biggest screen in Dublin.

While we have nothing of note to tell about the "Tivo" which was the nickname it earned from the locals, neither could we find an official closing notice. We did however come across this small advertisement on Saturday, September 26th 1964 which we believe was its last and we can only take it for granted that this then was its closing date.

TIVOLI—Glenn Ford, "All This And Money Too," also "The Lone Ranger and the Lost City of Gold."

Glenn Forde played opposite Hope Lange in this romantic farce ,which had many of great actors doing fun things, including Telly Savalas, Ricardo Montalban and Charles Boyer.
(This film was released in America as "Love is a Ball".)

The Tivoli now a theatre, this picture was taken Feb 10th 2005

We later came across this advertisement in the "Evening Press" on Wednesday, June 29th 1988.

Kevin Cunningham worked in the Tivoli cinema for a time and he told us that "Bang-Bang" was a regular visitor there and never ever gave an ounce of bother. "Bang-Bang, he said, was a gentleman and having purchased his ticket at the cash desk he would approach the doorman and in a nervous manner he would raise his hand to his forehead in a jerky manner and salute twice and say 'good night sir' good night sir". When the show was over Bang-Bang would exit the cinema almost unnoticed amongst the other cinema-goers.

When we met with Kevin, George asked him if he had ever been in the Princess Cinema where George had once worked and said Kevin yes' but only once and that was long after it had closed. Explaining, he told us that when the furniture and fitting of the Princess were being sold off the Tivoli owner bought the stall seats for the back end of the Tivoli as the Princess had had the best of seating.

Yes said George, I can vouch for that, because part of my job there was to care for the seating and the management in the Princess was very strict in their rules of behaviour in relation to the proper use of the seats. We in the "Prinner" considered it a serious offence if a patron attempted to put his/her feet upon the seat in front or for that matter jam their knees into the back of the seat in front.

Dublin born Thomas Dudley also known all over Dublin as "Bang-Bang" died on January 11th 1981 in Clonturk House for the Blind in Drumcondra. His home address was 50b Bridgefoot Street, Dublin 8.

Bang-Bang was a loveable Dublin character of the '50s and '60s, who while travelling on the platform of city centre buses would pretend to shoot all and sundry with a mock gun which was in effect a large old fashioned iron key. He would point this huge key at his intended victim and shout, "Bang, Bang".

Bus passes were not available then but Bang-Bang had no cause to worry, as no bus conductor ever sought to collect a fare from him. He could also alight from one bus and hop onto another at will.

~~~~~

When the Tivoli closed in 1964, it re-opened a short time later as a Bingo Hall and the odd one off concert, however following a fire the venue once again closed and it remained more or less derelict for many years.

Tony Byrne a very successful local businessman, who was born and reared in Winetavern Street, had a great fondness for the Tivoli cinema and as a child he and his pals used to attend every change of programme there. Tony was reared in the house that stood next door to the famous pawnbrokers that was known all over Dublin as the "Bicycle Pawnoffice" this pawnoffice also advertised "that one could pledge ones piano there if one had a mind to".

Tony was a man with two serious passions in life, with one being football and the other a love of theatre. As a child the Tivoli was one of his local cinemas and he and his close friend Johnny Giles never missed a programme there. Like most neighbourhood cinemas the "Tivo" had three changes of programmes every week and Tony and his friends were there for every change.

Tony pursued his love of football and on many occasions he played for both Shamrock Rovers and Shelbourne and for a period of four years he was the owner of the Shelbourne Football Club. He was also on the executive committee of the FAI. In the bread and butter department he made his way in the world of business and by sheer hard graft he became a successful businessman by the age of 40 years.

Having achieved this status, he was now in the position to pursue his other passion in life which was of course his love of the theatre and as he had always been conscious and saddened by the closure of the Tivoli cinema. He decided to buy these now derelict premises in 1986. This he did by taking over the Tivoli Cinema Company and its property. It could be envisaged that the Tivo had waited patiently over those long years for Tony, who was one of its most loyal patrons, to mature.
~~~~~

The cinema, a 1700 seater was in quite a bad condition and a lot of the seats, which included a number of wooden ners, were in serious need of replacing, in fact the whole building required refurbishing.

It wasn't Tony's idea to re-open the building as a cinema but rather as a theatre and even better still he decided to split the building in two by building a new floor between the roof and the ground floor that would support an overhead theatre and at the same time accommodate a separate music venue on the ground floor.

This was a brilliant idea that allowed Tony to put on two separate shows every night, a musical or play upstairs and a concert or top show band downstairs. Always mindful of others he had an Otis lift installed for the benefit of wheelchair users and the old and frail.
It was said that the Tivoli was one of the first theatres to have such a lift installed.

Tony Byrne at the drive-in entrance gates of his home in Dublin14

When the renovations were finished the bottom floor music venue had a capacity for 1000 patrons and the upper floor theatre had seating for 560 persons.

In 1896 the theatre was temporarily opened for the production of the musical "Carousel" and in 1987 it opened again during the Theatre Festival where a Swedish production company called the "Orion Theatre Group produced the play Pygmalion.

In 1988 the theatre officially opened on a permanent basis with the play "Bouncers" which starred Brendan Gleeson.

George had an interview with Tony Byrne in his house in Dublin14 on Thursday August 3rd 2006 and Tony told him so much about the history of the Tivoli theatre that George felt that its story deserved a book of its own.

Now being the proud owner of a premises with two separate venues Tony determined to engage top bands and artists for his music hall and the best of productions for the theatre. Many Oscar winners tread the boards of the Tivoli, including Jeremy Irons who won an Oscar for his role in "Reversal of Fortunes" and Oscar winner Jeffrey Rush. Sinead Cusack also performed in the Tivoli alongside her husband Jeremy. Tom Conti another Oscar nominee also did a stint there.

The Tivoli also had its fair share of dignitaries attending the theatre including Mary Robinson who as President of Ireland paid her first visit to a theatre there. When the late Dermot Morgan of Scrap Saturday fame opened his show "Jobs for the Boys" most members of the cabinet attended, including Albert Reynolds. "D'unbelievables" did a turn in the theatre from time to time and on each occasion they attracted packed houses, as did shows like "Annie" and plays like "Stones in his Pocket". Brendan Carroll played there many times and his play "the Curse" was premiered in the Tivoli and Niall Tobin often brought the house down with his outrageously funny acts.

Cyril Cusack took a small part as "Star Keeper" in the musical "Carousel" which was staged again in the Tivoli in 1991 and starred Michael Praed in the lead role. It was said that Cyril who died two years later, took the part to lend the show its much needed famous name. It was also said that it was Cyril's last stage appearance.

Shakespearian plays also went down well in the Tivoli and many foreign Shakespearian companies had great successes. The Tivoli was for many years "The Theatre" for students who were well catered with special productions to suit their curriculum such as the 2002 production of "Macbeth".

Brendan Behan's play the "Hostage" was amongst the top plays produced in the Tivoli

The Music venue was also a major success and attracted the best names in show business such as Sinead O'Connor, and groups like Oasis and Blur who played to capacity houses.

The Tivoli thrived for many years but in 2005 it appeared to go into decline for some unexplained reason and following its last production it remain closed. Tony is now pondering its direction and for the time being it is currently 'resting'.

~~~~

Dublin's Theatre Festival began in Marlborough Street in 1957 and George was its first Doorman, (See his book "The Prinner" for more details).
~~~~

TIVOLI THEATRE
Burgh Quay

The Tivoli Theatre was situated on Burgh Quay where the Irish Press once had their offices towards the end of the 20th century. This building started off its life as an old Corn and Flower Store and when it became vacant the Dublin architect William Henry Byrne was engaged to convert the premises into a music-hall .

It first opened as the "Grand Lyric Hall" on Friday, November 27th 1897 and was made most welcome by theatregoers as they packed its capacious environments. It was said to have a seating capacity for some 1,500 patrons.

Sometime later it had a name change to the "Lyric Theatre of Varieties" and in1899 the management ventured into Cinematograph Exhibitions and had a "Cinematograph Company present the story of "Dreyfus", his imprisonment and second trial.

This was the story of a French artillery officer named Captain Alfred Dreyfus who when accused of passing defence secrets to Germany, was arrested, tried, found guilty and sentenced to life imprisonment on Devil's Island. Within a few years following; pressure from a group who believed in his innocence the evidence against him was re-examined and he was brought back from Devil's Island to face a second trial in France. His film is the story of that trial.

While the second trial did not find him innocent he was later pardoned by President Emile Loubet and in 1906 he was exonerated by the French Supreme Court of Appeal and reinstated in the army, where he was promoted to the rank of Major and decorated with the Legion of Honour.

This was Victorian cinema at its earliest and best, but unfortunately we could not ascertain who had shot the footage of this film. However we believe it was one of three possibilities (a) Monsieur Orde, (b) George Melies, (c) Pathe, all of which were on the market in the autumn of1899.

~~~~~

In 1901 the theatre closed for redecoration and re-opened on Monday October 28th 1901 as the "Tivoli Theatre", and from then on it began to present nightly the Tivoli Grand Bioscope Pictures along with its usual fair. The Tivoli Theatre was now well on its way to becoming an established Cine-variety venue.

This cinema had the distinction of being the only place in Dublin projecting its pictures from behind the screen rather than from the front, which was of course the conventional way. Mr. Charles Jones was the manager and he was supplied with his films by Messrs Weisher of Liverpool.
~~~~~

TIVOLI TWICE NIGHTLY **TIVOLI**

THEATRE OF VARIETIES (LATE LYRIC).

TWO DISTINCT PERFORMANCES NIGHTLY.

TO-NIGHT AT **7** ....TO-NIGHT AT **9**

MISS SARAH BERRY,

The Greatest Contralto Vocalist ever in Dublin

Arthur Gilbert — Black and Dean

Victoria Monks — Ernestine Trio

CHARLES CRAWFORD,

Irish-American Comedian.

FOUR PICK ME UP GIRLS.

Tom Gilleno — Smith and Johnson

FOYS TROUPE,

The Greatest Comedy Acrobats in the World.

NOTE THE PRICES.

STALLS 1s. CIRCLE 6D.

PIT 4D. GALLERY 2D.

Doors Open—First House, 6.30 ; Second House, 8.45.
Early Doors, Open to all Parts 10 minutes before ordinary door. Gallery, 3d. ; Pit, 6d. ; Circle, 9d. ; Stalls, 1s. 3d.

The Bioscope and living pictures occupied only a small time slot in the advertised schedule of the "Tivoli Theatre" but as time went by and pictures became more and more popular, they began to take up more space and it wasn't too long before they became the main stay of each performance.

The "Tivoli Theatre" thrived and it was one of the most popular venues in Dublin for a nights entertainment, however it was twice brought to its knees by striking workers, with the first happening in 1924.

This strike came about when one of the six stage employees was dismissed because it was found that he was not working in harmony with the other members of the staff. When his position wasn't filled, The Workers Union", to which the sacked man had belonged demanded that his position be filled by another one of their union members with a view of keeping the number of stage hands at the level of six.

This the manager refused to do claiming as his reason, the fall off in trade. The Union then called out the other five workers and pickets were placed on the theatre. With the theatre heavily picketed every night attendances were seriously affected and at the end of the week management decided that their only course was to close the theatre.

This action was unfortunate for the remaining forty workers, who were not affected by the strike as they belonged to another trade union and now found themselves out of work.

TIVOLI THEATRE
MADGE GREY
COMEDIENNE & CHILD IMPERSONATOR
BILLY MOORE AND KIDDIES
THE PICHARD PLAYERS
JEAN FURNESS-GEO HYLTON
CHAS, CONLEY AND
THE FIVE FRISCOS

The theatre remained closed after Saturday night's last performance on November 1st 1924 and this was its last advertised programme. The quality of the advert was so bad that we have had to substitute one of our own making, as we have resorted to in many other pages of this book. We would tell you that if we can scan an advertisement and find it in any way legible we would prefer to print them as found rather than substitute them. After all no matter how bad they are, there is nowt like the genuine article.

The strike went on for many weeks and escalated when it spilled over and involved the "Queens Theatre" where five men ended up in court on November 25th and were charged with conspiring to obstruct the thoroughfare and refusing to disperse when requested.

The Carlton and Corinthian cinemas became involved and letters began appearing in the newspapers asking that something be done. The dispute then began to take another turn and it now appeared that there was a fight for supremacy between the Workers Union led by James Larkin and the Irish Transport and General Workers Union. (See "War of the Unions")

The Corinthian put on a bold front during the dispute by inserting large advertisements in the national newspapers

On the night of Tuesday, November 18th disorderly scenes were witnessed in O'Connell Street outside the "Carlton "cinema where seven men were arrested and brought before the Police Court the next morning. These men were all members of the Workers Union and all were charged with causing a breach of the peace.

While there was no more mention of the "Queens Theatre" the main three cinemas involved were the "Tivoli Theatre" the "Corinthian and the "Carlton" and though the "Tivoli" remained closed the other two closed and re-opened and between them they put the following advert in the national press on Thursday, November 20th 1924

CITIZENS! KEEP THE CINEMAS AND THEATRES OPEN

The right of employes to work in Cinemas and Theatres where there is no industrial dispute is being maintained by the people engaged in catering for you in the lin of popular amusements.

The CARLTON CINEMA, O'Connell Street, and the CORINTHIAN CINEMA, Eden Quay, are being kept open in defiance of the dictation of Larkinism and a small minority of the ex-employes.

It is the imperative duty of the public to maintain this right of work, and keep these theatres open.

This is where YOU come into the Picture.

No theatre or cinema will close down unless the citizens shirk their duty and refuse to enter. Citizens! Assert your Rights. Fulfil your duties.

Don't be intimidated. Don't be bullied. Don't be dictated to by a little gang of nois, disturbers of the peace.

Patronise the Carlton and the Corinthian. Get into the queue in your hundreds and bring your friends with you.

CITIZENS! KEEP THE CINEMAS AND THEATRES OPEN

Hearings and meeting were planned but as mentioned in the story on the "War of the Union" we never found the printed details of the outcome of the strike. It did, however, end as the "Tivoli Theatre" re-opened on Monday, December 22nd 1924.

Opening advertisement

TIVOLI THEATRE
RE-OPENING TODAY MONDAY DECEMBER 22ND 1924
Welcome return of the famous
DIXIE MINSTRELS
IN ALL THEIR LATEST SUCCESSES
MIRTH, MELODY AND HARMONY
STRONGER AND BETTER THAN EVER
NEILLE STOOLE-JOE MASTERSON-THE FANJACKS

7 - TIVOLI - 9

TO-NIGHT ... A GRAND REVUE ... TO-NIGHT

WORK AND WORRY.

SUNDAY at 8 p.m.,

PICTURES AND VARIETY.

Closed during Summer for Decorations, excepting Sunday Evenings at 8 p.m., when the Usual Pictures and Variety will be shown.

On Saturday May 28th 1928 this advertisement appeared in the "Evening Mail" which informed us that the theatre was closing for the summer months for the purpose of decorating, but that it would continue to run a cine-variety show every Sunday until further notice.

However, this is more or less the last we heard of the "Tivoli Theatre" other than the fact that it appeared to have become embroiled in another cinema dispute which this time around appeared to emanate from the "Grand Central" cinema, where it would seem that a number of cinemas belonging to the Irish Kinematograph Company which was headed by Alderman J.J Farrell as Managing Director was suffering under the effects of a lighting strike by its workers.

It would appear that the Tivoli belonged to this group, which also included the "Grand Central" "Pillar" and the Mary Street, picture House ("The Maro") within its ownership. Also affected was the "Plaza" and "Electric Theatres" which we understand meant the "New Elec"

This lighting strike, which J.J. Farrell claimed was in breach of an agreement between the Cinema Association and the men's union because an official strike was subject to a months notice to employers and ditto when an employer decided to impose a lock-out on employees. He also claimed that the strike was brought about because he refused to re-instate an employee whom he had discharged when this employee had threatened physical violence when he was being taken to task for misbehaviour. The newspaper article did not specify just what this misbehaviour was, however it was rumoured that he was caught smoking in the operating room and when challenged he attempted to strike his employer.

Alderman Farrell said that he could never keep in his employment an employee who threatened physical violence to him and that this strike was all about establishing this right for employees

When this dispute was settled, which eventually it was, it would appear that the "Tivoli Theatre" which had remained shut during the strike never again re-opened and the next we know the "Irish Press" had acquired the premises in 1930 for conversion to a workroom and offices for the production of their newspapers.

In 2006 the "Irish Press" is long gone as is their printing works and offices and a block of offices now occupies the site.

An old Tivoli poster.

Tivoli Burgh Quay (Picture courtesy National Library Dublin)

In 1915 A variety show was taking place in the Tivoli and topping the bill were Robb and Dixon, Scottish entertainers, George Leonard, Lilian Stevens, Fred Bluett and many more well known and much loved artists.

Prices of admissions were 6d, 9d and 1/- with special prices for children who attended the early show and it was said that juveniles having attended that show could then afford to eat a bag of chips from one of the many chip-carts which would station themselves at the corner of Burgh Quay and then round off the evening with a visit to the Theatre Royal which was just around the corner and all for the cost of less than 1/-

Daniel O'Connell held many a meeting in the Corn Exchange building in the 1840's where he knew that if there was trouble from nearby Trinity students there were some 150 sturdy coal porters within calling distance who wouldn't hesitate to throw troublemakers into the River Liffey!

TOWER CINEMA
Clondalkin.

In other parts of this book we have laboured on the difficulties of obtaining early release films for the smaller cinema and one could say that the Tower Cinema was developed because of this want. As we have already mentioned in another storyline, this unfair practice of film distribution caused many a smaller cinema to go under.

It would appear that in the 1930s Messrs Egan & Kelly of Portlaoise, had a large chain of cinemas spread across the country and were anxious to increase their holdings. The reason being that the more cinemas they controlled the better their chances of obtaining early releases. The number of seats on offer by any theatre group dictated their abilities to rent the best films as soon as possible after their release.

Whenever they opened, or caused to be opened a new cinema in a town or village it was their modus operandi to encourage local involvement and when they set their sights on the village of Clondalkin they sought out a suitable partner in that village.

Their next move however was to find suitable premises to house their new cinema and as luck would have it they came across an old bus garage which was well located in the village centre and was now in disuse, available and suitable for their intended purpose.

A view of Main Street, Clondalkin circa 1918
The building to the left of this picture would have formed a part of the site where the Omnibus garage and waiting room was built in 1924.

This old building was built in 1924 as a garage and waiting room for the Clondalkin Motor Bus Company, which had been launched in 1919 by T.F.Healy, proprietor of the Black Lion House and D.R. White, Managing Director of the Clondalkin Paper Mills. The purpose of this company was to provide an Omnibus link service between Clondalkin and Inchicore where the Dublin United Tramway had their No. 21 Terminus.

This was the first motor-bus company to operate in the Dublin area and the service was soon extended to Rathcoole, Saggart, Baldonnell and Nass. In 1924 the garage and waiting room was built in the village and the company's passengers were very appreciative.

In December of 1926 A Mr. F.T. Wood from Cheshire England bought the company for £5,000 and renamed it the "Irish Omnibus Company and in 1929 in an agreement with the Dublin United Tram Company they instituted the No 51 route.

Later again in 1929 the Great Southern Railways Company acquired control of the company and the garage and waiting room, no longer needed fell into disuse.

~~~~~

Mrs Mary O'Toole who was resident in Oak Lodge, a beautiful old house that stands on New Road across from the church gate, owned a lot of land in the Clondalkin area, including the land on which the garage was built. When Egan & Kelly approached her with a view to acquiring the old garage and waiting room they mentioned that they were going to set up a cinema in the village in partnership with a certain local businessman and Mrs O'Toole vetoed their proposal and suggested that they instead use Mr. Peter Ging.

~~~~~

While it never came to light why Mrs. O'Toole chose Peter Ging, it would seem that her choice was a shrewd one as Peter and his family made a good job of converting the old property into a beautiful and comfortable cinema.

~~~~~~

About Peter Ging

Peter Ging was a bar manager of two pubs which were owned by Guinan a well to do businessman. However Guinan was most unfortunate in that he died in his forties and Peter married his widow Rita who was only twenty at the time.

They sold all the pubs and bought Hatfield House in Drumcondra and ran it as a nursing home. Circa 1919 they sold the nursing home. They leased houses in Goatstown, Crumlin and finally bought the Laurels house in Clondalkin. They also bought a farm in Kilteel (near Saggart) and ran it from their home in the Laurels. In 1933 the Land commission acquired the farm in Kilteel.

1n 1936 they leased Diamond House, which was situated on the corner of Tower Road and Nangor Road. This was a complex building as it had originally been a girls school, then the Ace of Diamond Pub and then a general store. The house had good living quarters and this encouraged Peter and his family to vacate the Laurels and move into Diamond house.

The Laurels was then converted into a very profitable boarding house, which catered for the Clondalkin Paper Mill workers who came from all over the country to work in the Mills which had recently restarted. The re-opening of the Mill also augured well for the Diamond shop and it was from Diamond house that Pete, through the good graces of Mary O'Toole was linked to Egan & Kelly.

Laurence

Thomas

Peter and Rita had four sons, Laurence, Thomas, Peter and Patrick, and two daughters Margaret and Mary. It was to his two eldest sons, Laurence and Thomas that he assigned the task of converting the old garage and waiting room into a Cinema for the people of Clondalkin

The cinema which was named the "Tower" (after the 7th Century Round Tower which still stands complete in the Village) was finished in early 1939 and opened on April 9th with a 1933 horror film "The Mystery of the Wax Museum", which starred Fay Wray, Lional Atwill and Edwin Maxwell.
~~~~~~

Following the official opening of the cinema Peter threw a late night party in the Diamond House but Laurence and Thomas exhausted from their efforts fell asleep.

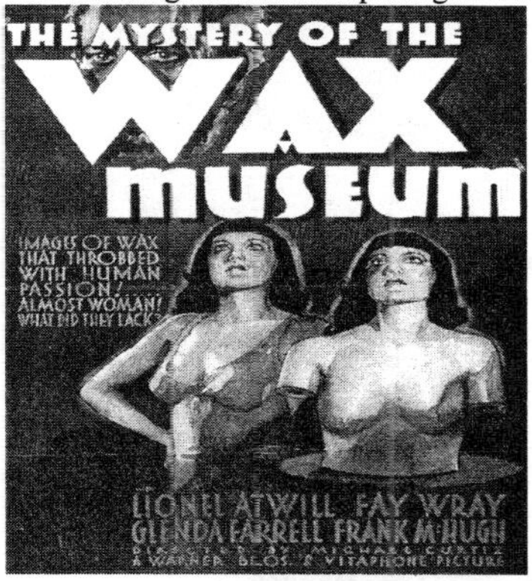

The "Tower" had seating for 350 persons and admission prices ranged from 1/- to 4d for the 'woodeners'

These woodeners as they were called were at one time covered with a reasonably comfortable padding, but the coverings received so much abuse at the children's matinees that it was considered more prudent to remove the covering and have simple plain wooden benches.

Rita Ging

Peter Ging

In the early stages programmes changed nightly and people came from all the surrounding areas to see a show, including Tallaght, Saggart, Newcastle Baldonnell, Drimnagh and Bluebell.

In the thirties and forties, attendances were excellent and those that didn't live within walking distance of the cinema would cycle, as the last bus from Clondalkin left at 9.30 pm. It was not uncommon to find the foyer of the Tower stocked with dozen of bicycles where patrons would leave them on arrival and then go out and join the queue of people waiting for admission. At times these queues would extend up the Monastery Road.

Sunday Matinees were generally for children only and suitable films and follow-uppers were specially chosen for them. The price of admission was 4d and miraculously the seating capacity of the cinema would somehow increase enormously on a Sunday afternoon...

In the early days the cinema did not have a shop or kiosk but sweets, cigarettes and other goodies could be had from a shop across the road, which was run by the Jacob sisters. Sweets were displayed in large glass jars and your penny or tuppence worth would be handed to you in a rolled paper cone. If you purchased a packet of five Woodbine cigarettes, five Maguire and Patterson friendly matches would be supplied free.

In the 1960's this Kiosk, pictured on the left, was added to the foyer and in later years when cinema business was declining the takings from this shop helped to keep the cinema open.
Mrs Ennis from Booth Road served in the shop as did Mrs. Lindsey.

Mrs Hoare was in charge of cleaning and housekeeping.

The Tower Cinema, under the management of the Ging family was, unlike other cinemas, very community orientated and considerate of its duties to its patrons and the parish of Clondalkin. When retreats were being held in the local church the Ging family would close the cinema for the duration, and on many occasions the cinema was given over for charity nights and local fund raising events for the local schools etc.

In order to keep the records straight and allow the charities to benefit from the proceeds tax free, special tax exemptions would be applied for.

In some cases the organiser of an event would be allowed to bring along a film for display and very often these films would arrive at the last minute and cause panic and delay because they would have to be rewound and put onto special spools before being shown.

On one occasion no film was brought and the organiser took to the stage and said to the audience," you're a poor audience if you can't entertain yourself" and with that, people from the audience took it in turns to do a piece on the stage and a great night was had by all.

Pictured standing beside the "Box Office" is Harry Wall and Miley Smith both of whom were long serving Doormen of the Tower, as were John Denton and Frank Goldsberry, all of whom would have doubled as house ushers. Eleanor Kelly (now Goodwin) was an usherette and also worked in the cash office.

Mary Ging was a cashier as was Tom Murphy (brother of Rita Ging) from Cappagh.

Changes and historical facts over the years.

Peter Ging bought out Egan & Kelly in January of 1941.
On the death of Peter Ging in January of 1942 the Tower closed for a week and the cinema was left to Larry and Tommy and in later years to Larry alone.

The cinema was extended in 1942 with the raising of the roof to the rear and the provision of extra seats, which brought the seating capacity up to 500.

A new sound system was installed by Cecil Napier of Tower Road and in 1957 the screen was enlarged and new projector lenses were purchased to enable Cinemascope pictures to be screened.

1964 Larry Ging died, leaving his wife Lily with four children aged 6 to 16. Lily took over as manager of the cinema and all four of her children served their apprenticeship in the cinema.

In the sixties, in an effort to attract customers the cinema underwent a major uplift, which included the refitting out of the foyer, new entrance doors and the fitting of poster display cabinets on the outside walls. Monthly programmes were introduced and these were hand-delivered to all the houses in the area. Advertisements were also placed in the daily papers.

Lily Ging with two of her doormen, Harry Wall and Miley Smith

In 1965/66 the war film "Blue Max" was being shot in Dublin and Baldonnell Airport was the base used for the storage of the airplanes used in the film. Stars of the film included James Mason, Ursula Andress and George Peppard who starred as Bruno Stachel the German pilot who was obsessed with winning the "Blue Max" a most honoured and sought after World War 1 medal which was awarded to pilots who had shot down 20 enemy aircraft.

Fantastic flying scenes and dog fights were enacted daily in the skies over Wicklow and the flight path of these planes passed over Clondalkin. It was rumoured that in some scenes George Peppard did his own flying. The Tower cinema was chosen by the film crew to allow John Guillermin, the Director, to view each day's 'rushes'.

This is a picture of the old oil-burning furnace that was used to heat the cinema. George reminisced that it was not unlike the old coal-burning furnace that he used to attend to in the Princess Cinema many moons ago.

TOWER CINEMA

Sunday, 24th August

Flanagan and Allen in

HERE COMES THE SUN

Full Supporting Programme

Monday, 25th August

Betty Grable John Payne in

THE DOLLY SISTERS

In Technioolor Full Supporting Programme

Wednesday, 27th August

Janet Blair Alfred Drake in

TARS AND SPARS

FULL SUPPORTING PROGRAMME

Thursday August 28th

Richard Crane in

JOHNNY COMES FLYING HOME

also "HONEYMOON AHEAD"

Friday 29th August

Orson Welles Joan Fontaine in

JANE EYRE

We believe that the poster behind the entrance door (left of photograph) is advertising "The Happiest Millionaire", With Fred McMurray & Tommy Steele
The poster on the right features "Shout at the Devil".

Interior shot (Small screen).

Auditorium Wide screen).

It was estimated that in its 38-year lifespan, 14,000 shows took place in the Tower.

The Tower closed on Saturday May 14th 1977 and its last picture was "Shout at the Devil".

Closed.

Extended Storyline

We have unashamedly extended our story on the Tower Cinema in order to share with you a series of unique behind the scene pictures that might never be shown anywhere again. These are simple pictures of the projection and rewind rooms of the Clondalkin Tower cinema, which were taken by members of the Ging family.

The scenes on show are unique because the items of equipment on display are of a bygone age and because the cinema industry is now in touch with a digital technique whereby the mere pressing of a button will beam down from a satellite a new release film at will, they are now totally redundant and obsolete.

No longer will reels of film have to be collected from the Renters and wound and rewound and duly returned or passed by freight onto the next cinema, no more waiting or struggling to be first in line for new releases. No more competition with the city cinemas or first class house for new releases, simply press a button and hey presto you are screening the latest.

* Note the bulb-like valves

Projection Room

Projector

A good insight into the intricate threading of the film through a projection machine.

One of the Ging brothers 'switching on'.

Nick Molloy Chief Operator 1961-1977

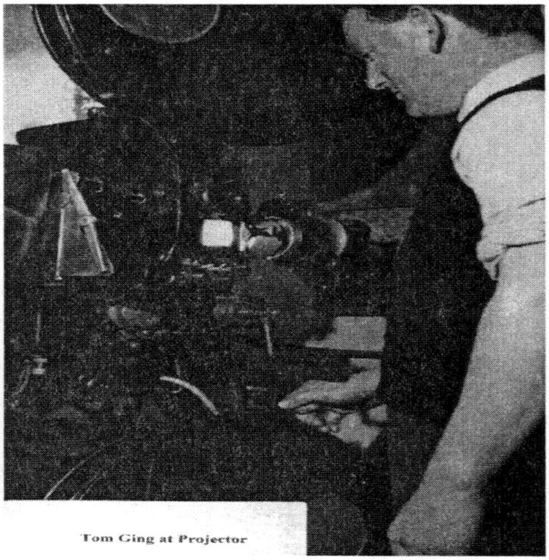

As evidenced by these pictures the Ging family were very much to the fore in the running of their family cinema and served in and learned all aspects of the business. However they were not alone in the operating room as they employed the best of technicians over the years such as Nick Molloy Chief Operator for sixteen years, Christy Hickey, Martin Kilduff, Cecil Cullinan and Eddie McGee.

The Story of Peter Ging, his family and their involvement with the building and running of the Tower cinema came to us courtesy of Patrick Ging who also provided us with the Tower and family photographs.

The following reasons and observations on the decline of the Tower were expressed by Patrick Ging.

The 40s, 50s and 60s, were good years for the cinema, mainly because people did not have cars and as such would look locally for their entertainment.

On New Years Eve, 1961, RTE opened.

Towards the end of the 60s and the beginning of the 70s lifestyles started to change. More and more people were getting televisions and it was proving to be cheaper and more convenient to stay at home and watch same.

City cinemas were converting to Twins and Multi-screen cinemas and small cinemas like the Tower could not get the latest films quickly enough.
Transport was easier and with more people buying cars, travelling to the city to see a new release was becoming much more convenient.

Small cinemas were being forced to take newer films for longer periods and at higher percentages but they did not have the population to support this demand and consequently profits dwindled until it became impossible to remain in business. In the 1960's some 160 cinema sites closed in the space of eight years.

In 1977 the cinema closed and the building was converted into shop units.

~~~~~

~~~~~

The site of the "Tower" cinema in June of 2006 and on the extreme left of the building stands, to the best of our knowledge, the original operating rooms.

The Main Street in June of 2006.
George positioned himself as close as he could to the spot where the photographer stood when he took the original picture circa 1918, which is on display at the beginning of this story.

TRINITY CINEMA
12 Trinity Street.

Never heard of it? Well, neither did we until we came across an article in the "Evening Herald" on August 7th 1945. This article was in fact a regular feature called "Town Topics" with the byline of Argus.

Argus it would appear wrote about all topics but on this particular night he devoted a section of his article to the passing on of old cinemas and in his opening column he suggested that a number of his older readers would be in shock when they read about the old Pillar Picture House being converted into another ice cream saloon and that this discovery made him wonder about how many of the earlier cinemas had survived in the Capital.

He reminisced about the Volta and told us that it was so called by its Italian Directors after the great 1800 Century Italian Physicist Count Alessandro Volta who invented the first battery and that the electric unit was named the Volt in his honour.

He also believed that the Pillar which specialised in first-run Charlie Chaplin films was one of the first three cinemas in Dublin.

Cinemas that had disappeared had numbered more than he had imagined and he mentioned the Coliseum of Redmond's Hill, the Dame St cinema which lay almost opposite the Olympia, the Brunswick of Pearse Street, the Picture Palace at 50 Thomas Street, the Coffee Palace of Townsend Street and the one he couldn't remember the name of was the Cosy / Corona of Parnell Street. However when he gave mention to a cinema called the Trinity in Trinity Street he gave us cause for hot flushes as we had never come across any mention of such a cinema before and we had fully believed that we had covered all old Dublin cinemas.

By sheer coincidence Argus also noted that the Coliseum was a rather unhappy name for a cinema as we have done and mentioned same as a snippet of information in another part of this book, however Argus didn't mention the Ranelagh Coliseum of 1924.

Argus also mentioned the possibilities of pre-fabricated cinemas heading our way. It would seem that at the time Charles Skouras brother of 20th Century Fox chief was forming a corporation in the United States to make and sell pre-fabricated steel cinema which would be complete with seating for between 600 and 3000 persons. The cost of one of theses units would be 60% less than the present style of cinema building.

So far we have failed in our efforts to unearth some further information on the Trinity, and fingers crossed that there aren't any more similar cinemas that have escaped our attention.

~~~~~
~~~~~

VOLTA

This cinema, it has been claimed, came to Dublin courtesy of James Joyce who together with a number of Italian investors organised the conversion and remodelling of an old provision shop, which they had just bought from a Mr. Boyd, into a cinema.

The "Volta", which was said to be Dublin's First Cinema.
(Picture courtesy of the National Library)

The building was situated at 45 Mary Street and was ideal for conversion into a cinema that would be capable of showing the most modern living pictures available.

It would seem that this all came about when James Joyce who was living in Trieste at the time learned from his sister that Dublin had no cinemas. That this news apparently encouraged him to set up a company with the help of a number of Italian businessmen which would enable him to bring cinema to Dublin.

With the company set up and money which had been invested by his Italian friends in the bank, James returned to Dublin and bought the Mary Street premises which he immediately had converted into a cinema.

When the work was completed the cinema was found to be attractively finished with a most decorative front entrance and a commodious auditorium that could hold a large number of people. The interior was richly decorated in a colour scheme of crimson and light blue and was furnished with every convenience for the comfort and safety of its patrons.

The cinema opened on December 20th 1909 with James Joyce as managing director and it was his decision to introduce Italian themed films to his Dublin audiences the first of which was "The Tragic Story of Beatrice Cenci", a most frightening story about the daughter of a violent and incestuous old man, with murder the only way out. A supporting programme was entitled "Bewitched Castle".

With the films being all Italian orientated, the manager Mr. Huish had leaflets printed explaining their storylines and these he would hand to the patrons as they entered the cinema. A small orchestra played suitable music.

A number of the worlds best known operas were also featured on the screen of the Volta and these would be accompanied by a specially prepared gramophone record recital of artist's representative of the numbers actually sung in the scenes depicted. When the records were not in play the in-house five-piece orchestra would accompany the unravelling of the plot.

Prices of admission were 6d, 4d, 3d and children could get in for 1d.

In conjunction with the opening of the Volta, a Bioscope Company under the name of "The International Cinematograph Society Volta" also set up offices in Dublin and this company had no less than 23 film producing factories in different countries across the globe. While branch offices existed in a large number of continental cities none existed in England and the company came direct to Ireland. It was the intention of the Society to introduce Dublin to the quick continental system of low prices, presenting only the newest films, and a constant change of subject. It was this Society that introduced Opera films to the Volta.

While we were led to believe that this was Dublin's first cinema proper, we must point out that there were many venues in Dublin that held Cinematograph and Bioscope exhibitions such as the Father Mathew Hall in Church Street. While this building was more a concert hall than a theatre, it had been providing pictures from as early 1909.

The Volta management were also generous in their attitude and on more than one occasion they entertained the boys from Artane School to an afternoon show in the cinema and the headmaster of the school wrote a letter of thanks to the proprietors and said that the pictures were very fine and most instructive.

However well intentioned the proprietors were, the business didn't go all that well and some blamed this on the management's choice of continental films and after a short seven months in business James Joyce sold the Volta to an English theatre company at a loss.

We would also bring to your attention the fact that the "Volta" opened in a very quiet manner with no big fanfare or gala opening to announce the coming of cinema to Dublin, instead it appeared to simply open for business without even a small advert in a Dublin paper. It was some days later when we came across an article in a newspaper which informed its readers that a new cinema had opened in Mary Street.

The "Bioscope" magazine made mention of the "Volta" some 10 days after it opened and referred to it as Dublin's Cinematograph Volta which had opened its show of "Living Pictures" at 45 Mary Street and here we would remind you that at that time there were many venues in Dublin showing "Living Pictures". The only real difference that distinguished the "Volta" from the other venues was that the pictures in the "Volta" were of an Italian origin.

The new owners "The Provincial Cinematograph Theatres Ltd", retained the name Volta, but changed the style of pictures and appeared to do al right. This company had already made inroads in Dublin by opening up the Sackville in Sackville Street and were soon to open the Picture House (Grafton) in Grafton Street.

In May of 1912 the company had to close the Volta when they failed to secure a renewal of its licence from the Recorder in Green Street Courthouse.

On May 24th 1912 the Provincial Cinematograph Theatre Company had reason to renew the dance and music licences for all its three cinemas and an application was presented to the Right Honourable The Recorder in Green Street Courthouse by Mr. Richard Bell the Volta manager that had succeeded Mr. Huish who had been promoted to the position of manager at the Grafton Cinema.

However because of complaints from the Rector of St Mary's Church who claimed the opening of the Volta on Sunday nights were attracting young people away from Sunday night church services, objections were raised against the renewal of the licence.

Mr. Robertson of the Chief Crown Solicitor's Office also lodged an objection because he said the previous licence issued to the Volta management was expressly given for six days a week only and that Sunday openings were forbidden.

The Recorder in his summoning up said that this was a case in which the Rector of the parish was very indignant and that this situation should not have been allowed to carry on so near a church. "In England, he said, this would not have been allowed".

Mr. Robertson also reiterated that the previous licence had been specially dealt with and the licence was granted on a distinct understanding that there would be no Sunday opening.

While The Recorder granted the licences in respect of the Sackville and Grafton Street cinemas he withheld for the present, the Volta licence.

On November 2nd 1912 the Volta management renewed their application to the Right Honourable Recorder and again there were objections and the hearing was adjourned. We have no follow-up to these hearings and can only assume that the Volta did eventually receive its music and dance licence; however whatever happened and whatever course justice took, we found that the Volta was taken over by Mr. James Jameson, director of the Animated Picture Company in 1913...

Mr. Jameson was a well known personality in the world of cinema and his company ran exhibitions in many Dublin venues, it was also active in the Rotunda Rooms cinema where it had been more or less resident for something akin to eleven years.

With James Jameson at the helm, the "Volta" was now on the right course.

Championship Fight

THE Volta Picture House has secured the Exclusive Film rights of the two Championship Fights, Bombardier Wells v. Colin Bell and Johnny Summers v. Harry Stone. This special attraction will be added to a big programme of interesting pictures.

Prices as usual 3d. 4d. and 6d.

Bombardier Wells

(Of ENGLAND)

v.

Colin Bell

(Of AUSTRALIA)

For the Heavyweight Boxing Championship of the British Empire and a purse of £2,000

July 16, 17 and 18

THE TRAGEDY AT THE "PEPPER BOX" INN

Thrilling Detective Drama in Three Parts.

Continuous Performance from 2 to 10.30

THE

Volta Picture House

MARY STREET, DUBLIN

In 1914 the Company managed to secure the exclusive rights for the film of the two Championship fights between:

Bombardier Wells
V
Colin Bell

This contest was for the Heavyweight Championship of the British Empire and a purse of £2,000.

and

Johnny Summer's
v
Harry Stone

This film ran for a full week and the programme included interesting pictures.

~~~~~

THE VOLTA PICTURE HOUSE,

45, MARY STREET.

Showing to-day

"THE BROKEN COIN."

TOMORROW (SUNDAY) AS USUAL

2.30 TILL 7, AND 8.30 TILL 10.30.

PEOPLE BEING ALLOWED OUT TILL MIDNIGHT

This Film "The Broken Coin" was advertised on May 13th 1916, but rather than a film, it was most likely one of the twenty episodes of an adventure/mystery serial that had begun in 1915 which starred Grace Cunard as Kitty Gray, Francis Ford as Count Frederick. Francis also directed these serials, which also cast his brother, John Ford.

* * * * *
~~~~~

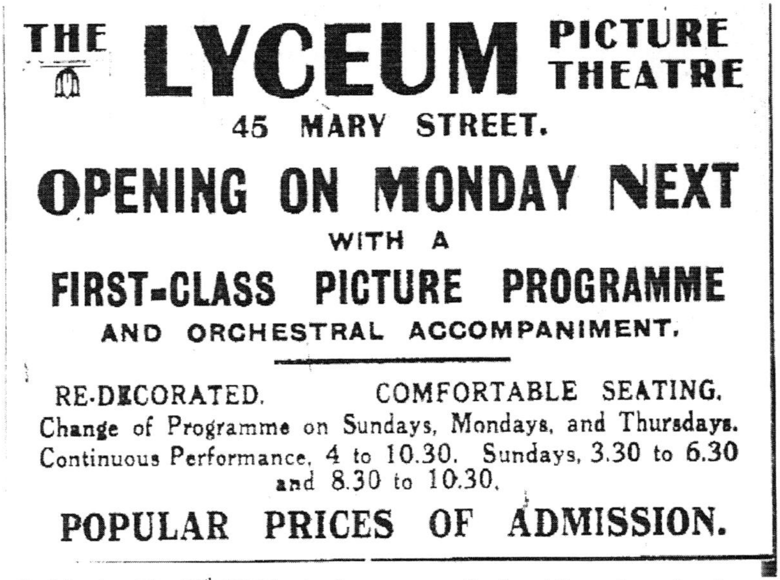
THE LYCEUM PICTURE THEATRE
45 MARY STREET.
OPENING ON MONDAY NEXT
WITH A
FIRST-CLASS PICTURE PROGRAMME
AND ORCHESTRAL ACCOMPANIMENT.
RE-DECORATED. COMFORTABLE SEATING.
Change of Programme on Sundays, Mondays, and Thursdays.
Continuous Performance, 4 to 10.30. Sundays, 3.30 to 6.30 and 8.30 to 10.30.
POPULAR PRICES OF ADMISSION.

On Monday, May 10th 1920 having been temporarily closed for re-decoration the Volta re-opened as the "Lyceum".

For the next twenty eight years the cinema continued to trade without bringing too much notice upon itself and we believe in latter years it again had a name change back to the "Volta".

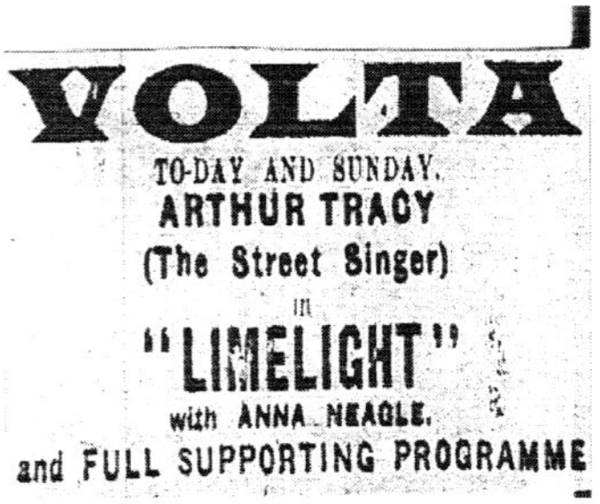
VOLTA
TO-DAY AND SUNDAY.
ARTHUR TRACY
(The Street Singer)
in
"LIMELIGHT"
with ANNA NEAGLE.
and FULL SUPPORTING PROGRAMME

On March 27th 1937 the Volta had the pleasure of featuring the beautiful musical "Limelight" which had just been released.

This film, which should not be confused with Chaplin's Masterpiece of 1952, starred Anna Neagle as Marjorie Kaye, a chorus girl who discovers Bob Grant (Arthur Tracy aka "The Street Singer"), when he sings for pennies to the queue outside the theatre where she works.

She introduces Bob to the producer of the show and when the male lead falls ill, Bob takes his place and gains fame. Ignoring poor lovelorn Marjorie he basks in the attention of his new female fans and dates one for a while. However, in true showbusiness style he soon realises that Marjorie is his true love and returns to her willing arms. Also starring were Tily Losch, Jack Buchanan, Ellis Jeffrey's and Hal Erickson.

Worth a mention

LYCEUM THEATRE
MARY STREET

Is by far the best War Picture that has been made . . . . so true, actual, and unforced.

—"DAILY NEWS."

Prices—4d., 9d. & 1/-.

Come Early to Avoid Disappointment

Doors Open at 2 o'clock.

On January 24th 1924 the Lyceum secured the war film "Verdun" for display and this film, which depicted horrific and bloody scenes from one of the longest battles of World War 1, attracted great attendances.

This film told the story of the Battle of Verdun, which was one of the longest and bloodiest engagements of World War 1 and it was said that over two million men were involved.

On February 21st 1916 Crown Prince Frederick Wilhelm under the direction of General Erich Von Falkenhayn, launched a massive offensive on Verdun, Douaumont and Hardaumont and while Douaumont and Hardaumont fell quite quickly the French rallied in Verdun under the command of General Petain with the now famous war cry,

"They Shall Not Pass".

The battle dragged for months with thousands being slaughtered on both sides and in July 1916 a British offensive in the Somme relieved some of the pressure on the French troops. By December 1916 the French had recovered most of the lost ground.

The German's had viewed this battle as one of attrition and they expected that the engagement would bleed the French army white: however at the end of the battle they had suffered almost as many losses as the French.

Casualties.
An estimated figure
French 400,000

German 380,000.
* * * * *

An unfortunate fact;
For some time before it closed the Volta earned the nick-name of the "Lousehouse".

To the best of our knowledge the Volta closed its doors circa 1947 or thereabouts and although we have no documentation to prove the exact date of its closure we have noted that according to Thom's Street Directory of 1949 the building was then vacant and remained so for a good many years.

In 1955 the premises was taken over by Hipp's Gents Tailors and outfitters and its upper floors were let to John L. Luck Gown and Mantle manufacturer.

Hipp's continued to trade there for nigh on 25 years but in 1980 the shop again fell vacant.

In 1983 it re-opened again as a Boot & Footwear shop and remained so until 1990 when it was taken over by Penney's Department Store.

An old photo of No 45, which mentions the name "Lyceum" on the banner above.
(Picture courtesy Dublin City Archives)

This very rare picture of the "Volta" came to us courtesy of Maurice Craig, who very kindly gave us permission to re-produce it in our book. We would also like to include in our gratitude David Griffin of the Irish Architectural Archives who organised this copy from the Merrion Square Archives.

While we had formed an opinion that the Volta had closed circa 1947 there is a possibility that the end came a wee bit earlier as evidenced by this advertisement, which appeared in the "Irish Independent" newspaper on May 17th 1947.

VOLTA CINEMA, 45 MARY STREET

The Volta is one of the oldest cinemas in Dublin, and enjoys a good steady patronage. It is situated in the best part of this leading city thoroughfare, where the traffic by day and evening is considerable.

The theatre is spacious and has all necessary accommodation—offices, lavatories, emergency exits, etc., and complies with the Corporation's requirements, and is suitable for factory, office or shop premises.

The premises are held for 21 years from November, 1942, at £450 and rates (P.L.V. £170), and are at present let to the Capitol and Allied Theatres, Ltd., at £728 (landlord paying rates) per annum, but vacant possession will be handed over on the 1st November next. In the meanwhile, the purchaser will be in receipt of the profit rent.

P. F. O'REILLY, Solicitor, 8 South Great George's Street.

(FROM GENERATION TO GENERATION)

ALBERT MacARTHUR, LTD.

'PHONE 76754 (2 Lines). MacARTHUR HOUSE, D'OLIER ST., M.I.A.A.

As can be seen by the wording of the advertisement, the premises though enjoying a good and steady patronage as a cinema was also said to be suitable as a factory, office or shop premises.

It would also appear, that the premises was handed over to its new owner on Saturday November 1st, and that the cinema was closed at that time.

However we have no way of knowing what the new owners had in mind for the building which still had sixteen years left of its 1942 twenty one year lease and it may well have been their intention to continue running it as a cinema.

Whatever happened between November 1947 and 1949, the building was listed in Thom's Street Directory of 1949 as being vacant and it appeared to remain in a vacant state until it was taken over by Hipp's in 1955.

This photo is courtesy of the Irish Times and it was taken circa early May 1947. We would assume that the picture advertised for the following Sunday nights performance was its last.
"High Powered" (1945), which starred
Robert Lowery and Phyllis Brooks

The Auction date was set for Tuesday June 3rd 1947.
On Monday, October 27th we came across an article in the "Irish Independent" which informed us that after catering to cinemagoers for over 40 years the Volta had finally closed and we thereby concluded that Sunday night October 25th was its last night as a cinema

WAR OF THE UNIONS.

We read an article in the Film Centre library in relation to cinemas, which informed us that in 1944 the trade unions had greater strength in Ireland than in any other country in the world. It also mentioned that all cinema workers in Ireland were members of the "Irish Transport & General Workers Union". However, this was not in evidence in 1924 when the Workers Union of Ireland and the Irish Transport & General Workers Union were fighting for supremacy in the world of cinema.

It would appear that in November of 1924 three cinemas were forced to close their doors because of inter union disputes. It was said that in all cases the cause of the trouble was exactly the same and was traceable to the persistent efforts of the Workers Union of Ireland under the direction of James Larkin to poach members from the I.T. & G.W U in the course of which all forms of intimidation were exercised and employers came to grief between the battling unions.

According to a newspaper report on Monday, November 17th 1924 there was no question of wages or conditions of employment being involved in the dispute. The whole issue was that the Workers Union of Ireland declared that unless members of the staff of theatres and picture houses who belong to the I.T. & G.W.U. withdraw their allegiance from that organisation and join the followers of James Larkin, the places of amusement will either be picketed or compelled to close down.

Already the Corinthian, Carlton and Tivoli were affected and had closed their doors. When the Tivoli closed some fifty people were deprived of their jobs and the Government was at a loss of revenue to the tune of £100 per week in amusement tax. In the case of the Tivoli the W.U.I demanded that a dismissed member of the staff should be replaced, though there was no work for him.

The Carlton management decided to brave it out and re-open for an afternoon performance whether or not the premises were picketed or intimidation was resorted to by the W.U.I. However, the dislocation of business was brought about by a lightening strike of three operators who refused to work alongside six members of the I.T & G.W.U. unless they agreed to join the W.U.I. The house was full at the time when the men withdrew their labour and management had no course but to shut down.

The situation was clearly getting out of hand and the I.T & G.W.U. determined to protect their workers gave an undertaking to the management to supply men in the places where Mr. Larkin's workers were on strike.

In the case of the Carlton cinema I.T & G.W.U. operators were in attendance later that afternoon and a performance was held.

~~~~

The Corinthian was in trouble when some members of the staff who were in the W.U.I. refused to work with the doorman who was a shop steward with the I.T & G.W.U. and rather than have an exhibition outside their doors, management suspended the man, and needless to say the I.T.& G.W.U. took a stand on this issue. The Corinthian closed and would not open until further notice.

Fears were entertained that there might be an extension of the trouble, but the action of the I.T & G.W.U. in staffing the Carlton was regarded as a hopeful sign.
~~~~

A meeting of the Theatre and Cinema Proprietors Association was called to deal with the situation and the I.T. & G.W.U. put the following advertisement in the local papers on Wednesday November 19th 1924:

IRISH TRANSPORT AND GENERAL WORKERS' UNION.

ALL MEMBERS AND TRADE UNIONISTS ARE HEREBY NOTIFIED THAT

NO TRADE DISPUTE

EXISTS IN

THE CARLTON CINEMA,

O'CONNELL STREET, or

THE CORINTHIAN CINEMA, Eden Quay,

and that full Trade Union Staffs under Union Conditions and the old Working Agreement, are employed there.

WORKERS: SUPPORT YOUR COMRADES WHO ARE FIGHTING FOR THE RIGHT TO WORK.

[illegible]

The Strike, Dispute or War of the Unions was settled, or appeared to be settled, for although we searched and re-searched the papers for the final outcome we never found it, but the "Tivoli Theatre" re-opened on December 22nd 1924.

WE BEG TO DIFFER.

When we decided to write about the history of all old Dublin cinemas we naturally enough mentioned our intentions to our friends and acquaintances and in almost every instance the question was thrown at us "Did you know about the "Volta" they would ask, and then they would proceed to tell us that that was the first cinema in Dublin. Yes we said we know all about the "Volta" and its connection with James Joyce.

On almost every corner we turned and every book we read that had something connected with cinemas in its pages we came across the confirmation, that the Volta was the first cinema in Dublin, and accepting this we wrote about the opening of the "Volta" at 45 Mary Street on December 20th 1909. He added to it, as much information as possible, i.e. that it failed under the management of Joyce and that the cinema was sold to an English Theatre Company, that it later had a name change to the "Lyceum" and later again it changed back to the "Volta" and finally became a "Penney's" shop.

We filed that story as finished and carried on with our search for other Dublin cinemas and the history of same, however as the months passed by we began to find discrepancies in dates and different versions of the history of cinemas in Dublin. A good example of this was the different versions of the ownership of the Sundrive Cinema Company and its three cinemas, The "Classic, Kenilworth and Sundrive". (See George's book "The Prinner").

Because of this, instead of working as a team and sharing the workload between us, we decided to work separately and compare and argue over our findings with the one view of establishing accuracy at any cost. This modus operandi appeared to work, but added seriously to our workload. We also discovered that we were now working as research investigators rather than just researchers.

We would also point out that in many instances while researching the history of a cinema we accidentally came across information on subjects that we had long finished with and in consequence we had to reopen our files on same and make amendments. This caused a great delay in finishing off our stories on Old Dublin Cinemas.

In January 2006 we were tracing articles in connection with the Coffee Palace cinema in Townsend Street, when we came across news item that told us that this cinema had also been known as the "Palace Cinema" which had shown a series of films for an American Company in 1908 long before the "Volta" had opened. This information brought about great pondering on our behalf. It would now appear that the much-acclaimed "Volta" was not Dublin's first cinema.

One of the first things we did following these findings was to look up the definition of the word 'Cinema' in our dictionary and on the internet, and the answer in all cases was that the word 'Cinema' meant a movie theatre, a picture palace or a location which was used as a building to view motion pictures.
We now present our finding that proves that the "Volta" was not Dublin's first cinema.

This advertisement, which appeared in the "Evening Herald" on April 2nd 1909, surely proves beyond all shadow of a doubt that there was life before the "Volta"

On top of which we give you the "Queen's Theatre" which its manager claims is the Peoples Popular Picture Palace and is said to be turning away hundreds of would be patrons nightly.

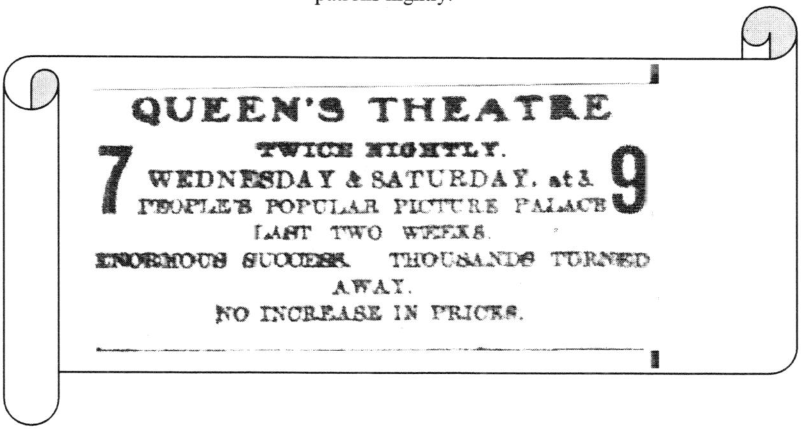

If that's not enough we would tell you that the "Tivoli" on Burgh Quay in January 1903 was showing "Bioscope "pictures nightly, the "Rotunda" was showing 'Living Pictures', the "Empire Theatre" was introducing a Grand New Series of "Empire Pictures" and the Worlds Fair Theatre and Waxworks had Cinematograph displays of all new pictures. So just where was Dublin bereft of a cinema, or, if you like, locations where one could view a motion picture?

In 1905 we had Hale's cinema in South Anne Street or would that be too small a venue to mention, though dedicated to cinema only, it did only accommodate twelve persons.

We also mentioned in another section of this book that the "Father Mathew Hall" in Church Street showed pictures on October 23rd 1909 before the opening of the "Volta" in December of 1909.

On Monday December 28th 1902 the Rathmines Town Hall had on display an Edison's extraordinary sensational animated picture by the name "A Trip to the Moon".

Not to be outdone, the Antient Concert Rooms in Great Brunswick Street also displayed wonderful films presented by the American Animated Photo Company and showing that night of Monday December 22nd 1902 was "Life at the Vatican" together with a series of animated pictures depicting incidents and ceremonies transpiring at the Vatican including living pictures of His Holiness Pope Leo XIII.

The Empire Theatre featured its own motion pictures, which were known as "Empire Pictures" and on display on October 2nd 1903 was their own film "Baldoyle Races". Come along, their advertisements said, and see yourself caught by the "Empire Cinematograph" in magnificent life sized pictures.

1903 saw the Tivoli Theatre introduce their "Grand Bioscope" on November 16th and the Rotunda had been showing their "Living Pictures" for quite some time.

A selection of movies that were doing the rounds during the years prior to December 20th 1909

THE NIGHT OF TERROR

THE BARONET COWBOY

AROUND NEW YORK IN 15 MINUTES

THE FLOWER GIRL LIFE STORY

HIS ONLY SON

THE HARBOUR PIRATES

THE STORY OF THE KELLY GANG (1905)
(This was the world's first feature length film)

And here
WE REST OUR CASE

We would, however, concede to the fact that the "Volta" although not Dublin's first cinema in out opinion, might instead have been the first building dedicated to film only shows, because as far as we know it never held a concert or variety performance.

~~~~~

Snippet
In 1913 the film entitled "Ireland the Nation" which was the subject of a private showing in a Dublin cinema was said to be the first full length film to be made in Ireland.
~~~~~

WHITEHALL GRAND
Collins Avenue.

The Whitehall Grand Cinema was officially opened by An Tanaiste Mr. W. Norton on Saturday, July 31st, 1954.

This is a new super-luxury cinema with the emphasis on everything modern and it has seating for over 1000.

The entrance is most inviting with the most modern décor, flooring and fittings. The auditorium is oval shaped with a modern type stadium which we believe was pioneered by the Sundrive Cinema Company in their trilogy of cinemas.

The seats are finished in cherry red and with their oak woodwork are in colourful contrast with the beautiful soft grey of the carpeted floor. The walls and ceiling are done in shades of grey, blue and oatmeal and all blend well and bring about a most comfortable ambience.

Air conditioning is provided by a filter system fitted underneath the stage and the fresh air emanates from a large grille running the length of this stage. The stale air exits through vents fitted around the stadium area and when necessary, the heating is supplemented by radiators.

Projection and sound equipment are of the most modern and a clear and bright picture with high fidelity sound is promised.

Prices of admission are 1/3 for the stalls and 2/3 for the stadium area.

The Whitehall Grand will service a huge catchment area which not only includes Whitehall, but Donnycarney, Larkfield, Beaumont and Santry and management is assured of full attendances nightly and in return they promise to provide the best films available.

The film chosen for the opening night was "Doctor in the House", starring Dirk Bogarde and our own Noel Purcell.

About "Doctor in the House".

Doctor in the House which stars, Dirk Bogarde, James Robertson Justice, Kenneth More, Kay Kendall, Muriel Pavlow and Noel Purcell is a medical comedy and was the first of a series of seven 'Doctor' movie's, all of which had much of the same cast and crew.

This film also launched the career of Dirk Bogarde who prior to this movie only played small supporting roles. The film was also nominated for four BAFTA's with Kenneth More wining "Best Actor".

In the seven 'Doctor' movies, Dirk played the lead role in four Doctor in the House 1954, Doctor at Sea 1955, Doctor at Large 1957 and Doctor in Distress 1963. Michael Craig took the lead in Doctor in Love 1960 and Leslie Philips finished off the series with Doctor in Clover 1966 and Doctor in Trouble 1970.

At that time in 1954 according to an "Evening Herald" reporter, it would appear that "Doctor in the House" film nearly broke a record in the world of Dublin cinema by running simultaneously in three houses, the Metropole in O'Connell Street where it had been running for the past three months, the State in Phibsboro and now in the Whitehall Grand.

Proceeds of the opening night were donated to the Cinema and Theatre Benevolent Fund.

To the best of our knowledge nothing untoward happened in or to the Whitehall Grand and it would seem that it enjoyed a good trade until the decline in the Dublin cinema business when it closed with all its sister cinemas on Saturday night June 29th 1974.

WHITEHALL (Over 15s) At 4.35, 7.00, 9.30 "KUNG FU THE HEAD CRUSHER". Plus! At 3.10, 5.40, 8.05. "HEADS I KILL YOU, TAILS YOU'RE DEAD".

Patrons please note that this cinema will remain closed as and from the end of this evening's programme.

The last two films to be displayed in the Whitehall Grand were,

"Kung Fu the Head Crusher", starring Yang Chun & Ingrid Hu And Chuei Fu Shang
&
"Heads I Kill You, Tails your Dead" Comedy Western with George Hilton as
Allelujah.

When it closed, the Whitehall Grand re-opened as a venue for Bingo and soon became one of the best known in the city and it is still functioning as such in this month of December 2005.

From what we hear, so popular is this venue that organised bus loads of Bingo players are ferried there on a regular basis.

The Whitehall Grand circa 2005.

Death of a Cinema.
(Picture: 'Sundrive', courtesy "Newspage" Passionist's Fathers, Mount Argus).

WORLD'S FAIR
Waxworks Exhibition, Cinema, Theatre, Palace of Variety's and the $6^{1/2}$d stores, 30 Henry Street.

(Not to be confused with Samuels Bazaar at number 6 Henry Street).

World's Fair Waxworks Exhibition
30 Henry Street
Open from 10am till 10pm
ENTIRE CHANGE OF PROGRAMME

THE AKHUROTS, SKETCH ARTISTE'S. EDIE D'ALLWOOD COMMEDIENNE.
MARK SELWYN, ACTOR VOCALIST. HOLLY CHAPMAN. SERIO AND DANCER; FRED RICHARDS, DESCRIPTIVE VOCALIST; FAY AND FOY, MUSICAL COMEDY ARTISTES;
CINEMATOGRAPH ALL NEW PICTURES

ADMISSION: TWOPENCE (CHILDREN - ONE PENNY).

As can be see from this advertisement a variety of entertainments were on offer from this building, including, Cinematograph Pictures. It was also Dublin's first Waxworks and we tell a story about these premises under the heading of "A Cinema in Disguise" in another section of this book which by now you will already have read.

We would also tell you that there appeared to be two $6^{1/2}$d shops in Henry Street, the other being Samuels which sold a variety of low priced goods, which would be on a par with a small Woolworth's type of shop. However to the best of our knowledge one shop had nothing to do with the other and it would appear that the story we tell about Victor M Wood's under the title of "A Cinema in Disguise" is also guilty of mixing these premises up. We could of course have deleted Victor Wood's version, but we would rather have you read our findings as found.

The Worlds Fair started off as a $6^{1/2}$d shop and why it was called this is beyond our knowledge. However, it must have had some significance at the time when we note that a similar named shop was operating further up the street, could it, we wondered, have been an early type of pound shop, the like of which we have in abundance today? We have this shop on record as having been in existence from 1893. However we later found that the Waxworks, which was said to be on the style of Madame Tussaud's in London had opened on December 29th 1892.

Alderman Charles James was the proprietor of this business, which he now advertised as the Worlds Fair Waxworks Exhibition and $6^{1/2}$d stores which he ran with the help of his wife and an adopted daughter. The building we might add was of some considerable size and it stretched as far as and backed onto Princes Street. The Waxworks was situated on the first floor and as there was plenty of space, the James's began putting on stage shows in which the daughter used to do an odd turn. In 1906 we found advertisements informing the public that Living Pictures were now on offer in the Worlds Fair.

Alderman Charles James unlike many business-men in the area did not live overhead. Instead he had quite a substantial house at 159 Strand Road, Sandymount, which was known locally as Wellington House.

The Worlds Fair was a most popular and varied place of entertainment and prospered on its policy of forever changing programmes which were on display five times daily during the hours of 10 am to 10 pm.

A sample programme for Tuesday, March 2nd 1908 advertised the following entertainment:

Van Gelder the peoples favourite Conjuror, Ernie Norman and Evelyn Belle Comedians and Dancers, Will Fox Novelty Ventriloquist.
Cinematograph Pictures, featuring "Burglary by Motor", "Wonderful Lantern Pictures" and "Travelling on the Cheap" on top of which you could view the Waxworks.

On a good day and if business in the $6^{1/2}$d stores permitted her absence, you just might get to view and hear Councillor James's adopted daughter Marcella the Midget Queen sing a song on the stage.

There is very little that we can add to the story of the Worlds Fair as told by Victor Wood's at the beginning of this book except to more or less corroborate his memories, however we would surmise that when the building was destroyed during the 1916 Rising that Councillor James and his good wife were of a respectable age and most likely retired to their home in Sandymount. To the best of our knowledge they personally did not rebuild or cause to be rebuilt new premises on the site. It would also be reasonable to assume that they were of comfortable means, as the business in Henry Street appears to have been good to them.

However the site was re-developed and when the Post & Telegraph Company rebuilt the General Post Office building they expanded their interest to include all of the overhead space as far as and including 24 Henry Street which was the site of the Coliseum Theatre which had also been destroyed in the Rising and all of the space to the rear which extended into Prince's Street. Other than the extended post office building only a row of retail shop units occupies that stretch of Henry Street in 2006. What was the site of the $6^{1/2}$d Stores and Waxworks prior to 1916 is now a retail shoe shop, as is by sheer coincidence the ground floor retail unit of 24 Henry Street and would you believe it so is the site of Samuel's Bazaar; with neither of the three connected in any way.

BEWITCHED, BOTHERED AND BEWILDERED AGAIN!

During our research, we came across some right tricky and often puzzling situations, where some news items or pieces of information that came our way via written reports and books dedicated to certain subjects etc, would to say the least contradict our findings and seriously add to our workload. This story of the 6 ½ d shops and entertainment centres is a good case in point and we would be failing in our efforts if we didn't bring it to our reader's attention.

The World's Fair story was, as far as we were concerned, finished and we fully believed that the reminiscences of Victor Wood were of the Worlds Fair theatre and Waxworks at 30 Henry Street rather than Samuels Bazaar at 6 Henry Street. We filed the story as such and moved on.

However as is often the case, we were checking through the Dublin Corporation Reports of October / December 1911 in relation to a caution which was issued to the "Coffee Palace Cinema", in Townsend Street when at the top of the page in question was a report on the Committee's approval for seating accommodation for 47 persons in Samuels's Exhibition Hall at No. 6 Henry Street which would fit in well with Victor telling us that the cinema had no seats. What can we do, 'but again rest our case'.

Our apologies, if we did indeed misinterpret Victor's memories. But in our defence we never ever came across an advertisement for Samuel's Exhibition Hall.

The Worlds' Fair and $6^{1/2}$d Store at 30 Henry Street.
(Picture courtesy of Seamus Kearns)

In late April 1902 a disastrous fire occurred in the Waxworks of 30 Henry Street and it would appear that all the wax figures melted which resulted in the closure of that section of the premises until further notice. Unfortunately, as that same upstairs floor also housed the stage and cinema, no entertainment of any sort was available for a time until repairs were carried out. However, the downstairs $6^{1/2}$d shop was unaffected and a notice on the shop window proclaimed that 'Eugenie' was still available and could be consulted daily from 12 noon to 9pm. For the moment we do not know who or what Eugenie was, but if we are lucky enough to find out we will include details at the end of the waxworks story

Nearly four months later on August 20th 1902 the upstairs section of 30 Henry Street having had extensive repairs and total refurbishment carried out, was re-opened for business.

The premises now had a spanking new look with an extra large stage where continuous performances with a grand array of talent took place every hour. (Cinema as yet had not entered the equation of the downtown waxworks in Henry Street). Eugenie was still available for consultations during the noon to 9pm period and the waxworks enjoyed all new figures, which were worthy of inspection.
Admission was 2d and children one penny

Some of the most popular artists to tread the boards of the Worlds Fair stage were as follows:
Marcella, Songstress and Hoofer and daughter of the James's.

Messrs Pettigrove & Sons with their marionettes and great dresses, scenes and effects provided wonderful and entertaining Cinderella pantomimes to the most appreciable of audiences.

George Harcourt, Conjurer

Mons Dugarde, Ventriloquist

Joe Kelly, Character comedian

Harry Sinclair, the Great Imitator

Ida Dalton Vocalist and Dancer

Lillie Hustler, Dancer

Van Gelder, Facial Artist

* * * * *

Eugenie was advertised in many ways, i.e. Eugenie receives clients, **Eugene is available for consultations and Eugenie will be here from 12 noon to 9pm, but there was no mention of Eugenie's abilities.**

An Extremely Rare Find!

This picture is a rare find indeed and we cannot tell you how elated we were when we stumbled across it in the Saturday's Evening Telegraph of December 21st 1912.

WORLD'S FAIR VARIETIES.

(Photograph Showing Front of Hall from Main Entrance.) Latest **Photograph** of the WORLD'S FAIR VARIETIES, 30 HENRY STREET, DUBLIN, **after recent** Alterations. The Proprietors have spared no Expense in making it the **Cosiest and** most Up-to-Date Hall in Dublin. Both the Variety Artistes and Animated Pictures are of Excellent Quality. Special Attractions have been secured for **XMAS** WEEK, including a Magnificent Pantomime Picture. Continuous **Performance** Daily, 3 to 5.30, and Twice Nightly, 7 to 9 o'clock. Price of Admission—Tip-Up Seats, 3D. and 6D. Children, 2D. 71298

In our search for information on Eugenie and her qualifications we finally discovered that she was a Scientific Palmist. This description of her abilities, were mentioned in a small advert in the Evening Telegraph of Thursday January 2nd 1901.

A long trawl, but finding the answer made the effort worthwhile.

SOME FINAL COMMENTS

(An opinion expressed by George)

Following the publication of Jim Keenan's "Pictorial Selection of old Dublin Cinemas" and of course my own book "The Prinner" which gave a good account of the history of a handful of old Dublin cinemas it would appear that every Tom, Dick and Harry were now about to put pen to paper to record their knowledge of old cinemas.

It would also appear that when I produced my first book on cinemas "The Prinner" in 2005 that I had inadvertently appeared to declare the "Season Open" for other cinema enthusiasts to have a go, and I now have whispers of some six writers in action.

When I began my research in early 2004 and approached a number of libraries for any information they had on file about their local picture palaces, I was very surprised to find that the information available was minuscule if indeed they had any at all. In fact the staffs of some libraries were totally unaware that a local cinema had actually existed in their area.

Dublin City libraries did feature an exhibition of old cinemas, which went on tour around their various branch libraries in the last few years. This display consisted of a large stock of photographs, some newspaper clippings, programmes and text, but up to that point in time nobody it would seem had attempted to record the history of cinemas in book form.

There was a rumour or two that someone was planning such a book, but so far nothing concrete has hit the bookshelves. My interest and investigations into local cinemas were welcomed with open arms and all that I met were most anxious to help. The fact that I planned to produce a book on my findings was much appreciated, so much so that the first batch of books I had printed were all on order

One librarian that I met with told me that I was an answer to a prayer I was also invited by the Rathmines, Ranelagh and Rathgar Historical Society to give an illustrated talk on the history of the Princess Cinema on November 25th 2004.

In my opinion, the more books that are published on the history of old cinemas the better, as there is so much interest, that library shelves are crying out for stock. The cost of publishing and in particular self-publishing a book is a problem and as I believe that the bulk of our readers will be golden oldies like yours truly, the cost of purchasing so many copies could well be a prohibiting factor and I would therefore remind would be readers that copies of most publications will be available for borrowing from library shelves.

It is now almost the end of August 2006, Saturday 26th to be precise and Patrick and I believe that we have given mention to every known cinema that operated in Dublin County prior to 1975 and we are now closing the covers of our manuscript.

Our book will be self-published and on Monday we will meet with a printer and discuss terms. It is our intention to publish our book both in hardback style and paperback. The hardback will be a first edition copy for the likes of collectors and libraries and the paperback for the comfort of easy reading etc.

The Gilbert Library and Dublin City Archives have kindly offered to launch our book from their premises in Pearse Street and we expect that most Dublin bookshops will stock a copy or two, as will most Dublin libraries.

I am not all that sure that the book will be ready for the Christmas market as our intention is more attuned to quality and accuracy rather than a race to achieve great sales.
Our goal is to promote copies of our book to as many Dublin library shelves as possible and our point of sales will be confined to the Greater Dublin Area.

The fact that others are researching cinema history will also pass on a message to our many friends, family members, colleagues and neighbours that we are not the only ones on Gods earth that appear to be totally preoccupied with old cinemas and their history.